THE COMPLETE
SAILING
MANUAL

THE COMPLETE
SAILING
MANUAL

STEVE SLEIGHT

CONTENTS

LONDON, NEW YORK, MUNICH,
MELBOURNE, DELHI

Senior Editor	Gareth Jones
Senior Art Editor	Michael Duffy
Project Editor	Hannah Bowen
Production Editor	John Goldsmid
Production Controller	Sophie Argyris
Jacket Designer	Mark Cavanagh
Managing Editor	Stephanie Farrow
Managing Art Editor	Lee Griffiths
US Editors	Rebecca Warren
	Margaret Parrish

DK INDIA

Managing Editor	Saloni Talwar
Managing Art Editor	Romi Chakraborty
Project Editor	Neha Gupta
Project Art Editor	Pooja Pipil
Editors	Rashmi Rajan,
	Suneha Dutta
Designers	Diya Kapur,
	Aanchal Awasthi
Production Manager	Pankaj Sharma
DTP Manager	Balwant Singh
DTP Designers	Shanker Prasad,
	Arjinder Singh,
	Tanveer Abbas Zaidi

Produced for Dorling Kindersley by
Schermuly Design Co.

Project Editor	Cathy Meeus
Project Art Editor	Hugh Schermuly

REVISED EDITION
First American Edition, 2012
Published in the United States by
DK Publishing
375 Hudson Street
New York, New York 10014

12 13 14 15 16   10 9 8 7 6 5 4 3 2 1
001—181268—January/2012

Copyright © 2012 Dorling Kindersley Limited
Text copyright © 2012 Steve Sleight

CONTINUED ▶

Published in Great Britain by Dorling Kindersley Limited.
A catalog record for this book is available from the Library of Congress

Printed and bound in Singapore by Star Standard Industries
ISBN 978-0-7566-8969-8

DK books are available at special discounts when purchased in bulk for sales promotions, premiums, fund-raising, or educational use. For details, contact: DK Publishing Special Markets, 375 Hudson Street, New York, New York 10014 or SpecialSales@dk.com

DISCOVER MORE AT www.dk.com

Author's Dedication
This book is dedicated to my mother, Irene.

PLEASE NOTE
As with many sports, there are inherent risks with sailing. Always wear a buoyancy aid or life jacket, and ensure that you have adequate supervision as a beginner. In this book the masculine gender is commonly used, for clarity only.

KEY
The following symbols appear throughout the book.

↓
WIND DIRECTION

⇊
TIDE DIRECTION

↓
BOAT DIRECTION

CONTENTS CONTINUED

FOREWORD

Sailing is in my blood. My father Roddy was a keen sailor, and he skippered *Second Life* in the first Whitbread Round the World Race in 1973–74. My own sailing career began at the age of eight when my family lived in Restronguet, Cornwall, England. My first boat was an Optimist dinghy, and I joined the local sailing club and began entering national youth events. What started as a hobby quickly turned into a way of life.

A large part of my early success was due to the fantastic teaching I received from my instructors and coaches. Sailing always centered around having fun, and I believe this is really important when training young people on the water. Whatever your age, it is vital you learn the correct techniques and improve your skills through good-quality training. This will help keep you safe and significantly increase the pleasure and reward you get from this pastime.

Sailing is a complex sport. Not all of us have easy access to instruction, but Steve's book solves this problem. Whether you want to sail dinghies or larger yachts, and whether you want to race or cruise, Steve's passion for sailing—and the comprehensive information presented here—will enable you to get the most from your time afloat.

Happy sailing!

Ben Ainslie, CBE
Triple Olympic gold and silver medallist
Three-time ISAF World Sailor of the Year
ISAF 2010 World Match Racing Tour Champion

THE **JOY** OF SAILING

Unlike any other sport or recreation, sailing offers a sense of freedom and independence that, once experienced, often leads to lifelong addiction. The sea always has something to teach and one never ceases to learn. What's more, as any sailor will tell you, boats have a life and personality of their own. This book is intended not only as a practical guide to a wonderful sport, but also aims to convey the joy of being afloat.

INTRODUCTION

Sailing is both the most relaxing pastime imaginable and the most complex sport in the world. It is a serious competitive sport for some, and recreation for others. But the origins of both forms of sailing lie in the distant past and the days of exploration, migration, and commerce and commerce across the oceans and seas.

The origins of sailing

For thousands of years, the world depended exclusively on sail power for long-distance travel across water. Whether on great rivers, seas, or oceans, sail power was the only alternative to muscle power applied to oars and paddles. In every part of the world, local populations devised their own solutions to the challenge of harnessing the wind and building boats capable of carrying people and goods long distances across bodies of water.

These local solutions created unique craft, some of which still survive. Viking longboats traveled thousands of miles under oars and their simple square sails. The huge lateen (triangular) sails, characteristic of Arabian dhows, were an efficient sailing solution for the waters in which they sailed. The Chinese solution to sail power was the Chinese lugsail, commonly called the junk rig, while the Polynesian islanders developed the proa—their unique multihulled craft.

Designs for warships, merchant ships, and fishing vessels all evolved to suit their function, resulting in many types of boat, each with special strengths and advantages. Hundreds, if not thousands, of boat designs evolved, each with its own specific advantages to suit local conditions and needs.

Perhaps the design pinnacle of cargo-carrying sailing ships was the magnificent clipper ship of the 19th century. Designed and built for speed, clippers raced across oceans to be first to market and capture the best prices for their precious cargoes of wool and tea.

Sailing today

Today, sailing throughout the world has evolved into a major sport and recreational activity. You can sail at any age; it doesn't matter if you are male or female, or if you are able-bodied or disabled. You can enjoy it for fun and freedom, or let the most complex sport in the world challenge your competitive skills.

The International Sailing Federation (ISAF), which is the world governing authority for the sport of sailing, has 137 member nations, each represented by a national body. ISAF is responsible for promotion of the sport internationally, managing sailing at the Olympic Games, developing the International Yacht Racing Rules and Regulations for all sailing competitions, the training of judges, umpires, and other administrators, and the development of the sport around the world.

Recreational sailing

Recreational sailing is less structured than the sporting side, although in many countries the ISAF Member National Authority is involved in promoting the sport, providing training programs, and representing

ROYAL YACHT
The Royal Yacht *Mary* firing a gun salute. The *Mary* was presented to King Charles II in 1660 and introduced the concept of yachting as sport in England.

AT THE LIMIT
Racing brings the thrill of
competition and the challenge
of pushing your boat to its limits,
whatever the conditions.

the interests of boat users at national government level and on a variety of international bodies. But, in general, boat owners do not have to belong to their national governing body—or even a club or association—to enjoy the recreational pleasures of sailing. In most countries, sailing and boating are relatively unregulated.

The rewards of sailing include the experience of self-reliance and responsibility, the learning of a multitude of skills that have been evolving for thousands of years, the sense of freedom of being away from the land—if only for a short time—and the joy of being close to the natural forces of wind and water.

These rewards make the sailing experience a perfect therapy for many people in recovery from illness or emotional trauma, and an excellent environment for pursuing personal development and as an activity for corporate team-building.

Small-boat sailing

Sailing in small boats—dinghies and small keelboats—is the core of the sport. If you learn to sail in a dinghy, you will learn faster than in a larger boat and will develop a more instinctive feel for a boat's behavior. Many people start as children, which is ideal, but it is possible to learn to sail small boats at almost any age.

The massive expansion of the sport in the mid-to-late 20th century came from the development of small-boat sailing for leisure and sport, and the story of its growth in popularity is linked to the development of stronger, lighter materials. First came plywood, followed by the introduction of fiberglass and more sophisticated construction using advanced resins and fibers, such as Kevlar and carbon fiber, and machine-molded plastics.

Today, dinghies are available for every type of sailing, from recreation to high-speed sailing and racing. At the highest level, the most advanced boats require athletic skills at least the equal of any other physical Olympic sport.

Cruising

The use of yachts to cruise coastal waters and undertake ocean passages dates back to the mid-19th century, a time when the large racing yachts of the day were sailed almost exclusively by professional crews. To such sailors, the idea of cruising offshore in a small yacht bordered on insanity, yet a few individuals, most notably British sailor Richard Tyrrell McMullen, pioneered yacht cruising and inspired thousands of others through their example. McMullen sailed thousands of miles around the British Isles from 1850. He died at the helm of his yacht in the English Channel in 1891.

Other notable pioneers include London lawyer John Macgregor, who cruised in a small sailing canoe, and American Joshua Slocum, who in 1898 became the first person to complete a single-handed circumnavigation of the globe, aboard the 36 ft (10.9 m) *Spray*.

Many influential cruising sailors followed over the ensuing decades and, today, more and more people

DEVELOPING SKILLS
Sailing in small boats is lots of fun and will teach you the basic skills faster than sailing in larger boats.

CRUISING FOR PLEASURE
The joy of cruising is quite different from racing. With cruising comes the pleasures of self-reliance, relaxation afloat, closeness to the environment, and the freedom to sail anywhere you choose.

are discovering the joys of cruising, whether on coastal or offshore passages, or ocean voyages.

Offshore racing

Offshore racing in boats that had a dual cruiser-racer role became very popular in the 1970s. Since then, this branch of the sport has seen many problems with handicapping rules, while escalating costs and increasing professionalism have had a negative impact on the sport. Today, there are signs of some resurgence in offshore racing, and the popularity of inshore Grand Prix-style events for one-design big-boat classes has increased considerably. At club level, cruiser

racing is still highly accessible and lots of fun, and the latest types of day-racing sportsboats have brought increasing numbers back to small keelboat racing.

Professional sailing

The growth in professional sailing in the past 20 years has been a major boost for the sport. Starting with the employment of top racing sailors by sail lofts and boatbuilders to help customers and promote their products, the professional scene has grown to include professional racers, instructors, coaches, yacht skippers, and crews, and a whole support industry built around the growth in

sailing, dinghy, and yacht racing, and the rapidly developing superyacht industry. Today, much of the focus of the sport's training industry in the leading sailing nations is on the creation of a pool of highly skilled professional yacht crew.

Technology and techniques

Another key element in contemporary sailing has been the development of new materials. Strong, stiff, and lightweight materials, such as carbon fiber, have enabled designers to build ever larger yachts with ever larger rigs. Lighter, larger boats now sail faster than ever before. Indeed, racing yachts now circle the globe nonstop

HIGH-PERFORMANCE THRILLS
Skiff-type dinghies provide the ultimate in speed and thrills. Here, the three-person 18-foot Skiff shows how exciting these boats can be.

faster than any commercial ship could manage. The development of much lighter and more powerful boats, both dinghies and large yachts, has brought about a new technique—that of apparent wind sailing—and the design of new rigs to handle it.

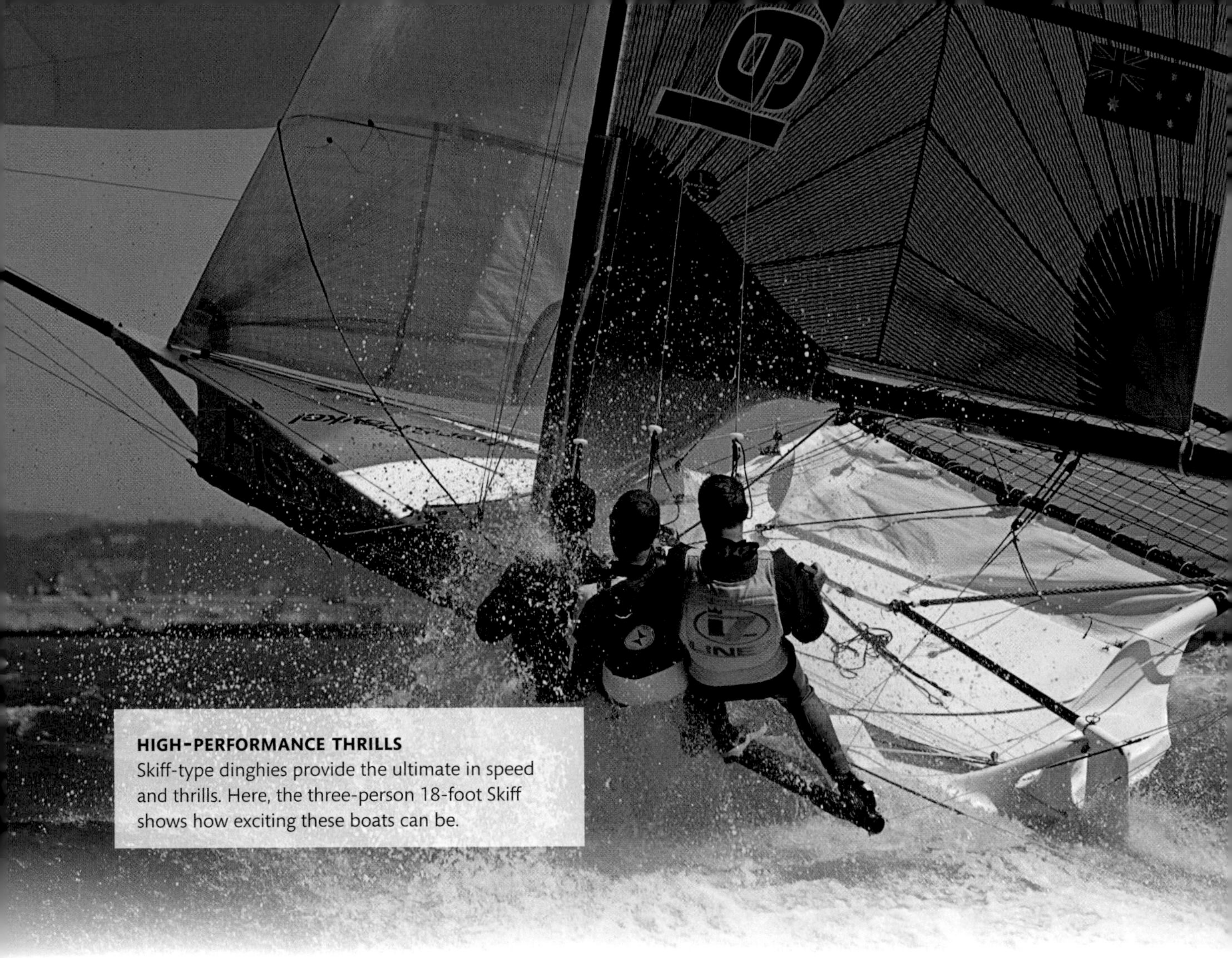

As boats go faster, their speed increasingly affects the strength and direction of the wind in which they are sailing. These boats generate so much wind from their own speed that in consequence they almost always sail with the apparent wind well forward. This phenomenon has brought about new methods of sailing and new boats and events to serve the sport.

Skiffs and multihulls

The fastest single-hulled small boats today are the "skiff" type of dinghies, which typically feature very lightweight, narrow hulls, large rigs designed for apparent wind sailing, and wide "wings," often with trapezes to allow the crew to balance the power.

Multihulls constitute another design approach, in which light boats with two (catamaran) or three (trimaran) narrow hulls provide a boat that has great stability, and can carry a very powerful rig. A further innovative development is that of foil-borne sailing, where the hull is completely clear of the water most of the time, with the International Moth leading the dinghy classes. Foils are even capable of lifting a large multihull completely clear of the water and allowing it to achieve unprecedented speeds.

Olympics

One of the pinnacles of the diverse sport of sailing is, of course, the Olympic Games. The Olympics have events for several different classes of boat for men and women, including dinghies, single- and double-handed, heavy and light. Catamaran and windsurfing disciplines are included, although after 2012, the keelboat event is to be dropped. The leading

Olympic sailors are full-time, professional athletes who spend hours in the gym and training on the water. A successful Olympic campaign can lead a top sailor into many other areas of the sport, including offshore and inshore yacht racing and the America's Cup.

Ocean racing

In its amateur heyday in the 1970s and 1980s, offshore and ocean racing thrived through the stimulus of adventure and competition. Offshore races in Europe, the United States, and Australia were highly popular and led to rapid design development and new equipment and techniques.

The highlight of this era was the Whitbread Round the World Race, which provided plenty of adventure and competition. Numerous amateur sailors made their names and reputations sailing in this race and many became members of the first generation of professional offshore sailors as sponsorship came to the sport of yacht racing.

Today, the Whitbread Round the World Race has evolved into the Volvo Ocean Race, an event owned by its sponsor in which there is no room for amateurs and no choice of yachts. The event is the summit of round-the-world, fully crewed racing, and is sailed on yachts in the Volvo 70 class. These yachts are extremely powerful, fast, and brutal to sail offshore. The crews are all full-time professional racers who are recruited by heavily sponsored teams. The focus of the race is now on delivering boat sponsors and audiences in key markets to the event, and the route of this race is quite different from the traditional round-the-world course.

A different formula has been followed by the French organizers of the premier single-handed,

RACING ACROSS OCEANS
Professional teams in the Volvo Ocean Race (such as Puma, pictured here), race around the world at speeds that can reach over 30 knots and provide intense competition.

nonstop, round-the-world race, the Vendée Globe. Sponsorship is still a crucial part of the staging of this event, especially for the competitors. This challenging competition is nonstop, starting and finishing in France, and follows the classic round-the-world sailing route south of all the great capes.

The yachts are built to the Open 60 rule, which allows freedom for development and a variety of design approaches. These boats are also very fast and powerful, yet have to be handled by a single sailor. This really is the ultimate race for the single-handed sailor; it provides the purest test of the individual against the elements, as well as against a large fleet of competitors. The Vendée Globe is hugely popular with the French public and, increasingly, with an international audience.

Offshore and round-the-world racing can be hard for the individual to get into. Individuals pay to race aboard a skippered yacht, with training before the race usually included in the price. The largest event of this type is the biennial Clipper Round the World Race.

EXTREME RACING

The Extreme 40 class is a fully professional series that performs in venues around the world. In this latest form of "stadium racing," the race takes place close to the shore to bring high-speed action within view of shore-side spectators.

In this event, a fleet of large one-design yachts, all owned by the event organizer and each with a professional skipper, races around the world on a course with a number of legs. Individuals can pay to compete in the whole race or individual legs. Each race yacht is usually sponsored by a city or region, which also hosts one of the race stopovers.

Stadium racing

At the opposite end of the sport from round-the-world racing, is the rapid growth in match racing and the new phenomenon of stadium-type events.

The professional Extreme 40 international circuit has brought high-octane racing in very fast Extreme 40 catamarans to shore-based audiences, with the racing taking place often within yards of the shore or harbor wall. These short-course, "crash-and-burn" events, with races lasting only a few minutes and plenty of high-speed incidents, have proven a hit with spectators and online audiences.

Match racing, with its one-on-one format is also ideally suited to the stadium environment and a professional match-racing circuit has evolved, complete with professional teams and sponsors, and live broadcast and online coverage.

America's Cup

The America's Cup is probably the best-known sailing event, since it is the world's oldest, continuously contested sporting trophy. Unlike any other sporting event, however, the

America's Cup is as much a contest about money, ego, and lawyers as it is about sporting prowess. In fact, for many followers, the lead up to the event as well as the event itself can be as compelling as a soap opera.

After over a century and a half of competition, the latest format is match racing in 72 ft (21.9 m) wingsail catamarans with a preliminary America's Cup World Series in a smaller, 45 ft (13.7 m) version.

America Cup teams are funded by a mix of superrich individuals and corporate sponsors and include the best design, support, and racing talent in the sport. The top sailors from other disciplines, including the Olympics and match racing, often lead these fully professional teams.

Superyachts and classics

The development of the superyacht sector has been a significant change in sailing in recent years. New materials and technologies have led to the ability to build much larger yachts than ever before. Wealthy individuals have worked with specialized designers to develop yachts, both power and sail, that are larger than anything previously seen, having more in common with commercial shipping than normal yachts.

The growing classic yacht sector employs significant numbers of professional sailors and support staff. Some of the most historic and beautiful yachts of earlier eras have been restored or re-created, using the best new materials. This has made it practical to cruise, race, and charter these yachts with relatively small professional crews.

Ocean cruising

While the competitive side of sailing gets the most attention, there are thousands of sailors for whom sailing

CLASSIC SUPERYACHT
Restored or modern classic yachts are often in the superyacht category and require large, professional crews to sail and race.

is a way of life and a means of traveling the globe. There has been a tremendous growth in the numbers of amateur sailors cruising the world on small and medium-sized yachts, enjoying the self-sufficient, nomadic lifestyle that only a cruising yacht can provide.

Getting started

In this varied sport, it can be difficult to know where and how to get started, but when you begin to explore the opportunities you are likely to find that there are lots of people and organizations ready to

help. If you have friends or family who sail, show your interest and ask them to take you sailing. Find a club in your local area and ask how to get involved. Read sailing books like this one, magazines, and online sources to find out more and see where your interest leads.

A good way to start is by taking a beginner's course at a club or sailing school. From there you'll find plenty of advice and assistance to take your interest further.

So, if you think sailing could be for you, don't hesitate, get started and join us on the water!

FIRST PRINCIPLES

There are a number of basic principles and terms that are common to all types of sailing—whether your boat is a small dinghy, an ocean-going yacht, or anything in between. If you are new to the sport, you should acquaint yourself with these principles so that you have a thorough understanding of the fundamentals of good sailing before you go afloat for the first time.

SAFETY AFLOAT

Water is a potentially hostile environment, so safety is an important consideration whenever you go afloat. Sailing is not a particularly dangerous sport as long as a few sensible guidelines are followed, including wearing suitable clothing and using appropriate buoyancy gear. You should aim to develop a healthy respect for the water and only sail within the limits of your experience. This will minimize any risks and help to ensure that your sailing is not marred by accidents.

Choosing clothing

There is a huge variety of modern clothing and safety gear now available for all types of sailing, from wind-surfing to offshore cruising. Do not be tempted to rush out and buy a whole new wardrobe of expensive gear as soon as you decide to try sailing. Gain some experience in a boat first. This will help you to decide what sort of sailing attracts you most and, from this, you can choose the kind of gear that will be most appropriate for your needs. What you wear when sailing will also depend on the weather and the air and water temperatures. Some boats are wetter than others, but whatever boat you are sailing, there is always a chance that you will get wet, if only from spray, so choose your clothing accordingly.

Staying warm

The key to comfort on the water is to stay warm. As a general rule, it is wise to wear one more layer than you think you will need. Do not go sailing in only swimming gear. It is never as hot afloat as you think, unless there is no wind and baking sunshine, in which case you risk severe sunburn.

For your first few sailing trips you can make do with comfortable pants and sweaters; avoid jeans and cotton tops as these become cold when wet. Wool is the best natural material, but most effective of all are garments made from synthetic pile, which are very light and warm. They wick water away from the skin and dry extremely quickly.

Heat loss is one of the biggest dangers that you face when sailing. Prolonged exposure to cold will quickly lead to exhaustion, and the speed with which this occurs always surprises the inexperienced. If immersed in water at 62°F (17°C), even a healthy person, clothed normally and not exerting himself, will lose consciousness in two to three hours. If the water is colder or rough, survival time will be considerably reduced. Even aboard the boat, energy levels quickly deteriorate if you allow yourself to get wet and cold.

Keeping dry

As a general rule, to stay warm while sailing you need to keep as dry as possible. This is achieved by wearing a waterproof layer over your warm

WEARING THE RIGHT GEAR
Always wear clothing that is appropriate to the type of sailing and the conditions. Here, the crew is wearing light, inshore sailing waterproofs and life jackets.

CONTROLLING HEAT
Wear several thin layers rather than one thick one. Layers increase insulation by trapping air; heat control is simply a matter of removing or adding a layer.

clothing. Multipurpose windbreakers and overalls will see you through your first few sails, but eventually you will want to buy sailing clothing suited to your specific requirements.

The alternative to keeping warm by staying dry is to wear a close-fitting neoprene wetsuit, which is designed to trap a thin layer of water between the material and the skin (*pp.64–67*). The water is quickly warmed to near body temperature by your body heat. Sailors in high-performance dinghies commonly wear wetsuits, but if you are sailing for recreation rather than racing, then you may choose to wear waterproofs. A wetsuit is not appropriate aboard a larger boat where you can more easily stay dry, so choose waterproof pants and jacket.

Avoiding sunburn
Protection from the sun is important when sailing because reflection from the water, even in overcast weather, quickly produces sunburn. Remember to apply a sunscreen of at least factor 15 to all exposed skin before you go afloat, and reapply it at intervals.

Sunglasses that filter out the sun's ultraviolet rays are essential to protect your eyes while sailing, and it is often worth wearing a hat to keep direct sunlight off your head. Use a suitable retainer, such as a length of cord, to keep your hat and sunglasses secure.

PERSONAL BUOYANCY
Personal buoyancy is essential for anyone using a small boat, whether rowing a tender to a larger yacht, dinghy sailing, or windsurfing. Do not go afloat in a dinghy unless you are wearing either a buoyancy aid or a life jacket, and make sure that it is properly fastened.

Types of personal buoyancy
A buoyancy aid is designed to provide some support when you are in the water with the minimum amount of physical restriction. A life jacket is more cumbersome to wear, but it provides total support. It is designed to turn an unconscious person face upward to facilitate breathing.

Buoyancy aids
Buoyancy aids (*p.67*) use closed-cell foam in a vest or waistcoat-type jacket that is comfortable to wear, which makes them the usual choice for racing-dinghy sailors or inland sailors. They are often worn over a wetsuit (which also provides a degree of buoyancy).

Life jackets
Sea sailors may choose the additional security of a life jacket (*p.216*). These These are available in a variety of styles to suit all shapes and sizes, but you must make sure you buy a size that is suitable for your body weight. Some life jackets use closed-cell foam to provide all the buoyancy, but most use manual or automatic gas inflation and are worn deflated until required.

SAILING ACCESSORIES
When sailing, it is important to consider protection for your head, hands, and feet. You will probably be able to make do with what you already own until you gain some experience; then you can buy extra gear as necessary to suit your needs.

Headgear
One-third of body heat is lost through the head, so a warm hat or balaclava will make a significant contribution to your comfort on colder days. On sunny days, a hat will help to prevent sunburn and sunstroke. Tie long hair back or secure it under a hat. This prevents it from blowing around and getting in your eyes or being caught in the rigging—which can be painful.

Gloves
Wear gloves to protect your hands and keep them warm. Specialized sailing gloves—which have nonslip, reinforced palms and fingers to help your grip—will resist wear from ropes. Open-fingered sailing gloves, which allow you to deal with more intricate tasks, are also available. Fleece-lined mittens can be used on cruisers when sailing in cold weather, but they are too restrictive for use in a dinghy.

Footwear
Correct footwear will protect your feet and provide the grip you need to stay upright and on the boat. Shoes and boots for sailing should have flat, nonslip soles without a heel. Do not sail in bare feet as you will risk injury from deck gear.

Sailing knife
A stainless-steel sailing knife with retractable blade and shackle key can be attached to a length of line and tied to your waist. Keep the blade sharp for cutting rope and use the key to fasten and undo shackles.

PARTS OF A BOAT

Knowing and understanding the names used for the different parts of a boat are important first steps in learning to sail. These names, along with the terms used to describe the various maneuvers, are part of the language of sailing, which has developed over centuries to define all aspects of seamanship. All sailing boats have a number of parts in common, and, while it is not necessary to memorize the contents of the nautical dictionary, it will help if you are familiar with the basic terms.

The hull and foils

The hull is the body of the boat, which provides the buoyancy to float itself, equipment, and crew. In most dinghies, and in many larger boats, the hull is commonly constructed of glass-reinforced plastic (GRP), but dinghies may also be built of wood or molded plastic. Cruiser hulls can also be made of aluminum, steel, or ferro-cement.

To reduce sideways drift (leeway), the hull of a sailing boat has a foil underneath called a keel. Dinghies usually have a movable keel called a centerboard or a daggerboard. Larger boats have keels that are usually fixed permanently under the boat and, unlike movable keels, provide stability through their weight.

A centerboard is adjusted by pivoting it within its case. It is brought up out of the way when launching or recovering a dinghy, and it is rarely removed from its case. A daggerboard moves vertically. It is lifted out of its case when the boat is not in use, and it is often stored in a protective bag.

The rudder

A rudder is used to steer the boat. In a dinghy, it is controlled with the tiller, which usually has an extension that allows the helmsman to sit on the side of the boat. Dinghy rudders can either have a lifting or a fixed blade. A lifting blade is useful as it can be raised when sailing to and from the shore. A fixed blade is common in racing dinghies as it is lighter and potentially stronger, but it makes the boat harder to sail in shallow water. In larger yachts, the rudder is often controlled by a wheel mounted on a pedestal in the cockpit.

The rig and fittings

The rig (p.26)—comprising a mast, boom, and sail or sails—harnesses the wind and converts its force into drive to push the boat forward. Details of rigs depend on whether the boat is a dinghy or a larger cruiser, and will also vary between individual models.

In most boats, the mast is supported by a system of wires called the standing rigging. However, single-handed dinghies often have a freestanding mast without any of the standing rigging found on other boats.

Sails are hoisted and controlled by ropes collectively known as the running rigging. Blocks (pulleys) and tackles (pulley systems) help to adjust and control the running rigging, while cleats are used to secure ropes. Control systems range from very simple on basic dinghies to highly complex on high-performance dinghies and cruiser-racers, on which the crew can adjust sail shape and mast bend to maximize performance.

A DINGHY HULL

Most dinghy hulls have a pointed bow, but some smaller ones have a square bow known as a pram bow, which increases buoyancy forward and adds room inside. Many have a foredeck covering the bow area, and sidedecks along the sides. A thwart provides a seat across the boat, and side benches often run under the sidedecks. A case for a centerboard or daggerboard runs fore and aft in the middle of the boat, with a slot that allows the board to project through the bottom of the hull.

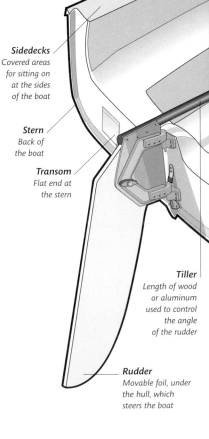

Sidedecks
Covered areas for sitting on at the sides of the boat

Stern
Back of the boat

Transom
Flat end at the stern

Tiller
Length of wood or aluminum used to control the angle of the rudder

Rudder
Movable foil, under the hull, which steers the boat

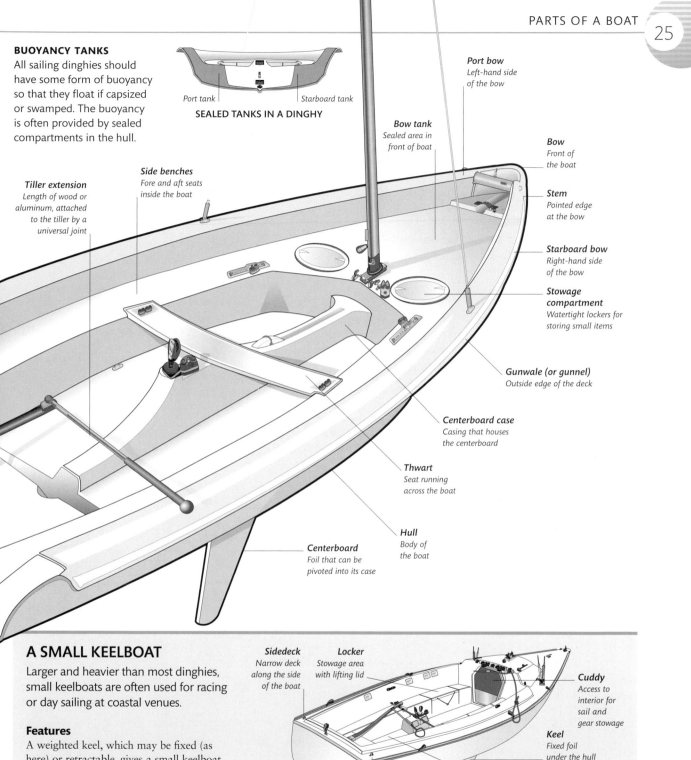

BUOYANCY TANKS
All sailing dinghies should have some form of buoyancy so that they float if capsized or swamped. The buoyancy is often provided by sealed compartments in the hull.

Port tank | *Starboard tank*
SEALED TANKS IN A DINGHY

Port bow
Left-hand side of the bow

Bow tank
Sealed area in front of boat

Bow
Front of the boat

Stem
Pointed edge at the bow

Starboard bow
Right-hand side of the bow

Stowage compartment
Watertight lockers for storing small items

Tiller extension
Length of wood or aluminum, attached to the tiller by a universal joint

Side benches
Fore and aft seats inside the boat

Gunwale (or gunnel)
Outside edge of the deck

Centerboard case
Casing that houses the centerboard

Thwart
Seat running across the boat

Hull
Body of the boat

Centerboard
Foil that can be pivoted into its case

A SMALL KEELBOAT

Larger and heavier than most dinghies, small keelboats are often used for racing or day sailing at coastal venues.

Features

A weighted keel, which may be fixed (as here) or retractable, gives a small keelboat greater stability than a dinghy and minimizes the risk of the boat's capsizing. The large cockpit provides room for several crew.

Sidedeck
Narrow deck along the side of the boat

Locker
Stowage area with lifting lid

Cuddy
Access to interior for sail and gear stowage

Keel
Fixed foil under the hull

Rudder
Movable foil under the hull

Mooring cleat
Used to secure a mooring rope

Cockpit
Area from which the boat is sailed

THE RIG

Many sailing dinghies are rigged as a Bermudan sloop with a mainsail and a jib, both of which are triangular in shape. The jib, which is set on the forestay, adds drive and makes the mainsail more efficient than it would be alone. In addition, many dinghies carry a spinnaker (*pp.144–155*) for increased sailing downwind. Standing rigging includes all the wires and ropes that support the mast and boom, while running rigging is used to hoist and control the sails.

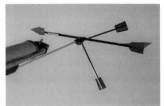

WIND INDICATOR

Small vane at the masthead to indicate wind direction. A burgee (small pennant) may be hoisted instead.

Battens
Strips of wood or fiberglass that slip into pockets on the sail to support its leech (curved outer edge). Battens can be short, as in the lower two here, or full-length as in the upper two

Jib
Triangular sail at the front of the boat, attached to the bow and hoisted in front of the mast

Forestay
Some small boats have a wire that runs from the mast to the bow to support the mast. Others (as here), use a thin rope, which is removable when the jib is hoisted

Gooseneck
Universal joint that attaches the boom to the mast

Spreaders
Aluminum or wooden tubes between the mast and shrouds for additional mast support

Mainsail
Large, triangular sail set behind the mast

Mast
Upright pole, usually aluminum, that supports the sails and may be stepped on the deck or the bottom of the hull

Boom
Horizontal pole, usually aluminum, to which the foot of the mainsail is attached

Shrouds
Wires on port and starboard sides that support the mast

Mast step
Socket in which the heel of the mast sits

SAILS

Most small boat sails are triangular and made from Dacron (a woven cloth) or Mylar (a laminated film material). They often have reinforced patches in high-load areas such as the three corners.

Head
Top corner

Leech
Aft edge

Luff
Front, leading edge

REINFORCED CORNER

Parts of a sail
Each edge of a sail has a name: the luff is the leading edge; the leech is the aft edge; and the foot is the bottom edge. The corners are also named: the head, tack, and clew.

Roach
Additional curved area on the leech outside a straight line from head to clew

Tack
Bottom, forward corner

Foot
Bottom edge

Clew
Bottom, aft corner

RUNNING RIGGING

Halyards hoist the sails, and sheets control them. The mainsheet controls the mainsail, and it usually has a tackle system that employs a combination of blocks to increase the power of the helmsman's pull on the sheet. The jib is a smaller sail, so the jib sheets, which control it, do not usually require a tackle system.

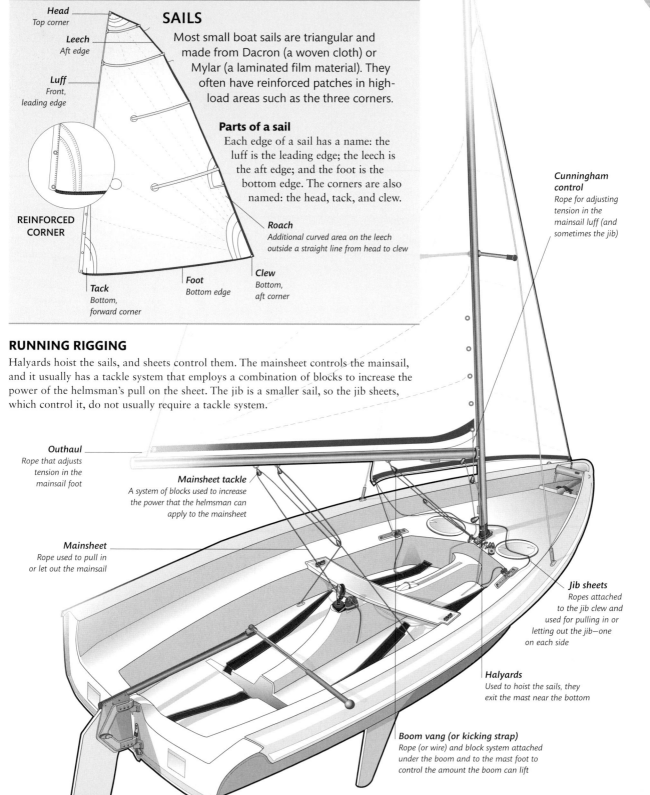

Cunningham control
Rope for adjusting tension in the mainsail luff (and sometimes the jib)

Outhaul
Rope that adjusts tension in the mainsail foot

Mainsheet tackle
A system of blocks used to increase the power that the helmsman can apply to the mainsheet

Mainsheet
Rope used to pull in or let out the mainsail

Jib sheets
Ropes attached to the jib clew and used for pulling in or letting out the jib—one on each side

Halyards
Used to hoist the sails, they exit the mast near the bottom

Boom vang (or kicking strap)
Rope (or wire) and block system attached under the boom and to the mast foot to control the amount the boom can lift

SMALL-BOAT FITTINGS

Various fittings are attached to the boat to help the crew control the rig and sails. Fairleads, which may be fixed, or mounted on a track for adjustment, are used to guide ropes. Cleats are used to secure halyards and control lines, and are also often used to secure the sheets so that the helmsman and crew are not required to hold them continuously. Other fittings include the toe straps, which allow the crew to sit out, and block-and-tackle systems that help to control the running rigging. Boats intended for novices usually have simple fittings but more complex equipment will be found on high-performance boats.

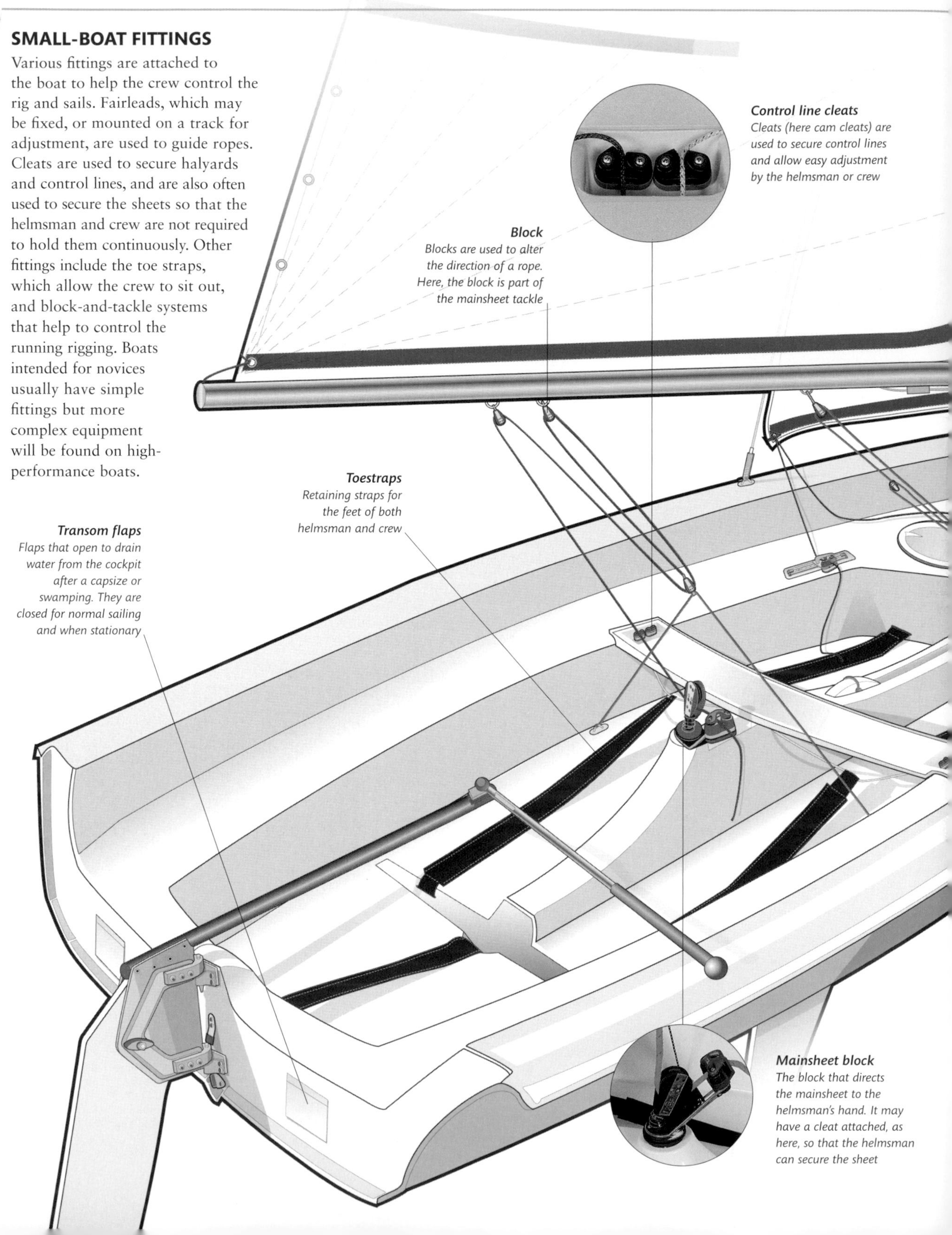

Control line cleats
Cleats (here cam cleats) are used to secure control lines and allow easy adjustment by the helmsman or crew

Block
Blocks are used to alter the direction of a rope. Here, the block is part of the mainsheet tackle

Toestraps
Retaining straps for the feet of both helmsman and crew

Transom flaps
Flaps that open to drain water from the cockpit after a capsize or swamping. They are closed for normal sailing and when stationary

Mainsheet block
The block that directs the mainsheet to the helmsman's hand. It may have a cleat attached, as here, so that the helmsman can secure the sheet

Jib fairlead
Smooth eye or rotating pulley for altering the direction of the jib sheet. The sheet is led through the fairlead to a cleat. The fairlead may be fixed, or mounted on a track for adjustment, as here

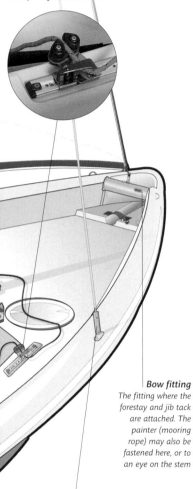

RELATIVE TERMS

On shore, we usually describe the position of things in relation to ourselves—"left," "right," "in front," or "behind." On the water, they are always described in relation to the boat or the wind.

The boat
The terms "port" and "starboard" relate to the boat. Facing the bow, the port side is to the left and the starboard side is to the right.

The wind
Windward and leeward relate to the wind. The windward side of the boat is the side toward the wind; the leeward side is the side away from the wind.

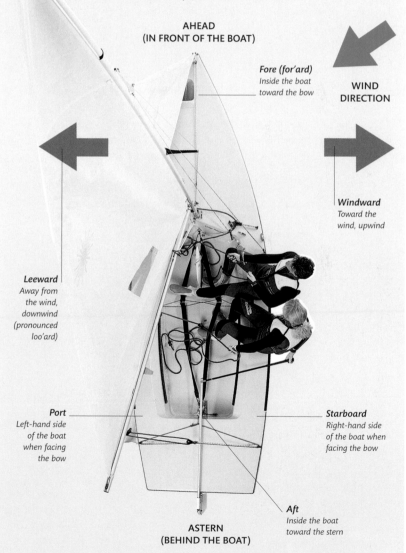

**AHEAD
(IN FRONT OF THE BOAT)**

Fore (for'ard)
Inside the boat toward the bow

**WIND
DIRECTION**

Windward
Toward the wind, upwind

Leeward
Away from the wind, downwind (pronounced loo'ard)

Bow fitting
The fitting where the forestay and jib tack are attached. The painter (mooring rope) may also be fastened here, or to an eye on the stem

Port
Left-hand side of the boat when facing the bow

Starboard
Right-hand side of the boat when facing the bow

Shroud adjusters
Metal plates that secure the shrouds to the hull and allow adjustment to rake the mast backward or forward

Aft
Inside the boat toward the stern

**ASTERN
(BEHIND THE BOAT)**

ESSENTIAL EQUIPMENT

As well as any removable rigging, there are several other items that should be aboard when you go afloat, especially if you are sailing without a safety boat present. In particular, there has to be some means of propelling the boat if you cannot sail. There must also be adequate buoyancy to keep the boat afloat in the event of a capsize, as well as bailing gear. An anchor and warp (anchor line) are also important if you sail on the sea. All equipment must be stowed safely so that it stays in place if the boat heels or capsizes.

Paddles or oars

You must always carry at least one paddle so that you can move the boat in a calm. A pair of oars is useful if you sail on the sea and have a larger, general-purpose dinghy with the space to stow them. They are more efficient than a paddle, but you will need a pair of rowlocks mounted in sockets on the gunwales. Some oars are jointed in the middle for easier stowage.

Buoyancy

Buoyancy must be sufficient, but not excessive, and it must be distributed so that the boat floats level when capsized. Buoyancy is usually provided either by tanks that are permanently built into the structure, as is the case with most modern dinghies, or by removable buoyant materials, such as inflatable airbags, which must be securely attached to the hull.

Bailers

All dinghies will get water in them even if they do not capsize, and it is important to be able to remove it easily. Apart from making you wetter than necessary, water that is allowed to build up in the bottom of the boat will slop from side to side and make the boat heel more.

Many modern dinghies have open transoms that allow any water in the boat to flow straight out through the stern. When the boat has a solid transom, bailing may be done automatically through retractable self-bailers, which are lowered when the boat is moving. The flow of water under the hull and past the bailer sucks the water out from inside the boat. Most have a nonreturn valve to prevent water from entering the boat when it slows down, but it is best to raise them if you stop. Remember to retract them to avoid damage when taking the boat out of the water.

Anchor and warp

An anchor can be an important piece of equipment, particularly for sailing at sea without safety cover. In the event of an accident, a foul tide, calm weather, or even if you just need a rest, it allows you to stop the boat in shallow water without drifting on the wind or tide.

A small, folding anchor (*opposite*) can be a good choice because it takes up little space, but when anchoring for any length of time, a small burying anchor should be used. A burying anchor digs into the seabed and provides more security than a folding anchor. You will also need an anchor warp, which can also be used if your boat needs to be towed. Be sure to stow the anchor and warp securely.

HOW TO BAIL

Automatic self-bailers fitted in the bottom can be opened to let the water out when you are sailing fast. Some boats have transom flaps that allow the water to flow out after a capsize. Alternatively, you can bail by hand using a scoop bailer.

SCOOP BAILER

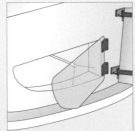

BAILING BY HAND
Always bail over the leeward side of the boat or else the water may be blown back on board (or into your face). A bucket is best for removing a large amount of water after a capsize; a scoop bailer is useful for smaller quantities. Get rid of the last few drops with a sponge.

TRANSOM FLAP
Hinged flaps in the transom get rid of water quickly after a capsize or swamping.

Stowing gear

There is very little room for extra items in a small boat, so store everything carefully. If the boat has a foredeck, use the area underneath for things that you want to keep dry, such as spare clothes, which are best put in waterproof bags beforehand. Place heavy items, including the anchor, near the middle of the boat, so that they do not affect fore and aft trim. Any space under the sidedecks can be used for storing oars or paddles.

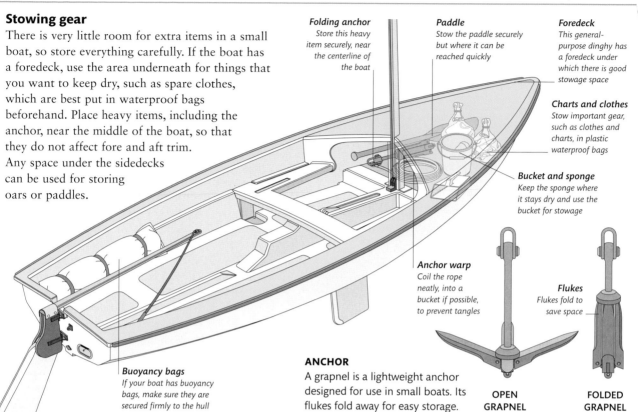

Folding anchor
Store this heavy item securely, near the centerline of the boat

Paddle
Stow the paddle securely but where it can be reached quickly

Foredeck
This general-purpose dinghy has a foredeck under which there is good stowage space

Charts and clothes
Stow important gear, such as clothes and charts, in plastic waterproof bags

Bucket and sponge
Keep the sponge where it stays dry and use the bucket for stowage

Anchor warp
Coil the rope neatly, into a bucket if possible, to prevent tangles

Flukes
Flukes fold to save space

Buoyancy bags
If your boat has buoyancy bags, make sure they are secured firmly to the hull

ANCHOR

A grapnel is a lightweight anchor designed for use in small boats. Its flukes fold away for easy storage.

OPEN GRAPNEL

FOLDED GRAPNEL

EFFICIENT BOAT BUOYANCY

The ideal amount of buoyancy will allow the boat to float level on its side when capsized, with the centerboard within reach. The boat will have relatively little water in it when righted.

Checking built-in tanks

Most built-in tanks have removable bungs that should be taken out when the boat is not being used, to allow trapped water to drain away. Any inspection hatches should also be removed when the boat is not afloat.

Checking buoyancy bags

Check buoyancy bags to be sure that there are no leaks and that the fastenings are firm; there should be at least three straps on each bag. When the boat is capsized or full of water, the fastenings take an enormous load. It is vital that they do not break, as the boat could then sink or be impossible to right.

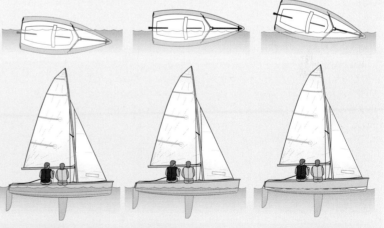

TOO LITTLE
With too little buoyancy, the boat floats low in the water. It is difficult to right when capsized because of the weight of water and comes up with a lot of water on board (*above*).

CORRECT
With the correct buoyancy in the hull, the boat floats level when capsized, and is fairly easy to right. When righted (*above*), the boat comes up with relatively little water on board.

TOO MUCH
With too much buoyancy, the boat sits high in the water and is likely to invert, which makes recovery harder. When righted (*above*), there will be little water on board.

HOW BOATS SAIL

When you begin sailing, it is not essential to know any of the theory of sailing but it is a great aid to learning if you have some understanding of how sails work to drive the boat. By studying some of the theory alongside sessions on the water, you will spend less time learning by trial and error.

Driving force

Sailing boats derive their power from the wind flowing across the curved surfaces of the sails. This is very similar to the way an airplane wing produces lift to keep the plane in the air. A sail, like an airplane wing, works at its best at one small angle to the wind. Therefore, efficient sailing requires constant sail adjustment (trimming) to keep the sails at the correct angle to the wind. If a sail is let out too far, it will simply flap like a flag and produce no forward drive. If it is pulled in too much, the airflow over the sail's surface will break down and the sail will stall—just like an aircraft that tries to fly too slowly.

Sideways force

Not all of the force produced by the sails pushes the boat forward, except when the boat is on a run with the wind directly behind it. At other times, the total force produced by the sail has a sideways element that attempts to push the boat sideways. The strength of the sideways force depends on the point of sailing the boat is on. The sideways force is at its greatest when the boat is close-hauled, and diminishes as the boat bears away from the wind (*p.35*).

On all points of sailing, if a sail is pulled in too far so that it stalls, the driving force drops rapidly, while the sideways force increases. The boat slows down and heels more.

Role of the keel

A keel, centerboard, or daggerboard, is used to resist the sideways force. The keel's area must be sufficient to resist the sideways force created when close-hauled. In dinghies, the keel's area can be varied by raising the centerboard, but a keelboat has a fixed amount of keel underwater.

Although the keel resists the sideways force, it is not completely eliminated, and on upwind courses, a sailing boat always slips sideways slightly. The difference between the course steered and the course actually sailed is called leeway (*opposite*).

Heeling force

Because the sideways force generated by the sails acts some distance above the waterline, it has the effect of trying to heel the boat. The keel resists the sideways force but acts under the water, so the sideways resistance provided by the keel increases the heeling effect. The heeling force has to be counterbalanced by a dinghy crew's weight or by the weight of the keel in a keelboat.

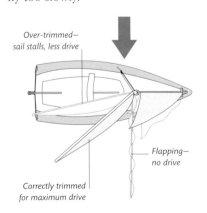

THE CORRECT TRIM
To find the correct trim for a sail, let it out until it begins to flap at the luff, then pull it in until the shaking just stops. Repeat regularly to check the trim.

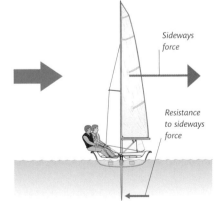

SIDEWAYS FORCE
Part of the total force produced by the sails pushes the boat sideways. The sideways force is resisted underwater by the centerboard or keel.

HEELING FORCE
The vertical separation between the sideways force from the sails and the resistance from the keel causes a force that acts to heel the boat.

TRUE AND APPARENT WIND

True wind is the wind which we feel when stationary. When we sail, we feel apparent wind, which is a combination of the true wind and the wind produced by our motion. Wind indicators on moving boats show apparent wind, while wind indicators ashore show true wind.

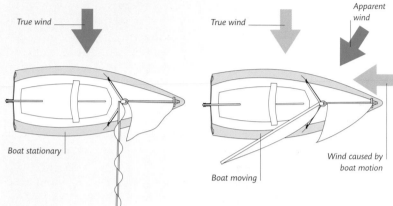

True wind

Boat stationary

True wind

Apparent wind

Wind caused by boat motion

Boat moving

TRUE WIND

The only time you feel the true wind afloat is when the boat is stationary. Check the true wind direction by using flags ashore or on moored boats, or by smoke from chimneys ashore.

APPARENT WIND

When the boat moves, it creates its own wind, which combines with the true wind to form the apparent wind. Apparent wind is always farther ahead than the true wind direction except on a dead run.

UNDERSTANDING LEEWAY

As you sail on upwind courses, you will notice that your boat slips sideways to some extent. Called leeway, this sideways drift is at its greatest when you are sailing close-hauled.

Minimizing leeway

Make sure that your centerboard or daggerboard is fully down when sailing close-hauled, and is set correctly on other points of sailing. Leeway is most noticeable when you are sailing slowly because the keel cannot work at maximum efficiency, so maintain speed to minimize leeway. When sailing close-hauled, do not try to steer farther to windward to counteract leeway as the boat will simply slow down and leeway will increase.

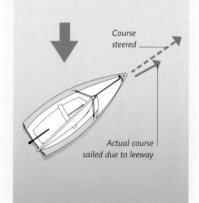

Course steered

Actual course sailed due to leeway

THE EFFECT OF LEEWAY

Leeway is the difference between the course steered through the water and the course that the boat achieves, which is to leeward of the course steered.

CLOSE-HAULED

The helmsman and crew of this dinghy are sitting on the sidedeck to use their weight to help balance the heeling force while sailing close-hauled.

THE DYNAMICS OF SAILING

Sail force

A properly trimmed sail deflects the airflow, which splits at the leading edge of the sail. The airflow moving across the convex (leeward) surface

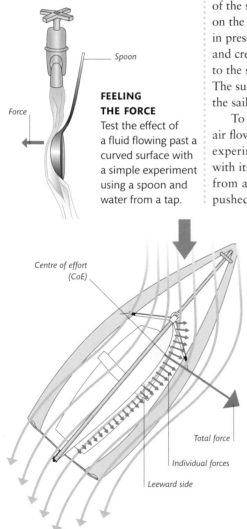

Spoon

Force

FEELING THE FORCE
Test the effect of a fluid flowing past a curved surface with a simple experiment using a spoon and water from a tap.

has to travel farther than that moving across the concave (windward) side and speeds up accordingly. When the airflow moves faster, its pressure drops and so the pressure on the convex side of the sail is lower than the pressure on the concave side. The difference in pressure sucks the sail to leeward and creates a force at right angles to the sail at all points on its surface. The sum of these individual forces on the sail drives the boat forward.

To understand the effect when air flows around a sail, try this simple experiment: hold a spoon lightly, with its back to the stream of water from a faucet. Rather than being pushed away from the stream, as

you might expect, the spoon will be sucked into the stream by the water flowing past the spoon's convex surface.

Sail shape

The curved shape of a sail determines the amount the wind must bend around it and the force it produces. The shape of a sail can be adjusted, within limits, by tensioning the outhaul, halyard or cunningham, and the sheet. Sails are adjusted to be flat in very light winds (when the wind has insufficient energy to bend around a full sail), full in light to moderate winds, and flat again in strong winds when the boat is over-powered.

Centre of effort (CoE)

Total force

Individual forces

Leeward side

AIRFLOW WITH ONE SAIL

As the wind flows across a sail, it moves faster on the leeward (convex) side, creating low pressure, and slower on the windward side, which creates a high-pressure area. This effectively sucks the sail to leeward and produces forces acting at right angles to the sail's surface at each point on the sail. The sum of these forces acts at what is known as the sail's center of effort (CoE).

AIRFLOW WITH TWO SAILS

When two sails are used, their interaction is critical to performance. Although the jib is much smaller than the mainsail, it is potentially a more efficient sail because it does not have a mast in front of it to disturb the airflow. The jib is trimmed so that the slot between the jib leech and the mainsail luff is parallel all the way up. The air flowing through the slot is compressed and will accelerate. This further decreases the pressure on the leeward side of the mainsail and so increases drive.

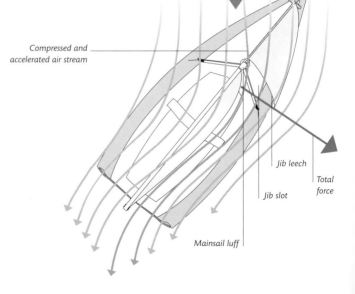

Compressed and accelerated air stream

Jib leech

Total force

Jib slot

Mainsail luff

Drive with two sails

When a jib is added in front of a mainsail, it creates its own drive in the same way as any single sail, but it also has the effect of increasing the efficiency of the mainsail. It does this by directing a stream of air along the convex (leeward) side of the mainsail. As the air flows through the slot between the jib leech and the mainsail luff, it is compressed between them and so it accelerates. This further reduces the pressure on the leeward side of the mainsail, and increases its drive significantly. This is the reason why most sailing boats are rigged with a mainsail and jib.

To work efficiently, the jib and mainsail must be trimmed so that the curve of the jib leech matches the curve of the mainsail luff on the leeward side. This produces a smooth slot between them and allows the air to flow smoothly and accelerate through the slot. If the jib is pulled in too much, or mainsail let out too much, the slot will be constricted and drive will be lost. If the jib is not pulled in sufficiently, or the mainsail is pulled in too much, the slot will be too wide, and drive will again be reduced.

Forward drive

All the individual forces that act on a sail's surface can be thought of as one force acting at a single point on the sail, which is known as the Center of Effort (CoE) of the sail.

To help understand the way in which the sails' force pushes the boat sideways as well as forward, the total force generated by the sails can be split into two elements at right angles to each other: a forward, driving force and a sideways force.

The relative sizes of the driving and sideways forces depends on the angle of the sails to the boat's centerline, which varies with the angle to the wind at which the boat is sailing. When sailing on a close-hauled course, the sails are pulled in tight, close to the centerline, and the sideways force is greater than the driving force. When the boat turns onto a reach, the sails are let out about halfway and the driving force increases, while the sideways force reduces. Turn further away from the wind, onto a run, when the sails are let out fully, and the driving force acts almost directly forward and the sideways force is zero.

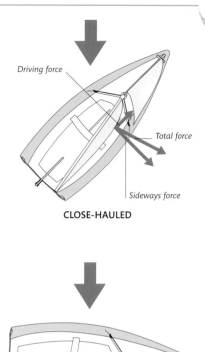

Driving force

Total force

Sideways force

CLOSE-HAULED

Driving force

Sideways force

Total force

REACHING

DRIVE AND SIDEWAYS FORCE
The relative strength of the driving and sideways forces depends on the angle of the sail to the boat's centerline, which varies with the point of sailing. When the boat is close-hauled (*top*), with the sails pulled in tight, drive is less than when reaching (*above*), and the sideways force is greater.

THE SLOT
Whatever the size of boat, the slot between the jib and the mainsail is vital for efficient sailing. Both sails must be trimmed together to keep the slot parallel between the jib leech and the mainsail through which the airflow can accelerate smoothly.

THE MAIN CONTROLS

Rudder, centerboard, sails, and crew weight are the main controls in a sailing dinghy. They need constant adjustment to keep the boat sailing efficiently, to steer, and to alter course. Knowing how to combine these controls to manage the movement of the boat is a very important aspect of learning how to sail. When sailing with a crew, the helmsman is usually responsible for the mainsail and the rudder (via the tiller and tiller extension), while the crew takes care of the centerboard and the jib.

Using the rudder
The rudder is moved using the tiller and the tiller extension, which the helmsman usually holds in the hand nearest to the stern. The extension is best held in a dagger-style grip with the end passing in front of your body. The rudder is effective only if it has water flowing past it, so you can only steer with it when the boat is moving. The quicker you are sailing, the more effective it becomes due to the speed of the water moving across it. When the boat is moving forward, the bow will turn in the direction opposite from the way in which the tiller is pushed. (When the boat is moving backward, the rudder action is reversed.)

Turning effect of the rudder
The rudder is the main control used to alter course. Practice using the tiller to turn the rudder, and

DAGGER GRIP
Hold the end of the tiller extension in a dagger-style grip and pass the end in front of your body.

familiarize yourself with its effects by sitting on the side of the boat opposite the sails and watching the direction in which the bow turns as you move the tiller.

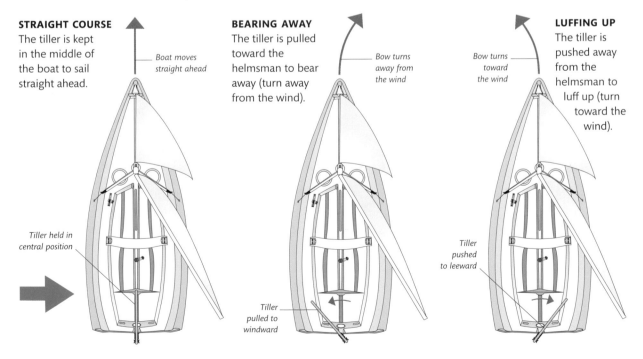

STRAIGHT COURSE
The tiller is kept in the middle of the boat to sail straight ahead.

Boat moves straight ahead

Tiller held in central position

BEARING AWAY
The tiller is pulled toward the helmsman to bear away (turn away from the wind).

Bow turns away from the wind

Tiller pulled to windward

LUFFING UP
The tiller is pushed away from the helmsman to luff up (turn toward the wind).

Bow turns toward the wind

Tiller pushed to leeward

Using the sails

A sail works best at a particular angle to the wind, known as the angle of attack (*p.32*), so it must be trimmed (adjusted) as you alter course, and checked regularly while sailing to be sure the setting is correct. To find the optimum angle, ease the sail out until it starts to shake at the luff (*p.27*), then pull it in again just far enough to stop it from shaking. Pull the sail in tight only when the boat is sailing close-hauled (*p.40*). As the boat turns away from the wind, the sails are let out (*p.40*) until, on a run, the sails are nearly at right angles to the centerline.

RUN
Sailing with the wind behind on a run (*p.40*), the sails are let out fully and the jib can be goosewinged.

CLOSE-HAULED
When sailing close-hauled, the sails are pulled in tight, close to the centerline, to achieve the correct angle to the wind.

Turning effect of the sails

To learn about the turning effects of the sails, let either sail out while keeping the other filled correctly and the boat upright. Allow the tiller extension to move freely in your hand and the boat will turn—toward the wind if the mainsail is full, and away from it if the jib is full.

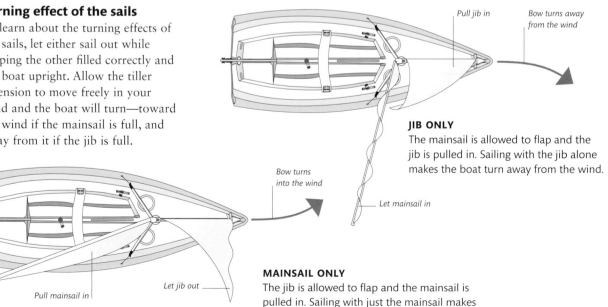

Pull jib in

Bow turns away from the wind

JIB ONLY
The mainsail is allowed to flap and the jib is pulled in. Sailing with the jib alone makes the boat turn away from the wind.

Let mainsail in

Bow turns into the wind

MAINSAIL ONLY
The jib is allowed to flap and the mainsail is pulled in. Sailing with just the mainsail makes the boat turn toward the wind.

Pull mainsail in

Let jib out

Using the crew's weight

A dinghy sails fastest when it is upright in the water, and when the heeling force (*p.37*) is balanced by the weight of the helmsman and crew. Their placement, fore and aft, also determines the boat's trim (how it sits in the water). The helmsman sits on the windward side, opposite the sails, so that he has a clear view of the sails and the course being steered. The crew moves his weight according to the point of sail and wind strength.

Depending on wind strength and the point of sailing, the crew may move from alongside the helmsman to sitting on the opposite side to balance the helmsman's weight to windward. By adjusting the position of his weight, the crew can also heel the boat to help it alter course.

SAILING UPRIGHT
Both the helmsman and crew use their weight to keep this dinghy upright. They sit out on the sidedeck with their feet under the toestraps to balance the boat.

Turning using the crew's weight

In addition to positioning the weight of helmsman and crew to keep the boat upright, their weight can also be used to help the boat turn when the helmsman wishes to change course. A boat will turn in the opposite direction from the way it is heeled; if the boat is heeled to windward by moving the crew's weight, it will turn to leeward. Heel it to leeward and it will turn to windward. Experiment by moving around the boat to see how it changes direction when it is balanced differently. When sailing with both a helmsman and crew, it becomes the responsibility of the crew to make any major adjustments to the boat balance.

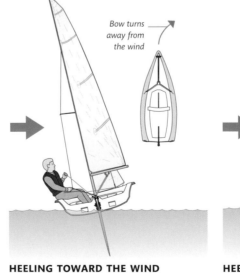

Bow turns away from the wind

HEELING TOWARD THE WIND
The helmsman moves his weight to heel the boat to windward so that the boat turns to leeward (away from the wind).

Bow turns toward the wind

HEELING AWAY FROM THE WIND
The helmsman moves his weight to heel the boat to leeward so that the boat turns to windward (toward the wind).

Using the centerboard

The effect of the centerboard (or daggerboard) is altered by moving the foil to different depths in the water. It is lowered when the boat is turned toward the wind and raised when the boat is turned away from the wind. The centerboard has a significant effect on the performance of the boat. It should be raised when you are sailing away from the wind, otherwise it will make the boat slower and more difficult to control. It must be lowered when turning toward the wind, otherwise the boat will simply slip rapidly sideways as there is nothing to counteract the sideways force of the wind (*p.33*).

DAGGERBOARD

A daggerboard moves vertically through its case and protrudes above deck as it is raised. Unlike a centerboard, it is not fixed in the case, so it can be removed and stored in a padded bag to prevent damage when the boat is not in use. It should have a retaining cord on its top edge so it cannot be lost in a capsize.

Fully down

Half down

Quarter down

DINGHY WITH DAGGERBOARD

CENTERBOARD

A centerboard pivots on a bolt through the centerboard case and rotates into its case as it is raised. As the centerboard is raised by pushing the top forward in the boat, so its tip moves aft in the water. Unlike a daggerboard, a centerboard's surface area moves aft as it is raised into its case.

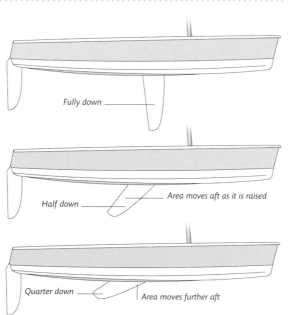

Fully down

Half down — Area moves aft as it is raised

Quarter down — Area moves further aft

DINGHY WITH CENTERBOARD

TACKING AND JIBING

The two most important maneuvers in sailing, tacking and jibing, involve using the main controls together to make a significant course change.

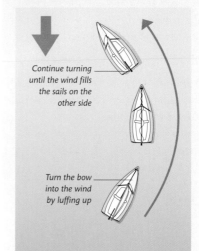

Continue turning until the wind fills the sails on the other side

Turn the bow into the wind by luffing up

TACKING

During a tack (*pp.90–93*), the bow of the boat is turned through the wind using the rudder, sails, and crew weight.

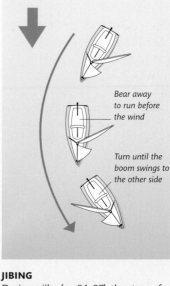

Bear away to run before the wind

Turn until the boom swings to the other side

JIBING

During a jibe (*pp.94–97*), the stern of the boat is turned through the wind using the rudder, sails, and crew weight.

POINTS OF SAILING

The direction in which a boat is being sailed is often described in relation to its angle to the wind. Collectively, these angles are known as the "points of sailing." When you change from one point of sailing to another, the sails, the centerboard, and the position of the crew all need to be adjusted to suit the new angle of the boat in relation to the wind.

SAILING COURSES

Various terms and phrases are used to clarify the direction and type of sailing course that you are on and to describe exactly what the boat is doing in relation to the wind.

Luffing and bearing away
If you turn the boat toward the wind you are luffing (or luffing up); if you turn away from it you are bearing away.

Upwind and offwind
All courses that are closer to the wind (heading more directly into it) than a beam reach are called upwind courses. Those farther away from the wind than a beam reach are known as offwind, or downwind, courses.

Port and starboard tack
The boom's position is used to describe which tack you are on. If it is over the port side of the boat, you are on starboard tack. If it is over the starboard side, you are on port tack. Even on a dead run with the wind directly astern you are still on one tack or the other, depending on which side your boom is on.

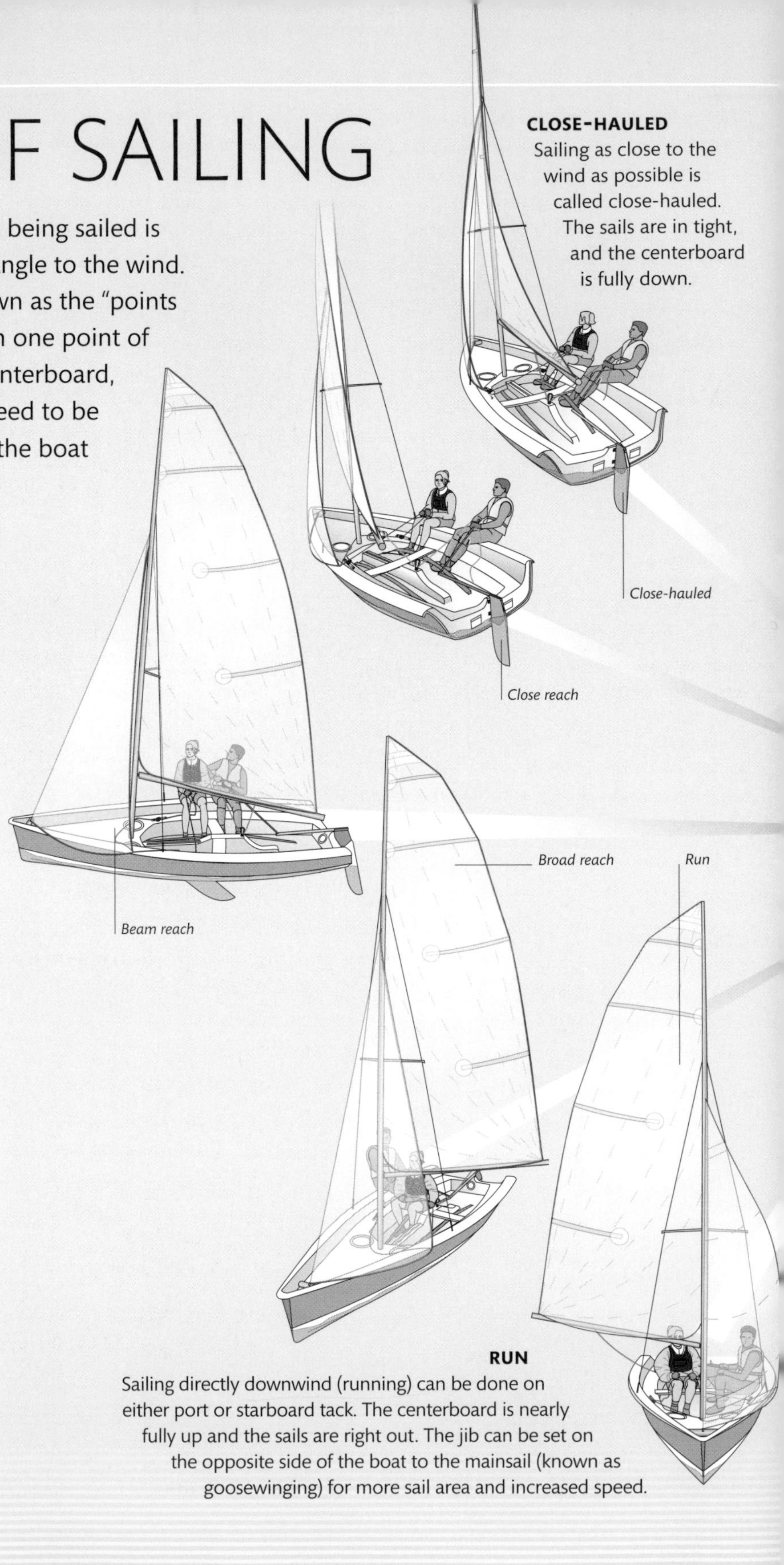

CLOSE-HAULED
Sailing as close to the wind as possible is called close-hauled. The sails are in tight, and the centerboard is fully down.

Close-hauled

Close reach

Beam reach

Broad reach

Run

RUN
Sailing directly downwind (running) can be done on either port or starboard tack. The centerboard is nearly fully up and the sails are right out. The jib can be set on the opposite side of the boat to the mainsail (known as goosewinging) for more sail area and increased speed.

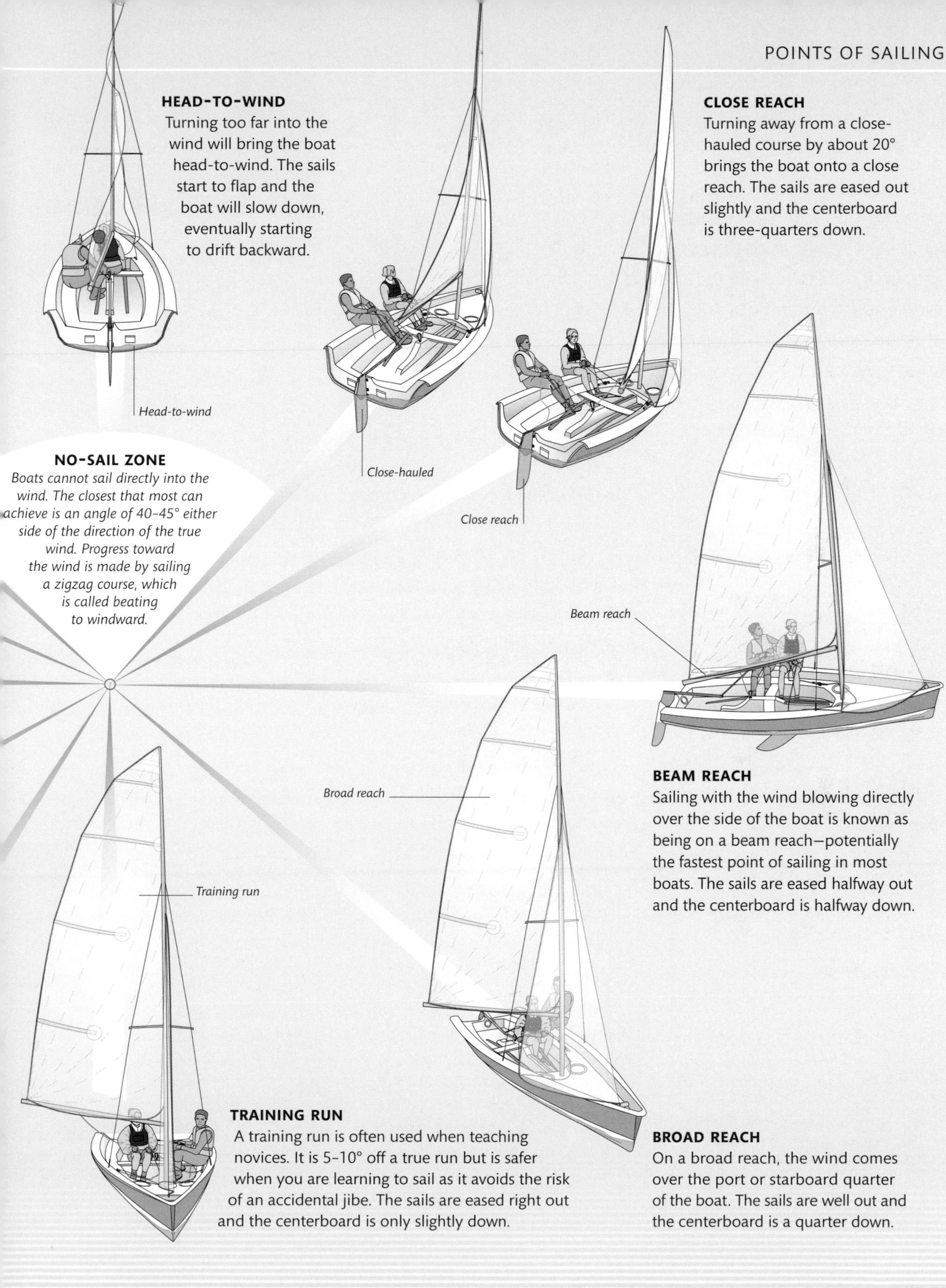

HEAD-TO-WIND

Turning too far into the wind will bring the boat head-to-wind. The sails start to flap and the boat will slow down, eventually starting to drift backward.

Head-to-wind

CLOSE REACH

Turning away from a close-hauled course by about 20° brings the boat onto a close reach. The sails are eased out slightly and the centerboard is three-quarters down.

Close-hauled

Close reach

NO-SAIL ZONE

Boats cannot sail directly into the wind. The closest that most can achieve is an angle of 40–45° either side of the direction of the true wind. Progress toward the wind is made by sailing a zigzag course, which is called beating to windward.

Beam reach

BEAM REACH

Sailing with the wind blowing directly over the side of the boat is known as being on a beam reach—potentially the fastest point of sailing in most boats. The sails are eased halfway out and the centerboard is halfway down.

Broad reach

Training run

TRAINING RUN

A training run is often used when teaching novices. It is 5–10° off a true run but is safer when you are learning to sail as it avoids the risk of an accidental jibe. The sails are eased right out and the centerboard is only slightly down.

BROAD REACH

On a broad reach, the wind comes over the port or starboard quarter of the boat. The sails are well out and the centerboard is a quarter down.

ROPES AND KNOTS

Used to secure the boat, and to hoist, trim, and adjust the sails, ropes are an essential feature of all sailing boats. To sail safely and efficiently, you need to understand how to handle rope and how to keep it neat when not in use. Learning a little about the different properties of the various types of rope will enable you to select the most suitable rope for any particular task. It is also vital to know how to tie the small selection of knots that are most useful for sailing.

CONTROL LINES
Racing boats typically have many control lines, which are often led to a central point where they are conveniently located for adjustment by the crew. It is helpful to color-code ropes and mark their cleats to avoid confusion.

TYPES OF ROPE

Rope can be made from many different fibers and in a number of ways. The material and the type of construction determine how the finished rope behaves in terms of stretch, strength, durability, and flexibility.

POLYPROPYLENE
Polypropylene is used to make low-cost, general-purpose, three-strand ropes that are light and will float.

POLYESTER
Polyester rope can be braided or three-strand. It is strong, with low stretch, and does not float.

NYLON
Nylon rope is strong and elastic. It does not float and loses strength when wet.

ARAMID AND HMP
Aramid fiber and high-modulus polyethylene ropes are very strong and light and have very low stretch. They are very slippery and require special splices and knots.

HANDLING ROPES

Modern sailing ropes are constructed using synthetic materials, which are lighter and much stronger than natural fibers. They are immune to rot caused by dampness—although nylon rope loses a significant amount of strength when wet—and are available in a range of colors for easy identification on the boat.

There are two main types of rope construction: three-strand rope, in which three sets (strands) of already twisted yarns are twisted together; and braided rope, in which the yarns and strands are braided together. Braided rope is taking over from three-strand for most uses on small boats, especially for ropes made from high-performance fibers.

The strength of a rope depends on the material, the construction method, and the diameter of the rope. High-performance ropes are exceptionally strong and have low stretch properties compared with older synthetic materials, so thinner ropes can often be used to handle the loads on sheets, control lines, or halyards. However, very thin ropes are hard to hold, and it may be impossible to pull effectively on a rope if its size is too small to handle comfortably.

Choosing rope
It is important to choose the right rope, and the right size, for a particular job. Polypropylene rope makes a cheap mooring line, and, because it floats, it is ideal for safety lines. However, it is not strong and stretches a lot, so it is not appropriate for sheets, halyards, or control lines.

Polyester rope is strong and has fairly low stretch properties, so it is suitable for mooring lines, sheets, and halyards. Prestretched polyester is also available for purposes, such as halyard use, that require minimum stretch, but it is less flexible and less comfortable to use than standard polyester rope.

Nylon rope is strong but stretches a lot. This makes it inappropriate for use in halyards or sheets, but it is often used for mooring or anchoring where stretch is an advantage, as it allows the rope to absorb shock loads. It does, however, lose significant strength when wet, and this must be allowed for when selecting the size.

Aramid and HMP ropes are very strong, light, and have minimal stretch, but they are more expensive than other types. They are excellent for halyards, control lines, and some sheets aboard high-performance boats.

Coiling rope

When ropes are not in use, they should be coiled and secured so that they are out of the way but easy to use when necessary. If they are left loose, they will tangle quickly and be difficult to unravel when they are needed. The way rope is coiled depends on the method of construction. Three-strand rope should be coiled in equal-sized loops (*below*), whereas braided rope is best coiled in figure-eights to balance the left and right twists of the braided strands (*bottom*).

COILING THREE-STRAND ROPE

To prevent kinks, three-strand rope is coiled in the same direction in which the strands are twisted, usually clockwise. As the loops are made, the rope must also be twisted slightly in the same direction to ensure that the coils lie flat.

❶ Hold the rope in your left hand and make loops with your right (reverse if you are left-handed). Twist the rope away from you between thumb and index finger.

❷ Finish coiling the rope, leaving a long working end. Wrap this several times around the whole coil to bind the individual loops together.

❸ Make a loop with the remainder of the working end and push this through the top of the coil, above the bound part.

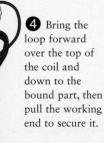

❹ Bring the loop forward over the top of the coil and down to the bound part, then pull the working end to secure it.

COILING BRAIDED ROPE

Coil braided rope in figure-eight coils that balance the left and right twists that are put into the rope during construction. Secure as for three-strand rope.

COILING
Coil the rope with your right hand, if right-handed, and make figure-eight coils into your left hand.

ROPE CONSTRUCTION

All rope, whether made from natural or synthetic materials, is made from short fibers that are spun into yarns, then collected into strands. The strands are then twisted or braided into the finished rope. The way the yarns are gathered into strands, and the way strands are formed into rope, help determine the rope's properties and how easy it is to handle, coil, splice, and knot.

Three-strand (laid) rope

Three-strand or laid rope is made by twisting yarns together in one direction to create the three strands. The strands are then twisted together in the opposite direction to create the rope. The opposing directions of the twists give it strength and the friction within the rope construction holds the rope in shape.

Yarns are twisted into strands

Three strands are twisted together to make rope

Twist remains in strand when it is unlayed

Braided rope

Most modern rope is made by a braiding process. A core of strands, which may be braided or lightly twisted together, is covered by a braided sheath, which, depending on type, can provide the strength for the rope, or may just protect the inner core.

Inner core is made from loosely braided strands

Seamless sheath is made from braided strands

Yarns, made from twisted fibers, are gathered or lightly twisted into strands

Cleating rope

A cleat is used to secure a rope and prevent it from slipping. Cleats may be of the cam, clam, or traditional horn variety. The clam and horn cleats have no moving parts.

Whichever type of cleat is used, it must be the right size for the size of the rope. If a rope is too large, it will not fit into a small cam or clam cleat, and there will not be enough space on a horn cleat to put on sufficient turns. If the rope is too small for the cleat, it is likely to slip through a cam or clam cleat, although it can be cleated on a large horn cleat provided sufficient turns are used to create the necessary friction to hold the rope in place.

A rope is cleated in a cam cleat by pulling it down and through the spring-loaded cam jaws, which hold it in place (*below*). To uncleat the

CAM CLEAT
A cam cleat has two spring-loaded cams with grooved faces that grip the rope when it is pulled down into the jaws. The rope must be sized correctly for the cleat. To uncleat, pull the rope upward.

CLAM CLEAT
A clam cleat has no moving parts but has a grooved, V-shaped body. The grooves grip the rope and, under load, it is forced farther into the cleat. To uncleat, pull the rope upward.

rope, pull the end upward, out of the cleat's jaws. If the rope is heavily loaded, it may need quite a sharp pull upward to release it.

To cleat a rope in a clam cleat, simply pull it down into the V-shaped holding grooves. To uncleat, pull the rope upward, out of the grooved body of the cleat. As with the cam cleat, uncleating a heavily loaded rope may require a sharp tug.

To secure a rope to a horn cleat, it must be wrapped around the cleat in a series of turns to create sufficient friction between the rope and the cleat (*right*). To uncleat a rope from a horn cleat, unwrap the turns.

Maintaining rope

During use, and when a boat is left unattended, rope collects dirt and salt particles, that become trapped within the rope's strands. Over time, the dirt causes abrasion, weakens the rope, and makes it stiffer and harder to handle. Taking care of your ropes will extend their life considerably and make them more flexible and easier to handle. Small ropes can be washed in a washing machine, while larger ones can be soaked in a bucket and scrubbed with a solution of warm water and mild detergent. Once they have been washed, coil the ropes and hang them to dry.

Knotting rope

Many thousands of knots have been developed over the centuries, each with its own name and practical or decorative use. Fortunately, you need to know only a few simple knots when you start sailing. In fact, the reef knot, the sheet bend, the figure-eight, the bowline, the round turn and two half hitches, and the clove hitch (*pp.46–47*) will take care of most of your needs throughout your sailing career.

Spend some time practicing tying the important knots so that your technique is smooth and you are able to tie and untie the important knots quickly and accurately.

CLEATING A ROPE ON A HORN CLEAT

The horn cleat is a common fixture on many sailing boats. Rope is secured on it by a round turn, followed by a series of figure-eight turns over and around its two horns.

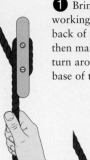

❶ Bring the rope's working end to the back of the cleat, then make a full turn around the base of the cleat.

❷ Take the rope across the top of the cleat, pass it behind the upper horn, and then bring it back across the front to form a figure-eight.

❸ Add several figure-eight turns to make sure the rope is secure. Finish off with another full turn around the base of the cleat.

ROPE AND KNOT TERMS

There are several terms that are used to identify the various parts of the rope during knot tying. Terms like the standing part, the working end, a bight, loop, or crossing turn, distinguish the parts and ends of a rope, and describe the different shapes that are made while knots are being tied. Learning to tie knots may seem confusing at first, but the process becomes much easier once these terms are understood.

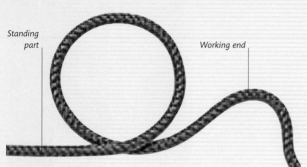

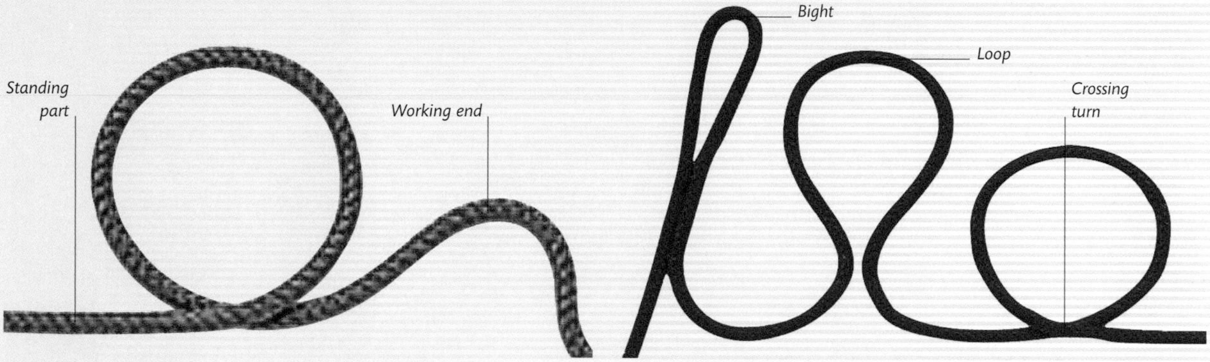

Standing part

Working end

Bight

Loop

Crossing turn

THE PARTS OF A ROPE
The part of the rope you are using to tie a knot is called the working end. The rest of the rope (the part that remains unaffected) is called the standing part.

BIGHTS, LOOPS, AND CROSSING TURNS
A bight is made by folding the rope back on itself; a loop is made by forming a circle without crossing the rope; and a crossing turn is made by crossing one part of the rope over or under another.

ROUND AND SIMPLE TURNS
A round turn takes the rope one-and-a-half times around the object, whereas a simple turn involves passing the rope around just one side of an object.

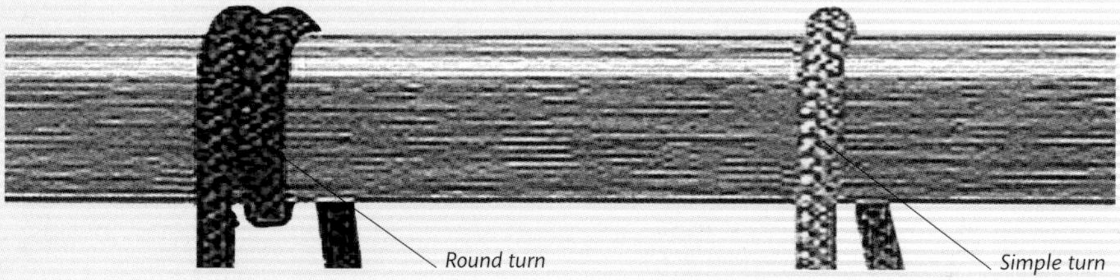

Round turn

Simple turn

Sealing rope ends

If a rope end is left unfinished, it will quickly fray. Frayed rope ends are not only messy-looking, but are wasteful of expensive rope, will jam in blocks and fairleads, and make knotting and cleating more difficult. If not dealt with promptly, the rope will continue to fray or unravel and may become useless. The best and most permanent way to seal a rope end is with a whipping (*p.222*), but a quicker, if less effective, seal can be made with adhesive tape, shrink tubing, and commercial sealants. Check all your rope ends at regular intervals and repair any fraying as soon as possible to avoid permanent damage.

LIQUID WHIPPING
Commercial liquids are available that will seal a rope's end. Simply dip the end in the liquid and leave to dry.

PLASTIC TUBING
Slide a suitably sized heat-shrink tube over the rope end and apply heat until it shrinks tightly around the rope.

GLUE
Dip thin ropes into a latex-based or polyvinyl acetate adhesive and leave it to dry for a short period.

ADHESIVE TAPE
Wrap adhesive tape tightly around the rope end to form a temporary seal. This is useful when splicing rope.

SIX BASIC KNOTS

REEF KNOT

Used for tying the ends of rope of equal diameter, the reef knot is named after its most common use: tying the ends of a sail's reef lines when putting in a reef (*p.74*). It is easy to tie it properly; just remember the rule: left over right, then right over left.

1 With the rope under the object, cross the two ends of the rope with the left working end over the right working end.

Left working end

Left working end

2 Now bring the left working end up, over, and pass it behind the right working end.

3 Bring both working ends up and tuck the now right working end over the left working end and through the middle.

4 Tighten the knot by pulling on both the working ends, producing the distinctive square-shaped reef knot.

SHEET BEND

A sheet bend is one of the best ways of joining two ropes together. If they are of different diameters, make the loop in the thicker rope. For more security, tie a double sheet bend by taking an additional turn around the loop (repeat steps 2 and 3).

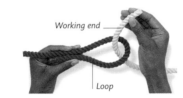

Working end

Loop

1 Make a loop in the blue rope, then pass the working end of the white rope through the loop from below.

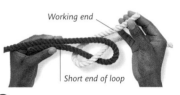

Working end

Short end of loop

2 Pass the working end of the white rope around and under the short end of the loop in the blue rope.

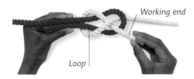

Working end

Loop

3 Bring the working end of the white rope over the long end of the loop, back to the top, and then under itself.

Standing part

Working end

4 Finally, tighten the sheet bend by pulling on the loop and the standing part of the white rope.

FIGURE-EIGHT

A figure-eight is a stopper knot used in sailing to stop a rope end from running out through a block or fairlead. It is simple to tie, does not jam, and is easily undone.

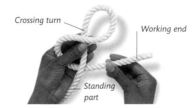

Crossing turn

Working end

Standing part

1 Make a crossing turn, bringing the working end of the rope over and then under the standing part.

Crossing turn

Standing part

2 Bring the working end up to the top of the knot and then pass it through the center of the crossing turn. Pull tight.

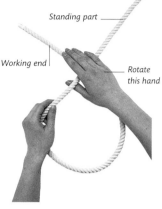

BOWLINE

If you learn only one knot before you go sailing, make it this one. The bowline (pronounced bow-lynn) is used to make a loop in the end of a rope or to tie to a ring or post. The bowline cannot be untied under load.

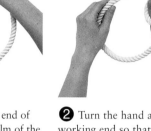

1 With the working end of the rope held in the palm of the hand over the standing part, rotate the hand so the working end is pushed under the standing part as the palm turns face upward.

2 Turn the hand and the working end so that a crossing turn is created around the hand and the working end.

3 Finally, pass the working end behind the standing part and then down through the crossing turn. Tighten the knot by pulling on the standing part and the doubled working end.

1 Form a round turn by bringing the working end of the rope up through the ring (or around a post or rail), from bottom to top, twice.

2 Take the working end over the standing part. Pass it below the standing part, then bring it to the top again and tuck it under itself, making a half-hitch.

3 Pass the working end below the standing part again, then bring it to the top and tuck it under itself again, making the second half-hitch. Pull both ends to tighten.

ROUND TURN AND TWO HALF-HITCHES

This knot is very useful for tying a rope to a post, rail, or ring. It is easily untied, even when under load, so it is good for moorings.

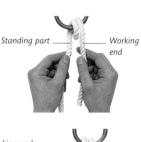

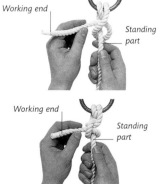

1 Make a turn around the post, bringing the working end up over the standing part.

2 Use the working end to make a second turn in the same direction, taking it behind the post and bringing it around to the front again.

3 Tuck the working end under the second turn. Pull on the working end and the standing part to tighten the knot.

CLOVE HITCH

The clove hitch is used for short-term mooring to a ring or post, or for hitching fenders to a rail. Make it more secure with a long working end.

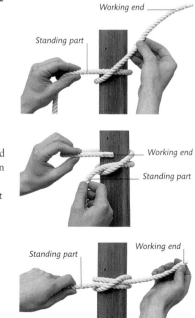

OARS AND PADDLES

The way in which you handle a dinghy under oars is one of the best indications of your seamanship skills. Rowing a dinghy that has been specifically designed for the purpose is a very satisfying exercise: good rowing boats are easy to row and move straight and well under oars. Larger rowing dinghies can also be moved with one oar, using the impressive art of sculling. However, sailing dinghies are rarely designed for rowing or sculling, and paddling may be the only viable option.

Rowing

The easiest craft to row are long, relatively narrow dinghies, which are stable in the water. The worst are inflatables, which are flat-bottomed and badly affected by wind. You will need the longest oars that can be used with the boat and a pair of oarlocks or crutches, which slot into plates on the gunwales and act as pivot points for the oars. Remove oarlocks when alongside a boat or pontoon, or else they may cause damage.

There are some basic points to bear in mind when rowing. To come alongside another boat or a pontoon, you must turn parallel to it and then unship the inboard oar so that it does not get trapped or broken. As soon as the boat is secured, unship the other oar.

If you are rowing in choppy water, the blades may get caught by waves as you swing them forward. To reduce this problem, feather them (turn them so that they are parallel to the water's surface) as you complete the stroke.

HOW TO ROW

Sit on the thwart in the middle of the boat facing the stern. If you have one passenger, he should usually sit in the stern. If you have several passengers, position them to keep the dinghy level.

Sculling

Sculling involves moving the boat by using a single oar over the transom. The sculling oar is retained in a oarlock, or in a sculling notch cut into the transom. If rowing is an art, then sculling is sublime. Little is more striking than watching an experienced boatman sculling a dinghy with casual aplomb. Sculling is best learned in a heavy dinghy when there is no wind or waves. It is one of those skills that seem to be impossible at first, but simply require some dedicated practice before you are rewarded with a great sense of achievement.

Paddling

With many dinghies, the most convenient alternative to sailing is paddling. Paddles take up less room than oars and do not need oarlocks. Paddling requires relatively little skill, but bear the following points in mind for increased efficiency: keep your arms straight as you pull on the paddle, lean well forward to put the blade into the water, and use your torso rather than just your arms to provide the power for each stroke.

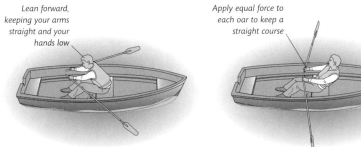

Lean forward, keeping your arms straight and your hands low

Apply equal force to each oar to keep a straight course

Lift the blades just clear of the water surface

❶ Place your hands a shoulder-width apart and lean forward. Then dip the oars into the water so that the blades are at right angles to the surface.

❷ Lean back, pulling on the oars and keeping your arms straight. As you lean fully back, bend your arms in to your chest to complete the stroke.

❸ Push down gently on the oars to lift the blades clear of the water, then lean aft, swinging the oars forward clear of the water, and repeat steps 1 and 2.

HOW TO SCULL

To scull, stand upright in the dinghy facing aft, with your legs apart so that you are balanced. The basic sculling stroke is a figure-eight made from side to side across the stern. Place passengers in the middle.

Sculler
Stand at the stern, legs apart

1 Hold the oar with both hands, thumbs underneath, at shoulder level. Make sure the blade is vertical and fully immersed; the oar should be balanced, its weight taken by the sculling notch or oarlock.

2 Twist the oar so that the blade is slanted to one side, then move your hands sideways—in the opposite direction of the way the oar blade is slanted.

3 At the end of the stroke, roll your wrists to twist the blade in the opposite direction and move your hands across your chest toward the other side.

4 Repeat steps 2 and 3 to keep the boat moving forward. The motion of the blade through the water should be smooth and steady throughout the stroke.

Twist your wrists

Pull the oar across your chest

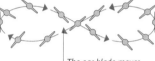

The oar blade moves through the water in a figure-eight motion

How to paddle

If you are alone, you can paddle facing forward, with the sails down and rudder stowed or held against your knee (*below*). Alternatively, paddle stern first, kneeling at the transom, and make drawing strokes that pull the boat backward. With two people, both can paddle, or else one person can steer using the rudder while the other paddles—the paddler sits forward, on the opposite side from the helmsman.

Sails
Lower the sails when paddling alone

Paddler
Start the stroke leaning well forward with arms straight, and keep knee against tiller

Sails
If sails are hoisted, allow them to flap

Crew
Take long, strong strokes

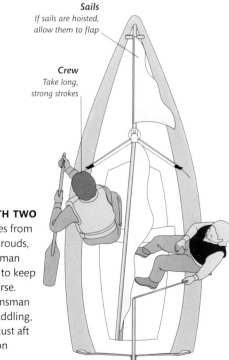

PADDLING ALONE

Sit well aft. Move the paddle through the water, turning the blade away from the side of the boat at the end of the stroke. This helps prevent the boat from turning away from the paddle—an effect that can also be reduced by lowering the centerboard or daggerboard.

PADDLING WITH TWO

The crew paddles from just aft of the shrouds, while the helmsman uses the rudder to keep the boat on course. When both helmsman and crew are paddling, both should sit just aft of the shrouds on opposite sides.

MOVING SMALL BOATS

The majority of small boats are kept ashore between sailing trips as they are not stable enough to be left on moorings and would be vulnerable to damage if left afloat. They are easily transported between venues on a car roof rack or a road trailer towed behind a car. However, the boat is at its most vulnerable to damage when it is on land, so it is important to know how to move it safely. Learning a few basic lifting and moving techniques will also protect you from personal accidents and injuries.

Road trailers

The road trailer should be designed for the boat, with plenty of chocks and rollers to provide adequate support. Overrun brakes, which cut in when the car brakes, should be installed on the trailer if it has to carry a heavy dinghy or keelboat. Always make sure the boat is securely attached before driving away. Tie the mast and any other removable equipment to the boat or the trailer.

Some road trailers have an integral launching cart that rides on top of the trailer when the boat is transported on the road. The boat sits on the cart, which is loaded and unloaded by lifting the cart handles and wheeling it onto or off the trailer from the back.

Roof racks

Smaller and lighter dinghies are usually transported on a roof rack, which should be sturdy and securely attached to the vehicle. Pad the rack and ropes to prevent damage to the boat. It is usually best to carry the boat inverted on the rack with the bow facing forward. Tie it securely to the rack, or strong points on the car, using rope or straps. Lash the mast and boom to the roof rack, alongside the boat, and stow all other removable equipment in the car.

USING ROOF RACKS
A roof rack should be fixed securely to the car so it cannot move under the weight placed on it. Lash the boat using ropes or specially made webbing straps.

Rollers

Solid or inflatable rollers are a good alternative to carts or trailers for short trips across beaches or up to boat parks. They are particularly useful for moving heavy boats across sand or gravel. At least three rollers are required. They are placed under the bow and the boat is pushed over them. Each roller is retrieved as it reappears behind the stern, and is placed in front of the bow to continue the movement until the destination is reached.

LIFTING A BOAT
Dinghies can be heavy and awkward to lift—several pairs of willing hands make lighter work of it. Some dinghies have lifting handles, but with most you will have to grasp the inside or outside edges of the sidedecks.

Place the boat at an angle to the car

❶ First turn the boat over. Make sure that the bow is facing forward before leaning the boat gently against the back of the car.

Then slide the boat on from the back

❷ Slide or lift the boat onto the rack either from the side or from behind the car, depending on which is easiest with your vehicle.

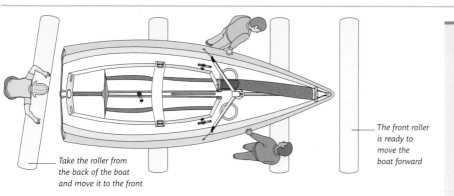

Take the roller from the back of the boat and move it to the front

The front roller is ready to move the boat forward

USING ROLLERS

At least three people and three rollers are needed to roll a boat smoothly. Place each in turn under the bow of the boat then roll the boat forward, removing each roller as it appears at the stern.

Launching carts

A launching cart is the usual means of moving a dinghy from the boat park to the water, and it is often used to store dinghies on the shore. Before moving a boat (or storing it) on its cart, make sure it is sitting correctly on the chocks and that it is tied securely with its painter to the cart handle. The ease with which your cart moves depends on the type of wheels. Small solid wheels work well only on hard surfaces. If you need to launch across a sand or gravel beach, choose larger wheels, preferably with inflatable tires.

To launch, push the cart into the water until the boat floats off. Make sure that someone keeps hold of the painter. Take the cart above the high-water mark, out of the way of others. Reverse this procedure to bring the boat ashore, tying the boat to the cart handle and making sure that it is on its chocks before pulling it out of the water.

COMBI TRAILER

Some road trailers incorporate a launching cart. Here, a small keelboat is easily launched on its cart without immersing the road trailer and risking water damage to the wheel bearings.

AVOIDING DAMAGE

A boat is most likely to be damaged when it is being transported on land, or when it is being launched or recovered from the water. Most damage can be avoided by following a few simple rules.

While launching

When you are launching the boat using a cart, always push the cart into the water until you can float the boat off. Never drag the boat off the cart, since this will scratch the hull. Similarly, when recovering, float the boat onto the cart rather than dragging it on.

While on land

Avoid stepping into a single-skin dinghy while it is ashore or on its launching cart. Without the support of the water underneath it, the bottom of the boat may be deformed or holed by your weight.

While carrying

You will need at least four people to carry an average dinghy. Most of the weight is concentrated in the front part of the boat, so if you need to carry it over any distance, make sure you distribute the lifting power accordingly.

While moving

Always look up before you move boats to check that your tall aluminum or carbon-fiber mast is not about to become entangled with a high-voltage cable. People have been electrocuted when moving their boats, so be aware of your surroundings.

While not in use

Whenever you leave the boat for any length of time, clean and dry the sails and all other equipment and stow everything neatly, then cover the boat to protect it from the elements (*pp.118–119*).

STAYING CLEAR OF OTHERS

Every type of craft on the water, from the smallest dinghy to the biggest supertanker, is governed by the International Regulations for Preventing Collisions at Sea, often referred to as the "Col Regs" or "the rules of the road." Additional rules, set by the International Sailing Federation (ISAF), govern boats when racing, but the Col Regs always take precedence. The full rules are complex and cover every eventuality, but when you start sailing you need to know only the basic rules covered here.

Keeping clear

Maintain a careful watch all around and try to anticipate the actions of others. Remember to look astern regularly—novices are often startled by unseen overtaking boats. When it is your responsibility to keep clear, it is important that you do so in plenty of time. Make a large alteration to your course so that your intentions are obvious to the other vessel, and pass astern rather than ahead of it. When you are underway, keep a safe distance from boats at anchor or on a mooring. Always give a wide berth to boats that are fishing or trawling to avoid the possibility of becoming entangled in nets or lines.

When one vessel is in the process of overtaking another, the overtaking boat must keep clear until completely passed, even if it is a sailing boat that is overtaking a powered vessel.

Negotiating channels

When proceeding along a channel or fairway, all boats should stay close to the starboard side of the channel in whichever direction they are going. Avoid crossing busy channels or shipping lanes. If you must do so, always cross as nearly as possible at a right-angle to the traffic flow. Do not pass close in front of vessels that are moving along the channel, and make sure that you complete the crossing as quickly as possible.

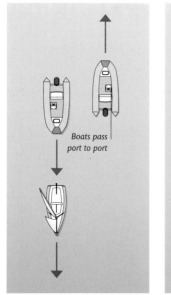

Boats pass
port to port

CHANNEL RULE
All vessels, whether under sail or power, must stay close to the starboard side of channels, so that they pass port to port.

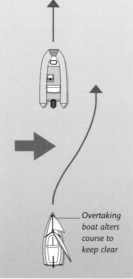

Overtaking
boat alters
course to
keep clear

OVERTAKING RULE
An overtaking vessel must keep clear of the one being passed even if it is a sailing boat that is overtaking a power boat.

STARBOARD-TACK RULE

A sailing boat that is on starboard tack (with the boom to port) has the right of way over a boat on port tack. A boat on port tack (with the boom to starboard) must give way to a starboard-tack boat. When you first start sailing it is sometimes difficult to remember which tack you are on. Solve this problem by marking the boom as shown below.

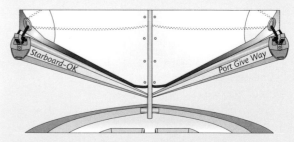

Starboard–OK
Port Give Way

MARKING YOUR BOOM
Mark your boom "Starboard–OK" on the starboard side and "Port–Give Way" on the port side. This will remind you which tack you are on and the right-of-way rule that applies.

AVOIDING COLLISIONS

Whenever two boats—whether under sail or power—meet in a potential collision situation, there is a rule that specifies which one has right of way. The boat with right of way, known as the "stand-on" vessel, must maintain its course, while the other boat, known as the "give-way" vessel, is obliged to keep clear.

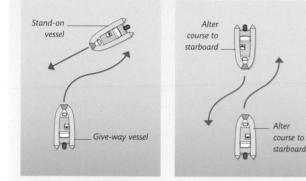

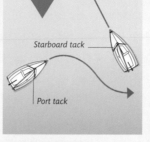

POWER BOATS CROSSING
The boat on the other vessel's starboard side has right of way, so the give-way boat alters course to pass behind it.

POWER BOATS HEAD ON
When power boats meet head on both, must give way—by steering to starboard so as to pass port to port.

SAILING BOATS ON OPPOSITE TACKS
The boat on the port tack alters its course to pass behind the boat on the starboard tack.

SAILING BOATS ON THE SAME TACK
The windward boat must keep clear and steers to pass behind the leeward boat.

Giving way

In general terms, a power vessel yields to a sailing vessel. However, in practice, this is not always the case. For example, the rule does not apply to large ships in confined waters, which are usually restricted in their ability to maneuver. Fishing boats are also a special case and you must stay clear of them. Large ships may have a blind spot under their bows, where a boat will be hidden. In such circumstances, it is the responsibility of the small-boat sailor to get out of the way as quickly as possible.

In a narrow channel, such as on the approach to a marina, even a small yacht under power may not have room to alter course, so dinghies should keep clear. In fact, unless the power vessel is about the same size as your boat, it is always best to stay out of its way. Remember, too, that a dinghy under oars is classed as a power-driven vessel and must keep clear of sailing boats.

IN A CHANNEL
In some sailing areas dinghies and yachts share the same waters as large vessels. If crossing a channel, pass behind ships and give them as wide a berth as possible.

WEATHER BASICS

The most important factor to take into consideration when you go sailing is the weather, especially the strength and direction of the wind. Once you are on the water, the complexity of the weather—how quickly it can change, and how variable the wind direction and strength can be—may surprise you if you are not used to sailing. You need to be able to recognize onshore and offshore winds because they determine the ease or difficulty of leaving and returning to shore, as well as conditions farther out.

WEATHERWISE

Study the strength and direction of the wind before you go afloat, and check local forecasts for any imminent changes in the weather.

Weather forecasts

Always check the weather forecast before you sail. Although forecasts are available from many different sources, not all will give specific information on wind conditions, so it is advisable to use a sailing forecast that covers your area in as much detail as possible. In ports or harbors, the offices of the harbor master often display the local forecast. Sailing clubs may also provide forecasts. At clubs, you can also seek information and advice from more experienced sailors with extensive local knowledge. Always bear in mind your sailing capabilities and the limitations of your experience. If in doubt, stay ashore.

Wind direction

It is always more pleasant to sail in warm sunshine than cold drizzle, but neither temperature nor rain are critical to sailing. The wind, on the other hand, is vital, and you should constantly be aware of its direction and strength. Check it before you go afloat, and continue to monitor it once you have set sail.

Wind indicators

As you gain experience, you will find that you automatically register wind direction by the feel of it on your face. Until this becomes second nature, however, you must try to estimate the wind direction and force by studying all available signs. Look at the wind indicator at the top of your mast, if installed, or those on other boats, and study the movement of flags ashore. Smoke from chimneys will blow in the direction of the wind, and the angle of the smoke will give an indication of its strength. Moored boats often point into the wind, but remember to take into account any tides or currents.

Bear in mind that the wind shifts very frequently, even if the weather is apparently stable, and it can be bent from its true direction by trees, tall buildings, or hills. A river valley will often affect the wind, causing it to blow up or down the river.

Offshore wind

When you are planning a sailing trip, do not underestimate the strength of a wind that is offshore (blowing from the land across the shore and out over the water).

CHANGEABLE CONDITIONS
Wind strength can increase quickly and dramatically. Make sure you and your crew are prepared for sudden changes in the conditions.

WIND STRENGTH

Learn to recognize when it is safe to set sail by studying the Beaufort Scale, which indicates the strength of the wind and describes its visual effects. For initial outings, a Force 3 is the ideal wind strength. Seven to ten knots will fill the sails but will be gentle enough to allow you to keep control of your vessel. Anything less than a Force 3 will cause the boat to move slowly and lack responsiveness; anything more and beginners should be wary of going out. A Force 6 is a dinghy-sailor's gale; only experienced crews should sail in winds that can reach 27 knots.

FORCE	DESCRIPTION	EFFECTS ON SEA	SIGNS ON LAND	WIND SPEED
0	Calm	Mirror-smooth water. Dinghies tend to drift rather than sail.	Smoke rises vertically and flags hang limp.	Less than 1 knot
1	Light Air	Ripples on water. Sufficient wind to maintain motion.	Smoke drifts slightly, indicating wind direction.	1–3 knots
2	Light Breeze	Small wavelets with smooth crests. Sufficient wind to sail steadily but upright. Wind is felt on the face.	Light flags and wind vanes respond with small movements. Leaves rustle.	4–6 knots
3	Gentle Breeze	Large wavelets with crests starting to break. Ideal conditions for learning to sail a dinghy.	Light flags extend fully, and leaves and small twigs are set in motion.	7–10 knots
4	Moderate Breeze	Small waves with fairly frequent whitecaps. The crew will be working hard. Boats plane easily. Beginners should head for shore.	Small branches move on trees, and dust and paper are lifted off the ground by the breeze.	11–15 knots
5	Fresh Breeze	Moderate waves with frequent whitecaps. High risk of capsize when dinghy sailing.	Small trees sway visibly and the tops of all trees are in motion.	16–21 knots
6	Strong Breeze	Large waves start to form and spray is likely. This is a dinghy-sailor's gale. Only experienced crews with good safety cover should race.	Large trees sway and the wind whistles in power lines. It becomes difficult to use an umbrella.	22–27 knots

Offshore winds can be quite misleading as there is likely to be a calm patch close to the shore, but beyond this the wind will be stronger and the waves much larger. If you set sail in an offshore wind and then discover that the weather conditions farther out are more severe than you anticipated, you may experience difficulties returning home.

Onshore wind
When the wind is onshore, you will feel its full force and waves may break on the shoreline. Onshore winds bring different sailing challenges. Attempting to launch the boat and leave the shore through breaking waves can be difficult with the wind against you. However, away from the beach the waves should calm down. You will also find that it is easier to return to base in an onshore wind.

INLAND OR SEA

Whether you sail on inland waters or on the sea depends on the type of sailing you want to do, as well as on where you live. Learning to sail is usually easier and safer on inland waters, but once you have gained some experience you will probably want to be more adventurous and try sea sailing. In many parts of the world, sailing on the sea involves dealing with tides. It is important for both your safety and enjoyment that you understand how to check tidal information and how tides affect sailing at sea.

Inland waters

Inland waters vary from small lakes and reservoirs, which are often made from flooded gravel pits, to more significant stretches of water, such as large lakes and wide rivers. Remember that some inland waters are privately owned, so if the stretch of water is new to you, find out whether you need to get permission to sail there. Look for notices on the banks and shorelines.

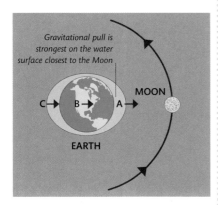

Gravitational pull is strongest on the water surface closest to the Moon

C → B → A →   MOON

EARTH

GRAVITATIONAL PULL

The gravitational pull of the Moon (strengthened or weakened by that of the sun) attracts the water on the near side (A), Earth itself (B), and the water on the far side (C) by decreasing amounts. This pull causes two bulges in the surface of the water on opposite sides of Earth. We experience these bulges as tides.

All types of inland waters have their own characteristics and potential hazards, so ask for advice at a local sailing club before you go afloat. If you plan to sail without safety cover on a large stretch of inland water, make sure that someone knows your plans before you set sail. Look for bridges and overhead power lines that may be lower than the mast, and check for signs indicating dams or locks.

The rules of the road (*pp.52–53*) apply wherever you are sailing. In constricted waters, such as a narrow river or small lake, you may find that the sailing conditions are congested, which will test your maneuvering skills. When you are sailing on a river, be aware that you are likely to have to contend with a current as the water flows downstream toward the sea. On some rivers these can get very strong, especially if there has been heavy rain upstream. Some rivers, especially large ones, also have a tidal flow that may reach some way inland from the sea.

Tides

Tides are vertical movements of the water due to the gravitational attraction of celestial bodies (primarily the Moon) on Earth's surface.

The horizontal movement of water produced by the tides is called a tidal stream. This flows along coasts and up and down estuaries and rivers. When the tide is rising, the stream is said to be flooding; when it is falling, the stream is said to be ebbing. Flood tides run up rivers and estuaries while ebb tides run back toward the sea. The speed of the tidal stream is affected by the difference in the height of the water surface between low tide and high tide. It runs much faster during spring tides than during neaps, and is at its strongest during the third and fourth hours of the flood or ebb.

Sea sailing

If you are planning to sail at sea, make sure that you have all the tidal information you need. Details about the times of high and low water can be found in a local tide table, and a tidal atlas for your area will show the direction of the stream for each hour of the tidal cycle.

Remember that when a tidal stream flows through deep channels or around headlands, it is at its strongest. If it is constricted in any way, such as by a headland, an uneven bottom, or rapidly shoaling water, then you can expect tidal races, eddies, and overfalls. Stay away from these in a small boat, especially if the wind is strong or is blowing against the stream. It will be apparent when the wind blows in opposition to a tidal stream, as it will kick up waves that are bigger and steeper than you would otherwise expect. When the tide turns to run with the wind, these waves will quickly die down again.

When going sailing in tidal waters, always make sure that someone ashore knows your plans, and store an anchor aboard so that you have the option of anchoring in shallow water if the wind drops or if you get into difficulties.

THE CAUSES OF TIDES

Tides are caused by the Moon's gravitational pull (and to a lesser extent that of the Sun) on the surface of the water. The combined influence of these two celestial bodies determines tidal ranges.

Tidal ranges

The gravitational pull of the Moon and the Sun produces two high tides and two low tides in most places every day. The difference in height between a low tide and the next high tide is called the tidal range.

Spring and neap tides

The juxtaposition of the Sun and Moon affects the height of the tides at different times of the month. At the times of a full and new moon, when the Sun, Earth, and Moon are in line, the gravitational pull is largest. This causes spring tides, with the largest range between high and low tides. When the Moon is in its first and last quarters, the Sun, Earth and Moon are at right angles to each other and cause neap tides, with the smallest range between high and low water. The strength of tidal streams depends on the range, so expect strong streams at spring tides and weaker ones at neaps.

SPRING TIDES
During spring tides, there is a significantly larger difference between the water's height at low tide and high tide.

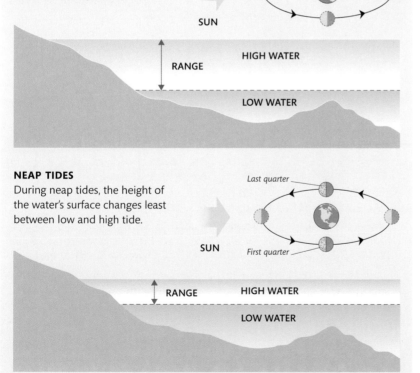

New moon   Full moon

SUN

RANGE   HIGH WATER

LOW WATER

NEAP TIDES
During neap tides, the height of the water's surface changes least between low and high tide.

Last quarter

SUN   First quarter

RANGE   HIGH WATER

LOW WATER

TIDE INDICATORS

When you are sailing in tidal waters, it is important to know when the tide turns. When the tidal stream runs in your favor, it is easy to make progress over the ground, but if it runs against you, progress may be slow or impossible until the tide turns.

Checking the direction

One of the easiest ways of checking the direction of the tidal stream is to look at boats at anchor or on a mooring. They will usually point into the stream, unless they have a shallow draft (like dinghies or motor boats), in which case they are more likely to lie head-to-wind, especially if the wind is strong. Look at deep-keeled cruisers for an accurate indication of the tidal stream. The tide also flows around buoys and posts, or any other fixed object in the water, and reveals its direction and strength by the wake that streams downtide of the object.

BUOY IN A TIDAL STREAM
Buoys are very useful indicators of the direction of a tidal stream because they often lean away from the direction of a strong stream. A tidal stream also produces a wake or bow wave as the water sweeps past the buoy.

SMALL-BOAT SAILING

Dinghies offer the best introduction to sailing because they are so responsive to wind and waves and to your actions on the tiller and sheets. General-purpose dinghies are ideal for learning the basics about rigging and launching, experiencing the different roles of the helmsman and crew, and becoming proficient in all the important sailing maneuvers.

CHOOSING A SMALL BOAT

There are literally hundreds of different types of dinghies and small keelboats on the market. They are available in a huge variety of designs for a wide range of sailing activities, from relaxed day-cruising to highly competitive racing. Most modern boats are built with strong, lightweight materials, and many offer tremendous performance potential while requiring little maintenance. You are bound to find one that will suit your level of skill, experience, and ambition, as well as your budget.

STARTER BOATS
Modern general-purpose designs are good for beginners to learn in, and are still rewarding for more experienced sailors.

First steps

General-purpose boats are usually the most appropriate type of dinghy when you are first learning to sail. These boats are relatively stable, so any mistakes are easier to rectify without mishap than they would be in a sensitive, high-performance dinghy. Most sailing clubs and schools use general-purpose dinghies for teaching because they often have enough space for an instructor and two students, but some also offer courses in single-handed dinghies. This is often the fastest way to learn, but it can be hard work sailing alone while learning.

Expanding your horizons

Once you have progressed and are sailing confidently, you will probably consider buying your own boat. Since the choice is so vast, it is best to draw up a detailed short list of your specific requirements. For a start, think about where you are going to do most of your sailing and what type of sailing you want to do. High-performance racing boats (*pp.122–125*) are huge fun

HULL SHAPE

The shape and depth of a dinghy's hull when seen from behind provides a good indication of the purpose for which it is designed. A flat, shallow, usually rounded hull shape indicates that the dinghy is intended for high-performance sailing and racing. Wider hulls are more stable than narrow ones, and deeper and heavier hulls are more often used for general-purpose boats that are ideal for beginners.

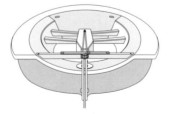

ROUND-BILGE HULL
If the hull is shallow, usually with a round bilge (curved shape), it is probably meant for racing. The shallower the hull the more likely it is to be designed for speed.

DOUBLE-CHINE HULL
If the hull is deep, the boat is likely to have been designed as a general-purpose dinghy. Also, general-purpose hulls may have one or two chines (angled, flat panels).

and very exciting to sail, but they are not suitable for family picnics or for use with oars or an outboard motor. If you want to race, make sure you choose a boat that is popular where you are going to do your sailing, and check that there is a good club fleet in which to start racing.

Do not pick a high-performance boat until you have the experience to handle it. It is certainly not necessary to choose a high-performance boat to get good racing. In fact, many general-purpose dinghies have very committed and competitive racing fleets and are a good option to start racing. If you are unsure as to whether you are ready to race your own boat, consider crewing for someone else in order to gain experience and develop skills.

If you want to day-sail or cruise, choose a strong and stable boat that is specifically designed for this type of sailing. A good cruising dinghy will have plenty of room inside a deep and stable hull, and will have space for stowing additional equipment you may need, such as a cockpit tent and cooking gear.

Joining a club

You will need to join a club in order to participate in races. In fact, it is worth joining one anyway, before

buying your own boat, because this will enable you to meet more experienced sailors who will usually have sailed in a range of small boats. Crewing for club members in as wide a range of boats as possible is a very good way of adding to your sailing experience at low cost. Depending on where you live, you may find several sailing clubs in your vicinity. Some may be primarily dinghy and small keelboat clubs, while others may concentrate on yacht racing and cruising. Before you join a club, visit the ones in your area and find out

MULTIPURPOSE BOATS
Some small multipurpose dinghies can be sailed single-handed or with a crew (with a jib fitted), as here.

what kind of sailing they focus on. Check out what types of boat they sail and talk to as many members as possible. Pick a club that sails small boats and try to find one that has a training program to introduce newcomers to small-boat sailing and help them develop their skills and broaden their experience.

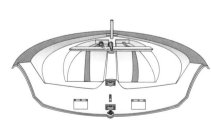

MODERN GENERAL-PURPOSE DINGHY
The hull is shallower, with a flatter bottom than older designs, but is quite wide and so has better stability than narrower types.

SINGLE-HANDED DINGHY
The hull shape is shallow and the bottom is quite flat at the stern. The narrower hull offers less stability than wider designs but offers higher performance.

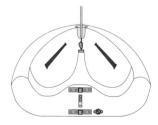

MODERN FUN BOAT
Some small, modern designs are designed for fun sailing and occasional racing. Some can be sailed by one or two people and are popular at vacation sailing centers.

Buying a small boat

When you first start sailing, it is not necessary to buy your own boat. In fact, it is best not to consider buying until you have some experience of different boats and have decided on the type of sailing that interests you most. Before you buy a boat, try to get some experience sailing as many different dinghies or small keelboats as possible.

When you decide to buy a boat, make a shortlist of the ones that seem suitable. Read boat reviews in sailing magazines, and on websites, and visit boat shows to view different boats. Try to pick boats for your shortlist that are popular and well established in the area you plan to sail, as these will maintain their value best and be easy to sell again.

Once you have a shortlist, arrange to take a trial sail in each of the boats you are interested in. If the manufacturer cannot arrange this, contact the class association, which will be able to help you set up a sail with an existing owner. Details of class associations can be found through your national sailing authority, or you can search for their websites online.

If you plan to buy a secondhand boat, which is often a very good way to get started, look in magazines and sailing websites for boats that match your shortlist and to find the average price for the types of boats you are interested in. When you have found one or more possible boats that seem to suit your requirements, ask an experienced small-boat sailor to view them with you and advise you on their condition and suitability for your experience and ambitions.

Once you have bought a boat, it is a very good idea to join the class association, as this will help you meet other owners, join in organized class racing, and learn tips about your particular boat. The association may also offer low-cost insurance policies and other benefits, such as organized training sessions, that make it well worth joining.

MODERN DINGHY
This modern, molded-plastic dinghy is a good dual-purpose boat. It is great for racing but the beamy hull is stable, with plenty of room for the crew, which also makes it a good all-purpose family boat.

TYPES OF DINGHIES AND SMALL KEELBOATS

There is a wide range of small boats that are suitable for beginners and recreational sailing, as well as a varied selection for single-handed sailing or for children and young adults. Although not necessarily designed for racing, there is no reason why a general-purpose boat cannot be raced; indeed, many of the popular classes have strong racing fleets. Small day-sailing keelboats are not classed as dinghies as they have weighted keels. However, they do offer good performance but with a much-reduced risk of capsize.

GENERAL-PURPOSE DINGHIES

WAYFARER The Wayfarer is a classic general-purpose dinghy. A relatively heavy boat, it is large and stable enough to be kept on a mooring. There is good racing, and Wayfarers have cruised long distances.

VANGUARD 15 The Vanguard 15 is a double-handed, one-design dinghy that is simple, durable, and lightweight. This easy-to-transport, popular boat can be used for racing or for family leisure sailing.

FEVA The Feva is a modern, multipurpose dinghy that has the option of being sailed single-handed or with a crew, with just a mainsail or with the addition of a jib and gennaker.

SMALL KEELBOATS

FLYING FIFTEEN The Flying Fifteen is a popular, double-handed international class that is used mainly for racing. It has a weighted keel yet it is light enough to plane. It has a mainsail, jib, and spinnaker.

SONAR The Sonar is a popular keelboat that is ideal for day-sailing and competitive racing. It is used for international women's, youth, and disabled racing in match, team, and fleet racing.

SQUIB The Squib was designed as a one-design keelboat for club racing and family sailing. It offers easy handling and good performance while its ballast keel removes the risk of capsize.

BOATS FOR CHILDREN

OPTIMIST The Optimist is a favorite for children. A small, light single-hander with a simple rig, it is ideal for starting to sail and is raced very competitively all over the world. It is an international class.

TOPPER The Topper is a very popular, international single-hander, which is particularly suitable for children. The Topper is built from molded plastic and it is virtually indestructible.

PICO The Laser Pico is a durable, plastic boat that can be sailed by everyone. It's ideal for children and entry-level sailors, and is equipped with a removable jib and reefing mainsail.

BOATS FOR YOUNG ADULTS

420 The 420 is an international class that is ideal both for beginners and for young sailors starting to race. The 420 provides a good introduction to the use of a trapeze and a spinnaker.

LASER RADIAL Based on the same hull and equipment as the Olympic Laser (pp.124–125), the Radial has a smaller sail and more flexible lower mast that makes it an ideal single-hander for young adults.

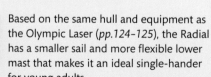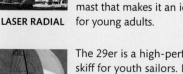
29ER The 29er is a high-performance skiff for youth sailors. It has a single trapeze and an asymmetric spinnaker. Sailing this exciting boat requires coordination and agility.

PROTECTIVE CLOTHING

When you sail in small boats, you are very exposed to the elements, so it is important for your comfort to wear clothing that keeps you warm. Although the choice of what to wear is very wide, there are only two basic approaches. One is to wear a drysuit or waterproofs over warm clothing; the other is to wear a wetsuit. If you sail a dinghy, it is inevitable that you will sometimes find yourself in the water, so it is also vital that you have a buoyancy aid to help keep you afloat if you capsize.

Starting off

If you learn to sail at a sailing club or school, you will probably be provided with waterproofs and a buoyancy aid. Normal casual or sports clothing will suffice under the waterproofs, and you can wear athletic shoes on your feet. If you learn to sail in a small dinghy, you may be provided with a wetsuit, as it is inevitable that you will get wet and waterproofs will not provide sufficient protection.

Once you start to sail your own boat or to crew for others on a regular basis, you will want to invest in some specialty clothing, but you should get some experience first so that you can choose the type of clothing that will suit the sailing you wish to do. Ask experienced sailors for their recommendations and visit a sailing pro shop to try on a range of types.

Wearing waterproofs

Waterproofs are most suitable for sailing in small keelboats or stable general-purpose dinghies that are unlikely to capsize. They have the advantage over a wetsuit or drysuit that they are easier to put on and take off, and it is easier to control your temperature.

If your boat is kept on a mooring or pontoon, it is practical to wear waterproofs, but if you have to launch from a slipway or beach, waterproofs will not keep your legs dry when you wade into the water to launch the boat. Even if you wear sailing boots, it is likely that the water will come over the top of your boots during launching. If this is the type of sailing you do, then consider wearing a wetsuit or drysuit, or be prepared to have wet legs before you start sailing. In a warm or hot climate, wet legs are no hardship, but if you sail in a cooler climate, you will want to stay as dry as possible, especially at the start of your trip afloat.

You can choose from a one-piece waterproof suit or separate jacket and pants. A one-piece suit has fewer water entry points, but separates allow you to wear the jacket or pants alone when required and so may be more useful if you are sailing for recreation rather than racing. Waterproof jackets are available with a front zipper or as a smock type. A zippered jacket is easier to put on and can be worn unzipped, when you need to regulate your temperature. The smock type is more waterproof, since it has no

zipper, but is harder to put on or take off, as it must be pulled over the head. Waterproof pants are available in waist-high or chest-high designs. Waist high are quicker to put on, but chest-high pants have suspenders that prevent them from slipping down and also offer extra protection that means they can often be worn without a jacket.

Materials

Waterproofs are usually made with an outer layer of nylon for extra strength, and an inner, waterproof layer that is bonded to the nylon. The waterproof layer might be PVC, which is fairly cheap, or a breathable fabric, which will be considerably more expensive. However, breathable fabrics do offer superior performance, allowing

HIGH PANTS
High-fit waterproof pants have suspenders for security and can be worn without the jacket if preferred.

water vapor and perspiration to escape rather than accumulate and eventually soak your clothing.

Wearing a wetsuit

When you are likely to get wet while launching or sailing, a wetsuit offers you a means of staying warm without worrying about how to stay dry.

Wetsuits are made from neoprene, which is composed of numerous small cells, each of which holds a small bubble of gas. These bubbles give the material its insulation properties, making it difficult for the cold to penetrate, or the heat from your body to escape.

Wetsuits are tailored to be very close-fitting to ensure that only a thin layer of water can penetrate between the neoprene and your skin. When you get wet, this thin layer of water is trapped between your skin and the layer of neoprene and is quickly warmed up by your body heat. The thin layer of warm water and the insulation of the neoprene protect you from the cold.

Types of wetsuits

Different weights of neoprene are available and suits for sailing usually range between 3 mm and 5 mm, although suits as thin as 0.5 mm are also available. Thicker suits are used for winter sailing, while the thinner ones are adequate for sailing from spring to fall in most climates. Some suits use thicker neoprene in the torso with thinner material in the arms and legs to allow for easier movement. Suits for small-boat sailing should have reinforced patches on the seat, shins, and knees.

Wetsuits are available in a variety of styles, including full-length, shortie, and long-john designs. Separate jackets are also available, which can be worn over a shortie or long-john

for extra warmth. Full suits have a zipper entry system, usually in the back of the torso, and good suits have adjustable ankles and wrists.

Most good wetsuits have thin inner and outer skins of a stretchy, nylon-based material bonded to the neoprene to protect it from damage.

It is advisable to wear a rash vest, made of Lycra or thin neoprene and Lycra, under a wetsuit to protect your skin from abrasion and rash.

Some sailors also wear a thin windproof vest over their wetsuit to protect it from damage and to prevent wind chill when sailing.

Wetsuit socks can be worn under dinghy boots to keep feet warm; neoprene sailing boots with zips and nonslip soles are also available. Neoprene gloves will keep the hands warm, and a wetsuit hood will prevent heat loss through the head in the coldest weather.

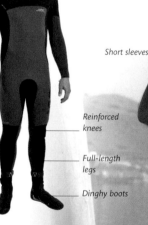

Latex seal at neck

Short sleeves

Reinforced knees

Full-length legs

Dinghy boots

FULL WETSUIT
Wetsuits are available in a variety of styles. Choose a good-quality, well-fitting suit to ensure that you stay warm and comfortable.

SHORT WETSUIT
For summer sailing, a shortie wetsuit is often more appropriate than a full suit. Wetsuit boots are ideal for dinghy sailing.

Neoprene boots

Wearing a drysuit

A drysuit is a type of waterproof suit that is designed to prevent any water entry, even when you are immersed in water. The drysuit prevents water from entering at the wrists, ankles, and neck by using seals, usually made of latex, that fit tightly to the skin. Drysuits are generally made as one-piece suits, but two-piece versions are also available. In this case, the pants and smock have latex seals at the waist that are rolled together to prevent water from entering between smock and pants. One-piece suits have a zipper system with the zipper sometimes fitted diagonally across the chest or the back. Zippers in the front make entry and exit. Good suits have reinforced seats, knees, and shins to protect these high-wear areas.

To control your body temperature when wearing a drysuit, you need to take care when choosing the clothing you wear underneath. Shorts and a T- shirt often suffice in warm weather, but thin thermal clothing is better in colder conditions. If you decide to use a drysuit, choose one made from breathable fabric, which allows your perspiration to pass through the suit. It is easy to overheat when wearing a drysuit, and if the material is not breathable, you will quickly become wet inside the suit from the perspiration you produce when you are working hard.

Hands and feet

It is very important to protect the extremities from injury and cold when sailing, so take care to choose good footwear, gloves, and a hat.

Footwear can consist of deck shoes, dinghy boots, or long sailing boots. Deck shoes and long sailing boots are fine for keelboat sailing, but for dinghy sailing it is better to choose a pair of dinghy boots or wetsuit boots, since you are likely to get your feet wet when you wade in the water to launch and recover your dinghy.

Gloves help protect the hands when handling ropes and help to keep them warm when sailing in cold conditions. Sailing gloves are available in short- or long-fingered varieties. The short-fingered ones allow you to handle intricate tasks, such as fastening a shackle or tying a knot, but long- finger ones provide better protection for the hands. A compromise is a pair with full-length fingers on all but the index finger and thumb. Most sailing gloves are made of a supple leather or synthetic alternative with an elasticated back and loop and hook wrist closure system.

Protect the head

A hat is useful for protecting the head from the sun in the summer and helping to prevent heat loss in colder conditions. A baseball cap is often

PROTECT THE HEAD AND EYES
A peaked cap will keep sun off the head and a good pair of sunglasses will protect the eyes from glare from the water.

used as its brim helps protect the eyes from glare. Add a retaining strap to stop the hat from being blown or knocked off your head while sailing. A wide-brimmed hat will provide more shade for head and shoulders in very sunny conditions, but is more vulnerable to being blown off your head in windier conditions. In winter, a thermal balaclava will help prevent heat loss from the head, which can account for 30 percent of the heat loss from your entire body.

In sunny conditions, always wear a pair of high-quality sunglasses to protect the eyes from glare from the water's surface, which can be considerable. Pick a pair that covers the eyes well to prevent light from seeping in around the edges, and use a retaining strap to prevent loss. Polarized lenses are best for reducing glare, and they also make it easier to see the signs that wind shifts and gusts make on the water's surface.

Caring for your equipment

Sailing clothing can be a considerable investment, so it pays to take care of your equipment. Always rinse out all your clothing thoroughly in fresh water after each sail and hang up to dry. Some clothing can be washed in a washing machine at low or medium temperature, but always check the manufacturer's instructions. Most clothing should not be tumble-dried. Never use solvent-based cleaners to remove stains, as these are likely to damage the fabric.

Do not leave your waterproofs, drysuit, or wetsuit in direct sunlight, as this will cause the fabric to deteriorate. Lightly lubricate zippers with petroleum jelly and close zippers and fold clothing neatly for storage. A light dusting of talcum powder inside a wetsuit makes it easier to put on.

DINGHY DRYSUIT

A one-piece drysuit has close-fitting latex cuffs, collar, and ankles, which are designed to form a waterproof seal, thus keeping the wearer dry.

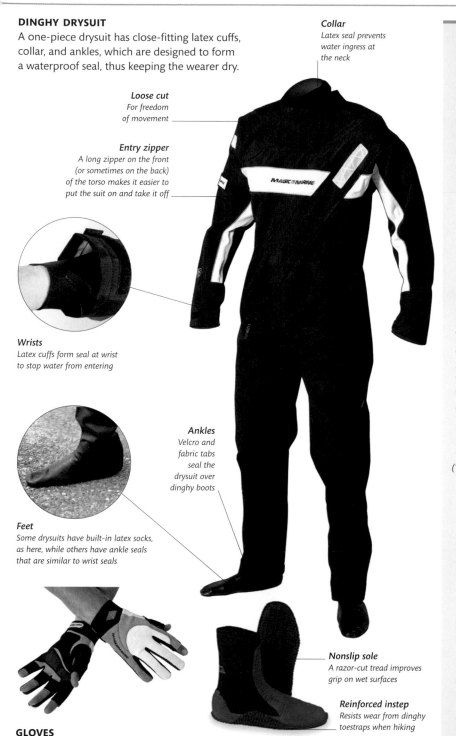

Collar
Latex seal prevents water ingress at the neck

Loose cut
For freedom of movement

Entry zipper
A long zipper on the front (or sometimes on the back) of the torso makes it easier to put the suit on and take it off

Wrists
Latex cuffs form seal at wrist to stop water from entering

Ankles
Velcro and fabric tabs seal the drysuit over dinghy boots

Feet
Some drysuits have built-in latex socks, as here, while others have ankle seals that are similar to wrist seals

Nonslip sole
A razor-cut tread improves grip on wet surfaces

Reinforced instep
Resists wear from dinghy toestraps when hiking

GLOVES

Good sailing gloves have reinforced palms and fingers for gripping rope securely—even when wet—and protecting the hands.

DINGHY BOOTS

Rubber sailing boots with molded soles are popular for dinghy sailing because they protect the feet and give good grip.

BUOYANCY AIDS

Buoyancy aids—as opposed to life jackets—are the usual choice for dinghy sailors, especially for racing and inland sailing. They are available in a variety of designs to suit all shapes and sizes.

Choosing a buoyancy aid

Make sure the buoyancy aid you choose is of a type that is approved by your national standards authority. Also, make sure that the size of the buoyancy aid is suitable for your body weight. A range of styles is available to suit all types of dinghy sailing and small-boat activity, with special sizes available for children (and even for pets). Try the buoyancy aid on before you commit to buying, and make sure it fits comfortably over your wetsuit, waterproofs, or drysuit. If you use a trapeze harness, check the buoyancy aid with the harness.

Closed-cell foam
Provides a minimum of 50 Newtons (11 lb/5 kg) buoyancy

VEST STYLE

Waist belt
Always fasten and tighten the waist belt for security

WAISTCOAT STYLE

RIGGING THE BOAT

Before going afloat you must rig the boat, which involves fully preparing it for sailing. If you sail a dinghy that is kept ashore, rigging is usually done in the dinghy dock before moving the boat to the water. If your boat is stored in a dinghy dock or kept afloat on a mooring, the mast is usually left in place. However, if you have transported the boat to the sailing area on a roof rack or trailer, you will need to step the mast and attach and adjust the standing rigging before the sails can be hoisted. The sails are then rigged, and all the running rigging (sheets, halyards, and control lines) are attached and checked to be sure that they are led correctly. Finally, you should gather up any other gear you need to take afloat and stow it securely in the boat.

Unstayed masts

Boats that have unstayed masts (*pp.130–131*) are usually stored with the mast unstepped, particularly if the mainsail is attached to the mast via a sleeve (the sleeve slides over the mast and the sail can be fitted or removed only when the mast is unstepped).

Unstayed masts are often made in two sections that are slotted together. The sail is fitted to the mast, which is then lifted vertically and lowered into the mast step. There is normally a locking arrangement fitted in the step, which is used to secure the mast in place. Alternatively, a rope downhaul or cunningham line is used to secure the sail and mast to the boat.

Stayed masts

Masts with stays can be stepped either on the keel, on the foredeck, or on a bow tank. In all cases, a mast step is attached to the boat to accept the mast's heel fitting. The fore-and-aft position of the step can sometimes be adjusted to allow alterations to the mast position and rake (lean). In all cases, the mast is supported by wires,

called standing rigging, which are attached to the mast at the hounds and to the boat at the chainplates. The shrouds brace the mast to port and starboard. They run through the ends of the spreaders, which are attached to the mast at about mid-height. Shroud

STEPPING AN UNSTAYED MAST
With the sail sleeved over the mast from the top, the mast is lifted into a vertical position and lowered into the mast step. Place your hands some distance apart on the mast to give more leverage.

length is adjusted with a rigging link or bottlescrew. A forestay, which runs from the hounds to the bow-fitting, stops the mast from falling backward. On some small dinghies the forestay is removable once the jib is hoisted.

Stepping the mast

Before you attempt to step the mast, make sure that it will not hit any overhead obstructions such as power lines when you lift it into place. It is quite often possible to step the mast on small dinghies on your own, but the job is much easier, and much safer, with two people. Although most dinghy masts are light in weight, their length and windage (resistance to the wind) can make them unwieldy to lift in and out of the boat. It helps to have the dinghy on its cart in a bow-down position so that the mast will lean forward against the support of the shrouds when it is placed in its step. Make sure that the tails of all halyards and other rope ends are tied out of the way so that they cannot be trapped under the mast heel. When lifting the mast, keep it as close to vertical as possible and position your hands quite wide apart on it to give better leverage. Check whether the design of your boat will allow you to stand in it when ashore. Modern, double-floored dinghies are usually strong enough, but older designs may be damaged if you stand in them.

Raking the mast

Once you have stepped the mast, you may need to adjust the shrouds and forestay to set the correct mast rake. Most boats sail best with their masts raked aft slightly, but the mast must be upright in a sideways direction. For general sailing, the amount of rake is not too critical, but when you start racing you should set the rake according to your class's tuning guide.

STEPPING A STAYED MAST

KEEL STEPPING

Boats with keel-stepped masts are usually quite easy to step because the mast heel can be positioned into its step before it is pulled into the upright position. Once the mast is in the mast gate, it is held quite securely.

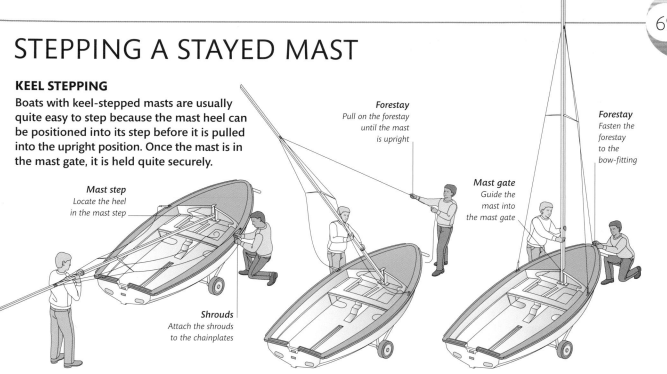

Mast step
Locate the heel in the mast step

Forestay
Pull on the forestay until the mast is upright

Forestay
Fasten the forestay to the bow-fitting

Mast gate
Guide the mast into the mast gate

Shrouds
Attach the shrouds to the chainplates

❶ Lay the mast and rigging on the boat, with the mast heel resting on the mast step and with the front side of the mast uppermost. Attach the two shrouds to the chainplates on the sidedecks.

❷ One person lifts the mast and positions the heel into the mast step. When the mast heel is in the step, the other pulls on the forestay. The person supporting the mast guides it into the mast gate.

❸ Attach the forestay and close the deck-level mast gate. Check the mast rake. Make sure that the halyards are not twisted around the rigging, and that they are led correctly to their respective cleats.

DECK STEPPING

Deck-stepped masts do not have the additional support of a mast gate. They must be lifted vertically before being located into the mast step, and have less support until all the rigging is secured.

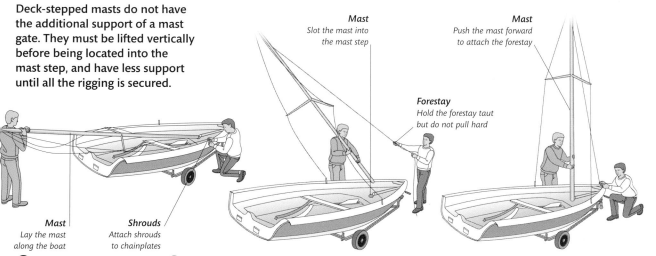

Mast
Slot the mast into the mast step

Mast
Push the mast forward to attach the forestay

Forestay
Hold the forestay taut but do not pull hard

Mast
Lay the mast along the boat

Shrouds
Attach shrouds to chainplates

❶ Lay the mast on the boat with the fore side uppermost and the heel toward the bow. Attach the shrouds to the chainplates.

❷ If the boat has a double floor, one person can get into the boat to lift the mast into position. In an older boat with a single floor, do not get into the boat when ashore. Lift the mast in from the side of the boat.

❸ Allow the mast to lean forward, held by the shrouds, and attach the forestay to the bow-fitting. Next, adjust the shrouds and forestay to get the desired rake. Finally, make sure the halyards are not twisted and that they are led correctly to their respective cleats.

MAINSHEET SYSTEMS

The mainsheet is used to adjust the position of the boom and to help control the shape of the mainsail. When the mainsail is full of wind, there can be quite a heavy load on the mainsheet, so it is run through a system of blocks, called a mainsheet tackle, to make it easier for the helmsman to hold and adjust.

There are two main types of mainsheet systems: center and aft. On the former system, the end of the sheet leads to the helmsman's hand from a block forward of the helmsman. In aft-mainsheet systems, the sheet is led from aft of the helmsman. Either type may have a traveler on a track, which can be used to position the mainsheet athwartships. Center mainsheets are common on racing boats as they offer more control of the sail. Boats with aft-mainsheet systems have more room in the cockpit, which makes them the most popular design for general-purpose dinghies.

Mainsheet systems are usually left in place when the boat is not being sailed. When rigging, make sure the fittings are secure and the sheet runs correctly and smoothly through the various blocks in the tackle. Also, make sure the mainsheet has a figure-eight knot (*pp.46–47*) in the end to prevent it from running out through the mainsheet blocks.

Aft-mainsheet systems

In an aft-mainsheet system, the top block of the tackle is normally attached to a swivel plate at the end of the boom. The bottom block is often attached to a traveler that runs on a track across the transom. Other, simpler designs may be found: sometimes the lower mainsheet block is attached to a rope bridle attached to the transom corners. If a traveler is used, it may have control lines to adjust its position on the track.

Aft-mainsheet systems do not usually have a jamming block for the mainsheet, but they may have a ratchet block to reduce the load that the helmsman has to hold. Because the mainsheet leads from aft, he must face aft when tacking.

Center-mainsheet systems

In most center-mainsheet systems, the top block of the mainsheet tackle is attached to the middle of the boom. This means it has less leverage and more load than an aft mainsheet, so extra blocks are needed in the tackle. The lower block may be attached to an athwartships-track, which runs across the middle of the boat, or it can be fitted on the floor, on a raised hoop, or on the centerboard case. There is usually a cleat attached to the lower mainsheet block so that the sheet can be cleated when the helmsman chooses. If an athwartships track is fitted, the mainsheet tackle's lower block is attached to a traveler that runs on the track. The position of the traveler is usually controlled by lines led from the traveler to the sidedeck within easy reach of the helmsman.

CENTER-MAINSHEET TRAVELER
This center mainsheet has an athwartship track with a mainsheet traveler, the position of which is adjusted by control lines.

CENTER LEAD WITH AFT TACKLE
In this Laser II, the mainsheet tackle is attached near the end of the boom with the lower block on an adjustable rope-bridle system. The sheet then leads forward along the boom to a central block.

AFT MAINSHEET
In this conventional aft-mainsheet arrangement, the lower block is attached to a traveler running on a track mounted on the transom. The traveler position may be adjusted using control lines.

RIGGING THE JIB

Rigging the jib is a one-man job that is usually carried out by the crew, who is responsible for handling the sail. It is always good practice to check the sail for damage as you unfold it and while you are attaching it to the boat. In particular, check the corners and seams for worn or frayed stitching.

Jib fittings

The details of jib fittings and the way it attaches to the boat vary according to the design and size of the boat. In all cases, the jib tack is attached to the bow fitting, usually with a shackle, and its head is attached to the jib halyard, using a shackle or by tying a knot (usually a bowline). Jib sheets are attached to the clew and led through the fairleads on each side of the boat.

On many boats the jib luff is attached to the forestay, using webbing straps, or metal or plastic clips called hanks, that are clipped around the forestay. Alternatively, the jib may not be attached to the forestay, which may be removable once the jib is hoisted. In this case the jib will usually have a wire sewn into the luff to take the high loads. In other cases, a low-stretch tape or rope reinforcement is used. Some jibs are fitted with a roller device at the tack to allow them to be rolled up around their luff when not in use.

Start rigging the jib by removing it from its bag and finding the tack, which can usually be identified by the sailmaker's label. Attach the tack to the bow fitting, then hank the jib luff to the forestay if this system is used in your boat. Start hanking from the tack and work upward, making sure the luff is not twisted between the hanks. Attach the sheets to the clew. Finally, attach the halyard to the sail when you are ready to hoist it.

ATTACHING THE JIB

Remove the sail from its bag, and lay it on the foredeck. A wire-luffed jib will have been stowed by coiling the luff in circles to prevent the wire from kinking. Uncoil it carefully, and make sure that there are no twists in the sail by running your hand along the luff from tack to head. Take care that the sail does not blow off the boat, and try to keep the sail clean while you are handling it.

❶ Attach the tack of the jib to the bow fitting on the dinghy, usually just behind the point where the forestay is fastened. This is usually done with a shackle or lashing. On some boats, as here, the forestay is removed once the jib has been hoisted.

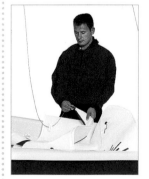

❸ Run a hand along the luff to make sure it is not twisted. If your jib has luff hanks, attach them to the forestay. Check the halyard for tangles and attach it to the head of the sail.

ROLLER FURLING

Some dinghies and small keelboats have a jib roller furling system that allows the jib to be rolled up when not required.

❷ Attach the jib sheets. If they are one piece, as here, make a loop in the middle of the sheet, push it through the cringle, then pass the ends through the loop. Pull the rope through to tighten. If there are two sheets, tie them to the clew cringle.

❹ Hoist the jib by pulling on the halyard. Make sure the sheets are loose so it can flap. Some small dinghies have a simple cleat for the halyard, but others, as here, have an adjuster.

❺ Cleat the halyard or attach it to the adjuster. Here, the adjustment tackle is hooked into a loop in the end of the wire part of the halyard. Coil up the rope tail and stow neatly.

RIGGING THE MAINSAIL

If you are sailing a boat with an unstayed mast (*p.68*) and a sleeved sail, you must fit the mainsail onto the mast before it is stepped. In most boats, however, the sails are attached only after the mast has been stepped. A mainsail is attached to the mast along its luff and to the boom at its foot. There are two methods that are used to attach the mainsail to the boom. In many boats, the mainsail is fitted by sliding its foot into a groove in the top of the boom. In this case, the sail will have a boltrope sewn in a hem at the foot. Other designs have a loose-footed mainsail, which means that the sail is attached to the boom only at the tack and clew.

Mainsail fittings

A mainsail usually has three or more battens that support the roach (the curved shape of the leech). Without them, all the sail that is outside a direct line between head and clew would curl over and be ineffective. Some mainsails have full-length battens that run from the leech to the luff, while others use short battens or a combination of both. Some jibs are also fitted with battens.

Battens may differ in flexibility, depending on which batten pocket they are made for, and the inner end of the batten may be more flexible than the outer end to match the curve in the sail. If this is the case, the battens should be marked to show which pocket they belong in and the end that should be inserted first.

Boom fittings

The boom is attached to the mast via a gooseneck and a boom vang. The gooseneck locates it and allows it to pivot from side to side, while the boom vang prevents it from lifting.

BATTENS

Battens are made of wood, fiberglass, or plastic. They slot into pockets sewn into the sail and are either tied into the pocket or slipped under a flap sewn into its outer end. Battens are often made for specific pockets, so make sure that they are inserted the right way around and in the correct pocket.

Slide batten, most flexible end first, into pocket

Make sure batten is properly secured in its pocket

1 Insert the batten, inner end first, into the correct pocket and slide it in to its full length.

2 Push the batten firmly in and secure it in place with the fastener provided, here a Velcro strip.

Full-length batten

Short batten

MAINSAIL BATTENS
This mainsail has two full-length battens at the top and two short battens lower down the leech.

ATTACHING A CONVENTIONAL SAIL TO THE BOOM

Take the mainsail out of its bag and unroll it inside the boat, with the luff closest to the mast. Make sure you have the requisite number of battens and that they are all in place (*above*). Once you have fitted the mainsail to it, put the boom inside the boat until you are ready to hoist the sail. Do not put the boom onto the gooseneck until after the sail is hoisted. The boom is likely to slide off the gooseneck if it is fitted before the sail is hoisted.

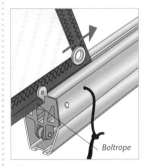

Boltrope

1 Holding the clew, slide the boltrope into the groove at the forward (mast) end of the boom. Make sure that none of the sail cloth gets caught in the groove with the boltrope.

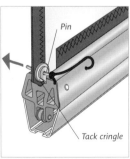

Pin

Tack cringle

2 Pull the clew until all the foot of the sail is in the groove. Fix the tack to the forward end of the boom (often by sliding a pin through the tack cringle and the boom).

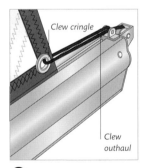

Clew cringle

Clew outhaul

3 Pull the foot of the sail so that it is taut, and fasten the clew outhaul which is used to adjust the tension in the foot of the sail. It is usually adjustable but may be fixed at the boom end.

ATTACHING A LOOSE-FOOTED SAIL TO THE BOOM

Unroll the sail and make sure the battens are in their pockets. Because the foot of the sail is not attached to the boom along its length, you need only attach the clew and the tack. The clew is attached to the outer end of the boom with the clew outhaul, while the tack is either fastened to the gooseneck, with a pin or a lashing, or secured with an adjustable rope called a tack downhaul. Do not put the boom onto the gooseneck until the sail is hoisted.

❶ Remove the sail from its bag and unroll it on the boat. Find the two lower corners, the clew, and the tack.

❷ Put the metal "slug" fitted at the clew into the cutout in the boom's groove. Slide it out to the end of the boom.

❸ Pass the clew outhaul through the clew cringle and fasten its end at the end of the boom, here by hooking a knot into a slot.

❹ Attach the halyard to the head. If a ball is fitted, as here, push a loop through the cringle, then put the end through the loop.

❺ To hoist the sail, one person pulls on the halyard while the other feeds the sail's boltrope into the mast groove.

❻ Attach the boom to the gooseneck (*above*). Pass the tack downhaul through the tack cringle and secure the end.

The gooseneck

The gooseneck is a hinged fitting that attaches the boom to the mast. It can pivot to left and right, and up and down, and allows the boom to move freely in these directions. When fitted into a socket in the boom end, it prevents the boom from rotating.

FITTING THE BOOM

The gooseneck is usually fixed in position, although some can be slid up or down to adjust the boom's height. Its pin is inserted into the socket on the boom end.

The boom vang

The boom vang, or kicking strap, usually consists of an adjustable tackle of rope (or wire) that stops the boom from rising under the pressure of wind in the mainsail. The vang is attached to the boom some way back from the gooseneck, and to the mast just above the heel, making an angle of about 45 degrees between mast and boom.

Hook fits into eye

THE VANG TACKLE

The boom vang usually consists of a rope tackle attached to the boom by a hook (*above left*) or a key and slot system. The other end of the tackle is attached near the base of the mast, and the control line runs aft (*above right*).

SOLID VANG

Some boats have a solid vang fitted above the boom, between it and the mast. The mast end is pivoted, and the boom end runs on a track along the boom. The vang is adjusted by a tackle running between the lower end of the vang and the gooseneck.

REEFING A DINGHY

If the wind increases beyond Force 3, many sailing dinghies start to become harder to handle. Reducing the sail area, known as reefing, makes the dinghy more stable and easier to control in stronger winds. There are three main methods of reefing a mainsail: traditional slab reefing; rolling the sail around the boom; and rolling the sail around the mast. The method you use will depend on the design of your dinghy. A jib can be exchanged for a smaller one or rolled around the forestay.

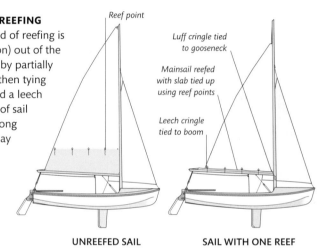

A MAINSAIL REEFED ASHORE

When to reef

Racing dinghies are hardly ever reefed, and races are frequently postponed in strong winds. When sailing for recreation, however, reefing allows you to sail under control in strong winds and reduces the risk of capsize. You can reef while you are afloat if your boat has slab or boom roller reefing, but it is much easier to reef ashore before you set sail. A single-handed dinghy with a sleeved sail should be reefed before sailing.

When reefing a dinghy that has a mainsail and a jib, you should change to a smaller jib, if possible, when you reef the main in order to keep the sail plan balanced.

Methods of reefing

Slab reefing involves taking a portion out of the mainsail, and dinghies designed for this method will have one or two rows of reef points (thin ropes stitched to the sail) or cringles (reinforced eyes in the sail) for lacing a reefing line. Dinghies with unstayed masts can be reefed by rolling the sail around the mast, although this is not easy to do afloat. Dinghies with aft-mainsheet systems are most commonly reefed by rolling the sail around the boom—a method that cannot be used when the mainsheet is attached in the middle of the boom.

TRADITIONAL SLAB REEFING

The traditional method of reefing is to take a "slab" (portion) out of the mainsail. This is done by partially lowering the sail and then tying down a luff cringle and a leech cringle, leaving a fold of sail parallel to the foot, along the boom. The fold may be left hanging, or it can be tied up using reef points, or laced with a line led through a row of reef cringles across the sail.

Reef point

Luff cringle tied to gooseneck

Mainsail reefed with slab tied up using reef points

Leech cringle tied to boom

UNREEFED SAIL

SAIL WITH ONE REEF

ROLLING THE SAIL AROUND THE BOOM

Rolling the mainsail around the boom is used for aft-mainsheet systems (*p.70*). It requires one person at the gooseneck and one at the aft end of the boom. A tuck is put in the leech to stop the boom from drooping after reefing. The rolled sail covers the boom vang fitting, so a replacement is created using a sail bag, a length of rope, or a webbing strap tucked into the sail as it is rolled.

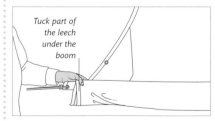

Tuck part of the leech under the boom

❶ Slacken the halyard. Take the boom off the mast, make a 6-in (15-cm) tuck in the leech, pulling it tightly aft, and wrap it around the boom. Holding the tuck in place, rotate the boom, pulling the sail taut at both leech and luff as you go.

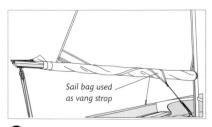

Sail bag used as vang strop

❷ Three turns before you finish the reef, insert the temporary vang strop. Complete the reef, replace the boom on the gooseneck, tighten the halyard, and tie the vang to the strop.

REEFING A CENTER-MAINSHEET BOAT

Some dinghies with a center-mainsheet system are designed to be reefed. They often have a loose-footed mainsail that attaches to the boom only at the tack and clew. To reef with this system, hoist the sail part way up the mast and, with one person at the tack and the other at the clew, tightly roll the sail up from the foot until you reach the leech and luff cringles. Slide the new clew slug into the boom and attach the clew outhaul through the leech cringle, then attach the tack downhaul through the luff cringle. Hoist the sail until the luff is taut and cleat the halyard.

1 With one person at the luff and one at the leech, roll the sail up tightly parallel to the foot, and smooth out any creases.

2 Holding the rolled-up sail, put both the clew slug and the reefing slug into the groove in the top of the boom.

3 Pass the clew outhaul through the leech reef cringle and fasten its end back at the boom end. Pull the clew outhaul tight.

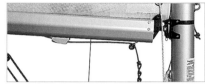

4 Pass the tack downhaul through the luff reef cringle and the old tack cringle and fasten its end under the gooseneck.

ROLLING THE SAIL AROUND THE MAST

A mainsail rigged on an unstayed mast (*p.68*) is reefed by rolling the sail around the mast. Boats with unstayed masts usually have a loose-footed mainsail, which is attached to the aft end of the boom by the clew outhaul. The outhaul must be released before the sail can be reefed. With the sail free to flap like a flag, it can be passed around the mast a number of times, or the mast can be rotated to roll it up. Once sufficient sail has been rolled around the mast, the clew outhaul is reattached and the clew pulled out to tighten the foot. The clew outhaul should be fastened around the boom as well as to the end to hold the clew close against the boom.

Roll the mainsail around the mast

REEFED SAIL

UNREEFED SAIL

1 Release the clew outhaul and remove the boom from the mast. Wrap the sail around the mast or rotate the mast to roll the sail up. In the latter case, release the mast lock or the downhaul (depending on which system the boat employs) to allow the mast to rotate, resecuring the mast when the sail has been reefed.

Clew

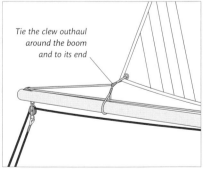

Tie the clew outhaul around the boom and to its end

2 Fit the boom back onto the mast and refasten the clew outhaul, ensuring that you pass it around the boom to hold the clew close to the boom. Tighten the boom vang.

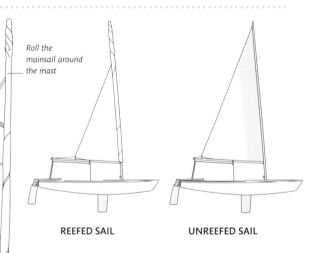

HELMSMAN AND CREW

In a two-person boat, both crew members have distinct roles that must be carried out if the boat is to sail safely and efficiently. The helmsman is in overall charge of the boat. He is also responsible for steering the boat and trimming the mainsail. The crew follows the helmsman's instructions and is responsible for trimming the jib and adjusting the centerboard. Both crew members must be prepared to move their weight to keep the boat balanced and correctly trimmed, although the main balancing work is the responsibility of the crew.

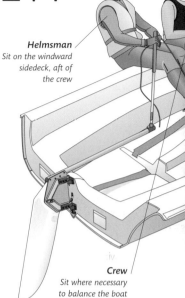

Helmsman
Sit on the windward sidedeck, aft of the crew

Crew
Sit where necessary to balance the boat

The helmsman's role

The windward sidedeck is the best position for the helmsman. He should sit far enough forward to be clear of the end of the tiller, while holding the tiller extension in his aft hand and the mainsheet in his forward hand. This position allows him the clearest view of the water all around the boat, as well as affording a clear view of the sails. It is the most comfortable place from which to control the rudder and trim the mainsail. To perform his role as chief decision-maker, the helmsman must have a good knowledge of the rules of the road (*pp.52–53*) so that he knows when to keep clear of other boats and when he has right of way.

His instructions to the crew must be clear; they must be loud enough to be heard over the noise of wind and water. They must also be given early enough for the crew to be able to respond in good time. Although he is in charge of the boat, the helmsman should encourage input from his crew, and must be prepared to listen to information and advice.

The crew's role

The crew sits just forward of the helmsman but must be ready to move in and out of the boat to keep it upright, while allowing the helmsman to stay on the windward sidedeck. He must learn to anticipate changes in the direction or strength of the wind; and should be ready to counteract their effects by altering his position quickly.

When sitting out, helmsman and crew tuck their feet under toestraps to allow them to lean out without over-balancing. The toestraps should be adjusted so that both can sit out.

The crew should trim the jib to match any changes in wind direction or the boat's course. He should raise

COMMUNICATION
The helmsman and crew should aim for good communication to help them coordinate their movements to keep the boat upright and balanced.

22

POSITION OF THE CREW
When sailing in medium conditions, the helmsman and crew usually sit side by side on the windward sidedeck, with the crew being prepared to move as necessary to keep the boat balanced.

and lower the centerboard (or daggerboard) to suit the point of sailing. He should also keep a good lookout all around the dinghy, especially to leeward, where it can be difficult for the helmsman to see. He must warn the helmsman about any potential collision situations in good time. An experienced crew will also discuss sail trim with the helmsman.

Coordination

It is important that the helmsman and crew learn to coordinate their movements. When the boat heels, the crew should move first to adjust the balance—the helmsman moves only if there is a large change in trim. When a course change is required, good crews move together smoothly to assist the turn and to maintain balance and speed. This teamwork becomes increasingly important when sailing in high-performance dinghies and when racing.

UNDERSTANDING HEEL AND TRIM

One of the most important factors contributing to fast, efficient, and easy sailing is the correct sideways balance, and fore-and-aft trim of the boat. Much of the effort expended by the helmsman and crew during sailing goes into maintaining the ideal balance.

Correcting heel

When sailing in light winds, upwind, or on a reach, the helmsman sits to windward and the crew corrects heel by sitting to leeward. If the wind increases, the crew moves first into the middle of the boat, then to sit out beside the helmsman. When sailing downwind, the heeling force is almost zero, so the crew sits in the middle of the boat or to leeward, opposite the helmsman.

Correcting trim

In moderate winds, the boat should be level fore and aft when the helmsman and crew sit side by side, with the crew sitting just behind the windward shroud. By sitting close together, they reduce the windage of their bodies and also keep their weight centered, which allows the bow and stern to lift easily to pass over waves. If their weight is too far forward, the bow is depressed and steering can become difficult. If their weight is too far back, the stern is depressed and the transom digs into the water, which makes the boat slow down and difficult to sail upwind.

When sailing upwind in very light winds, the helmsman moves forward to just behind the shroud, and the crew sits in the middle or to leeward. This lifts the flat, aft sections of the boat and reduces drag. When sailing downwind in strong winds, the helmsman and crew move aft to lift the bow, but not so far as to make the stern drag.

CORRECT TRIM
The helmsman and crew sit close together to minimize the windage of their bodies. They position themselves to trim the boat fore and aft so that the transom is just clear of the water. In lighter winds they would move forward slightly to lift the stern, and in stronger winds they would move aft to lift the bow.

CORRECT BALANCE
The crew moves her weight to balance the boat and allow the helmsman to sit to windward from where he has the best view of the sails and course. Here, the boat is on a broad reach in light airs, so the crew sits to leeward, under the boom, to balance the boat. From here, she can see the jib trim and hazards to leeward.

TURNING FORCES

A sailing boat's performance is determined by the efficient interaction of the main controls—hull balance and trim, sails, rudder, and centerboard. When used correctly, these make the boat easy to steer and sail efficiently. However, the hull, sails, and centerboard can produce powerful turning forces, which, in extreme cases, may overcome the effects of the rudder. You need to learn how to keep all these forces in balance; otherwise, the boat will slow down and become more difficult to sail.

Balance and trim

Although the sensation of speed may be greater when your dinghy is heeled well over, sailing this way is actually slower than sailing with the boat upright. A dinghy hull is designed to be at its most efficient when it sits on its natural waterline, level sideways (balance) and fore and aft (trim). When it is balanced and trimmed in this way, the boat will sail fast and will tend to move in a straight line.

Balance is achieved by the crew moving their weight in and out of the boat to port and/or starboard in order to counteract the heeling force of the sails. When the boat is upright, the shape of its underwater section is symmetrical and it will move in a straight line, and when allowed to heel the shape changes and it will try to turn.

The fore-and-aft trim of the boat is just as important as its sideways balance. The amount of the hull in the water—its waterline shape—can be altered by the crew moving forward or aft, and this shape will have an effect on the way the boat handles. If the crew moves forward in the boat, this will depress the bow while lifting the stern. This can be useful to reduce hull drag in very light winds, but it is slow in other conditions, and the boat will

tend to turn toward the wind. If the crew moves their weight aft, the stern will be depressed and the bow raised. This is often done when sailing downwind in strong winds or when planing (*p.126*) to prevent the bow from digging into the water. In other situations, however, it will slow the boat down and tend to make it turn away from the wind.

The sails

A boat's sails are trimmed to create the force that drives the boat forward, but they can also be used to help change direction. Most small boats have two sails—a mainsail behind the mast and a jib forward of it. When both are trimmed correctly (and the hull is upright and the centerboard in the correct position), the boat will be well balanced and will require little use of the rudder to keep it on course.

Most of the time you will trim the sails to work efficiently together and eliminate their turning effects. When you want to change course, however, the sails can be a very useful aid in making the maneuver as smooth and efficient as possible. By using the sails to help turn the boat, you will reduce the amount you need to use the rudder (*p.81*). The helmsman and

crew must coordinate their actions in trimming the mainsail and jib in order to achieve the desired turning effect.

The centerboard

A centerboard or daggerboard is used to resist sideways force (*pp.34–35*). It also acts as the pivot point around which the boat turns.

Most dinghies are equipped with a centerboard that pivots inside a case. When it is raised and retracted, its tip moves back and upward. This decreases the area of centerboard under the boat and also alters its position along the fore-and-aft line, which affects steering. When it is in its correct position, the turning forces of the jib and mainsail are balanced around the pivot point. If the centerboard is raised, the boat will turn away from the wind as the pivot point moves aft. If it is lowered, the pivot point moves forward and the boat will tend to turn into the wind.

Daggerboards move vertically inside their case. When a daggerboard is raised, the area under the boat is reduced but its position along the fore-and-aft line remains the same and has no turning effect.

The rudder

The primary control for changing direction is the rudder. In addition, whenever it is moved off-center by more than four degrees, it acts as a brake as well as a turning control. The farther the rudder is turned, the greater the braking effect. Rudders work most efficiently when the boat is moving quickly. The braking effect is, likewise, most dramatic at high speed, when careful handling is required. At slow speeds, the rudder's effect is reduced because the water moves past it more slowly, and it has no effect when the boat is stopped. Its effect is reversed when the boat moves backward.

Boat trim

The natural tendency of most beginners is to sit too far aft in the boat. In normal conditions the helmsman should sit forward of the end of the tiller so that he can move it freely without it hitting his body. The crew should sit just forward of the helmsman, which in most dinghies will mean he sits just aft of the shrouds. Helmsman and crew should sit close together to keep their weight centered in the boat and to reduce the wind resistance of their bodies. In light winds they should move forward to lift the stern and reduce hull drag, especially when sailing on a windward course. In strong winds, and especially when sailing downwind, they should move aft to lift the bow.

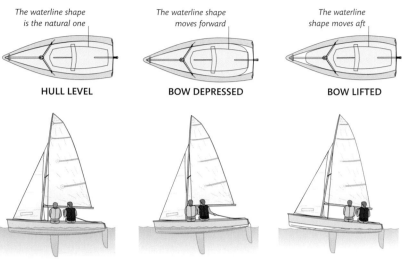

The waterline shape is the natural one

HULL LEVEL

The waterline shape moves forward

BOW DEPRESSED

The waterline shape moves aft

BOW LIFTED

HULL LEVEL
The crew trims the boat so that it sits in the water on its natural waterline. This is the best trim in most conditions.

BOW DOWN
The crew moves forward to depress the bow and lift the stern. The boat will tend to turn toward the wind.

BOW UP
By moving aft, the crew depress the stern and raise the bow. The boat tends to turn away from the wind.

Boat balance

When the hull is level in the water, sideways as well as fore and aft, it has a symmetrical waterline shape and will tend to sail in a straight line. However, if the boat heels to windward or to leeward, the shape of the waterline becomes asymmetrical, which makes the boat try to turn.

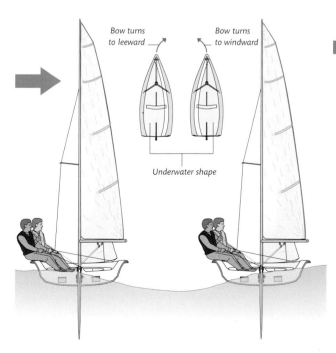

Bow turns to leeward

Bow turns to windward

Underwater shape

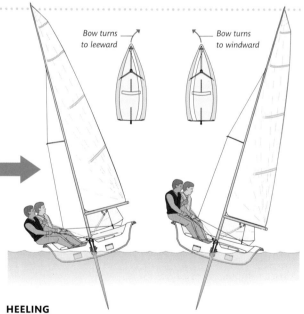

Bow turns to leeward

Bow turns to windward

HEELING
As the boat heels, the underwater shape changes and the rudder and centerboard become off-center in the underwater area. This makes the boat try to turn in the direction opposite of the heel.

WAVES ON THE BEAM
The turning effect also occurs when a wave passes under the hull from the side. First, the windward side is more immersed and the boat tries to turn away from the wind; then, the leeward side is more immersed and the boat tries to turn toward the wind.

Using the sails

Both the mainsail and the jib can be used separately to create a force that will turn the boat. Because the jib is smaller than the mainsail, its turning effect is not quite as large as the mainsail, but it will still be significant. The jib used alone acts in front of the centerboard's pivot point, so pulls the bow away from the wind. The mainsail used alone acts behind the pivot point, so pulls the stern away from the wind and the bow toward it. The turning effect of each depends on the other sail being let out.

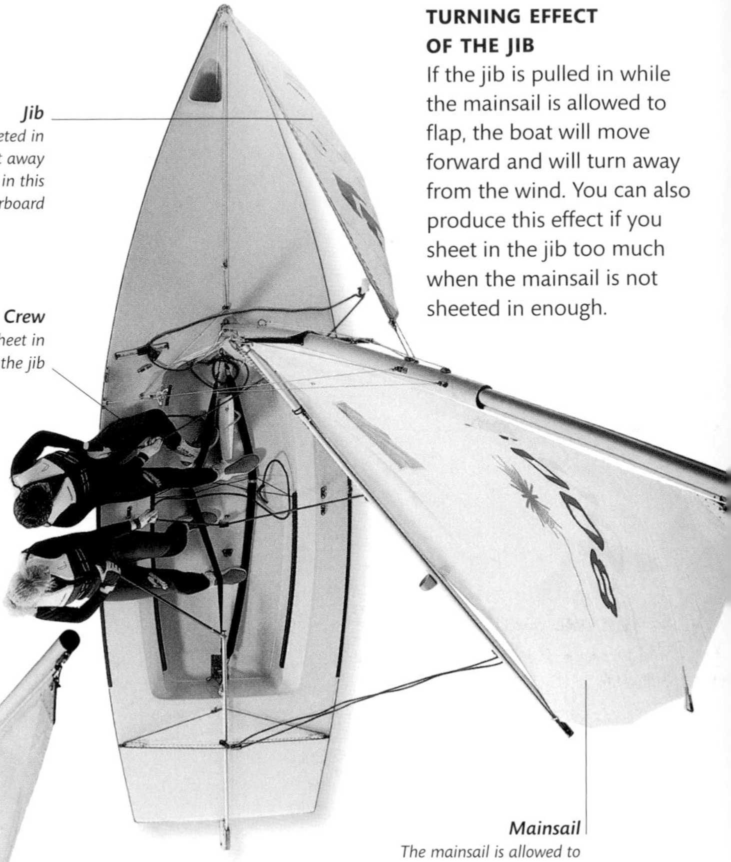

TURNING EFFECT OF THE MAINSAIL

If the mainsail is pulled in while the jib is allowed to flap, the boat will move forward and turn to windward. The more quickly you pull in the mainsail, the faster the boat turns. You will also produce this effect by sheeting in the mainsail too much when the jib is not sheeted in enough.

Jib
The jib is sheeted in to turn the boat away from the wind; in this case, to starboard

Crew
Sheet in the jib

TURNING EFFECT OF THE JIB

If the jib is pulled in while the mainsail is allowed to flap, the boat will move forward and will turn away from the wind. You can also produce this effect if you sheet in the jib too much when the mainsail is not sheeted in enough.

Mainsail
The mainsail is allowed to flap freely, so that it has no turning effect on the boat

Jib
The jib is allowed to flap freely, so that it has no turning effect on the boat

Mainsail
The mainsail is sheeted in to turn the boat into the wind; in this case, it will turn to port

SAIL SETTING USING TELLTALES

Telltales are light strips of wool or nylon, sewn or glued about 6–9 in (15–25 cm) in from the luff on both sides of the sails. They indicate whether the air stream at the sail surface is smooth or turbulent.

How telltales work

If the sail is trimmed correctly, the telltales on both sides will fly parallel. If those to windward fly higher, pull in the sheet; if those to leeward fly higher, let out the sheet.

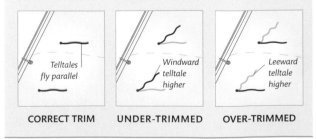

Telltales fly parallel

Windward telltale higher

Leeward telltale higher

CORRECT TRIM   UNDER-TRIMMED   OVER-TRIMMED

Using the centerboard

The centerboard or daggerboard provides most of the resistance to sideways movement, so it is vital that the centerboard or daggerboard is used properly, especially if you are sailing close-hauled (when it should be fully down). Beginners often forget to lower the board when sailing away from land, or when turning onto a close-hauled course. If you try to sail close to the wind with the board up, the boat will move as fast sideways as it does forward, resulting in a crab-like course and making it difficult for the helmsman to steer a course.

CENTERBOARD

If the centerboard is not lowered sufficiently, the sideways force will not be resisted and the boat will slide sideways. This leeward motion is most apparent when sailing upwind, when full centerboard is needed.

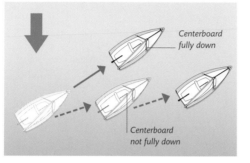

Centerboard fully down

Centerboard not fully down

CENTERBOARD MARKING

Marking the centerboard case, quarter down, half down, and so on, is a good way to indicate how much of the centerboard is protruding below the hull at any given time. Position the leading edge against the marks. If your dinghy has a daggerboard, mark the daggerboard itself, not its case.

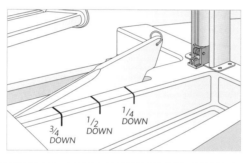

3/4 DOWN

1/2 DOWN

1/4 DOWN

Using the rudder

Sitting in the helmsman's position on the windward side of the boat, push the tiller away to turn the boat toward the wind. As the boat turns, the sails should be trimmed for the new course. If the turn continues, the boat will reach head-to-wind and stop. To turn away from the wind, pull the tiller toward you. As the boat turns farther downwind, the sails must be let out to keep them set correctly.

Keep your actions smooth. When the rudder turns, it acts as a brake as well as a turning device, so avoid jerking it backward and forward.

STEERING

Sit to windward opposite the sails when steering. Gently push or pull the tiller to move the rudder and turn the boat. When moving forward, the bow always turns the opposite direction from the way you move the tiller.

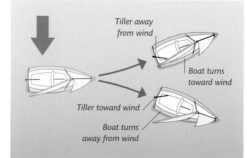

Tiller away from wind

Boat turns toward wind

Tiller toward wind

Boat turns away from wind

USING ALL THE TURNING CONTROLS

To understand fully how all the turning forces work in practice, try the following exercises when you go afloat. Start by sailing on a beam reach, then make sure that both sails are only partly full of wind, the centerboard is half down, and the rudder is centered. Now run through these two sequences.

Turn toward the wind

• First, the helmsman gently pushes the tiller away from him.
• The crew lowers the centerboard.
• Next, the helmsman pulls in the mainsheet to trim the mainsail, and the crew lets out the jib.
• At the same time, heel the boat slightly away from the wind.

Turn away from the wind

• The helmsman gently pulls the tiller toward him.
• The crew raises the centerboard.
• The crew pulls in the jib and the helmsman lets out the mainsail.
• At the same time, heel the boat slightly toward the wind.

UNDER CONTROL

Here, the crew is sailing fast downwind under full control by keeping the boat correctly trimmed and balanced, and using sail trim to help steer the boat as it surfs down a wave front. The boat is well balanced, so it is easy to steer.

GOING AFLOAT

The first time you set sail, whether it is alone or with an instructor, you will begin to appreciate the challenges, rewards, and responsibilities of sailing. When you are learning with an instructor you need concentrate only on acquiring new skills, leaving the safety aspects to him. If you sail off alone, however, you are in sole charge of your destiny. This is one of the greatest attractions of sailing, but you must be aware of the risks and take sensible precautions if you want to enjoy the experience.

Before launching

Whenever you decide to go sailing, choose a suitable location and only go afloat when the weather and water conditions are appropriate to your level of expertise. When you arrive at your chosen sailing area, be prepared to ask local sailors for their advice before you go afloat, since they will have experience of the prevailing conditions. Make sure that they are aware of your level of experience.

Many people start learning to sail on inland waters as they are generally more sheltered than the sea and there are no tides to complicate matters. Help is usually close at hand, too, should you find yourself in difficulties. However, there is no reason why you should not learn how to sail on the sea, provided that you are prepared to take sensible safety precautions.

Assessing the wind

For your first trip alone, pick a day when the wind is Force 3 or less. Check the weather forecast, paying most attention to the local area sailing forecast. Do not hesitate to cancel your trip if you are not sure that the conditions will be right.

When you arrive at the sailing area, take a careful look at all the wind indicators to help you build a picture of the conditions. Check flags, both ashore and on moored boats, and the direction of any smoke from chimneys, and the way trees move in the wind. Look at the waves on the water, which usually run at right angles to the wind. It is also very important that you know whether the wind is onshore or offshore as it can make a great difference to your trip.

Sailing in onshore winds

If the wind is onshore, it will feel stronger. If it is moderate or strong, it will cause waves to break on the beach. An onshore wind makes it harder to launch and sail off because it will tend to blow you back onto the shore. On the other hand, it is easy to return to the shore in an onshore wind, and you will not be in danger of being blown away from your base.

Sailing in offshore winds

If the wind is offshore, it can be very difficult to judge its true strength while you are on land. As you sail farther from the shore, its strength is likely to increase and may be more than you are happy with. In an offshore wind it is easy to launch and sail away as there are no waves on the beach and you will be blown clear of the shore. Getting back, on the other hand, could be more difficult and there is a danger of being blown away from your base and unable to return.

If you are sailing on the sea, avoid going afloat in offshore winds on your first few trips. On inland waters, make sure that another boat is nearby or that a safety boat will be available if you need a tow back to base.

NO WIND
If there is no wind, wait until it rises, especially if a tidal stream is present, as shown here by the moored boats.

ONSHORE WIND
Even a Force 3 blowing onshore will cause waves to break on the lee shore. If the water is shallow a long way out, the waves will break first some distance from the beach; if the shoreline is steep, the waves will break on the shore.

OFFSHORE WIND
A Force 3 wind causes quite different conditions when blowing offshore than it does blowing onshore. Close to land, the sea is sheltered and there will be no waves. Farther out, the conditions may be much rougher than they appear from the beach.

Checking the tide

If you are sailing on a river or the sea, you may have to deal with tidal conditions (*pp.56–57*). Obtain a copy of the local tide tables and check it for the times of high and low waters. Again, experienced local sailors will be able to give you advice.

Before you go afloat, make sure that you know the state of the tide. Find out the direction of the tidal stream and what time it will turn. Plan your trip so that you can sail back to your base with the tide when you are ready to return.

Avoiding collisions

Before you go afloat, remind yourself of the procedures for the prevention of collisions on the water (*pp.52–53*). It is your

TIDAL TIPS

Verify information given in tide tables by observing the shoreline: a wet shoreline means that the tide is going out, a dry one signals that it is coming in.

responsibility as skipper of your own boat to be familiar with these rules of the road.

When you are learning to sail, avoid busy shipping channels. Keep to the shallower water at their edges where you will not meet larger boats. If you do have to cross a channel, remember to do so at right angles so you get across as quickly as possible.

If you think you are in a potential collision situation and you are not sure of the rules that apply, then it is safest to assume that you have to keep clear. Make a large alteration of course to pass behind the other boat so that your intentions are obvious to the other skipper.

Remember to check regularly all around the boat. Beginners often forget to look astern and are startled when another vessel suddenly appears. The area behind the jib and mainsail can be hidden from helmsman and crew when they are sitting out to windward. Check this area regularly, asking your crew to move to leeward briefly for a clearer view if necessary.

FINAL PREPARATIONS

Before you go afloat there are several checks that you should run through to ensure you have a safe, enjoyable sail and an easy return. Do not be tempted to ignore these, even if you are in a hurry—your safety may depend on them.

Conditions check
Before you decide to sail, ask yourself about the conditions.
• Is the wind strength suitable for your level of experience?
• Is the wind onshore or offshore?
• Is the wind strength forecast to increase or decrease?
• Do you know the state of the tide, and will you be able to return without having to fight the current?
• Are there other sailors nearby who can help you if necessary?

Tell someone your plans
Once you have decided that it is safe to sail, you need to make sure a responsible person knows your plans—where you expect to sail and when you plan to return. When you do get back from your sail, remember to tell them you are back safely or they may notify the rescue services unnecessarily.

Equipment check
When you are at the shoreline and ready to sail, make sure you are fully prepared to go afloat.
• Is your clothing adequate?
• Are all the crew wearing personal buoyancy—fastened correctly?
• Is all the sailing gear rigged properly and in good condition?
• Are all the bungs and hatches in position?
• Are the oars or paddles on board and tied securely?
• Are there an anchor and warp aboard tied in securely?
• Is all personal equipment stowed neatly in waterproof containers tied in securely?

LAUNCHING A DINGHY

A well-planned routine for preparing and launching your dinghy will ensure that you rig it properly, and that all the necessary equipment is on board and in good working order. A launching trolley is the usual means of moving a dinghy to the water, and how you launch from there depends on whether it is a beach or slipway launch, or a pontoon launch. Whichever it is, work out a system with your sailing partner to build on the teamwork that will make you good sailors on the water.

Using a launch trolley

Most damage is done to dinghies when they are moved while ashore, so it is important to move the dinghy and launch it in a way that prevents the hull from coming into contact with the ground (*pp.50–51*); a launching cart is ideal for this. Dinghies are quite heavy and awkward to lift, so if it has been transported on a roof rack or road trailer, find a few people who are willing to help lift it onto its cart to make the job easier.

Position the boat so that there is not too much weight on the front of the cart when you lift it by the handle, and tie the painter around the cart handle to prevent the boat from sliding off. If the cart has a T-shaped handle, you can secure the rope with figure-eight turns.

Preparing the boat

Step the mast if necessary (*pp.68–69*), and make sure all the bungs are in position. Collect all the equipment, including the sails, rudder, paddles, and any other important removable gear, before you move the boat close to the launching point.

Sails are usually rigged (and lifting rudders fitted) before launching but, in some circumstances, such as launching from a pontoon, you may wish to rig them after launching. A lifting rudder can be fitted before launching, but a fixed blade must be left until you are afloat. Only fit a fixed rudder when you have moved the boat into water deep enough to take the rudder blade without it hitting the bottom. If you put the rudder in the boat for launching put it under the boom and mainsail, otherwise it may be thrown about when the sail is hoisted. The centerboard should be up when you launch; if you have a daggerboard, lay it in the bottom of the boat, under the boom and mainsail, until you go afloat. In most situations, hoist the jib before you launch unless its flapping will be a nuisance while launching.

If the boat can be kept head-to-wind when launching, you can also hoist the mainsail; otherwise, it is hoisted when you are afloat. Do a final check around the boat to ensure you have everything you need. Wheel the boat to the water, and launch, following the instructions for a beach, slipway, or pontoon (*pp.102–105*).

FITTING THE RUDDER

Both fixed and lifting rudders are secured to the boat by means of fittings on their stock. Fit a lifting rudder before launching. Fit a fixed rudder after launching, making sure the water is sufficiently deep first. If it has a removable tiller, fit the rudder to the boat, then fit the tiller. If you fit the rudder and tiller before hoisting the mainsail, make sure that the sail and boom do not catch under the tiller when the sail is hoisted.

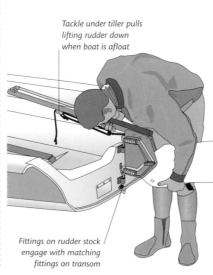

Tackle under tiller pulls lifting rudder down when boat is afloat

Fittings on rudder stock engage with matching fittings on transom

❶ Slide the fittings on the stock onto their counterpart fixings on the boat's transom. Make sure that the blade is held up so it cannot scrape on the ground. If you have a removable tiller, go on to steps 2 and 3.

 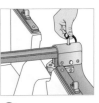

❷ Slide the tiller into the fitted rudder head and make sure it is a tight fit.

❸ Secure the tiller—usually with a pin that passes through the rudder head and the tiller.

Hoisting the sails

With the boat head-to-wind, the sails can be hoisted ashore. To hoist the jib, one person pulls on the jib halyard until the sail is up and then secures it to its cleat or other fitting provided. Some boats have a jib furling system so the jib can be rolled up once it is hoisted (*right*). To hoist the mainsail, one person guides the boltrope into the mast groove while the other hoists the sail with the halyard. Once the sail is fully up, the boom is slid onto the gooseneck. Make sure both main and jib sheets are free to run so the sails do not fill.

One person feeds the sail into the luff groove

Jib hoisted and rolled up

One person hoists the mainsail by pulling on the halyard

Boom lying in boat, not attached to mast until sail is hoisted

HOISTING SAILS ASHORE
If you are able to launch the boat while keeping it head-to-wind, you can hoist the sails ashore. Turn the boat head to wind so the sails can flap freely.

BEACH OR SLIPWAY LAUNCH
To launch from a beach or slipway, use the cart to wheel the boat into the water. Wheel it deep enough for the boat to float clear of the cart. As soon as the boat floats free, it will come under the influence of the wind and waves, so hold it firmly by the bow. For beach launches, you will need balloon tires on the cart to cope with the soft surface.

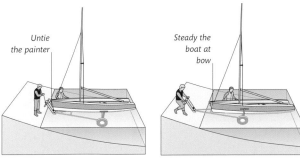

Untie the painter

Steady the boat at bow

1 Push the cart into the water until the boat floats off. Never push or drag the boat off or you will scratch its hull. Untie the painter to release the boat from the cart.

2 One person holds the boat by the bow, to one side of the slipway and clear of other users. The other takes the trolley to above high-water level and parks it clear of the slipway.

PONTOON LAUNCH
If you have to launch over the side of a pontoon, it is best to do it before hoisting the sails. Pontoon launches need at least two people, one on either side of the boat.

1 With one person holding the painter, lift the boat until its stern is over the water. Lower the stern into the water, then gently push the boat back until the bow can be lowered over the side. Launch the boat gently to avoid water flooding in over the transom.

2 Lead the boat to the end of the pontoon and turn it head-to-wind. Secure the painter on the pontoon before hoisting the sails and fitting the rudder.

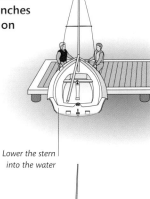

Lower the stern into the water

Turn the boat head-to-wind

BASIC TECHNIQUES

In order to become proficient at handling a boat, you need to practice using the main controls (*pp.36–39*). You must learn how the boat reacts to the wind on all points of sailing, and you must be able to change course smoothly and efficiently. You will also want to know how to stop the boat. When you start sailing, you will not yet have the skills needed to leave and return to the shore under sail, so on your first few trips afloat, row or paddle away from shore, then hoist the sails once you are in clear water.

FIRST SKILLS

As soon as you launch a dinghy, the wind will act on it and it will begin to move. There are three basic ways of stopping it from moving in the water, each of which involves making the wind work in your favor. The most controlled method, but also the most complicated, is heaving-to. Two further simple techniques for stopping a boat are the lying-to method and the head-to-wind method, both of which work by emptying the sails of wind so that they flap and lose forward drive. Lying-to is the more stable option as the boat will simply drift until you pull in the sails. In a head-to-wind position, the wind will push the boat backward due to the windage of the flapping sails, and the bow will start to turn in one direction or the other (depending on the position of the rudder) until the sails fill and the boat starts to sail. This method is used mainly when you need to stop alongside a mooring or pontoon or other boat.

When you are confident with these two ways of stopping, you can try the more controlled heaving-to (*p.100*).

No-sail zone
The head-to-wind method of stopping exploits the fact that there is an area of about 45° on either side of the wind direction into which it is impossible to point the boat and keep sailing. This area is known as the no-sail zone. When the boat is close-hauled, you are sailing along

Using the wind to stop and start
To lie-to, turn the boat onto a close reach (*p.41*) and let both sails out fully. It is not possible to lie-to when the boat is pointing farther offwind because, as you let out the mainsail, the boom hits the shrouds and the sail refills with wind. To sail away from the lying-to position, sheet in both sails and the boat will move forward.

To stop head-to-wind, turn the dinghy until the bow points into the wind. This makes the sails shake along the centerline of the boat and it will come to a stop. To sail away from a head-to-wind position, decide which way you want the bow to move and pull the jib across to the opposite side. This is known as backing the jib and will push the bow in the desired direction. When the boat has turned, trim both sails correctly and sail off.

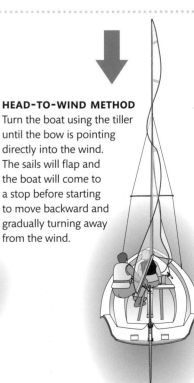

HEAD-TO-WIND METHOD
Turn the boat using the tiller until the bow is pointing directly into the wind. The sails will flap and the boat will come to a stop before starting to move backward and gradually turning away from the wind.

LYING-TO METHOD
Turn the boat using the tiller until the wind is blowing from a point just forward of abeam. Let both sails out fully so that they flap. The boat will stop and drift gently until you pull in the sails.

the edge of the no-sail zone. If you try to point closer to the wind, turning into the no-sail zone, the sails will shake and the boat will slow down and stop.

To get to a point upwind within the no-sail zone, it is necessary to sail a series of zigzags, first on one tack, then on the other, making progress to windward with each tack. This process is called beating to windward (*p.92*).

Starting to sail

When you first start sailing, it is easiest to get accustomed to using the main controls while sailing on a beam reach. This is the fastest and easiest point of sailing. It does not demand very accurate steering, sail trimming, centerboard positioning, or crew balance.

BOAT SPEED

The speed at which you can sail is dependent on a number of factors, including the strength of the wind, the point of sailing you are on (*pp.40–41*), the type of boat you are sailing, and how well you are sailing it. Tidal streams and waves will also affect speed (*pp.56–57*).

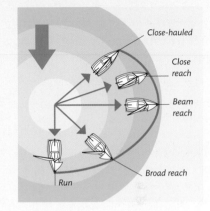

SPEED VERSUS POINT OF SAIL
Potential boat speed on specific points of sailing and in a particular wind strength are shown using a polar diagram. The concentric circles represent potential boat speed. The farther away from the central circle you are, the faster the boat is sailing. The precise shape of the performance curve depends on the design of boat. The diagram shows the performance curve of a typical general-purpose dinghy. It reaches its maximum speed on a beam reach and moves slowest when sailed on a run.

Close-hauled

Close reach

Beam reach

Broad reach

Run

THE FIVE ESSENTIALS

There are five essential elements to sailing efficiently: sail trim, centerboard position, boat balance, boat trim, and the course made good. Whenever one changes, you should quickly review the other four and correct them if necessary. Remember to check the five essentials every time you make a course alteration.

Sail trim
To check trim, ease the sails out until they shake along their luffs, then pull them in until the shaking just stops. Make it easier to check trim by fitting telltales, which show the wind flow across the sails (*p.80*).

Centerboard position
The centerboard is used to counteract sideways force (*p.81*), which is greatest when you sail close-hauled. So the closer you sail toward the wind, the more you must lower the centerboard, and the farther you turn away from the wind, the more you must raise the centerboard, until it is almost fully up on a run. Always keep it down at least a small amount to provide a pivot point around which the boat can turn.

Boat balance
The heeling force increases as you sail closer to the wind, so the helmsman and crew must both sit out in most wind strengths to keep the boat upright. If the wind strength or the course change, the crew should move first to balance the boat.

Boat trim
Always make sure the boat is trimmed correctly in a fore and aft direction. In light winds, trim the boat slightly down by the bow; in strong winds, move back slightly. Check that the wake is not very disturbed, which indicates that you are sitting too far aft. Helmsman and crew should sit close together to keep their weight concentrated in the middle of the boat. This allows the bow and stern to lift easily with the waves.

Course made good
Always remember to keep an eye on your course. Your objective is to sail the fastest route to your destination. This is not necessarily the straight-line course. If your objective is to windward, for example, you will have to sail a zigzag course to reach it. This means that you must decide when to tack and you will also have to allow for leeway. Even when you are sailing on a reach, the sideways force will cause a small amount of leeway, and your actual course through the water will be slightly to leeward of the course you are steering. Allow for this by steering upwind of your objective by a small amount. Be aware, too, of any tidal stream that may push you off your intended course.

CHANGING COURSE

Learning to change course introduces you to all the different points of sailing (*pp.40–41*). The best way to go through a complete change of course—from sailing toward the wind (an upwind course) to sailing away from it (a downwind course)—is to start on a beam reach with the boat sailing directly across the wind.

Starting to luff

Turning the boat toward the wind is known as luffing (or luffing up). Whenever you want to turn onto a more upwind course, you have to luff.

To luff, the helmsman pushes the tiller gently away from him and sheets in the mainsail. The crew sheets in the

jib and lowers the centerboard. As the boat turns toward the wind, the apparent wind (*p.32*) increases in strength and the heeling force (*p.32*) also increases, so the crew needs to sit out even farther to keep the boat upright and sailing at its best speed. Continue to luff until the boat is on a close-hauled course.

Starting to bear away

Turning away from the wind is called bearing away. Whenever you want to turn onto a more downwind course you have to bear away.

To bear away, the helmsman pulls the tiller gently toward him and lets the mainsail out. The crew

lets out the jib and raises the centerboard. As the boat turns further away from the wind, the apparent wind decreases in strength and the heeling force reduces, so the crew must move inboard to keep the boat level or prevent it from heeling to windward. Continue to bear away until the boat is sailing on a run.

Helmsman
Adjust the mainsheet and tiller continually

LUFFING: TURNING TOWARD THE WIND

Luffing up requires coordinated action with the tiller, centerboard, sail trim, and boat balance. The crew should lower the centerboard before the turn, and then concentrate on keeping the boat level and sheeting the jib in as the helmsman turns the boat and sheets in the mainsail.

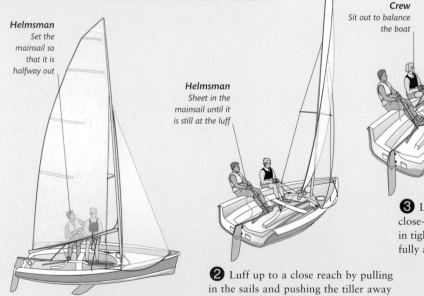

Helmsman
Set the mainsail so that it is halfway out

Helmsman
Sheet in the mainsail until it is still at the luff

Crew
Sit out to balance the boat

❶ Sail on a beam reach with the sails set correctly (*p.41*), the tiller centered, the boat upright, and the centerboard halfway down.

❷ Luff up to a close reach by pulling in the sails and pushing the tiller away from you. Lower the centerboard until it is three quarters down, and sit out more to counterbalance the increased heeling force in the sails.

❸ Luff up to very nearly close-hauled, sheeting both sails in tightly. Lower the centerboard fully and sit out even farther.

❹ Steer along the edge of the no-sail zone by alternately luffing up and bearing away slightly. Luff up until the jib luff starts shaking, and then bear away slightly until the shaking just stops.

BEARING AWAY: TURNING AWAY FROM THE WIND

Make sure the boat is upright before the maneuver because any heel to leeward will make it difficult to bear away. Let the sails out as the boat turns, and raise the centerboard.

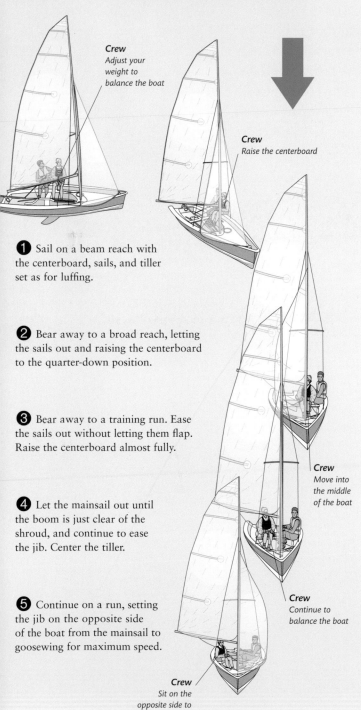

Crew
Adjust your weight to balance the boat

Crew
Raise the centerboard

1 Sail on a beam reach with the centerboard, sails, and tiller set as for luffing.

2 Bear away to a broad reach, letting the sails out and raising the centerboard to the quarter-down position.

3 Bear away to a training run. Ease the sails out without letting them flap. Raise the centerboard almost fully.

4 Let the mainsail out until the boom is just clear of the shroud, and continue to ease the jib. Center the tiller.

5 Continue on a run, setting the jib on the opposite side of the boat from the mainsail to goosewing for maximum speed.

Crew
Move into the middle of the boat

Crew
Continue to balance the boat

Crew
Sit on the opposite side to the helmsman

TECHNIQUES FOR SHEETING THE MAINSAIL IN AND OUT

The technique for sheeting the mainsail in and out varies according to your mainsheet system. Both methods require the helmsman to make adjustments while keeping the tiller still to avoid altering course unintentionally. To ease the sheet, let it slide out through your hand.

Center mainsheet

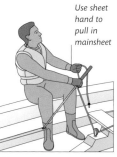
Use sheet hand to pull in mainsheet

Grasp the sheet near the block and pull

1 Pull in the mainsheet using your sheet hand. Holding the tiller extension in your tiller hand as if it were a dart, swing the extension across your body and down to grasp the sheet.

2 With sheet and tiller extension in your tiller hand, swing the extension aft. With your sheet hand, grasp the sheet at a point near the block and pull as far as you can. Repeat as necessary.

Aft mainsheet

Pull in the mainsheet as far as possible

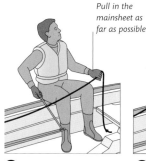
Secure sheet under the tiller thumb

1 Keep your tiller hand steady on the tiller extension. With your sheet hand, pull in the mainsheet as far as possible, bringing the sheet across your body from the stern.

2 Trap the sheet under the thumb of your tiller hand. Let go of it with your sheet hand, and then reach across your body to grasp the sheet and pull it again. Repeat these steps as necessary.

TACKING

One of the key sailing maneuvers, tacking is used to change direction by turning the bow of the boat through the eye of the wind. It requires good coordination between helmsman and crew. A tack can be performed from any upwind course but is most often employed to change direction from one close-hauled course to the other. When tacking an aft-mainsheet boat, the helmsman faces aft; if a center mainsheet is fitted, he must face forward to handle the mainsheet. The movements of the crew remain the same.

Tacking roles

The helmsman decides when to tack. He and the crew must turn the boat, trim the sails, and move their weight across the boat while keeping it as upright as possible. The helmsman checks that the new course is clear and that the crew is ready. During the tack, he must change hands on the tiller and mainsheet while moving across the boat, controlling both at the same time. After the tack, he must check sail trim, boat balance, and the new course.

The crew is responsible for releasing the jib sheet, picking up the new one, and moving across the boat to sheet in the jib on the new side as the boat completes the turn. The crew must be alert to helmsman's instructions, and must confirm that the new course is clear before committing to the turn.

The tacking maneuvre

Tacking is actually a prolonged luffing maneuver in which the boat turns sufficiently for the sail to fill on the opposite course. The maneuver begins with luffing up (*p.88*). The tack itself occurs when the bow of the boat passes through the eye of the wind, and the maneuver is complete when you are sailing on the new course.

TACKING FROM A REACH TO A REACH

When you are learning to tack, you will start by sailing on a beam reach with the wind on one side of the boat, and then tack onto the opposite beam reach with the wind on the other side.

BEAM-REACH TACK

Tacking from a beam reach to the opposite beam reach involves a turn of 180°. Turning through such a large angle gives the helmsman and crew more time to cross the boat before the sails fill on the new side. It does, however, require the boat to be sailing fast before the tack so that it has sufficient momentum to complete the turn. The helmsman must make sure the tiller is held over until the boat has passed head-to-wind.

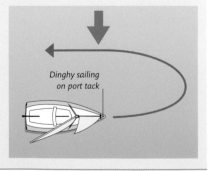

Dinghy sailing on port tack

7 Helmsman and crew trim the sails to suit the new course and balance the boat accordingly.

Rudder is centered

TACKING A CENTER MAINSHEET BOAT

This sequence shows a boat with a center mainsheet being tacked from a reach to a reach. The boat must be sailing fast before the tack, and you must steer it firmly through the turn, or else it may fail to complete the tack, stopping head-to-wind—a position known as being "in irons" (*p.93*).

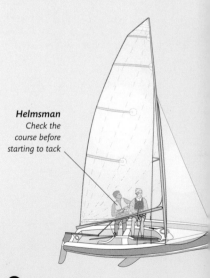

Helmsman
Check the course before starting to tack

1 Sail on a beam reach, trim the sails, and put the centerboard half-down. The helmsman checks that the course is clear of obstructions, then calls "ready about" to warn the crew.

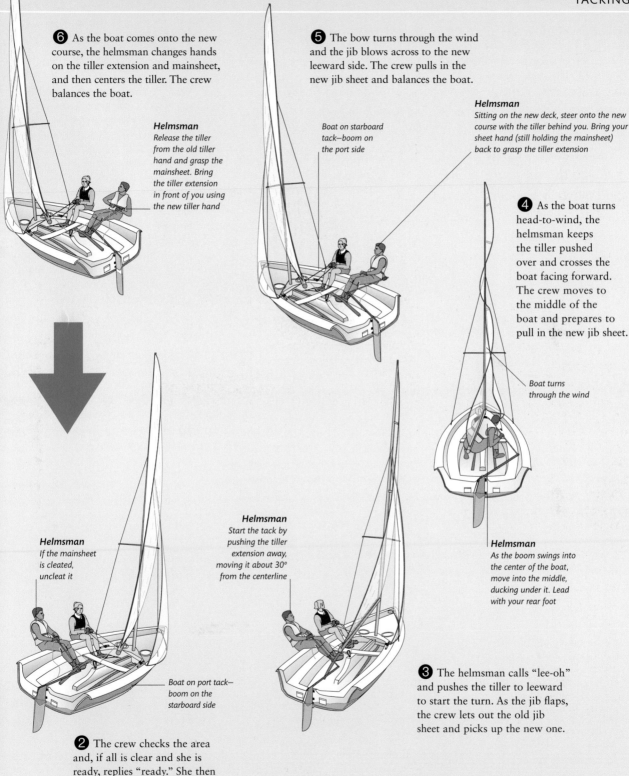

6 As the boat comes onto the new course, the helmsman changes hands on the tiller extension and mainsheet, and then centers the tiller. The crew balances the boat.

Helmsman
Release the tiller from the old tiller hand and grasp the mainsheet. Bring the tiller extension in front of you using the new tiller hand

5 The bow turns through the wind and the jib blows across to the new leeward side. The crew pulls in the new jib sheet and balances the boat.

Boat on starboard tack—boom on the port side

Helmsman
Sitting on the new deck, steer onto the new course with the tiller behind you. Bring your sheet hand (still holding the mainsheet) back to grasp the tiller extension

4 As the boat turns head-to-wind, the helmsman keeps the tiller pushed over and crosses the boat facing forward. The crew moves to the middle of the boat and prepares to pull in the new jib sheet.

Boat turns through the wind

Helmsman
If the mainsheet is cleated, uncleat it

Helmsman
Start the tack by pushing the tiller extension away, moving it about 30° from the centerline

Helmsman
As the boom swings into the center of the boat, move into the middle, ducking under it. Lead with your rear foot

Boat on port tack—boom on the starboard side

3 The helmsman calls "lee-oh" and pushes the tiller to leeward to start the turn. As the jib flaps, the crew lets out the old jib sheet and picks up the new one.

2 The crew checks the area and, if all is clear and she is ready, replies "ready." She then uncleats the jib sheet but does not let it out.

Sailing to windward

Once you have learned how to tack, you can experiment with sailing to windward. Although you can sail close-hauled along the edge of the no-sail zone (*p.40*), if you turn closer to the wind, into the no-sail zone, the luffs of the sails will start to flutter and the boat will eventually stop.

Pull the tiller gently toward you to turn away from the wind and resume sailing efficiently. Do not bear away too far, however, or you will give up valuable distance. To reach a point upwind, within the no-sail zone, you will need to follow a zigzag course—a process that is known as beating to windward.

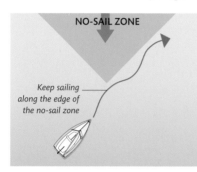

NO-SAIL ZONE

Keep sailing along the edge of the no-sail zone

EDGE OF THE NO-SAIL ZONE
To sail as close to the wind as possible, sheet in both sails tight and luff up gently until the luff of the jib starts shaking. Bear away slightly to stop the shaking, then repeat to sail along the edge of the zone.

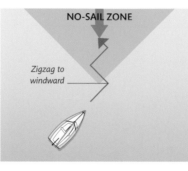

NO-SAIL ZONE

Zigzag to windward

BEATING TO WINDWARD
To sail upwind or get to a point that is within the no-sail zone you have to tack and sail a zigzag course. Here, the boat starts on port tack, then tacks onto starboard tack, making progress to windward with each turn. The helmsman can choose to make a series of short tacks or a smaller number of longer ones depending on the distance to his objective.

TACKING FROM CLOSE-HAULED

Tacking is most often used to turn from one close-hauled course to the other as part of the process of beating to windward. The boat turns through only 90 degrees, so the tack is relatively quick.

A CLOSE-HAULED TACK
Tacking from close-hauled to close-hauled involves a turn of only 90° and will happen much more quickly than when tacking from a reach to a reach. You should avoid turning too far after the tack, otherwise you will end up farther off the wind than the intended close-hauled course and will sail a longer distance.

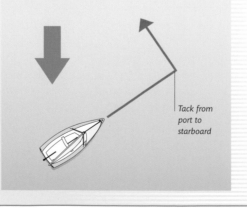

Tack from port to starboard

TACKING AN AFT-MAINSHEET BOAT

This sequence shows an aft-mainsheet boat tacking from close-hauled on port tack to close-hauled on starboard tack. Because it is an aft mainsheet, the helmsman must cross the boat facing aft and change hands on the tiller extension and mainsheet before the tack. The crew crosses the boat facing forward as usual. The boat turns through only 90 degrees, so the maneuver happens very quickly compared with tacking from a beam reach to a beam reach (*p.90*). The crew and helmsman must cross the boat swiftly before the sails fill.

1 The helmsman prepares to tack by checking that the course is clear. If it is, he calls "ready about." The crew makes sure that the centerboard is fully down, checks for obstructions, and replies "ready." He uncleats the jib sheet, but does not let it out.

Boat on port tack with the boom on the starboard side

Helmsman
Hold the tiller extension in a panhandle grip, ready to transfer the mainsheet to the aft hand and the iller extension to the forward hand

Crew
Uncleat the jib sheet

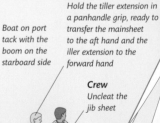

Helmsman
Steer onto the new course, then center the tiller

Boat on starboard tack with the boom on the port side

Helmsman
Sit on the new windward side, keeping the tiller extension over to continue the turn

Mainsail is sheeted in

5 As the boat comes onto the new course, the helmsman trims the mainsail and centers the tiller. The crew pulls the jib in tight, then cleats the jib sheet and balances the boat.

4 The bow of the boat moves through the wind, and the helmsman sits down on the new windward side. The crew sheets in the jib as it blows across the bow, and moves to balance the boat.

2 The helmsman changes hands on the extension and mainsheet, calls "lee-oh," and pushes the tiller to leeward. As the jib flaps, the crew releases the old jib sheet and picks up the new one.

3 As the boat turns head-to-wind, the helmsman keeps the tiller pushed over and crosses the boat facing aft. The crew moves to the middle and prepares to pull in the new jib sheet.

Boom swings to the center

Crew
Prepare to move across the boat

Helmsman
As the boom swings, move into the middle of the boat, ducking under it. Lead with your tiller hand

Helmsman
Push the tiller to leeward, and move your forward foot to the middle of the boat

A FAILED TACK

When a boat fails to tack, it may end up "in-irons." There are several reasons why a tack fails: the boat is sailing too slowly, the helmsman is steering badly, or the crew has pulled in the new jib sheet too early, making it fill on the wrong side.

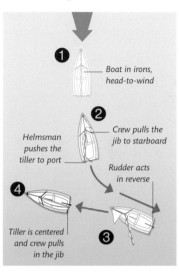

1 Boat in irons, head-to-wind

2 Crew pulls the jib to starboard

Helmsman pushes the tiller to port

Rudder acts in reverse

4 *Tiller is centered and crew pulls in the jib*

3

ESCAPING FROM "IN-IRONS"

1 To escape from being in-irons, the helmsman must push the tiller toward the side of the boat in the direction he wants the bow to go. Here, the tiller is pushed to port.

2 At the same time, the crew must pull the jib to the opposite side of the boat so that it fills with wind on its reverse side—a technique known as "backing the jib."

3 The boat will move backward and the rudder acts in reverse. The backed jib will help to push the bow in the desired direction.

4 As soon as the boat is pointing the right way, the helmsman centers the tiller and the crew sheets in the jib on the correct side. The boat is now ready to continue its course.

JIBING

Like tacking, jibing involves turning the boat to change tack and bring the wind on the other side. In jibing, however, it is the stern, rather than the bow, that turns through the wind. When you jibe, the mainsail stays full of wind throughout the maneuver, and its swing across the boat can be sudden and violent. This is very unlike tacking, where the sails lose drive and flap harmlessly until the turn is complete. Unless the boat is correctly balanced throughout, you may lose control or capsize.

Jibing roles

The helmsman decides when to jibe. He is responsible for making sure the new course is clear, and for making sure that the crew is ready. During the jibe, the helmsman must change hands on the mainsheet and tiller, while keeping control of both. He must also move across the boat during the turn. After the jibe, he has to steer onto the new course and check the sail trim and boat balance.

The crew is responsible for releasing the old jib sheet, picking up the new jib sheet, and moving across the boat to sheet in the jib on the new side as the boat completes the jibe. He must concentrate on balancing the boat throughout the jibe.

Preparing to jibe

Jibing begins with bearing away until the jib hangs limply behind the mainsail, indicating that you are on a dead run (*p.40*). You then luff up very slightly so that the jib just fills on the same side as the mainsail. This is a training run, which, when you are learning how to jibe, is the correct starting point for the maneuver.

JIBING FROM A TRAINING RUN

When you are learning, you will start by sailing on a training run with the wind behind you at an angle of 5–10 degrees off a run. After the jibe, you will probably be sailing on a broad reach.

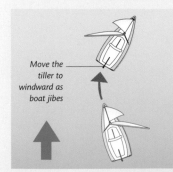

Move the tiller to windward as boat jibes

TRAINING-RUN JIBE

Learning to jibe by starting from a training run gives you more time to prepare for the maneuver and to adjust your weight to balance the boat. The boat will turn through quite a wide arc and, if you are not quick enough to straighten the tiller as the boom swings across, may turn onto a broad reach on the new tack. The helmsman should watch the mainsail leech carefully for signs that it is about to jibe. He should be in the middle of the boat as the boom comes across, with the tiller centered.

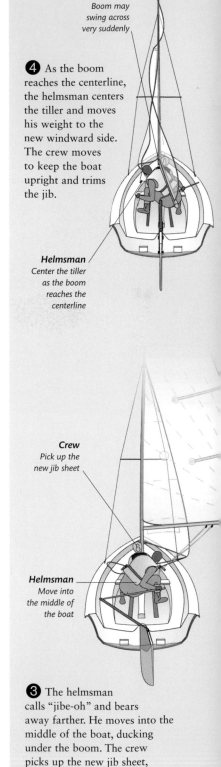

Boom may swing across very suddenly

❹ As the boom reaches the centerline, the helmsman centers the tiller and moves his weight to the new windward side. The crew moves to keep the boat upright and trims the jib.

Helmsman
Center the tiller as the boom reaches the centerline

Crew
Pick up the new jib sheet

Helmsman
Move into the middle of the boat

❸ The helmsman calls "jibe-oh" and bears away farther. He moves into the middle of the boat, ducking under the boom. The crew picks up the new jib sheet, while balancing the boat.

Mainsail immediately fills with wind and the boat accelerates

5 The helmsman changes hands on the tiller extension and mainsheet. The crew moves to keep the boat upright. In light winds, he will sit on the new leeward side. In stronger winds, he will move to the middle or to windward to keep the boat level.

Helmsman
Change hands on the tiller extension

Crew
Adjust the centerboard and jib as necessary

6 Once the boat is level, the helmsman can steer onto the new desired course. The boat will have turned through quite a wide arc, especially in light winds, and it is now likely to be sailing on a broad reach on the new tack. The sails are trimmed correctly and the centerboard adjusted, if necessary.

Helmsman
Steer onto the new course

JIBING A CENTER-MAINSHEET BOAT

In a boat with a center-mainsheet system, the helmsman faces forward during the jibe and changes hands on the tiller and mainsheet toward the end of the maneuver. From the helmsman's forward-facing position, he is able to watch the course and the mainsail. When the helmsman is competent in jibing, he can initiate the boom's swing by tugging on the mainsheet when he sees that the jibe is imminent. The crew's main task is to keep the boat balanced.

Crew
Move to balance the boat

Helmsman
Sheet in the mainsail to bring it off the shroud

Crew
Keep the boat balanced

Helmsman
Move the tiller to windward

2 The crew makes sure the centerboard is no more than a quarter down. He confirms the course is clear, and replies "ready." The helmsman then swings the tiller extension to the leeward side and moves his aft foot into the middle.

1 The helmsman luffs up from a run to a training run. He checks that the new course is clear, sheets in the mainsail to bring the boom just off the leeward shroud, and calls "stand by to jibe."

Jibing safely

Make sure that the boat is upright before the jibe. If it heels to leeward, it will be harder to jibe as the boat will try to luff up and turn in the wrong direction.

The centerboard must be no more than a quarter down when you jibe. If it is any lower, the boat will try to luff as the boom swings across and, as a result, may trip over the centerboard and cause the boat to capsize. If your dinghy has a daggerboard, make sure that it will not catch on the boom or boom vang as the mainsail swings across, otherwise you will capsize.

Jibing in strong winds can be hazardous and can be avoided by luffing up to a reach, then tacking around before bearing away to the desired course. If you choose to jibe in strong winds, do so when the boat is sailing as fast as possible. Because the boat is sailing away from the true wind, the apparent wind is reduced by the speed of the boat's movement. This reduces the forces on the sail and makes jibing easier. Pick a time when the boat is surfing down the front of a wave and jibe when the boat is at its maximum speed.

Jibing tips

Once you are committed to jibing, do not hesitate or change your mind. Turn the boat smoothly and be prepared to move fast as the boom comes across.

You can obtain advance warning of when the boat is about to jibe by watching the leech of the mainsail, about one-third up from the boom. When the jibe is imminent, the leech folds back to windward, showing that the wind is getting behind the sail.

As the boat jibes and the boom swings across the centerline, it is very important that both the helmsman

and the crew are in the middle of the boat, and that the tiller is centered. It is often necessary to turn the boat through quite a wide arc before the boom starts to move across the boat, particularly in light winds. You can get around this by giving a sharp tug on the mainsheet when you see the jib blow across the bow. This will start the boom moving across the boat earlier than it would do otherwise.

Accidental jibes

If you continue to bear away from a broad reach to a run, sailing farther and farther away from the wind, the boat will eventually jibe on its own as the wind swings across the stern. As this is an uncontrolled jibe, it can result in your taking an unexpected swim. Make sure you do not jibe accidentally by continually checking the wind direction whenever you are sailing downwind. An early warning sign of an unplanned jibe is when the jib tries to blow across to the windward side of the boat. This means that you are on a dead run, so if you bear away any more, then the boat will jibe.

4 As the boom reaches the centerline, the helmsman quickly centers the tiller and moves his weight to the new windward side. The crew keeps the boat upright and trims the jib as it reaches the new side.

Crew
Keep your weight central as the boom crosses the center

Helmsman
Move to the new windward side as the boom crosses the centerline

JIBING FROM A DEAD RUN

Although you will usually learn to jibe by starting on a training run and ending on a broad reach, it is possible to jibe while sailing on a dead run with no course alteration at all, or only a minor one.

A DEAD-RUN JIBE

To jibe on a dead run with minimal course alteration, it is necessary for the crew or helmsman to pull the mainsail across to the new leeward side, rather than using the wind to move it by turning the boat during the jibe. Sail on a dead run with the helmsman in the middle of the boat and the crew balancing it as necessary. When the helmsman calls "jibe-oh," the crew grasps the boom vang and swings the boom across. In a center-mainsheet boat, the helmsman can grasp the mainsheet tackle and use it to swing the boom over instead.

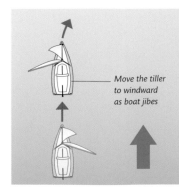

Move the tiller to windward as boat jibes

⑤ The mainsail fills at once on the new side and the crew moves to keep the boat upright. In light winds, he sits on the leeward side but in stronger winds he will need to be in the middle or on the windward sidedeck.

Helmsman
Trim the mainsail as it fills with wind and the boat accelerates

⑥ Once the boat is level, the helmsman can steer onto the new desired course. The boat is now likely to be on a broad reach on the new tack. The sails are trimmed correctly and the centerboard adjusted if necessary.

Helmsman
Steer onto the new course, adjusting the tiller and mainsheet

Crew
Move to balance the boat, and pick up the new jib sheet

Helmsman
Crouch to avoid the boom as it swings over

JIBING AN AFT-MAINSHEET BOAT

Executing a jibe in a boat with an aft mainsheet differs from jibing a center-mainsheet boat in that the helmsman changes hands on the mainsheet and tiller before the jibe, and he faces aft during the jibe. This means that he cannot see what is in front of the boat during the maneuver, so it is important that the jibe is completed as quickly as possible. The crew, as in all maneuvers, crosses the boat facing forward.

❶ The helmsman luffs up to a training run, checks the new course, sheets in to bring the boom clear of the shroud, and calls "stand-by to jibe." The crew checks the course and centerboard and calls "ready."

❸ When the helmsman sees that the mainsail is about to swing across, he moves to the middle of the boat, pivoting on the balls of his feet to face aft.

Helmsman
Swing the tiller extension to the other side of the boat

❷ The helmsman calls "jibe-oh," changes hands on the tiller and mainsheet, and puts his front foot into the center. He swings the extension to leeward and pushes the tiller to windward.

Crew
Check the centerboard is no more than a quarter down

Helmsman
Pull the boom off the shroud

SAILING A COURSE

One of the best ways to develop your skills is to sail a course that requires you to tack and jibe, and encompasses all the points of sailing (*pp.40–41*). How you arrange your course depends on your sailing area. A small island would be ideal to sail around. Alternatively, you could use a few buoys as your turning points, or else simply sail an imaginary circuit to bring you back to your starting point. Whatever course you set, try to sail out of the way of other boats on your first few attempts. As you sail, concentrate on sail trim, centerboard position, and boat trim and balance.

SAILING UPWIND

Start by sailing on the upwind courses (beam reach, close reach and close-hauled). On these courses you can slow down and stop, if necessary, simply by letting out the sails until they shake and lose power.

Beam reach
Steer onto a beam reach with the centerboard half down. Trim the sails and move your weight to keep the boat upright. If it heels significantly even though you are sitting out fully, consider reefing (*p.74*). Experiment with moving the tiller until you are happy with the way it alters the boat's course. Watch its effect by looking at how the bow moves in relation to the horizon. Keep checking the trim of the sails. In moderate winds, this will be the fastest point of sailing (*pp.40–41*).

Close reach
When you have gotten the feel of the boat sailing on a beam reach, you can luff up to a close-reaching course. Lower the centerboard to the three-quarters-down position and sheet in the sails to keep them full. You will need to sit out harder to counter the increased heeling force. In light winds this will be the fastest point of sailing.

Close-hauled
Sailing close-hauled is difficult to get right and requires plenty of practice. Lower the centreboard fully and luff up to a close-hauled course. Ask the crew to pull the jib in tight and cleat the sheet. Next, sheet the mainsail in tight and steer the boat by watching the luff of the jib. Your aim is to sail along the edge of the no-sail zone, making as much distance to windward as possible. Gently ease the tiller away from you, luffing up slowly, and watch for the moment when the jib luff shakes. At that point, pull the tiller towards you very slightly to bear away until the luff just stops shaking. To maintain an accurate close-hauled course, you must constantly repeat

SAILING A COURSE
Once you understand the basic maneuvers, the next step is to put them all together by sailing around a course. Here, Optimist dinghies sail around a course marked by inflatable buoys.

this gentle luffing up and bearing away, which demands concentration when you are learning. If you lose concentration you will find that you are sailing either too close or too far off the wind. The former is obvious as the jib will shake and the boat will slow down; the latter is more difficult to spot unless you have tell-tales fitted to the luff of your jib (p.80).

Avoid oversteering as you luff up and bear away. The boat should only turn a few degrees each time you move the tiller, so make only gentle steering movements.

If you find that the boat heels too far in gusts of wind, even though you are sitting out, reduce the heeling force by easing the mainsheet slightly to bring the boat upright again. When the gust passes, pull the sheet in again or the boat will heel to windward.

STEERING A COURSE

You will need to luff up, bear away, tack and jibe to complete this course. It is advisable to try to pick light to medium winds for your first few outings. Sailing in strong winds is obviously tricky, but very light winds can also be difficult—the boat will be slow to react and will require skillful sailing to keep it moving.

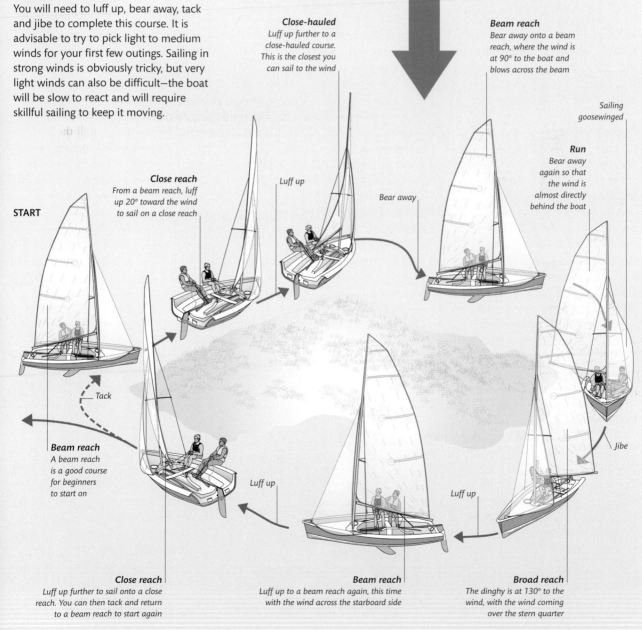

Close-hauled
Luff up further to a close-hauled course. This is the closest you can sail to the wind

Beam reach
Bear away onto a beam reach, where the wind is at 90° to the boat and blows across the beam

Sailing goosewinged

Run
Bear away again so that the wind is almost directly behind the boat

Luff up

Bear away

Close reach
From a beam reach, luff up 20° toward the wind to sail on a close reach

START

Tack

Beam reach
A beam reach is a good course for beginners to start on

Luff up

Jibe

Luff up

Close reach
Luff up further to sail onto a close reach. You can then tack and return to a beam reach to start again

Beam reach
Luff up to a beam reach again, this time with the wind across the starboard side

Broad reach
The dinghy is at 130° to the wind, with the wind coming over the stern quarter

SAILING DOWNWIND

After the upwind courses, you will notice a big difference as you sail onto the downwind courses (broad reach, training run, and dead run). The difference is especially obvious in moderate to strong winds. The wind strength will seem to decrease due to the effects of apparent wind (*p.33*). You will not have to sit out so hard to balance the boat; and you will not be pushing into the waves but sailing with them. Any spray that was flying upwind will disappear and the environment will seem warmer.

Broad reach

From a beam reach, bear away to sail on a broad reach. Ease out both sails until they set correctly, watching the luffs or telltales (*p.80*) to see when the optimum trim is achieved. Raise the centerboard so that it is a quarter down and move inboard to keep the boat level (shift your weight back slightly to lift the bow if it seems to be burrowing into the waves). In strong winds a broad reach is likely to be the fastest point of sailing.

Training run

From the broad reach, bear away to a training run so that the wind comes over one stern quarter, and ease the sails out as far as possible. Remember that you cannot ease the mainsail fully because the boom will hit the leeward shroud. Keep it just clear of the shroud to prevent chafe. If the boom seems to be rising too high at the outer end and the boat is rolling, tighten the boom vang to hold it down.

Unlike the mainsail, the jib is not limited in how much it can be let out. It should be set using the telltales or by watching for a shaking luff. If the jib collapses behind the mainsail, you have turned the boat too far from the wind, so luff up slightly until the jib fills again.

To sail efficiently on a training run, you need to raise the centerboard until little more than the tip protrudes below the dinghy. If the boat rolls and feels unstable, put a bit more of the centerboard down

to help stabilize it. Depending on the strength of the wind, the crew should sit in the middle of the boat or to leeward to balance the weight of the helmsman. To have a good view of the sails and the course, the helmsman should remain seated on the windward sidedeck.

Dead run

Sailing on a dead run is the trickiest point of sailing for the helmsman and crew. With the sails eased out fully and the wind blowing from straight behind the boat, there is no heeling force to balance against and the boat will tend to roll from side to side. The maximum speed is obtained by pulling the centerboard almost fully up, but this will increase the tendency to roll. If rolling becomes a problem, lower the centerboard to the quarter-down position.

The helmsman should sit on the windward side, but the crew will usually have to move right across to leeward to balance the helmsman's weight. The crew must be ready to move quickly but smoothly if the boat rolls either way. The helmsman must concentrate carefully on his course to avoid an accidental jibe.

Goosewinging

Once you have gained confidence on a run, you can try goosewinging by setting the jib on the opposite side of the mainsail. This will increase your speed and also help to balance the pull of the mainsail and make the boat easier to steer on a straight course.

To goosewing, bear away to a dead run so that the wind is coming directly over the transom. This makes the jib collapse as it is now in the wind shadow of the mainsail. Pull it across the foredeck using the windward jib sheet until it sets with wind and sets on the opposite side of the boat.

HEAVING-TO

Heaving-to, or the hove-to position, is more effective than lying-to (*p.86*) if you need to halt for anything longer than a few moments. It is a good position if you need to reef or if you want to rest.

HOW TO HEAVE-TO

Begin by tacking without freeing the jib sheet. Then let the mainsail out until the front half flaps. Push the tiller to leeward and keep it there. Raise the centerboard to about two-thirds down to prevent heeling. The force in the wind-filled jib is counteracted by the mainsail and rudder.

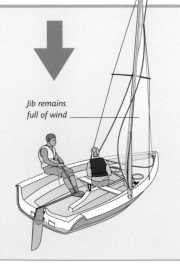

Jib remains full of wind

Whisker poles

Some boats that are not designed to have spinnakers (*pp.144–151*) have a pole, known as a whisker pole, that is used to boom out the jib when it is goosewinged. The whisker pole is clipped to a ring on the front of the mast and usually has a point on the other end that is pushed into the cringle at the jib clew. Tension is maintained on the jib sheet to prevent it from slipping out.

The whisker pole can be a very useful accessory if you have some distance to sail on a dead run. It keeps the jib goosewinged even if the helmsman luffs to a training run or even a broad reach. Without the help of the whisker pole, it is much harder for the crew to keep the jib set in this way. Make sure that you remove and stow the whisker pole safely before you jibe or luff up.

USING A WHISKER POLE
This Sharpie is a traditional dinghy class that does not use a spinnaker. Instead, a long whisker pole helps boost speed downwind and reduce rolling by poling out the jib on the windward side.

SAILING IN TIDES

When you sail in tidal waters, it is important to allow for a tidal stream, which will make your boat drift in relation to the seabed. It will influence how you steer to follow your course.

Tidal effects

To get a better idea of how the tide affects your boat, imagine you are walking on a moving walkway. If you walk in the direction in which it is moving, you will travel faster than you would if the walkway were static. If you turn around and walk in the opposite direction, it is harder to make forward progress and will take you longer. Walk across the walkway and its movement will take you sideways, away from your destination. These effects are identical to what happens to your boat when you sail in tidal waters.

Tidal direction

If you are going to sail in tidal waters, make sure that you know the direction of the tidal stream before you go afloat. Also, find out whether the direction is due to change while you are sailing.

Coping with tides

When you find yourself in a tidal stream, the following few tips will help you to keep out of trouble.
• Remember that the strongest tidal stream is usually found in the deepest water, while the weakest streams occur in shallow water.
• If the tide is going with you, maneuver into the strongest stream to maximize the benefit.
• If the tide is against you, get out of the strongest stream by heading for shallow water, but be careful not to run aground.
• If you have to sail across the current, head upstream of a straight-line course to allow for the tide's sweeping you sideways.

FROM AND TO THE SHORE

Setting off for your sailing trip and returning from it afterwards are usually the trickiest parts of the day. The shoreline is a solid obstacle that is a potential hazard to you and your boat if you do not know how to deal with it. Beaches, pontoons, and slipways require certain skills if you are to leave them and return to them without problems. You also need to know how to cope with onshore and offshore winds and changing tidal conditions, as well as obstacles, such as other sailing or power boats.

Weather shore

The main factor that will determine the ease or difficulty of leaving and returning to the shore is the wind direction in relation to the shoreline.

If the wind is blowing off the land, the shore is called a weather shore and the wind, an offshore wind.

In this situation, it is easy to leave the shore, since not only do you have the wind blowing you off the shore, but the water will be flat, with no waves breaking close to the land. To return to the shore, beat to windward (*p.92*). To stop the boat, turn head-to-wind when you reach shallow water.

Lee shore

When the wind blows onto the land, the shore is called a lee shore and the wind is referred to as an onshore wind. Leaving a lee shore can be difficult, especially in strong winds from a beach with breaking waves. Once launched, beat to windward to get away from the shore. To return, simply sail downwind. Landing on a lee shore can be difficult—especially in breaking waves—and should be avoided if possible.

Along the shore

If the wind is blowing along the shoreline, you have an easy launching situation—you can simply sail from and to the shore on a beam reach.

LAUNCHING FROM A SLIPWAY
A slipway is an easier launching point than a beach. Once the dinghy is afloat, park the cart, and sail or paddle off.

Leaving a beach

Most dinghies can be launched from a beach, but this is not normally as easy as launching from a slipway or pontoon. To move the boat across soft sand, you will need several people to carry it, or a cart with large tires. A stone or gravel beach is also difficult to negotiate, and you may damage the hull on the stones. Some beaches, usually sandy ones, have a shallow slope into the water, which remains shallow for a long way out, making it difficult to fit the rudder and use the centerboard or daggerboard. Stony or gravelly beaches often have a steeper slope where the water depth quickly increases. However, beaches with steep slopes are more prone to large, breaking waves in an onshore wind, which make launching more difficult.

Leaving a slipway

Using a proper slipway is easier, but be sure to examine the type of shoreline that lies to either side of it. You may discover that the slipway is just a ramp between two sections of sea wall, which will present a significant hazard when returning to shore—or even as you are leaving—should you make a mistake. Beware of slipways that end suddenly with a steep drop into deep water. If you are launching at low tide you may find yourself unexpectedly falling off the end.

Aptly named, slipways are often covered in algae and other slimy weeds, so take care not to lose your footing. Always hold onto the boat's painter so that the dinghy does not sail off without you, should you slip, and be wary of losing control of the cart.

Leaving a pontoon

A pontoon is usually the easiest launching point, especially if there is a slipway alongside to get the boat into and out of the water. Once your boat is in the water, you can move it to a berth alongside the pontoon and take your time leaving. When you return, you can lower and stow the sails at leisure before taking the boat out of the water. If the pontoon protrudes into deep water, consider any tidal stream effects (*opposite*).

Leaving a weather shore

Before you decide to leave from a weather shore, check the forecast. Because the wind is blowing off the land, it will be extremely difficult to judge how strong it is farther away from the shore, and beyond the sheltering effects of the land. There will not be any significant waves close to the shore, but as you sail farther out, you may get a nasty surprise as the wind increases and the waves grow in size. You sail away from a weather shore on a broad reach or run, but to return you will need to beat to windward. This may be difficult if conditions farther out are worse than you anticipated. Be prudent when sailing from a weather shore, and sail only when certain that the conditions offshore are within your capabilities.

Leaving a lee shore

You will probably be fully exposed to the prevailing conditions on a lee shore. In fact, the wind and waves may seem to be more daunting when you are on the beach than they actually are when you sail farther out. This is especially likely if the shore is steep, in which case waves will break onto it even in moderate winds. In this case, the hardest part of the sail is getting off the beach and sailing through the surf line to calmer water.

LAUNCHING IN TIDES

The presence of a current or tidal stream in the launching area may complicate leaving and returning maneuvers. In some circumstances, its direction and strength will determine the way in which you should leave or approach the shore.

Shallow water

When sailing off a beach, you do not usually have to worry about the effect of a tidal stream along the shoreline because you are launching into shallow water where the stream, if any, will be minimal. Be aware, however, of the direction and strength of the stream offshore and plan your course accordingly.

Deep water

In deep water, the tidal stream will affect how you sail away and return. Except when the tide is weak in relation to the wind, you should always treat it as the most significant force. If in doubt, sail away from the pontoon or slipway pointing into the tide and using just the jib if the wind is behind the beam. When you are returning, plan ahead and aim to turn into the tide to stop when you reach the pontoon or slipway. If this means that the wind will be behind the beam on your approach, lower the mainsail and sail in under the jib.

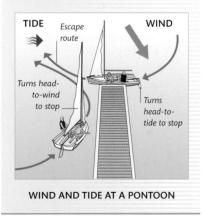

WIND AND TIDE AT A PONTOON

WEATHER SHORE

LEAVING A BEACH

When you leave a weather shore from a beach, begin with the usual launching procedure, preparing the boat and moving it to the edge of the water (*pp.84–85*). Turn the dinghy so that it is head-to-wind and hoist the sails (*p.85*). Launch the boat carefully, then, while one of you holds the boat by the painter, the other parks the cart up the beach and out of the way. You are now ready to get on board and sail away.

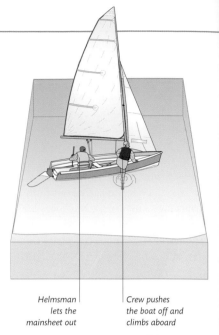

Helmsman boards and fits the rudder

Crew holds the boat by the painter and bow

Helmsman lets the mainsheet out

Crew pushes the boat off and climbs aboard

❶ The crew holds the boat while the helmsman boards, checks that all gear is stowed, and fits the rudder. The helmsman lowers the rudder blade (if it is the lifting type) and puts the centerboard about a quarter down if the water is deep enough.

❷ The crew turns the boat until he is by the windward shroud, pushes off, and climbs aboard. He then pulls in the jib to turn the boat further from the wind. The helmsman trims the mainsail and steers onto their chosen course.

Leaving a pontoon

Launch the boat down a slipway, if available, or over the edge of the pontoon if necessary (*p.85*). Move the boat to the part of the pontoon from which it will be easiest to leave— usually at an end on the leeward side. The helmsman gets aboard and fits the rudder and tiller. He hoists the jib, then the mainsail, and lowers the centerboard about half way. Before the crew can untie the boat and get aboard, he and the helmsman must plan their course to open water.

Check to see if there is any tidal stream affecting the boat. If the tidal stream is significant, plan to leave pointing into the stream. Look around before you sail off to be sure there are no other boats or obstructions in your path. Make sure that your crew understands the planned maneuver before you cast off.

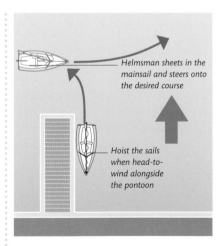

Helmsman sheets in the mainsail and steers onto the desired course

Hoist the sails when head-to-wind alongside the pontoon

Sails are set to sail on a reach

CLEAR WATER ASTERN

The crew unties the painter and steps aboard, pushing the boat backward. The helmsman pushes the tiller in the direction he wants the bow to move (here, to port) while the crew backs the jib. The boat moves backward and turns. Finally, the crew sheets the jib in on the leeward side of the dinghy to sail away.

OBSTRUCTION ASTERN

The crew pushes the boat forward and away from the pontoon. He gets aboard and then backs the jib, while the helmsman turns the boat away from the wind. As soon as the boat has turned, the crew sets the jib on the leeward side to sail away on a broad reach. The helmsman lets the mainsheet to help bear away.

Arriving at a beach

When you return to a weather shore, you will need to tack in toward the beach or slipway. The way you approach will depend on whether the water close to the shore is shallow or deep. If you are going to sail into shallow water, the crew must be prepared to raise the centerboard just enough to clear the bottom and the helmsman must be ready to lift the rudder blade if necessary. After you have raised the rudder blade, make only very gentle movements with the tiller because when the blade is in the raised position it is very vulnerable to breakage. Remember, too, that once the centerboard is raised, the boat will make more leeway, so do not expect to be able to sail efficiently on a close-hauled course.

Plan your course into the beach, and discuss the plan of approach with your crew so that he understands what is required. Make sure there are no other boats or obstructions in the way. If you are approaching a slipway, wait until it is clear of other users. When you reach the shore, the crew should step out on the windward side and hold the boat by the bow.

DEEP WATER

Where the water is deep at the shoreline, tack in close, then sail parallel to the land until you reach your chosen landing point. The helmsman turns the boat head-to-wind to stop. The crew gets out just behind the shroud, taking care to avoid stepping into deep water, and holds the boat while the helmsman lowers the sails, removes the rudder, and raises the centerboard fully.

SHALLOW WATER

Tack in to the shore, aiming for your chosen landing spot. As the water gets shallower, the crew raises the centerboard and the helmsman lifts the rudder. Make the final approach on a close reach. At the landing point, turn head-to-wind. The crew gets out and holds the boat, while the helmsman lowers the sails, removes the rudder, and raises the centerboard fully.

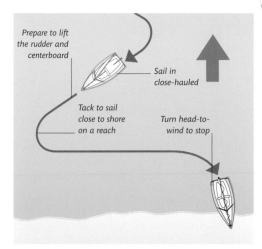

Prepare to lift the rudder and centerboard

Sail in close-hauled

Tack to sail close to shore on a reach

Turn head-to-wind to stop

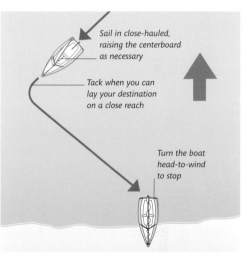

Sail in close-hauled, raising the centerboard as necessary

Tack when you can lay your destination on a close reach

Turn the boat head-to-wind to stop

Arriving at a pontoon

Approach the pontoon by sailing on a close reach. As you near the pontoon, ease out the sails to slow down, then turn head-to-wind to stop alongside. Pontoons usually have plenty of depth of water beneath them so you do not need to raise the centerboard or the rudder until you are safely alongside.

If there is a tidal stream present, consider its effects on your boat and, if it is strong, plan to turn into the tide to stop. Always plan an escape route in case you arrive at the pontoon going too fast to stop. Once alongside, the crew gets out to secure the boat.

STOPPING AT A PONTOON

As you reach the pontoon, turn head-to-wind so that the boat comes to a stop alongside. The crew secures the dinghy while the helmsman deals with the sails and other equipment. It is important that you do not approach the pontoon sailing too quickly.

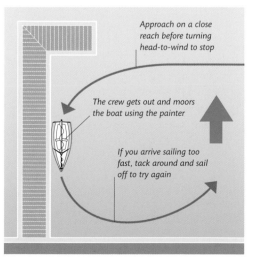

Approach on a close reach before turning head-to-wind to stop

The crew gets out and moors the boat using the painter

If you arrive sailing too fast, tack around and sail off to try again

LEE SHORE

Leaving a lee shore is complicated because you are obliged to sail close-hauled or on a close reach, which is difficult, especially if you cannot lower the centerboard fully due to shallow water. If the wind is directly onshore, you have no choice but to start on a close reach until you can lower the centerboard fully and head up to a close-hauled course.

Fortunately, the wind often blows onto the shore at an angle, giving a larger angle between the shore and one edge of the no-sail zone. Choose the tack that allows you to sail in the larger angle. Curved shores usually produce the same effect by providing a greater angle to sail in on one tack.

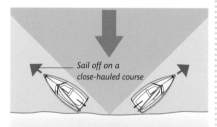

Sail off on a close-hauled course

WIND DIRECTLY ONSHORE

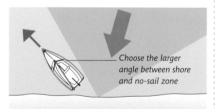

Choose the larger angle between shore and no-sail zone

WIND AT AN OBLIQUE ANGLE

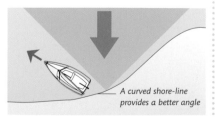

A curved shore-line provides a better angle

WIND ON A CURVED SHORELINE

Leaving from a beach

When leaving from a beach in deep water, turn the boat head-to-wind and hoist both sails ashore. When you are ready to launch, put the boat half in the water and wait for a suitable wave to lift the boat, then push off and sail away. In shallow water, hoist the jib before launching the boat, then hoist the mainsail. Lower the rudder and centerboard as soon as possible but be careful not to let them hit the bottom or they could break or stop the boat.

DEEP WATER

Lift the boat so that its front half is in the water. Decide on your leaving direction, then both stand by the side that will be to windward. Watch the waves as they approach. When one floats the boat, push it into deep water and climb aboard. Sheet in both sails, and lower the centerboard and rudder blade as soon as possible. Sail fast on a close reach to get through the waves and clear of the beach. Luff up to sail over each wave crest, then bear away.

Leaving from a pontoon

Launch the boat and turn it head-to-wind. If the wind is at an angle, put the boat on the leeward side of the pontoon. The helmsman steps aboard, hoists the sails, fits the rudder, and lowers the centerboard. He tells the crew how he wants to leave.

SAILING AWAY

The crew pushes the bow away from the pontoon and steps aboard. The helmsman sheets in the mainsail and the crew sheets in the jib to sail away on a close reach.

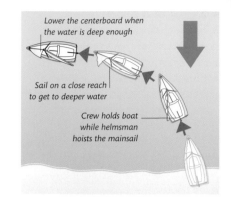

Lower the centerboard when the water is deep enough

Sail on a close reach to get to deeper water

Crew holds boat while helmsman hoists the mainsail

SHALLOW WATER
The crew holds the boat by the bow and walks the boat out until the depth is about 3 ft (1 m). The helmsman climbs aboard and hoists the mainsail.

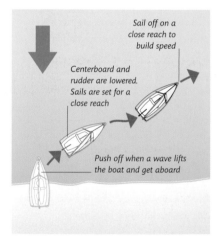

Sail off on a close reach to build speed

Centerboard and rudder are lowered. Sails are set for a close reach

Push off when a wave lifts the boat and get aboard

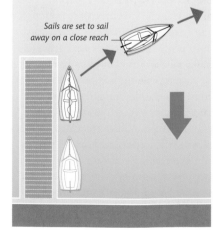

Sails are set to sail away on a close reach

Arriving at a beach

With the wind behind you, it is easy to approach a lee shore, but you must be careful with your stopping techniques. Arriving at a lee shore in strong winds is dangerous because the waves are likely to be steep and breaking, especially if the shore slopes sharply into deep water. Always keep to the windward side of the boat when jumping out, otherwise breaking waves or a strong gust of wind could push the boat on top of you, causing injury. Get the boat ashore quickly. In areas where a dinghy club sails from a steep beach, a shore team will often be present to help crews land and lift boats out of the water quickly.

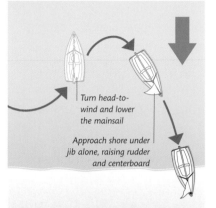

A SHALLOW WATER APPROACH

In shallow water, approach on a broad reach under full sail. When the water is about 3 ft (1 m) deep, turn into the wind to stop. The crew steps out on the windward side to hold the bow while the helmsman lowers the sails, and removes the rudder.

DEEP WATER SAFE APPROACH

Some way offshore, turn head-to-wind and lower the mainsail. Approach the shore under jib alone on a run or broad reach. Close to the shore, let the jib flap and drift in. Helmsman and crew jump out when the water is shallow enough.

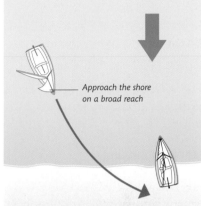

DEEP WATER FAST APPROACH

To land in large waves, approach fast on a broad reach and raise the rudder blade at the last moment. Just before the boat hits the beach, both crew jump out on the windward side, run the boat up the beach, and turn it head-to-wind to lower the sails.

Arriving at a pontoon

You often have a choice when approaching a pontoon on a lee shore. You can decide to lower the mainsail and approach under just the jib or, provided there is a pontoon at right angles to the shore, you can come in with both sails set. If in doubt, it is safest to lower the mainsail and come in under jib alone.

If the pontoon is in tidal waters, consider whether the tidal stream will affect your approach. If it is strong, plan to turn into it to stop. If possible, plan an escape route in case the boat is moving too fast to stop in the final approach, although this can be difficult when approaching a lee shore. Drop the sails and paddle in if it will be difficult to retain control under sail.

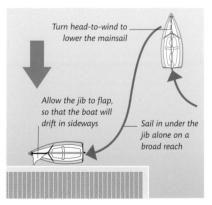

PARALLEL TO THE SHORE

Where there is nowhere to moor head-to-wind, sail upwind of your destination and lower the mainsail before approaching under the jib alone. Let the jib flap in the last stages so that you drift in slowly. Once alongside, the crew secures the boat to the pontoon.

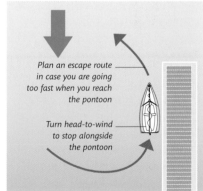

RIGHT ANGLES TO THE SHORE

Sail on a broad reach close to the shore, then turn head-to-wind to stop alongside. This requires good judgment, so plan an escape route; then you can go around and try again if necessary. If in doubt, lower the mainsail and come in under the jib alone.

MOORING AND ANCHORING

Some larger general-purpose dinghies and small keelboats are kept permanently afloat on moorings, which are often laid in rows called trots. Design varies, but most moorings have heavy concrete sinkers or anchors to secure them to the seabed. Some mooring buoys have a light pickup buoy, while others have a ring on top to which you secure the boat. Anchoring is rarely used in small boats nowadays, and more rarely in high-performance boats, but it can be useful in an emergency, for a brief stop, or when dinghy cruising.

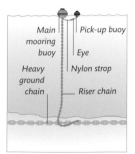

Main mooring buoy | Pick-up buoy
Eye
Heavy ground chain | Nylon strop
Riser chain

A MOORING

Nontidal waters

If you are moored or anchored in nontidal waters, the boat will always lie head-to-wind, making it simple to sail off with both sails set.

To sail away from the mooring, hoist the sails, lower the centerboard, and fit the rudder and tiller. The dinghy is turned to the desired direction for leaving, by backing the jib. Once the backed jib has pushed the bow around, the helmsman can sheet in the mainsail and the crew can then sheet the jib on the leeward side.

If it is important to turn sharply as soon as the mooring is dropped, the crew can help the turn by pulling the buoy aft, down the windward side. The farther aft it is released, the more the boat will turn downwind.

Tidal waters

In tidal waters, the direction and relative strength of the wind and tide determine how you leave a mooring. If the boat is lying head-to-wind, you can leave in the same way as you would in nontidal waters. But if the wind is not well ahead of the beam, it will not be possible to hoist the mainsail without it filling immediately and causing the boat to sail around the mooring. In this case, leave under the jib alone.

Preparing to leave a mooring

Prepare to leave a mooring by "singling up" the mooring line: run the working end of the painter through the eye on the mooring buoy, bring it back aboard, and make it fast. Undo the permanent mooring line, and release it. The dinghy can now be released simply by freeing the working end of the painter and pulling it back through the mooring eye.

LEAVING WITH BOTH SAILS

If the dinghy is head-to-wind, leave with both sails hoisted. The helmsman picks the direction to leave. The crew backs the jib on the other side of the boat and slips the mooring. If it is important to turn sharply away from the mooring, the crew passes the buoy along the windward side to the helmsman, who then releases it at the stern.

LEAVING WITH JIB ALONE

If the wind is not ahead of the beam, leave the mooring under the jib alone. Prepare both sails for hoisting, fit the rudder and tiller, and single up the mooring. Hoist the jib but let it flap, and lower the centerboard. The helmsman chooses the course to sail away and the crew slips the mooring and sheets in the jib. When clear of obstructions, luff up so that you are head-to-wind, and then hoist the mainsail.

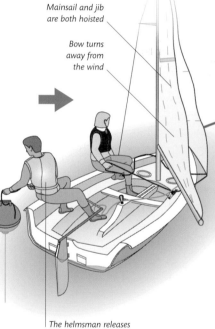

Mainsail and jib are both hoisted

Bow turns away from the wind

The helmsman releases the mooring at the stern to help the boat turn

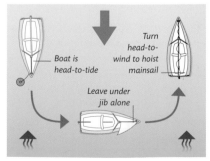

Boat is head-to-tide

Turn head-to-wind to hoist mainsail

Leave under jib alone

Picking up a mooring

Before you commit to an approach to a mooring, look at other boats already on the moorings, especially those that are similar to your own, to see if they are head-to-wind or being influenced by the tide. Assume that your boat will take up a similar position, and decide where the wind will be. If it will be well ahead of the beam, you can approach under both the mainsail and jib. However, if it is farther aft, you should approach under the jib alone.

Taking into account the proximity of other boats or obstacles, plan your approach to the mooring. If there is a tidal stream, make sure that you will pass other boats on their down-tide side to avoid being swept onto them.

At the mooring, pick up the buoy on the windward side, ahead of the shroud. Fasten the painter to the buoy and lower the sails. Then make fast securely with the mooring rope.

APPROACHING DOWNWIND

If the wind and tide are opposed or at an angle to each other, so that the boat will not lie head-to-wind when it is moored, you should approach under the jib alone. Lower the mainsail while you are still in clear water, and then approach downwind under the jib, aiming to arrive at the mooring pointing into the tide. Control your speed by using the jib sheet, and let the jib flap to slow down at the mooring.

APPROACHING UPWIND

If the boat will face the wind when it is moored, approach the buoy on a close reach, easing out the sails to slow down, and then luff up so that you are head-to-wind at the mooring. If the wind and tide are together but the wind is light, it may be better to approach on a beam reach to avoid getting swept down-tide

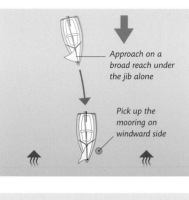

Approach on a broad reach under the jib alone

Pick up the mooring on windward side

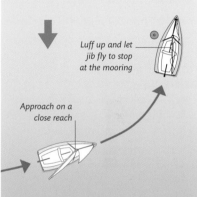

Luff up and let jib fly to stop at the mooring

Approach on a close reach

ANCHORING A DINGHY

You will need an anchor warp that is 3–5 times longer than the depth of water. Tie the warp to the mast and coil the bulk of it into a bucket. Take the other end out through the bow fairlead and back in around and behind the windward shroud. Tie it to the anchor using a round turn and two half hitches (p.47).

❶ Sail up to your anchorage site and stop exactly as you would at a mooring.

❷ Lower the anchor over the windward side. Quickly lower the jib.

❸ Lower the mainsail, paying out the anchor warp as the boat drifts back. Raise the centerboard and remove the rudder.

❹ Now make sure the anchor is holding by using a shore transit (p.333), and then stow the sails.

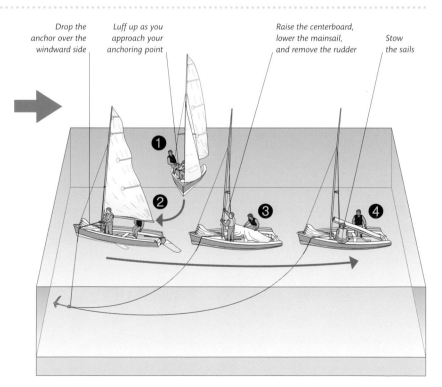

Drop the anchor over the windward side

Luff up as you approach your anchoring point

Raise the centerboard, lower the mainsail, and remove the rudder

Stow the sails

COPING WITH CAPSIZE

The stability of a dinghy depends largely on the movement of crew weight, which means that a capsize is always possible. It is a common mishap in most dinghies, so practice recovering your dinghy from a capsize until you are fully competent in the procedure. Get used to being in the water so that you feel relaxed when dealing with a capsize. If you fail to right a capsized boat, climb onto the hull, tie yourself on with the end of a sheet, and wait for rescue. Never try to swim to shore. A capsized boat is far easier for rescuers to spot than a swimmer's head.

Avoiding a capsize

The easiest way to avoid capsizing, and the need to recover a capsized boat, is to sail a small keelboat or one of the stable general-purpose dinghies that are less prone to capsizing than most other dinghies. However, if you do sail a more responsive and hence less stable dinghy, you can reduce the chances of capsizing by always sailing within the limits of your experience and ability, and by avoiding going afloat if the wind is strong. Even then, a change in conditions while you are afloat may catch you out.

If your dinghy can be reefed (*pp.74–75*), then make sure that you know how to reef it, while afloat if possible, so that you can adjust the sail area to suit the conditions. If reefing afloat is not possible and you are caught out by rough conditions, aim to sail the boat as upright as possible, while still sailing fast, by spilling wind from the sails to reduce heeling. Flatten the sails as much as possible (*pp.180–181*) and raise the centerboard or daggerboard slightly when sailing to windward, or on a close reach or beam reach, to reduce the heeling effect. Do not let the boat heel and slow down, as that will make it more vulnerable to capsizing. Head for shore as quickly as possible and, if you cannot reach your base, consider landing elsewhere to reef the boat ashore, or to wait for the conditions to ease.

If, despite all your efforts, you make a handling mistake, or a gust overpowers the boat and it heels to the point of a capsize, it may still be possible to recover the situation if you let go of the tiller and the sheets and quickly move your weight to the high side. There is a fair chance that, left to itself, the boat will round up rapidly into the wind and remain upright.

Leeward capsize

The most common type of capsize is when the boat tips over to leeward, away from the wind. This typically happens when the wind overpowers the righting effect of the crew's weight, and the boat heels so far that water floods in over the leeward gunwale. A typical leeward capsize occurs when the boat jibes and the crew are not quick enough to move their weight to the new windward side, or if the helmsman allows the boat to continue turning, and it is overpowered before it can accelerate on its new course. Once a leeward capsize becomes inevitable, the helmsman and crew should slip into the water between the boom and the hull. If they try to avoid getting wet, by hanging onto the side of the boat, they will probably invert the dinghy (*pp.114–115*).

LEEWARD CAPSIZE
This single-handed dinghy is about to capsize to leeward. The boat has been overpowered and the helmsman was slow to ease the mainsheet. With the boom end in the water, a capsize is almost inevitable.

Windward capsize

A windward capsize is somewhat less common than a leeward capsize. It usually occurs when a dinghy is sailing on a run or broad reach and it rolls heavily toward the wind. As it rolls, the part of the hull that is in the water becomes unbalanced (p.79) and makes the boat turn further away from the wind. The boat continues to roll and then tips over, toward the crew. This sort of capsize is usually considerably quicker and more violent than a leeward capsize and the crew may not have time to react. A typical occurrence is just before a jibe in strong winds. As the boat capsizes on top of them, the crew will usually fall backward into the water.

WINDWARD CAPSIZE

This single-handed dinghy is in the final stages of a windward capsize. The helmsman has let go of the tiller and dived toward the high side, but it is too late to prevent the capsize.

Staying safe

Capsizing inevitably has an element of danger because there is a small risk of being separated from the boat, trapped underneath it, or entangled in the rigging. The type of dinghy you sail will partly determine the level of risk. Many lightweight designs are prone to invert (pp.114–115)—turn completely upside down—and may do so quickly once they are on their side in the normal capsized position. When inverted, many high-performance boats do not have sufficient space in their shallow hulls for an air pocket in which a person caught under the boat can breathe. Older designs tend to have sufficient depth to their hulls to trap a sizable air pocket in which it is easy to breathe before making your escape from under the boat.

It is important, therefore, that you know the characteristics of the boat and brief your crew accordingly.

Another risk is the danger of entanglement in ropes or rigging. This is particularly dangerous if the boat inverts and a person is entangled underneath it. If there is an air pocket under the boat, the problem is less serious, as the person can breathe while he disentangles himself, but in the absence of an air pocket, any entanglement could prove fatal.

This risk of entanglement is greatest in high-performance boats where trapezes are used and where there is a greater number of control lines among which a person could get trapped. Such boats are usually more prone to inverting and are unlikely to have an air pocket under the upturned hull. When sailing a boat of this type, it is even more important to assess the dangers in advance, and to carry a very sharp knife that can be used to cut yourself free if you are caught among control lines (pp.136–139).

Whatever type of dinghy you sail, it is vital that in the event of a capsize, you stay in contact with the boat. Always keep a hand on the boat as you move around it, and if you have to swim around the boat to the centerboard, always take the end of the mainsheet with you to act as a safety line. Never attempt to leave a capsized boat and swim to the shore. Remember, the shore is much farther away than it looks, and an upturned boat is far easier to spot from a rescue boat than a swimmer's head.

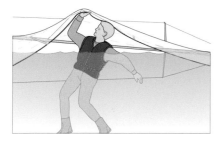

CAUGHT UNDER A SAIL
To escape from under a sail, lift the sail off the water to create an air pocket. Paddle out, keeping your hand up.

IN AN AIR POCKET
When under a boat with an air pocket, there is no rush, as you can breathe. Take a breath and pull yourself under the gunwale.

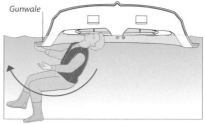

WITHOUT AN AIR POCKET
When under a boat without an air pocket, hold your breath, move quickly to the edge, then pull yourself under the gunwale.

CAPSIZE RECOVERY

Righting a capsized dinghy

The standard way for righting a capsized two-person dinghy is to use the scoop method, so named because one person is scooped aboard as the other pulls the boat upright. The scooped person's weight in the boat helps to prevent it from capsizing again once it is righted.

While the boat is capsized, both helmsman and crew must avoid putting weight on the boat, which could make it invert. During a capsize recovery, the helmsman and crew will be of sight of each other for most of the time. They must keep talking to each other so that both know what is happening.

Always try to right the boat with the mast coming up against the wind to avoid another capsize. If you capsized to windward, wait until the boat swings around with the mast downwind. If you fail to do this and try to right the boat with the mast pointing into the wind, the wind will get under the sail as soon as the mast is lifted off the water and the boat will come upright very rapidly, and will probably capsize again on top of the person who was standing on the centerboard.

Once the boat is righted, bail out the water, if necessary, before sailing off. If you are sailing a modern boat with a high floor, it will probably self-drain as soon as you start sailing, but an older design may need you to bail some of the water out by hand (*p.30*). A high-performance boat (*pp.120–189*), with a trapeze system and a spinnaker, may require the righting system to be modified, but the same principles apply, and it is always best if one person can be scooped aboard if possible.

RIGHTING THE BOAT
The heaviest person should right the boat by standing on the centerboard or daggerboard. The lighter person lies in the water alongside the boat, just behind the mast, holding onto a toestrap. When lying alongside the boat, do not put any weight on it, as this will make it much harder to right. Make sure that the mainsheet and both jib sheets are released.

SCOOPED ABOARD
As the boat comes upright, it will do so more quickly as the water drains from the mainsail. The crew in the water will be scooped aboard and their weight will help stabilize the boat. The helmsman can often climb aboard unaided as the boat comes upright.

USING THE SCOOP METHOD

The scoop method relies on one person standing on the centerboard to pull the boat upright. Often it is the helmsman who rights the boat while the crew is scooped aboard, but if there is a significant difference in their weights, the heavier person should right the boat, leaving the lighter one to be scooped aboard. If the centerboard is not fully down, the crew can push it down from inside. To avoid breaking the centerboard, the person righting the boat should stand on the part nearest the hull. While waiting to be scooped up, the other person should make sure the mainsheet is free and the boom vang is released so that the mainsail can flap loosely when the boat is righted.

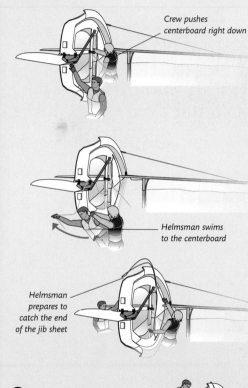

Crew pushes centerboard right down

Helmsman swims to the centerboard

Helmsman prepares to catch the end of the jib sheet

Helmsman climbs on the centerboard

Crew is scooped aboard

❶ The crew pushes the centerboard down fully, then joins the helmsman at the stern. The helmsman checks that the rudder is still in place. If it has floated off, he secures it with any available line.

❷ The crew passes the end of the mainsheet over the top of the rudder to the helmsman. Using this as a safety line, the helmsman swims around the bottom of the boat to the centerboard.

❸ From inside the boat, the crew throws the end of the uppermost jib sheet over the boat to the helmsman. The crew then floats inside the hull, head toward the bow, holding onto a thwart or toestrap.

❹ Using the jib sheet to help him, the helmsman climbs up onto the centerboard, positioning his feet close to the hull. He then leans back with straight arms and legs, pulling steadily on the jib sheet.

❺ The boat comes upright, scooping up the crew. If possible, the helmsman scrambles aboard by the windward shroud as the boat rights itself, or the crew helps him aboard, moving slowly to avoid another capsize.

RIGHTING A SINGLE-HANDED DINGHY

Many single-handers float quite high when capsized, so the daggerboard can be difficult to climb onto. Wrap your arms over it and hang your weight on it to make the boat come slowly upright. Alternatively, push the bow deeply into the water, which may make the boat rotate into its upright position.

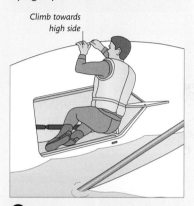

Climb towards high side

❶ In a leeward capsize, you may be able to avoid getting wet. As soon as a capsize appears inevitable, let go of the mainsheet and tiller and climb up over the top gunwale to reach the daggerboard.

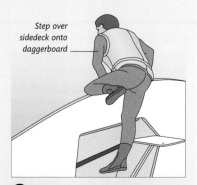

Step over sidedeck onto daggerboard

❷ Step over the sidedeck and onto the daggerboard. Turn around to stand on the daggerboard and hold the gunwale. Pull the boat upright, climbing back in as it is righted.

MAST IN THE MUD

If you capsize in shallow water, there is a possibility that the mast will catch on the bottom. The mast may get stuck if it hits soft mud, and you will have problems pulling it upright using only your body weight. In this case, you may have to ask for a tow. Make sure the helmsman of the tow boat knows what he is doing, or you may damage the mast.

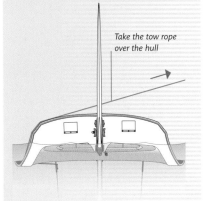

Take the tow rope over the hull

POSITIONING THE TOW ROPE

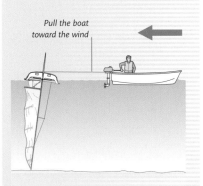

Pull the boat toward the wind

HOW TO TOW UPRIGHT

Take the tow line over the hull and tie it to a chainplate or other strong point that is within reach. If possible, attach the line to a leeward chainplate and prepare to pull the boat up against the wind. Motor very slowly at right angles to the boat, and toward the wind, until the boat rotates to lie on its side.

INVERSION

Dealing with an inversion

Many modern dinghies are prone to quickly turn completely upside down when they capsize. This is because they usually have a lot of built-in buoyancy distributed along the bottom and sides of the hull. This means that they float high on their sides and easily tip (or are blown over) to the inverted position. In this position their decks often form a seal with the water. This makes it even more difficult to bring them upright, because the water seal has to be broken first. If you sail this type of dinghy, it is imperative, when it capsizes, to avoid putting any weight on the hull and to get both people clear of the boat by moving to the transom. Then, if it inverts, the crew will not become trapped underneath the hull.

Dinghies differ in how they are best righted from an inversion. Some can be pulled upright by both crew standing on one gunwale or kneeling on the hull. With others, it is easier if one crew member pushes down on a corner of the transom to break the deck seal with the water while the other crew member pulls the boat upright. You should get to know the best way to right your boat by asking experienced sailors in your class.

Inversion in shallow water also brings the risk of that the mast will hit the bottom. Be careful not to put any weight on the boat if the mast is touching the bottom, as it may break. Lie in the water with your feet against the hull while pulling on the jib sheet to try to right the boat, or ask a safety boat for help in towing the boat into a normal capsized position.

INVERTED
If the centerboard retracts, as here, stand on one gunwale and pull on the opposite jib sheet or fixed righting line.

Losing the centerboard

Sometimes the centerboard will retract into its case when the boat turns upside down, or a daggerboard will fall out entirely. If the centerboard retracts, one of the crew will have to stand on the lip of the gunwale instead of the centerboard and pull on a jib sheet to bring the boat back to a horizontal position.

In a boat that traps an air pocket under the inverted hull, it is possible for one person to dive underneath to push the centerboard out, but you should not attempt this in a boat that does not have space for an air pocket. In the case of a daggerboard that is not secured and falls out during an inversion, it is possible to use it in the righting procedure if you can reach it easily. If so, climb onto the upturned hull and place the daggerboard into its slot from the bottom. Lean on it to bring the boat to the horizontal, then replace it in its normal position in the case from the inside before continuing with the righting procedure. Avoid this problem in the first place by having a retaining line on the centerboard or daggerboard that prevents it from fully retracting while you are sailing.

RIGHTING FROM INVERSION

The technique for righting an inverted dinghy is to bring it up to the normal capsized position, lying on its side, before proceeding with the scoop method of recovery (pp.112–113). When bringing the boat up to the normal capsized position, try to make sure that the mast comes up against the wind. Otherwise, the wind will get under the sails and cause the boat to immediately capsize again on top of you. Avoid this by standing on the windward side of the inverted hull when righting it.

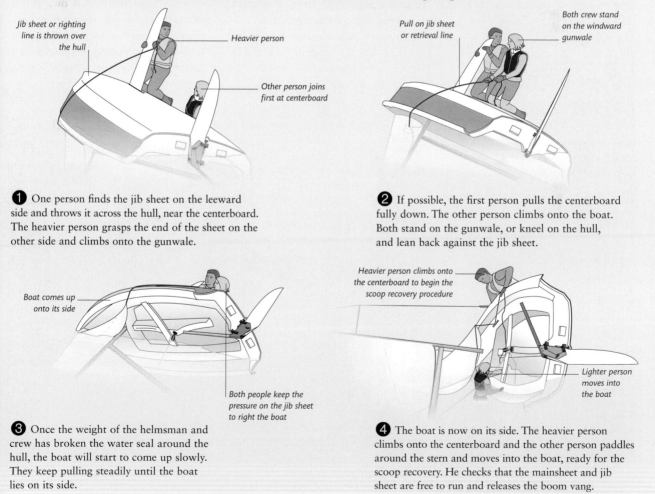

Jib sheet or righting line is thrown over the hull

Heavier person

Other person joins first at centerboard

Pull on jib sheet or retrieval line

Both crew stand on the windward gunwale

❶ One person finds the jib sheet on the leeward side and throws it across the hull, near the centerboard. The heavier person grasps the end of the sheet on the other side and climbs onto the gunwale.

❷ If possible, the first person pulls the centerboard fully down. The other person climbs onto the boat. Both stand on the gunwale, or kneel on the hull, and lean back against the jib sheet.

Boat comes up onto its side

Both people keep the pressure on the jib sheet to right the boat

Heavier person climbs onto the centerboard to begin the scoop recovery procedure

Lighter person moves into the boat

❸ Once the weight of the helmsman and crew has broken the water seal around the hull, the boat will start to come up slowly. They keep pulling steadily until the boat lies on its side.

❹ The boat is now on its side. The heavier person climbs onto the centerboard and the other person paddles around the stern and moves into the boat, ready for the scoop recovery. He checks that the mainsheet and jib sheet are free to run and releases the boom vang.

MAN OVERBOARD

It is fairly rare for someone to fall overboard from a dinghy. However, when it does happen, whoever is left in the boat needs to know how to sail it alone and how to turn around to recover the person overboard quickly and efficiently. The most common reason for falling into the water is a toestrap breaking or coming undone. To avoid accidents, check yours each time you go afloat, and practise your recovery techniques until you are confident that you could act safely in an emergency.

The recovery procedure

When someone falls overboard, it is vital that you keep him in sight at all times and get back to him, under full control, as quickly as possible. If you are the crew and your helmsman has fallen overboard, you must immediately let the jib sheet go and move aft to take control of the tiller and mainsheet. The procedure used for recovering a man overboard has the added advantage of teaching you how to sail slowly, under full control, and how to stop exactly where you want to.

The departure

The safest method of recovery is to put the boat on a beam reach and sail away from the person in the water. This gives you room to maneuver back to pick him up. Do not jibe to get back more quickly—it is too easy to capsize the dinghy, which will cause even more problems.

When you have some sea room between you and the man overboard, tack around and sail back toward him on the opposite beam reach.

The approach

From a beam reach, bear away onto a broad reach before luffing up onto a close reach for the final approach. This point of sailing is the only one on which you have complete control of your boat speed as you make the final approach to the person.

MAN-OVERBOARD RECOVERY

Release the jib sheet so that the jib flaps (leave it loose for the entire recovery), and steer the boat onto a beam reach. Position the centerboard about three-quarters down. Keep an eye on the person.

❶ Sail away on an accurate beam reach. Make sure that the wind is coming directly over the side of the boat.

❷ Sail about 10 to 15 boat lengths to give yourself room to maneuver during the next part of the recovery. Keep a constant eye on the person in the water.

❸ With the jib flapping, tack the boat onto the opposite beam reach, making sure you still have the person in sight.

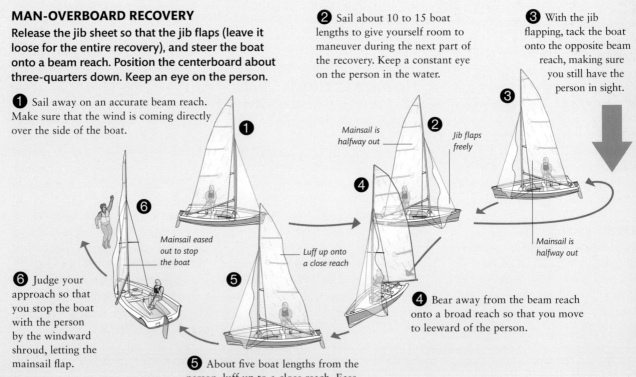

Mainsail is halfway out

Jib flaps freely

Mainsail is halfway out

❻ Judge your approach so that you stop the boat with the person by the windward shroud, letting the mainsail flap.

Mainsail eased out to stop the boat

Luff up onto a close reach

❹ Bear away from the beam reach onto a broad reach so that you move to leeward of the person.

❺ About five boat lengths from the person, luff up to a close reach. Ease the mainsheet to slow down if necessary.

PRACTICE TECHNIQUES

It is important to practice man-overboard recovery regularly. You will not want to use a real person for practice sessions, so make a substitute using a fender and a large water container (at least 6 gallons/25 liters), or several smaller ones tied together. Fill them almost full with water so they drift in a way similar to a person.

Learning

Throw the containers overboard on each of the points of sailing until you are confident that you can return accurately on each occasion. Practice until you can bring the boat to a complete stop with the bottles alongside the windward shroud on virtually every attempt.

Practicing the drill

Even when you are confident in your abilities, practice man-overboard recovery occasionally to keep up your skills. Run through the drill when you sail a new boat to get an idea of its characteristics. Use it to learn how to sail slowly under control—the skill that defines the expert sailor.

RETRIEVING CREW
Once you have returned to the person in the water, stop the boat with him at the windward shrouds. Move forward and grasp him under the armpits. Lean back to drag him into the boat.

As you approach the person in the water, make sure that you can stop with him on the windward side of the boat. If you try to pick him up on the leeward side, there is a real danger that the boat will drift on top of him or that you will capsize as you try to get him aboard.

Coming alongside

Once you are alongside the man overboard, tell him to grasp the gunwale at the windward shroud. In this position you can leave the boat to lie quietly with the sails flapping as you bring him aboard. If you try to bring him in too far aft, the bow will probably blow downwind and the boat will start sailing.

When he has a firm hold of the gunwale, give the tiller a flick to windward before letting go of it and moving forward to help him aboard. This flick helps to stop the boat from turning head-to-wind or even tacking around him in the water.

The rescue

Move to the windward shroud and grasp the person under the armpits. Lean toward him to push the side of the boat toward the water and then lean back and pull. You should now be able to drag his upper half into the boat. From there he can be rolled into the boat. If you have trouble getting him aboard, tie a bowline (p.47) in the end of the jibsheet and drop the loop over the side for him to use as a

step. If he is unconscious or too heavy to lift into the boat, tie him alongside and sail slowly for shore, keeping him on the windward side.

Once you have the sailor back aboard, check carefully for any injuries or signs of exposure or hypothermia (pp.430–431). If the person is wearing a wetsuit or drysuit, he should be no worse for the experience; otherwise, he will be wet and may be suffering from the cold. In this case, lay the person in the boat to warm up, and get to shore as quickly as possible. Seek medical help if necessary.

STOWING AFTER SAILING

Once you are back ashore, you will probably want to head straight for a hot shower. Before you do, however, it is a good idea to spend a few minutes making sure that the boat is clean and neat. Make a quick inspection for any damage, and then stow the sails and other removable gear. Finally, make sure the boat is well secured. A few minutes spent now will prevent damage and stop deterioration, and will ensure that the boat is ready to sail the next time you want to take it out.

Washing the dinghy

Wash the boat thoroughly with fresh water as soon as you bring it ashore. Pay extra attention to the blocks, as any traces of dirt or salt will damage the bearings. Rinse the centerboard casing, then wash all the equipment, including the sails and rudder.

Derigging

Derig the boat by going through the rigging order in reverse. First, take out the bungs in the buoyancy tanks or transom and allow any water to drain away, and open any hatches in the tanks to allow air to circulate. If you have a padded rudder-stowage bag, put the rudder into it as soon as you have washed it. Never lay it down on hard surfaces or where it might be stepped on. Be particularly careful with the blade—it is easily damaged. If the centerboard is removed between trips, it is also best stored in a padded bag. A daggerboard is always removed between trips, and this, too, should have its own protective bag.

Stowing the sails

If possible, allow the sails to dry before stowing them in the sailbag. Sails made of modern sailcloth will not be damaged if they are put away wet, but they should still be dried at the earliest opportunity to avoid mildew growth.

Remove the mainsail from the boom and unhank the jib from the forestay. Undo any shackles used to attach the sails to the halyards and reattach them to the fittings so that they cannot be lost. Remove the jib sheets and coil them up neatly. Stow them in the sailbag or tie them in the boat. If your jib has a wire luff, coil this up, making the jib into a smooth tube, to avoid kinking the wire. Once the sail is rolled up, it can be loosely folded so that it fits into the sailbag.

Fold the head in, then start rolling

❶ If you roll the sail carefully, the battens can be left in their pockets. Lay the sail flat and fold the head over onto the body of the sail. Then start rolling the sail, keeping the roll at right angles to the leech.

STOWING THE MAINSAIL AND JIB

Because the mainsail is large, it is easier to roll if it is laid out on a clean patch of ground, such as on grass or a concrete or wooden surface. If the ground is dirty, lay the sail over the boat to roll it. Roll the jib in the same way.

Keep the roll parallel to the battens

❷ Continue rolling the sail, making sure to keep the roll parallel to the batten pockets if the battens are left in. If the sail creases at the luff or leech, unroll it a bit and remove the creases.

Keep sails in bags for protection

❸ When the whole mainsail is rolled in a tight, neat tube, slide it into its sailbag. If the battens have been removed, stow them in the bag with the sail. Roll the jib in the same way and stow in its bag.

FITTING THE COVER
Put removable items into the dinghy, making sure that they are secure, then fit the cover over the top. Secure it under the hull at the bow and the sidedecks.

If the sail has a tape luff, roll it down the leech in a neat roll that fits easily into the sail bag. Roll the mainsail and stow it in its sail bag.

Checking for wear

To keep the boat in top condition, be prepared to spend a few minutes after each sail checking it over. Inspect each piece of gear for wear or damage. If you find any problems, deal with them at once, if possible. Otherwise, make a note to remind yourself of what needs to be done, and note the tools or materials for the repair. Always deal with repairs as soon as possible; otherwise, it is inevitable that the damaged item will fail at the most inopportune moment.

Storing the dinghy

After you have removed and stowed the gear and sails, you will need to put your boat somewhere, so that it is safe until the next time you go sailing. Many sailing clubs have dinghy docks in which you can leave your dinghy, and this is certainly more convenient than trailering the boat to and from the sailing area each time you use it. Very small boats can be stored in dinghy racks, which save space and provide good protection and support. More usually, dinghies are stored on their launching carts.

If you are storing your boat on a cart, the stern should rest on a soft support, such as a car tire, and the front of the cart should also be supported, so that the dinghy cannot tip forward and damage its hull. This will also allow any rainwater that gets in the hull to drain out through the transom or bung holes. Tie the boat securely to the cart with the painter, then fit the cover. All boats should have a cover that fits well and can be fastened tightly to provide complete protection from the elements. Even fiberglass boats can be damaged by sunlight, so a good cover is a sound investment. It will also discourage the theft of any equipment that you leave in the boat. Tie the cover firmly under the hull, and make sure that it cannot come loose in high winds. Then tie the boat down to securing points set into the ground, or to heavy blocks, which will prevent it from being blown over.

HOSING DOWN

As soon as you bring the boat ashore, hose it down with fresh water. Wash all the equipment, including the sails and rudder.

ADVANCED
SMALL-BOAT SAILING

When the basic skills of dinghy sailing have been mastered, they can be refined and new ones acquired, by moving up to a high-performance dinghy or a small keelboat. Once you have mastered the necessary skills, you will find that these boats provide exhilarating sailing.

HIGH-PERFORMANCE BOATS

If you have learnt to sail in a general-purpose dinghy, you will notice a tremendous difference when you first try sailing in a high-performance boat. High-performance boats are far more sensitive to changes in wind strength, accelerate faster, and require quicker reactions from helmsman and crew than general-purpose dinghies. Fast boats make more demands on your abilities and are more difficult to sail well, but they will teach you about the finer points of boat handling far more quickly than a slower boat.

Design advances

The development of the planing dinghy occurred in the 1930s, and by the 1960s, dinghy shapes and light weight had evolved sufficiently to allow some designs to plane when sailing to windward. Dinghy design then remained fairly static until the early 1990s, when modern materials and lightweight construction methods created a revolution in the small-boat market. Now, there is a range of dinghies available that are capable of much higher speeds than conventional dinghies and test helmsmen and crews to the limit of their abilities. The performance of the fastest dinghies has now entered the high-speed world previously shared by catamarans and windsurfers. Along with these extreme dinghies has come crash-and-burn-type, short-course racing, which offers plenty of thrills and spills.

The small keelboat market has also developed thanks to new designs and the use of lightweight materials. Now there are many more small keelboats available that are designed to provide fast and competitive racing for sailors who prefer to sail fast in a boat with a keel rather than in a high-performance dinghy, which is likely to capsize quite frequently.

Apparent wind sailing

The biggest difference between sailing a conventional and a high-performance boat is the effect of boat speed on the apparent wind.

FOIL-BORNE SAILING
Some modern boats are so light and powerful that they can rise above the water on foils and reach very high speeds.

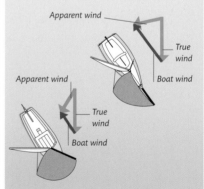

EFFECT OF APPARENT WIND
The extra speed (and resulting boat wind) of the faster boat (*top*) causes the apparent wind to increase and come from further forward than for the slower boat (*bottom*).

Because high-performance boats plane upwind and downwind even in quite light winds, their speed has a major effect on the strength and direction of the apparent wind. Sailing upwind, their speed increases the strength of the apparent wind, while sailing downwind, it reduces the apparent wind strength. Because the apparent wind is always shifted farther forward than the true wind, high-performance boats usually sail with the apparent wind coming from ahead of the beam even when sailing downwind, and have to sheet their sails in tighter than slower boats.

Crewed or alone

If you are considering a high-performance dinghy, you have a choice between a single-hander, a two-person, or even a three-person boat. The purest form of sailing is undoubtedly single-handing, and there is a range of high-performance boats available for the single-hander, including boats with a trapeze and even an asymmetric spinnaker. Most dinghy designs cater to two people, and you can choose between single or double trapezes, and a conventional or asymmetric spinnaker. The 18-foot Skiff is sailed by a crew of three, all on trapezes, and has a powerful rig that includes a very large asymmetric spinnaker.

SPEED COMPARISONS

A polar diagram is used to show the potential speed of a boat for a particular wind strength. For every wind strength, each design of boat will have a unique polar curve. Racing yachts use polar curves to predict the speed they should attain on any point of sailing, and to trim and tune the boat accordingly. Here, the curves illustrate the differences in performance between types of small boats.

Factors affecting speed

Speed is determined by the strength of the wind, the amount of sail area, and the weight of the boat, complete with its crew. In short, the more sail area you have and the less your boat weighs, the faster you will go. High-performance boats are generally much lighter than general-purpose dinghies. They have larger, more powerful rigs and much shallower hulls. They typically have little natural stability and rely entirely on the weight of the crew to keep them upright when they are being sailed. Their sole purpose is fast sailing, and they are used only for racing or thrill-seeking sailing.

Points of sailing

A general-purpose dinghy will be slower on all points of sailing than a high-performance dinghy. And a high-performance catamaran will generally be faster than a high-performance dinghy because it is wider and more stable, allowing the crew to make better use of the sail power available to them. All types of sailing boats will perform better on some points of sailing than others, and reaching courses are nearly always faster for most boats than close-hauled or running courses.

However, the latest generation of high-performance, skiff-type dinghies tend to be faster on a broad reach. They develop so much power on a beam reach in moderate to strong winds that it is almost impossible to sail at 90 degrees to the wind. These boats will generally capsize if you try to sail on a beam reach, so high-performance skiff sailors tend to call this point of sailing the "Crash Zone."

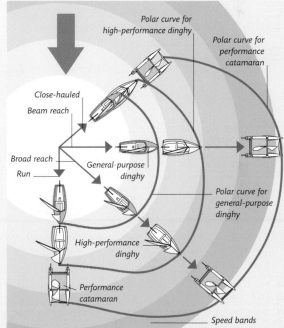

POLAR DIAGRAM
This polar diagram compares the potential speeds of a general-purpose dinghy, a typical high-performance dinghy, and a performance catamaran. In the diagram, the farther a boat is from the center, the faster is its speed. The catamaran is fastest on all points of sailing, with the greatest gains on beam- and broad-reaching courses. Skiff-type dinghies are closer in performance to a catamaran than to a conventional high-performance dinghy.

TYPES OF HIGH-PERFORMANCE DINGHIES

High-performance dinghies typically have shallow, narrow, and lightweight hulls with large rigs. They often have at least one trapeze, but the fastest boats have both helmsman and crew on trapezes. The fastest dinghies have large asymmetric spinnakers, often flown from the masthead, to increase speed downwind. High-performance boats are available to suit a range of skill levels and physical sizes and abilities. Small keelboats offering high performance are also available (p.161).

DINGHIES

OLYMPIC 470

The Olympic 470 is a good introduction to high-performance sailing. It has a spinnaker and one trapeze and is ideal for lighter crews. It provides close racing with separate fleets for male and female sailors.

B14

Developed from the 18-foot Skiff, this lightweight two-handed dinghy relies on wide wings rather than trapezes from which the crew can hike out. The B14 requires good fitness and boat handling skills.

RS800

The RS800 is arguably the easiest of the twin-trapeze boats to sail. It offers many of the thrills of higher-performance skiffs without as many spills. Like the Laser 4000, this class is particularly suited to lighter teams.

OLYMPIC 49ER

The Olympic 49er is one of the skiff-type, high-performance boats with huge rigs and twin trapezes. Inspired by the 18-foot Skiff, it uses a large asymmetrical spinnaker set on the end of a long retractable bowsprit.

INTERNATIONAL 505

The International 505 is a classic high-performance boat with a large spinnaker and a trapeze for the crew. The 505 gives close racing in large, competitive fleets. It is more suitable than the 470 for heavier sailors.

RS500

The RS500 is a single-trapeze boat that provides exciting performance, while being relatively easy to handle. It is suitable for crews looking to progress their sailing skills to the more advanced requirements of handling a high-performance dinghy.

INTERNATIONAL 14

The International 14 is one of the oldest racing classes, and has been developed over the years to keep ahead of the opposition. It now has twin trapezes and is a very demanding boat to sail.

18-FOOT SKIFF

The 18-foot Skiff is the classic high-performance dinghy. It has been developed over decades to the state-of-the-art boat it is today. Now sailed by three-man crews, the Skiff is the pinnacle of high-performance boats.

SINGLE-HANDERS

INTERNATIONAL MOTH

The International Moth is a radical, foil-borne, single-handed, development class. The modern design is a carbon fiber hydrofoil-borne craft that weighs just 66 lb and is only about 13 inches wide, testing the skills of even the best sailors.

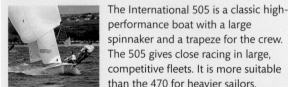

INTERNATIONAL CANOE

The International Canoe is one of the fastest single-handed dinghies. It has an extremely narrow hull inherited from its ancient canoe origins, with a sliding seat on which the helmsman balances the boat. There is an option to use an asymmetric spinnaker.

Making a choice

If you learned in a general-purpose dinghy and want to progress to sailing faster boats, the next step is to sail in a moderately high-performance class that uses a conventional or asymmetric spinnaker (*pp.144–155*) and a trapeze (*pp.136–139*) for the crew. Crew for someone else before buying a boat, just to make sure you like this type of sailing. If you want to sail as fast as possible—and spend a lot of time capsizing in the early days—you may like to consider one of the faster classes, which are generally characterized as skifflike, after the 18-foot Skiff, which first pioneered multiple trapezes, asymmetric spinnakers, and the use of racks on the hull sides to allow the trapezing crew to create more leverage to balance the very powerful rig.

Most of these skiff-types are two-person boats, like the 49er, the Olympic two-person, high-performance dinghy class, but extreme high-speed single-handed dinghies, like the Musto Skiff, are also available. Remember, though, that any of the more extreme designs

HIGH-PERFORMANCE KEELBOAT
If you want the thrills of high-performance without the spills a dinghy provides, you can choose a performance keelboat.

will require a considerable amount of time and effort to learn to sail and will involve a lot of capsizing while you are learning. The process is made considerably easier, and more enjoyable, if you pick a class that is popular in your sailing area so that you will have plenty of similar boats to sail against and experienced sailors to ask for advice.

Another way to get high-speed sailing, with less risk of capsize, is to pick from one of the catamaran classes (*pp.166–173*) or to choose a performance-orientated small keelboat (*pp.160–165*).

Racing

The most sensible and convenient approach to racing is to pick a class that is already being actively raced in the area that you want to sail. Most popular classes have good club-level racing, and some provide world-class competition. You will also need to choose between speed and tactics. Very high-performance dinghies are great for sheer speed but not ideal for close, tactical racing because of the difficulty in handling their power. In fact, some of the best racing is often to be found in slower boats in which the racing is closer and more interesting tactically. Many of the largest racing fleets are found among the older, general-purpose dinghies that offer the closest tactical racing.

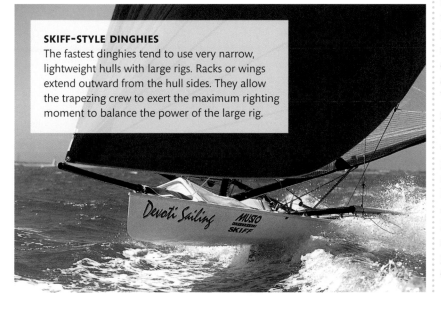

SKIFF-STYLE DINGHIES
The fastest dinghies tend to use very narrow, lightweight hulls with large rigs. Racks or wings extend outward from the hull sides. They allow the trapezing crew to exert the maximum righting moment to balance the power of the large rig.

IMPROVING YOUR TECHNIQUE

Once you have mastered the basic sailing techniques, you will be able to rig and launch your boat, handle it on all points of sailing, and return safely to your starting point. When you feel that these basic techniques are second nature, it is time to consider progressing to a faster and more responsive boat. There are several techniques for performance sailing that you will need to learn. These include understanding how and when a boat planes, how to refine sail trimming for better performance, how to balance the helm, how to sail close-hauled efficiently, and how to maintain the speed of your boat while changing course.

rise out of the water when planing to the point where the hull forward of the mast is out of the water, but the fastest planing dinghies rise out of the water significantly more, often to the point where they plane on just the aftermost sections of the hull just forward of the transom, with the rest of the boat clear of the water.

Most dinghies, even heavier general-purpose ones, will plane if there is sufficient wind and the crew understands planing techniques, but light boats with a large sail area will plane readily even in quite light winds. Although slower dinghies and most small keelboats may only plane on a beam or broad reach in strong winds, high-performance dinghies are capable of planing when sailing to windward.

Planing

When a boat rises up on its own bow wave and skims across the water like a speedboat, it is said to be planing. A boat will plane when it is traveling fast enough to create lift under the hull, raising the boat onto its own bow wave. The shape of the hull is an important factor in planing.

Boats that plane well have broad, flat sections in the aft half of the hull. It is on these that the boat rides when it is planing. Most planing boats

Planing tips

There are several techniques that you can use to encourage your boat to plane. The first is known as pumping. If the boat cannot quite rise onto the plane, wait for a gust of wind, sit out hard to keep the boat upright while

HOW TO PLANE

Start on a beam reach in a wind of at least Force 3. Be ready to move your weight aft to help lift the bow onto the plane. Speed will increase quickly as you plane and the apparent wind will shift forward, so be ready to sheet in both sails. Extra speed will make the rudder more efficient; small movements of the tiller will be enough to keep the boat on course. The boat will slow down quickly if it slips off the plane. Ease the sheets as the apparent wind shifts aft, and move your weight forward again.

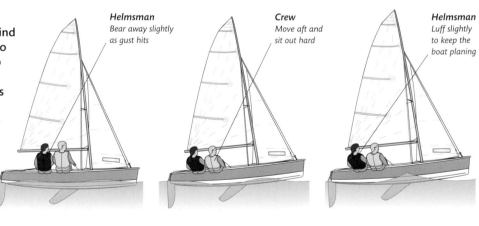

Helmsman
Bear away slightly as gust hits

Crew
Move aft and sit out hard

Helmsman
Luff slightly to keep the boat planing

❶ Sail on a beam reach with the centerboard no more than half down. Wait for a gust of wind and, as it hits, bear away slightly and ease both sheets a little. Keep the boat upright.

❷ Move your weight aft a little as you feel the boat accelerate. The bow will lift as it begins to plane. If the boat heels when you are sitting out hard, raise the centerboard a little.

❸ Remain planing as long as possible by luffing slightly to keep the apparent wind forward. This may enable you to continue planing until the next gust arrives.

rapidly trimming both sails in, then out again. This produces a burst of extra power, which should help the boat to rise onto the plane.

Another way of helping the boat to plane is to use a wave to help you accelerate. Sailing downwind in waves, wait until the stern lifts on a wave, then bear away to surf down its front. As the boat accelerates, luff up slightly and sheet in the sails. It is important to keep the boat upright throughout this maneuver. The speed gained from surfing down the wave may create enough wind pressure to keep you on the plane as the apparent wind shifts forward. If the boat begins to plane, the apparent wind will stay forward, and you will need to trim the sails correctly to the new apparent wind direction in order to maintain planing.

Sail setting

One of the hardest things to get used to when you start sailing is having to adjust sail trim. However, as you develop your skills, trimming the sails to suit even small changes in wind direction becomes almost automatic.

When you sail fast dinghies, you will find that they are very responsive to changes in wind strength and will accelerate or slow down very quickly. As they alter their speed, the apparent wind (p.34) will shift forward (accelerating) or backward (slowing down), and sail trim must be adjusted each time this happens. The apparent wind will also shift aft when a gust hits the boat, so be ready to ease the sails as you see a gust approaching, sheeting them in again as it eases.

Balancing the helm

When a boat is sailing upright, trimmed correctly fore and aft, and the sails are accurately set, there should

be little or no tendency for it to turn. If you let go of the tiller, the boat will continue on a straight course. This condition is referred to as a balanced helm. If the boat turns to windward when you let go of the tiller, it has weather helm. If it turns to leeward, it has lee helm. In practice, it is easier to sail a boat that has a small amount of weather helm, since this gives some feel to the steering and, in particular, makes it easier to steer the boat accurately on a close-hauled course. When you are learning, it is also a safety factor, since, if the tiller is let go by accident, the boat will turn into the wind and stop.

Lee helm is to be avoided because it makes the boat difficult to sail; if the tiller is let go, it will not turn into the wind and automatically stop.

You can alter the balance of the helm while sailing by adjusting the centerboard if your boat has one. Lift the centerboard slightly to reduce weather helm and lower it to eliminate lee helm. When you

tune your boat (pp.138–141), you can also adjust the rake of the mast to produce the desired helm balance.

Sailing at speed

Assuming that the boat is tuned correctly, the achievement of optimum speed depends on the skills of the helmsman and crew. Concentration and constant attention to sail trim, boat balance, and course steered are necessary to achieve top performance. When you first sail a high-performance boat, it will take time and practice to get used to the faster reactions that are required to sail it efficiently.

Take care to avoid violent changes of course, especially when sailing offwind, because it will be hard to keep the boat balanced through sharp turns. Remember that the rudder is much more efficient when you are traveling at high speed, so much smaller tiller movements are needed than when you are sailing slowly.

PLANING
This lightweight sportsboat is planing well under an asymmetric spinnaker. The crew are well aft, and to windward, to keep the boat level and help the bow lift.

USING TELLTALES

The easiest way to check whether you are trimming the sails correctly and have the right twist and leech tension is to attach telltales (*p.80*) to the sails.

Mainsail telltales

Stick nylon telltales on the mainsail leech. When the sail is correctly set, for medium wind and flat water, all the telltales will stream aft, with the one near the top batten periodically folding behind the sail.

Jib luff telltales

Twist in the jib can be checked by using the luff telltales. When the top, middle, and lower windward telltales all stream aft together, the sail has the correct amount of twist. If the top windward telltale lifts before the middle and lower windward ones, it has too much twist; the fairlead should be moved forward. If the bottom or middle windward tell-tales lift before the top one, move the lead aft to increase twist.

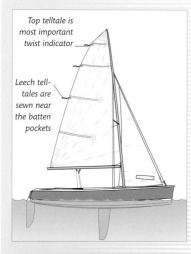

Top telltale is most important twist indicator

Leech tell-tales are sewn near the batten pockets

READING LEECH TELLTALES
When all the telltales stream aft with the top one occasionally folding behind the leech, the sail is set correctly for medium wind and flat water. If the top telltale remains folded behind the leech, ease the mainsheet or boom vang.

Controlling twist

As well as setting the sails at the correct angle to the wind using luff telltales (*p.80*), you also need to adjust the leech tension in each sail to control the amount of twist (the difference between the angle of the sail at the foot and the head). Adjusting twist is important for boat speed. In most conditions, twist is adjusted to maximize power, but in strong winds it is used to reduce heeling. Excessive heeling makes the boat slower and harder to steer.

Leech telltales (*left*) are a useful indicator of the amount of mainsail twist. The amount needed depends on the conditions and the cut of the sail. In general, you should have some twist in very light conditions, less twist in light-to-moderate winds, and more twist again in strong winds.

Mainsail twist is controlled by tension in the mainsheet or vang. The more tension there is in either, the less twist there is. Jib twist is controlled by the fore-and-aft position of the fairleads and jib-sheet tension. Move jib fairleads forward to reduce twist, and aft to increase it.

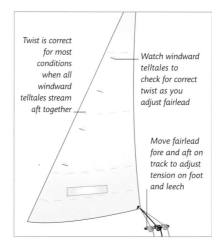

Twist is correct for most conditions when all windward telltales stream aft together

Watch windward telltales to check for correct twist as you adjust fairlead

Move fairlead fore and aft on track to adjust tension on foot and leech

ADJUSTING JIB TWIST
Increase twist in the jib by moving the jib sheet fairlead aft. Reduce twist by moving the fairlead forward.

REDUCING HEELING WITH TWIST
These boats are racing in a fairly strong wind with their crews fully extended on the trapeze. Their sails are set with quite a bit of twist to reduce the heeling force.

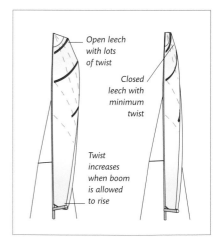

Open leech with lots of twist

Closed leech with minimum twist

Twist increases when boom is allowed to rise

MAINSAIL TWIST
Ease the mainsheet and/or the vang to allow boom to lift and increase twist (*left*), and tighten them to reduce twist (*right*).

MAINTAINING BALANCE AND TRIM

To achieve maximum performance, it is essential that the dinghy is sailed upright and level fore and aft. Sitting out will help to maintain balance, and sitting together in a central position will keep the boat level fore and aft. By sitting together, the helmsman and crew also reduce windage and so increase their possible speed.

BALANCE
Sit out or trapeze (pp.136–137) to keep the boat upright. If it still heels, ease the mainsheet or increase twist to spill some wind. Weight distribution and sail trim require constant attention to maintain balance.

TRIM
Keep the boat level fore and aft by sitting close together. In strong winds, move aft slightly to allow the bow to lift and pass over waves smoothly; in light winds, move forward to keep the transom clear of the water and reduce drag.

TURNING THE BOAT
Bearing away around a racing mark, the helmsman eases the mainsail to start the turn while the crew prepares to come in but heels the boat to windward.

Changing direction
One sure sign of a skilled sailor is the ability to change course without slowing the boat unnecessarily. A good helmsman and crew will always prefer to use sail trim and boat balance to turn the boat (pp.78–81) and reduce the need to use the rudder. This is because each time the rudder is turned more than 4–5 degrees off the centerline, it causes drag and slows the boat. Using heel and sail trim is especially important when bearing away, as the rudder may prove ineffective, especially in strong winds, if the boat heels to leeward, or if the mainsail is not eased before the turn. Keep the boat upright, or heeled to windward slightly, and ease the mainsail to bear away successfully.

Sailing close-hauled
Sailing close-hauled is usually the biggest challenge for the novice. The helmsman must keep the boat sailing as close to the wind as possible without letting speed drop by sailing too close (known as pinching). He must also avoid erring in the other direction and losing ground to windward by sailing too far off the wind. Practice sailing close-hauled using the telltales on the jib luff (p.80) to follow the best course. Both windward and leeward telltales should be kept streaming aft for the best balance between speed and pointing. The windward set can be allowed to rise occasionally, but the leeward ones should not lift, as this indicates that the boat is sailing too far off the wind.

COPING WITH WIND SHIFTS

Spotting and using wind shifts are essential skills, particularly if you want to race. A header is when the wind moves forward; a freer (or lift) is when it moves aft. Dealing with wind shifts effectively can significantly reduce the distance sailed.

Exploiting wind shifts

If you have to tack upwind, you will sail the quickest course if you tack when you are headed. If the wind shifts back, it will head you again on the other tack. You can then tack again and make more ground to windward. Remember that a wind shift that is a header on port tack is a freer on starboard tack.

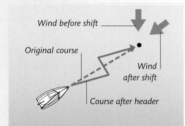

HEADER

A header will force you to bear away from your course in order to keep the sails full. You will then have to tack to reach your destination.

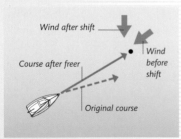

FREER

When the wind moves aft, it is a freer. To prevent your boat from sailing too far off course in a freer, you should luff up as soon as the wind shifts.

Understanding the wind

The wind rarely blows consistently from one direction. In fact, you will often find that the wind oscillates around a mean direction, perhaps shifting 10–20 degrees on either side of the mean, and sometimes producing considerably larger shifts. In an oscillating wind, the shifts will occur at reasonably regular intervals and it is possible to time how long the wind takes to shift from one side of the mean to the other, and back again.

At other times, the wind may shift from one direction to another due to a change in the weather pattern, perhaps the passage of a front (*pp.368–369*), and then, rather than oscillating backward and forward, it will move from the old direction to the new one, sometimes rapidly and at other times in small, incremental movements. In some localities, the proximity and shape of the land causes the wind to bend across an area (*opposite*).

When you are sailing, and especially when racing, it is very important to work out how the wind is shifting or bending so that you can take advantage of the shifts or bend to reduce the distance you need to sail. Spotting wind shifts may be quite easy if the shift is a large one, if you know the waters on

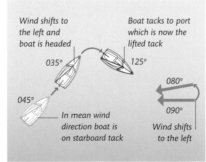

WIND SHIFTS TO THE LEFT

Boat on starboard tack sees compass heading change from 045° to 035°, showing a 10° header, and tacks to port tack.

which you sail well, or if there are clear and obvious landmarks near the race course that you can use to check your heading. However, the easiest way to spot small shifts that can otherwise go unnoticed is to use a compass.

Velocity shifts

Be aware that changes in the true wind's speed will create velocity shifts that are easily confused with true lifts or headers. If you notice a lull in the wind followed by your tell-tales lifting, suggesting a wind shift, the cause is likely to be a velocity header. This occurs when the apparent wind shifts forward because of a drop in true wind speed, while the boat speed has yet to drop. Hold your course, do not bear away as you would in a true header until the boat speed drops and the apparent wind moves aft again.

Similarly, expect a lift when the wind speed increases and, if possible, anticipate it by luffing up slightly as the gust arrives to take advantage of the velocity shift moving the apparent wind aft temporarily.

Using a compass

Small-boat sailors use a compass tactically, to spot changes in wind direction. If the wind is blowing from

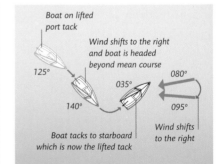

WIND SHIFTS TO THE RIGHT

Boat now on port tack sees compass heading change from 125° to 140°, showing a 15° header, and tacks to starboard tack.

MECHANICAL COMPASS
A mechanical compass uses a permanent magnet fixed to a pivoted compass card in a chamber filled with a damping liquid.

an average direction of 090° (an easterly direction), and your boat sails close-hauled at an angle of 45 degrees to the wind, then the boat's course on starboard tack will be 045° and 135° on port. If the wind then shifts 10 degrees to the left, to blow from 080°, then a sailor traveling on starboard tack will notice that his course has changed from 045° to 035°. This is a good time to tack on to port, where his heading will now be 135 − 10 = 125°. This is a good

tack to stay on unless the number on port increases to more than the average heading of 135°.

If the wind then shifts to the right and the sailor finds himself on a new heading of 140°, the compass is now telling him that he is on a 5° header, and it is time to tack once again onto starboard, which is the new "lifted tack." Identifying such subtle changes in wind direction would be very difficult without a compass.

Types of tactical compass

The conventional type of compass uses a magnet under a card engraved with compass degrees. The card is mounted on a pivot in an oil-filled bowl that acts as a damping mechanism to minimize excessive movement of the card in rough seas.

An electronic compass does not require damping in the same way, and it is possible to read changes in heading to the nearest degree, rather than the 5 degrees that is the practical limit of accuracy of a conventional compass. Some tactical electronic compasses are solar-powered. Not all classes allow them to be used, so check before buying one.

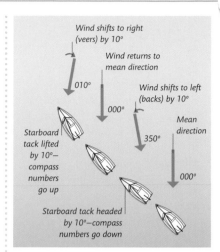

OSCILLATING WIND SHIFTS
An oscillating wind shifts either side of a mean direction. Remember the rule about compass numbers increasing or decreasing (*below*) to quickly spot lifts and headers.

FORCE		LIFT	HEADER
PORT TACK		Compass number goes down	Compass number goes up
STARBOARD TACK		Compass number goes up	Compass number goes down

WIND BENDS

Sometimes the wind can curve across the course, particularly when it is blowing around a high headland or over a large obstacle like a hill or mountain in the vicinity of the course. In a wind bend, the shortest route upwind is achieved by sailing toward the inside of the bend on the headed tack, and then tacking onto a lift that takes you up the inside of the curve. In this case, tacking at the first sign of a header would be the wrong course of action.

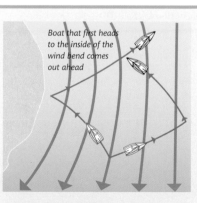

USING A WIND BEND
If a wind bend is the cause of a shift in wind direction, stay on the headed tack to get to the inside of the bend before tacking onto the lifted tack.

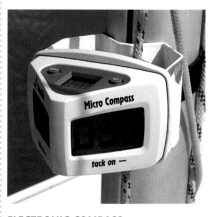

ELECTRONIC COMPASS
An electronic compass is easier to read than a conventional compass. This unit is mounted on the mast and is self-powered by a solar cell on the top of the compass.

SAILING EXERCISES

Confident boat handling is a sure sign of a good sailor. It can be developed only through practice on the water, preferably in a range of dinghies, since this will show how different characteristics influence handling. The best way to learn the finer points of controlling a dinghy is to experiment with a few boat-handling exercises. The first time you attempt the exercises described here, choose a gentle Force 2–3 wind and sail to a clear stretch of water, free from obstructions or other boats.

IN REVERSE
A keelboat can be sailed backwards in the same way as a dinghy, but more than one person may need to hold the boom out.

Sailing with one sail

If you have a two-man dinghy with the standard arrangement of mainsail and jib, you will usually use both sails when sailing. The rig is designed for both sails to work together and to balance their forces around the centerboard. However, when a two-sail dinghy is sailed under a single sail, its handling characteristics change considerably, and it may be difficult to complete some maneuvers.

Try sailing on all the points of sailing (pp.40–41), first under mainsail alone and then only with the jib. This exercise teaches you about sail balance and how your boat reacts under a single sail. You will also find out how your boat handles at slow speeds, which will be useful when you are sailing to and from the shore or when you are in competition and maneuvering at the start of a race.

Mainsail alone

Start by lowering the jib and sailing under mainsail alone. Without the jib in front of it, the mainsail is less efficient (p.33) and the boat will sail more slowly, especially on upwind courses. The boat's sail plan is designed to balance around its pivot point (at the centerboard or keel); removing the jib moves the center of effort aft, giving the boat weather helm (p.128). It therefore tries to turn into the wind. The helmsman must counteract the weather helm by moving the tiller farther to windward to keep the boat on course.

The boat will sail reasonably well on a beam reach, but with more weather helm than normal. If you sail a dinghy that has a centerboard, you can reduce excess weather helm by raising it more than usual to move the pivot point aft. If you sail a keelboat or a dinghy with a daggerboard, this option is not available to you.

As you turn toward the wind to a close-reaching course, the lack of a jib will impede performance even more. By the time you reach close-hauled, the boat will feel quite sluggish. When you tack, the boat will turn into the wind easily, but it will be slow to bear away on the new tack. Ease the mainsheet after the tack to bear away to a close reach. This will increase speed before you attempt to sail close-hauled on the new tack. Be careful not to let the boat slow down too much when sailing closehauled or you will not have enough speed to be able to steer with the rudder. If this happens, the boat will turn into the wind and stop. Keep the boat moving as fast as possible, sailing just off a closehauled course to make progress to windward without stalling.

The lack of the jib will not be so apparent on downwind courses, because it is the size of the mainsail that contributes most to speed and, on a run, the jib is often blanketed behind the mainsail.

Jib alone

Once you have mastered sailing under mainsail alone, try the exercise under jib alone. Without the mainsail, the boat will suffer from lee helm on a beam reach or upwind courses. It will be considerably slower than usual on all points of sailing. Sailing downwind is easy but slow, but sailing upwind will be difficult. Some boats will sail upwind under jib alone, but with a considerable amount of lee helm. Sail with the centerboard or daggerboard farther down than usual to help counter this. Tacking under the jib is difficult or impossible in some boats or weather conditions, such as strong winds. Experiment to see how your boat behaves in a range of conditions.

SAILING BACKWARD

Remember that when the boat is moving backward through the water, the flow of water over the rudder is reversed, so its action is also reversed, and the bow will move in the same direction in which you move the tiller. With the rudder now leading the boat as it moves backward, its effects are exaggerated. Make only small movements with the tiller, or the boat will swing quickly to lie at an angle to the wind. Keep the crew weight well forward to stop the transom from digging in, which will also make the boat turn. When you want to sail forward again, push the tiller in the direction you want the bow to move. Wait until the boat turns, then center the tiller, sheet in the sails, and sail off.

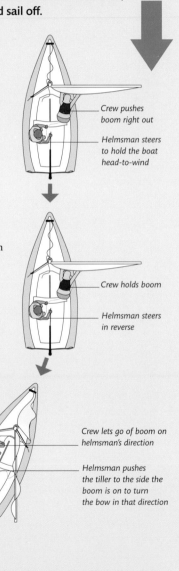

1 Point the boat directly into the wind so that the jib flaps on the centerline, and have your crew push the boom out fully on one side. Let the mainsheet run out to allow the boom to be pushed all the way out. Watch the water flowing past the boat to gauge when the boat has stopped. Until it stops, the rudder will work in the normal way. Use it to hold the boat head-to-wind.

Crew pushes
boom right out

Helmsman steers
to hold the boat
head-to-wind

2 When the boat starts moving backward, the rudder will work in the opposite way from normal. To steer in reverse, push the tiller a small amount in the direction you wish the bow to turn. Do not make large movements with the tiller or the boat will turn violently.

Crew holds boom

Helmsman steers
in reverse

3 To sail forward again, push the tiller in the direction you want the bow to go. It is usually best to turn the bow to the side the boom is on. If you turn the other way, the boom will swing rapidly across the boat when it is released. Tell your crew to let go of the boom.

Crew lets go of boom on
helmsman's direction

Helmsman pushes
the tiller to the side the
boom is on to turn
the bow in that direction

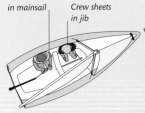

Helmsman
centers tiller
and sheets
in mainsail

Crew sheets
in jib

4 When the boat has turned sufficiently—to a close reach or beam reach course—the helmsman moves the tiller to the centerline and he and the crew sheet in the sails to sail off forward.

Sailing without a centerboard

Centerboards or daggerboards rarely break (although it is possible to lose a daggerboard during a capsize if it is not secured to the boat). However, it is useful to try sailing without one so that you can see just how much they influence the way a dinghy behaves under sail. Stop the boat on a close reach and raise the centerboard completely. Now sail off on a beam reach and watch the way in which the boat slides sideways, making considerable leeway (p.69) as it sails forward.

Tacking is difficult or impossible without a centerboard to pivot around. Before attempting to tack, get the boat sailing as fast as possible on a close reaching course and push the tiller away farther than usual to try to get the bow through the wind as quickly as possible. If, despite this, the boat fails to tack, you will have to jibe around to change tack.

On upwind courses it is hard to make headway because the dinghy will crab sideways as fast as it goes forward. Experiment with heeling the boat to leeward slightly and moving the crew's weight right forward to depress the bow and the Veed sections of the front part of the hull. If you sail a deep-hulled, general-purpose type dinghy, especially one constructed with flat panels and chines (p.60), the shape of the hull may provide sufficient lateral resistance to allow you to make some progress to windward. If you sail a dinghy with a very shallow hull, however, it is likely to be impossible to make any progress upwind. Even on a beam reach, the boat will make considerable leeway. It is only when you are on downwind courses, when the centerboard would usually be only slightly down, that the boat will sail normally.

Sailing without a rudder

Another good exercise is to sail around a triangular course without the rudder. Either remove the rudder completely or, if it is a lifting type, raise the blade out of the water. Sailing without the rudder teaches you the importance of sail trim, centerboard position, and boat balance and trim. Remember, to luff up trim in the mainsail, let out the jib, heel the boat to leeward, and trim it down by the bow. To bear away, reverse these instructions. Without the rudder, the effects of the other controls become more obvious. It is usually best to try this in light winds with only one person in the boat. This gives you total control over all turning forces and avoids confusion between the helmsman and the crew. A triangular course will seem impossible at first, as you will tend to sail in circles, but with practice you should be able to achieve it in moderate conditions. You will find you will need to raise the centerboard quite considerably to rebalance the boat. Once you are proficient at sailing on your own without a rudder, practice the exercise with your crew so that you learn to coordinate your movements.

PRACTICING WITHOUT A RUDDER

Take the rudder off the boat. Keep the centerboard half down to start with and use the jib and mainsail, together with boat heel, to turn the boat.

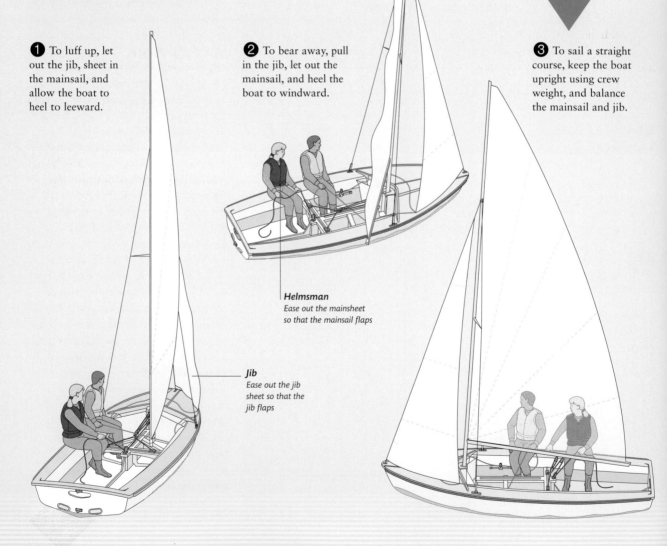

❶ To luff up, let out the jib, sheet in the mainsail, and allow the boat to heel to leeward.

❷ To bear away, pull in the jib, let out the mainsail, and heel the boat to windward.

❸ To sail a straight course, keep the boat upright using crew weight, and balance the mainsail and jib.

Helmsman
Ease out the mainsheet so that the mainsail flaps

Jib
Ease out the jib sheet so that the jib flaps

Fixing the rudder to the centerline

An alternative to sailing without the rudder is to leave the rudder in position and to secure the tiller on the centerline by tying shockcord (elastic line) from the tiller to both gunwales or to the toestraps. Tie the shockcord fairly tightly so that it takes some force to move the tiller off the centerline. Now, practice sailing without holding the tiller. The advantage of this method is that it more accurately reflects the normal sailing situation, where the area of the rudder blade assists the centerboard in preventing leeway and influences the boat's balance. It also means that if you need to use the rudder in a hurry, it is already in place and you only need to remove the shockcord from the tiller to regain full control.

Blindfold sailing

There are some excellent blind sailors in the world who have learned to rely on their other senses for sailing. Try sailing with a blindfold and see what you can learn from touch and sound. This exercise is best tried in a double-handed boat where helm and crew can take it in turns to wear the blindfold, with the sighted sailor giving feedback to the blindfolded sailor. Try this exercise only in a clear stretch of open water, with no other boats or obstructions in your way. This exercise will assist you to develop the "feel" necessary to sail the boat automatically, while maintaining full speed, which is an essential skill when you are racing.

Although you will initially feel very disoriented when deprived of vision, try to focus on how the boat feels through the tiller, the sound of the bow wave, and the angle of heel. Get used to these sounds and sensations when the boat is sailing well and try to replicate them to achieve the same performance. This helps you get to know your boat and the way it handles in the water.

FIXING THE RUDDER
To sail with the rudder fixed in a central position, use a length of heavy shockcord to lash the tiller on the centerline.

Switching places

Another exercise that is only relevant to boats with two or more crew is to change places among the crew. Switching places allows everyone to learn what it is like to do the other jobs in the boat and is equally valuable whether you sail a two-person dinghy or a keelboat with a crew of four or more. It helps give you a much greater understanding of your sailing partner's role and might help you appreciate how you can adjust your technique to make his tasks easier. Try this exercise in a Force 3 or less, when the boat is relatively easy to handle and capsizing is unlikely. If you have spent the day racing in one role, use the sail back into shore as an opportunity to switch positions.

It is a nice change to do something different, and you will become a more complete sailor if you can master both roles. Once ashore, discuss your perceptions of the tasks your partner normally undertakes, and explore ideas for making each other's jobs easier or faster.

RUDDERLESS SAILING
If your boat has a lifting rudder, you can simply lift the blade rather than remove the rudder completely.

USING TRAPEZES

Sailing dinghies rely on the weight of their crew to keep them upright when they are being sailed. In many general-purpose dinghies, this is achieved by the helmsman and crew sitting out as far as possible with their feet under toestraps. However, high-performance dinghies usually have a much larger sail area than general-purpose dinghies and in most conditions sitting out is simply not sufficient to balance the power of the sails. Trapeze systems are used in these boats to increase the righting power.

SWINGING OUT AND IN

Practice getting out onto the trapeze and back into the boat until your movements are smooth and confident. Then practice while tacking until you can swing in, unhook, move across the boat while trimming the jib, and swing out on the trapeze on the new windward side.

1 Hook the trapeze to the harness and sit out, allowing the trapeze wire to take your weight. Hold the handle lightly in your front hand for control and security.

Hold the jib sheet in your aft hand

2 Put your front foot on the gunwale and push yourself out, keeping your body at right angles to the boat. Bring your aft foot up so that you are standing on the gunwale.

Shockcord runs around mast and tensions leeward trapeze

Place your front foot on the gunwale

3 Lean back at full stretch with your feet about a shoulder-width apart. To come in, reverse the procedure. Take your aft foot off the gunwale first.

Stretch out supported by the trapeze

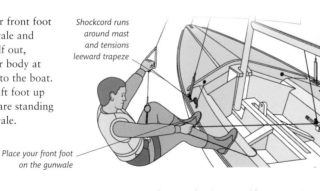

Trapeze systems

A trapeze system consists of a trapeze harness attached to a trapeze wire suspended from the hounds. It enables sailors to hang out over the side of the boat, moving their weight farther outboard and adding to the boat's stability. Formerly, the standard arrangement was a single trapeze for the crew only. This is still used in many dinghies, such as the 505 and the 470. With the appearance of ever-larger rigs, however, twin trapezes have become common. The Olympic 49er and International 14 are examples of twin-trapeze boats.

Good communication between helmsman and crew is vital in a trapeze boat. The helmsman must give the crew plenty of warning of a tack or jibe to allow him time to come in off the trapeze. Good coordination is also essential, as the use of a trapeze accentuates the crew's effect on the boat's balance. In particular, the helmsman must be ready to ease the mainsheet to keep the boat upright as the crew swings in and must be prepared to give the crew time to get out on the trapeze after a tack or jibe before sheeting in or altering course.

Single trapeze

On a single trapeze system, wires run from just above the hounds, one on each side of the mast, to suspend the crew outside the gunwale. The end of the wire comes down just aft of the shrouds. The wire has a handle and, usually, a stainless-steel ring for attachment to the trapeze harness. The trapeze ring often has an adjustment system to allow control of the height at which the trapeze is held. A length of stretchy shock cord connects the two trapeze wires and runs around the front of the mast. It keeps the leeward wire taut and neat when the crew is on the windward trapeze.

Trapezing techniques

When you are out on the trapeze, you must be ready to move your weight in and out quickly to react to gusts or lulls, and to move your weight fore or aft to keep the boat trimmed properly.

Your weight will be most effective if you trapeze as low as possible, parallel to the water when the boat is upright, but this is only practical in flat water and steady conditions. When there are big waves or if the wind is gusty and shifty, raise your position using the adjustment system on the trapeze wire to keep your body clear of the water. Not only is the boat slowed significantly if your body hits a wave, but the impact could cause you to lose your footing and be knocked off the side of the boat.

Heel and trim

Adjust to changes in heel by stretching outward to help the boat sail through gusts and bending your knees to swing your weight inboard if the wind dies. Maintain correct fore-and-aft trim by moving your weight along the gunwale. As the boat bears away, move aft to help the bow lift. This is especially important when planing under a spinnaker (*p.145*).

Balance

The trapeze wire leads upward and forward from your body, so it will pull you forward. Resist this tendency by keeping your front leg straight and bending your aft leg to remain balanced. If the boat slows rapidly for any reason, such as plowing into a wave, the force trying to pull you forward will increase quickly, so be prepared to swing your weight aft. Many boats have footstraps on the gunwale toward the stern to allow the trapezing crew to secure their aft foot and avoid being pulled forward.

HARNESSES

The secret to being relaxed on a trapeze is a comfortable harness. Choose one with a high, broad back to give good support. Many top trapeze sailors have a "diaper" harness tailor-made to fit their body snugly. Alternatively, you can buy an adjustable harness that can be altered with buckles or laces. Some harnesses use a spreader bar arrangement for the hook, or a simpler, square metal plate. The most important thing is to select a harness that will keep you comfortable during whole day's sailing.

Fitting and maintenance

Make sure that the harness fits well over your sailing gear and that it evenly spreads the load of your weight hanging from the trapeze into your back and lower body. The trapeze ring is attached to a hook on a metal plate on the harness. If possible, adjust the harness so that the hook is just below the waist, at your body's point of balance. Check the harness's stitching regularly and wash it thoroughly in fresh water after each sail.

Alternative types of harness

A potential problem when using a traditional trapeze harness is that the large metal hook on the front of the harness can get caught on ropes and rigging, and in rare cases can present a serious safety problem when the hook snags on rigging during a capsize or inversion.

A safer alternative to the fixed hook is a trapeze harness fitted with a quick-release system that allows the hook to be detached from the harness when needed. Although many harnesses are still sold with a fixed hook, a buckle with a quick-release hook can be bought separately to replace the standard buckle.

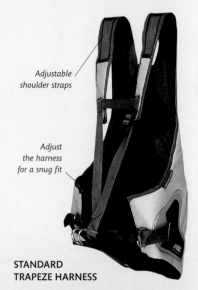

Adjustable shoulder straps

Adjust the harness for a snug fit

STANDARD TRAPEZE HARNESS

QUICK-RELEASE HOOK
Some trapeze harnesses come complete with a quick-release hook but the buckle can be retrofitted to standard harnesses.

RELEASING THE HOOK
If the quick-release hook becomes snagged, it can be instantly detached from the harness by pulling on the release cord.

Multiple trapezes

Some high-performance boats are fitted with multiple trapeze systems to enable both the helmsman and crew to trapeze. Although most high-performance dinghies sail with a crew of two, the 18-foot Skiff sails with three crew on trapezes. Some of the extreme boats designed to sail on Swiss or Italian lakes have as many as nine crew, all on trapezes. Sailing a boat with multiple trapezes requires great skill, coordination, and plenty of practice, as well as very good communication between all crew.

Boats with multiple trapeze systems often have racks or wings that extend out from each gunwale. Racks are made of aluminum or carbon fiber tubing, whereas wings may be of solid construction. The crew stands on these when trapezing to move their weight even farther outboard. Trapeze wires and rings are the same as on a single trapeze, although the helmsman's trapeze may not have a handle, as both his hands are full with the mainsheet and tiller extension. When trapezing, the helmsman uses a very long tiller extension. He passes this aft when

tacking and jibing. Some boats have two tiller extensions, one for each side of the boat, which makes it faster to run across the boat when tacking and jibing.

One noticeable difference between sailing a Skiff-type dinghy and a more traditional design, is the way the crew moves around the boat. In a modern design, the helmsman and crew are usually trapezing, and they rarely sit in or on the boat. During tacks and jibes they stand up, moving quickly from one side to the other, often running across the boat and out onto the rack or wing on the other side.

SAILING WITH TWIN TRAPEZES
Some high-performance dinghies sail with both helmsman and crew on trapezes. The helmsman steers using a very long tiller extension. Skiff-type dinghies are usually narrow and have wings or racks to increase the righting power of the trapezing crew.

Going out on the handle

The safest way to go out on the trapeze is by hooking on first and then pushing off the side of the boat with your front foot (*p.136*). Once you are comfortable and confident with this technique, you can try holding on to the handle and pushing out in the same way with your legs, before clipping the hook on to your harness, once you are fully trapezing. This requires good arm and shoulder strength, but enables you to move out on to the trapeze more quickly. When you become confident with this technique, you can try "handle-to-handle" tacking, the fastest method used by the best sailors. This keeps your weight out on the old tack until the last minute and gets it out on the new tack as fast as possible. However, a loss of strength or a failure in coordination as you tack, will result in an unexpected swim.

Using your arms

The trapeze is a useful way of creating more righting moment and being able to harness more of the wind's power. If, as your confidence increases, you can stand on tiptoe, then you can increase your righting moment in gusts by a few percent more. Putting one or even two arms behind your head will further increase your righting moment and help the boat go a little bit faster in strong winds. In order to do this, you need good balance because you can no longer use the jib sheet in your hand to steady yourself in rough conditions. Rather than dropping the jib sheet altogether, however, fasten it loosely through one of the straps in your harness so that it is close at hand should you need to adjust it.

Helming from the wire

Helming from the trapeze is easier than it looks, but it is wise to get some experience on the trapeze by

FLY BY WIRE
Sailing a high-performance, single-handed trapeze dinghy, which has little natural stability, requires a great deal of practice and excellent coordination.

crewing for someone else first so that you can develop good technique before combining it with helming.

In many boats, the helmsman holds the mainsheet in his front hand. In other boats, like the 49er or the 18-foot Skiff, the crew controls the mainsheet (it often comes straight from the boom rather than a block on the floor), leaving the helmsman free to concentrate on steering. The important thing is to anticipate any changes about to affect the boat, such as a gust, a lull, a windshift, or another boat nearby.

Think ahead, and try to spot situations before they arise. By spotting a gust or lull before it arrives, you can bend your knees, ease the mainsheet, steer the boat, or do whatever else is necessary to cope with the change of situation. If you leave the decision too late, you can end up getting wet. When the boat heels to windward—typically in a lull or a heading wind shift—the crew can be dumped very rapidly into

the water while still attached to their trapeze wires. Among high-performance sailors this is known as "tea-bagging".

Single-handed trapezing

Single-handed trapezing is very similar to helming from the trapeze in a double-handed boat, except that you do not have the luxury of a crew to run around to keep the boat balanced. This means that sailing a trapezing single-hander requires extra vigilance to spot any change in the conditions and respond quickly in order to keep the boat sailing upright. Be ready to bend your knees and swing back into the boat quickly if you think you are about to sail into a lull or a heading wind shift, or to ease the mainsheet to cope with strong gusts. It helps if you adjust the length of your trapeze wire so that you trapeze a bit higher than usual, as this enables you to respond more easily to an unexpected change in wind conditions and boat heel.

TACKING AND JIBING

When you tack and jibe in a high-performance dinghy, your balance and boat-handling skills are really put to the test. Your movements must be smooth and quick, and they must be timed carefully. A tack nearly always slows the boat, and a jibe can result in a capsize. In light winds, you can try roll tacking and roll jibing to ensure that you maintain speed through the maneuvers. However, this is only possible in conventionally shaped dinghies—not skiff or foil-borne types.

4 The crew then swings out on the trapeze, hooks on, and sheets the jib fully home.

Helmsman
Sheet in the mainsail as the crew swings out

Helmsman
Ease the mainsheet when the boat is head-to-wind and move to the new side

TACKING

High-performance boats are very sensitive to weight distribution and turn very quickly. The fastest dinghies are inherently unstable and are not forgiving of mistakes. They have more stability when sailing fast than when moving slowly, such as during a tack. The helmsman and crew must aim to complete each tack, and get the boat sailing fast on the new tack, as quickly as possible.

Good communication between helmsman and crew is vital. In a single-trapeze boat, the helmsman has to pace the turn to suit the speed of the crew. In a twin or multiple-trapeze boat, the helmsman may also be trapezing, and cannot tack as fast because he has to move across the boat, and out onto the new trapeze, while handling a long, single tiller extension or twin extensions.

TACKING WITH A TRAPEZE
When learning to tack a boat with single or multiple trapezes, the helmsman should start by tacking fairly slowly. Too fast a tack will make it difficult for the crew to get across the boat—and out on the new trapeze—before the sails fill again. This will cause the boat to heel and slow down considerably.

3 As the boat passes head-to-wind, the crew sheets the jib partly in on the new side.

Crew
Move into the boat

2 As the helmsman starts the tack, the crew swings into the boat and moves into the middle, keeping the jib sheet taut.

Crew
Unhook and prepare to move in

1 When the helmsman calls a tack, the crew unhooks while remaining on the trapeze using the handle.

MULTIPLE-TRAPEZE TACK
In a boat with multiple trapezes, the helmsman has to deal with a trapeze, tiller extension, and possibly the mainsheet. With a double extension, he releases the old one and picks up the other when he has crossed the boat.

ROLL TACKING
In most conditions, a tack causes the boat to slow down. However, in light airs, speed can be maintained (or even increased) by roll tacking. Rolling the boat through a tack in light winds drags the sails through the air, increasing the speed of the airflow, and accelerating the boat. Roll tacks (and jibes) are not used in skiff-type dinghies, since their racks hit the water and slow the boat down.

Crew
Adjust weight to balance the boat

❹ Once the boat is upright, the crew moves quickly back to the middle or to leeward to balance the helmsman's weight to windward.

Helmsman
Change sides and sit down

❸ When the boat is halfway between head-to-wind and the new close-hauled course, both helmsman and crew move up to the new windward side and pull the boat upright. As they do so, the helmsman sheets in the mainsail to its correct setting.

Crew
Heel the boat to windward

❷ As the boat comes up into the wind, both helmsman and crew lean out hard on the windward side, rolling the boat toward them. As the boat passes head-to-wind, the crew sheets the jib to the new side and the helmsman eases the mainsheet.

Helmsman
Allow boat to heel to leeward and let the tiller move naturally to leeward

Crew
Heel the boat to leeward

Helmsman
Steer into tack and heel the boat

❶ Just before a roll tack, bear away slightly to increase boat speed, then heel the boat to leeward and steer into the tack.

JIBING

When you jibe a high-performance boat, the keys to completing the maneuver successfully are speed and boat balance before the jibe. You should also take care to check the centerboard position before you jibe. High-performance boats sail downwind under a spinnaker or asymmetric, and you need to learn how to handle these sails during a jibe (*p.94*). Twin- or multiple-trapeze boats sail downwind with the crew trapezing, and require even greater skill and agility when jibing than other high-performance boats (*p.122*).

Speed and balance
Speed before the jibe reduces the strength of the apparent wind, which makes it easier to bring the mainsail across to the new leeward side and reduces the wind pressure on the rig.

When sailing in waves, you should jibe when the boat is on the face of the wave, as this is when it will be sailing at its fastest. Wait until the boat's bow drops down the face of a wave (and the boat accelerates) before turning into the jibe. Never jibe on the back of a wave, when the boat will be slowing down, causing the apparent wind to increase.

Keeping the boat balanced will help you to avoid a windward capsize before the jibe, or a leeward capsize after it. Heeling to windward too much, as you bear away into the jibe, can result in a rapid wipeout to windward. Alternatively, if the boat is allowed to heel to leeward, it will be harder for the helmsman to turn into the jibe. In boats with a low boom, there is also a risk of the boom hitting the water, possibly causing a capsize.

Centerboard position
The risk of capsizing is increased if the centerboard or daggerboard is too far up or down. In most boats, it pays to have the board about one quarter down during the jibe. Any farther down and it will be difficult to bear away into the jibe when sailing fast. There is also a risk of the boat "tripping" over the board and broaching (turning rapidly to windward) after the jibe. If the board is too far up, the boat may roll as you bear away into the jibe, making it hard for the helmsman to retain control, and risking a capsize. Experiment with your boat to find the optimum centerboard position for jibing in a range of wind strengths.

Jibing with a trapeze
Single-trapeze boats with a spinnaker often sail downwind on broad-reaching courses, which do not require the crew to be on the trapeze except in strong winds. In this case, the helmsman and crew jibe in the standard way. Twin- or multiple-trapeze boats, however, usually sail downwind with an asymmetric on a shallower course, with the crew trapezing. In this case, the boat must turn through a broader angle in the jibe and the crew has to move quickly to jibe, and get out on the trapezes on the new side.

TWIN-TRAPEZE JIBE
On a twin-trapeze boat, the helmsman steers onto a run and moves into the boat just after the crew. He swings the long tiller extension aft and around to the new side during the jibe. He then changes hands on the extension and mainsheet, and hooks on to the new trapeze, ready to move out as he luffs onto the new course.

ROLL JIBING

For boats without a spinnaker, a roll jibe is a very effective technique for maintaining speed in light winds. When using a spinnaker or asymmetric, you can use a small roll to help the boom over in light winds. A large roll may make the spinnaker collapse. Keep your use of the rudder to a minimum by using sails and heel to steer the boat.

❸ The boat will accelerate out of the jibe, helped by the lowered centerboard. Once the jibe is completed, set the centerboard for the new course.

Helmsman
Change sides and pull the boat upright

Helmsman
Bear away into the jibe

❷ The boat should be heeled enough so that the end of the boom just touches the water after the jibe. As it does so, pause until the mainsail fills, then pull the boat upright using crew weight.

Crew
Prepare to roll the boat

❶ Before the jibe, lower the centerboard fully. With the boat on a run, the crew rolls it to windward and prepares to pull on the vang to swing the boom across.

Helmsman
Rotate the tiller extension to leeward

TIPS ON ADVANCED TACKING AND JIBING

Tacking and jibing are always a good test of skill, and you can judge a dinghy or keelboat crew's teamwork by how they tack and jibe, especially in very light or very strong winds. Both these extremes demand excellent "feel," good communication, and quality boat handling.

Communication

Tacking or jibing requires very close coordination between the helmsman and crew. A wrong move by either, or poor synchronization during the turn, can unbalance and slow the boat. In light airs, this will stop the boat, and in strong winds it risks a capsize. If you race a high-performance boat, you will quickly discover that quite small mistakes mean the difference between winning a race or being a runner-up. Improve your performance by good communication in the boat and by discussing maneuvers, and your technique, when ashore.

Practice

The quickest way to improve your skills is by spending lots of time practicing on the water. Leading Olympic and international crews spend several hours on the water nearly every day, honing their skills. Normal club sailors cannot devote so much time, but even a few hours of serious practice will be rewarded by smoother and faster maneuvers.

Feel

The elusive skill you should seek is called "feel." It tells you how the boat is about to react and how to "find the groove"—the fine, ever-changing edge on which a boat sails when perfectly balanced; with a light helm, little heel, and a willingness to accelerate.

SPINNAKERS

Loved by artists, photographers, and spectators because of their shape and their bright colors, spinnakers often cause concern for the crews who have to trim them. In fact, if a simple routine is followed, these large, lightweight sails are not difficult to fly, and they add tremendously to the sail area, providing much-increased power. A spinnaker brings a performance boat alive.

Anatomy of a spinnaker

Spinnakers were originally used only on downwind courses, but modern sailcloth and sail shapes allow high-performance boats to carry spinnakers even on a beam reach.

A variation of the conventional spinnaker, called an asymmetric spinnaker or, sometimes, a gennaker, has become popular on many high-performance boats (*pp.152–155*), but conventional spinnakers are still widely used on all types of boats.

A conventional spinnaker is attached only at its three corners, rather than to a spar or stay along any of its sides, and it relies on the force of the wind to keep it in position when hoisted. It requires skill and practice to hoist, set, and lower a spinnaker properly while avoiding twists and tangles.

Apart from the spinnaker itself, you will need a spinnaker pole, a halyard and hoisting system, and sheets. The sheets lead from each clew, outside all the rigging, to blocks and cleats on the sidedecks. The sheet on the windward side of the boat is known as the guy. When you jibe, the old sheet becomes the new guy and vice versa. Many crews use a continuous sheet system in which a single piece of rope is attached at each end to the clews.

Head of sail
Hoisted close to the halyard sheeve

Sail panels
Dinghy spinnakers are often cross-cut

Uphaul
Line that holds the spinnaker pole up

Spinnaker pole
Projects the clew away from the boat

Downhaul
Holds down spinnaker pole

Sheet
Leads from the clew to a block at the stern, then forward to a cleat

Guy
Spinnaker sheet to windward

Reaching hook
Holds guy down clear of the crew

PARTS OF A SPINNAKER
The spinnaker is set ahead of the forestay with its windward clew extended by the spinnaker pole. Two sheets, attached to the clews, control the sail.

USING A SPINNAKER
A spinnaker adds considerably to the sail area when sailing off the wind. Here, an International Dragon keelboat sails on a run with the spinnaker set.

Spinnaker design

Spinnakers are made from lightweight nylon sailcloth. Downwind spinnakers are generally cut with a full shape, a wide midsection, and a broad head, whereas those for reaching, have a flatter and narrower design. Dinghies usually have one all-around spinnaker, whereas small keelboats may have a choice of two, for running or reaching courses, and larger racing yachts may have several spinnakers for use in a range of conditions.

Spinnaker pole

The spinnaker pole is used to extend the spinnaker clew away from the boat. It is usually made of aluminum or carbon fiber. The pole's inner end clips onto a bracket on the front of the mast, and the outer end is clipped onto the spinnaker guy. The pole is held vertically by an uphaul and downhaul with which you can alter its angle and the height

of the outer end. The fittings on the ends of the pole have retractable plungers, which are controlled by a light line that runs along the pole from one end-fitting to the other. In some boats the pole is stowed in the boat, whereas in many high-performance boats it is stowed in brackets that are fitted to the boom.

Sheet leads

The arrangement for the sheets varies between different boat designs, but the turning blocks for the sheets are usually placed on the sidedecks near the stern. The sheet then leads forward to the crew, often through a ratchet block, to ease the load the crew must hold. The guy usually has a system to allow it to be held down near the shroud, out of the way of the crew, when they are sitting out or trapezing. On some dinghies, a reaching hook is used for this purpose. On others, and on small keelboats,

twinning lines are used. A twinning line comprises a small block with a light line attached to it. The block runs along the spinnaker sheet, and the line leads through another block, mounted on the gunwale, near the shroud, and then to a cleat where it can be adjusted. In use, the twinning line on the guy is pulled tight to hold the guy down; the twinning line on the sheet is left slack.

Marking the sheets

Setting the spinnaker can be made simpler by marking the sheets, so that you can effectively preset the sail for hoisting and jibing.

To mark the sheets, first hoist the spinnaker in light winds, with the boat stern-to-wind. Set the sail square across the bow, without the pole, and with neither sheet under a reaching hook, then cleat the sheets. Use a permanent marker to mark each sheet at the point where it passes through its cleat. In the future, when you prepare to jibe the spinnaker, simply cleat each sheet at its mark to set the sail correctly for the jibe.

To make it faster to set the spinnaker after hoisting, put another set of marks on the sheets. Hoist the sail and set the pole with the outboard end just off the forestay. Then mark the guy at its cleat. Before a hoist, cleat the guy at its mark and the pole will be set correctly for a reach.

Stowage systems

Methods of stowing, hoisting, and lowering the spinnaker vary, but a good system allows you to hoist and lower the spinnaker quickly, with the minimum chance of a foul-up, and stow it neatly without twists, ready for hoisting again. Most small boats have either a pouch stowage system on either side of the mast or a chute system (*pp.146–147*).

SPINNAKER CHUTES

Many high-performance dinghies, as well as some catamarans and small keelboats, use a spinnaker chute to stow a conventional or asymmetric spinnaker because a chute allows fast and easy hoisting and lowering.

Chute systems

Spinnaker chutes are often built into the boat. They have a bell-shaped mouth set into the foredeck just ahead of, or to one side of, the forestay. If there is no room ahead of the forestay for the chute mouth, it is usually set on the port side, immediately behind the forestay. This means it is easier to hoist and lower the spinnaker when on starboard tack, which is usually the tack on which you round the windward mark when racing. On catamarans, the chute mouth is often mounted on the crossbeam or under a bowsprit (pp.166–167). A fabric sock or rigid plastic tube runs from the mouth of the chute back into the boat. This holds the spinnaker when it is stowed.

Chute systems are useful because the spinnaker cannot become twisted when it is hoisted and lowered and both maneuvers become easier, although it is possible to drop the sail in the water under the bow when lowering if the correct procedure is not followed (p.149).

Spinnakers designed to be used with a chute are often given a silicone finish to reduce friction and to shed water rapidly, as a chute often funnels water over the sail when it is stowed. A spray-on finish is also available.

Using a spinnaker chute

A chute system allows the spinnaker to be hoisted and lowered relatively easily, even on a beam reach, but it is safest to steer onto a broad reach or run before hoisting or lowering. If the chute mouth is offset on the port side of the forestay, it is easier to hoist and lower the spinnaker when on starboard tack so the chute mouth is to leeward of the forestay. You can hoist and lower on port tack, but if you do so, bear away to a broad reach or run before the hoist or drop to minimize friction between the sail and the forestay.

The big advantage of a spinnaker chute is that it relieves the crew of the need to help with the hoist or the drop. When hoisting, the helmsman pulls up the sail and the crew can concentrate on fitting the spinnaker pole, setting the spinnaker as soon as it is hoisted, and balancing the boat. During the drop, the spinnaker is automatically gathered into its sock, so the crew is free to stow the pole.

CHUTE MOUTH
Here, the chute mouth is ahead of the forestay, so the asymmetric spinnaker fitted to this boat can be hoisted easily on either port or starboard tack.

PACKING THE SPINNAKER IN A CHUTE

It is important that the spinnaker is packed correctly in its chute before the boat goes afloat. It must be packed without twists, or it will be difficult for the crew to set the sail when it is hoisted.

Packing procedure

Before you go afloat, attach the halyard, sheets, and downhaul to the spinnaker and hoist the sail to make sure it is not twisted. Pull on the downhaul as you lower the spinnaker so that the sail is drawn into the chute. Keep pulling steadily until all the spinnaker has disappeared completely into the mouth of the chute. Take all the slack out of the halyard and the sheets and cleat them.

STOWING THE SPINNAKER

When the spinnaker is stowed, by pulling it into the chute using the downhaul, the head and two clews should be the last parts of the sail to disappear into the chute mouth. When the helmsman pulls on the halyard to hoist the spinnaker, it should slip smoothly out of the chute without any twists, and will set easily as the wind fills it.

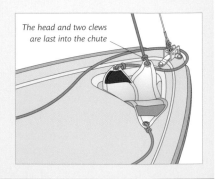

The head and two clews are last into the chute

SPINNAKER POUCHES

Stowing a spinnaker in a pouch, bag, or locker requires a little more care than when using a chute system. If the spinnaker is not packed correctly, it can develop a twist that becomes apparent when the sail is hoisted, preventing it from being set correctly.

Using pouches

With a pouch system, the boat is equipped with light fabric pouches, one either side of the mast. The spinnaker is best stowed in the pouch that will be to leeward when hoisting, as this allows for an easier hoist. When the sail is stowed, the halyard is hooked under the reaching hook to keep it neat.

Bags and lockers

Some boats have a single bag behind the mast for stowage. The sail can be hoisted and dropped to leeward or windward as needed. Some small keelboats have lockers on either side of the cockpit that work like pouches. The sail is best stowed in the locker that will be to leeward when hoisting the spinnaker.

PACKING THE SPINNAKER

Whether a boat has a bag, pouches, or lockers, the spinnaker is stowed in exactly the same way. The middle of the spinnaker is packed first so that the three corners attached to the sheets and halyard end up on top of the packed sail.

PACKING THE SPINNAKER IN A POUCH

It is important to ensure that the spinnaker is correctly packed into its pouch, bag, or locker so that it can be hoisted quickly and easily. If possible, the best way to do this is to hoist the sail while the boat is ashore or moored and then lower it into the pouch or locker. To do so, pull down one luff and pack it into the pouch, then gather in the rest of the sail until the three corners lie on top of the sail bundle.

1 Attach the halyard and sheets to the spinnaker and then hoist the sail.

Hoist the sail by pulling on the halyard

2 As one person slowly lowers the sail, the other grasps one clew and gathers in the luff, gradually packing it into the pouch.

Pull the sail down by the luff

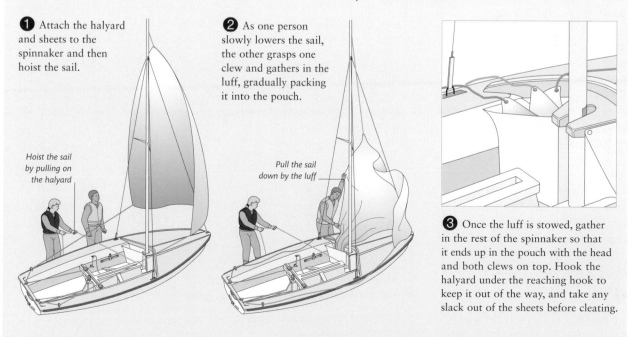

3 Once the luff is stowed, gather in the rest of the spinnaker so that it ends up in the pouch with the head and both clews on top. Hook the halyard under the reaching hook to keep it out of the way, and take any slack out of the sheets before cleating.

HOISTING AND LOWERING

Generally, a chute makes it easier to hoist and lower a spinnaker than with a pouch system, which requires more manual dexterity from the crew, and good timing and understanding between helmsman and crew. Some boats' class rules allow only one or the other method of spinnaker stowage system, but others allow a choice. If you do have the choice of opting for either chute or pouch system, find out what the top sailors in your class are using and copy their systems first, before experimenting with alternative ideas.

POUCHES

HOISTING FROM A LEEWARD POUCH

A spinnaker is easier to hoist from a leeward pouch or locker because the helmsman can usually hoist it directly out of the pouch without help from the crew. Bear away to a run or broad reach to hoist the sail.

1 The crew releases the halyard from the reaching hook and pulls on the guy to draw the windward clew towards the forestay. As the helmsman hoists the sail, the crew clips the pole to the guy.

Spinnaker pole

Guy

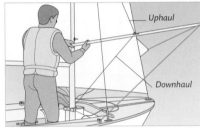

Uphaul

Downhaul

2 The crew attaches the uphaul and downhaul, and clips the inboard end of the spinnaker pole onto the mast bracket, which is positioned above the boom.

3 The helmsman controls the sheet and guy while the crew sets the pole, slips the guy under the reaching hook, or adjusts the twinning line, then trims and cleats the guy.

HOISTING FROM A WINDWARD POUCH

Good coordination and teamwork are needed when hoisting from a windward pouch. Ensure that the sheets are marked correctly (*p.145*), so that you can cleat the guy in the correct position beforehand. Bear away to a run before the hoist. The crew has to take the bundled spinnaker out of the pouch and throw it up and forwards, while the helmsman rapidly hoists it.

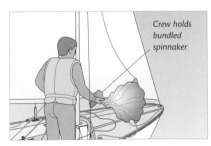

Crew holds bundled spinnaker

1 The crew frees the halyard and cleats the guy so that the clew will clear the forestay. He removes the spinnaker from the pouch, holding it tightly.

Crew throws bundle up and forward

2 The helmsman hoists rapidly as the crew throws the sail forwards. The crew pulls on the sheet to bring the sail around to leeward of the forestay.

Helmsman trims sheet and guy

3 The helmsman controls the sheet and guy while the crew rigs the pole. The crew slips the guy under the reaching hook and cleats it, or pulls on the twinning line.

Lowering the spinnaker

You can choose between lowering the spinnaker into either the windward or leeward pouch, although the safest and quickest method, in a dinghy, is to drop the spinnaker into the windward pouch, as this keeps the crew's weight on the windward side. In a dinghy, only drop the sail into the leeward pouch if you need it in that pouch for a later leeward hoist. For either method, the crew's job is made a lot easier if the helm steers onto a broad reach or run for the maneuver.

WINDWARD DROP

For a windward drop, the crew must remove and stow the pole before lowering the sail. He then pulls on the guy until the clew is in his hand and pulls the sail down by its luff, stuffing it into the windward pouch. He stows the halyard under the reaching hook.

LEEWARD DROP

The crew pulls hard on the sheet until he can reach the clew, then releases the guy and pulls the sail under the boom and into the leeward pouch. Once all the sail is in the pouch, and the halyard is hooked under the reaching hook, the crew removes and stows the spinnaker pole.

❶ The crew unclips the pole from the mast, removes the uphaul and downhaul, and unclips the pole from the guy.

Crew removes and stows the pole

❷ As the helmsman lowers the sail, the crew pulls down on the luff, stuffing it into the pouch. When the luff is stowed, he pulls in the rest of the sail, hooks the halyard under the reaching hook, and cleats the sheets.

Crew pulls the sail into the pouch

CHUTES

Hoisting and lowering

The spinnaker is hoisted from the chute using the halyard attached to the head of the sail. This halyard, which is often operated by the helmsman in a two-person dinghy, runs down inside the mast, then to a jamming cleat within reach of the person who will hoist and lower the sail. The spinnaker is lowered using a downhaul, which is attached to a reinforced patch in the middle of the spinnaker and runs down through the chute mouth and tube. The halyard and downhaul usually consist of one continuous piece of rope. When the halyard is released and the downhaul is pulled, the sail collapses and is drawn down into the chute, ready to be hoisted once again. When dropping, the crew should pull on both sheet and guy to hold the foot in and allow the middle of the sail to enter the chute first.

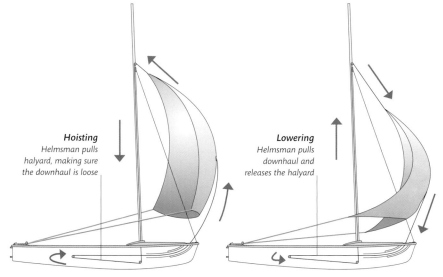

Hoisting
Helmsman pulls halyard, making sure the downhaul is loose

Lowering
Helmsman pulls downhaul and releases the halyard

HOISTING FROM A CHUTE

The helmsman hoists the sail by pulling on the halyard, while the crew sets the sheet and guy to their marks and attaches the pole. The helmsman then cleats the halyard and trims the sheet and guy while the crew is dealing with the pole.

LOWERING INTO A CHUTE

The crew sheets the foot of the sail tight against the forestay. Uncleating the halyard, the helmsman pulls on the downhaul. As soon as the middle of the sail enters the chute, the crew releases the sheet and guy, and removes the pole.

HANDLING A SPINNAKER

Successful spinnaker work demands plenty of practice and good communication between the helmsman and crew. Once set, the spinnaker has an enormous effect on the handling of a small boat, and it must be kept under control at all times. This is primarily the crew's job, and it requires great concentration. The crew must learn to trim the spinnaker correctly and should understand how to cope with gusts. Spinnaker jibing requires slick crew work if it is to be completed without mishap.

Playing the sheet

Each spinnaker shape needs trimming in a slightly different way, but there are some general rules to help you get the best out of your boat. The most important thing is to keep the sail symmetrical about its centerline; this involves keeping the clews level, at the same height above the water. You must also encourage the spinnaker to fly as far as possible from the mainsail so that air can pass freely between the two sails. When the spinnaker is set correctly, the crew will be able to ease the sheet until the luff starts to curl back on itself about halfway up. A well-designed, stable spinnaker can be sailed with some luff curl without collapsing. The point at which the luff starts to curl is the optimum trim in any particular wind strength and point of sailing. As the boat speed changes, the apparent wind shifts forward or backward, and the sheet must be trimmed continually to keep the spinnaker on the edge of curling.

Handling gusts

You must know how to handle gusts, to keep the power in the spinnaker from overcoming rudder control. As a gust hits, the crew eases the spinnaker sheet to curl the luff and allows the boat to accelerate. Failure to do this will make the boat heel and develop considerable weather helm (*p.128*), making it hard for the helmsman to stay on course or bear away. The apparent wind will shift forward as the boat accelerates, and the crew must be ready to sheet in to prevent the spinnaker collapsing. When the boat slows down, the apparent wind will shift aft and the sheet must be eased.

POLE ANGLE AND HEIGHT

The pole angle and height must be adjusted correctly so that the sail is set at its most efficient position and can be trimmed effectively. The crew adjusts the pole angle using the guy, which is cleated once the correct angle has been set. The height of the pole is altered, usually by the crew, using the uphaul and downhaul.

Pole angle

Set the angle of the pole just greater than a right angle to the apparent wind. This means bringing the pole aft as the boat sails farther downwind, and easing it forward as the boat turns onto a reach. Always keep the pole off the forestay or it may bend or break. Remember to adjust the guy after putting it under the reaching hook or tightening the twinning line.

Pole height

When the pole is horizontal, it holds the spinnaker as far away as possible from the rest of the rig, but it is even more important to make sure the clews of the sail are kept level, at the same height above the water. The windward clew (attached at the pole end) is held in place by the pole, but the clew to which the sheet is attached is free to move up and

down, depending on the strength of the wind and the boat's course. If the leeward clew is lower than the tack, lower the pole. If it is higher than the tack, raise the pole.

CORRECT   **TOO LOW**   **TOO HIGH**

POLE SETTING
When the spinnaker pole is set correctly (*above left*), the sail is most efficient and easier to trim; if too low or too high (*above center and right*), the sail shape is inefficient and it may collapse.

JIBING THE SPINNAKER

Successful jibing with a spinnaker set requires a standard routine and plenty of practice. It is vital to keep the boat upright and to complete the jibe quickly to prevent the spinnaker from getting out of control. To prepare for the jibe, the helmsman bears away to a run and the crew removes the guy from the reaching hook and sets the sail square across the bow. If the sheets are marked (*p.145*), they can be set at the jibing position quickly and easily. The boat is now ready to be jibed.

JIBING

Ideally, at the point of jibing, the crew weight is in the middle, the pole is being switched across, and the sail remains full.

POLE HEIGHT

Adjust the pole height using the uphaul and downhaul to keep the clews level and the spinnaker symmetrical.

3 Removing the old guy from the pole end, the crew fits the pole onto the mast bracket. He then puts the guy under the reaching hook, cleats it in the correct position, and takes the spinnaker sheet from the helmsman.

Crew
Clip the inner end of the pole to the mast

2 Standing in the middle of the boat, the helmsman takes control of the guy and sheet to keep the spinnaker full. The crew removes the pole from the mast, clips it onto the new guy, and pushes it out to the new side.

Helmsman
Steer the boat with the tiller between your knees

1 With the boat pointing dead downwind, the mainsail and jib (if hoisted) are jibed. The crew helps the boom over by pulling on the vang, and sheets the jib to the new side.

Crew
Pull on the vang to help the boom over

ASYMMETRIC SPINNAKERS

Asymmetric spinnakers look like a cross between a large jib and a spinnaker. They are sometimes also known as "gennakers," the word derived from "genoa" and "spinnaker." They are commonly used on high-performance dinghies and catamarans, and some sportsboats. An asymmetric spinnaker is set from a long bowsprit (a spar projecting from the bow) rather than a spinnaker pole, which makes it much easier to handle when hoisting, jibing, and lowering, as the crew does not need to handle a pole. The bowsprit, which is nearly always retractable, is usually made from carbon fiber for strength, stiffness, and lightness; the sail is made from lightweight nylon or polyester sailcloth.

MASTHEAD ASYMMETRIC SPINNAKER

Handling asymmetrics

An asymmetric spinnaker is usually larger than a conventional spinnaker and is often flown from a point higher on the mast, with the halyard exiting at the masthead or slightly lower, between the hounds and the masthead. These large sails generate considerable power but in many ways are easier to handle than a conventional spinnaker because the tack is attached to the end of the bowsprit, and they do not require adjustments to a spinnaker pole. They are controlled by two sheets, both of which are attached to the clew, just like a jib.

Sail trimming

An asymmetric sail is trimmed using two sheets. The sheets lead to the aft quarters of the boat and may have twinning lines (*p.145*) to move the lead forward when sailing on a broad reach. An asymmetric is inefficient when sailing on a dead run, so sailing

HOISTING AND LOWERING

An asymmetric spinnaker is stowed and launched from a chute or pouches, depending on the specific boat design. The bowsprit is normally retracted when the asymmetric is not being used, so it has to be extended before the sail is hoisted. To hoist, the crew pulls a line to extend the bowsprit. In many boats, the bowsprit is extended by a single-line system, which also pulls the sail's tack to the outer end. In other boats, separate lines are used and the crew first extends the bowsprit, then pulls the tack to its outer end. The halyard is then pulled to hoist the sail. The process is reversed to drop the sail.

HOISTING FROM A CHUTE
To hoist from a chute, the crew extends the bowsprit and pulls the tack of the sail to its end, then hoists the sail with the halyard.

LOWERING INTO A CHUTE
To lower into a chute, the crew pulls on the downhaul to pull the sail into the chute, then retracts the bowsprit.

LOWERING INTO A BAG
When the asymmetric is stowed in a bag or pouch, one crew member must gather the sail as it is lowered and stow it in its bag.

downwind is done in a series of jibes and reaches to maximize the effect of apparent wind (*pp.124–125*). The crew must avoid oversheeting the sail and try to keep it trimmed with a slight curl in the luff for top speed.

Asymmetric sails are at their most efficient when the boat is planing fast, as this is when the effect of apparent wind is at its strongest, allowing the boat to head downwind, while sailing in an apparent wind that is on or ahead of the beam. To achieve this, the helmsman must first steer on a reach to build speed and bring the apparent wind forward, before bearing away to a more downwind course while maintaining the speed and apparent wind angle.

Light wind trimming

In light wind conditions, when planing is not possible, particularly in the heavier types of sportsboats, it pays to steer the boat farther downwind and sail a shorter course to the next mark, without losing pressure in the asymmetric sail. This calls for good communication between helmsman and crew. The crew can feel the pressure in the sail through the tension in the sheet. When the crew says "good pressure," the helmsman knows he can continue to steer the same course. If the crew says "bad pressure," the helmsman may choose to luff up to create more apparent wind and put more pressure in the sail.

Strong wind trimming

Normally, it is fastest to trim an asymmetric with an inch or two of curl on the luff. Even the slightest amount of oversheeting can make the boat slower, and the helmsman will feel the difference as the rudder loads up with more lee helm. As soon as the crew eases the sheet, so that the sail's luff curls again, the helmsman will feel

the rudder become less loaded and the boat will accelerate again. However, in some high-speed skiff classes, the asymmetric develops so much power, and the boat accelerates so fast, that there is a danger of "pitchpoling"— capsizing stern over bow. To avoid this, overtrim the asymmetric to the point where you feel comfortable with your speed once more. When you feel confident to sail faster, the crew eases the sheet a little, and the boat will accelerate once more. In strong winds, think of the asymmetric spinnaker sheet as the throttle. The more you release the sheet to the point of curl

on the luff, the faster you will sail. Overtrimming the sheet is a useful technique when sailing in strong wind and waves, when there is a danger of plowing the bow into the back of a wave. It is much safer to travel a little slower with an overtrimmed sail than to risk a pitchpole capsize.

FLYING AN ASYMMETRIC
This 49er's crew are sailing under their large asymmetric. Both sailors are trapezing high for better visibility and control, and the crew has the asymmetric trimmed with a slight curl in the luff for maximum speed.

JIBING ASYMMETRIC SPINNAKERS

Jibing an asymmetric spinnaker is a relatively simple process compared with jibing a symmetrical spinnaker, but it is still a maneuver that requires good timing and coordination between helmsman and crew.

When sailing a dinghy fitted with an asymmetric, especially a high-performance dinghy, it is important to keep the boat upright throughout the jibe, with minimal heel to windward or leeward. The helmsman must avoid using too much rudder during the jibe, keeping the turn slow and gentle. If the helmsman steers too rapidly, the boat will turn too far after the jibe, with a high risk of a capsize. It is better to start off by turning too little than too much when you are learning to jibe an asymmetric.

From the crew's point of view, jibing an asymmetric is much simpler than a conventional spinnaker, since there is no pole to handle and the bowsprit remains fully extended. However, in order to execute an efficient jibe, timing on the sheet is critical. There are two slightly different techniques you can use, depending on whether you are jibing at speed in medium or strong winds, or more slowly in light winds.

High-speed jibes

In planing conditions, the helmsman starts the maneuver by warning the crew so that he has sufficient time to come in off the trapeze or, in a non-trapeze boat, to move in ready for the jibe. As the helmsman begins to bear away into the jibe, the crew should move toward the centerline and hold the old sheet where it is, or even pull in an extra handful if he has time to do so. This means that the asymmetric will be pulled quite taut to leeward, which will prevent the sail from "hourglassing" (tying itself in a twist) when the boat is pointing dead downwind in the middle of the jibe.

At the same time, the crew picks up what will become the new sheet and takes it across the boat to the new side. As the mainsail jibes, and the crew reaches the new side, he releases the old sheet and pulls in the new one. With good timing, a crew can have the asymmetric set on the new side without its collapsing.

Survival jibing

A variation to the high-speed jibing technique, which is appropriate for the most unstable high-performance dinghies, is for the crew to keep the old sheet pulled on hard as the boat turns out of the jibe, holding the sail tight on the new windward side. The wind will now blow the wrong way across the sail, from leech to luff. This keeps the boat surprisingly stable and in control, while traveling quite slowly. Only when both helmsman and crew are settled on the new jibe and ready to accelerate should the crew release the old sheet and pull on the new one. This is a highly effective technique for surviving windy jibes in high-performance dinghies.

Low speed jibes

The high-speed jibing technique is appropriate in all but light winds when the boat is not planing. In these lighter conditions there is a variation to the crew's jibing technique that helps the boat accelerate more quickly out of the jibe. When the helmsman warns the crew of the imminent jibe, the crew picks up the new sheet and immediately starts to pull on it, while releasing the old sheet. As the boat goes through the middle of the jibe, the clew of the asymmetric should already be passing the forestay, and by the time the boat exits the jibe, the crew will already have the sail set and filling on the new leeward side. It is important, for the success of this light-wind jibe, that the helmsman does not start turning the boat into the jibe until he sees the crew take the first one or two pulls on the new sheet. This will ensure that the sail sets properly on the new jibe.

ASYMMETRIC JIBING
The helmsman and crew are in the middle of the boat and the crew is ready to sheet the asymmetric across to the new side.

❺ The crew hooks on and swings out onto his trapeze and trims the asymmetric. The helmsman also moves out on his trapeze and steers onto the new course, sheeting in the mainsail to suit the new course and apparent wind.

Helmsman and crew move onto trapezes

Helmsman moves across boat

Crew pulls on new sheet

❹ As the mainsail jibes, the crew releases the old sheet and rapidly pulls in the new sheet to move the asymmetric around the forestay to the new leeward side. The helmsman moves to the new side, picks up the new tiller extension, or swings the single extension around to the new side, and hooks onto his trapeze.

❸ The helmsman moves into the boat, picks up the mainsheet and uncleats it, and continues to turn the boat in a gentle curve. The crew picks up the new sheet on his way across the boat and holds the old sheet or pulls it in slightly.

Helmsman moves into boat

Crew moves into boat

❷ As the crew moves off the trapeze, the helmsman eases the mainsheet, cleats it and drops the end in the boat, and starts to move in off his trapeze. At the same time, he steers gently into the jibe.

❶ The helmsman warns the crew by calling "ready to jibe." The crew moves in to the boat first and prepares to jibe the asymmetric.

JIBING AN ASYMMETRIC

Jibing an asymmetric spinnaker is easier than jibing a conventional spinnaker, as the sail is jibed just like a jib and there is no spinnaker pole to switch from side to side. Stop twists from developing in the sail by holding the old sheet in tight until the boat has jibed, then pulling quickly on the new sheet to pull the sail around the forestay to the new leeward side. In light winds, start pulling the new sheet before the boat jibes to move the sail around the forestay more quickly so that it fills earlier on the new course.

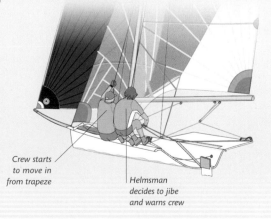

Crew starts to move in from trapeze

Helmsman decides to jibe and warns crew

SINGLE-HANDED SAILING

The purest form of sailing is when you go afloat alone and are solely responsible for balance, trim, and handling. You learn quickly when you sail single-handed, and you can sail whenever you want to, without having to find a crew. Single-handed boats are usually cheaper and simpler than two-person dinghies. They are normally lighter and can often be transported very easily on a car roof rack. Another benefit is that they are usually quick to rig, so you can be sailing within minutes of arriving at the venue.

Choosing a single-hander

Sailing single-handed a quite different experience from sailing in a double-handed dinghy or among a larger crew in a small keelboat, and you should be certain that this type of sailing is for you before you buy your own boat. Some sailing schools offer instruction in single-handed dinghies, and most watersports centers have single-handed boats available. It is a good idea to try as many as possible and to do some research; talk to sailors at your local club, visit boat shows, and explore manufacturers' and class websites online.

Remember that most dinghies have an optimum size and weight range for their crew, and single-handed dinghies are the same. You should make a shortlist of dinghies that are appropriate to your height, weight, and degree of skill and athleticism. Single-handed dinghies are available to cater to a wide range of ages, physical attributes, and levels of skill, and you should be able to find a class that suits your needs. As with double-handed dinghies and small keelboats, it is best to choose a single-handed dinghy that is popular at your local club. This will ensure that there is a fleet to sail and race in without the need to travel.

SINGLE-HANDED DINGHY
A common and popular single-hander has an unstayed mast and a single, sleeved sail that slips over the mast. It is designed to be straightforward to rig, launch, sail, and recover alone.

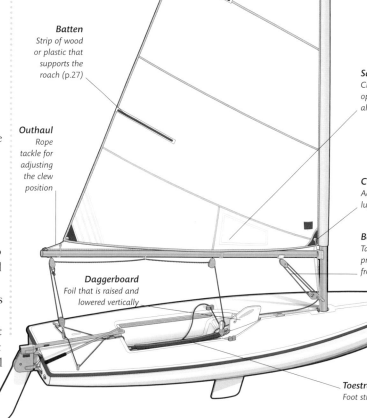

Batten
Strip of wood or plastic that supports the roach (p.27)

Outhaul
Rope tackle for adjusting the clew position

Daggerboard
Foil that is raised and lowered vertically

Webbing strap
Fits over the top of the mast to secure the head of the sail

Sleeve
Cloth tube sewn into the luff, into which the mast is fitted

Sail window
Clear plastic opening for better all-around vision

Cunningham
Adjusts mainsail luff tension

Boom vang
Tackle that prevents the boom from lifting

Toestrap
Foot strap for helmsman

TYPES OF SINGLE-HANDER

Most single-handed dinghies have a single sail and are designed for hiking (sitting out) rather than trapezing. However, some designs have a mainsail and jib, a mainsail and asymmetric spinnaker, or even all three sails. Some dinghies use a trapeze to increase righting power and some incorporate wings or racks to increase the righting power when the helmsman is hiking or trapezing. One of the oldest, yet most extreme designs, requires the helmsman to deal with a mainsail, jib, asymmetric spinnaker, and a sliding seat that is swung across the boat when tacking and jibing.

SINGLE-HANDED DINGHIES

LASER

The men's Olympic single-hander, the Laser is the world's most popular single-handed dinghy. Used for all types of sailing, from beach sailing to Olympic-class competition, it requires good fitness but offers excellent competition for all levels of ability.

FINN

The FINN dinghy is the heavyweight single-handed dinghy in the Olympics. Events for this boat, designed in 1949, have been included in every Olympic Games since 1952. It is a challenging boat to sail, popular around the world, and suitable for larger sailors.

RS600

The RS600 is a good introductory boat to modern, skiff-type single-handed trapezing. It has a carbon-fiber mast with a removable mast extension and reefing system that allows the sail area to be reduced by 20 percent when learning or for strong winds.

RS700

The RS700 is a demanding single-hander with skiff-style performance, a trapeze, and asymmetric spinnaker. The boat has a performance equalization system with adjustable width wings to allow equal competition for sailors of different weights.

INTERNATIONAL MOTH

The International Moth is one of the oldest single-handed designs but is also one of the most innovative. A development class since the 1920s, the Moth has led the way with design ideas and is now leading the way in the development of fully foil-borne sailing.

INTERNATIONAL CANOE

The origins of the International Canoe date back to the 1850s. It still has the distinction of being the fastest single-handed monohull dinghy in the world. It has a sliding seat arrangement, a mainsail, jib, and an asymmetric spinnaker.

Rigging and launching

Most single-handed dinghies have a mainsail only. This is set on a mast that is stepped farther forward than on a two-sailed dinghy.

The mast may be unstayed (*p.68*) for easy rigging, and flexible so that it can be bent to provide an efficient sail shape and to release excess power in strong winds. Whereas a stayed mast and sail arrangement allows you to hoist the sail before or after launching, as conditions dictate, an unstayed mast with a sleeved mainsail must be rigged before launching and the boat kept close to head-to-wind.

A single-hander is launched in the same way as a two-man dinghy. You usually have to do the job on your own, although it is easier to launch and recover the boat if someone else is available to deal with the cart.

Sailing

Single-handed dinghies are usually light and thus sensitive to changes in trim and balance. The helmsman must move his weight in and out, and fore and aft, to keep the boat upright and correctly trimmed without the help of a crew. It is important that the sail is set correctly, and you must get used to adjusting its shape using the outhaul, cunningham control (*p.177*), mainsheet, and vang.

Downwind courses reveal the biggest differences between a single-hander and a two-man boat. When there is only one sail, there is an increased weather helm and a constant tendency for the boat to turn to windward. This can be reduced by heeling the boat to windward until the helm is balanced, but skill is required to maintain this position without risking a windward capsize. Single-handers usually plane easily and are fun to sail downwind in waves, as they react instantly to the tiller and accelerate rapidly.

Tacking

Tacking a single-hander well requires good timing and smooth actions. The helmsman's movements are the same as in a two-man dinghy (*pp.90–93*). The boom is often very low, so you will have to duck even lower under it. Ease the mainsheet as you turn through the wind to make it easier to avoid the boom and to reduce the chance of getting stuck in-irons (*p.159*). Do not move off the windward side too early. Wait until the boom is approaching the centerline with the boat heeled toward you, then cross quickly and get your weight out over the new windward side as the boat completes the tack. Sit out hard and sheet in as the boat comes upright. Change hands on the mainsheet and tiller extension after the tack.

Jibing

Raise the daggerboard until it is just clear of the boom and vang. If the vang is tight, ease it to keep the boom from hitting the water and capsizing the boat. The helmsman's actions through the jibe are the same as they are in a two-man dinghy (*pp.94–97*). Sailing fast on a very broad reach or a run, turn into the jibe and give a sharp tug on the mainsheet to start the boom swinging across. As it does so, straighten the tiller and get your weight out on the new side. Change hands on the tiller and mainsheet.

TACKING
This skilled solo sailor is tacking. He allows the boat to heel toward him and waits for the boom to reach the centerline before he begins to move across the boat.

Sailing skiff-type dinghies

Some of the fastest single-handers have many of the characteristics of the double-handed skiff-type dinghies. They have very light, narrow, and shallow hulls with wings or racks sticking out from the hull's sides to increase the righting power of the helmsman who trapezes to keep the boat upright. This type of single-hander is extremely fast but requires extra skill and agility to sail well.

When tacking a singlehanded trapeze boat, take extra care to avoid stopping in irons (*right*) during a tack. Just before the tack, bear away onto a close reach, ease the mainsheet and cleat it, and start stepping into the boat with your back foot as you begin steering into the tack. Aim to keep the boat as flat as possible throughout the maneuver. Unclip from the trapeze wire and move smoothly to the new

side, picking up and uncleating the mainsheet on the way. As you sit on the new side, steer on to a close reach with the mainsail well eased. When the boat is under control and moving forward on the new course, stand up, hook on, and push out on the new side as you pull in the mainsail and start to steer up to a closehauled course again.

To jibe a trapeze single-hander, treat it as if it were a non-trapeze boat. Bear away to a run, swing in from the trapeze, get settled and fully prepared, and then jibe as you would any single-hander. Get settled on the new jibe, and then hook up onto the trapeze again, if required. Take your time over this maneuver in the beginning. As you become more proficient, you can start practicing wire-to-wire jibes, at which point you can call yourself an expert.

RIGGING AN UNSTAYED MAST

Some single-handed dinghies have stayed masts, and their mainsails are rigged like a two-man dinghy (*pp.68–73*). However, many small single-handers have unstayed masts, which are light and easy to rig, although it is helpful if someone can assist you. The mast usually comes in two pieces, for easy storage and transportation, that are slotted together before the sail is fitted. Most single-handed dinghies use a daggerboard rather than a centerboard. Make sure that this and the rudder are in the boat before you launch it.

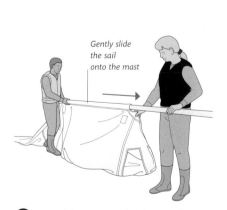

Gently slide the sail onto the mast

❶ Assemble the mast by slotting the two pieces together. Unfold the mainsail and find the sleeve in the mainsail luff. Slide the mast into the sleeve.

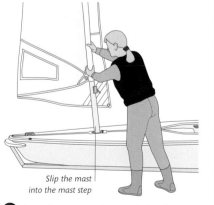

Slip the mast into the mast step

❷ Step the mast and secure it in place. Attach the boom to the gooseneck and attach the mainsail's clew to the boom using the outhaul. Fit the boom vang.

GETTING OUT OF IRONS

Tacking can be difficult in some single-handers because there is no jib to help pull the bow away from the wind onto the new tack. When you tack, a single-hander can sometimes refuse to go through the eye of the wind, and instead get stuck head to wind "in-irons" (*p.93*).

Avoiding the problem

Getting stuck in-irons in a single-hander can occur for a number of reasons. Lack of speed before the tack will make it difficult for the boat to complete the turn. Avoid this by bearing away slightly before the tack to build speed.

When tacking in waves, the bow may hit a wave, which will stop the boat. Minimize this risk by watching the waves and tacking when the bow is rising up the face of a wave. The boat should complete the tack before the next wave arrives. Another cause is tacking with the mainsheet too tight. This keeps the mainsail leech tight which causes the boat to try to turn into the wind. Cure this by easing the mainsheet quite a lot as you tack. If stalling out head-to-wind is still a problem in your boat, try easing the vang, increasing cunningham tension, or pulling up the daggerboard slightly, or doing a combination of all three.

Recovering from in irons

If the boat stops head-to-wind, push the boom away from you so that it fills on the reverse side and pushes the boat backward. At the same time, push the tiller away from you. The twin actions of pushing the boom and tiller will turn the boat quickly to a close-hauled course.

SMALL KEELBOATS

The principles of sailing a small keelboat are not so different from those of a dinghy. Unlike a dinghy with a lightweight centerboard, however, the lead bulb of the keel will make it very difficult to capsize a keelboat. In many ways this makes a small keelboat a more forgiving type of boat to sail, and a good choice for learning the basic skills of sailing.

Keelboat differences

A keelboat is heavier than a dinghy, so the working loads on the sails, sheets and blocks are all much higher. You may have to use tackles or winches instead of ratchet blocks to be able to cope with the extra loads of the jib or spinnaker sheets.

Some keelboats have lifting keels, but these are only intended to make launching and recovery easier and are not designed to be adjusted while sailing. This means that you will need to be more aware of the depth of water that you are sailing in. Whereas on a dinghy you can lift the centerboard in shallow water, this isn't possible in a keelboat, and if you run aground it might be difficult to get off.

Keelboats tend to have more crew than dinghies, so crew members often specialize in a particular role rather than multi-tasking as in dinghies. Keelboats also tend to be more expensive to purchase and maintain.

POPULAR SMALL KEELBOAT
This 23-ft (7-m) keelboat is suitable for day sailing with the family, or racing with a crew of between three and five.

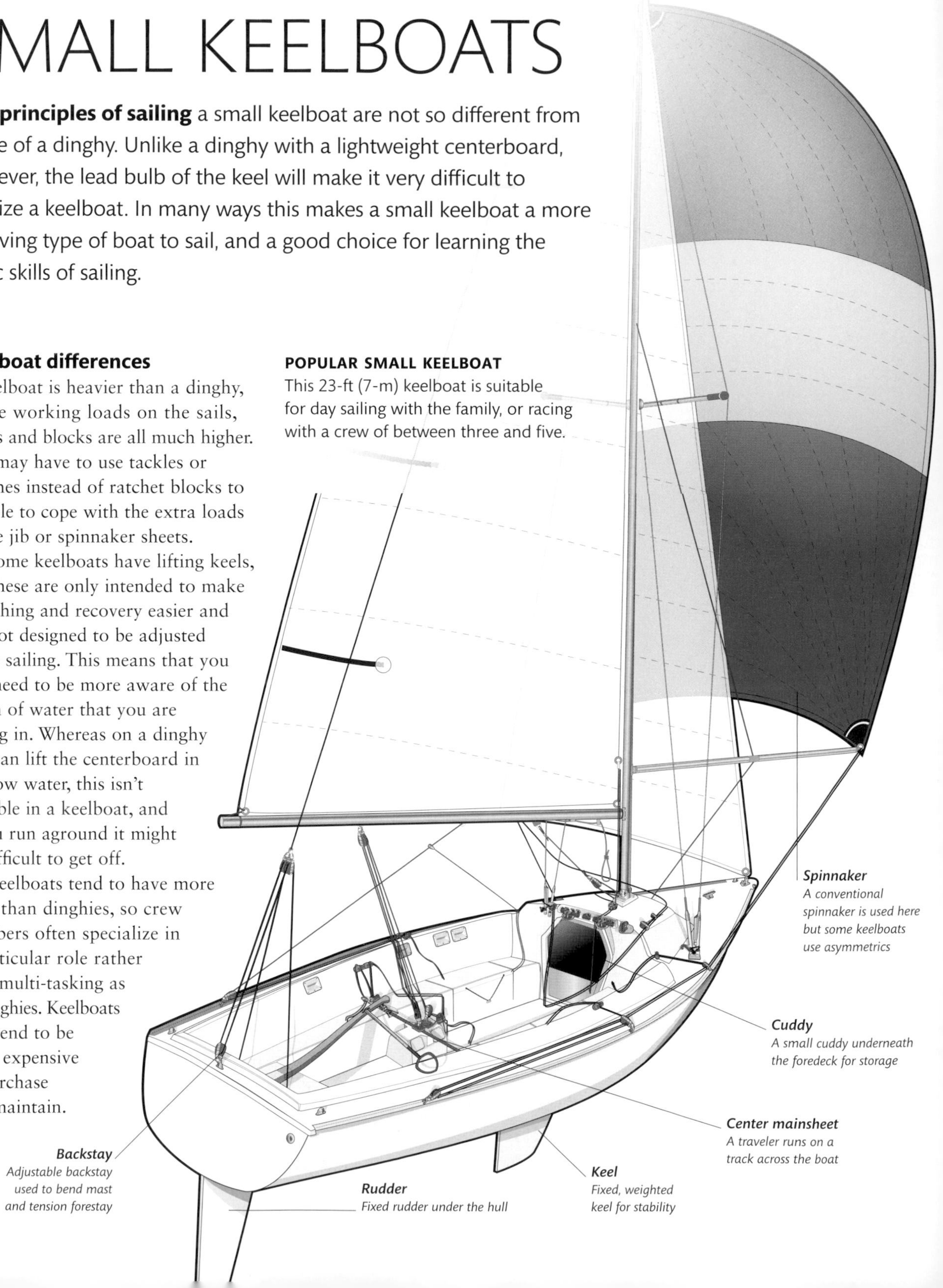

Spinnaker
A conventional spinnaker is used here but some keelboats use asymmetrics

Cuddy
A small cuddy underneath the foredeck for storage

Center mainsheet
A traveler runs on a track across the boat

Backstay
Adjustable backstay used to bend mast and tension forestay

Rudder
Fixed rudder under the hull

Keel
Fixed, weighted keel for stability

TYPES OF SMALL KEELBOAT

CONVENTIONAL KEELBOATS

Designed for racing or day sailing, this type of keelboat generally carries between three and five crew, and has a rig that consists of mainsail, jib, and a conventional spinnaker that is hoisted to hound height. Boats range from the heavier, classic keelboats such as the Dragon, to the lighter, modern types that offer dinghylike handling and planing performance, such as the Sonar.

SPORTSBOATS

Another type of keelboat, known as sportsboats, typically use asymmetric spinnakers. Although most are no faster than conventional keelboats upwind, they are designed to plane downwind under asymmetric spinnakers, often flown from the masthead. The Melges 24 was one of the first sportsboats on the market and remains among the most popular choices.

Its dinghylike performance and handling, plus great versatility, has made the Sonar very popular with all types of sailors, as well as the keelboat of choice for the Paralympic Games.

SONAR

The Laser SB3 is a three-person sportsboat with a large asymmetric spinnaker for high speeds downwind. It has a no-hiking rule and a weight limit.

LASER SB3

The Dragon is a classic keelboat with a long, thin, and heavy hull with a long keel. It offers excellent international competition and remains very popular.

DRAGON

The J80 is easily controlled, but exciting to sail and race. The advanced composite construction ensures that for their size, these boats are fast, light, and strong enough to be sailed hard.

J80

The Etchells 22 measures 30 ft (9 m) long, and is raced by a crew of three or four. The class offers some of the toughest international racing outside of the Olympic arena.

ETCHELLS 22

With its carbon mast and very light all-up weight, the Melges 24 is one of the fastest sportsboats available and is also one of the most demanding. Teams sail with either four or five crew.

MELGES 24

The two-man Star is one of the oldest racing classes, and until recently was the men's Olympic keelboat. It provides some of the toughest sailing competition in the world.

STAR

This type of sportsboat is modeled on the Open 60 and Open 70 race yachts and features wide hulls, rotating rigs, asymmetric kites, and masts that are set well back.

OPEN 5.7 AND 6.5

SAILING SMALL KEELBOATS

The heavier weight of a keelboat requires a different approach to sailing compared to the lighter weight of an unballasted dinghy. It takes more time to accelerate and to slow down, so every time you tack, jibe, or do any maneuver that requires a change of direction or speed, you must allow more time for things to happen and for the boat to regain speed.

Sailing upwind

How a keelboat performs upwind and how it should be sailed depends on its particular design characteristics. Classic keelboats, such as the International Dragon (*p.161*) tend to have long, narrow hulls and deep keels, and are designed to sail to windward at quite a large angle of heel. More modern designs, such as the Sonar (*p.161*) with its dinghylike hull shape and short keel, and all sportsboats, sail much faster if they are kept as upright as possible. This means that their crews must hike (sit out) as far as is allowed under their class rules to help keep the boat upright when sailing to windward. Some classes put no restriction on hiking, while others require the crews to remain seated inside the gunwale.

Many keelboats point quite high when sailing to windward, sometimes tacking through as little as 50 degrees from tack to tack. This can make it quite hard to tell whether you are ahead or behind another yacht when racing on windward legs, and many helmsmen use sight lines drawn on the deck to help them gauge how they are doing compared with other boats.

Because sails on a keelboat are heavily loaded, and require multipurchase blocks or winches to adjust them, it is often simpler to set the sails to a good average position

and for the helmsman to steer the boat around any changes in wind or wave condition. A good helmsman can build up speed by bearing away a tiny fraction before luffing up slightly to gain ground to windward. As he does so, the speed will drop, and the skill lies in recognizing at what point to bear off again and get the boat up to speed once more before repeating the process.

Unlike a dinghy, easing the sails slightly and footing off (bearing away a little bit) for speed does not tend to make a keelboat sail much quicker.

Because a keelboat is relatively heavy, it usually pays to point as high into the wind as possible without losing too much speed, except in choppy or rough water when it is best to bear away slightly to maintain speed. Good helmsmen know instinctively when the boat is in "the groove," the correct balance of speed and pointing for the best performance to windward.

Sail setting

Many of the same principles of sail setting apply as in dinghies (*pp.174–183*). Adjust the sails to be full for choppy seas and/or medium wind strength conditions, and flatten them for flat water and/or windy weather. The vang and cunningham tend to be less important controls on a keelboat. Mainsheet tension and traveler position tend to be the main controls for the mainsail, along with the backstay. The tighter you pull the

SAILING UPWIND
Many modern keelboats, like this Sonar, need to be sailed as upright as possible, just like a dinghy, so it is important that all the crew sit out as far as is allowed by class rules—which vary from type to type.

backstay, the more the mast bends and at the same time tightens the forestay. This will flatten both the mainsail and the jib, and will also alter the feel of the steering. A general rule is: the windier it is, the more backstay you should pull on, although this varies depending on the particular type of keelboat.

Tacking

All maneuvers in a keelboat require good communication and some advance warning. The helmsman should keep the rest of the crew well informed about his intentions. When planning to tack, give the crew enough warning, especially when they are sitting out hard. This will give the jib trimmer time to get in position to release the jib sheet.

The smooth transition of the jib from one side to the other is the most important factor in a good tack. If the jib fails to release smoothly from the old side, then when the boat tacks the jib will back and virtually stop the boat dead in its tracks. It is a good idea for the helmsman to watch the jib trimmer as he steers the boat into the tack. When he sees that the jib sheet is releasing satisfactorily, he can safely continue with the tack.

The helmsman can also make the jib trimmer's job easier if he steers slowly through the tack. This will give the trimmer time to pull most of the jib sheet in, using the winch or multi-part sheet, before the sail fills with wind and becomes much harder to pull in. Once the helmsman sees that the jib is most of the way in on the new tack, he can steer fully onto his new course to get the boat back up to full speed. Easing a little mainsheet after the tack will also help accelerate the boat, gradually sheeting the mainsail back in as the boat accelerates up to full speed.

Sailing downwind

Weight is the important difference between a dinghy and a keelboat when sailing downwind. Even sportsboats, and other keelboats that are able to plane, will need more wind to get up on the plane than will a dinghy. Older designs of keelboats, most of which do not have the flat aft hull sections needed for planing, will surf in waves but are unlikely to rise up onto the plane except, perhaps, in the strongest of winds.

While a dinghy with an asymmetric spinnaker will usually sail fastest downwind if it sails a series of reaching courses, jibing downwind in a manner similar to tacking upwind, in many keelboats it pays to sail straight downwind. This is because the extra speed gained by sailing a series of reaching courses is not sufficient to make up for the extra distance sailed. However, in medium to strong wind conditions, some of the faster keelboats with asymmetric spinnakers respond well to heading up a few degrees to get them planing. The extra distance sailed is then more than offset by the large increase in speed.

Whether you sail a conventional keelboat or sportsboat, the principles of sail setting downwind are very similar to those used for a dinghy. However, because the loads in the sails are much greater, adjustments cannot be made so easily or so frequently as in a dinghy. As with upwind sailing, the helmsman may find he has to steer to suit the set of the sails rather than have the sails trimmed to suit the course he wishes to steer. If the crew is strong, fit, and well-practiced, however, they will be able to make more rapid adjustments and will be able to follow the helmsman's course changes. If this is the case, the boat will sail much faster than those with a less able crew.

SAILING DOWNWIND
Sportsboat-type keelboats are designed to plane quickly downwind under their large asymmetric spinnakers.

Jibing

This is usually the most challenging maneuver in keelboat sailing. Safety is the primary consideration here, and it is vital that all the crew keep their heads down as the boom swings across during the jibe. You can minimize the risk of the boom crashing across by sheeting the boom almost to the centerline as you prepare for the jibe. As the boat jibes, and the wind fills the sail on the new side, let the mainsheet run out rapidly on the new side.

Jibing an asymmetric spinnaker is very straightforward, and very similar to the process described for dinghies (*pp.154–155*). Handling a symmetrical spinnaker is made more complicated by the need to switch the spinnaker pole from one side to the other. Although the technique used in most small keelboats is the same as used in dinghies (*pp.150–151*), it requires good understanding and timing between all the crew. In most keelboats the foredeck crew must move onto the foredeck to jibe the spinnaker pole. In strong winds, do this after the mainsail is jibed.

MOVING SMALL KEELBOATS

Small keelboats have some advantages over dinghies; they are larger and more stable and usually have more room for the crew, but their size also makes them a bit more difficult to launch and recover and to move around on shore. Some smaller keelboats minimize these disadvantages by having lifting keels and rudders so that they can be launched and recovered from a trailer only slightly larger than used by many dinghies. Larger keelboats, with fixed keels and rudders, require more substantial trailers for moving ashore and are usually launched and recovered using a small crane. Many small keelboats are kept ashore when not sailing.

DRY SAILING
Keelboats kept ashore are easily accessible for maintenance and less vulnerable to damage than those kept on moorings.

Dry sailing

In areas where small keelboats are popular, it is common for them to be dry-sailed—that is, kept ashore on a trailer or cart and launched only when needed. Keelboats can also be left afloat on a mooring in a sheltered harbor, but dry sailing has some advantages.

Dry sailing is easier on the boat than mooring it afloat because it is not subjected to pitching and rolling loads on its rig, and it will not risk water absorption into the fiberglass laminate of which most are built.

Also, it is not necessary to apply antifouling paint to the hull to prevent fouling. This has particular merit for race boats, which benefit from the smoothest possible hull finish. Storage ashore allows for easy access for maintenance and race preparation. Boats that are dry-sailed are usually stored ashore with their masts stepped, so they only need to be lifted into the water to be ready to sail.

Many clubs and boatyards in areas where small keelboats are popular offer dry sailing facilities, and some provide a complete service

that includes launching your boat in time for you to go sailing and lifting it ashore again when you return.

Launching and recovery

A keelboat with a lifting keel and rudder is relatively easy to launch and recover. It can sit ashore on a road trailer or launching cart and be launched from a slipway in the same way as a dinghy. Its draft will be deeper than a dinghy, even with the keel raised, so the trailer must be taken farther into the water to float it off.

Once in the water, the boat must be maneuvered into water deep enough to allow the keel and rudder to be lowered. If the wind is offshore, the crew can paddle out; otherwise a tow, or the use of an outboard engine, may be necessary. These boats are not suitable for launching off a ramp or beach on a difficult lee shore, but a sheltered slipway poses few problems. Most lifting keels are raised vertically

USING A SLIPWAY
Keelboats that have lifting keels and rudders can be launched from a trailer. Pick a sheltered slipway with a gentle slope.

through the hull and cockpit floor in the same way as a dinghy's daggerboard, but their weight means that a winch or tackle must be used.

A keelboat with a fixed keel generally requires the use of a crane, although it is possible to launch some from a trailer on a suitable slipway.

Boats that must be craned in and out often have a lifting point fitted in the hull above the keel, usually attached to the bolts that fasten it to the hull. To lift the boat, a strop is attached to the lifting eye and hooked onto the crane hook. It may be necessary to unfasten the backstay at its lower end to keep it clear of the crane jib or wire.

If the boat does not have a center lifting point, two straps are used, led under the hull with one forward and one aft of the keel. The ends of each strap are attached to the crane hook for lifting, and the straps may need to be lashed in position to stop them from slipping backward or forward, depending on the shape of the hull.

TOWING A KEELBOAT
Boats with fixed keels sit high on a trailer and need strong supports. They must be lashed down tightly, with the mast also well secured to its supports.

A center point lift has the advantage of giving complete access to the hull when scrubbing or polishing the bottom, but either system works well.

When ashore, a keelboat usually sits on a road trailer or wheeled cradle to allow it to be moved between the crane and its storage slot. For dry sailing, keelboats usually have their mast left stepped when they are brought ashore, but if they are to be towed on a road trailer, the mast must be lowered and it, the boom, and all other loose equipment must be stowed securely for the journey. In some designs, it is possible to lower the mast manually, but many require the use of a crane to lift the mast in or out.

Using a road trailer
Even a small keelboat is likely to be longer than the vehicle used to tow it, and many will be significantly larger and much heavier. Towing a large boat on a long trailer is not as simple as moving a dinghy, and the towing vehicle should be more powerful and capable of towing the combined weight of the boat and the trailer.

Boats with fixed keels sit much higher than those with lifting keels and require more substantial trailers.

CRANING IN AND OUT
A center lifting point makes craning easier. The alternative is to use webbing straps ahead of and behind the keel.

Double-axle trailers are needed for the larger keelboats, and an overrun braking system on the trailer should be fitted. The boat must be very securely tied down, with the mast stowed on deck. This will usually require mast supports at bow and stern and, preferably, in the middle. The boom and spinnaker pole must also be lashed securely, with plenty of padding to protect against movement and chafe that would otherwise damage the equipment very quickly.

Sails and loose gear are best carried in lockers on the trailer or in the towing vehicle, but if they must be stowed in the boat, they should be secured so that they cannot roll around. When towing, stop and check all lashings regularly.

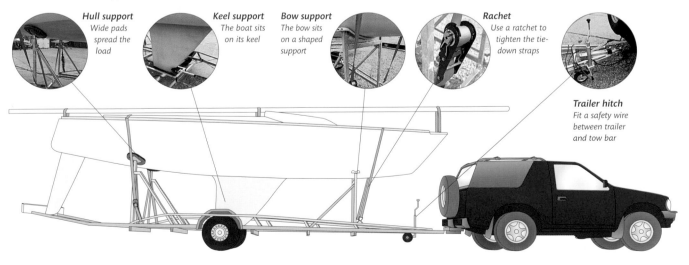

Hull support Wide pads spread the load

Keel support The boat sits on its keel

Bow support The bow sits on a shaped support

Rachet Use a ratchet to tighten the tie-down straps

Trailer hitch Fit a safety wire between trailer and tow bar

CATAMARANS

If you want exciting, high-speed sailing, try a catamaran. Frequently referred to by their shorter nickname of "cats," they consist of two hulls connected by two beams and a trampoline to allow the crew to move from side to side. Their wide beam makes them more stable than single-hulled dinghies, while their narrow hulls and light weight offer little resistance and make them very fast. Catamarans come in a variety of sizes and shapes to suit all ages, sizes, and skill levels.

Catamaran rigs

Most catamarans have a large, fully-battened mainsail, and a much smaller jib that is usually tall and narrow. However, single-handed catamarans are usually sailed without a jib. Some use a loose-footed mainsail, set without a boom, in which case the multipart mainsheet tackle attaches directly to the clew. The lower end of the mainsheet runs on a full-width traveler on the rear beam.

The mast is normally designed to rotate so that it can take up an efficient angle to the wind on all points of sailing. The angle of rotation is controlled by a device called a mast spanner that is adjusted by the crew.

The rotating mast arrangement makes the rig very efficient at the high speeds that catamarans can achieve. Because of these high speeds, catamaran sails tend to be cut very flat, and catamaran sailors pay a lot of attention to the stiffness of their full-length battens. Some expert sailors even change battens for different wind conditions. Softer, more flexible battens create a fuller sail, suitable for conditions where the crew wants to develop maximum

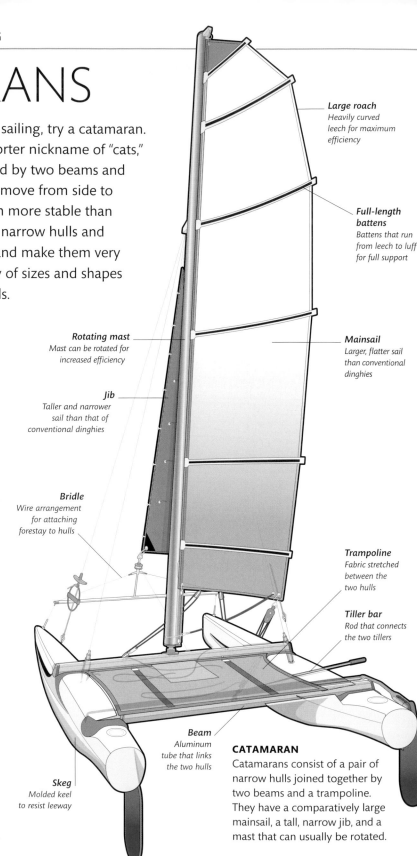

Large roach
Heavily curved leech for maximum efficiency

Full-length battens
Battens that run from leech to luff for full support

Rotating mast
Mast can be rotated for increased efficiency

Mainsail
Larger, flatter sail than conventional dinghies

Jib
Taller and narrower sail than that of conventional dinghies

Bridle
Wire arrangement for attaching forestay to hulls

Trampoline
Fabric stretched between the two hulls

Tiller bar
Rod that connects the two tillers

Skeg
Molded keel to resist leeway

Beam
Aluminum tube that links the two hulls

CATAMARAN
Catamarans consist of a pair of narrow hulls joined together by two beams and a trampoline. They have a comparatively large mainsail, a tall, narrow jib, and a mast that can usually be rotated.

TYPES OF CATAMARAN

There are many types of catamaran on the market, so you should be able to find one that is suitable for your particular requirements. If you want to race, choose a boat that has a good fleet near you. Before you make your decision, ask the opinion of expert sailors and have a trial sail in a few different types.

HOBIE

The Hobie range of catamarans is intended for fast, fun sailing, but there are also good racing fleets in many parts of the world. Hobies have asymmetric hulls without centerboards or daggerboards.

DART 16

The Dart 16 and its larger brother the Dart 18 are excellent boats for fast sailing and competitive racing, and are extremely popular with catamaran sailors. The Dart uses symmetrical hulls with skegs.

F18

F18s are a class of high-performance boats with asymmetric spinnakers. This is a Formula class, which means that any boat that meets certain design specifications may compete in F18 races.

power from the rig. When conditions are stronger and the crew needs to take power out of the sail, they exchange the flexible battens for a stiffer set, which helps keep the sail flatter and less powerful.

Because catamarans travel at such high speeds, the strength and angle of the apparent wind means that the sails are always sheeted quite close to the centerline, even on downwind courses. This is the reason why many catamaran classes do not use a vang, or even a boom for the mainsail, as the mainsheet tension suffices for controlling the shape of the sail.

Some high-performance catamarans are equipped with asymmetric spinnakers to further increase speed downwind. These tend to be very flat compared with asymmetric spinnakers on dinghies or keelboats, because of the high speeds that catamarans achieve when sailing downwind.

Hull design

Catamaran hull shapes vary quite considerably, depending on their design purpose. Some catamarans have hulls that are identical and are symmetrical around their centerline. Symmetrical hulls are usually fitted with a centerboard or a daggerboard in each hull, to resist leeway.

Alternatively there may be a skeg (a molded-in keel) about two-thirds of the way aft on both hulls. The skeg resists leeway without the need for a centerboard or daggerboard. Other catamarans have asymmetrical hulls with a fatter shape on the outboard side of each hull, in which case the two hulls are mirror images of each other. These do not usually need centerboards or daggerboards. The lack of centerboards or daggerboards is an advantage for catamarans designed for fun sailing, where excellent upwind performance may not be of great importance, or for boats that are likely to be sailed from a beach, where the lack of centerboards or daggerboards makes launching and recovery easier.

Catamarans have twin rudders, one at the stern of each hull, with their tillers connected by a tiller bar. The long tiller extension is attached to the middle of the tiller bar. Many catamarans are fitted with one or two trapezes for extra power.

Most of the sailing techniques already described can be used to sail catamarans, but some aspects are different (pp.168–173).

RIGGING AND LAUNCHING

ASSEMBLING A CATAMARAN

Because of their width, catamarans usually have to be dismantled to be transported. Once at the sailing venue, they have to be reassembled on a flat surface. Grass is best, since it will not cause damage to the hulls; otherwise, protect the hulls with something soft, such as a roll of old carpet.

The assembly process consists of attaching the beams to the hulls, fitting the trampoline and toestraps, stepping the mast, and attaching any removable equipment.

Two-person catamarans are best assembled by two crew members, but single-handers can be assembled by one person, although it is easier with a helper. Once assembled, the catamaran is placed on its cart, ready to be rigged and moved to the water.

CATAMARANS ON LAND

Catamarans can be unwieldy on land because of their width. However, they are very light, so moving them is quite easy, even with only two people.

Moving

Most catamarans are moved on a specially built cart with two wheels and two chocks under each transom. The cart is placed under the hulls at the point of balance and the bows are used as the handle for pushing and pulling the catamaran around the boat dock.

Securing

If you leave a catamaran with the mast stepped, fasten it very securely to the ground at both shroud points, to stop it from blowing over in strong winds.

1 Lay out the hulls, preferably on a soft surface, with the inner sides uppermost and about a beam length apart.

2 Slide the main and rear beams into their sockets in one hull. Ensure the clips engage to fully secure the beams (*inset*).

3 Roll the hull onto its keel and fit the second hull to the other end of the beams. Check that the locking system is secure.

4 Fasten the trampoline to the hulls and beams and make sure it is laced very tightly. Fit the toestraps and tie tightly.

5 Step the mast by laying it on the trampoline and temporarily pin the heel onto the mast support while it is raised.

6 Fasten the shrouds to the chainplates, lift the mast upright, attach the forestay to the bridle, and unpin the heel to let it rotate.

7 Attach both rudders with the blades in the raised position. Connect the tillers with the tiller bar and fit the extension.

8 Fit loose gear like the jib sheet fairleads and cleat, mainsheet, and downhaul. The boat is then ready for sails to be rigged.

LAUNCHING A CATAMARAN

When sailing a double-handed catamaran, decide which of you is going to hold the boat and which will take the wheels back up the beach. It usually makes sense to have the taller or heavier person hold the boat so that they can control it while standing in the water.

If you sail a single-handed catamaran, it will make launching easier if you have a helper to take the wheels ashore, or collaborate with other sailors to help each other. Before you push the boat into the water, make sure all the sheets are uncleated and the mainsheet traveler is free to run

from side to side. Alternatively, leave the mainsheet disconnected from the mainsail clew, or boom if your boat is fitted with one, until you are afloat and ready to leave the beach.

Fit the rudders in their raised position and place daggerboards, if used, on the trampoline until the boat has been launched. Always launch the boat with the bows facing into the wind so that the sails can flap freely.

1 Wheel the catamaran into the water with the jib, if fitted, rolled up or flapping, the mainsheet disconnected from the boom, and the rudders raised.

2 One person holds the catamaran by a bow or the bridle while the other goes between the hulls to remove the wheels and take them back up the beach.

3 The helmsman climbs aboard and attaches the mainsheet to the boom, positions the daggerboards, if fitted, in their slots, and partly lowers the rudders.

4 The crew pushes the bows in the direction they wish to sail off and climbs aboard as the helmsman lets the traveler slide to leeward to sail off slowly.

5 With the mainsheet traveler right down to leeward, the boat sails slowly away from the beach. The helmsman lowers the rudders as the boat reaches deep water.

Lee shore

The hardest launching situation is when the wind is blowing onto the shore. This means that the catamaran must be launched bows first into the waves, which may be breaking on the beach or slipway. Controlling the boat when you push off will be more difficult because it will not be possible to lower the rudders until you have sailed beyond the shallow water.

The helmsman decides which tack to leave the beach on, and pulls in the jib sheet until the jib is half full. He makes sure the mainsheet traveler is free to run all the way to leeward. As the jib fills, the catamaran will move

forward slowly, and at this point the crew can pull himself onto the trampoline. The crew then pulls in the jib sheet farther, while the helmsman uses the mainsheet traveler to control the direction of the catamaran. He pulls the traveler to windward to luff up, or eases it to leeward to bear away. Once in deep water, he pushes the rudders fully down and cleats the traveler on the centerline.

Windward shore

Launching from a windward shore is straightforward. Hoist the sails ashore and launch the catamaran stern first. Once the cart has been

returned to the shore, the helmsman and crew take a bow each and sit on it in front of the trampoline.

With the sails flapping and rudders raised, the catamaran will drift backward. Once the boat has reached deeper water, move aft, lower the rudders and centerboards, and push the tiller over to turn the boat away from the wind so that you can sail off.

The same technique can be used to land on a lee shore. Turn the boat into the wind a few boat lengths from the beach, lift the rudders and centerboards, and sit on the forward sections of the hulls to reverse the boat safely to the shore.

SAILING CATAMARANS

Dinghy sailors who decide to sail catamarans need to learn a few new techniques; they will also have to be prepared for the much greater speed potential that is offered by a catamaran. Heading upwind is more difficult in a catamaran than it is in a conventional dinghy and requires a good deal of practice. It is when sailing on downwind courses at speed that catamarans really perform. They are more stable than dinghies and are easier to jibe, but they can still be capsized.

Wind and speed

Because catamarans sail so fast, there is a much bigger difference in the direction of true and apparent wind (*p.32*) than in most dinghies. A wind indicator is usually installed on the forestay bridle so that the helmsman can constantly check the direction of the apparent wind.

A dinghy sailor must also get used to the high speed of a catamaran, which means that you need to allow more space for maneuvers, especially passing other boats. Be prepared for gusts, too, as the catamaran will accelerate rapidly when they hit.

Setting sail

The first time you sail a catamaran, you should start on a beam reach, just as you would with a single-hulled dinghy. Put the boat beam-on to the wind and slowly sheet in both sails. The faster acceleration and the forward shift of the apparent wind mean that the sails have to be sheeted in closer than they would be on a slower-moving dinghy. The load on the sails will also be greater than that in a dinghy. The jib sheet usually has a tackle to make it easier to trim, and the mainsheet on most catamarans requires at least a seven-to-one tackle.

This makes it easier for the helmsman to handle the large loads. Use the mainsheet to control leech tension, and adjust the angle of the sail with the traveler. Set the mainsail twist by using the leech telltales as you would in a dinghy (*p.128*). Although the rudders are small, they are efficient at high speeds, when you will need only small movements of the tiller extension to adjust the course. When you tack or jibe, however, the boat slows down and considerable force may be needed to turn the boat.

Daggerboards or centerboards (if fitted) should be lowered about halfway on a reach. The leeward board is usually lowered first and kept at a lower position than the windward board. As you turn onto a close reach, lower the boards farther still and sheet in the sails, using the traveler to bring the mainsail closer to the centerline.

Flying for speed

Catamarans sail fastest when the windward hull is kept flying, just skimming the water's surface, giving minimum resistance. However, this slight heel is difficult to maintain and takes a lot of practice. Even in medium winds, the helmsman and crew will have to sit out or trapeze hard to keep the boat balanced. Once the helmsman and crew are fully extended, heel is controlled by the helmsman's trimming the mainsail with the traveler and adjusting the course. Luff to maintain heel and bear away to reduce it.

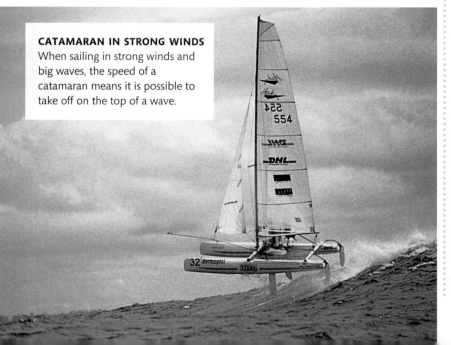

CATAMARAN IN STRONG WINDS
When sailing in strong winds and big waves, the speed of a catamaran means it is possible to take off on the top of a wave.

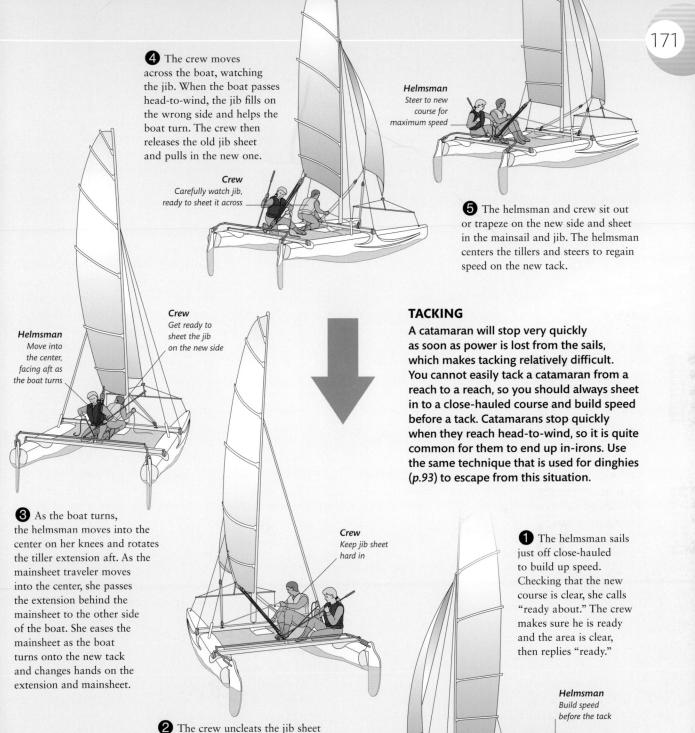

4 The crew moves across the boat, watching the jib. When the boat passes head-to-wind, the jib fills on the wrong side and helps the boat turn. The crew then releases the old jib sheet and pulls in the new one.

Crew
Carefully watch jib, ready to sheet it across

Helmsman
Steer to new course for maximum speed

5 The helmsman and crew sit out or trapeze on the new side and sheet in the mainsail and jib. The helmsman centers the tillers and steers to regain speed on the new tack.

Helmsman
Move into the center, facing aft as the boat turns

Crew
Get ready to sheet the jib on the new side

TACKING

A catamaran will stop very quickly as soon as power is lost from the sails, which makes tacking relatively difficult. You cannot easily tack a catamaran from a reach to a reach, so you should always sheet in to a close-hauled course and build speed before a tack. Catamarans stop quickly when they reach head-to-wind, so it is quite common for them to end up in-irons. Use the same technique that is used for dinghies (*p.93*) to escape from this situation.

3 As the boat turns, the helmsman moves into the center on her knees and rotates the tiller extension aft. As the mainsheet traveler moves into the center, she passes the extension behind the mainsheet to the other side of the boat. She eases the mainsheet as the boat turns onto the new tack and changes hands on the extension and mainsheet.

Crew
Keep jib sheet hard in

1 The helmsman sails just off close-hauled to build up speed. Checking that the new course is clear, she calls "ready about." The crew makes sure he is ready and the area is clear, then replies "ready."

Helmsman
Build speed before the tack

2 The crew uncleats the jib sheet but keeps it hard in. The helmsman calls "lee-oh" and pushes the tiller extension away until the rudders are at an angle of 45° to the transoms. She sheets in the mainsail to help the boat turn into the wind.

Upwind sailing

When you turn to a close-hauled course, sheet the sails right in and steer using the telltales on the jib and the wind indicator. Fully lower both centerboards. Be careful not to pinch (sail too close to the wind), as this makes speed decrease rapidly.

Catamarans are sensitive to fore-and-aft trim, so the helmsman and crew must sit close together, near the middle of the boat, to keep it level. In light winds, move forward to lift the transoms clear of the water—the crew usually lies on the trampoline in the middle of the boat. In stronger winds, move farther back to help keep the bows from burying as the boat accelerates.

Downwind sailing

In light or moderate winds, fast catamarans can sail faster than the true wind speed, and this speed can be fully exploited downwind. It is more efficient to sail downwind in a series of broad reaches, much as you would tack upwind. Sailing dead downwind is slow, but on a broad reach, the speed of the catamaran pulls the apparent wind forward until it is on the beam, thus increasing its strength. The fastest speed downwind is usually achieved by steering to keep the apparent wind, shown by the wind indicator, blowing at right angles to the boat.

Moderate winds

Downwind in moderate winds, the helmsman sets the mainsail by letting the traveler out and uses the mainsheet to adjust the twist in the mainsail. Trim the sail to keep the top leech telltale just streaming. The crew eases the jib out as far as possible, keeping all the telltales streaming. The helmsman steers to keep the apparent wind at 90 degrees to the boat. The helmsman and crew may have to sit on opposite

CATAMARAN COMFORT

Catamarans tend to be wet because they are so fast. Buy good-quality waterproofs or a wetsuit to enjoy the sailing fully.

sides of the boat to keep the weight balanced between the hulls, but the crew moves to windward if the boat starts to heel. If the wind is strong enough, the boat is sailed with the windward hull just touching the water to achieve maximum speed. Where centerboards or daggerboards are fitted, raise them as much as possible; if steering becomes difficult they can be lowered slightly. The helmsman and crew must be prepared to move around the boat to keep it level fore and aft. If the wind drops, move forward to lift the transoms; if it increases, move aft to stop the bows from depressing and slowing the boat.

Light winds

Downwind in light winds, both crew and helmsman sit well forward to lift the transoms and depress the bows, and the crew sits on the leeward hull to balance the helmsman on the windward side. To keep the jib from sagging under its own weight, the crew should hold its clew to keep it trimmed, rather than using the sheet.

The helmsman should steer with gentle movements and concentrate on building and maintaining boat speed. In these conditions, it is very easy for the sails to stall, which will make the boat slow dramatically. If this happens, the helmsman must luff until the apparent wind moves forward again and boat speed increases. When the boat is moving fast again, the helmsman can bear away gently to progress farther downwind while maintaining speed.

Strong winds

Catamaran sailing is at its best downwind in strong winds, when the boat reaches its maximum speeds and accelerates rapidly every time a gust hits. The power in the sails depresses the bows, so it is vital that both the helmsman and crew sit out, or trapeze, at the stern of the windward hull. The bows must be prevented from diving underwater or you will capsize. The high boat speed increases the apparent wind speed, so the helmsman can steer farther downwind while maintaining the apparent wind at right angles to the boat. As gusts hit, the boat will accelerate and the apparent wind will move farther ahead, so the helmsman should bear off to retain the constant apparent-wind angle. In lulls, he must head-up to maintain the angle. Be ready to ease the jib in serious gusts to prevent the bows from digging in.

CAPSIZE RECOVERY

Catamarans are very stable, but can capsize if the crew makes a mistake. This is especially true in strong winds, when capsizes can be spectacular.

Righting a catamaran

You must react quickly in a capsize to prevent inversion; an inverted boat is difficult to right without outside assistance. With most larger catamarans, one crew member should stand on the lower centerboard while pulling on a jib sheet, as when righting a dinghy (*pp.112–113*). The other crew member should depress the bow or stern of the lower hull to sink it, which will assist righting. Some smaller catamarans can be righted by pushing the stern or bow under-water to rotate the boat upright.

3 As the sail swings across, the helmsman briefly stops the mainsheet from swinging to leeward so that the mainsail battens flick to their new shape. She then releases the tackle and moves to the windward hull. She steers onto the new course while the crew trims the jib.

Crew
Sheet jib across and move to balance the boat

Helmsman
Move to the new windward side and steer to the new course

2 Keeping the boat turning, the helmsman swings the tiller extension behind the mainsheet to the new windward side. She changes hands on the mainsheet and tiller, putting her new forward hand on the mainsheet tackle between clew and traveler.

Crew
Watch jib and prepare to sheet it across

Helmsman
Steer through the jibe and take hold of mainsheet tackle

JIBING

A catamaran is easier to jibe than a dinghy because of the stability created by the two hulls, and because its speed reduces the strength of the apparent wind. The catamaran moves quickly, so you must make sure that you have plenty of room for the maneuver and make sure the boat is under full control before you start the jibe. Jibe with the centerboards or daggerboards fully raised. Catamarans rarely sail dead downwind, so you will jibe through a wide angle, from one broad reach to the other.

1 The helmsman bears away from a broad reach to a run and makes sure that the area that the boat will turn into is clear. When ready, she calls "stand by to jibe." The crew also checks the new course. If the crew is ready and the area clear, he replies "ready."

Helmsman
Bear away from a broad reach to a run

Crew
Pick up new jib sheet and prepare to move across the boat

TUNING YOUR BOAT

In order to get the best from your boat, especially if you want to do well in racing, you have to set it up to suit your combined crew weight and the type of mast and sails you use. Many factors contribute to the way a sailing boat performs, and you need to understand each one of them—and how they work together—to tune it effectively for a wide range of conditions. Your aim is to set it up to achieve maximum speed in light, medium, and strong winds, so that you can concentrate on boat handling and tactics.

How to start

Before tuning your own boat, find out how the fast sailors in your class set up theirs. Many top sailors are happy to help novices learn how to tune their boats. Initially, it will be sufficient to aim to set up your boat so that it is exactly the same as the best performer in your class. This will help you achieve a good performance quickly and will prevent you from getting too confused by all the variables that combine to make a fast setup.

Once you are more familiar with tuning techniques, try experimenting with other adjustments. Your class association may be a good source of further information—many of them publish tuning aids to help people who are new to the subject. The main reason for varying your settings from the top sailors in your class is because your combined crew weight differs from their crew weight.

In general, if you and your crew are heavier than the average weight of the top sailors, you will want to develop more power from your rig by setting the mast up for fuller sails. If you are lighter, your boat will be over-powered earlier, and so you may want to sail with

BOAT PREPARATION
Some high-performance dinghies, like this 18-foot Skiff, are placed on their side to make it easier to rig and tune the mast and sails prior to a race.

flatter sails, or adjust your rig to allow you to flatten the sails more than your competitors.

The hull and foils

It is very important that all the underwater parts of the hull, including the centerboard and the rudder, have a perfect finish, free from any blemishes that would disturb the flow of water across their surfaces. Check them regularly and repair any damage immediately, lightly sanding away imperfections. In light winds and flat water, when the boat is not sailing at its maximum speed, the drag caused by underwater blemishes is a very significant part of the total drag.

While you are working on the underwater surfaces, turn the boat on its side and lower the centerboard fully. Make sure it is held rigidly in its case and does not bend when you lean on its tip. If there is any give in it, replace it with a stiffer board, as any deflection as it moves through the water will slow the boat. Next, turn the boat upside down, and check the alignment of the centerboard with the rudder and the centerline of the hull. If the centerboard leans one way or the other, out of line with the rudder tip, then use packing strips (toestrap webbing or thin plastic strips) to pack out one side of the case until the centerboard is in line with the rudder.

The bottom of the centerboard case should be fitted with rubber or plastic strips, which seal the slot and prevent water turbulence—another source of drag. Make sure the strips are in good condition and fit flush with the hull, molding smoothly around the board when it is lowered. If your dinghy has a lifting rudder, check that the blade fits tightly in the stock and that there is no sideways movement that will cause drag and make it harder to steer accurately.

TUNING FOR SPEED
This 470 is sailing fast upwind in medium to strong conditions. Mast bend, clew outhaul, and the cunningham are being used to flatten the mainsail and allow the top to twist, thus reducing power. The jib fairleads have been moved aft to open the slot between mainsail and jib.

The rig

Most high-performance dinghies have large, powerful rigs with a variety of controls to allow the amount of power delivered by the sails to be adjusted to suit the conditions. Boats that are less focused on performance have fewer controls, but significant changes to the rig can still be made.

The rake (lean) and bend—fore and aft as well as sideways—of the mast is used to alter the shape, and thus the performance of the sails. Full sails deliver maximum power, but as the wind increases, the crew's weight, and their ability to keep the boat level, will be overpowered. In strong conditions, the crew needs to be able to flatten the sails to reduce power.

THE MAST

Masts are usually made from aluminum or carbon fiber, and are strong and light. They are also designed to have a certain amount of flexibility, so that they can be bent to adjust the shape of the mainsail. Masts come in a variety of cross-section shapes and weights, and each one will bend in a different way. If you have a choice, use a mast of the same type used in the top boats in your class. Choosing a different mast type from the experts' choice will usually be because of crew weight differences. Light crews tend to use more flexible rigs than heavier crews, so follow the example of a crew of a weight similar to your own.

Mast rake

It is easier to alter the rake and bend of the mast if it is keel stepped (p.69), as the gate at deck level usually has some form of control that can be adjusted. A mast that is stepped on deck can be adjusted only via the spreaders and the shrouds, unless it also has wires running to mast at the gooseneck that control the amount of bend at this point in a way similar to a mast gate. Before adjusting your mast's bend, you need to check its rake. This is usually measured between the top of the mast and the top of the transom on the centerline. Again, follow the example of leading sailors in your class and record the measurements for use in the future.

Sails and pre-bend

It is very important that the amount of pre-bend in your mast matches the shape your sailmaker has built into the luff of the mainsail. Pick a leading sailmaker for your class, tell him your crew weight, and ask for the fast

settings for pre-bend and mast rake. Use these as a starting point for your rig setup and only deviate from these settings when you are confident that you have explored other areas of tuning, such as sail setting.

Mast bend

A key part of setting up the rig for maximum performance is adjusting the pre-bend. This is the amount of bend set in the mast before you start sailing, and it directly influences the mainsail shape. Tuning the mast involves deciding how much you want it to bend and adjusting the controls accordingly.

The rigs of many dinghy classes are set up with about 3–4 in (75–100 mm) of pre-bend in the mast. If you have no other figure to go on, from your class association or sailmaker, use this measurement as a reasonable starting point for experimentation.

MAST BEND
This small keelboat's mast bend flattens the mainsail to reduce power and eases leech tension by flexing in the gusts.

Spreaders and shrouds

The main factors that affect mast bend are the tension in the shrouds and the length and angle of the spreaders. Typically, spreaders are set up to push the shrouds out and aft of a direct line from the hounds to the chainplates. Increasing tension in the shrouds causes the spreaders to stiffen the mast sideways and push its middle forward, thus putting more bend into the mast. Before the mast is stepped, the length or angle of the spreaders can be altered. Some boats have adjustable spreaders that allow the angle to be changed afloat. However, in the early stages, avoid getting involved in such complex adjustments. Use the same measurements as the fastest sailors.

Keel-stepped masts

If your mast is keel-stepped, it will have some form of control to adjust its fore-and-aft position in the mast gate. This might be a strut or a ram, or it may be a set of simple chocks that can be removed or added as required. All these systems are designed to hold the mast back, at gate or gooseneck level, to stiffen it and limit bend, or to allow it to move forward to increase bend.

Deck-stepped masts

Some of the newer skiff-type classes favor deck-stepped masts. In this case, the lower mast bend is controlled by an extra set of wires that run from the chainplates up to gooseneck level. These wires, most commonly referred to as the "lowers," operate in a fashion similar to the keel-stepped mast controls acting at the mast gate. Tighten the lowers to limit lower mast bend, slacken the lowers to increase mast bend.

Rig measuring tools

To be able to copy other sailors' settings and replicate them on your own boat, you will need three tools: a logbook, a measuring tape calibrated in metric and imperial units, which is at least a yard longer than your mast height, and a rig tension gauge. The latter is a simple device that uses the resistance of a strong spring, or length of metal, to measure the tension in the standing rigging. The most popular types are made by Loos and SuperSpar, and you will find that many tuning guides refer to a "Loos" number of say, "35," rather than the actual tension in pounds or kilograms.

The tape measure and the tension gauge will help you find the right combination of mast rake and rig tension for your boat. If you are serious about improving your boat speed, then keep a written record in the logbook of the rig settings that you use for every racing and training session, and your impressions of how your speed compared with others'.

MAST BEND

The amount of mast bend controls the fullness of the mainsail. Use a straight mast for maximum fullness and power in light to moderate winds. In very light, drifting conditions, increasing pre-bend will flatten the sail and make it easier for the wind to flow around it. As soon as there is a perceptible breeze, however, straighten the mast. In medium to strong winds, when the wind increases to the point where the crew's weight is no longer sufficient to hold the boat upright, the mast should be bent to flatten the sail and reduce power.

Straight mast gives full mainsail

Full mainsail for maximum power

STRAIGHT MAST

Bent mast flattens mainsail

Mainsail is flatter to reduce power

MAST WITH PRE-BEND

SPREADERS

The length and angle of the spreaders help control mast bend. Long spreaders push the shrouds outward and stiffen the mast sideways. Angling the spreaders aft causes the shrouds to push the middle of the mast forward. This increases mast bend. When the jib halyard is tightened, the shrouds are tensioned and the effect of the spreaders on the mast is increased.

Spreaders angled aft push shrouds backward

Long spreaders deflect the shrouds sideways

SPREADER ANGLE

SPREADER LENGTH

MAST-GATE CONTROL

A keel-stepped mast usually has some form of fore-and-aft control at the mast gate to adjust mast position and bend. In this small keelboat, plastic chocks are used. Chocks can be moved in front of the mast to push it aft, or behind it to push it forward.

THE SAILS

Most high-performance dinghies have a number of controls that can be used while sailing to adjust the shape of the sails and thus to increase or decrease power. These controls are best rigged so that the helmsman or crew can adjust them while sitting out, or trapezing. Mark all your controls so that you can record the fast settings in your logbook for easy replication.

Mainsail adjustments

As well as holding down the boom, the boom vang pulls it forward into the gooseneck. If this force is not resisted by chocks, a mast ram, or lowers, it will cause low-down mast bend. This flattens the mainsail in the lower half and increases twist in the upper leech, thereby reducing power in the top of the sail in strong winds.

The clew outhaul controls tension in the foot of the mainsail. Easing it increases the sail's fullness in the lower third of the sail and closes the lower leech. Tightening it flattens the sail and opens the lower leech.

Tensioning the cunningham tightens the mainsail luff, opens the upper leech and increases twist. It also pulls the point of maximum camber forward to counteract the effect of stronger winds that push the camber aft in the mainsail.

Jib adjustments

The position of the jib fairleads and the tension in the jib sheet control the jib's shape and the slot between jib and mainsail. Fairleads should be adjustable fore and aft and, ideally, sideways, so that you can alter their position to suit all wind conditions. In general, they are moved forward and inboard to increase power and narrow the slot, and back and out to open the slot and flatten the sail. Make sure that the slot stays parallel all the way up. Jib luff tension is set by the jib halyard. In dinghies, adjusting the jib halyard also alters tension in the shrouds and effects mast bend. Adjust it to minimize luff sag when close-hauled in medium winds. Ease it in light winds and tighten it in stronger winds.

SAIL CONTROLS

Modern sailcloths are very stable, allowing sail shapes that perform well in a wide range of conditions. As wind strength increases or decreases, however, the crew needs to maintain top performance by using the sail and rig controls to adjust the fullness of their sails and to control the position of maximum draft. Remember that changing one control is likely to have an effect on one or more of the others.

EQUIPMENT	ACTION	RESULT
Jib halyard	Increasing tension	Reduces sagging in jib luff. Tightens leech
Jib fairleads	Adjusting fore and aft, and sideways	Alters shape of jib, twist in leech, and adjusts slot between jib and mainsail
Cunningham	Increasing tension	Pulls maximum camber forward in sail, opens upper leech, increases twist
Boom vang	Increasing tension	Reduces mainsail leech twist and bends mast low down
Mainsheet	Adjusting sheet tension	Controls boom angle and leech tension
Mainsheet traveler	Adjusting position	Controls boom angle
Clew outhaul	Increasing tension	Flattens lower third of mainsail and opens lower leech

Tuning small keelboats

Many of the same principles of tuning dinghies apply to keelboats, but the controls may vary. Many keelboats have an adjustable backstay, which is a useful tool for adjusting mast bend. In medium airs, the backstay tends to be slack, with the crew using large amounts of mainsheet tension to create maximum leech tension for power. In light winds of less than 4 knots, however, the backstay can be used to flatten the mainsail, to encourage airflow over the sail. In strong winds when it is necessary to depower the rig, increasing backstay tension will help flatten the mainsail and open the upper leech. Remember to release backstay tension when you bear away downwind, to put power back into the mainsail and avoid excess load damaging the mast.

Most of the techniques described for dinghies also work for keelboats, although the mainsheet traveler tends to be more of a primary control in keelboats. Keep the boom on the centerline in light to medium winds, but as the wind increases, it usually pays to let the traveler down to leeward to help depower the mainsail. Easing the traveler on a keelboat will also help reduce weather helm. The aim of many of the tuning adjustments on a keelboat is to reduce weather helm to a minimum. A boat that is easy to steer also tends to be fast through the water.

TO INCREASE POWER
- Ease the jib sheet slightly
- Move the jib fairleads forward
- Ease the mainsail outhaul
- Ease the cunningham control
- Bring the boom closer to the centerline
- Stiffen the mast at deck level using the mast-gate control

MAXIMIZING PERFORMANCE IN ALL CONDITIONS

Start tuning afloat by sailing close-hauled in medium winds of about 7–16 knots, Force 3–4. In these conditions, your boat will be fully powered up, with you sitting out or trapezing as hard as possible to keep the boat level. Experiment with the controls one at a time.

Light winds

In medium winds, the maximum fullness of the sails is used to develop power. In very light winds of 4 knots or less, however, the wind does not have enough energy to bend easily around full sails. Therefore, you need to flatten the sails.

Remove the mast chocks in the mast gate or ease off the ram to allow the mast to bend forward at deck level and pull the clew outhaul to its maximum extent. Leave the cunningham and vang slack and adjust the mainsheet and traveler to keep the boom close to the centerline with the top leech telltale on the point of stalling.

Flatten the jib by moving the jib fairleads aft and out, but ease the jib sheet slightly. If the wind strength increases, the mast will try to bend further and creases will appear from the luff of the mainsail. At this point, start restricting mast bend using the chocks or the ram to increase the power in the sail.

Medium winds

In medium winds, aim to achieve maximum power from the rig. Set the jib fairleads in their middle position and sheet the sail so that all the windward telltales (p.80) break together. Use the mast-gate chocks or ram to prevent the mast from bending beyond the set amount of pre-bend. Ease the clew outhaul by about 1–2 in (2.5–5 cm) from its maximum position and leave the cunningham slack. Sheet the mainsail using the mainsheet and leaving the vang slack. Sheet it hard enough to have the top leech telltale (p.128) on the point of

stalling. If your mainsheet runs on a traveler, pull it to windward until the boom is on the centerline. The boat should now be fully powered up, with you and your crew sitting out as hard as possible, or trapezing, to keep the boat upright.

If the mainsail develops large creases running from the clew to the middle of the luff, it is an indication that your mast is bending too much and you need to adjust the spreaders or shroud tensions to reduce the bend.

Strong winds

When you sail upwind in strong winds, you need to reduce power to sail fast and stay in control. If you can adjust the rig before sailing, it usually helps to increase the mast rake and the shroud tension. You may also decide to alter the spreader angle to prevent excessive bend. If the boat becomes overpowered, tension the cunningham and pull the outhaul tight. The Cunningham pulls the draft in the sail forward and helps flatten it, while the outhaul flattens the lower part of the sail.

Use the vang to hold the boom down and increase low-down bend in the mast, and use the mainsheet to trim the sail. You can ease the vang in the lulls to increase power and tighten it in the gusts to reduce power. Move the jib-sheet fairleads aft and tighten the sheet to flatten the sail, open the slot, and allow the head to twist slightly. If you are still overpowered, it can help to pull up the centerboard or daggerboard as much as halfway. This is an often-overlooked method of depowering the boat.

ROUGH-WEATHER SAILING

The definition of rough weather is subjective—in conditions that are too difficult for novice sailors, an expert crew will be able to enjoy fast and exhilarating sailing. The design of the boat influences the way you experience the conditions, as does the wind direction in relation to the shore and any tidal stream. Winds of Force 5 to 6 can be considered rough weather, but a Force 4 against a strong tide can kick up large waves and make sailing more difficult than a Force 6 in flat water.

Gaining experience

As you develop your sailing skills, it is important that you learn to handle your boat in strong winds. It is often best to gain experience while racing, because racing fleets still sail in rough weather and always have safety boats available. When you sail just for fun, however, it will be your decision whether to venture out.

Before you go afloat, check all your gear to make sure it is in good condition and that nothing is likely to break. Rough weather imposes considerable loads on the boat, sails, and equipment, and it is vital that they are strong enough to handle the stress. Make sure that your clothing is

adequate (*pp.64–65*). Sailing in these conditions can be very tiring and requires concentration, stamina, and endurance. If you find that you are getting tired or cold, come ashore immediately, as your strength will decrease rapidly and you could easily find yourself in trouble.

You will notice that the boat reacts much faster and more violently in rough weather than it does in lighter winds. You will need to react quickly to changes in wind strength and direction. The heeling force will be considerable, and you will need all your strength and agility to keep the boat under control. Depending on your boat and the wind strength, you

may find that you plane on many points of sailing. Speed is your ally in these conditions—when the boat is upright and moving fast, it is easier to control and requires smaller tiller movements to keep it on course.

Reaching

Start by sailing on a reach to get the feel of the conditions. The boat should be planing and the helmsman and crew should move well aft to keep the bow up and the rudder immersed. If the boat heels, ease out both sails to keep the boat upright, allowing the luffs of both sails to "lift"—shake or backwind—if necessary. If the boat is overpowered, move the jib sheet fairleads back to allow the top of the jib to twist, and ease the vang to twist the mainsail. Watch for gusts, easing the sails and bearing away to keep the boat upright as they pass.

Broaching

One of the hazards of rough-weather reaching, particularly when flying a spinnaker, is broaching. When a gust strikes the sails, there is often a tendency for the boat to round up into the wind without much warning. The helmsman may try to fight the weather helm by pulling hard on the tiller, but at this point it is often too late and the boat will round up uncontrollably into the wind. Prevention is the best policy, and both helmsman and crew should look frequently over their shoulder to see when the next gust is about to strike. Just as a gust—indicated by a dark patch on the water—is about to reach the boat, make sure the boat is absolutely upright and bear away slightly, with the crew ready to ease

ON A REACH
Reaching in strong winds, this Laser sailor eases the vang so that the mainsail twists off and heeling is reduced. This also keeps the boom end clear of waves.

PLANING TO WINDWARD
This helmsman and crew are working hard to keep the boat upright and planing to windward. The mainsail is eased slightly to reduce heeling.

the spinnaker sheet at least an armful. If the gust is bigger than expected, bear away even more and ease even more spinnaker sheet, and the boat will accelerate rather than heel.

Easing the vang, sometimes all the way off, can also help the boat cope with a big gust on a reach. If you are sailing on a keelboat with four or more people, assign one person to be solely responsible for controlling the vang, pulling it on in the lulls and easing it rapidly in the gusts.

Close-hauled

Luff up to a close-hauled course, being careful to sheet in gently as the boat turns so that it stays upright. It is important that heeling is kept to a minimum, and the helmsman must constantly trim the mainsheet to achieve this. In the strongest gusts, the mainsail may have to be let out until it backwinds (flaps) across most of its width to spill wind and prevent the boat from heeling. Keep the jib sheeted in tight except in the strongest gusts, when it should be eased out a little way until the gust passes.

High-performance dinghies will plane to windward, and the mainsail should be eased as necessary to keep the boat upright. Slower dinghies, which do not plane to windward, can use the no-sail zone as a way of decreasing power. As a gust hits, the helmsman eases the mainsheet a little

and steers closer to the wind until the jib luff starts to backwind. This reduces the power in the rig, and gains ground to windward. Do not sail too close to the wind, however, or the boat will slow down and heel more when you try to bear away to the correct course. Steer through big waves by luffing up as you climb them, then bearing away as the bow passes through the crest.

Downwind courses

In strong winds, the boat will plane continuously on a broad reach—and possibly even on a run. Sailing on a run in very strong winds is difficult because there is no heeling force to balance against, and there is always the danger of an unplanned jibe. The boat will sail faster and will be more

stable on a broad reach. There will be sufficient heeling force to allow both the helmsman and the crew to sit to windward (well aft to prevent the bow from digging in). When sailing in waves, you must anticipate each wave and bear away down its face as the stern lifts. The boat will accelerate, and you should then luff slightly to ride the face of the wave as long as possible, avoiding digging the bow in at the bottom of the trough.

If the bow does dig in to a wave, it may nosedive and suffer a pitchpole capsize. Avoid this by reducing the efficiency of the sails to slow the boat. In a singlehander, tighten the vang and oversheet the mainsail. In a boat with an asymmetric spinnaker, oversheet the sail as much as necessary to slow down to the point where you feel safe. In a dinghy or keelboat with a conventional spinnaker, head up to a broad reach so that you sail down the waves at an angle rather than straight down them.

NOSEDIVING
Sailing a high-performance boat very fast downwind in waves brings the risk of nosediving into a wave and pitchpoling.

TACKING AND JIBING IN STRONG WINDS

In rough conditions, your boat is vulnerable at slow speeds, especially when tacking and jibing. The helmsman and crew must work hard to keep the boat balanced through these maneuvers, which must be completed as quickly as possible so that the boat can get back to full speed with minimum delay.

Tacking

Before tacking, the helmsman must ensure the boat is moving as fast as possible and should look ahead of the boat to find a stretch of flat water in which to tack. However rough it is, the size of waves always varies, so look for a long valley between two swells, or a wave with a smallish peak, around which to time the tack.

Give the crew plenty of warning when tacking in rough weather, and time the start of the tack so that the bow passes through a wave crest as you luff into the tack. This will ensure that the boat is on the new tack and moving again before the next wave arrives. Timing of body movement is crucial. The aim is to keep the boat flat throughout the maneuver.

In a dinghy, as the helmsman starts to luff up slowly, both helmsman and crew should come in from their hiking or trapezing positions, but remain on the windward side, ready to move smoothly and swiftly across to the new windward side as the boat tacks.

Once the boat is through head to wind, helmsman and crew should move to the new side as quickly as possible. The mainsail and jib should be sheeted only three-quarters of the way in, with both sails luffing slightly. This will help the boat accelerate and make it less likely to capsize if a gust hits the sails. Once you are both fully

hiking or trapezing and the boat has accelerated, sheet the sails back into their normal position.

Some boats sail best upwind in windy weather, using a lot of tension in the boom vang, but this can sometimes cause a problem when tacking. The tension in the boom vang causes the mainsail leach to be very tight during a tack, and this can make the boat stall head-to-wind. It can also make it quite hard for the crew to get under the boom. If you have problems with getting caught in-irons, or getting under the boom during a tack, ease the vang before the tack, and pull it on again only when the boat is fully up to speed again.

This problem of getting stuck head-to-wind is particularly common in single-handers, that rely on large amounts of vang to flatten the sail but have no jib to help pull the bow away from the wind (*p.159*). It can help to bear off slightly onto a close reach to build speed and then tack the boat onto a close reach on the other tack, before sheeting in and luffing up to a new close-hauled course. If you still have problems, then try these solutions in order of importance:

increase cunningham tension, raise the daggerboard, and ease the vang. As you become more adept at rough-weather tacking, you should need to rely less on these techniques, but be aware that older sails are harder to tack than new ones, because the sail's center of effort moves aft as the sailcloth ages and stretches out of shape.

Jibing

Jibing in any boat must be completed quickly and smoothly. It should be attempted only when the boat is moving at top speed—when the apparent wind is least—and never when it is slowing down—when the apparent wind pressure increases. For this reason, jibing is much easier when the boat is surfing down the front of a wave or planing at high speed. Do not be afraid to jibe when sailing fast; it really is the safest way to handle the maneuver.

Take great care with the boom in rough conditions, as it can fly across the boat with great force. Make sure that you and your crew have your heads down before you jibe. Some sailors even wear protective head gear for this reason.

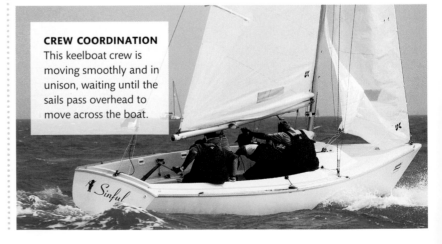

CREW COORDINATION
This keelboat crew is moving smoothly and in unison, waiting until the sails pass overhead to move across the boat.

ROLLING DOWNWIND
Non-planing, classic keelboats tend to roll heavily when sailing in strong winds. Beware of unintentional jibes when sailing on a run in strong winds.

Conventional spinnaker

In a boat sailing with a conventional spinnaker, which will run straight downwind, the jibing technique is very similar to that used for lighter conditions. With the boat sailing on a run, roll the boat slightly to windward, about 5 degrees, just to help the rudder steer the boat through a gentle arc. At the same time, grasp all the parts of the mainsheet tackle and "throw" the mainsail over to the new jibe. This allows you to avoid a large change of course to get the mainsail to jibe, and means you are less likely to broach after the jibe. At the moment the boom swings across the boat, the helmsman should reverse the helm and steer the boat back to a run. The course steered through the jibe will resemble an "S" shape, ensuring that the boat sails dead downwind as much as possible. Once the boat is steady, the crew can move forward to change the spinnaker pole to the new side.

Asymmetric spinnaker

Subtlety of steering is essential to jibing an asymmetric spinnaker successfully. It is surprising just how little steering a planing dinghy requires. Make sure the boat is flat or even heeled slightly to leeward throughout the maneuver, as any windward heel will mean that the asymmetric, pulling at the top of the mast, will capsize the boat as it exits from the jibe. This angle of heel is a very important distinction between jibing a symmetric or asymmetric spinnaker dinghy. As you steer into the jibe, move your body weight over as quickly or as slowly as is required to match the speed of the turn through the jibe. A rapid turn will require rapid movement across the boat.

Jibe the asymmetric spinnaker as normal or consider using the survival jibe technique in heavy weather (*pp.154–155*), as it is much quicker to jibe safely and remain upright than it is to deal with a capsize.

Single-hander

Jibing a single-hander with just a mainsail can be quite tricky because there is no spinnaker to keep the boat moving through the jibe. This means it is very hard to avoid the boom slamming across on the new side, which can easily lead to a broach.

The key to successful jibing in a non-trapeze single-hander is to use a version of the roll jibe (*p.141*). As you steer into the jibe, heel the boat to windward and, as you feel the mainsheet tension become light (the sign that the sail is about to jibe), give it a quick tug to help it on its way. At the same time, transfer your weight rapidly to the new side to bring the boat level again, while steering back onto a downwind course as quickly as possible. Again, the aim is to steer an S-shaped course

to instigate the jibe and then bring the boat back to a dead run straight after the jibe.

The added difficulty is that the helmsman must steer with the tiller extension held behind his back at this stage. Once the boat is under control on the new jibe, the helmsman can change hands on the extension and get settled on the new course.

Keelboats

Jibing a keelboat in rough weather is, in principle, the same as jibing a dinghy, but it is important to remember that all the loads are much higher. This means that all crew members must be aware of these extra loads on sails, sheets, tackles, and winches. Be particularly wary of the boom as it flies across, and ensure that everyone keeps their heads well down below its swinging arc. When sailing a keelboat with a conventional spinnaker in strong conditions, jibe the mainsail first. The foredeck crew only goes forward to jibe the spinnaker pole once the boat is under control again. Be sure to keep steering the boat straight downwind to keep the loads on spinnaker sheet and guy to a minimum until the pole has been attached on the new side.

PHYSICAL FITNESS
Rough weather is physically demanding and quickly saps strength, so it pays to make sure you are fit for the conditions.

RACING

There is no better way to learn to sail a boat well, and to build on your existing skills, than to race against other boats that are in the same class. Racing quickly teaches you the intricacies of good boat handling, and you will also learn how to tune your dinghy or keelboat for a wide range of wind conditions. Join a club that supports the class of boat you are interested in, or, if you already own a boat, but your club does not support its class, consider racing in a mixed, handicap fleet.

Starting to race

Racing is organized through sailing clubs at a local level, and through class associations on a national or international basis. You will need to join your class association, which will arrange for your boat to be measured and certified within the class rules.

The association will also be able to provide you with tuning data and can advise you on which clubs provide fleet racing for your type of boat.

At club level, each fleet normally has a class captain who organizes the racing calendar and who is usually an experienced sailor in the class.

You will nearly always find that the class captain and other owners are welcoming to newcomers and will be pleased to help you get started.

If you do not own your own boat, you will often find that you can get a crewing position quite easily. Crews are often in short supply, and it is a great way to learn racing skills.

Making a choice

If you have ambitions to reach the top in dinghy racing, you should choose one of the recognized International- or Olympic-class boats and be prepared for a long, hard, and expensive route to the top. If, on the other hand, your ambitions do not extend beyond becoming a good club racer or a competitor in a national championship fleet, you will have a wider choice of boats. Narrow down your options by deciding whether you want close, tactical racing or speed, and whether you want to sail with a crew or prefer to sail a single-handed dinghy.

SAILING CLUBS

By far the best way to meet other sailors and develop your skills is to join an active sailing club. These range from dinghy clubs to those that embrace dinghies, small keelboats, and larger yachts.

Clubs and racing

To improve your dinghy sailing skills, find a local club dedicated to dinghy sailing. The club will probably provide fleet racing for several classes and will also have a handicap fleet in which other less popular dinghies can race. Dinghy clubs often have junior or cadet sections that provide training courses and racing for young members. If you have your own boat and want to race against others of the same class, make sure you join a club that has a strong fleet of your class.

SAILING IN A CLUB
Club racing forms the backbone of dinghy sailing and is the starting point for all who wish to race. Once a sailor has become proficient enough to reach the top of a good club fleet, he or she can progress to Class Open Meetings and National Championships.

TACTICAL RACING

For close, tactical racing, pick a class such as the Laser—the Olympic single-hander. It has large and very competitive fleets worldwide and is challenging to sail. It is also relatively cheap to buy and run. Whatever your level of skill or ambition, you will always find Laser sailors of your standard to ensure good close racing.

HIGH-SPEED SAILING

For high speeds and an adrenaline rush, consider a boat like this F18 Hobie Wildcat catamaran or a single-hulled dinghy such as the Olympic 49er, the International 14, or the Foiling Moth. These are extreme machines that demand great skill, coordination, and agility to sail, but deliver a fantastic return in performance and fun.

Tactics versus speed

You do not need to sail the latest high-performance dinghy to enjoy very competitive racing. In fact, many of the largest and most competitive racing fleets are found in classes that were designed many decades ago and which, by modern standards, are quite slow. They may not offer the ultimate in speed, but the racing is often very close and tactically intense.

For speed, look at catamaran designs or modern monohull dinghies with multiple trapezes and large, asymmetric spinnakers. If you prefer not to sail in one of the high-performance dinghies but still want speed, you should consider a small keelboat or a sportsboat. These will provide exciting sailing without the level of physical exertion a high-performance dinghy requires.

If you do not want to have to find a crew, consider a single-handed class, which will provide the ultimate test of your individual racing skills.

COURSES AND STARTING

Racing can take place around any shape or length of course, but there are a few common types of courses used for Club and Championship racing. Most courses are set to ensure that the first leg after the start is to windward. Races can start with a downwind leg, on a reach or a run, but this is far less common and is mostly restricted to yacht races.

Most courses for dinghy, small keelboat, or catamaran races are set with marks rounded in a counter-clockwise direction, or with "marks to port," as it is often described. This is because it ensures that the final approach to the windward mark will be on starboard tack, which is the tack with the right of way under the racing rules. If a course is set with marks rounded to starboard, there is a higher chance of collisions.

Old Olympic course

Otherwise known as a Triangle-Sausage course, this used to be the standard course for Olympic class boats, but is still very popular with some of the more traditional dinghy classes, including some singlehanders and boats with conventional spinnakers. The race starts with a windward leg, and then moves on to two reaching legs. After a second windward leg, the course then turns directly back downwind on a run.

Windward leeward

The simplest configuration is a windward leeward course. This has become the course of choice for the asymmetric dinghy classes, and many of the sportsboat classes. On the old Olympic course there are not many overtaking opportunities on the reaches, which can be quite processional. Instead, the windward leeward configuration offers the challenge of the windward legs plus the tactical options of jibing downwind on the run, where place changes are more common, which makes the racing more interesting.

Square course

This has become a popular course configuration since it allows a race committee to race two separate fleets on the same course. The race officer can send the first fleet off on the "outer loop," and the second fleet can start five minutes later and race on the "inner loop."

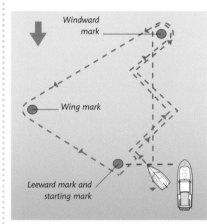

Windward mark

Wing mark

Leeward mark and starting mark

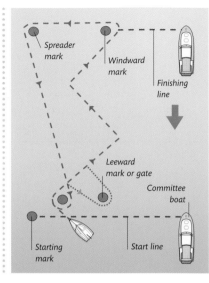

Spreader mark

Windward mark

Finishing line

Leeward mark or gate

Committee boat

Starting mark

Start line

WINDWARD LEEWARD COURSE
Ater a beat to windward, there is a very short reach to a spreader mark, if used, then a run to the leeward mark or gate.

OLD OLYMPIC COURSE
The windward leg is followed by a reach to the wing mark and another reach to the leeward mark, then a beat and a run.

SQUARE COURSE
This course allows the race committee to race two fleets, using the inner and outer loops, to separate the two.

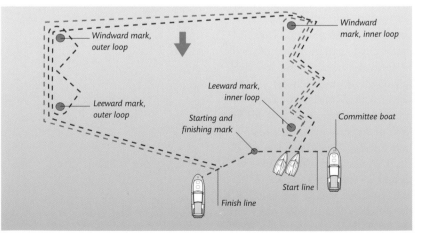

Windward mark, outer loop

Windward mark, inner loop

Leeward mark, inner loop

Leeward mark, outer loop

Starting and finishing mark

Committee boat

Start line

Finish line

STARTING

A race committee will set a start line between two points, usually the mast on a race committee boat at the starboard end of the line, and another boat, or an inflatable buoy, at the port end of the line, which is often referred to as the "pin end." The race officer will usually aim to set a start line that is square—at 90 degrees—to the average wind direction. The aim of the racing sailor is to start at the favored end of the line (below), as close to the line as possible, without being over the line at the start signal. The race officer will watch the line at the start time to see if any boats are over. If there are, he will sound a further signal and fly an individual recall flag, indicating that the offending boats must return to the line to start correctly. If there are many boats over the line, he may choose to have a general recall, in which case that start will be abandoned and the whole starting procedure will commence once more.

Starting procedure

Sailors need to stay close to the race committee vessel during the minutes before the start of a race, so that they can see the flags and hear the sound signals, which will be made by whistle, horn, or starting gun. It is important to know that the flags are the definitive signal; the sound signal is only to draw attention to the flags. So if the flag movements and the sound signals do not happen at the same time, set your watch by the flag signal. The most common timing sequence is 5-4-1-Go, although others may be used.

SIGNAL	FLAG AND SOUND	MINUTES TO GO
Warning	Class flag + 1 sound	5
Preparatory	Flag P (or flag I, Z, Z with I, or black flag) + 1 sound	4
One-minute	Preparatory flag removed + 1 long sound	1
Start	Class flag removed + 1 sound	0

| INDIVIDUAL RECALL | GENERAL RECALL | POSTPONEMENT | PREPARATORY (P) | DISQUALIFICATION (BLACK FLAG) | I (ONE MINUTE RULE) | Z |

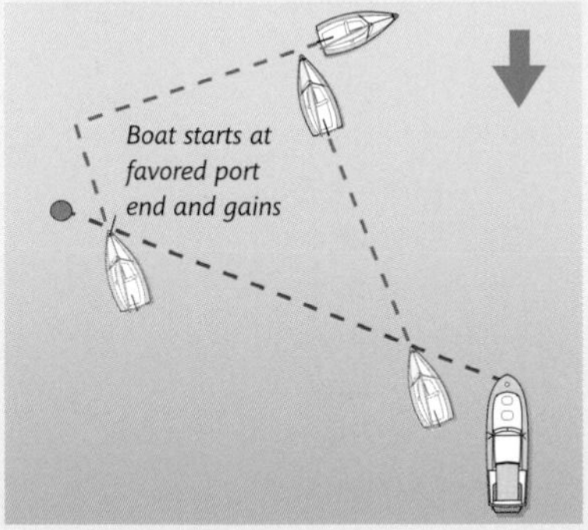

PORT END BIAS
If the port end of the line is closer to the wind, a boat starting there will be ahead of a boat starting at the other end of the line.

Boat starts at favored port end and gains

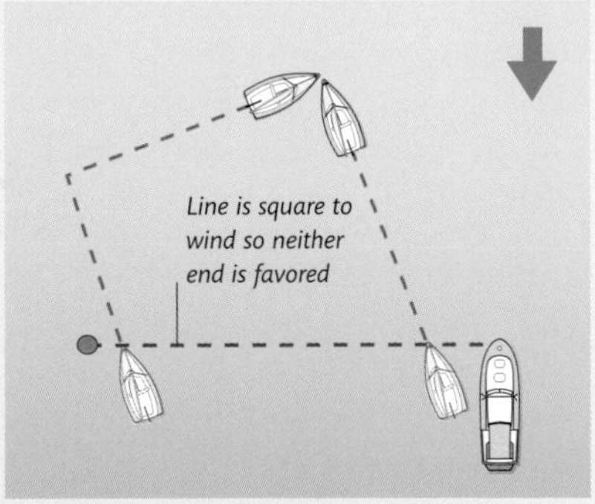

SQUARE LINE—NO BIAS
When the line is square to the wind, neither end is closer to the wind and there is no advantage for either end of the line.

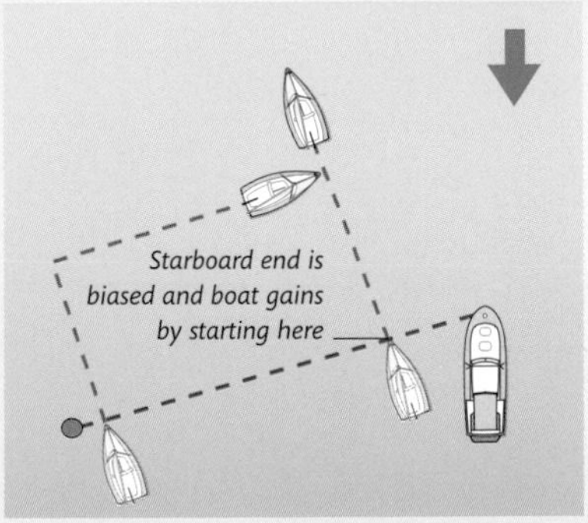

Line is square to wind so neither end is favored

STARBOARD END BIAS
If the starboard end of the line is closer to the wind, a boat starting there will be ahead of a boat starting at the other end of the line.

Starboard end is biased and boat gains by starting here

FROM START TO FINISH

The racing day begins long before the starting gun sounds. Most sailors check the weather forecast the night before racing, and the times of the tide if they are racing in tidal waters. On the morning of the race, it is a good idea to read the sailing instructions very carefully, and also to find out what the wind is actually doing compared with the forecast. If you have a choice of sails for different wind conditions, then you will need to make a decision about which to use for the day.

Check how far away the race course is, and how long it is likely to take to get there. You need to arrive in the starting area at least 10 minutes before the 5-minute starting sequence begins to have time to check the line bias, and it is much better if you can arrive half an hour or more before the start. This will allow time for doing some practice tacks and jibes and to check that the boat is tuned correctly for the wind and wave conditions.

Check the wind

Use the time before the start to check the wind shifts and to plan a strategy for the first beat. From the starting area, sail off on port or starboard tack and sail as well as you can to windward. Constantly check the compass to find out how the wind is shifting. Write down (use a non-permanent marker on any handy surface) the average heading, then tack and do the same on the other tack. Sail about halfway up the beat, if time allows, then head back to the start line, taking the opportunity to hoist the spinnaker, check that it is not twisted, and do a couple of practice jibes.

Check the line bias

Back at the starting area, the Race Committee should have laid the starting line, and now is the time to check the line bias (*p.187*). While most race committees will attempt to set a start line at 90 degrees to

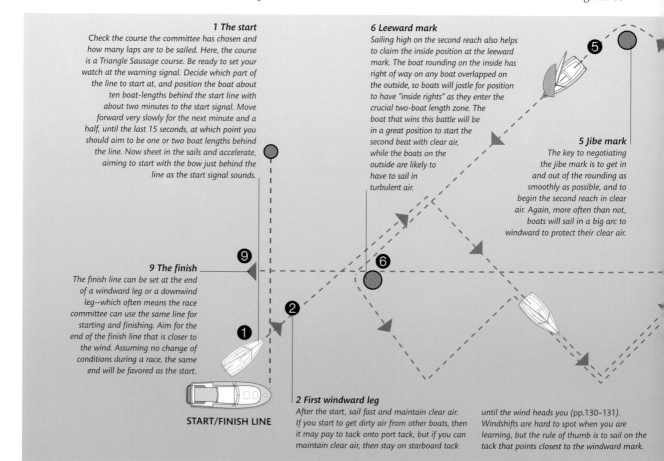

1 The start
Check the course the committee has chosen and how many laps are to be sailed. Here, the course is a Triangle Sausage course. Be ready to set your watch at the warning signal. Decide which part of the line to start at, and position the boat about ten boat-lengths behind the start line with about two minutes to the start signal. Move forward very slowly for the next minute and a half, until the last 15 seconds, at which point you should aim to be one or two boat lengths behind the line. Now sheet in the sails and accelerate, aiming to start with the bow just behind the line as the start signal sounds.

6 Leeward mark
Sailing high on the second reach also helps to claim the inside position at the leeward mark. The boat rounding on the inside has right of way on any boat overlapped on the outside, so boats will jostle for position to have "inside rights" as they enter the crucial two-boat length zone. The boat that wins this battle will be in a great position to start the second beat with clear air, while the boats on the outside are likely to have to sail in turbulent air.

5 Jibe mark
The key to negotiating the jibe mark is to get in and out of the rounding as smoothly as possible, and to begin the second reach in clear air. Again, more often than not, boats will sail in a big arc to windward to protect their clear air.

9 The finish
The finish line can be set at the end of a windward leg or a downwind leg—which often means the race committee can use the same line for starting and finishing. Aim for the end of the finish line that is closer to the wind. Assuming no change of conditions during a race, the same end will be favored as the start.

START/FINISH LINE

2 First windward leg
After the start, sail fast and maintain clear air. If you start to get dirty air from other boats, then it may pay to tack onto port tack, but if you can maintain clear air, then stay on starboard tack until the wind heads you (pp.130–131). Windshifts are hard to spot when you are learning, but the rule of thumb is to sail on the tack that points closest to the windward mark.

the wind direction, the wind is nearly always shifting one way or the other. This means that one end of the line is likely to be closer to the wind than the other. It is called the favored end because a boat starting at this end has less distance to sail than a boat at the other end. A simple way to identify the favored end is to sail along the start line with the bow pointing toward one end of the line. Sheet the mainsail, with the traveler cleated on the centerline, so that it is set correctly for the course. Cleat the mainsheet and tack around to sail the opposite way along the line. Look at how the mainsail is setting now. If it is oversheeted and needs to be eased, then you are pointing away from the favored end. But if

it is flapping slightly and needs to be sheeted farther in, then you are pointing toward the favored end. Use this method two or three times to make sure you are clear about which end is favored. If you can't tell the difference between one tack and the other, it probably means the line has been set square to the wind and neither end is favored.

Choose where to start

To achieve a successful start, your aim should be to position your boat:
• just behind the line (but very close to it) at the starting signal
• traveling at full speed
• with space around you, especially close to leeward
• at the favored end of the line

The vast majority of boats cross the line on starboard tack, as this tack has right of way. It is possible sometimes to start on port tack, but it is a high-risk maneuver and is best left until you are more experienced.

Starting well and consistently requires a lot of practice, but by concentrating on these four priorities, in the order shown, you will make a reasonable start most of the time.

Although starting right at the favored end offers the most potential advantage, it is difficult to achieve in practice. Many boats will try for the ideal spot, but only one boat will make it. It is better to start just along the line from the favored end where it will be easier to find clear space and get a clean start.

8 The run
After the second windward leg and windward mark rounding, the race nears its conclusion with a run to the finish. One of the biggest priorities on the run is to find the bands of strongest wind. Wind strength often varies across the course. Windshifts are also important downwind, except that now you want to sail in the headed wind, rather than the lifts that you were looking for upwind. Remember the basic rule of taking the jibe that points you closer to the finish. All these considerations are even more important in asymmetric spinnaker boats, which sail large angles downwind. Remember also that the more separated you are from another boat, the bigger the relative gain or loss if the wind strength or direction changes.

4 The reach
There are many tactics that can be used on the reach, but one of the highest priorities is to keep clear wind. This is why many boats sail on a big arc to windward, to protect their wind from boats trying to overtake them. Normally, place-changing is quite limited on the reach, with superior boat speed or boat-handling being the main reasons for any place-changing.

3 The windward mark
The safest approach to the windward mark is on starboard tack, as coming in on port tack brings a risk of collision. Before you round the mark, look to see if any of the leading boats are flying spinnakers on the first reach, or if it is too close to the wind or too windy to fly a spinnaker safely. Assuming that it is possible to carry a spinnaker on the reach, bear away around the mark, and once you have space around you to hoist safely, set the spinnaker as quickly as possible.

7 Second windward leg
By the time you sail the second windward leg, the fleet will have spread out and there will be more room to choose your own course. Try to find clear lanes to sail, free of interference of other boats, and concentrate on sailing fast, heading to whichever side of the course you think is favored from earlier experience on the previous windward leg. If the wind is oscillating backward and forward around a mean direction, concentrate on always sailing on the lifted tack.

CRUISERSAILING

Many people who learn to sail in small boats eventually move on to larger ones, perhaps because of a desire to sail longer distances, cruise foreign shores, or even adopt the live-aboard lifestyle. It is useful to have learned basic skills in a small boat first, but there are many new skills that a cruiser sailor needs to master, and some people choose to start their sailing in a cruiser, which is a perfectly valid approach.

STARTING TO CRUISE

The best way to start cruising is to sail on a friend's boat or to find a skipper in need of crew. Try a few day-sails and at least one overnight or longer passage to help you decide if you like cruising. If you do, take a course in skippering skills, boat-handling, or navigation at a sailing school. If you are used to sailing a dinghy, you will need to learn to handle a larger and heavier boat, and how to function well as part of a team. It is not necessary (or advisable) to buy a boat before you start cruising.

What is a cruiser?

A cruiser need not be especially big—some, indeed, are little more than large dinghies, although they have a cabin to accommodate the crew. Most have some form of weighted keel, although cruising catamarans do not use keels but rely on their large beam for stability. All cruisers obey the basic rules of aerodynamics and hydrodynamics that affect all sailing boats. There are, however, major differences between various types, in the way they behave under sail and power and in the manner in which their rigs, sails, and equipment are arranged and handled by the crew.

There is a significant difference in handling and performance between a general-purpose dinghy and a high-performance one, but the differences between types of cruisers are even more notable. This is why there is no substitute for on-the-water experience, and why you should try to sail as many different types of cruisers as possible before deciding on the one that will best suit you.

Passage-making

Skippering a boat on passage requires a wide range of skills. Boat-handling skills are needed to get the boat into and out of harbor and to ensure a fast and comfortable passage. Pilotage and navigation skills take the boat safely and efficiently between ports, and boat-management skills ensure that the boat and its gear are kept in good order. Finally, crew-management skills ensure that yours is a happy ship with a well-rested, well-fed, and highly motivated crew performing at their optimum. A good skipper has all these skills at his disposal and, most importantly, understands that their relative importance changes at different times in each passage.

Cruising lessons

Sailing has up until now avoided excessive bureaucracy, but there is a growing trend toward regulation: some countries require skippers to hold recognized certificates. You should check with your national authority to see which rules apply.

If you aspire to own your own cruiser or sail long passages aboard other people's boats, you can (and should) extend your knowledge in a number of ways. Take a sailing

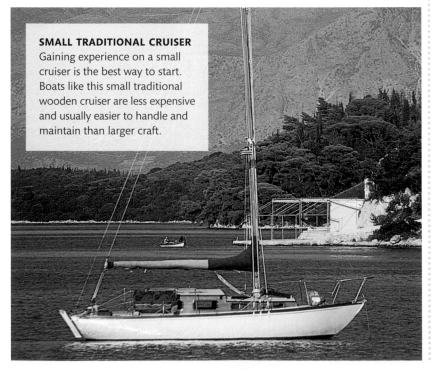

SMALL TRADITIONAL CRUISER
Gaining experience on a small cruiser is the best way to start. Boats like this small traditional wooden cruiser are less expensive and usually easier to handle and maintain than larger craft.

course at a school recognized by your national authority, and read as much and as widely as possible on the subject. Once again, and most importantly, it is advisable to get as much sea-time as you can aboard as wide a range of boats as possible in different waters and conditions.

Dedicated theory courses at a local night school or college are usually very good, but there is no substitute for hands-on experience, and that can only be obtained by time on a cruiser at sea.

Teamwork

More and more people are now learning to sail in cruisers, rather than starting in dinghies as was the traditional route. This is not ideal, as the basic sailing skills are easier, and safer, to learn aboard a small boat. The average size of cruisers is also increasing, and a growing number of people buying their first cruiser choose a boat of about 35 ft (11 m).

Few of these boats are designed to be sailed single-handed; many need a crew of three or more to sail them efficiently without tiring the crew. Cruiser sailing, therefore, requires more of a team effort than dinghy sailing. It also involves living, eating, and sleeping in cramped quarters with several people for extended periods; the ability to get along with others is crucial. Whereas it is easy to put up with someone's annoying habits when you do not have to see them all the time, trivial things can cause arguments and friction aboard a small boat. A good skipper will be aware of this danger and will attempt to put together a compatible crew, but it is up to each crew member to show tolerance in order to preserve harmony aboard.

BOAT HANDLING

Handling a cruiser requires much greater care than a dinghy because of its larger size and, importantly, its much greater weight. Cruisers also require both skipper and crew to acquire a range of skills that can only be learned on the job.

Cruiser size

If you make a mistake coming alongside in a dinghy, a collision can usually be prevented by use of a well-placed foot. Even if a collision occurs, the damage is unlikely to be serious. However, a cruiser's extra weight and momentum make close-quarter maneuvering far more difficult and mistakes much more expensive. Another significant difference between a dinghy and a cruiser is the weight of the gear and the load on the sails and sheets. Although it is easy to hold a dinghy's jib sheet in your hands or hoist a sail by hand, a cruiser's sheets and halyards require the use of winches and can impose considerable loads. Learning how to handle ropes and sails under load is an important part

of cruiser sailing: correct techniques are essential to avoid injury to yourself or others and to prevent damage to gear.

New skills

The dinghy sailor, who is used to lightweight gear, has to become accustomed to handling much larger and heavier sails and ropes. The correct, and safe, way to use winches must be learned (p.228), and a sailor new to cruisers must understand the potential danger of more highly loaded gear. New seamanship skills must be acquired to enable the sailor to sail, berth, and moor the yacht safely, and essential navigation skills need to be learned to allow comfortable and safe offshore passages.

Smaller cruisers

It is not necessary to have a large boat to go on long-distance voyages. Although larger boats are increasingly popular, the average-size cruiser sailing the world's oceans is still only about 35 ft (11 m), and many considerably smaller boats have taken their crews around the world. Most long-term voyagers cruise with just two people on board, sometimes with their children or an additional crew member. This means that they are sailing short-handed most of the time, so a smaller boat has advantages in terms of easier boat-handling and in the lower cost of ownership. Cruising with a simpler and cheaper boat also means that you can head off sooner than if you were to wait until you could afford your dream boat.

Buying a cruiser

If you do decide to invest in your own cruiser, it is in your own best interest to keep the boat as simple as possible. Keeping the boat simple reduces costs, makes the boat easier to sail, and lessens the likelihood of equipment failure ruining a cruise.

Bargains can often be obtained by purchasing a second-hand cruiser, especially one that has a good inventory of the equipment you want on board. When buying a used boat, however, always have it surveyed to be sure that there are no hidden defects and that the sale price is not excessive. Look for second-hand boats in sailing magazines and by talking to brokers, who will also be able to give you useful advice on financing and surveys.

CHOOSING A CRUISER

All cruising boats are a compromise—most commonly between cost, performance, and comfort. You need to be realistic in your ambitions, and your budget, when you set out to choose a cruiser. Even a small cruiser represents a considerable investment, both in purchase price and in maintenance and running costs. Before you buy, decide what kind of cruising or cruiser-racing you want to do, and the areas in which you plan to sail. Get some experience in different boats before you buy.

Cruising

Many people dream of long-term voyaging, but relatively few of us leave our onshore responsibilities and escape to sea full-time. If you are one of the lucky ones who are free to sail away, you have a wide choice of boats that can take you on long voyages for months at a time.

Be realistic about your onshore commitments, however. The reality for most of us is that career and family ties prevent us from achieving more than a few weeks' cruising every year, interspersed with weekend cruising or racing. This type of cruising does not require an ocean cruiser equipped with every conceivable luxury.

You must also consider how many people will be on board most of the time. Many cruising boats sail with a crew of only two or three, so you do not need a particularly large boat to enjoy good cruising.

At least when you start cruising, try to keep things as simple as possible: a small boat equipped with only the basic gear will be less expensive to buy and maintain. It will be much cheaper in mooring and insurance costs, and easier to handle, yet it will deliver just as much pleasure as a larger, more

complex yacht. The very simplicity of the yacht means that you are likely to spend more time sailing.

Sailing area

The most practical type of cruiser for you will be determined by the area and conditions in which you will do most of your sailing. If you plan to sail in shallow waters, consider the option of a cruiser with bilge keels or a centerboard (*p.152*), for example. If you plan to undertake long offshore voyages, many standard production cruisers are quite adequate with a little modification. Unless you are

very experienced, you would be wise to select a well-built production boat from a reputable builder, rather than having a boat built from scratch.

Racing

Some people enjoy mixing cruising with club or regatta racing. If you want to race, look at the types of boats that are raced at clubs in your sailing area. A few cruiser-racers race in one-design fleets but club races for cruisers are usually sailed under a handicap system so you might want to consider a boat's rating when buying.

You will need to have more crew on board for racing than for cruising, so ensure that the boat has safety gear for everyone on board. Racing will add to the costs of equipping and maintaining the boat.

A good cruiser-racer is also often well-suited to leisure cruising, allowing you to mix the excitement of racing with the relaxation of some longer cruising passages. When cruising, use smaller sails than you would if you were racing.

TRY BEFORE YOU BUY

Many people dream of sailing away on ocean voyages and save for years to buy their "ideal" boat, only to discover that that type of boat is not for them. It is a costly mistake that is easy to avoid.

Gaining experience

Before buying your own cruiser, get as much experience as possible of the type of cruising that you hope to do. Sail aboard as many different boats as you can, on both short and long passages. When you decide on your ideal boat, arrange a substantial sail in it in order to assess how it handles under power and sail. If you are uncertain, ask an experienced sailor to advise you.

Chartering and time-sharing

It is not always necessary to buy your own boat to enjoy cruising. You could crew on other people's boats to gain experience, or charter different boats to compare them. Chartering is a low-cost way of building cruising experience. It also gives you the opportunity to sail in exotic cruising areas. Time-sharing a cruiser is also an option that is becoming increasingly popular.

TYPES OF CRUISER

The term "cruiser" covers a vast range of boats, from the smallest trailer-sailers to the dedicated long-distance cruiser that is capable of taking its crew safely across oceans. Some are designed to mix leisure cruising and racing. They can offer a level of performance that was unknown a few years ago, even from dedicated racing boats. The range of cruisers available includes older, traditional-design sailing boats, built a century or more ago and still going strong; one-of-a kind designs built in wood, fiberglass, steel, aluminum, or even ferro-cement; and a huge number of production boats and family cruisers.

TRADITIONAL CRUISERS

TRADITIONAL YAWL

The term "traditional cruiser" usually means that the yacht is of a heavy-displacement type. It could be gaff or Bermudan rigged, and will have a long keel. An older boat will be wooden, whereas more recent types may be built of fiberglass or steel. Older designs are typically narrower, and often deeper, than modern cruisers.

TRAILER-SAILERS

26-FT (8-M) CRUISER

Trailer-sailers offer the advantage of being small enough to move by road on a dedicated road trailer. This opens up new cruising areas without the need to sail the boat on long passages to get there. Most trailer-sailers have a lifting centerboard or daggerboard, usually weighted for stability, to allow them to fit on the trailer.

PRODUCTION CRUISERS

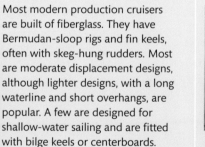

40-FT (12-M) CRUISER

Most modern production cruisers are built of fiberglass. They have Bermudan-sloop rigs and fin keels, often with skeg-hung rudders. Most are moderate displacement designs, although lighter designs, with a long waterline and short overhangs, are popular. A few are designed for shallow-water sailing and are fitted with bilge keels or centerboards.

LONG-DISTANCE CRUISERS

STEEL CRUISER

For sailors looking for a long-distance, live-aboard cruiser, there is limited choice, as most production yachts are not designed or built for this role. This steel, gaff-rigged Wylo 11 epitomizes an ideal, simple, and reliable go-anywhere voyaging yacht. It provides generous accommodation and has larger hatches than most cruisers of its size.

CRUISER-RACERS

CRUISER-RACER

A modern cruiser-racer combines fast, efficient cruising with good maneuverability and speed suitable for racing. These designs are much lighter than a pure cruising yacht. They have efficient Bermudan-sloop rigs, and are likely to have shorter overhangs, larger rigs, and more efficient keels and rudders than cruisers.

MULTIHULLS

CATAMARAN

Most cruising multihulls are catamarans rather than the trimaran configuration, which is more popular for racing. Multihulls offer speed (provided they are kept light), the ability to dry out easily, and upright sailing. Catamarans also have a lot of space on deck and in the accommodation down below.

CRUISER DESIGN

With the development of large, production-line boat-builders, many yachts today look very similar. A typical modern cruiser has a Bermudan rig and a fin keel, usually with a freestanding rudder (called a spade rudder) or a rudder that is mounted on a skeg. This configuration originated with racing yachts, and it is highly efficient, especially upwind. For cruising, however, it is not necessary to stick with this conventional approach. Many other rig and keel configurations are available.

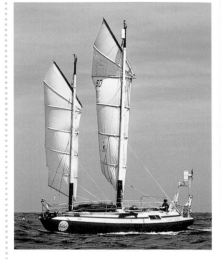

JUNK SCHOONER
The ubiquitous Bermudan sloop rig is not the best rig for long-distance cruising. The junk rig makes it simple to hoist, trim, reef, or lower the sails.

Making a choice

Nothing is guaranteed to excite passions as much as a discussion among cruising sailors of the relative merits of the various design types. Proponents of traditional design maintain that only a long keel (*p.197*) is a suitable choice for an offshore cruiser, and some argue that this should be combined with a gaff rig (*p.199*) for best results. The fact is that traditional cruising yachts were developed to suit the materials their builders had available. New materials and construction techniques offer other design and building methods that traditional builders would surely have used had they been available. Before you can realistically assess the merits or otherwise of different types of cruising boat, it is necessary to get as much cruising experience as possible, preferably in a wide range of boat types. Key to assessing the merits of the various options is a clear understanding of the type of cruising you plan to do.

Hull shape

Traditional, wooden cruising yachts invariably had a long keel that was an integral part of the hull structure. Today, most hulls have a canoe-type body to which a separate keel is bolted (*opposite*). Hulls have gotten wider, lighter, and shallower underwater but with higher topsides, and there has been a move away from elegant overhangs at bow and stern to short overhangs, with near-vertical bows and reverse-angle sterns becoming fashionable.

Bow and stern shapes

The traditional and elegant spoon and raked bow shapes are still common, but vertical or near-vertical bows are also seen, following their use on racing yachts to maximize the speed-producing waterline length. At the stern, many production cruisers are now produced with scoop sterns to give a bathing and boarding area. Traditional stern shapes, such as transom, counter, and canoe sterns, are still used on some new cruisers but are more likely to be found on older yachts that date from an era when there was more variety in yacht design.

RAKED BOW

VERTICAL BOW

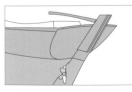

FLAT-TRANSOMED STERN

SCOOP STERN

CANOE STERN

COUNTER STERN

TYPES OF KEELS

Keels and rudders

Keel and rudder design has evolved over the years as new materials have provided greater strength and stiffness. Traditional yachts developed from working boats and used long keels that were an integral part of the structure. Most modern yachts are now built with variations on the fin keel, although a number of other keel types are also available.

Whatever its type, a conventional keel has two purposes: to resist leeway (*pp.32–33*) and to provide stability (*pp.200–201*). Similarly, a conventional rudder fulfills two roles—it provides the steering control and helps the keel resist leeway. Recently, race yacht design has separated the conventional keel's functions by developing the concept of a canting keel—which provides stability—and twin foils—which provide the steering and resistance to leeway function.

Stability, leeway, and draft

A weighted keel provides most of a yacht's stability (the rest is provided by form stability, which depends on the beam and shape of the hull). The keel's effectiveness depends on its weight, its center of gravity, and its depth. The lower its center of gravity, the greater the stability it provides.

Modern materials allow racing yacht designers to create very deep, narrow fin keels that carry their weight in a torpedo-like bulb at the bottom of the keels. A racing keel's efficiency at resisting leeway is high because it is very deep, even though it is narrow—known as having a high aspect-ratio. It has very little wetted surface drag, so it is a fast design. Rudders on racing yachts are also very deep yet narrow for racing efficiency. However, these developments are poor solutions for a cruising yacht, as they are expensive, vulnerable to damage, and require expert steering. Also, a very deep keel denies the yacht access to shallow water areas.

The latest racing developments separate the stability and leeway-resisting functions by using a strutlike keel that cants from side to side to provide a massive righting force, while a daggerboard and a rudder resist leeway and provide steering. A refinement has fore and aft steerable foils—both resist leeway and provide steering control, so you can steer the bow and the stern.

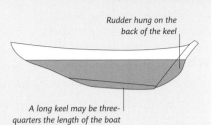

Rudder hung on the back of the keel

A long keel may be three-quarters the length of the boat

LONG KEEL
A traditional long keel adds strength to a wooden hull. It runs for up to three-quarters the length of the vessel. The rudder is often hung on the back of the keel.

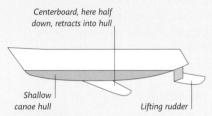

Centerboard, here half down, retracts into hull

Shallow canoe hull

Lifting rudder

CENTERBOARD
A centerboard and lifting rudder allow a yacht to float in very shallow water. It requires a centerboard case and adds complexity, but can be a good solution.

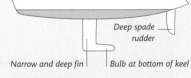

Bilge keels project from each side

Rudder supported by a full skeg

BILGE KEELS
Twin keels, known as bilge keels, allow a yacht to sit upright when dried out. They are less efficient than a fin keel but are simpler than a centerboard arrangement.

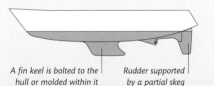

A fin keel is bolted to the hull or molded within it

Rudder supported by a partial skeg

CRUISING FIN KEEL
A cruising fin keel is usually fairly wide for strength and simplicity. Some are quite short but have a heavy bulb at the bottom to minimize draft for shallow water cruising.

Deep spade rudder

Narrow and deep fin

Bulb at bottom of keel

RACING FIN KEEL
Racing yachts use very deep and narrow fin keels with heavy bulbs at the bottom for maximum efficiency, but they are not a good solution for most cruising yachts.

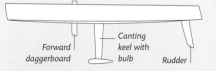

Forward daggerboard

Canting keel with bulb

Rudder

CANTING KEEL
The canting keel has a heavy bulb at the end of a thin keel that can be canted from side to side to maximize righting moment.

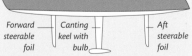

Forward steerable foil

Canting keel with bulb

Aft steerable foil

CANTING KEEL PLUS TWIN FOILS
Two steerable foils give leeway resistance and steering control while the thin, strutlike canting keel provides the stability.

Cruiser attributes

The attributes you require in a cruising yacht depend on both your personal preferences and the type of cruising you intend to do. If you expect to do mainly weekend cruising with the occasional week or two-week cruising vacation, you will be well served by many production cruisers that are optimized for day sailing with nights spent in a marina berth, with the ability to undertake the occasional offshore passage.

If, however, your plans include some serious offshore cruising, with passages lasting a number of days, or perhaps an ocean crossing, you will have to look for different attributes. Comfort at sea becomes much more important, along with characteristics such as being easily steered by hand or autopilot, comfortable motion in a seaway, stable and dry, with well-laid-out deck gear, and a safe and secure cockpit. Speed is much less important to the offshore cruiser than comfort and security. Although a fast cruiser gives you more options when passage-making, and can help you escape from bad weather, comfort and safety are much more important for a long-term, live-aboard cruiser. Also important is a simple boat that does not require a lot of specialist and expensive maintenance.

If you can afford a larger cruiser, over about 50 ft (15 m), then it is possible to find safe, comfortable cruiser designs that are also capable of fast offshore passages, but they will be significantly more expensive than smaller or slower cruisers.

Monohull or multihull

One debate that will never end regards the relative merits of monohull and multihull configurations for a cruising yacht. Monohull adherents point out that a multihull (a trimaran or catamaran) can capsize in very rough weather, whereas a monohull will usually right itself if it capsizes (*pp.200–201*). They say that the additional speed of a multihull is only appropriate for coastal cruising as the extra weight of stores and equipment needed when offshore cruising means that a multihull is overloaded and cannot achieve the speed which is its main selling point. Multihull proponents respond that even if a multihull capsizes, it will not sink, unlike a monohull with a weighted keel, which will sink if its hull or deck is breached by the sea. They also point out the extra comfort of sailing upright rather at an angle of heel, and the safety benefits of having the speed to make fast passages and escape bad weather systems. The debate will rage forever, but it is worth trying both types, perhaps on chartered vacation sails, to make up your mind.

Choice of rig

Almost as much as the multihull debate, the choice of rig also excites the passions of long-distance cruisers. Although the Bermudan sloop rig is almost universal on production cruisers, this has as much to do with ease of building and production economics as the particular merits of the rig for long-distance cruising. Again, it is worth trying to get some experience sailing with different rigs if possible. The gaff rig has some benefits for offshore cruising, as does the junk rig, and even if you prefer to stick with the Bermudan mainsail, a cutter is more appropriate for offshore sailing than the standard sloop configuration (*opposite*).

CRUISING CATAMARAN
Catamarans offer considerable room above deck and below, the ability to dry out easily, and sailing without heeling. Cruising catamarans can be faster than monohull cruisers, but only if they are kept light and not overloaded.

TYPES OF RIGS

A rig is categorized by its mainsail type and the number of masts and headsails (jibs) carried. Early yachts often had two masts and a gaff rig, as this was the easiest way to handle heavy sails. Improvements in sail materials and rig engineering have made single masts with Bermudan sails today's most popular rig.

Sloop

The sloop is the most common and simplest rig. It has one mast, one mainsail (either gaff or Bermudan), and one headsail. A Bermudan sloop can be described as masthead or fractional. A masthead sloop has a larger headsail with the forestay attached at the top of the mast. A fractional sloop has a smaller headsail set on a forestay fixed to the mast some way down from the top. Fractional sloops allow the mast to be bent for sail control. Most dinghies are fractional sloops, but many cruisers are masthead sloops.

Cutter

The cutter rig remains quite popular, especially for long-distance cruisers. It has one mast but carries two headsails, each on their own stay. This reduces the size of each headsail and makes them easier to handle. A cutter can have either a gaff or a Bermudan mainsail.

Two-masted boats

Boats with more than one mast are not common today, but ketch or yawl rigs can be found on older boats more than 35 ft (11 m) long. In both the ketch and the yawl, a mizzen mast is stepped some way aft of the main mast. The ketch has a larger mizzen mast (stepped farther forward) than the yawl. The schooner is another two-masted yacht. Its taller main mast is stepped aft, with a smaller foremast ahead of it.

Una rig

In the una, or cat, rig, the mast is stepped forward and is usually unstayed. The mainsail is often rigged with a sleeve around the mast. There is no headsail. On larger boats there may be two masts, in a schooner or ketch arrangement.

BERMUDAN MAINSAIL

A Bermudan mainsail has three sides. It is by far the most common mainsail on modern boats of all sizes.

Head — Leech — Luff — Tack — Clew — Foot

GAFF MAINSAIL

A ggaff mainsail has four sides. It is set on a comparatively short mast, with a boom at its foot and another spar (the gaff) along its head.

Peak — Head — Throat — Luff — Leech — Tack — Clew — Foot

BERMUDAN SLOOP

The Bermudan sloop has a triangular mainsail and a single headsail. A masthead sloop has the forestay attached at the top of the mast, as here.

Headsail — Mainsail

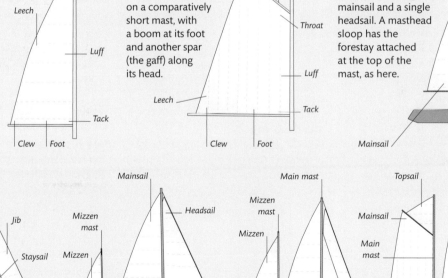

BERMUDAN CUTTER

Cutters have two or more headsails, each set on its own stay. The inner headsail is called the staysail, the outer is the jib.

Mainsail — Jib — Staysail

BERMUDAN YAWL

The yawl rig is characterized by a small mizzen mast stepped aft of the rudder post. It may have any number of headsails.

Mainsail — Mizzen mast — Headsail — Mizzen

BERMUDAN KETCH

On a ketch rig, the mizzen is stepped aft of the main mast but ahead of the rudder post. It may have one or more headsails.

Main mast — Mizzen mast — Mizzen — Main mast

GAFF SCHOONER

On a schooner, the main mast is stepped behind the shorter foremast. A gaff schooner has a gaff-rigged mainsail, as here.

Topsail — Foresail — Foremast — Mainsail — Headsail — Main mast

STABILITY

Few things are more disastrous for a yacht than for it to suffer a knockdown, turn turtle, and remain floating upside down. Among other tragedies, the disasters of the 1979 Fastnet Race and the 1998 Sydney–Hobart Race have put considerable pressure on regulatory bodies to agree appropriate international standards for boat stability, and on designers and manufacturers to design and build boats that stay upright in the conditions for which they are designed.

As the boat heels farther, the righting moment rises to maximum before decreasing again as the center of buoyancy moves back toward the center of gravity. Eventually a point is reached where the center of gravity and the center of buoyancy are again vertically aligned. This angle of heel is known as the Angle of Vanishing Stability (AVS), but is sometimes also called the Limit of Positive Stability. This is the last point at which the boat can right itself. If it heels any

Weight and buoyancy

When a boat is upright its center of gravity, the point at which all its weight can be considered to act, is vertical, above its center of buoyancy. When the boat is at rest, such as on a mooring or in a marina berth, the opposing effects of its weight and buoyancy are in equilibrium and determine how high the boat sits in the water.

As the boat heels, its center of gravity remains in the same spot, but the center of buoyancy, acting at the center of the submerged area, moves as the underwater shape changes due to the boat's heel angle. Now the forces of weight pushing down, and buoyancy pushing up, are no longer vertically aligned. The two forces combine to create a rotational moment (turning force), which works to try to return the boat to an upright position.

The righting moment

The rotational or righting moment (RM) is calculated as the overall boat weight multiplied by the distance between the centers of gravity and buoyancy. When upright, the righting moment is zero, but when the boat heels the center of buoyancy moves away from the center of gravity and the righting moment rises.

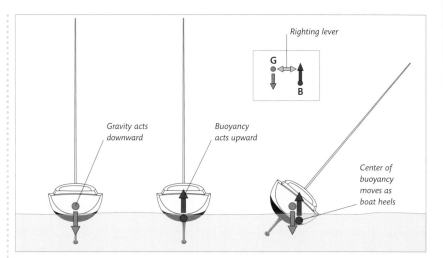

Righting lever

Gravity acts downward

Buoyancy acts upward

Center of buoyancy moves as boat heels

RIGHTING FORCES
When a boat heels, the center of buoyancy moves away from the centerline as the underwater shape changes, forming a righting moment with the center of gravity that is proportional to the distance (righting lever) between them.

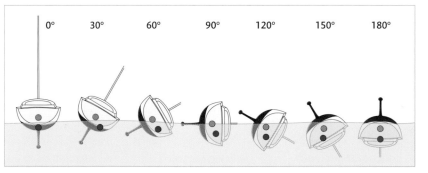

0° 30° 60° 90° 120° 150° 180°

STABILITY AND HEEL ANGLE
The righting moment increases until it reaches a maximum at some angle of heel, here at 60°, and then decreases as the center of buoyancy moves back in line with the center of gravity, here at 120°. Beyond this point, the righting moment is negative.

farther, then the righting moment will operate in the wrong direction, pulling the boat over until it is fully inverted. Finally, floating totally upside down, the righting moment becomes zero again and the boat may remain inverted if the AVS is low and there are no outside factors, such as wave impact, to help it right itself.

Angle of Vanishing Stability

If you purchase a new boat, the manufacturer should be able to provide you with a graph that plots the righting moment against the angle of heel (below). If a manufacturer is reluctant to provide such a graph, be cautious—the boat's stability may be lower than you require.

When the righting moment is plotted in graphical form against angle of heel, the resulting graph can tell you a lot about how the boat will react. When the slope of the graph is steep, the righting moment is in command and it is more difficult for the boat to heel. Where the graph's curve is shallow, the boat will heel more easily. The point on the graph at which the curve cuts the horizontal axis represents the Angle of Vanishing Stability. The greater this angle, the more effort is required to invert

the boat and the more likely it is to come back upright if it should suffer a knockdown.

Modern cruising yachts are light and designed for good accommodation below. This results in a broad beam, helping make them more resistant to heeling, initially, than narrower boats, but it can also reduce the AVS and make them more stable in the fully inverted position. Many cruising yachts are designed with a minimum draft to allow easy access to shallow areas. Combined, broad beam and shallow draft reduce a boat's AVS, making it more vulnerable to a knockdown or total inversion than narrower, heavier, and deeper drafted designs.

Practical considerations

You can help to keep your yacht's stability as high as possible by avoiding fitting heavy equipment high up. Fitting a radar scanner on the mast, or an in-mast or jib furling system, will raise the center of gravity and reduce stability. Keep this in mind when stowing items of gear on deck.

Once at sea, remember that boats are most vulnerable to capsize through wave action rather than the effects of wind. The worst case for

BREAKING WAVES
Even quite a small breaking wave can cause a knockdown if it catches a boat beam on. The power of the wave may be enough to roll the boat.

any boat is when caught side-on by a breaking wave. Once a wave starts to break, the energy released can capsize a yacht caught side-on by the breaking top.

You may encounter breaking waves in tide rips or overfalls even in moderate conditions, so try to avoid these areas, which are often marked on charts. In rough seas, avoid being caught side-on by a breaking wave by turning into or away from breakers. A breaking wave, no higher than your boat's beam, could have enough energy to cause a knockdown.

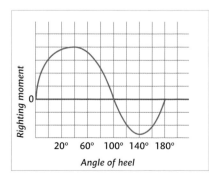

STABILITY CURVE
A manufacturer should be able to provide a stability curve for each model that shows the Angle of Vanishing Stability.

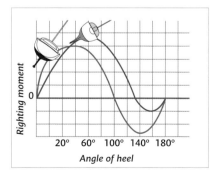

DIFFERENT DESIGN TYPES
Modern light, wide, and shallow draft boats often have less ultimate stability than many older designs.

REDUCING STABILITY
Any heavy equipment on or above deck will reduce stability. The higher the equipment, the greater the effect.

RIGGING AND SAILS

The Bermudan-sloop rig as easily identifiable characteristics— a single mast with triangular headsail and mainsail. This configuration is by far the most common for large-scale production boat-building. However there are a number of variations on this arrangement designed in accordance with the boat's intended purpose and level of performance. The number of sails used on a modern sloop rig is relatively limited, but all have a mainsail and one or more headsails. The mast, usually made of aluminum, is supported by an arrangement of wires, called the standing rigging.

RIGGING

Rigging falls into two categories: standing rigging and running rigging. Standing rigging supports the mast, holds it upright and controls its bending characteristics, and transfers the loads from the sails into the hull. Standing rigging is tightened when the mast is stepped in the boat, and adjusted on the first few sails as the rig is tuned, but is then usually locked in place so it cannot work loose. Running rigging comprises the ropes and wires that are used to hoist and adjust sails or make adjustments to the rig. Running rigging may be made of rope or wire, depending on the job it has to perform.

Standing rigging

Most types of cruiser masts are held firmly upright by standing rigging that supports the mast on its four sides. A forestay, attached at the masthead or lower down, at the hounds, prevents the mast from falling backward and a backstay

Masthead instruments
The masthead houses a range of instruments, usually comprising wind-speed and direction sensors, a VHF radio aerial, and a tricolor navigation light

Forestay
The forestay runs from the bow-fitting to the masthead and supports the mast fore and aft together with the backstay

Cap shrouds
The main sideways supports for the mast, the two cap shrouds run on either side from the chainplate, over the spreader end, to the masthead

Spreaders
These widen the angle of the cap shroud to the mast and help to support the mast

Topping lift
The topping lift runs from the boom end up to the masthead, then down to deck level, where it is adjusted. It supports the boom when the mainsail is lowered but is left slack when the sail is hoisted

Boom vang
Used to prevent the boom from rising due to wind pressure in the mainsail, the boom vang can be a rope tackle or an adjustable, rigid strut that also supports the boom

Boom
Attached to the mast by the gooseneck fitting, the boom supports the mainsail's foot

Mainsheet
This sheet controls the angle of the mainsail

Lower shrouds
One or two lower shrouds support the lower mast

Halyards
Used to raise and lower sails, halyards are usually led inside the mast and emerge at deck level, where they are led aft to winches for adjustment

Bottlescrews
Fittings to adjust the tension in shrouds and forestay

Keel
The keel resists leeway and provides stability

Rudder

Propeller

keeps it from falling forward. Two main shrouds called the cap shrouds hold the mast sideways. They run from each sidedeck up to the masthead (or the hounds, depending on the design of the rig), passing over the ends of one or two sets of spreaders. On masthead rigs the spreaders are usually set at right angles to the mast, but on a fractional rig—where the forestay and cap shrouds terminate at a point below the masthead—the spreaders are often swept aft.

Spreaders hold the shrouds away from the mast and increase the angle of support between the shrouds and the mast. They also stiffen the mast in a sideways direction and allow the use of a thinner mast section. For this reason, racing boats may have three, four, or more pairs of spreaders, but most cruising boats have one or two. If two pairs of spreaders are used, a diagonal shroud (or intermediate shroud) is likely to be fitted, running from the end of the lower spreader to the mast near the root of the top spreader.

In addition to the cap shrouds, other, lower shrouds are likely to be fitted. A common arrangement is a pair of lower shrouds on each side, one running from forward of the mast up to a point near the lower spreader root, the other from aft of the mast to the same point. Sometimes a pair of aft lowers is fitted, but the forward lowers are replaced by a single forward lower that run from the centerline up to the mast near the aft lowers.

Most standing rigging on cruising boats is made of stranded stainless steel wire, although solid rod rigging is also encountered, and it is also possible to use high-performance rope thanks to its low-stretch and low-weight characteristics. Standing rigging is adjusted by terminal fittings called bottlescrews. These fit between the shroud and the chainplate attached to the hull and allow the wire to be tightened or loosened. Once each bottlescrew has been adjusted, when the rig is being tuned, it should be locked in place so that it cannot turn unintentionally and slacken the rigging while the boat is sailing.

Rigging variations

The standard masthead configuration provides a secure and balanced geometry to resist the loads imposed on the mast, but other configurations are used, including freestanding rigs that have no standing rigging.

Some cruisers are designed with a fractional sloop rig, in which the forestay does not run to the masthead but attaches some way down the mast. A fractional sloop rig is often used on performance-oriented cruisers or cruiser-racers, because it allows for the mast to be bent under sail to help flatten the mainsail in stronger winds. The headsail is also smaller and the mainsail larger on a fractional rig compared with a masthead rig, making it easier for a small crew to handle.

Larger boats may be cutter-rigged (p.199) with a smaller staysail between the headsail and the mast. This rig requires an inner forestay, onto which the staysail is hanked, balanced by an additional backstay. Often in pairs, these "running backstays" are adjustable so they can be stowed away from the boom and mainsail when not in use.

Running rigging

Ropes and wires that require constant or regular adjustment are known as running rigging. The most common types of running rigging are halyards and sheets. Most sheets on cruising boats are made from low-

FRACTIONAL RIG
A fractional rig, which typically has a larger mainsail and smaller headsail than a masthead rig, may be found on smaller cruisers, cruiser-racers, and multihulls.

stretch polyester rope, usually in braided form, while halyards may be made from rope or wire with a rope tail spliced into it. If made of rope, halyards can be made from polyester or, for better performance and much less stretch, from a high-performance, very-low-stretch fiber such as PBO. Like standing rigging, running rigging should be regularly inspected for wear and damage. Fraying can occur if a rope is regularly cleated, jammed, or winched in the same part of the rope. If possible, minimize local wear by moving the rope slightly to spread these loads. This may not be possible with halyards but can usually be achieved with sheets.

SAILS

Every cruiser requires a selection of sails, but their number and type will depend to some extent on the size and type of the cruiser, together with the kind of cruising it is intended for. At a minimum, it must have enough sails to keep the boat sailing efficiently in all conditions, including strong winds.

The standard production cruiser is rigged as a Bermudan sloop and has one mainsail that is reefed to suit the wind strength (*pp.246–249*). A Bermudan sloop also has either a selection of different-sized headsails to cope with a range of wind strengths, or a roller-furling system on the forestay to reduce the size of the headsail as the wind increases. The Bermudan sloop rig is not as efficient downwind as it is upwind, so many cruisers use a spinnaker or gennaker (sometimes called a cruising chute) to add sail area when sailing downwind in light to moderate winds.

Most mainsails and headsails are made from Dacron, although some large cruisers and cruiser-racers use cloth with Aramid fibers for its strength and weight advantages. Spinnakers and gennakers are made from lightweight nylon sailcloth.

Mainsail

The mainsail is the hardest-working sail on a cruising boat, as it has to cope with a wide range of wind strengths, from a flat calm to a full gale. It has to be strongly constructed, with ample reinforcement around its corners and other stress points, and be able to withstand wind loads, chafe, and damage from extensive exposure to sunlight. In some areas, weakening of the cloth due to ultraviolet light may be among the worst damage-inducing factors to

SAIL WARDROBE
A typical sail wardrobe for a Bermudan sloop not fitted with headsail roller furling has a selection of headsails, a mainsail, a spinnaker, a trysail, and a storm jib.

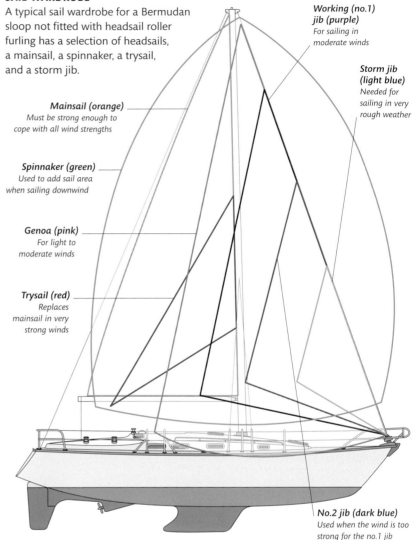

Mainsail (orange)
Must be strong enough to cope with all wind strengths

Spinnaker (green)
Used to add sail area when sailing downwind

Genoa (pink)
For light to moderate winds

Trysail (red)
Replaces mainsail in very strong winds

Working (no.1) jib (purple)
For sailing in moderate winds

Storm jib (light blue)
Needed for sailing in very rough weather

No.2 jib (dark blue)
Used when the wind is too strong for the no.1 jib

which the sail is exposed. Despite all the loads and wear and tear it must be able to withstand, the mainsail must not be too heavy or it will not set well in light winds and will be difficult for the crew to handle, stow, and hoist.

If the boat is equipped with a trysail, the mainsail will be furled on the boom in the worst conditions and replaced with the trysail, but in less extreme weather the mainsail will be reefed to suit the conditions.

Most mainsails on cruising boats have three reefs that allow you to reduce the sail's size in steps down to about one-third of its full size, although smaller boats may have only two rows of reefs fitted as standard.

Battens

Cruising mainsails are usually fitted with battens just like a dinghy's mainsail (*p.72*). Their purpose is the same; to support the roach—that part of the mainsail that extends beyond a straight line from clew to head. Modern cruisers often have mainsails with quite bit of roach, because it provides extra power, so effective battens are important to ensure that the sail sets properly.

Many cruising mainsails are fitted with full-length battens. These battens run from leech to luff and have the advantage of giving good control over sail shape. They also prevent the sail from flogging when the sheet is eased; instead, the sail lies quietly and less damage is done to the cloth than when a conventional sail flogs noisily in the wind. To use full-length battens effectively, however, does require a properly designed system with free-running sliders attaching the luff to the mast. Specially designed sliders with ball bearings handle the loads of a fully battened mainsail and make lowering and hoisting much easier.

Fully battened mainsails have the advantage of stacking neatly on the boom when lowered, much like a Venetian blind, but will only do so if a lazyjack system is fitted. Lazyjacks are light lines, on each side of the boom, that run from the boom up to the mast. Usually adjustable from the boom, the lazyjacks act as guides and hold the battens between them as the sail is hoisted and lowered.

Headsails

Roller-reefing headsail equipment is convenient, but the shape of a partly rolled headsail is rarely good enough to make an effective sail shape for sailing to windward. However, the gear is easy to use, convenient, and it is a simple and quick job to reduce sail area in strengthening winds.

Despite the convenience, many people prefer not to compromise performance, or risk those occasions when the equipment jams, and choose to sail with headsails attached to the forestay by hanks. With hanked-on headsails, the headsail is changed according to wind strength.

Headsails can be categorized as genoas or jibs: a genoa is a large headsail that overlaps the mast, while a jib is smaller, does not overlap the mast, and is usually cut with a higher clew and foot.

A typical cruiser that does not use a roller-reefing headsail will carry a selection of headsails, usually including a genoa for use in light winds, a working jib for moderate conditions, plus one or more other smaller jibs to use as the wind rises.

Every cruiser should carry a storm jib. This is much smaller than the others, and is made to cope with the strongest winds. If the normal headsail is set on a roller furler, the storm jib should have its own, removable stay that is attached to a strong deck fitting on the foredeck when it is needed for hoisting the storm jib.

FULLY BATTENED MAINSAIL
Full-length battens give more control over sail shape, help the sail stack easily on the boom, and make the sail quieter.

ABOVE DECK

The deck and cockpit areas are the parts of a cruiser where the practical business of sailing and boat-handling is conducted. Deck layouts vary, but most modern cruisers have fairly similar arrangements. Once you are familiar with one boat, you will find it quite easy to get used to another of a similar type. There are two main layouts: one has an aft cockpit, and the other has a center cockpit. The aft cockpit layout is the most common, especially in cruisers under about 40 ft (12 m).

Foredeck

The foredeck, ahead of the mast, is the most exposed working area on deck. Common procedures carried out near the bow include changing the headsail, anchoring, and picking up a mooring buoy. If fitted, a windlass, an electric winch principally used for raising the anchor, will be positioned on the foredeck. Great care should be taken when working on the foredeck as it is the area of the boat where the most motion is felt when sailing in waves, and it is easy to lose your footing.

Sidedecks

Aft of the mast, most small and medium-sized boats have a central cabin trunk raised above the level of the side decks and foredeck to give increased headroom below. In this arrangement, sidedecks run between the cabin trunk and the deck edge. Some larger boats are flush-decked, with no cabin trunk, giving wider decks that are easy to work on.

Some sidedecks on smaller boats are quite narrow, and care is needed when moving along them. Tracks for the jib-sheet fairleads usually run fore and aft along both sidedecks. The cap and lower shrouds terminate at

chainplates that are fitted either at the deck edge or inboard on the sidedeck. Jackstays should run along the length of both sidedecks: these are lengths of webbing or plastic-covered wire, to which the crew attach their harnesses when working on deck.

Coach roof

The coach roof is the top of the raised cabin trunk in the middle of the boat. The mast is either stepped on the coach roof or passes through it to be stepped on the keel. Halyards and other control lines emerging from the mast are often led aft across the roof to winches at its aft end. Hatches and ventilators are fitted to let light and air into the cabin. A life-raft or tender may also be stowed here. There should be handrails running the length of the roof on either side to provide a secure handhold for crew making their way along the sidedecks. The main hatch is positioned in the aft end of the coach roof, just in front of the cockpit.

Hatches and ventilation

All cruising yachts should have some form of ventilation in addition to the main companionway hatch and the fore hatch. Smaller hatches may be fitted in the coach roof, to

give light and ventilation, over the heads compartment, the galley, and saloon. Best of all are true ventilators that can be left open in rough conditions, when hatches must be shut.

CRUISER FITTINGS

A typical modern, fast offshore cruiser is designed to make quick passages that are also safe and comfortable. The boat is sturdily constructed with strong, well-fastened deck gear. It has a deep, comfortable cockpit for crew security, which is sheltered by a large spray hood to offer protection from the elements. There is a stern platform that gives the crew access to the tender.

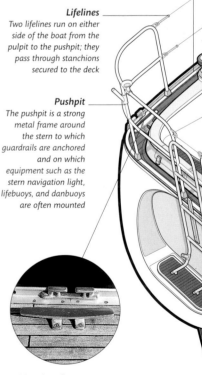

Toerail
An aluminum rail is often fitted to the edge of the deck to strengthen the hull-to-deck joint and to provide a restraining bar to stop feet from slipping off the deck

Lifelines
Two lifelines run on either side of the boat from the pulpit to the pushpit; they pass through stanchions secured to the deck

Pushpit
The pushpit is a strong metal frame around the stern to which guardrails are anchored and on which equipment such as the stern navigation light, lifebuoys, and danbuoys are often mounted

Mooring cleat
Warps are led through fairleads before being secured on the deck cleats

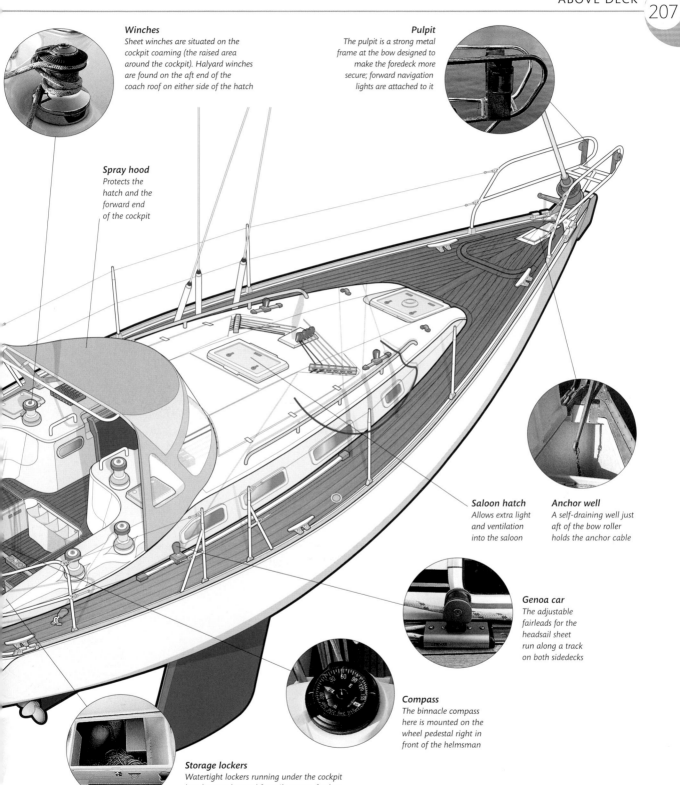

Winches
Sheet winches are situated on the cockpit coaming (the raised area around the cockpit). Halyard winches are found on the aft end of the coach roof on either side of the hatch

Pulpit
The pulpit is a strong metal frame at the bow designed to make the foredeck more secure; forward navigation lights are attached to it

Spray hood
Protects the hatch and the forward end of the cockpit

Saloon hatch
Allows extra light and ventilation into the saloon

Anchor well
A self-draining well just aft of the bow roller holds the anchor cable

Genoa car
The adjustable fairleads for the headsail sheet run along a track on both sidedecks

Compass
The binnacle compass here is mounted on the wheel pedestal right in front of the helmsman

Storage lockers
Watertight lockers running under the cockpit benches can be used for sails, warps, fenders, gas bottles, and other boat gear

Cockpit

The cockpit is the main working area of the boat, and the most secure place on deck. The boat is steered from the cockpit, by a wheel or a tiller, and it has become standard for most sail controls to be led to this area. Most importantly, the cockpit footwell should be self-draining, with large drains in the floor quickly shedding any water that finds its way aboard.

The cockpit is separated from the cabin by a raised area called a bridge deck, and by washboards (removable wooden partitions) that close the companionway, the entrance to the cabin. Many cruisers have a spray hood over the companionway to protect it and the forward part of the cockpit from spray and to provide shelter for the crew in rough conditions. Weather cloths, known as dodgers, can be laced along the lifelines for added protection.

The cockpit should be kept uncluttered and tidy. It is good practice to leave sheets and other ropes neatly coiled or flaked ready for quick use. Be cautious about sitting near the mainsheet traveler if it is sited in the cockpit. If the locking device or control line on the traveler were to slip or fail, the traveler and mainsheet block could crash across the boat, causing damage or injury if anyone is in its way.

Steering position

Steering is usually handled through a tiller on smaller boats and a wheel on larger ones. Wheels operate just like a car's steering wheel; rotate to the left and the boat turns to the left, or to port; rotate to the right and the boat turns to the right, or to starboard. A tiller works just as it does in a dinghy—it is pushed in the opposite direction of the way you wish the bow to move. Although

WHEEL STEERING
A wheel is usually mounted on a pedestal and is large enough to allow the helmsman to steer from the side, where he can see the jib luff. Instruments and engine controls are usually mounted on the pedestal.

a wheel may seem more natural to anyone used to driving a car, its arrangement is more complex and expensive than a tiller, gives less feedback from the rudder, and takes up more room in the cockpit.

If a wheel is used, it is usually fitted to a pedestal in the middle of the cockpit. The pedestal can also act as the boat's dashboard by housing the main steering compass and display screens for electronic performance and navigation instruments (*pp.328–331*). Alternatively, the compass and instruments may be mounted on a bulkhead or other convenient vertical surface near the helming position. This is usually the arrangement when tiller steering is used. Do not sit in the cockpit in a way that obscures the instruments from the helmsman, who may need to continuously monitor one of the instruments.

The engine throttle and gear shift will usually be located near the steering position, on the pedestal if a wheel is used, and on the side of the cockpit footwell or coaming if a tiller is used. Sometimes, the engine control panel with warning lights, tachometer, and other instruments is also situated close to the steering position. Alternatively, it may be fitted down below, where it is away from exposure to the elements or accidental damage.

Lockers

Most cruisers have one or more stowage lockers located under the cockpit seats. These are used for the stowage of items that are regularly needed on deck, including fenders, boathook, mooring warps, safety equipment, and sails. Gas bottles for the galley stove should be stored in a separate self-draining deck locker so that any leaking gas drains overboard rather than into the boat.

Locker lids should have strong and secure latches to lock them shut. They should also have a securing system to hold them when opened, otherwise they can easily crash shut, pinching fingers, if the boat heels or pitches.

Some cockpit lockers are very deep and equipment stored there can be hard to find. Keep lockers tidy and be consistent about where everything is stowed so you can find things easily.

Moving around on deck

The decks of most boats are cluttered with an array of hardware, all of it important to the functioning of the boat but also a potential trap for the unwary crewmember moving around on deck. If the decks were level and stable, there would be less of a problem, but a yacht at sea is constantly moving under the influences of wind and waves. Moving around on deck when the yacht is pitching and heeling is

hard enough, but there are also many obstacles to avoid. Stubbed toes are very common sailing injuries, and it is also easy to lose your footing by tripping on a piece of deck hardware. Remember that if you sail at night you will need to be able to move around the deck in the dark, so try to get accustomed to the deck layout of a new yacht before taking it to sea in rough conditions or at night.

Most modern boats have their halyards and control lines led back to the cockpit in order to minimize the amount that the crew has to go on deck to accomplish tasks. However, there are always some occasions when it is necessary to leave the cockpit, and then it is prudent to wear and use a safety harness in all but the most benign conditions.

All cruising boats should have jackstays rigged when going to sea. Made of webbing or plastic-covered wire, they should run from the cockpit,

along each sidedeck, to the foredeck. It should be possible for a crewmember to clip onto a jackstay while still in the cockpit and make his way to the bow without needing to unclip his safety harness.

Before going forward to handle a job, consider whether you need to wear waterproofs. Although it may be dry in the cockpit, the foredeck is much more exposed and it takes only one wave to come over the bow while you are working there to soak you. Always wear proper footwear, either deck shoes or sailing boots with nonslip soles.

If you will need tools or equipment, make sure you have everything with you, and confirm the instructions if you are unsure of your task, as it can be very difficult to communicate back and forth from foredeck to cockpit.

At all times be particularly attentive to the position and potential movement of the boom. If you are caught unawares, it could cause a nasty blow to the head and possibly knock you overboard. It is advisable to squat, keeping your center of gravity low, when moving around a boat, and always to move along the windward, uphill, side of the boat. This way, if you trip, you will fall into the boat, not over the leeward rail. Always keep one hand free for gripping a handrail or other secure fitting. The shrouds, designed to take heavy loads, may be used as handholds when moving forward, but do not grasp sheets or other running rigging that may be suddenly adjusted by the crew back in the cockpit. When you reach your work station, remember to think of your own safety as well as the job to be done. When you finish, make your way carefully back into the cockpit before unclipping from the jackstay.

MOVING ON DECK
If you need to move around on deck when under sail and well heeled, stay on the windward side if possible unless, as here, it is necessary to work on the leeward side.

DOWN BELOW

The accommodation in a cruiser is determined by its length, beam, and freeboard (height out of the water). In small cruisers under about 33 ft (10 m), there is little space for anything more than basic accommodation. In larger cruisers, there is room for more berths, greater privacy, and more luxury. Most cruiser interiors are based on an arrangement that has a separate forward cabin, a main saloon, a separate heads (toilet) compartment, a galley, and a chart table. Some also have one or two aft cabins.

SEA-GOING INTERIOR

A typical sea-going interior on a medium-sized offshore cruiser includes a good working area in the galley and at the chart table, a comfortable saloon, and a separate heads compartment. There are at least two secure sea berths.

Navigation instruments
The navigator has navigation instruments, VHF radio, and an electrical panel within easy reach of the chart table

Comfort in port

When looking at the internal layout of a cruiser, consider the type of sailing you plan to do. If you intend mostly to cruise by day and overnight on moorings or in marinas, then an accommodation layout optimized for comfortable use when upright rather than when sailing may be appropriate. You will have plenty of choice, as most production cruisers are designed with interiors that are more suitable for use in port than at sea.

Comfort at sea

Good seagoing interiors provide comfort and security by having lots of handholds, enough secure berths for the off-watch crew, and no sharp corners that can cause injury. The galley should be laid out for safe use when underway, the countertops should have good fiddles (rails) that are effective when the boat is heeled, and the navigation area should allow the navigator to be braced securely while working at the chart table.

The main working areas below are the galley and chart table. Both should be designed to be safe and secure for the cook and navigator when the boat is heeled and allow easy access to any equipment

needed. The galley should have deep single or double sinks to retain water when the boat is heeled, and there should be adequate counter space for preparing meals at sea. The stove should be hung in gimbals to allow it to swing and remain upright when the boat heels. A restraining bolt should secure the stove in a fixed position when it is not needed to swing with the boat's motion.

Hanging locker
Hanging storage space for clothes or waterproofs

Heads
The heads contains a toilet, sink, and shower

Aft cabin
The separate aft cabin has a double berth

Saloon table
A fixed table with folding leaves; it also has bottle storage in a built-in locker that is reached through a lid in the table top

Fire extinguisher
The saloon fire extinguisher is stowed out of sight but within easy reach in its own dedicated stowage space

Saloon berths
The forecabin contains two single berths or a double for use at sea

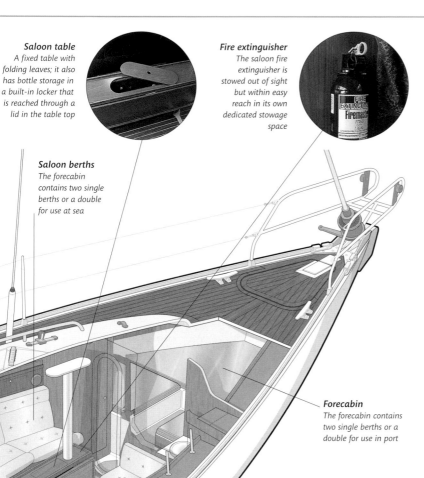

Forecabin
The forecabin contains two single berths or a double for use in port

Shelving
Shelf space in the forecabin, saloon, and working areas adds to the storage space

Fiddles
All horizontal surfaces should have high fiddles to stop items from sliding off at sea. Corner gaps between fiddles allow the galley counters to be cleaned

Galley
A good seagoing galley has a gimbaled stove, plenty of locker and drawer space for food and utensil stowage, and provides a secure and safe place for the cook to work

STOWAGE

Stowage space is always limited in small boats. It should be arranged so that each member of the crew has sufficient storage space for personal gear situated close to their bunk.

Stowing the gear

In a well-designed cruiser, there should be a variety of storage areas to cater to the enormous diversity of gear that finds its way aboard a cruising boat. There should be areas, often under bunks, suitable for bulky gear, and individual lockers and drawers for smaller items. All lockers should be closed with positive catches, to prevent their doors from bursting open when the boat heels. Dedicated stowage should be provided for items such as glasses and crockery, safety gear, and, where possible, waterproofs and boots. It is useful to prepare a stowage plan and write down where every item is stowed. Otherwise, it can be difficult to find an item in a hurry.

TIDY STORAGE
There is limited storage space on most cruisers. It is important, therefore, that crew members stow their own gear neatly and ensure that the boat is kept tidy; otherwise, it could deteriorate into an unpleasant mess in rough conditions.

Galley

The galley should be equipped with a small stove, usually fueled by bottled gas or, sometimes, kerosene. The stove is normally mounted on gimbals so that it remains upright when the boat heels, but it is possible to use a fixed stove fitted with high rails to keep cooking pans in place while in use. If gimbals are fitted, they should allow the stove to swing freely through as wide an arc as possible, and it should also be possible to lock the stove upright for use in port. Ideally, the stove should be placed where spillages will not land on the cook, but this is not always possible in a small boat. A restraining strap is useful for the cook to lean against when the boat is heeled, and there should be a crash bar in front of the stove to prevent the cook from being thrown onto the hot burners. For added protection, wear waterproofs when using the galley in rough weather.

The sink should be deep but narrow for use at sea. Twin sinks are useful if space is available. The fresh-water supply can be delivered by hand or by electric pump. However, the convenience of electrically

GALLEY
A galley that will be used at sea should have deep sinks situated near the boat's centerline and deep fiddles on the counter tops. A crash bar should be fitted in front of the stove to protect the cook.

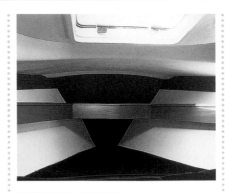

FORECABIN BERTHS
Forecabins on small yachts often have a V-shaped berth in the bows. These berths are not comfortable at sea but are used in port.

pumped water can lead to waste of a limited water supply. If an electric pump is fitted, there should be a manual back-up. Some yachts also have a hot-water supply to the galley and the heads compartment. A seawater faucet in the galley is useful for use away from land, when clean seawater can be used for washing dishes and cooking vegetables.

A small freezer or refrigerator may be fitted, though this is costly in terms of electrical generation, and there must be sufficient stowage for crockery, pans, and supplies within easy reach. Work space is often limited, but there should be enough room to prepare a meal without using the chart table.

A fire extinguisher and fire blanket must be easily accessible, as the galley represents a fire risk. If gas is used, the bottle should be stored in its own self-draining, gas-tight compartment. The supply should be turned off at the bottle when not being used. This can be done by hand or, more conveniently, by fitting a solenoid valve near the bottle, with its control switch in the galley. Make a habit of turning off the gas when you have finished cooking.

Berths

On a cruiser intended for offshore passages, there should be a sea berth available for every off-watch crew member. Berths for use at sea should be arranged so that they are parallel to the fore and aft line of the boat, and not too far toward the bow or stern, where the motion at sea will be worse than near the middle of the boat.

Canvas lee-cloths or solid wooden leeboards should be fitted to all sea berths. These ensure that you cannot roll or be thrown out of the berth in rough conditions. Lee-cloths are more comfortable to use than solid leeboards and can be easily removed and stowed under the mattress when not in use. Either type should be securely fastened, since they can be subjected to considerable loads.

Heads

The toilet compartment is often situated between the main saloon and the forecabin in a small compartment, although some boats have sufficient space for a heads sited near the companionway. The position

HEADS
Make sure you understand how to use the marine toilet, as incorrect usage can lead to a blockage. Good ventilation and regular cleaning will keep unpleasant odors to a minimum.

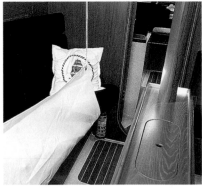

LEE-CLOTHS
To prevent yourself from falling out of your bunk when the boat heels, rig up a canvas lee-cloth or leeboard on the open side of the bunk to keep you secure.

SALOON
The saloon is the relaxation and entertainment center of the yacht. It should be comfortable, well lit and ventilated, and have secure handholds.

---

farther aft has the benefit of being situated conveniently for the cockpit and is in the area where the motion of the boat is felt least, making the heads more comfortable to use.

Most heads contain a marine toilet, a small sink, and lockers for personal items. Some also have a shower facility with hot and cold water. The heads can be a convenient spot for oilskin stowage if there is space for a hanging locker. The seacocks for the inlet and outlet pipes must be easily accessible and should be kept closed when the heads is not in use. This is essential if the toilet bowl is installed on or below the waterline; otherwise, flooding could occur.

Make sure that all crew and visitors understand how to operate the heads. Mistakes here can cause much misery, especially for the crew member (usually the skipper) who has to unblock or repair the toilet. Put instructions for use near the toilet.

Chart table
The chart table should be close to the companionway, so that the navigator can communicate easily with the cockpit crew. It should be a self-contained area out of the way of the main living spaces and the galley. All instruments and radio sets should be situated here, where they can be easily accessed. Most navigators prefer to sit at the chart table, usually facing forward. The chart table should be large enough to hold a chart folded no more than once, and there should be secure stowage for pencils, plotters, and other navigation equipment.

Charts are usually stored in the space under a lifting chart-table top, or in a drawer underneath. Space is also needed for reference books, many of which will be quite large. The main electrical switch panel is often mounted in this area. Avoid using the chart table as a general dumping area.

Saloon
The saloon, usually situated in the center of the cabin, is the area reserved for relaxing, eating, and entertaining. It is the largest interior space in the boat, and should have plenty of good handholds to make it easy to negotiate at sea when the boat is heeled. Handholds should be placed at various heights, so that they can be used when sitting or standing—by children or adults. The corners of all furniture should be rounded so that there are no sharp edges to injure people falling against them.

Good lighting and ventilation help make the interior more pleasant. Natural light is supplied by plenty of ports, windows, and hatches, all of which should be strong and well fastened. Ventilation should be provided by hatches, opening ports, and special ventilators that can be used at sea without letting in water.

PROTECTION AFLOAT

Having the right clothing and safety equipment is always important when you go afloat, but especially when you are cruising. The dinghy sailor can look forward to a hot shower at the end of a trip, but the cruising sailor may be at sea, sometimes in unpleasant conditions, for hours, days, or even weeks. In these circumstances, the only way to ensure your continuing comfort is to wear the right clothing. It is also essential to have proper safety gear, such as harnesses and life jackets, on board.

CRUISER CLOTHING

It is always cooler afloat than ashore, and, for those sailing in temperate areas, the key requirement is to stay warm. Cold reduces your ability to think and act efficiently and can also increase the risk of seasickness. When sailing in anything other than perfect conditions, it is vital to wear the right clothing in order to maintain a comfortable working temperature. On the other hand, a gentle breeze on a hot day can mask the sun's true power, so keep a good supply of sunblock on board, stowed in the cockpit.

To stay warm, your clothes should provide sufficient insulation, with a barrier layer to stop the warm layer from getting wet and eliminate wind chill. Silk and wool are the best natural insulators, but modern synthetic fibers are the usual choice. They are very light, dry quickly, and wick moisture away from the skin, keeping the wearer dry and warm.

Marine-clothing manufacturers make special multilayered clothing systems. These consist of a thin, light, underwear layer, over which is worn a thicker, warm layer. Either layer can be worn separately to suit different temperatures. A top, waterproof layer keeps the wearer dry. The latest designs use waterproofs made of breathable material. These are intended to keep water out and allow perspiration trapped inside to pass through, keeping the wearer dryer than with conventional waterproofs. These designs are expensive, but the best systems do deliver extra comfort.

Hats and gloves

A hat protects you from the sun in hot weather, reduces heat loss in cold conditions, and can keep rain out of your eyes. A thermal balaclava provides warmth when sailing in the coldest weather. Whatever headgear you choose, make sure it fits comfortably under the hood of your waterproof jacket.

Sailing gloves protect your hands and keep them warm in cold weather. Gloves are available with nonslip palms to grip ropes, and with cut-off fingers for delicate tasks. In very cold weather, fleece-lined gloves or mittens keep the hands warm but must be removed when handling ropes.

HANDLING HEAT
Shorts and T-shirts are the best clothes in hot weather, but take precautions against sunburn and wear sunglasses to protect the eyes; a hat will help prevent sunstroke.

Waterproofs

There are many types of waterproofs available to suit all conditions. The main difference between waterproofs designed for coastal sailing and those intended for offshore or ocean passages is in the weight and strength of their material. Ocean-grade waterproofs will probably have a better hood arrangement and more storm seals on cuffs, ankles, neck, and zip openings. They will also be more expensive. Be realistic about the type of sailing you intend to do, and choose your waterproofs accordingly.

OFFSHORE WATERPROOFS

Heavy duty waterproofs designed for offshore use are made of tougher material than inshore or coastal styles. Breathable materials can give added comfort but are not essential.

THERMALS

Thin, light, multilayered thermals worn underneath waterproofs will keep the wearer dry, warm, and well insulated from the elements.

Thermal all-in-one
Thermals are light, warm, and comfortable to wear

Loose cut
Allows freedom of movement

COLLAR AND HOOD

The hood folds into the collar when not in use. High collar protects the face in cold weather.

Breathable inner layer
Helps feet stay warm and dry

High leg
Gives maximum protection

Nonslip sole
For security on deck

BREATHABLE BOOTS

Boots that breathe are the ultimate in foot comfort in wet and cold weather. This type has a leather outer layer.

Double-wrist seal
The inner latex seal is adjustable with Velcro, as is the outer sleeve's wrist seal

Pockets
Zipper pockets provide a secure place to keep small items handy

Long jacket
Gives extra protection and does not ride up when seated

Reinforced knees
Reduce wear when kneeling on decks

Loose cut
Allows easy movement and fits over boots

CRUISER BOOTS

Waterproof, high-leg boots protect the feet and provide grip on wet decks.

SAFETY MATTERS

All cruisers should carry sufficient safety equipment to cope with an emergency involving either boat or crew. All responsible skippers should run a safe boat where all on-watch and off-watch practices are designed to minimize risks.

Danger can come in a number of ways: a crewmember can fall overboard or be injured; fire can break out on board; or the boat can be holed and take on water. Safety equipment must be stowed in a place where it can be reached quickly when needed, and the crew must know where it is, how it works and understand the correct procedure for using it.

Safety starts even before you get onboard. Care should be taken when climbing onto a boat, especially when stepping up from a pontoon or from an unstable tender; it may be the skipper's first duty to demonstrate how to get on and off the boat safely.

Staying out of danger

It is important that all crew members are aware of the potential dangers on deck and down below, and understand how to move safely around the yacht. The cockpit is the safest place on deck when under way, and offers security to the on-watch crew. There should be plenty of strong, dedicated attachment points for the crew's safety harnesses; and in challenging conditions, crewmembers should always clip on before leaving the companionway.

Jackstays (safety lines) should be installed along each sidedeck so that it is possible to move all the way from the cockpit to the bow without unclipping the harness line. When moving on deck, each crew's line should, ideally, be short enough to prevent them from going overboard in the event of a fall. Remember that the jackstays and the fittings to which they are attached will take a tremendous load if a person does fall overboard, so make sure their strength is sufficient.

When standing and sitting on deck, always be aware which sheets, blocks, and other fittings are under load at the time. Never place yourself in the way of a loaded sheet; if anything failed, it could whip toward you and cause injury. When walking on deck, do not stand on ropes or sails, as they may move underfoot and throw you off balance.

In rough weather, only move from the cockpit to the deck if really necessary. Plan your movements in advance and, when possible, use the windward sidedeck to move fore and aft. A yacht's motion in rough weather can be very lively, so keep your weight low to aid balance; don't be ashamed to crawl along the deck and sit on the foredeck to reduce the risk of falling overboard.

Moving around down below can be difficult in bad weather. There should be ample handholds at heights to suit all the crew. In rough weather, when the boat is heeling and pitching, move from handhold to handhold and try to anticipate the boat's movements to avoid losing your balance and being thrown across the boat.

Safety equipment

Any cruising boat, even one used just for day sailing, should carry a variety of safety equipment to help the crew deal with potential problems. The farther afield you plan to cruise, the more extensive your safety

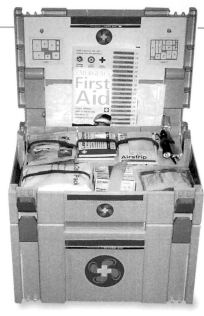

FIRST-AID KIT
First-aid kits designed for long-distance cruising are more comprehensive than those intended for coastal cruising.

equipment will need to be. Among the equipment carried aboard should be a first-aid kit, personal safety equipment (*opposite*), equipment to repair hull damage and minimize flooding (*p.418*), fire-fighting equipment (*p.218*), attention-getting devices (*p.210, pp.422–423*), emergency steering equipment (*p.419*), heavy weather sails and, when all else fails, means for abandoning ship (*pp.426–427*).

First-aid kit

Make sure that you have a well-stocked first-aid kit on board in case a crew member is injured. The first-aid kit should reflect the type of sailing you do. A simple kit containing some adhesive and cloth bandages is all you need for day sailing and short cruises. Longer passages, however, require a more comprehensive kit so that you can deal with any injuries onboard until you can obtain medical assistance.

PERSONAL SAFETY EQUIPMENT

The best way of keeping safe at sea is by staying on the boat. This makes a safety harness the most important item of personal safety gear. A life jacket will keep you afloat if you go overboard, but it is best to avoid falling in the water in the first place. A combined harness and life jacket is a good option.

Safety harnesses

There are several types of safety harnesses. Some waterproof jackets have a built-in harness to protect you whenever you are wearing the jacket. However, a separate harness may be more useful, as it can be worn at any time—even in conditions where you do not want to wear a waterproof jacket. Some life jackets, usually the inflatable type, have an integrated safety harness. These are popular as they are easy to put on, reasonably comfortable to wear, and do not require you to don two separate items of equipment. Whatever type you choose, make sure it has wide, comfortable straps that are easily adjusted for a personal fit and be sure to pick one that has a crotch strap. This holds the harness down and prevents it from being pulled over your head if you fall over the side and find yourself being towed at the end of your harness tether.

Life jackets

The most popular and practical life jacket for small-boat cruising is the inflatable type. These are available with manual inflation only, or manual plus automatic inflation. Do not rely on a manual-inflation-only type, as there is a risk that you will not be conscious when you fall overboard, in which case you will need an automatically-inflating jacket. Buy the best life jacket you can afford—your life may depend on it. Look for a well-made life jacket with a built-in splash guard to protect the face from water and spray, crotch or thigh straps to hold the jacket down, attached whistle and light, and a strong attachment point for a safety tether. Check the fit of the jacket before you buy, trying it on over your waterproof outer clothing to get a comfortable fit that does not restrict your movement.

Other equipment

It may also be prudent to carry a small personal torch (those with LED bulbs are a good choice) and a multipurpose tool or a simple knife. If you choose a knife, make sure it can be closed or sheathed so it cannot cause accidental injury. A personal man-overboard (MOB) beacon is also an option if the boat has a MOB receiver.

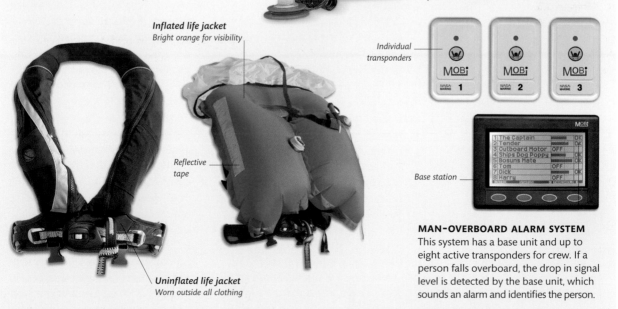

LIFE JACKET
Be prepared to pay for the best quality life jacket. Choose one with a sprayhood and thigh straps, which are more comfortable than a crotch strap.

Battery and water activation unit

Light

Inflated life jacket
Bright orange for visibility

Reflective tape

Uninflated life jacket
Worn outside all clothing

LIFE JACKET LIGHT
An automatic, water-activated light fitted to a life jacket for night sailing gives a much better chance of being spotted if you fall overboard in the dark.

Individual transponders

MOB¡ NASA MARINE 1
MOB¡ NASA MARINE 2
MOB¡ NASA MARINE 3

Base station

	MOB¡
1 The Captain	OK
2 Tender	OK
3 Outboard Motor	OFF
4 Ships Dog Poppy	OK
5 Bosuns Mate	OK
6 Tom	OFF
7 Dick	OK
8 Harry	OFF

MAN-OVERBOARD ALARM SYSTEM
This system has a base unit and up to eight active transponders for crew. If a person falls overboard, the drop in signal level is detected by the base unit, which sounds an alarm and identifies the person.

Fire prevention

Fire is one of the worst emergencies that can happen afloat. If not dealt with very quickly and effectively, it can cause the boat to burn to the waterline and sink. As usual, prevention is better than cure, and cruising sailors should understand the causes of fire and how to minimize the risks, as well as what to do if a fire does break out.

Common causes of fire on boats are smoking, ignition of flammable materials stowed on board, gas buildup in the bilges, faulty wiring, escaping gasoline (if kept for an outboard engine) or flames from the galley. Rules for smoking on board should be set and adhered to. Some skippers insist that no one should smoke anywhere other than on deck, by the leeward rail, where ash and cinders will blow straight over the side. If you have recently used solvents or paints on board, consider whether there is any need for their containers to remain on board. While they are unlikely to spontaneously combust, they could turn a minor incident into a major explosion.

If gas is used for cooking, every crew member should understand the risks associated with it and the routine to be used to minimize risks. Gas is heavier than air, so every time the stove gas valves are opened, a tiny amount of gas is expelled before ignition. This gas can only sink into the bilges. A gas alarm that detects a build up is a sensible addition for any boat using gas, but in any case it is good practice to regularly pump the bilges and, when prudent to do so, flush the boat with fresh air by opening hatches and creating a flow of air through the boat. Keep the gas supply turned off at the bottle as well as at the oven when not in use. Regularly check gas fittings, tubing, and pipework to test for leaks.

Fire extinguishers (*p.422*) must be situated where they are most likely to be needed: close to the galley and the engine, in the saloon, and up forward. Correct siting of extinguishers should also make it possible for any crew member down below to secure a safe exit route for themselves from the cabin.

Dry powder extinguishers work on all fires and a foam extinguisher is good for oil or fat fires. The engine space should have a dedicated extinguisher that can be activated without opening the engine compartment. All extinguishers have instructions for use printed on them, but familiarize yourself with these before you need to use them in a real emergency. Stow a fire blanket close to the galley, where it is useful for smothering a pan fire. Use it by grasping the blanket at the corners, turning your wrists back toward you

LIFEBUOY AND DANBUOY
A cover over the lifebuoy helps protect it from UV light. It should be fitted with a nylon drogue to reduce its drift in the water, a strobe light for visibility at night, and a danbuoy (a brightly colored marker pole with code flag O—the man-overboard signal), which is more visible than a person or a lifebuoy in the water.

so that the blanket covers and protects your hands. Turn your head away or keep your face as far from the flames as possible. A blanket is an effective way of smothering a fire, so it can also be used if clothing catches fire.

Fighting a fire is not a time for heroics. A calm, measured, and safe strategy should be adopted. The number of crew at risk should be kept to a minimum. When a crew member detects a fire, he should immediately shout to alert everyone, including the off-watch crew that may be sleeping. The crew should assemble on deck, don life jackets, and make preliminary preparations for abandoning ship. If possible, a mayday call should be made at once; be sure to keep handheld radio equipment where it can be used if the main radio is unreachable.

Lifebuoys

Every cruiser should have a couple of lifebuoys stowed for immediate use in case someone goes overboard. They

FIRE EXTINGUISHERS
A small foam extinguisher is handy to have in the galley, while larger dry powder extinguishers should be available in each cabin and near the engine compartment.

FLARE
Carry flares to suit the type of sailing you do. For offshore sailing, have a full set of flares stored in a watertight container.

are only effective if they are thrown at once. Stow the lifebuoys—most cruisers carry two—in quick-release brackets on the pushpit. To be useful in a nighttime man-overboard situation, a lifebuoy should be equipped with a flashing strobe light. Most are of the floating type that attaches to the lifebuoy by a floating line. In its holder, the light is held upside down; when it is thrown into the water, it floats the right way up and an internal switch turns the light on. Check the light regularly and replace the batteries before they run out.

To increase the effectiveness of a lifebuoy, attach a danbuoy—a weighted, floating marker pole about 6 ft (2 m) high. Danbuoys are available in solid or inflatable form and have a flag at their top, usually code flag O, which means man overboard. A danbuoy should be stowed along with the lifebuoy on the pushpit.

Another type of lifebuoy is attached to a very long floating line, the other end of which is secured to the boat. The lifebuoy in this arrangement is often a soft-collar type that the person in the water can easily pass over their head and under their arms.

In use, this system is designed to be thrown toward the man overboard. If the person cannot reach it, the boat is then steered in a circle around the casualty. The lifebuoy, at the end of the long floating line, follows along behind the boat, encircling the man overboard. When the person can reach the floating line, he can easily pull the lifebuoy toward him. Once in the lifebuoy, the casualty can be pulled to the yacht by the remaining crew and secured alongside. The lifebuoys usually have a lifting strop to which a tackle can be attached to lift the casualty out of the water.

Flares

You should have a number of flares on board suitable for the type of sailing you do (p.423). If you are out sailing for the day in coastal waters, several red parachute flares and a few hand-held red flares, together with a couple of orange smoke flares, will be sufficient. If you sail at night, carry a few white flares to signal your position in the event of a potential collision (a powerful flashlight is also useful here). If you sail farther offshore, increase the number of parachute flares you carry and add a floating dye marker.

Make sure that you, and your crew, have studied the instructions printed on the flares before you need to use them, and that you can demonstrate their usage during your safety briefing to the crew. Before using any flare consider the conditions and decide which type of flare is most appropriate. If cloud cover is low, there is no point in firing a parachute flare through the cloud base. In these conditions, fire at an angle to keep the flare under the cloud and maximize the visible burn time.

EPIRBs and SARTs

If you plan to spend a lot of time offshore, you should consider equipping your vessel with an EPIRB—emergency position indicating radio beacon. In an emergency, it is triggered manually or automatically and sends information about your position to a network of satellites. Your EPIRB is registered to your vessel, and when a distress message is received, the emergency services know what type of boat they are looking for. A search and rescue transponder, SART, transmits directional signals that are displayed on rescue service's radar screens, which helps approaching vessels to home in on your position.

Life raft

If you sail offshore, you should carry either a dedicated life raft or a dual-purpose tender that can serve in this important role. Life rafts should be professionally serviced annually to be sure that they meet current safety standards. Carry an emergency grab-bag filled with food, water, flares, and other essential survival equipment in case you need to abandon ship in an emergency, and store it where you can find it in a hurry.

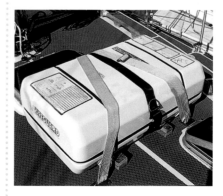

LIFE RAFT ON DECK
A life raft is packed inside a canister or case. It is often stowed on deck, lashed down with quick-release fastenings.

CRUISER ROPEWORK

Learning basic rope skills is an essential first step for anyone who aspires to become a good seaman. An experienced sailor will perform these skills naturally, as proficiency in rope-handling forms the basis for much of the work involved in sailing a yacht. It is not necessary to be a knot-tying expert to become a good seaman. However, you should know how to tie a few essential knots quickly and accurately, how to coil, handle, and stow ropes of all sizes, and how to heave a line.

USING ROPES

A typical cruiser will have many different ropes on board, ranging from light line up to heavy mooring and anchor warps. Ropes found on cruisers are larger and heavier than those used on dinghies and can be more difficult to handle because of their extra weight and length. Each rope has its use and place on board, and each will require handling in a way determined by its size and purpose. Practice tying a few essential knots, and coiling, cleating, stowing, and heaving these larger ropes. Proficiency in these skills can be critical when mooring, as well as in other situations. You should be able to complete these tasks quickly and efficiently, even in the dark when you cannot see the rope you are handling. The basic knots and rope-handling skills (*pp.42–47*) must become second

nature. You should then extend your ability by learning the additional knots shown (*opposite*). Always ensure that ropes are coiled and stowed neatly to avoid tangles, and never leave mooring ropes lying around the deck or pontoon, where someone could trip over them. Wash all ropes once a year with mild detergent to remove salt and grease.

Heaving a line
Sometimes you will need to heave (throw) a line to someone on another boat or on the dock. If there is a tangle in the line, your throw will fall short. Do not rely on a previously coiled rope, but re-coil it before the throw. Make sure that the rope is long enough to reach your target. On larger boats, there may be a heaving line of

light rope with a weight spliced into one end to help it travel. Once caught, it is used to pull over a heavier warp.

Working with rope
When you start whipping, splicing, or seizing rope (*pp.222–223*), the tasks will be easier if you have some simple tools. A sharp knife is needed for cutting rope and trimming ends, and adhesive tape is useful for temporarily binding the ends of strands. A fid or marlinspike are helpful when splicing, and a sailmaker's palm and needle are useful for whippings and seizings.

SWEDISH FID
Hollow blade is used for threading strands when splicing.

FID
Pointed end separates strands of stiff three-strand rope.

SAILOR'S KNIFE
Sharp, straight blade gives neat cuts.

ADHESIVE TAPE
Adhesive tape is used for temporary whippings.

SAILMAKER'S NEEDLE
Sharp triangular point is easily inserted into rope.

MARLINSPIKE
The blunt point is used to release a tight knot.

Metal patch

PALM
Metal patch is used to push on needle.

Throwing hand

PREPARING   **THROWING**

The throw
Heave the line underarm and aim above the target, letting the line uncoil from your other hand. Hold on to the end

READY TO THROW
Coil the rope neatly and split into two coils, half in your throwing hand and the rest in the other hand. Stand with your non-throwing shoulder toward the target.

CRUISER KNOTS

Many of the knots used on cruisers are identical to those required to sail a dinghy, so reacquaint yourself with them (*pp.44–47*). Two other knots—the fisherman's bend and the rolling hitch—are often used onboard a cruiser, especially when mooring, and should be included in your rope-handling skills.

FISHERMAN'S BEND

This knot is similar to the round turn and two half-hitches (p.47), but is more secure. It can be used for tying an anchor warp to the anchor or a mooring warp to a ring.

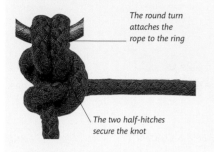

The round turn attaches the rope to the ring

The two half-hitches secure the knot

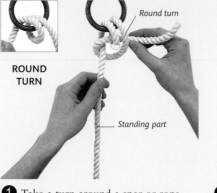

ROUND TURN

Round turn

Standing part

❶ Take a turn around a spar or rope, taking the working end up on the right side of the standing part. Bring the working end across the standing part.

Working end

❷ Take a second turn identical to the first turn. Take the working end up between the standing part and the second turn.

ROLLING HITCH

The rolling hitch is a very useful knot when you want to tie a rope around a spar or to take the strain off another rope. It grips very tightly and is valuable in an emergency, when you can use it to take the load off another line to pull along the spar.

The three turns of this hitch secure the rope to a spar

Rope pulls along spar

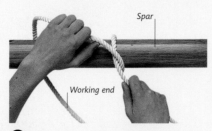

Spar

Working end

❶ Make a turn around a spar or rope, bringing the working end up on the right side of the standing part. Take the working end across the standing part.

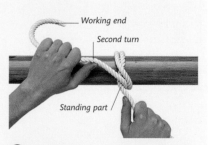

Working end

Second turn

Standing part

❷ Make a second turn identical to the first turn, bringing the working end up between the standing part and the second turn.

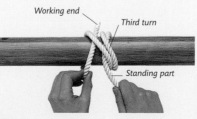

Working end

Third turn

Standing part

❸ Take a third turn, and then bring the working end up on the left side of the standing part. Next, tuck the turn under itself.

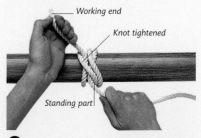

Working end

Knot tightened

Standing part

❹ Pull on both the standing part and the working end to tighten the knot. Pull the standing part over the first two turns before putting strain on the rope.

WHIPPING, SEIZING, AND SPLICING

Whipping

A good method of binding the end of a rope to prevent the strands from fraying or unraveling is to whip it. With modern synthetic ropes, you can accomplish the same thing by heat-sealing the ends (*p.45*), but whipping the rope using thin twine is much stronger and neater.

SAILMAKER'S WHIPPING

The sailmaker's whipping is a secure method of binding the end of three-strand rope without needing to sew the twine using a sailmaker's needle. Make the whipping about one and a half times the diameter of the rope.

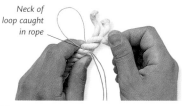

Loop of whipping twine — Strand end

1 Unlay the end of the rope and pass a loop of whipping twine over one of the strands.

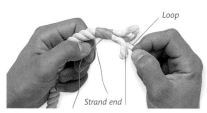

Neck of loop caught in rope

2 Relay the strands of the rope with the loop protruding from the rope. Leave a short tail on the loop.

Loop

Strand end

4 Take the loop and pass it over the end of the strand that the loop was placed over in step one.

Whipping turns

3 Wrap the twine tightly around the rope in a series of whipping turns. Work toward the end, leaving the loop and tail free.

Whipping — Strand end

Short tail

5 Take the short tail and pull until the loop is tightened over the strand end and the whipping.

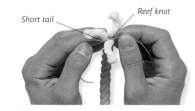

Short tail — Reef knot

7 Tie a reef knot, with the tail and the working end of the twine, in the center of the strand ends. Trim the strand ends.

Short tail

6 Take the tail along the groove from which it emerges to the other end of the whipping.

COMMON WHIPPING

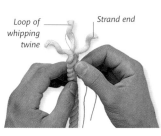

The common whipping is the simplest to learn and is suitable for both braided and three-strand rope. It is not as secure as some other whippings but is quick and easy to complete.

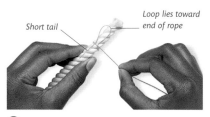

Short tail — Loop lies toward end of rope

1 Form a loop in the end of the twine and lay it along the rope with the loop toward the end of the rope.

Whipping turns — End of loop

2 Wrap the long end of the twine around the rope, moving toward the rope end. Pull each turn tight.

Loop

3 When the turns approach the end of the rope, pass the end of the twine through the loop.

Loop is pulled under whipping

Short tail

4 Pull hard on the short tail of the loop to bury it under the turns. Trim both twine ends close to the whipping.

SEIZING

Seizing is used to bind two parts of a rope alongside each other. The friction created by the seizing between the two parts of the rope is able to hold very high loads. A seizing can be used to create a loop in the end of braided rope.

Clove hitch

Whipping twine

1 Form an eye in the end of the rope and, with the end of a length of whipping twine, tie a clove hitch around the two parts of the rope to be seized to each other.

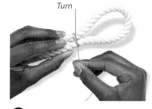

Turn

2 Pass the whipping twine around the two parts of the rope to make a series of turns. Pull each turn tightly and make sure it sits neatly alongside the preceding turns.

Seizing

Pull whipping twine through

3 Continue making turns until the length of the seizing is three times the diameter of the rope. Now create a frapping turn by taking the twine down between the two parts of the rope.

Frapping turn

Seizing

4 Pass the whipping twine over the seizing and down between the two parts of the rope. Pull the twine tight to complete the first frapping turn then repeat for a second.

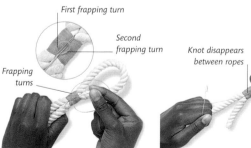

First frapping turn

Second frapping turn

Frapping turns

5 Pass the twine up between the two parts of the rope and between the frapping turns. Pass it under one of the turns, then over both turns, and under the other frapping turn.

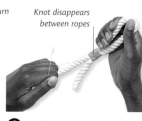

Knot disappears between ropes

6 Pull the whipping twine tight until the knot disappears between the two ropes. Trim the end of the whipping twine but leave a short end so that the knot cannot untie itself.

Splicing

Splicing is used to join two ropes (or to join a rope tail to a length of wire), to bind the end of a rope, and to form a fixed eye in the end of a rope (*below*). Once completed, a splice is stronger than a knot and is permanent. Splicing three-strand rope is fairly straightforward, but braided construction (*pp.42–45*) is more complex to splice.

All splices require the rope to be unlaid so that the individual strands can be manipulated and inserted under and over laid strands in the body of the rope. When unlaying a rope to work with individual strands, always seal the ends of the strands temporarily to prevent them from fraying. Plastic tape makes a useful temporary seal. It is also sensible to secure the rope at the point to which you have unlaid the strands. Use a few turns of twine tied tightly around the rope.

EYE SPLICE

An eye splice is used to form a fixed eye in the end of a three-strand rope such as a mooring warp. Three rounds of tucks can be sufficient in natural fiber rope, but use five tucks in synthetic fiber ropes to compensate for their slippery surface.

Standing part

Loop

1 Unlay the rope strands some way back from the end and form a counterclockwise loop of the size required for the eye.

First strand end

2 Take the end of the top strand and tuck it under a strand on the standing part, tucking against the lay.

Second strand end

Standing part

3 Turn the splice over and tuck the end of the second strand under the next strand in the standing part.

Third strand end

4 Turn the splice and tuck the third end under the third strand on the standing part. Repeat five times.

USING WARPS

Warps are mooring ropes used to tie a boat to a pontoon, dockside, mooring buoy, piles, or other boat. Knowing how to use warps is an essential part of cruiser handling. The size of warp will depend on the size and, most importantly, the weight of your boat: large yachts will have big warps that are heavy to handle. All warps should be strong enough to hold your boat and long enough to allow for the rise and fall of the boat in tidal waters.

Nylon is the most common material for warps, since it is strong. It also stretches well to absorb shock and reduce loads on fairleads and cleats. Warps should always be coiled when not in use, and stored, preferably hanging up, in a locker from where they can easily be retrieved.

When mooring alongside, a number of warps are needed to hold the boat safely and to prevent it from ranging back and forth and causing damage. The precise arrangement depends on whether you are tied to a dockside (and have to allow for the tide), or to another boat or floating pontoon that also moves in response to changes in tidal height.

Avoiding problems

The best way to avoid problems when mooring with warps is to have one rope for each job and to make each one up on its own cleat. Always make up the end to a cleat ashore or on the pontoon or a neighboring boat, and bring the rest of the warp back on board where it can be cleated and stowed. This avoids leaving rope ashore and makes it easy to adjust your warps on board when necessary. Sometimes you may make fast with a slip line led through a ring or around

---

TURNING WITH WARPS

There are times when it would be much easier to leave a berth if the boat was facing the other way, particularly if you want to leave under sail. This can be achieved by the use of warps.

USING WARPS

The best way to turn a boat using warps is to make use of the tide or wind to help the maneuver. Start by placing fenders on the far side of the boat and at the bow and stern to protect the boat when it turns. The boat shown here is lying stern-to-tide, so the stern will be moved away from the pontoon to turn the boat. If the boat was lying the other way around, the bow would be turned first.

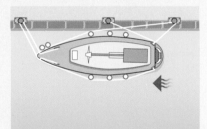

❶ Rig a stern line outside all rigging on the far side. Move the bow spring to a cleat on the far side, and the shore end to a cleat aft of the boat.

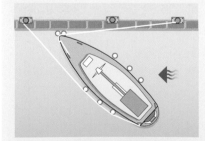

❷ Release the bow line and stern spring. Release the stern line and push the stern out, or pull on the bow spring. The tide will start to swing the boat out. Take up the slack on the new stern line.

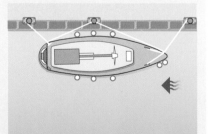

❸ The turn will slow down as the boat lines up with the tide. Make fast the new bow and stern lines and rig new springs. For short stays, you need only rig a bow line and a stern spring.

MOORING WARPS

Each mooring warp has a different function, and it is important to know which warp does what. If you leave your boat alongside in tidal waters, make sure that there is sufficient slack in the warps to allow for the lowest level of tide; otherwise, the boat will end up hanging from its warps and could be damaged.

Bow line
The bow line (or head rope) and the stern line position the boat. They must be strong enough to take the main load and long enough to allow for the rise and fall of the tide. The farther away they are taken from the boat, the less adjustment is needed as the tide rises or falls

a cleat ashore with both ends brought back aboard (*opposite*). This is only suitable for temporary stops, as a warp rigged in this way is likely to chafe where it passes through the ring or cleat. When chafe occurs in the middle of a long warp, it becomes useless unless you can cut it in half and make it into two shorter warps.

Cleats

All mooring cleats and fairleads must be large enough for the job. They should be securely bolted to the deck, and have smooth, rounded edges to prevent chafe on the warps. Generally, the larger the cleat, the less it will wear the rope and the easier it will be to make up a rope with sufficient turns. Some yachts have a central bollard, the Samson post, on the foredeck together with a pair of cleats, one on either side of the bow, and a pair at the stern. If there is no central bollard, there should be at least three cleats on the foredeck. A pair of midship cleats on the sidedecks is useful when mooring alongside.

Fairleads

Fairleads should be fitted on either side of the bow and stern and alongside each midship cleat, if attached.

SLIP LINES

A slip line is a warp led through a ring or around a cleat or bollard ashore, with both ends made fast on board. It allows the crew to release the warp from on board and is particularly useful when berthed alongside a quay wall. Never rig a warp permanently as a slip: this can lead to chafe in the middle of the warp and ruin it.

Using rings

If a slip line is rigged through a ring ashore, it is important to lead it through the ring in the right way. Lead the end of the warp that will be released up through the ring if it is lying on top of the quay, or down through the ring if it is hanging on the quay wall. In this way, the warp lifts the ring away from the quay as it is pulled, preventing the warp from jamming as you pull it on board. Make sure there are no knots or splices in the warp to snag, and pull the line steadily to avoid tangles.

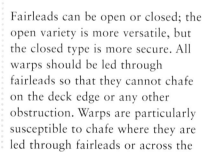

Warp led up through ring

Warp led down through ring

SLIP LINES THROUGH RINGS

Fairleads can be open or closed; the open variety is more versatile, but the closed type is more secure. All warps should be led through fairleads so that they cannot chafe on the deck edge or any other obstruction. Warps are particularly susceptible to chafe where they are led through fairleads or across the edges of dock walls. They can be protected by feeding the warp through short lengths of plastic tubing, which can then be positioned at likely chafing points. Check that your fairleads do not have any sharp edges, or these will quickly damage your warps when they are under heavy strain.

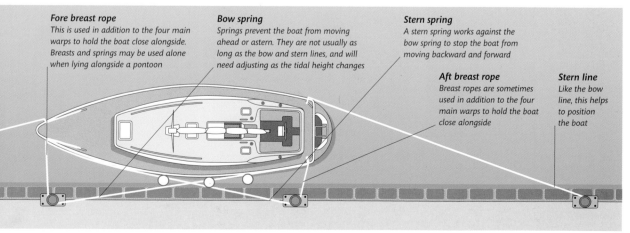

Fore breast rope
This is used in addition to the four main warps to hold the boat close alongside. Breasts and springs may be used alone when lying alongside a pontoon

Bow spring
Springs prevent the boat from moving ahead or astern. They are not usually as long as the bow and stern lines, and will need adjusting as the tidal height changes

Stern spring
A stern spring works against the bow spring to stop the boat from moving backward and forward

Aft breast rope
Breast ropes are sometimes used in addition to the four main warps to hold the boat close alongside

Stern line
Like the bow line, this helps to position the boat

BASIC SAIL SKILLS

Sails on a modern cruising yacht aare similar in most respects to those found on a dinghy, but they are both larger and heavier. Also, a cruiser's sail wardrobe is more extensive than a dinghy's, because it must have sails suitable for a wide range of conditions, from light airs to storm-force winds. Many modern cruisers are fitted with a headsail roller-reefing system, which allows one sail to be used in a range of wind strengths, but some follow the traditional approach of having several sails of different sizes.

Bending on sails

"Bending on" is the traditional term used to describe fitting the mainsail onto the boom. It is usually done only at the beginning of the sailing season, as the mainsail on most cruisers is stowed on the boom and removed only at season's end. Headsails are traditionally bent on when needed, being stowed at other times, but many modern cruisers use a roller-reefing system that allows the headsail to be furled tightly around the forestay when the boat is not sailing. With this system, the headsail is often left bent on throughout the season.

Mainsail foot

Most cruiser mainsails are attached to the boom either by sliding the bolt rope out along the groove in the boom, as is done with many dinghies (p.72), or with slides that are attached to the sail and run in the boom groove. The tack is fastened to the gooseneck using a shackle or lashing. The clew is pulled toward the outer end of the boom using the outhaul, which, if it is adjustable, runs inside the boom, to a winch or cleat at the forward end.

Mainsail luff

The luff is usually attached to the mast by slides that run in the mast groove. With a fully battened mainsail, the battens run from the leech to the luff. They fit into special low-friction sliders that enable the sail to be hoisted and lowered easily despite pressure from the battens.

Reefing lines

Lines to reef the mainsail (pp.246–247) are usually led from the end of the boom through the reef cringles in the leech. They are then led back down to the boom before being led forward to a winch and cleat at the forward end of the boom, or through turning blocks back to a winch in the cockpit. Similar lines are sometimes rigged at the luff unless the luff cringles are fixed onto inverted hooks known as ram's horns.

HOISTING THE MAINSAIL

Before hoisting the mainsail, make sure that the boat is facing head-to-wind. If it is not, the sail will fill as it is hoisted, making the job difficult, if not impossible, and the boat will start sailing before you are ready.

❶ Check that the halyard is clear aloft. Remove the ties that hold the stowed sail in place on the boom, fully release the mainsheet, and pull on the halyard. As you hoist, keep an eye aloft to make sure that the sail does not snag on anything.

❷ If the halyard is led aft to a winch in the cockpit, as here, one crewmember at the mast can pull on the halyard to help hoist the sail more quickly. The person at the winch takes in the slack, only winching the halyard when the sail is nearly hoisted.

❸ Put enough pressure on the halyard to pull a light crease into the sail parallel to the luff—this will disappear when the sail is full of wind. Cleat, coil, and stow the halyard, ease off the topping lift and leave it slack, and tighten the boom vang.

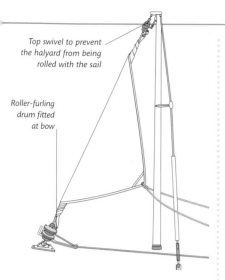

Top swivel to prevent the halyard from being rolled with the sail

Roller-furling drum fitted at bow

ROLLER-FURLING HEADSAIL
The luff of a roller-furling headsail runs in a foil fitted to the forestay. The tack is fixed to a drum that turns to roll the sail.

Furling headsails

In roller-furling and reefing headsail systems, a headfoil is fitted over the forestay. The headfoil has a groove (or two) in the aft edge, into which the sail's luff is fed. The tack is shackled to the roller-furling drum at the base of the headfoil, and the head is shackled to a halyard swivel that slides over the headfoil. The sheets are attached to the clew in the usual way, using a bowline on each. They are then led aft through their turning blocks or fairleads. Remember to tie a figure-eight knot (*p.46*) in the end of each sheet. After the sail is hoisted, it is furled by pulling on the furling line wound around the furling drum. This rotates the headfoil, and thus furls the sail.

Other headsail systems

If a furling system is not used, the yacht will have a number of headsails of different sizes to suit a range of wind strengths. These sails are stowed in a sail locker, and are rigged when needed. This type of headsail is rigged exactly like the jib of a dinghy (*p.70*). Remove the headsail from its bag and attach the tack to the stemhead fitting with a shackle, or by hooking it over a ram's horn. Next, clip the luff hanks onto the forestay and attach the sheets to the clew. Shackle the halyard to the head. The sail is now ready to hoist.

Hoisting the headsail

Unlike the mainsail, the headsail can be hoisted in any wind direction. Make sure, however, that the sheets are free so that the mainsail can flap freely until you are ready to sheet in. If you have a roller-furling headsail, it will already be hoisted and stowed in its furled state. To unfurl it, make sure the furling line is free to run and pull on the appropriate jib sheet.

If you have hanked-on headsails, hoist the sail using the halyard and halyard winch. Before hoisting, untie any sail ties securing it, and make sure the halyard is not tangled aloft. Hoist the sail by hand, with one turn around the winch drum (*p.228*), adding turns and using the handle only when needed. Tighten the halyard until a small crease appears in the sail, parallel to the luff. This will disappear when the sail is full of wind. Cleat the halyard and coil and stow the tail.

STOWING THE HALYARD

If your halyard winches are mast-mounted, you will have a long length of halyard when each sail is hoisted. A good way to stow them, after cleating (*p.44*), is to coil them and hang them on their cleats. If your halyards lead aft to winches in the cockpit, their tails are more effectively dealt with by stuffing them into bags mounted on the bulkhead for this purpose. Alternatively, coil on their cleats or winches.

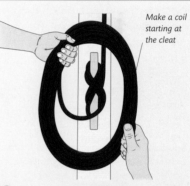

Make a coil starting at the cleat

1 Once the halyard has been cleated, coil up the tail, starting from the cleat end to avoid putting twists in the rope.

Pull a bight of halyard through the coils and twist it once or twice

2 Grasp the part of the halyard that leads to the cleat and bring it through the coil center, twisting it once or twice.

Slip the loop over the cleat

3 Pull the twisted loop over the coils and drop it over the top horn of the cleat to hold the coils securely.

USING WINCHES

The sails on a cruiser are larger than those on a dinghy and, therefore, exert much more force on their sheets and halyards. Winches are an important part of the sail-handling equipment, as they provide the mechanical advantage to control large loads. On traditional craft, however, tackles are sometimes used to perform the same function. Winches positioned in the cockpit are used for handling sheets, control lines, and halyards that are led aft. Mast winches are used for any halyards and reefing lines that are not led aft.

There are two types of winches—the standard winch and the self-tailing winch. A standard winch usually requires two people: one to load and wind the winch, and the other to tail

(pull) on the free end (the tail) of the sheet or halyard. On a self-tailing winch, there is a circular grooved cleat running around the top. This retains the tail of the rope and allows one person to operate the winch. Some winches have two or three speeds.

Manual or electric

Most winches are manually operated, using a handle. Longer handles give more power than shorter ones. Electric winches are common on larger yachts with hydraulic winches used on the largest. Both types are operated by push buttons and great care must be taken when using them because of the enormous loads that can be involved.

SELF-TAILING WINCH
Most modern yachts have self-tailing winches for one-person operation. Load the rope onto the winch and feed it into the self-tailing jaws. Wind the handle with your shoulders positioned over the winch.

WINCHING-IN USING A STANDARD WINCH

To use a winch, one person loads the rope, inserts the handle, and prepares to wind in, while another prepares to tail. When working with sheets or halyards under load, be careful to avoid pinching your fingers between the rope and the drum. The best way to protect your fingers near the winch is to keep the back of the hand facing the drum. To winch efficiently, adopt

a stable stance with your shoulders over the winch. Use your body weight and both hands on the handle whenever possible, as this exerts the maximum amount of force. Always check what you are about to do before you do it; a winch makes it possible to apply big forces very quickly, and sails and gear can be damaged by over-enthusiastic winching.

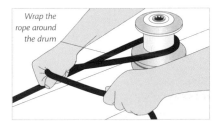

❶ If there is strain on the rope, use two hands to load the winch. Load in the direction in which that the drum rotates.

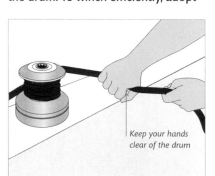

❷ Make at least three full turns. As you wrap the rope around the winch, rotate your hand to make sure you keep your fingers clear of the drum.

Keep your hands clear of the drum

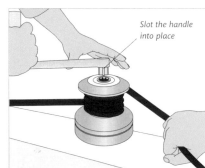

❸ Insert the handle into the winch once the turns have been wound on. Make sure that the handle is seated fully into the socket or it may slip as you wind.

Slot the handle into place

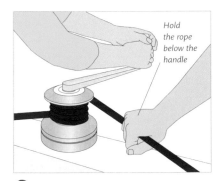

❹ Turn the handle clockwise for high speed, and counterclockwise for slow speed. The person tailing must maintain a steady pull on the tail.

Hold the rope below the handle

Loading a winch

Loading a winch means putting turns of rope on it before it can be used. Usually, at least three full turns are needed to provide sufficient friction between the rope and the winch drum. The rope must be wound on in the same direction that the winch drum rotates. Nearly all winches rotate clockwise, but you can quickly check an empty winch's rotation by seeing which way it spins freely.

Using a winch

Once the winch is loaded, a handle, inserted in a socket in the top of the winch, is used to wind in the rope. Some handles have a locking system that prevents them from being knocked out of the winch. With these, you must operate a small lever on the handle to insert and remove it.

Winch in the rope, and cleat it securely once you have finished. Cleating is not always necessary with a self-tailing winch, because it has a circular cleat mounted above the drum. However, it is safer to secure the rope on a separate cleat or to pass a final loose safety turn around the entire winch which will prevent the rope from being

accidentally knocked out of the self-tailer. With the rope cleated, remove and stow the handle. Never leave a handle in a winch when it is not in use.

Easing a sheet

Headsail sheets impart high loads on their winches, and you must be very careful when easing or fully releasing one. If you need to ease the sheet, undo it from its cleat, keeping it taut to prevent it from slipping prematurely. Press the heel of your other hand against the turns on the winch to increase the friction of the rope against the drum, and keep the sheet under control as you ease the turns slightly.

Releasing a sheet

To fully release a loaded sheet (when you are tacking, for example), do not unwind the turns from the drum or the sheet will kink and jam. Pull the sheet sharply upward and release it as the turns come off the drum.

EASING THE SHEET
Ease the sheet on both manual and power winches in the same way. Hold the tail in one hand, while pressing the other hand against the turns on the drum in order to prevent a riding turn. Allow the rope to slide gradually around the drum.

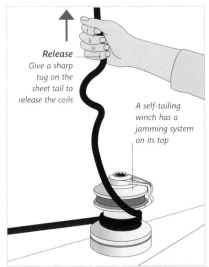

Release
Give a sharp tug on the sheet tail to release the coils

A self-tailing winch has a jamming system on its top

RELEASING THE SHEET
When you need to release the sheet from the winch, uncleat the tail and pull the sheet upward sharply so that the coils are freed from the drum without getting twisted or jammed. Let go of the rope end as soon as the coils leave the winch.

RIDING TURNS

Riding turns occur when the coils on the winch become crossed over each other. This will jam the rope and prevent it from being released. Riding turns usually occur on a sheet winch when too many turns have been put onto the winch drum before the slack in the sheet has been pulled in.

Clearing a riding turn

To clear a riding turn on a working sheet or halyard, you must first remove the load from the winch, but do not try to do this by hand. Instead, tie another line to the sheet or halyard ahead of the winch. Attach this line with a rolling hitch (*p.221*), and then lead it to another winch (positioned in the direction in which you need to pull to relieve the load on the first winch). Load the second line onto the new winch and wind it in until it takes all the pressure off the riding turn. Now return to the jammed winch and release the riding turn. Reload the sheet and winch it in. Release the rolling hitch and the second line.

Riding turn prevents sheet from being eased

RIDING TURN
A riding turn occurs when the rope turns become crossed. The load on the rope locks the turns, preventing the rope from being released. If the load is light, it may be released by hand, but usually another line must be used to relieve the load.

LOWERING AND STOWING SAILS

Lower the sails by reversing their hoisting procedures. Before you lower the mainsail, remember to tighten the topping lift to take the weight of the boom if it is not supported by a solid vang. Otherwise, the boom will come crashing down onto the deck and may cause injury or damage.

Make sure that the boat is head-to-wind so that the mainsail cannot fill with wind, then ease the mainsheet and allow the sail to flap. Lower the mainsail, keeping the halyard under control so that it does not rush out. When the sail is down, secure the halyard and tighten the mainsheet to prevent the boom from swinging around. The mainsail can now be stowed. Rigs other than Bermudan may require different procedures.

If you have a headsail-furling system, you can roll the sail around the forestay simply by easing the sheet and pulling on the furling line. If you have a hanked-on headsail, send a crewmember forward to stop it from falling into the water,

then ease the halyard and lower the headsail onto the foredeck. Secure the halyard, and then stow the sail.

Headsails can be lowered or furled with the boat at any angle to the wind. When using roller furling, it is best to keep some wind pressure in the sail to be sure the sail rolls up tightly.

Stowing the mainsail

During the sailing season, the mainsail is usually left stowed on the boom, shielded from the elements by a sail cover. Sailcloth is damaged by long-term exposure to ultraviolet light, so it is important to protect the sail with its cover whenever it is not being used.

Rope guides called lazyjacks will stow a fully battened main neatly on the boom as it is lowered. Lazyjacks run from the mast to the boom. They control the sail and stack it like a Venetian blind, requiring only the sail ties to secure it. The sail cover must be designed to fit around the lazyjacks, or they must be pulled forward out of the way before the cover is fitted.

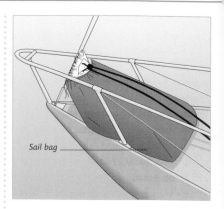

Sail bag

TEMPORARY HEADSAIL STOW
Hanked-on headsails can be temporarily stowed in their bag on the foredeck. The sail can remain hanked on, ready to hoist, with sheets attached. The bag protects the sail and keeps the decks clear.

Stowing headsails

A headsail that is stowed furled on the forestay needs to be protected from ultraviolet light, which will degrade the exposed parts of the sail. Many sail-makers allow for this by building in a sacrificial strip of material along the leech. Alternatively, you can hoist a cover over the furled sail.

A furling headsail is easily stowed; simply roll it away around the forestay by pulling on the furling line. A hanked-on headsail can be stowed neatly on the foredeck so it is ready for reuse. To do this, pull the sail out along one sidedeck and furl it parallel to its foot into a neat roll that can be secured to the lifelines or stanchions clear of the deck. Always carry extra sail ties for jobs like these.

SECURING THE MAINSAIL
When the mainsail has been lowered and flaked over the boom, it is secured with sail ties and the halyard is removed from the sail and stowed.

Alternatively, you can use the headsail bag to cover and protect it while it is still hanked to the forestay. Fold the sail in half by pulling the clew up to the tack and head. Now pack the bulk of the sail into its bag; you should end up with just the tack, clew, and head protruding. The sheets can be left attached, but the halyard should be removed. The halyard end should then be stowed on the pulpit to keep it out of the way. If the headsail is not to be used again in the near future, it should be removed and stowed in its bag in the sail locker.

When you sail with hanked-on headsails, you will change them to suit the wind strength. When you remove a sail, it is best to stow it immediately in its bag in the sail locker, if you have one, or pass it down the forehatch and stow it in the forepeak. In rough weather, bring it aft and pass it down the main hatch. Occasionally, however, you may stow it temporarily on the foredeck if you are likely to use it again soon. Make sure that it is lashed securely to the stanchions so that it cannot slip overboard. Never leave a sail on deck in rough weather.

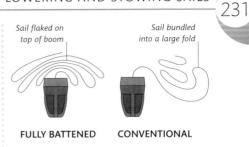

Sail flaked on top of boom

Sail bundled into a large fold

FULLY BATTENED   **CONVENTIONAL**

STOWING MAINSAILS

A fully battened mainsail will stow itself in Venetian-blind-like folds as it is lowered. A conventional mainsail is pulled over to one side of the boom after being lowered and is stowed neatly.

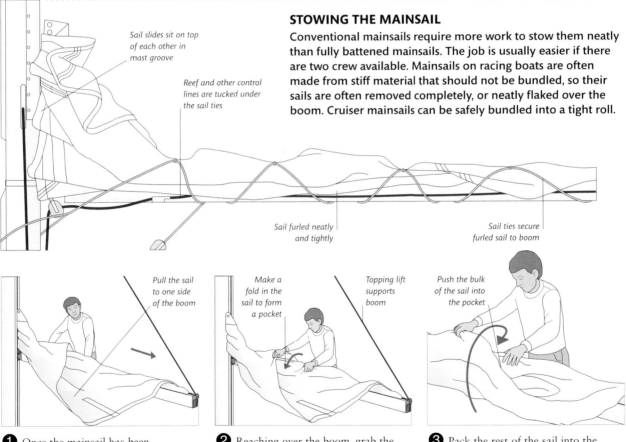

Sail slides sit on top of each other in mast groove

Reef and other control lines are tucked under the sail ties

STOWING THE MAINSAIL

Conventional mainsails require more work to stow them neatly than fully battened mainsails. The job is usually easier if there are two crew available. Mainsails on racing boats are often made from stiff material that should not be bundled, so their sails are often removed completely, or neatly flaked over the boom. Cruiser mainsails can be safely bundled into a tight roll.

Sail furled neatly and tightly

Sail ties secure furled sail to boom

Pull the sail to one side of the boom

❶ Once the mainsail has been lowered, pull it over to the leeward side of the boom. Move around to the windward side of the boom so that you are in the best position to stow it neatly. Make sure the mainsheet is pulled in and cleated before you start.

Make a fold in the sail to form a pocket

Topping lift supports boom

❷ Reaching over the boom, grab the leech of the sail some way up from the foot. Pull it aft and toward you to form a pocket. If there is more than one crew member available, one should stand at the aft end of the boom, where it is easier to create the pocket in the sail.

Push the bulk of the sail into the pocket

❸ Pack the rest of the sail into the pocket, pulling the leech aft as you go to create a neat bundle. When all the sail is inside, pull the pocket tightly around the sail and secure it with sail ties tied around the bundle and the boom. Put on the sail cover to protect the sail from UV light.

USING THE TENDER

Although the principal use of a tender is to transport you to and from the shore when anchored or moored, it can fulfill several other roles. It can be used, along with the life raft, in the event of abandoning ship, and it can be used for pottering, fishing, and exploring shallow harbors. There are many types, solid, folding and inflatable, but the choice often comes down to the space available to stow it on the cruiser. All tenders should be easy to handle under oars, but many owners also carry a small outboard engine for use with the tender.

USING THE TENDER
Rowing is quieter but many cruisers fit an outboard on the tender, especially if it is an inflatable type which is harder to row than a solid dinghy.

Types of tender

The vast majority of cruisers carry an inflatable dinghy, because it is easy to stow when deflated. A traditional inflatable is, however, difficult to row even in ideal conditions and can be impossible in a strong wind and choppy water. A small, solid dinghy makes a far better tender if you have the space to stow it on deck, but few modern yachts have this facility.

Other choices include a small rigid inflatable boat (RIB) with a solid bottom and inflatable topside tubes, or a folding or sectional dinghy that requires less space than a solid dinghy. Also, newer types of inflatables have improved floor arrangements—either roll-up, inflatable, or solid—that make them more stable, dryer inside, and easier to row than the older, single-floor type. In the end, the space you have for stowage, and the price, are likely to be the key factors.

Buying a new tender can be expensive, and its glossy finish will not survive long if it is used regularly. Tenders take a lot of punishment when cruising and are attractive to thieves and children looking for amusement. Mark the name of your cruiser on the tender, and use a padlock and chain to secure it when leaving it ashore.

Stowing the tender

Most inflatables are stowed deflated in a cockpit locker or on deck, and are inflated by a foot or electric pump when needed. This does mean, however, that they are not available for instant use, such as in an emergency. Solid or folding tenders, RIBs with their tubes deflated, or inflated inflatables, can be lashed down on the coachroof or foredeck, as long as they do foul any gear or restrict the crew's movement around the decks and coachroof.

Some cruisers carry their tender in davits at the stern; an inflatable can also be carried on short trips by lashing it across the rear of the pushpit. Both these arrangements create a lot of windage, however, and can form an obstruction when the boat is tied up alongside.

If an outboard engine is carried for the tender, this is often stowed on a mounting pad on the pushpit. A fabric cover over the engine will help to protect it from the elements when not in use. Be careful when lifting the outboard and when passing it up or down between the tender and the yacht; an outboard is awkward to lift and is easily dropped. Attach a safety line to prevent it from being dropped overboard.

Towing a tender

An alternative to stowing the tender aboard is towing it behind. You will lose a little cruising speed, but this may be an acceptable compromise. Use two towing lines; the tender's painter secured to a towing point on the tender's stern and another towing warp attached to a separate strong point at the tender's bow. If the painter breaks, the secondary line will stop the tender from being lost.

Do not underestimate the load on the line or risk losing the tender by using a weak deck fitting. Adjust the length of the tow to position the tender on the front of your stern wave so that it minimizes drag and the tendency to veer from side to side. If the tender surfs down waves and rides up to your stern, lengthen the tow rope considerably to drop the tender well behind.

Always remove all equipment from the dinghy before towing it, and never allow anyone to ride in the tender when it is being towed.

Getting a tender aboard

If your tender is stowed on deck when not in use, you need to have a routine for lifting it aboard. If it is an inflatable it can simply be hauled aboard when it has been emptied of its gear, but a heavier dinghy will need the use of a lifting tackle.

First remove the outboard engine, the oars, and any loose gear. Secure a line to the tender's outboard engine before attempting to lift it, and tie the other end to a strong point onboard the cruiser so that if the engine is dropped, it won't be lost underwater.

To lift the tender, tie a rope bridle to the bow and stern and attach a halyard—the spinnaker halyard is often the best choice—to the middle of the bridle. Winch on the halyard to lift the dinghy while another person holds it away from the cruiser's side with a boathook. Position the dinghy on deck, preferably in permanent chocks, and lash it down very securely.

Using the tender

Be cautious when using the tender, and never overload it; make two trips if necessary to transport the crew and their gear. Make sure you have sufficient equipment to cover all eventualities, even if you are going only a short distance. The equipment list could include an anchor and line, spare oar or paddle, handheld radio, torch, mini-flare pack, extra gasoline for the outboard, a means of bailing, and an air pump if it is an inflatable tender. In some dinghies these items can be stowed permanently in a small locker.

Get to know how your tender handles under outboard engine, and practice rowing it as much as possible (*p.48*). Make sure that the oars are long enough to give a good performance under oars. Do not, however, choose oars that are too long to stow inside the dinghy.

When rowing in tidal waters, take note of the direction and strength of the tide to avoid getting swept downtide of your destination. If you are rowing across the current, aim uptide so that you are swept down to your destination. If you have to row against the tide, row into shallow waters where the tide is weakest. Head out into the current, if necessary, only when abreast of your destination.

When leaving the dinghy at a landing spot, pull it ashore, if possible, and leave it well above the high tide level so that it cannot float away before you return.

GETTING IN AND OUT

More sailing accidents happen using the tender than on the cruiser itself. Always wear a life jacket when using the tender, and carry a flashlight at night to warn other boats of your presence. Be especially careful when getting into and out of the tender. Inflatables seem quite stable, but they can invert like any dinghy if you put your weight in the wrong place. Inflatables also flex and move as you shift your weight, as they are not as rigid as a solid dinghy. Some cruisers have a stern platform, from which the dinghy can easily be boarded in calm water. If your boat has this arrangement, tie the dinghy at the cruiser's stern with its painter and a stern line so that it is held securely.

❶ The person rowing should get into the tender first. Boarding is made easier if you have removable steps or a boarding platform at the stern and if the tender is secured at both its bow and stern. Step into the middle of the dinghy and sit down at once to get your weight low in the boat. Sit on the middle thwart, which is the usual place to row from. Other crew members pass the oars down into the dinghy, then climb aboard when the rower is ready. The oarsman can put the outboard oar in its oarlock, ready to cast off.

❷ Do not risk an accident by trying to cram too many people or too much gear into the tender: make two trips if necessary. Arrange passengers and gear equally fore and aft to keep the dinghy level. Once the rower has the outer oar in place in its oarlock, untie the tender and push off before the inner oar is fitted into its oarlock. Reverse the procedure when coming alongside. If using a dinghy with metal, removable oarlocks, always remove the oarlock on the side next to the cruiser; otherwise, it may scratch the topsides.

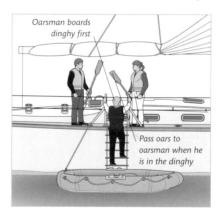

Oarsman boards dinghy first

Pass oars to oarsman when he is in the dinghy

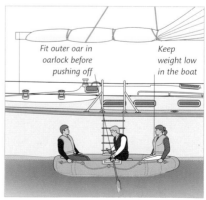

Fit outer oar in oarlock before pushing off

Keep weight low in the boat

PREPARING TO SAIL

Sailing a boat is not like driving a car. A motorist can pull over to get help if there is a mechanical problem, ask directions, take a rest, or eat a meal. On a boat none of this is possible. So before you go sailing, even for a short trip, you should check that the boat is ready for sea, that all its equipment is in place and in working order, and that all the crew understand its use. It is crucial that the safety equipment is fully functional, and that the crew know what it is for and how and when to use it. Problems can occur even on a short trip in good weather, so do not be complacent. Make sure you let someone ashore know of your plans and when you expect to return.

Before you set sail
Even if you are just heading out for a few hours in familiar home waters, spend a few minutes planning the trip and briefing the crew. Make an outline plan of where you expect to sail and when you will return. Check the weather forecast, and have a contingency plan prepared if the weather looks changeable. Make sure you know the state of the tide and what it will be doing over the period of your trip. Make sure you have enough provisions on board for the crew, sufficient to last the length of the trip with some spare.

If you are heading off on a longer cruise, your pre-passage planning needs to be more thorough. You can gain much pleasure from planning a passage at home; work done at this stage makes it more likely that your trip will go smoothly and efficiently.

On the boat, make a visual check of all equipment and systems and investigate in detail if any system appears deficient in any way.

Decide on how you wish to leave your berth and brief the crew on how the maneuver will be performed, their roles, and what jobs need to be done as soon as you have cleared the berth.

If you are going to be out for more than a few hours, prepare a snack and a hot drink in a Thermos flask before you sail. If conditions are rough, you may not feel like preparing food once you are under way; it will make life much more pleasant for the crew if this has been done before you set sail.

Stowing gear
The motion aboard a small boat in a seaway can be quite rough, and will dislodge all but the best-stowed gear and equipment. A boat's interior quickly becomes very squalid when gear breaks loose and is scattered around the cabin, especially if it gets wet. Spend some time before you set sail ensuring that everything is stowed securely and cannot move, however far the boat heels. Impress on your crew the need for neatness below and on deck, give them some stowage space for their personal items, and make sure they understand where all important equipment is stowed and how it should be secured. Take a final look around below and on deck before you leave your berth. Make sure all hatches are securely closed.

The safety briefing
It is normal for the skipper to brief the crew before heading out, even if there are only two of you or if a larger crew has sailed together often. In these circumstances, a quick rundown of the passage plan and how you plan to leave the berth may be sufficient, but if there are novices on board, or experienced crew who are new to the boat, a more extensive briefing will be necessary. Tailor the

SKIPPER'S BRIEFING
Before leaving the berth, the skipper should give a thorough briefing on all the boat's systems and safety equipment.

briefing to the experience of the crew, prevailing conditions, and intentions for the passage ahead. Things to cover include: use of the galley, gas and water supply discipline, use of the sea toilet or holding tank system, locations and instructions for fire extinguishers and blankets, whether smoking is permitted on board and if so, where and when this is allowable, location and use of flares, first-aid kits, radio equipment, man-overboard gear, and life raft.

The safety briefing should also include information about the weather conditions predicted and sensible sun protection and clothing options. The secret of a good safety briefing is to judge just how much information is needed to keep boat and crew safe without adding to any uneasiness among a novice crew.

Each crew member should be issued a life jacket and harness, which they should adjust to fit them tightly. On the skipper's instructions, they should then either wear them right away or keep them somewhere where they can be easily reached.

The skipper should also check if any of his crew are taking special medication or have health issues and whether they can swim, have any personal anxiety about being afloat, or have skills that could help in emergency situations.

If anyone suffers from seasickness, this is a good time to remind them to take their preferred treatment. Always carry a stock of seasickness tablets with the first-aid kit and make sure the crew knows they are available. There should always be more than one crewmember on board who knows some of the distress signals for use in an emergency and, in particular, can operate the radio equipment and follow the protocol for making an emergency call (*p.424*).

EQUIPMENT CHECK LIST

Make sure you have all the basic equipment on board that you need for the trip, and check that it is in working order before you set sail. Take the time needed to do a visual check of all systems.

Checklist

Most cruising boats have a surprising amount of equipment that should be checked periodically. Not all checks will be necessary every time you set sail, but a comprehensive checklist acts as a good memory aid. You should be sure to check all points on the list at intervals during the sailing season as part of a regular inspection and maintenance schedule.

The engine

• Check fuel, oil, and water systems, and the tightness of drive belts, seawater intake, impeller, and filter.
• Run the engine to warm it up before you cast off. Check that cooling water is being discharged.
• Check the propeller shaft's stern gland and greaser, if fitted.
• Make sure batteries are fully charged.
• Is a suitable tool kit on board, with sufficient spares for your engine, and other vital pieces of equipment?

Boat equipment

• Check the condition of the anchor chain. Know how much is available. Check that the end of the chain is secured on board to a strong point that is easily reached.
• Know your bilges—is it a dry or wet boat? What level of water is normal in your bilge?
• Check gas bottle fittings and piping, and test the gas alarm.
• Operate all seacocks. Be sure you have correct size bungs available.
• Do you have a waterproof flashlight with spare batteries and bulbs?
• Are your navigation lights and VHF radio in working order?
• Have you closed all hatches and ventilators that may let in water?

Safety equipment

• Is your first-aid kit complete and up to date? Have you briefed the crew on its location and composition?
• Check that you have safety harnesses and life jackets in working order for every member of the crew.
• Has the life raft been serviced recently? Are its lashings secure?
• Are there sufficient flares within their expiration date?
• Is there a foghorn on board?
• Check firefighting equipment. Are extinguishers fully charged?

Rig and sails

• Check masts and spars—look for broken strands in standing rigging, cracks in fittings, loose pins or joints, damage, and metal fatigue.
• Check running rigging for fraying and chaffing. Are the bitter ends and whippings in good condition?
• Check the sails especially the seams, stress points, cringles, strengthening patches, batons and any earlier repairs.

Navigation equipment

• Do you have an up-to-date chart on board for your sailing area?
• Do you have local tide tables, tidal atlas, and local sailing instructions?
• Are all the navigation instruments in working order?

General checks

• Check all hatch seals for signs of leaks.
• Is all your deck hardware in proper working order?
• Have you completed all necessary repair jobs?
• Do you have sufficient water and provisions on board, with enough to allow for an unexpectedly long trip?

HANDLING UNDER POWER

Pressures of time, busy sailing areas, and crowded marinas mean that most cruisers are now equipped with engines. Modern marine engines are far more reliable than their predecessors, and usually work when required. However, you should still allow for a possible engine failure. Have an anchor ready to let go, and sails ready to hoist, whenever engine failure could cause problems. A boat under power does not steer like a car, and factors such as prop walk and windage will affect the boat's handling.

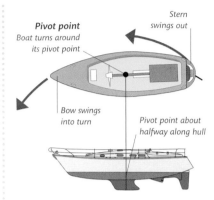

Pivot point
Boat turns around its pivot point

Stern swings out

Bow swings into turn

Pivot point about halfway along hull

THE WAY BOATS TURN
When a boat is turned, its stern does not follow the bow through the turn. Instead, the boat pivots and the stern swings out.

Boat handling

People who are new to sailing often make the mistake of assuming that a boat steers in the same way as a car. In fact, when a boat turns, it pivots around a point near its center, and the stern swings out away from the direction of the turn. When handling the boat in a confined space, you should be aware of the stern's swing as you turn the boat.

Propeller effects

The key to handling a boat well under power is understanding the propeller effect called "prop walk." Water density increases with depth, so the lower blade of a propeller is always in denser water than the upper blade, creating a paddlewheel effect, which pushes the stern sideways in the same direction in which the propeller rotates. A typical right-handed or clockwise-rotating

propeller tends to "walk" the stern to starboard when moving forward. With most gearboxes, the direction of rotation reverses when going astern, "walking" the stern to port.

When going ahead, the rudder is more efficient and will easily counter prop walk as soon as you have steerage way. When going astern, however, the rudder is less effective on most boats, especially at the slow speeds normally used in reverse, and prop walk will be more apparent. You can discover the extent and direction of prop walk in reverse before you leave your berth. With the boat tied up securely, put the engine in reverse at half throttle. Look over the side to see from which direction water turbulence appears. This is the flow off the propeller. If free to move, the stern will swing away from the disturbance.

Boat characteristics

How a boat handles under power depends on a number of factors. These include engine size, propeller location

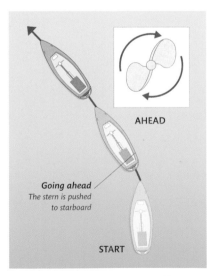

AHEAD

Going ahead
The stern is pushed to starboard

START

PROP WALK AHEAD
With a clockwise-rotating propeller, the stern will tend to move to starboard when the engine is running ahead.

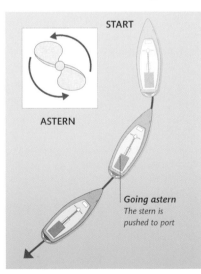

START

ASTERN

Going astern
The stern is pushed to port

PROP WALK ASTERN
With a conventional gearbox, the propeller rotates counterclockwise when running astern and pulls the stern to port.

and direction of rotation, type of keel and rudder, and the amount of windage above decks. A long-keeled boat with its rudder hung on the back of the keel is usually difficult to steer when going astern. In some cases, it may be impossible to get such a boat to go astern in a straight line.

It is important to know your boat's limitations so that you can plan your maneuvers to avoid such situations. The effect of wind on the boat can also help or hinder your maneuvers. A wind blowing from the side tends to push a boat's bow downwind when moving at slow speed. If this effect counteracts the effect of prop walk, you may be able to reverse in a straight line. If the wind contributes to the prop walk effect, you will not be able to stop the bow from turning rapidly downwind.

Steering under power

Many modern fin-keeled cruisers, especially those with a spade rudder, steer astern well, even at slow speeds. If you are steering this type of boat using a tiller, however, beware when motoring quickly astern. The forces on the rudder can be strong and will be transmitted to the tiller. Unless you hold it firmly and avoid large movements, the tiller may be wrenched from your grasp and swing violently to one side. If this happens, the boat will turn rapidly, and you may get trapped by the tiller unless you stand clear of its end.

You will be using the engine to maneuver in confined spaces, so you must learn how your boat behaves in different conditions. Experiment in a stretch of clear water to find out how it handles. Try steering in a straight line astern at different speeds, check the extent of prop walk, and see how tight a turning circle you can achieve under full power, half power, and at

low speed. Prop walk will result in a tighter turning circle in one direction, often when turning to port going ahead or astern.

When motoring astern, remember that the effect of moving the tiller is reversed: the bow will swing in the direction in which the tiller is moved, whereas the stern moves in the opposite direction. Keep practicing your handling skills until you are fully proficient at turning the boat in tight spaces. Even then, always plan for the unexpected, and have an anchor and sails ready for instant use.

TURNING UNDER POWER

Turning in a confined space is usually the most difficult maneuver under power. Unless you have the space to execute a power turn with the helm hard over, you will need to use your slow-speed handling skills and any wind effects to help you turn safely under full control. Prop walk can be very helpful for this kind of maneuver.

Prop walk

If the stern moves to port under prop walk when you go astern, start your turn to starboard. Put the tiller hard over to port and hold it there. Power the engine for a few seconds to start the boat turning. With the rudder hard over, the water pushed by the propeller is deflected by the rudder. This makes the stern move in the opposite direction. Shift to neutral when the boat moves forward. Reverse and give another burst of power, keeping the tiller hard over to port. Prop walk in reverse moves the stern to port. As the boat moves astern, shift into forward gear and give another burst of power.

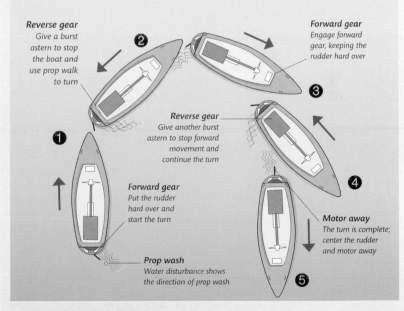

TURNING WITH PROP WALK
Use alternating ahead and astern bursts of power from the engine to turn, with the tiller held hard over. The aim is to use the propeller thrust to turn without moving the boat forward or backward significantly.

HANDLING UNDER SAIL

The handling characteristics of a cruiser depend on a number of factors, including its hull and keel shape and its rig configuration. Every class and design of cruiser is different and will behave in its own particular way under sail and power. The differences are apparent when you are sailing or motoring at normal speed, but they are much more obvious when it comes to handling the boat at slow speeds and in confined spaces, such as when entering or leaving harbor or berthing. It is these occasions that usually cause the most difficulty for inexperienced skippers and crews. The only way to become fully proficient in handling your boat is to learn how it behaves at all speeds, including when you are sailing and motoring very slowly.

Drifting characteristics

To start learning about your boat, take it to an area of clear water, away from other boats, and see how it behaves when left to drift. Go out under engine with the sails stowed. When you are clear of other boats, put the engine into neutral, turn the boat into the wind, and let it come to a stop. Let go of the tiller and see how the boat behaves. The bow will blow off downwind and the boat will pivot around its keel until it takes up its natural drifting position. Watch carefully to see how quickly the bow blows downwind—you will need to know this for situations when you must maneuver at slow speeds.

Some boats will lie naturally beam-on to the wind, but most point farther downwind. If the wind is strong enough, you will find that you can steer the boat downwind with the windage of rig and hull giving steerage way. You should experiment to see how broad an angle either side of dead downwind you can sail under bare poles, and how quickly the boat

moves through the water. Next, check to see how quickly your boat will stop when put head-to-wind. Motor head-to-wind and put the engine in neutral. The boat will slow down and eventually stop.

Take note of how far you have traveled before you lose rudder control and the boat comes to a complete standstill. You should repeat these exercises with a range of starting speeds, and in different wind and sea conditions, to build up a complete picture of your boat's behavior.

Mainsail alone

Once you have explored how your boat stops and drifts, hoist the mainsail alone and try sailing on all points of sailing. How well or badly your boat sails with only the mainsail will depend on the rig configuration and the underwater hull shape. Many modern cruisers sail well under mainsail alone. This is especially true of those with a fractional sloop rig, which has a proportionally larger mainsail and relies less on the headsail than a full masthead design.

You will probably find that the boat will sail downwind very easily with only the mainsail, but will perform less well on a reach or when close-hauled. The lack of a headsail will cause the boat to sail slowly on a reach. You will probably experience considerable weather helm as the boat tries to turn up into the wind and you are forced to counter this direction with a large amount of rudder.

You may find that sailing close-hauled is even more difficult. Try tacking the boat to see if it will turn through the wind and bear

HEADSAIL ALONE

Some well-balanced yachts will sail to windward under headsail alone. Try out different sizes of sails in different wind strengths to see how your boat responds.

away onto the new tack. If your boat will tack and sail slowly to windward under mainsail alone, this will be helpful when you need to sail slowly in confined spaces. Try turning the boat in as tight a circle as possible. You will find it easy to luff up, especially if you pull in the mainsheet rapidly as you start the turn, but bearing away will be more difficult without the headsail to assist the maneuver. The boat will need to be moving as fast as possible, and you must let the mainsheet all the way out before you try to turn, or the boat will respond very slowly, if at all.

Being confident in your ability to sail the boat slowly but in full control under mainsail alone is a valuable skill. It allows you to lower the jib and clear the foredeck before picking up a mooring, laying an anchor, or coming alongside, which makes life much easier for the foredeck crew.

MAINSAIL ALONE
Knowing how your boat handles under mainsail alone can be particularly useful when dealing with rough weather. Here, a small cruiser is using a deep-reefed mainsail alone in heavy conditions.

Headsail alone
Now try sailing the boat under headsail alone. Set the largest headsail you can for the prevailing conditions, and put the boat on each point of sailing in turn. The boat will sail well downwind and should be comfortable all the way up to a beam reach. It will sail more slowly on a reach than it would with full rig, and will probably demonstrate lee helm. Try sailing on a close reach and then close-hauled, if possible, but do not be surprised if your boat will not respond well to sailing close-hauled under headsail alone. Much will depend on the amount of wind and the size of the headsail. Try changing down to a smaller headsail and see what difference that makes. Experiment with all your headsails in turn. You should repeat the exercise with different headsail sizes in as many different wind strengths

and sea states as possible to determine how your boat handles. What works in ideal cruising conditions may not work in light or strong winds, or in rough seas. It is far better to find this out in an exercise than in a situation where the boat's safety depends on it. Finally, try turning the boat in fairly tight circles under headsail alone, trying different sized headsails in turn. The boat will bear away readily, but luffing up may be difficult as the headsail attempts to counteract the force of the rudder. Get the boat moving as fast as possible before luffing; pull in the headsail sheet slowly, letting it shake at the luff, to reduce its countereffect on the rudder. You will probably not be able to turn a full circle, as the boat may not tack. However, at least you will find out how close to the wind you can luff while still retaining control. Beware

of letting the boat slow down too much when trying to sail close-hauled under headsail alone. If it slows too much, the bow is likely to blow off quickly downwind, and you may find it difficult to regain control quickly.

Putting it all together
For most of the time when cruising you will use both sails together. In a properly tuned cruiser, the turning effects of the mainsail and headsail, when correctly set, will counteract each other and result in a balanced helm, without significant weather helm or lee helm. If the sails are trimmed properly, it should also be possible to steer a cruiser using sail trim alone, just as you can with a dinghy (*pp.134–135*). Experiment with sail trim to see if your boat can be steered in this way.

TACKING

The principle for tacking a cruiser is the same as for tacking a dinghy (*pp.90–93*), but in practice the maneuver has to take into account the facts that a cruiser is much heavier, slower to turn, and has a lot more load on its sails and sheets than a small boat. Tacking a larger boat takes longer than a small one, and requires a routine that will depend on the type of rig, the number of sails to be handled, and the size of the crew that you have available.

TACKING WITH A FULL CREW
When racing, it is important to tack efficiently, and the crew must work together to sheet the sails onto the new tack and move themselves across the boat.

Know your boat

Each cruiser will handle slightly differently, depending on its weight, type of keel, hull shape, and rig type, so it is important to get to know your own boat's handling characteristics. Once you know how your boat handles in a range of conditions, you will be able to tack the boat with confidence, knowing how to avoid getting stuck in irons (*p.93*) or stalling so that the boat sails slowly and slides sideways after the tack. This is important if you have to tack in confined situations, such as when sailing in to a harbor or approaching a mooring or anchorage.

Most production cruisers are fin-keeled, Bermudan sloops and, despite many other differences, they tend to have very similar handling characteristics. In general, the longer the keel on a cruiser, the slower it will tack, so a long-keeled traditional cruiser can be expected to tack more slowly than a modern cruiser with a fin keel that is quite narrow in a fore and aft direction. Different rigs also have different handling characteristics and are likely to effect the way a boat tacks. Cruisers with complex rigs, perhaps with two masts and a bowsprit, have more windage aloft than a Bermudan rig and may be more

prone to stopping head-to-wind during the tack. Multihulls, too, are often reluctant to tack as the windage of their topsides and cabin structure, combined with their very light weight and lack of momentum, conspire to stop the boat quickly as it turns into the wind to tack.

Tacking procedure

When tacking a cruiser, your aim is to turn the bow through the wind and sail the boat onto the new course with a minimum loss of speed. You will usually tack from a close-hauled course on one tack to a close-hauled course on the other tack while beating to windward, but you may also need to tack from a reach to a reach in other situations, such as when maneuvering in confined waters.

The cruiser's size and weight mean that tacking will be much slower than in a dinghy. There will also be more work for the crew because the sails are bigger. There may be more crew aboard, which will make the job easier, but they need guidance from the helmsman to coordinate their actions effectively. If you are a member of the crew, make sure that you know how the helmsman likes to perform the tack and, if you are unsure, ask how the boat handles

during a tack. If you are the skipper, brief the crew beforehand to avoid confusion. For example, if the boat's design characteristics make it difficult to tack, you may prefer the headsail to be backed to help the bow turn through the wind, so be sure to brief the crew on how and why you want the jib to be handled during the tack.

Slowing the turn

The ease or difficulty the crew face when handling the jib during the tack is often dependent on how the helmsman chooses to steer the boat through the tack. By slowing down the turn, once the bow has passed through the wind, the helmsman can give the crew more time to sheet in the headsail before it fills with wind. If the helmsman is not careful or considerate, the boat may turn too far on the new tack, and it will be more difficult for the crew to sheet in the sail when it is full of wind. However, holding the boat close to the wind after the bow has passed through head-to-wind is difficult in some boats or conditions, and if not done properly may result in the boat ending up in irons, so the helmsman should practice the technique and take account of the boat's particular characteristics. This is not a technique that will work well in a light boat, such as a catamaran, or when tacking in steep waves.

In all cruisers, remember to get the boat sailing at full speed before you attempt to tack, and do not ease the jib sheet until the sail shakes at the luff. Speed before the tack helps ensure you do not get stuck in-irons, and keeping the jib sheeted in until it loses drive will help power the boat into and through the tack.

Short-handed tacking

Most instructions for tacking a cruiser are given assuming that a full crew is available. In practice, however, this is rarely the case. Most cruisers sail with a couple, or a family crew, and even if a full crew is on board, some may be off watch, leaving just one or two people on deck. Sometimes there may be only one person in the cockpit, and it may be necessary to tack the boat singlehanded.

If the boat is steered with a tiller, it is often quite easy for the helmsman to push the tiller to leeward and hold it there with a hip or a foot, while he casts off the old jib sheet as the boat reaches head-to-wind, and pulls in the new one. The task is made easier if the boat is fitted with self-tailing winches (*p.229*) and if the cockpit is laid out so that the sheet winches are in reach of the helmsman. If the boat is fitted with a wheel, it is more difficult to steer without using your hands, but it can often be achieved. If an autopilot is fitted, you may be able to use its tack function to steer the boat through the tack while you handle the jib sheets.

Tacking in rough weather

Sailing in strong winds and large waves adds to the risk of getting caught in-irons and being blown back onto the old tack. Make sure to have the correct sail area for the conditions so that the helm is balanced, and make sure that the boat is moving fast before the tack. Try to pick a flat spot between waves in which to complete the tack.

If you sail a boat that is difficult to tack, you may wish to back the jib to force the bow through the wind and onto the new tack. In this case, hold the old jib sheet in until the jib fills on the wrong side, then release it. The backed jib will force the boat's bow onto the new tack, at which point you can release the old sheet and winch in the new one.

TACKING

Prepare to tack by sailing on a close-hauled course. The skipper must make sure the new course is clear. If there are enough crewmembers, it is best to have one manning each jib sheet winch. Otherwise, a single crew must prepare the new winch before releasing the old jib sheet.

❶ The helmsman calls "ready about." A crewmember puts two turns of the new sheet on its winch, and pulls in the slack. The other crew then uncleats the working jib sheet, but keeps it tight to prevent it from slipping on the winch.

❷ The crew calls "ready," and the helmsman, calling "lee-oh," starts to turn the boat into the tack. The crew on the working sheet watches the luff of the jib, and, as it starts to flap, eases and then releases the sheet.

❸ When the jib blows across to the new side, the new sheet is pulled in. When load comes on the sheet, the crew takes another turn or two on the winch. Then the handle is inserted and the crew winches the sheet to trim the sail.

JIBING

Like tacking, the principle for jibing a cruiser is the same as for a dinghy (*pp.94–97*) but the different size, weight, and handling characteristics mean that more care must be taken and an allowance made for the much higher loads that act on the larger boat's sails, sheets, winches, and cleats.

STAYING IN CONTROL
The most important part of jibing a cruiser is preventing the boom from swinging across the boat out of control.

Know your boat

As with tacking a cruiser (*pp.240–241*), there is no substitute for knowing the characteristics of your boat, although there is less difficulty when jibing, since there is no danger that the boat will stop during the maneuver. In many ways, jibing is a simpler process than tacking, but it can also be more violent, especially in strong winds, and has inherent dangers for the crew, who must be prepared for the maneuver.

When jibing a Bermudan sloop, you only have to deal with a mainsail and a jib, or possibly a spinnaker or gennaker (*pp.250–257*), but if you sail a ketch, yawl, or schooner (*p.199*), you will have two boomed sails to deal with, and with some rig types you may have two or more headsails to handle. Whatever the rig arrangement, the principle of jibing remains the same, and if you have more than one boomed sail, treat it as you would a normal mainsail. If you have more than one headsail to deal with, and are limited in the number of crew available, jibe the largest sail first.

Jibing procedure

When jibing a cruiser, your aim is to turn the stern through the wind safely and smoothly without the wind's causing the boat to broach out of control (turn rapidly toward the wind) as the steering effect of the sails and the heeled hull overcome the power of the rudder to steer the boat. Although the same procedures apply to jibing a cruiser and a dinghy, a cruiser has much heavier gear. It is vital, therefore, to control the boom through the jibe. Do not allow it to sweep across from one side to the other (known as jibing all standing), except in light winds.

If the headsail is poled out, the pole must be removed before the jibe. The mainsheet traveler should be cleated in the middle of its track to prevent it from slamming along the track from one side of the boat to the other, which can be very dangerous to any crewmember in its path.

When you are ready to jibe, steer onto a run and sheet in the mainsheet to bring the boom into the middle of the boat. In small cruisers, or if you are sailing a larger boat in light winds, sheeting in can be done by hand. However, larger boats usually have a mainsheet winch to handle the high loads. Make sure the mainsheet is cleated before the jibe. Continue the turn slowly until the mainsail fills on the other side. Sheet the jib to the new side when it blows across the bow.

In medium and strong winds, the boat will try to turn to windward as soon as the mainsail is jibed. The helmsman should anticipate this and counteract the turn by ensuring that the rudder is centered when the boom crosses the centerline. If the boat still tries to turn, he must be ready to steer back downwind to prevent the boat from turning toward the wind.

Once the boom has swung across under control, the mainsheet should be eased rapidly to set the mainsail at its correct angle. On all but the smallest cruisers, it is easier if a crewmember handles the mainsheet, rather than the helmsman, who should be free to concentrate on steering through the jibe.

Jibing in rough weather

Jibing is easy in light winds when the boat speed is low and the loads on the sails and sheets are light, but in strong winds and rough seas, the maneuver becomes harder and more dangerous.

Before you start a jibe in rough weather, consider whether it is necessary, or whether it would be safer to luff to a close reach before tacking around and bearing away to the new course. Tacking puts less pressure on the rig than jibing in rough weather, but it does involve turning into the wind and waves to complete the tack.

If you decide to jibe, brief the crew before starting the maneuver and make certain that the person handling the mainsheet fully understands their task. It is important in strong winds to sheet the mainsail in tight to the centerline before the jibe, then let it run out quickly after the jibe to ease the loads on the rudder that will try to turn the boat to windward. Remind everyone to keep their heads below the level of the boom during the jibe.

Like dinghies, a cruiser will be easier to jibe when it is moving fast, since this is when the loads on the rig will be least. Pick a time to jibe when the boat is on the face of a wave, possibly surfing, and make your steering actions positive to force the boat to turn where you want it to go. As soon as the boat has turned to bring the wind onto the new side of the mainsail, tell the crew handling the mainsheet to ease it out rapidly to set the mainsail correctly on the new jibe.

The jib can be jibed either before, after, or at the same time as the mainsail depending on the availability of crew. If headsail roller furling is fitted, it can be easier to roll away the headsail, then jibe the mainsail before unrolling the headsail on the new side.

Avoiding an accidental jibe

An accidental, "all standing" jibe is potentially dangerous, but when the boat is on a run, quite a small wind shift or deviation from course may cause an unintentional jibe. You can avoid this problem by not sailing on a dead run, especially in choppy conditions. If you sail on a training run (p.40), you will be less at risk from an unexpected wind shift or a wave pushing you off course. Alternatively, rig a preventer line to lock the boom in position and stop it from swinging across, even if the wind does get behind the mainsail. A preventer is a rope attached to the aft end of the boom, led forward to a turning block on the foredeck, and back to the cockpit where it can be adjusted, or released quickly, if necessary, in an emergency.

Short-handed jibing

If you have to jibe without help, take your time and deal with the mainsail first. Sheet it in tight to the centerline, turn the boat through the jibe, then ease out the mainsheet fully on the new side. Then jibe the headsail.

JIBING

Prepare to jibe by sailing on a run. In anything but light winds, the boom should be pulled in tight to prevent it from sweeping across the boat as you jibe, which may cause damage or injury. On larger boats, the mainsheet is often led to a winch and the sheet must be winched in.

❶ The helmsman warns the crew by calling "stand by to jibe." The mainsheet is pulled in to bring the boom to the centerline. If the mainsheet runs on a traveler across the cockpit, the traveler is cleated in the center before the jibe.

❷ While one crewmember prepares the new jib sheet by taking a turn or two on the winch and pulling in any slack, the other uncleats the working sheet and prepares to release it. When the crew is ready, they tell the helmsman.

❸ The helmsman starts a slow turn into the jibe, calling "jibe-oh." As the jib blows across the bow, the crew releases the old sheet as the new one is pulled in. The helmsman steers carefully downwind as the mainsail is let out on the new side.

SAIL BALANCE

Keeping a sailing boat balanced is as important in a cruiser as it is in a dinghy. When a dinghy gets out of balance, it is usually quickly apparent as the boat heels, slows down, and develops more weather or lee helm (*p.127*). The same occurs in a cruiser, but, because of its greater size and weight, and its relatively slow response, you may find it harder to spot when the boat is not well balanced. Get to know your boat so that you understand the best sail trim for all conditions.

achieving better speed while heeling less will allow the cruiser to make faster, and more comfortable, passages. Good balance can also be a distinct safety feature, since it is easier to handle heavy weather in a boat that is balanced correctly. A cruiser's rig and sails are tuned using the same principles that apply to tuning a dinghy (*pp.174–179*). If you find it difficult to tune your boat, ask your sail-maker to sail it and advise you on any changes that may be required to mast rake, mast bend, and sail shape.

Boat tuning

Many cruising sailors think that boat tuning is only of interest to racing sailors. Nothing could be farther from the truth. A well-tuned cruising boat will sail faster, heel less, and exhibit much less weather helm than a boat whose owner has not taken the trouble to ensure that the rig and sails are working in harmony. While ultimate speed is not the cruising sailor's main objective,

Weather and lee helm

Most yachts have a degree of weather helm, but it should never become so great as to require large angles of rudder deflection to keep the boat on course. Similarly, lee helm should not be permitted as it makes it very

GOOD SAIL BALANCE
This cruiser is sailing fast with little heel while close-hauled in moderate to strong winds. The mainsail has been reefed and sail balance has been maintained by partly furling the roller-reefing headsail.

BEARING AWAY
The crew is using the sails correctly to help the boat bear away smoothly without heeling. A crew lets out the mainsheet as the helmsman bears away, while the headsail is kept full to assist the turn.

difficult to keep the boat on course and can be dangerous. If the boat has lee helm and the wheel or tiller is released for any reason, the boat will bear away and keep sailing, possibly accelerating as it does so, rather than turning head-to-wind and stopping as it should. This can lead to accidents and should be avoided.

Try your boat on a close-hauled course in a good Force 3–4 breeze. With the boat sailing properly to windward, there should be a small amount of weather helm. If there is too much weather helm or, worse still, lee helm, you must tune your boat to get the desired balance.

Turning forces

The sails on a cruiser create exactly the same turning forces as they do on a dinghy (pp.78–81), but many cruising sailors fail to use (or to make allowances for) the effects of these forces. Instead, they rely solely on the rudder to turn the boat. This can lead to loss of control in strong winds. Therefore, you should always remember to use the sails to assist you when altering course. This is especially important when bearing away in strong winds.

HEAVING-TO

Heaving-to can be a very useful technique in a cruiser. You can heave-to to stop the boat in order to prepare and eat a meal in comfort, or to take in a reef if the wind strength increases. Heaving-to is also often a good tactic for riding out rough weather.

How to heave-to

The procedure for heaving-to in cruisers is the same as that for dinghies (p.100)—tack the main but don't touch the headsail or its working sheet; finally, lash the tiller to leeward. This arrangement balances the actions of the sails and rudder. Traditional long-keeled craft often heave-to very well, typically lying with the wind between 45 and 60 degrees off the bow. Modern cruisers, with shallower hulls and shorter keels, do not always heave-to so steadily, but you should be able to achieve an angle of about 60 degrees off the wind. Experiment with your boat and try different combinations of mainsail and rudder position. A typical arrangement has the jib sheeted hard aback, with the mainsail eased slightly, and the tiller lashed to leeward. If the boat will not lie close to the wind, try using a smaller headsail. A boat hove-to drifts at between 90 and 135 degrees to the wind direction, but it will lie much more quietly than if it were sailing.

Heave-to by backing the headsail to windward

HOVE-TO
A cruiser is hove-to by tacking while leaving the headsail sheet cleated on the old side. The tiller should be lashed to leeward (or the wheel lashed to windward) so that if the boat does try to sail, it will turn toward the wind and stop.

REDUCING SAIL AREA

For all sailing boats, there is a certain wind strength in which the boat is fully powered up. Beyond this optimum wind speed, the boat will be overpowered, will heel excessively, slow down, and be harder to steer. The wind speed at which this overpowering occurs varies according to boat type, size, rig, and keel shape. It also depends on sea conditions and air temperature. Cold air is heavier and exerts more force on the sails and rough seas throw the boat about and make it harder to steer.

Know your boat

Novices often think that a boat that is heeled sharply over, throwing lots of spray across the decks, naturally sails faster than a boat that is more upright. In fact, most modern boats sail faster if they are sailed as upright as possible and will slow down if they are allowed to heel too much. Excessive heeling also makes it much harder to steer, as weather helm increases to the point, in some boats, where it can be difficult or even impossible to hold the boat on course.

Whether a boat can cope with a lot of heel depends predominantly on its hull shape. A relatively narrow, moderate, or heavy displacement yacht (*pp.196–199*) with a long keel will sail to windward well heeled, and will be comfortable with the lee rail down to the water. On the other hand, the majority of modern mass-produced cruising boats are relatively wide, light or moderate displacement designs and are better sailed much more upright. Such boats will become increasingly uncomfortable if pressed

beyond about 20 degrees of heel, so you should reef earlier than you might if sailing a more traditional design.

Get to know your boat's sailing characteristics and how it behaves in rough weather so that you can reduce sail in good time, before the boat starts to struggle.

Shorten sail early

The easiest time to reef the mainsail or to change to a smaller headsail is before you leave your berth. Before any trip, remember to get an up-to-date forecast just before departure. If conditions appear borderline for reefing your boat, it is good seamanship to reef before leaving harbor rather than wait until you are at sea to assess the conditions.

Remember, it is much easier to take in a reef while still in sheltered water than when the boat is heeled and pitching in a rough sea. If, when you reach open water, conditions are not as rough as you expected, it is easier to shake out (take out) a reef than to put one in while being buffeted by wind as you try to leave harbor.

If you are at sea and the wind starts to strengthen, take in a reef or change to a smaller headsail as soon as you think it may be needed. It is very natural to delay the task in the hope that it will not be necessary, but this very often proves to be wishful thinking. Any delay will give time for the conditions to deteriorate further, which will make it harder to do the job when you finally decide it must be done.

Another time when you should reef early is if night is falling and you suspect conditions will worsen. In this case, it is much easier to reef in daylight than to have to complete the job in the dark.

SAILING IN ROUGH WEATHER
In high winds and large seas, a yacht should be reefed sufficiently to allow it to sail efficiently and comfortably.

Maintaining balance

When it becomes necessary to reduce sail, it is very important that you do so in a way that maintains the balance between the area of the mainsail and the jib. The pivot point of most sailboats is just behind the mast, and your aim should be to reduce the sail areas in front of and behind the mast in proportion to each other. If the jib is reduced too much in proportion to the mainsail, the sailplan will not be balanced and the boat will develop a lot of weather helm and tend to turn toward the wind. If the mainsail is reduced too much in proportion to the jib, the opposite will occur. The boat will develop lee helm and will try to turn away from the wind.

Most boats handle best if the jib is reefed first as the boat becomes overpressed. If the wind continues to increase, the next step is to take the first reef in the mainsail. Continue to reef both sails as necessary, to maintain the balance between them as the wind increases.

REEFING BOTH SAILS

Many modern cruisers are rigged with a roller-reefing headsail and a fully-battened mainsail. The first step when reefing is usually to roll away some of the headsail before taking a reef in the mainsail.

Full mainsail

Full-size headsail

UNREEFED

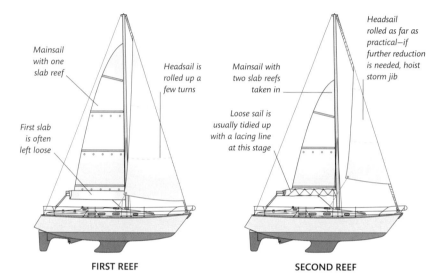

Mainsail with one slab reef

Headsail is rolled up a few turns

First slab is often left loose

FIRST REEF

Mainsail with two slab reefs taken in

Loose sail is usually tidied up with a lacing line at this stage

Headsail rolled as far as practical—if further reduction is needed, hoist storm jib

SECOND REEF

Storm sails

Cruising boats that make long passages should carry separate storm sails that can be used when conditions go beyond those for which your normal sails are designed. Storm sails are much smaller and tougher than normal sails. They are made of heavier cloth (which is usually orange for high visibility) with additional reinforcement and seam stitching.

A small triangular sail called a trysail is set in place of the mainsail, which is stowed on the boom. The trysail is usually set loose-footed with two sheets led to blocks on each quarter. A small storm jib is hanked to the forestay or, on a boat with a roller headsail, onto a specially rigged stay just aft of the furled jib on the forestay. You should practice rigging the trysail and storm jib in calm conditions to be sure that everything works and you understand how to set them efficiently before you need to use them in earnest in gale- or storm-force winds.

TRYSAIL AND STORM JIB

An offshore cruising boat should always carry sails designed for storm conditions. A small trysail replaces the mainsail, while a storm jib is set on the forestay, or on a removable stay if the forestay has a roller jib. Both sails are made from orange cloth so the boat can be seen easily.

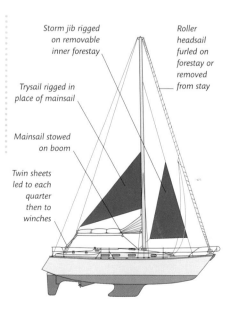

Storm jib rigged on removable inner forestay

Roller headsail furled on forestay or removed from stay

Trysail rigged in place of mainsail

Mainsail stowed on boom

Twin sheets led to each quarter then to winches

Reducing headsail size

How you reduce headsail area depends on the type of headsail system on your boat. If you sail with a roller-reefing headsail, you simply need to take a few rolls in the sail by easing the sheet and pulling in on the furling line. When sufficient sail has been rolled away, the furling line is cleated and the sail sheeted in again. The main problem with this system is that it rarely results in a well-setting sail once a few rolls have been taken in. Roller-reefed headsails usually develop a baggy shape that makes them inefficient when sailing to windward and adds to the heeling forces (which is the opposite of what is required). Nevertheless, many coastal cruising sailors choose to sail with this equipment because of the ease with which the sail can be reefed and furled on the forestay.

Changing headsails

The alternative to a roller-reefing system is to have a number of headsails of various sizes to suit different wind strengths. Each jib is hanked onto the forestay when in use. If you plan to sail far offshore, or expect to have to deal with rough weather on a regular basis, this system offers the advantages of being simple, efficient, and less prone to equipment failure.

To change a hanked-on headsail, the old sail is lowered, unhanked from the forestay, and the sheets removed from its clew. The old sail is stowed away in its bag and moved below, and the new sail is attached and hoisted in the normal way.

Changing a hanked-on headsail requires at least one crew member to go forward and work on the foredeck, which will be wet and moving quite violently in rough weather. The job is made easier if two crew are available to work together. One works at the mast handling the halyard and changing the sheets, while the other works at the forestay.

MAINSAIL SLAB REEFING

Slab reefing is a common system on production boats. If the reefing gear is properly organized, reefing should be quick and easy. In many boats, reefing can be carried out from the cockpit. In this case, each reef has luff and leech reefing lines led back to a cockpit winch. In some systems, a single line system is used for the first and second reefs. This system connects the luff and leech lines to an adjusting tackle within the boom. Both can then be tightened or released by adjusting a single line.

1 First, ease the mainsheet to spill all the wind from the mainsail. Then ease the boom vang. Take the weight of the boom on the topping lift, unless you have a solid vang that will safely support the boom.

2 Ease the halyard to bring the first reef down to boom level. Pull the luff reef cringle down to the boom by using a reef line, or by hooking it under a ram's horn at the gooseneck, and tighten the halyard.

3 Pull the leech reef line tight to pull the leech cringle down and out toward the boom end. There must be no wind in the sail while doing this, and the vang must be loose or the sail may tear.

4 Keep winching in the leech reefing line until the reef cringle is pulled down tightly to the boom. Release the topping lift, trim the mainsheet, and tighten the vang. Check that the halyard tension is sufficient.

5 There is now a fold of sail hanging down along the length of the boom. This can be left free, or tidied into a neat roll and secured by a light line laced through the reef cringles from leech to luff.

If you are sailing upwind when you need to change a headsail, you should slow the boat down to make the task easier and safer before you send someone forward. This can be done by easing the sails, heaving-to, or by altering course downwind, which will bring the boat upright and reduce the strength of the apparent wind. The crew going forward should always move along the windward sidedeck and be clipped on. Drag the sailbag rather than carry it and brace yourself securely before starting the job.

MAINSAIL REEFING

A mainsail has to be able to work as efficiently as possible in a wide range of conditions, from no wind to a full gale. This is achieved by reefing it as the wind strength increases. There are a number of reefing systems available; the most popular on modern boats is slab reefing (*below*). An alternative is roller reefing where the mainsail is rolled around the boom, or its modern version where the sail is rolled up around a tube inside the boom. Another system is in-mast roller reefing where the sail rolls around a tube inside the mast. Here, the mainsail is loose-footed with the clew attached to a car running in the top of the boom. The mainsail is often cut with a hollow leech so that it does not require battens. An alternative arrangement is to use vertical battens.

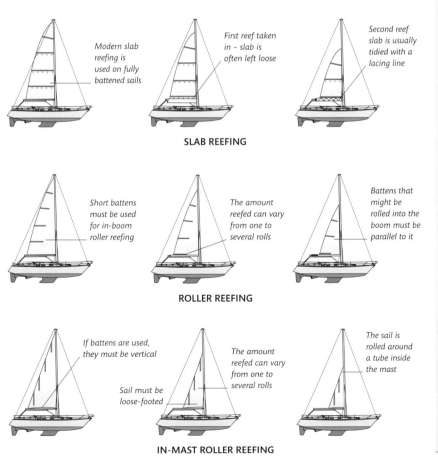

Modern slab reefing is used on fully battened sails

First reef taken in – slab is often left loose

Second reef slab is usually tidied with a lacing line

SLAB REEFING

Short battens must be used for in-boom roller reefing

The amount reefed can vary from one to several rolls

Battens that might be rolled into the boom must be parallel to it

ROLLER REEFING

If battens are used, they must be vertical

Sail must be loose-footed

The amount reefed can vary from one to several rolls

The sail is rolled around a tube inside the mast

IN-MAST ROLLER REEFING

REEFING HEADSAILS

Some jibs designed for heavy weather have a row of reef points so that they can be reduced in size quickly and easily. To reduce their area, the sail is partly lowered, the new tack is attached to the bow, the sheets are moved to the new clew, and the sail is re-hoisted.

Area of sail to be reefed

Upper tack, clew, and reef points

UNREEFED
A reefing headsail is made slightly heavier and stronger than a normal sail of the same size, but is set in the usual way if unreefed.

Line furls middle of sail

New tack attached to stem

Sheets attached to new clew

REEFED
When reefed, the upper tack and clew fittings are used. The bundle of loose sail along the foot is laced with a light line.

INCREASING SAIL AREA

The modern Bermudan sloop is the most efficient rig upwind, but it tends to be underpowered downwind in light and moderate breezes. In these conditions, it is necessary to increase the sail area to maintain a reasonable performance. This can be achieved by hoisting a special downwind sail such as a conventional or asymmetric spinnaker, or a gennaker (sometimes called a cruising chute).

DOWNWIND SAILS

In light to moderate breezes, the modern Bermudan rig is not very efficient downwind. In fact, gaff-rigged cruisers often perform better downwind, and even on reaching courses, as the gaff rig allows more sail to be carried for a given boat length and mast height. Although the Bermudan rig is the most efficient on upwind courses, sailing a Bermudan-rigged cruiser downwind in light conditions can be frustrating unless one or more special sails are carried to improve performance. Fortunately, there are several types of light-air and downwind sails to choose from to improve performance at varying costs and levels of complexity.

Spinnakers

A spinnaker is the traditional, light air, downwind sail used on Bermudan-rigged racing boats and many cruisers. It is essentially the same as a dinghy or small keelboat spinnaker but will be bigger, more powerful, and made of heavier sailcloth. There is a range of sail shapes, cloth weights, and construction methods available depending on the type of boat, whether the sail is for racing or cruising, and the wind strength in which the sail will be used.

Many cruisers have a single, general-purpose spinnaker (usually a tri-radial sail; *pp.144–155*), used when reaching or running. For light weather, some cruisers also carry a lighter crosscut or radial headsail. Cruiser-racers carry a number of different spinnakers for running or reaching in various wind strengths. These sails are built to work in a certain maximum apparent wind strength, so care should be taken to select an appropriate sail for the wind strength to avoid an expensive repair.

Asymmetrics

Some modern, fast cruisers follow the lead of high-performance dinghies and small keelboats and use asymmetric spinnakers. An asymmetric does not use a spinnaker pole, but requires a bowsprit—often made of carbon fiber for lightness—to hold the sail's tack ahead of the bow. The bowsprit is usually extended and retracted by control

SPINNAKER
A spinnaker adds considerably to the sail area of a Bermudan sloop and increases the boat speed on downwind courses.

ASYMMETRIC
Some fast cruisers use an asymmetric spinnaker with a retractable bowsprit, just like a high-performance dinghy or sportsboat. This offers good performance without the complexity of a spinnaker.

GENNAKER
A gennaker is smaller than an asymmetric and does not require a bowsprit. It is easier to handle than a spinnaker, but is less efficient, especially on a run. It is the favorite choice of many cruiser sailors.

TOPSAIL
A gaff-rigged cruiser can increase sail area by hoisting a topsail to fit in between the yard and the topmast. Some also carry a downwind foresail, called a balloon jib, which can be flown from a pole, as here.

lines. The lack of a pole makes an asymmetric much easier to use than a conventional spinnaker. An asymmetric uses two sheets, like a headsail, but the lazy sheet is led around the forestay rather than between the stay and the mast.

An asymmetric is efficient on a beam or broad reach but less so on a dead run, because it falls into the wind shadow of the mainsail. Cruiser-racers that use an asymmetric tend not to sail dead downwind. Their light weight and surfing ability make it far more effective to sail downwind on a series of broad reaches in most conditions, which is easily achieved as jibing (*pp.256–257*) is much easier than with a spinnaker and pole.

Gennakers
Like an asymmetric spinnaker, a gennaker does not use a spinnaker pole and is sheeted in the same way

as a headsail. It is not usually as large or as powerful, however, and is attached at the tack to the bow-fitting rather than to a bowsprit. This makes it easy to use. However, a gennaker is inefficient on a dead run, as it is blanketed behind the mainsail. To overcome this, the gennaker's clew can be held out to windward with a pole.

Reachers
A reacher is a light sail designed for use on courses between a close reach and a broad reach. Jibs and genoas are designed primarily for good performance on upwind courses, and are less efficient on reaching courses, especially in light winds. By comparison, a reacher is usually made from much lighter cloth and has a fuller shape. It is usually flown loose-luffed, attached only by its head (to the halyard) and tack (to the bow), but versions that hank to the forestay can be easier to handle.

A conventional spinnaker can be used on reaching courses but is harder to handle and cannot usually be flown above a beam reach, and then only in light winds. An asymmetric or a gennaker can be flown more easily on a reach and will usually suffice for most cruisers, but a specialist reacher can still be a good addition to the sail wardrobe for a long distance cruiser.

Sails for other rigs
Although the Bermudan sloop is the most common rig, other rigs can also increase their sail area in light winds. Gaff-rigged cruisers often hoist a topsail above the mainsail and may also carry a lightweight reacher. Ketches, yawls, and schooners (*p.199*) can utilize both masts to hoist various offwind sails, and often carry a large reaching sail between the two masts in addition to a spinnaker, asymmetric, gennaker, or reacher at the bow.

ADDITIONAL EQUIPMENT

All downwind sails require some additional equipment, even if it is only a halyard to hoist them and sheets to trim them. A conventional spinnaker requires the most complex arrangement with the asymmetric spinnaker and gennaker requiring much less equipment. Reaching sails require the least as they can often be hoisted on a jib or spinnaker halyard and only need a single sheet.

Spinnaker equipment

A conventional spinnaker is flown from a spinnaker pole attached to a bracket on the mast. The height of the pole's outer end is controlled by an uphaul and downhaul, or an uphaul and foreguy (p.254).

The spinnaker is controlled by a sheet attached to its clew and a guy attached to its tack. The guy is led through the end of the spinnaker pole and controls how far forward or aft the pole is set. Except on small cruisers, twin sheets and guys are used, with one pair rigged on each side. Only one pair is used at any one time. The windward guy leads from the tack, through the pole end, then through a block ahead of the cockpit, and to a winch. The leeward sheet runs from the clew through a block at the stern and onto a winch.

Asymmetric and gennaker equipment

The equipment required by an asymmetric spinnaker or a gennaker is much simpler than a conventional spinnaker. The gennaker has the simplest system. Here, the sail's tack is attached by a rope strop to the headsail's tack fitting or to the anchor roller on the bow fitting. One end of the strop can be tied or spliced to the gennaker's tack while the other is usually tied or spliced to a quick-release snap shackle. A spinnaker halyard is attached to the head, and two sheets are tied to the clew. The sheets are led outside everything to turning blocks located near the stern on each side deck. From the blocks, the sheets lead forward to cockpit winches for adjustment. The sheets of a gennaker usually pass between the mast and the forestay (below).

An asymmetric has an arrangement similar to a gennaker's, except that its tack is usually held out ahead of the boat by a retractable bowsprit. The bowsprit is pulled in and out by two control lines and a tack line usually runs through the pole and exits at its end. It is attached to the asymmetric's tack and is used to pull the tack out to the end of the pole. The sheets of an asymmetric are led the same as on a gennaker, except that they must pass around the forestay and not between the forestay and the mast. They may also have to pass around the sail's luff (below).

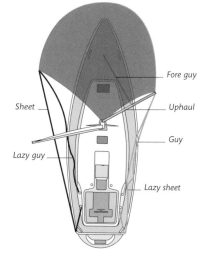

SPINNAKER EQUIPMENT
A spinnaker requires a pole with uphaul and downhaul, and a sheet and a guy that may be duplicated on each side.

Labels: Fore guy, Sheet, Uphaul, Guy, Lazy guy, Lazy sheet

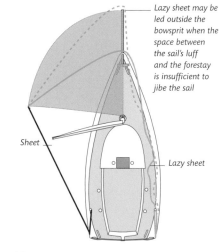

Lazy sheet may be led outside the bowsprit when the space between the sail's luff and the forestay is insufficient to jibe the sail

Sheet

Lazy sheet

ASYMMETRIC EQUIPMENT
An asymmetric is usually flown from a retractable bowsprit and has two sheets that are led to winches in the cockpit.

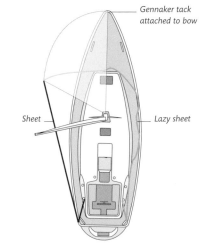

Gennaker tack attached to bow

Sheet

Lazy sheet

GENNAKER EQUIPMENT
A gennaker has its tack attached to the bow and is controlled by two sheets that are led to winches in the cockpit.

Packing a spinnaker

The key to trouble-free spinnaker hoisting is a well-packed sail. Any twists, tangles or misidentification of the clew, tack, and head while packing will cause problems when the sail is hoisted.

Unless the sail is hoisted in a sock (*below*) it will be packed in a bag or "turtle." The best place to pack the spinnaker into its bag is down below where it cannot be caught by a gust of wind. Because the spinnaker is the biggest sail on board, it will usually require the full length of the interior to lay out and pack it.

Identify the head of the sail, pull it out to one end of the interior, and temporarily fasten it to any convenient fitting to hold it in place. From the head, work down one luff tape until you reach one of the bottom corners. Fasten that

corner temporarily to hold it free of the bulk of the sail. Now follow along the foot tape to find the third corner and fasten it with the previous corner.

If the boat and spinnaker are small, the sail can now be packed into its bag, starting with the bulk of the middle of the sail between the head and the clews. Push the sail into the bag until only the three corners remain outside it. Keeping the corners correctly oriented to each other, tie them together with the tapes inside the bag, and fasten the bag's lid over the sail.

If the boat is larger than about 33 ft (10 m), the sail's size will make it difficult to pack this way without creating a twist in the sail. In this case, the sail is best "stopped" with yarn or elastic bands at intervals of about 6.5 ft (2 m) working down

from the head. The objective is to gather the sail into a long sausage between the head and the two clews. If using yarn, start at the head and work toward the foot, tying a length of yarn around the sausage at regular intervals. An easier way is to use a bucket with the bottom cut off. Slip a number of elastic bands over the bucket, then pull the sail through the bucket, starting at the head. At regular intervals, slide an elastic band off the bucket and around the sail.

With the spinnaker gathered into a long sausage, pack it into its bag, starting in the middle of the sausage so that the head and two clews are the last part of the sail packed into the bag. Secure with tapes as before to hold the three corners in their correct orientation to each other.

USING A SOCK

The trick to handling all lightweight, downwind sails is to keep them under full control during hoisting and lowering. The easiest way to do this on a short-handed cruising boat is to use a sock. This is a lightweight nylon tube, with a bell-shaped opening at the lower end, and two light control lines to pull the bell up and down. The sock can be used with a conventional spinnaker, an asymmetric spinnaker, or a gennaker. The sock covers the sail during hoisting and lowering, being pulled up out of the way when the sail is set.

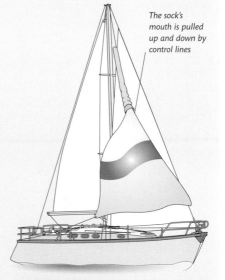

The sock's mouth is pulled up and down by control lines

Hoisting with a sock

With the sail stowed in its sock, the top of the sock is attached to the halyard, and the sail's sheets and guys are rigged. The head of the sock is then hoisted to the masthead. When the halyard has been cleated, pull the sock up clear of the sail using its uphaul, and set the sail in the normal way.

Lowering with a sock

To lower the sail, first steer onto a broad reach and hoist the headsail. The aim is to collapse the spinnaker,

asymmetric, or gennaker in the lee of the mainsail. To collapse the sail, ease the guy of a spinnaker, the tack line on an asymmetric spinnaker, or the sheet on a gennaker. Then pull the sock down using the sock's downhaul until it encases the sail. Once all of the sail is in the sock, lower the halyard and gather the sock tube onto the foredeck. Remove and stow the sheets, guys and halyard. The sock is stowed with the sail left inside it ready for use.

USING A SOCK
A sock makes it far easier to hoist and lower any downwind sail because the sail is held under control inside the sock during these tricky procedures. Make sure that the sail is fastened firmly to the top of the sock, and fit a swivel between the sock and the halyard to prevent the sock from twisting in use.

HOISTING AND TRIMMING

Before hoisting a downwind sail its sheets must be rigged and other equipment prepared for use. In the case of a spinnaker, the pole must be set and the sheets and guys led, outside everything, through their respective turning blocks and to their winches. If a retractable bowsprit is used with an asymmetric spinnaker, it must be extended and the tack line and sheets attached to the sail.

Rigging a spinnaker pole

The spinnaker pole should be rigged before the sail is hoisted. Attach the pole's inner end to the mast fitting, then attach the uphaul and downhaul to the pole's outer end. Place the working guy—the one on the side opposite the main boom—into the pole's outer end fitting, and hoist the pole into a horizontal position with the uphaul so it projects on the side opposite the main boom.

Preparing a spinnaker

When you are ready to hoist the spinnaker, attach its bag to the pulpit or to the leeward guardrail. Unfasten the top of the bag, then attach the halyard to the head of the sail.

If your sail uses twin sheets and guys, fasten a guy to each clew, and a sheet to each guy shackle (not to the clews). When the sail is hoisted, its windward sheet and leeward guy are left slack, or "lazy," while the sail is controlled by the "working" guy to windward and the "working" sheet to leeward. If your sail uses a dinghy-type system, with a single guy and sheet, attach them to the tack and clew, respectively.

If your sail is fitted with a sock (p.253), attach the halyard, sheet, and guy with the sail in its tube.

Preparing an asymmetric spinnaker or gennaker

If the sail is to be hoisted from a bag, fasten the bag to the pulpit or the leeward guardrail. Pull the tack out of the bag and attach it to a tack line from the stem fitting (for a gennaker) or to the tack line from the end of the bowsprit (for an asymmetric). If a retractable bowsprit is used, this must be extended before the sail is hoisted.

Attach the leeward sheet, which will be the working sheet when the sail is hoisted, and lead it outside everything to a turning block on the sidedeck near the stern, then to a winch. If it is not intended to jibe, it is not necessary to attach a windward, lazy sheet. If it is required later, it can be attached while the sail is flying by sheeting in on the leeward sheet until

the clew can be reached and the sheet tied on. If the lazy sheet is rigged, it is led forward and around the front of the forestay then back, outside everything to its turning block and onto a winch. On some boats, it is easier to jibe the gennaker or asymmetric if the lazy sheet is led around the sail's luff as well as the forestay.

Hoisting the sail

When all is ready, the sail can be hoisted. The helmsman should sail on a broad reach during the hoist to keep the sail in the lee of the mainsail. Aim to get the sail to the masthead (or hounds on a fractional rig) quickly and the halyard cleated before the sail can fill with wind. Trim the sheet to fill the sail, then neaten up the halyard tail and lower or furl the headsail.

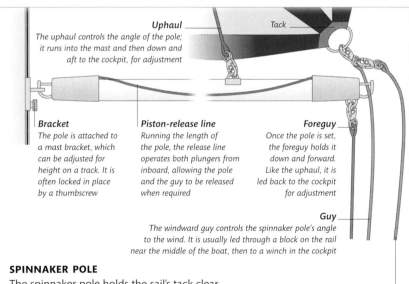

Uphaul
The uphaul controls the angle of the pole; it runs into the mast and then down and aft to the cockpit, for adjustment

Tack

Bracket
The pole is attached to a mast bracket, which can be adjusted for height on a track. It is often locked in place by a thumbscrew

Piston-release line
Running the length of the pole, the release line operates both plungers from inboard, allowing the pole and the guy to be released when required

Foreguy
Once the pole is set, the foreguy holds it down and forward. Like the uphaul, it is led back to the cockpit for adjustment

Guy
The windward guy controls the spinnaker pole's angle to the wind. It is usually led through a block on the rail near the middle of the boat, then to a winch in the cockpit

SPINNAKER POLE
The spinnaker pole holds the sail's tack clear of the boat on the windward side. It is held by an uphaul and a foreguy. The inner end fits onto a mast bracket, which may slide on a track. A piston-release line allows a crewmember standing at the mast to release the guy from the pole.

Lazy sheet
The windward sheet is left slack (as is the leeward guy) and is called the lazy sheet. The sheet and lazy sheet are usually led through a block near each quarter and then to a cockpit winch

HOISTING A SPINNAKER

Steer onto a broad reach with the headsail still hoisted. Then hoist the sail, and cleat its halyard. Pull the guy to get the clew to the pole end, but leave the sheet slack. Then trim the guy to set the pole at right angles to the apparent wind. Then cleat the guy and trim the sheet to fill the sail.

1 Attach the spinnaker bag to the pulpit (as here), or to the leeward guardrail if more convenient. Fasten the bag in position with its straps and open its top.

2 Atttach the halyard to the head of the sail and a sheet and guy to both clews. Check that the sheets and guys are led correctly and run freely.

3 Rig the spinnaker pole with the windward guy led through the end of the pole, and make sure the halyard is clear.

4 Pull the halyard to hoist the sail to the masthead as quickly as possible. Pull the guy to bring the clew tight to the pole end.

5 Once the spinnaker is hoisted and sheeted, furl or lower the headsail. Stow it ready to be hoisted again when needed.

TRIMMING DOWNWIND SAILS

The secret to trimming all downwind sails is to ease the sheet as much as possible without collapsing the luff of the sail. With a gennaker or an asymmetric spinnaker, the tack is fixed to the bow or to the end of a bowsprit, and only the sheet needs adjusting. A conventional spinnaker is more complex, as the guy and sheet, together with the pole uphaul and downhaul, must be adjusted to trim the sail.

Adjusting the halyard

The halyard of a conventional spinnaker should be hoisted as high as possible to prevent the sail oscillating from side to side, but the halyard of an asymmetric or a gennaker may need to be eased to allow the sail to fly with the correct shape in its luff. Experiment with the halyard setting in various wind strengths, and ask your sail-maker for advice if necessary.

Adjusting the pole angle

With a conventional spinnaker, the pole is trimmed aft by easing the foreguy and pulling on the guy, and trimmed forward by easing the guy and pulling on the foreguy. Trim the guy to set the pole just forward of a position at right angles to the apparent wind. Check the apparent wind direction by looking at the masthead wind vane or burgee. With the pole set at right angles to the apparent wind, cleat the guy, tighten the foreguy, and use the sheet to trim the sail. If the apparent wind moves forward or aft, adjust the pole angle to match.

Adjusting the pole height

In light winds, a spinnaker pole must be lowered to keep the clews level. As the wind increases, the free clew will rise under wind pressure. The outer end of the pole should be raised to lift the tack of the sail until it is level with the clew. If the mast end of the pole can be raised and lowered, usually by sliding its fitting on a track, adjust it to keep the pole horizontal so it has maximum projection from the mast. If you sail with an asymmetric, you will not have to adjust a pole, but will have to extend and retract a bowsprit. Since a gennaker does not require a pole or a bowsprit, there is nothing to adjust except the halyard and sheet.

Playing the sheet

For maximum performance, the sheet on all downwind sails should be adjusted constantly to keep the sail eased as much as possible without collapsing. Most well-cut downwind sails can be eased until they curl at the luff, indicating the sail is perfectly trimmed. You should still be able to ease more sheet before the sail collapses. If it does collapse, it will be necessary to pull the sheet in quite vigorously before the sail fills again. Once the sail has filled, ease out most of the sheet you have just pulled in. Unless you do this, the sail will be overtrimmed, and the boat will slow down, heel more, and be harder to steer, which could possibly lead to a broach in stronger winds (*p.257*). In most situations, a cruiser's crew will not wish to constantly play the sheet of the downwind sail. In this case, the sheet should be slightly overtrimmed and then cleated.

JIBING AND LOWERING

When a jibe is required, downwind sails must be changed from one side to the other. The technique used to do this varies, depending on the type of downwind sail being used.

Jibing a gennaker or asymmetric spinnaker

Jibing a gennaker or an asymmetric spinnaker is quite easy, as both are controlled by two sheets just like a headsail. The lazy, windward sheet of the gennaker leads from the clew forward around the back of the sail and around its luff and the forestay, and back to its fairlead and winch.

An asymmetric's windward sheet can be rigged in the same way, or it can lead inside the sail's luff (but outside the forestay), in which case it will jibe inside its luff (like a headsail), rather than outside it. In either case, the sail is jibed by easing the old sheet as the boat jibes, and pulling in the new one. Where an asymmetric has to pass between its luff and the forestay, the new sheet should be pulled in as much as possible before the old one is eased.

Jibing a spinnaker

A spinnaker is more difficult to jibe because the spinnaker pole has to be moved from one side to the other during the maneuver, which can be difficult or even hazardous as it requires working on the foredeck.

Small cruisers may have a dinghy-like double-ended pole system, in which case the jibing method for dinghies (*p.151*) is used. More often, they have a single-ended pole, with the uphaul and foreguy led to the outer end of the pole (*p.254*). This system requires the more complex dip-pole method of jibing (*right*).

DIP-POLE SPINNAKER JIBE

It is important that both the spinnaker and the pole are kept under full control throughout the maneuver. During a dip-pole jibe, the inner end of the pole remains attached to the mast, while the outer end is released from the old guy, lowered so that it can be "dipped" inside the forestay, attached to the new guy, and hoisted up to its horizontal position on the new side. Depending on the particular arrangement, the inner end may have to be raised up the mast on its track temporarily to allow the outer end to dip inside the forestay.

❶ The foredeck crew releases the old guy from the pole end by pulling the piston-release line. The inner end of the pole is raised, and the uphaul eased, to drop the outer end of the pole inside the forestay.

❷ The foredeck crew takes a bight of the old lazy guy forward, and guides the pole end inside the forestay. He clips the new working guy into the pole end fitting.

❸ The inner end of the pole is now lowered to its normal position and the outer end is raised with the uphaul. The guy is trimmed to pull the pole end aft.

❹ The mainsail was sheeted near the centerline during the spinnaker jibe to avoid it blanketing the spinnaker. The mainsail is now jibed (*p.243*).

❺ With the boat on its new course, the mainsail is let out to its correct position. The guy is used to set the pole angle, and the spinnaker is trimmed with the sheet.

Lowering

When lowering a downwind sail, it must be kept under complete control until it is in its bag or below deck. Always steer onto a run or broad reach before lowering the sail so that it can be lowered in the wind shadow behind the mainsail. A headsail is usually hoisted or unrolled before lowering the downwind sail as it prevents it from wrapping around the forestay. There are two ways to lower the sail: trip (release) the sail's tack and pull the sail down by its sheet; or grasp the foot of the sail and pull it down as the sheet, halyard, and tack line (or guy) are eased. The sail can be dropped onto the foredeck and down the fore hatch, or under the main boom, and down the companionway. Do not lower the sail faster than it can be gathered in.

TRIPPING A SPINNAKER
Ease the guy to let the pole move forward and ease the uphaul to lower the end of the pole to within reach of the foredeck crew. He should brace himself securely and keep his head safely below the pole so that it will not hit him as it springs back when the sail is tripped. He releases the sail by tripping the snap shackle that attaches the guy to the tack of the sail.

MAINSAIL AND HEADSAIL ALONE

In moderate to strong winds, most cruisers will not use additional downwind sails, but will sail downwind under mainsail and a headsail. Many cruisers suffer from a rolling motion sailing downwind if these sails are not set correctly.

Mainsail control

Set the mainsheet so the boom is just clear of the shrouds. Then tighten the vang. This prevents the boom from lifting, and stops the mainsail from twisting forward at the top. This will reduce rolling.

In light to moderate winds, ease the mainsail outhaul to make the sail fuller. In strong winds, tighten it as much as possible to flatten the sail. When sailing in strong winds, rig a line as a boom preventer to avoid an accidental jibe (p.243). Run it from the end of the boom, outside all the gear, to a block on the foredeck, then back to a cleat in the cockpit.

BROACHING

Broaching may occur when the boat is sailing under a downwind sail in moderate to strong winds and the sail is sheeted in too hard. The boat heels, and rounds up very quickly toward the wind.

Avoiding a broach

The best way to avoid a broach is to reduce sail area in good time when sailing in moderate to strong winds. A broach occurs when the boat is pressed too hard and turning forces develop that overcome the effect of the rudder.

A broach is most likely to occur in large waves, which make it difficult to keep the boat balanced. Once a broach begins, the helmsman will have no control over the boat's direction as the boat spins around toward the wind and heels violently. Even in moderate winds, a broach can occur when sailing on a reach under spinnaker if the sheet is pulled in too much, causing the boat to slow down and heel—the first signs of a broach. Drop the spinnaker if a rising wind threatens a broach, and sail under mainsail and jib (right).

REGAINING CONTROL
This cruiser-racer has broached violently under spinnaker. Now beam-on to the strong wind, with her boom end in the water, the boat is heeling heavily. In order to regain control, the crew must let go of the boom vang and spinnaker sheet.

Pole holds headsail to windward to increase effective sail area

POLING OUT
If the wind is too strong for a spinnaker, pole the headsail out to windward when on a run or broad reach, to add speed and reduce rolling.

BERTHING

It is very common for cruisers to berth alongside a pontoon or dock. Pontoons tend to be preferred in tidal waters because they float, and are thus able to move up and down with the rise and fall of the tide. This means that you do not have to adjust your warps to allow for changes in the water level. With dock walls, however, your boat will rise and fall in relation to the wall as you lie alongside, and may even dry out if the harbor is shallow. In addition, docks are often busy with fishing boats and other craft. This makes maneuvering more difficult, and yachts may have to raft alongside one another in order to save space. All alongside berths present different challenges, but the basic methods of coming alongside and leaving are the same.

CHOOSING A BERTH

Your choice of berth will determine the comfort of your stay. If possible, choose a berth that is sheltered from the wind and any swell. If the berth is affected by a swell rolling into the harbor, the boat could be damaged. Always lie on the lee side of a pontoon or dock if possible, so that the yacht is pushed off by the wind rather than being pressed against the berth. This will make it easier to leave and will provide a more comfortable stay. If you cannot lie on the leeward side of a berth, the next best option is to lie head-to-wind, as this keeps the companionway sheltered. If strong winds are forecast and you need to be able to leave quickly, avoid lying on the windward side of a pontoon.

Be aware of your boat's handling characteristics at slow speed, and do not attempt to enter a tight marina berth if it is too difficult to leave safely. Alongside berths have obvious attractions, but it is often safer, more comfortable, and cheaper to anchor or pick up a mooring elsewhere.

Effects of wind and tide

When approaching or leaving an alongside berth, the most important factor is the combined effect of wind and tide on your boat. As usual when handling a boat in close quarters, you should always try to leave or arrive at a berth pointing into the strongest element. If in doubt, assume that the tide will have the greatest effect. When approaching

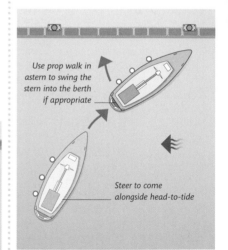

Use prop walk in astern to swing the stern into the berth if appropriate

Steer to come alongside head-to-tide

HEAD-TO-TIDE
Approach a berth into the tide, using it to stop the boat by the dockside. Use prop walk to swing the stern into the berth.

LEEWARD BERTH
It is more comfortable to berth on the leeward side of the pontoon, where the boat is held off by the wind instead of being pushed against the pontoon.

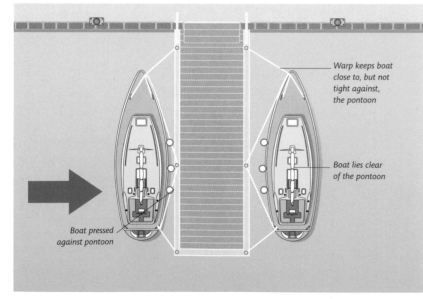

Warp keeps boat close to, but not tight against, the pontoon

Boat lies clear of the pontoon

Boat pressed against pontoon

a berth under power or sail, the aim is to stop the boat in the chosen position alongside the berth so that the crew can step—not jump—safely ashore and secure the lines. In the absence of any tide, head into the wind, if possible, and use the boat's wind resistance to help you slow down and stop. When a tidal stream is present, this will usually have the strongest effect on the boat. Except in a strong wind and weak tide, you should choose to stem the tide in your final approach.

Never attempt to come alongside a berth downtide in a strong stream. Even with a powerful engine, it will be very hard to stop the boat where you choose. The same considerations apply to leaving a berth: always leave pointing into the strongest element if possible. Sometimes you will find that you are berthed stern-to a strong tide. In this situation, you will have to leave astern or turn the boat in its berth using warps (*p.222*).

USING FENDERS

Fenders are used to protect the boat from contact with whatever it is lying alongside. They should be concentrated around the point of maximum beam, not spaced at even intervals along the hull.

Types of fenders

Plastic fenders are made in a variety of shapes and sizes. You should use at least four when lying alongside, and have some spare in case someone berths alongside without enough fenders to protect both craft. The movement of fenders can itself damage the gel coat or paint on the hull. You can avoid this by hanging a fender skirt between the hull and the fenders. When mooring alongside an uneven wall, it can be difficult to keep the fenders in position; a fender board (a wooden plank) hung outboard of the fenders solves this problem.

ATTACHING FENDERS
Attach the fenders to the coachroof handrails or the toerail. If possible, avoid attaching them to the lifelines or stanchions, which may be damaged by their movement.

DRYING OUT ALONGSIDE

It is sometimes necessary to dry out alongside a dock, either to work on the hull or because the harbor dries at low tide. How well a boat behaves depends on its keel shape and configuration. Multihulls sit happily upright on their hulls, and long-keeled boats dry out well sitting on their keel and leaning against a wall. Fin-keeled boats with narrow keels are less stable and are prone to tipping down at bow or stern.

Initial check

Ask the harbormaster about the state of the bottom before you dry out. Debris on the seabed can damage a hull or keel. If the seabed slopes steeply away from the wall, the keel could slip outward and cause damage to the hull.

Correct angle

Once in the berth, ensure that the boat leans slightly in toward the wall as it drops on the ebbing tide. Achieve this by placing heavy gear, such as the anchor and chain, on the sidedeck closest to the wall, or by leading a halyard to a strong point

on shore. Tighten the halyard as the boat drops to keep it heeling slightly toward the wall. You must also ensure that the mooring warps are arranged so that the boat cannot move too far from the wall as it drops, otherwise it will lean in at a large angle and could damage its topsides or rigging. Make sure that all warps lead out through fairleads so they cannot foul the guardrails; lash the warps into open fairleads if there is a danger of lines lifting out of them. The farther you can lead your warps fore and aft of the boat, the less you will need to adjust them as the tide falls.

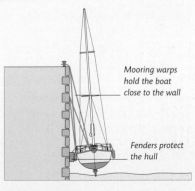

Mooring warps hold the boat close to the wall

Fenders protect the hull

DRYING BERTH
Secure your boat close to the quay wall with warps and use plenty of fenders to protect the hull while drying out.

LEAVING A BERTH

When you are preparing to leave an alongside berth, make a careful observation of all the factors that could affect the maneuver. Assess the strength and direction of wind and tide and their relative effects on your boat. Sound knowledge of your boat's handling characteristics will be of value here, especially with regard to its behavior at slow speed, its drifting characteristics, and how it reacts to wind on the beam. Look for any obstructions in the vicinity, and decide how to clear them. Consider the strength and experience of your crew. If the wind is light, there is little tide running, and there are no obstructions nearby, it is often easy to untie the warps, push the boat off, and sail or motor away. Most situations are more complex, however, and it takes careful preparation and execution to avoid damaging the boat.

Preparing to leave

After taking all the factors into consideration, decide on a plan to leave the berth and brief the crew. The task will be easier with a full crew, but if you sail single-handed or with just one other person, you should work out routines that suit your particular boat and crew.

In many cases, it is easiest and safest to leave under power, as this can give you greater control. Do not, however, assume that you must always use the engine. Many berths can be left safely under sail, and it is satisfying and instructive to do so when possible. If you do need to use your engine, start it and leave it ticking over in neutral to give it time to warm up before departure. Check which warps are under the most load, and plan to cast these off last.

Leaving under power

If the tide is the strongest element affecting you and it is on the bow, then you should leave bow first. If the tide is from astern, then leave stern first or turn the boat using warps. If the tide is not significant, leave into the wind if possible: bow first if the wind is forward of the beam, stern first if it is aft of the beam. However, these rules cannot be rigidly applied, since much depends on the boat's particular configuration, its engine power, and the strength of the wind.

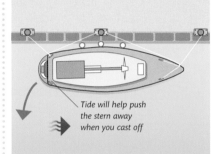

Tide will help push the stern away when you cast off

WIND AHEAD

If the wind is the significant factor, and it is forward of the beam, leave bow first. If the wind is off the dock, it will push the bow away. If it is onshore, spring off.

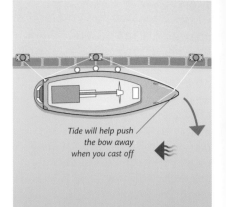

Tide will help push the bow away when you cast off

BOW INTO TIDE

When the boat is facing into a tidal stream, leave bow first. The bow line and stern spring will take the load of the boat; the stern line and bow spring will be slack and can be cast off first when you are preparing to leave the berth.

STERN INTO TIDE

When the stern is facing into a tidal stream, leave stern first. If your boat does not handle well in reverse, turn the boat using warps (p.224) and leave bow first, as above. If leaving stern first, cast off the bow line and stern spring first.

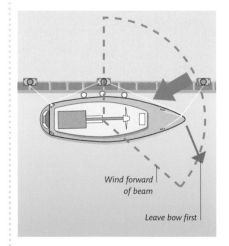

Wind forward of beam

Leave bow first

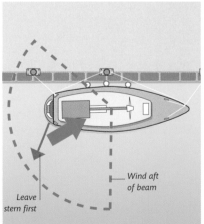

Wind aft of beam

Leave stern first

WIND ASTERN

If the wind is aft of the beam, leave stern first, or turn the boat using warps if handling astern is a problem. If the wind is onshore, use a spring to help you.

Pushing off

If you were to try to leave—even with no wind or tide to cause problems—by casting off your lines and motoring away, the boat's stern would hit the dock or pontoon as you turned. The way to avoid this is to turn either end of the boat away from the dock before motoring off. In small, light boats, this can often be achieved by simply pushing the bow or stern off with a boathook. In strong, offshore winds, the boat will drift clear of the dock once the warps are released, making it a simple matter to motor away.

Using springs

A more controlled departure can be achieved by using one of the springs to help turn the boat, enabling you to leave bow or stern first. Once you have cleared the berth and are in open water, stow the warps and fenders, making sure that all lines are kept out of the water and clear of the propeller.

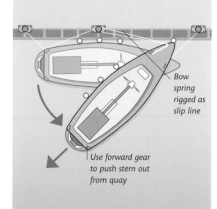

Stern spring rigged as slip line

Use reverse gear to pull bow out from quay

Bow spring rigged as slip line

Use forward gear to push stern out from quay

LEAVING BOW FIRST
Rig the stern spring as a slip line (p.225) and position a fender right at the stern. Cast off the other warps and motor gently astern, steering the stern in toward the dock as the bow begins to swing out. Once the bow has swung far enough to clear any obstructions, engage neutral, slip the spring, and motor away slowly in forward gear.

LEAVING STERN FIRST
Rig the bow spring as a slip line, position a fender at the bow, and cast off the other warps. Motor slowly ahead and steer carefully toward the dock. When the stern has swung out far enough, engage neutral, slip the spring, and motor slowly astern until you are away from the dock and able to engage forward gear.

Leaving under sail

It is often possible to leave a berth under sail, but if the wind is light and the tide is strong, you will have reduced control: it is usually easier to leave under power. If the wind is blowing onto the berth you will not be able to sail off at all. Use an engine, warps, or lay an anchor using the tender, to get yourself out of the berth. If tide is present, always leave bow-into-tide for best control. If the boat is lying stern-to-tide, turn it using warps before you attempt to sail off.

Once you are lying head-to-tide, sail off under jib only if the wind is on or aft of the beam. If the wind is from ahead, sail off under mainsail alone, or mainsail and headsail together if the wind is light. If the wind is from directly ahead, hoist and back the headsail to push the bow off.

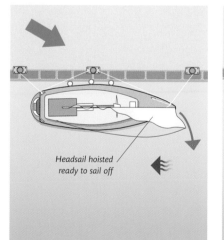

Headsail hoisted ready to sail off

OFFSHORE WIND AFT OF BEAM
Hoist the headsail but let it flap freely. First cast off the warps not under load, then cast off the others. Trim the headsail, and sail off under headsail alone. Once clear of the dock, turn head-to-wind before hoisting the mainsail.

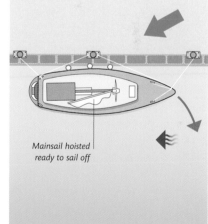

Mainsail hoisted ready to sail off

OFFSHORE WIND AHEAD
Hoist the mainsail and let it flap. Prepare the headsail for immediate hoisting. Cast off all warps, starting with those not under load, and push the bow off, with a boathook if necessary. Trim the mainsail and sail off, then hoist the headsail.

ARRIVING AT A BERTH

Approaching an alongside berth can be a complicated maneuver that requires thought, planning, and a well-briefed crew. If possible, take a practice run to assess the situation. Check the wind and tide effects at the berth and look for any nearby hazards that you will have to avoid on the approach. Remember to allow for last-minute problems by planning an escape route that will take the boat safely back to clear water. Check which side will be alongside the berth. If it is necessary to raft alongside another boat, ask permission first.

Once you have decided on your strategy, brief the crew and give them plenty of time to get the gear ready, particularly the fenders and warps. If you have sailed into harbor but intend to come alongside under power, start the engine in plenty of time to allow it to warm up. Drop the sails and loosely stow them before you approach the berth.

Preparation

Get the warps ready on deck; when you are berthed you will normally lie to at least four warps (pp.224–225).

Rig fenders and prepare the bow and stern warps by leading an end out through their fairleads, pulling sufficient through and making them fast to deck cleats. Take the outer ends of the bow and stern lines outside everything to the middle of the boat just aft of the shrouds. The crew should normally step off from here when taking their lines ashore, as it is the widest part of the boat and should be closest to the berth when coming alongside. You may not need to rig the springs until you are alongside and secured by bow and stern lines. However, a stopping spring can be a very useful aid (p.263), especially if the engine is not efficient in reverse.

Once you are alongside, secure the bow and stern lines. The stern spring is usually rigged next, if the wind or tide are on the bow, as this warp will take much of the load and will hold the boat parallel to the berth. Finally, rig the other spring and neaten up all warps, making sure that there are no loose coils of rope left lying on the quay or pontoon where passers-by may trip over them.

Arriving under power

If wind and tide effects are not significant, choose to come alongside on the side toward which prop walk (p.236) will push the stern when you engage reverse gear to stop. This will help you end up alongside, parallel to the berth. Once the boat is close alongside, the crew steps ashore and makes fast. When the wind or tide are significant, however, approach by heading into the strongest element. This gives you greater slow-speed control and will help you stop accurately at the berth. Do not approach down tide or with a strong wind behind, if it can be avoided (and never attempt this maneuver without a powerful engine).

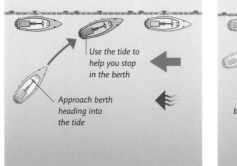

WIND AND TIDE TOGETHER OR OPPOSED
Use the tide to stop the boat by putting the engine into neutral as you approach the berth. Use reverse gear to help stop the boat if prop walk will act to pull the stern into the berth, but use it sparingly if prop walk acts in the opposite direction.

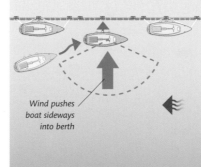

ONSHORE WIND
Approach into the tide, but aim to stop your boat a few feet to windward of the berth. Allow the effects of windage to push the boat gently sideways into the berth. If the bow blows quickly downwind, stop the boat with the bow slightly upwind to allow for the effect.

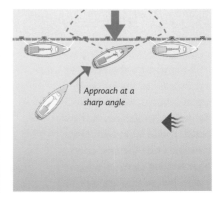

OFFSHORE WIND
In a strong offshore wind, the bow tends to blow downwind when you stop alongside. Counter this by leading the stern line farther forward than usual, and approach at a sharper angle. The crew must get the lines ashore quickly and straighten up the boat in its berth.

Arriving under sail

Berthing a cruiser under sail, especially in a confined space, requires skill and good judgment. The success of the maneuver will depend on your knowledge of your boat's handling characteristics and on the efficiency and speed of the crew. The choice of approach is much the same as when approaching under power. Always head into the strongest element of wind or tide so that you can use it to stop you when you reach the berth. If you approach too fast in the final stages, back the mainsail (if you are approaching into the wind), or lower the headsail (if you are approaching downwind). The crew will need to hold the leech of a partly lowered headsail to keep it drawing.

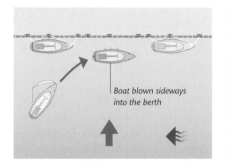

ONSHORE WIND

Approach downwind under headsail alone, turning into the tide to stop to windward of the berth so that the boat blows sideways into its berth. Stop the boat with the bow pointing slightly upwind to allow for its drifting faster downwind than the stern. Lower the headsail and get the warps ashore.

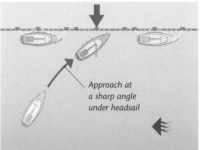

OFFSHORE WIND

Come in against the tide with the mainsail alone if the wind is forward of the beam. Use the headsail alone if the wind is on or aft of the beam. Approach at a sharp angle and lead the end of the stern line farther forward so that the crew can step ashore from ahead of the shrouds. Get the warps ashore and make fast quickly.

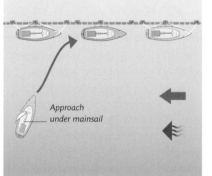

WIND AND TIDE TOGETHER OR STRONG WIND OPPOSED

If wind and tide are together, or if a strong wind is opposed by a weak tide, approach on a close reach under mainsail alone. Ease the mainsheet to slow down and turn into the wind when you reach the berth. Get the bow and stern lines ashore and make fast.

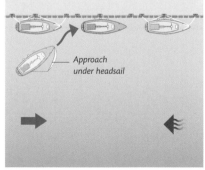

STRONG TIDE OPPOSING WEAK WIND

Approach from upwind under headsail alone. If the headsail alone will not push you over the tide, try hoisting just the head of the mainsail to provide extra drive. Slow down by letting the headsail flap. Get the warps ashore quickly.

SHORT-HANDED TECHNIQUES

Approaching a berth is relatively easy with a full crew to handle all the warps, but it can be tricky with the typical short-handed crew—often only two people on board.

Using an amidships spring

One way of entering a berth when short-handed is to use an amidships spring to control the boat. A line is led from a sidedeck cleat just aft of amidships to a cleat ashore that is level with the stern or farther back. This allows the boat to be held in position, parallel to its berth, by putting the engine slow ahead. If the boat swings toward or away from the berth, counteract this with the tiller.

When coming alongside, all the lines are rigged as normal with the addition of the amidships spring. As the boat stops alongside, the crew steps ashore with the spring only and makes it fast on a cleat or bollard. The helmsman puts the engine into slow ahead and adjusts the tiller to hold the boat parallel to its berth. The boat is now secure and the shore crew can make fast the normal mooring warps.

Stopping springs

The amidships spring can be used as a stopping spring if the boat is moving too fast when it comes alongside. To do this, the shore crew takes one full turn around a cleat or bollard before strain comes onto the line. As the line becomes taut, he eases it under control (known as surging a line) to slow the boat down. Do not let the warp jerk tight or it may break. Surging a line is a good way to stop even a large boat. Using a bow spring as a stopping spring does not work as well since it will pull the bow into the berth once strain comes on it, but the amidships spring will keep the boat straight.

MARINA BERTHS

Common in busy sailing areas, marinas provide a large number of sheltered berths, usually with good shoreside facilities, such as fuel and fresh water, showers, stores, restaurants, bars, pro shops, and repair yards. Marinas are therefore very popular and tend to be crowded in the busiest months of the sailing season. Boats are berthed very close together, on a network of floating pontoons, so maneuvering space is limited. Good boat handling is essential. You should always enter and leave a marina with caution, especially if your boat does not handle well under power. Be well prepared before you enter a marina, brief your crew, and have your warps and fenders rigged before you start the approach.

Choosing a berth

Before approaching a marina, it is vital that you know your boat's characteristics at slow speed and are able to turn in tight spaces using the effects of prop walk (*p.236*). If your boat does not handle well in reverse, you should avoid particularly tight or difficult berths. Marinas usually have a number of outside berths near the approach channel, with additional berths inside the network of pontoons. They are usually reached through narrow channels between pontoons that are often crowded with boats. If you are uncertain of the marina layout, or if your boat is difficult to handle, choose an outside berth if possible, perhaps maneuvering into an inside one later using warps. Most marinas have reserved berths for permanent berth holders, with others for use by visitors. Make sure you select a visitor's berth when visiting a marina for the first time. It is not usually wise to attempt to sail into a marina because of the confined space, although you may be able to pick up an outside berth under sail.

Preparing to berth

Before you arrive, contact the marina's berthing master by VHF radio to obtain directions to a suitable berth. Remember to ask which side of the boat you will berth on, so that you can prepare warps and fenders on the correct side.

If you have enough fenders, hang them on both sides of the boat so that you are well protected. This will also give you a choice of berthing on either side if the situation changes at the last moment or you find the planned berth too difficult to enter.

Marinas are often located out of the main tidal stream, so the effects of tide may not be significant in your final approach. Study the situation carefully, however, because if a pontoon sticks out into the tide, it may have a significant effect that you will have to allow for. When preparing to berth, you should assess the situation and pick the best approach method (*pp.262–263*).

BUSY MARINA
Marinas are popular because they provide safe berths and numerous useful facilities. They can be crowded and noisy, however, and charges can be quite high.

TURNING IN A NARROW CHANNEL

Sometimes you may need to turn in a very narrow channel between pontoons, without enough space to execute a normal turn under power. On many occasions, you can use prop walk to turn the boat in nearly its own length (*p.236*), but a strong wind or poor boat performance under power may render this impossible.

Using the anchor

Sometimes, when negotiating a marina to find a berth, you may find yourself heading down a narrow channel that turns out to be a dead end. In such circumstances, you need to be able to turn the boat or to reverse out the way you came. However, many sailing boats do not reverse well under power, and a strong following wind may make it difficult, or impossible, to turn in the space available. If you cannot use prop walk to assist you, you should consider using the anchor to help turn the boat. Use the depth sounder to check the depth of water and prepare the anchor for dropping as you motor slowly along the channel. When you reach the point at which you want to turn, drop the anchor but continue moving slowly ahead.

Allow the anchor chain to run out freely until you have paid out about twice the depth of water. Now put the engine into neutral, start the boat turning in the desired direction and, at the same time, secure the anchor chain by taking a turn around a foredeck cleat or bollard. The anchor chain will draw taut and pull the bow around until the boat has turned through 180 degrees. You can now motor slowly forward, recover the anchor, and make your exit safely.

TURNING WITH AN ANCHOR
Using an anchor to turn is an easy and effective technique. Most marinas are dredged regularly, so there should be no bottom obstructions to foul your anchor.

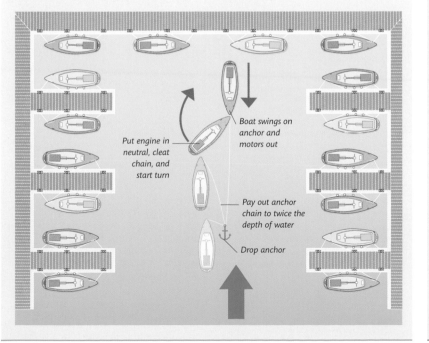

Put engine in neutral, cleat chain, and start turn

Boat swings on anchor and motors out

Pay out anchor chain to twice the depth of water

Drop anchor

DIFFICULT BERTHS

Marina berths in confined spaces can be very difficult to enter or leave in certain conditions of wind or tide. If you are concerned about whether you have enough room to maneuver, or that the wind or tide may cause you to lose control, use your warps to help you arrive or leave safely.

Using warps

The exact method of using warps will depend on the particular berthing situation; no hard and fast rules can be given. The skipper has to assess the effects of prop walk, wind, and tide on the boat while it is moving slowly into or out of its berth. He should plan to use the appropriate mooring warp to prevent or promote turning as required. A mooring warp used in this way should be rigged as a slip line so that it can be released quickly and easily from on board.

Into the wind

You may often find that you have to reverse out of a berth against a strong wind. Windage on the bow will tend to keep it downwind, and engine power may not be sufficient to turn in the space available. Use a spring to help you turn.

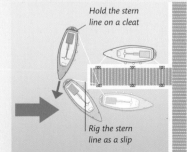

Hold the stern line on a cleat

Rig the stern line as a slip

REVERSING OUT
Rig the stern line as a long slip, and reverse out slowly. Cleat the stern line to hold the stern as the bow swings out. Slip the line and motor away.

Leaving a marina berth

Before leaving the marina, start the engine and allow it to warm up in neutral while you assess the situation and plan your exit. Consider how the wind and tide will affect the boat as you leave the berth and as you maneuver within the marina. Brief the crew thoroughly and get them to make ready any slip lines you may need to control the boat as you leave. They should be told in what order the lines are to be released, and must make sure that no warps are left in the water where they might foul the propeller. Take your time and proceed carefully.

EXITING THE BERTH

Your position in relation to the wind and tide, and whether you are bow-in or stern-in to your berth, will determine how you leave. Be aware of other boats on neighboring pontoons, and of boats entering or leaving the marina at the same time that may interfere with your plans.

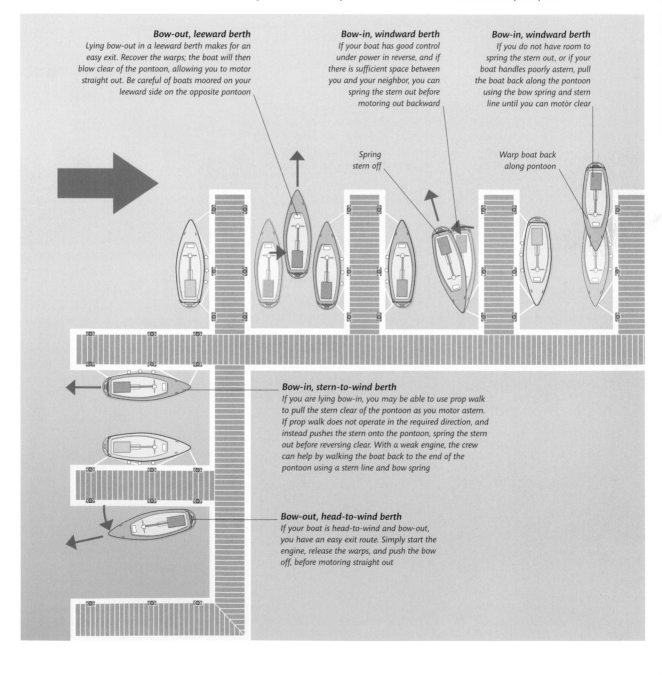

Bow-out, leeward berth
Lying bow-out in a leeward berth makes for an easy exit. Recover the warps; the boat will then blow clear of the pontoon, allowing you to motor straight out. Be careful of boats moored on your leeward side on the opposite pontoon

Bow-in, windward berth
If your boat has good control under power in reverse, and if there is sufficient space between you and your neighbor, you can spring the stern out before motoring out backward

Bow-in, windward berth
If you do not have room to spring the stern out, or if your boat handles poorly astern, pull the boat back along the pontoon using the bow spring and stern line until you can motor clear

Spring stern off

Warp boat back along pontoon

Bow-in, stern-to-wind berth
If you are lying bow-in, you may be able to use prop walk to pull the stern clear of the pontoon as you motor astern. If prop walk does not operate in the required direction, and instead pushes the stern onto the pontoon, spring the stern out before reversing clear. With a weak engine, the crew can help by walking the boat back to the end of the pontoon using a stern line and bow spring

Bow-out, head-to-wind berth
If your boat is head-to-wind and bow-out, you have an easy exit route. Simply start the engine, release the warps, and push the bow off, before motoring straight out

Arriving at a marina berth

Give yourself plenty of time to pick a berth. If necessary, sail past the marina a few times to get a good idea of its layout and the location of any likely berths. Call the marina on VHF and ask them to allocate you a berth. Tell them if your boat is difficult to handle and ask for a suitable berth.

When you have found a berth, plan your entry with care. Brief the crew and give them time to prepare the gear. They should know on which side to secure fenders and which warps are to be secured first. They must also check that no warps are trailing in the water where they might foul the propeller as you maneuver.

ENTERING THE BERTH

The direction of the wind and the angle of the berth to the wind will determine how you arrive at your berth. Your boat's ability to perform well at very low speeds and to prop walk will also have a bearing on your choice of berth and the way in which you enter it.

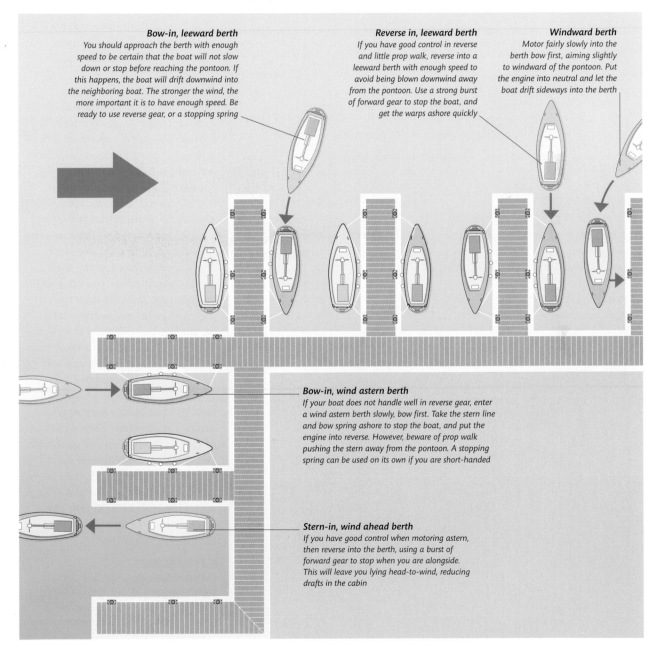

Bow-in, leeward berth
You should approach the berth with enough speed to be certain that the boat will not slow down or stop before reaching the pontoon. If this happens, the boat will drift downwind into the neighboring boat. The stronger the wind, the more important it is to have enough speed. Be ready to use reverse gear, or a stopping spring

Reverse in, leeward berth
If you have good control in reverse and little prop walk, reverse into a leeward berth with enough speed to avoid being blown downwind away from the pontoon. Use a strong burst of forward gear to stop the boat, and get the warps ashore quickly

Windward berth
Motor fairly slowly into the berth bow first, aiming slightly to windward of the pontoon. Put the engine into neutral and let the boat drift sideways into the berth

Bow-in, wind astern berth
If your boat does not handle well in reverse gear, enter a wind astern berth slowly, bow first. Take the stern line and bow spring ashore to stop the boat, and put the engine into reverse. However, beware of prop walk pushing the stern away from the pontoon. A stopping spring can be used on its own if you are short-handed

Stern-in, wind ahead berth
If you have good control when motoring astern, then reverse into the berth, using a burst of forward gear to stop when you are alongside. This will leave you lying head-to-wind, reducing drafts in the cabin

RAFTING ALONGSIDE

Stacking boats, one outside the other, beside a pontoon or dock, in between piles, or around a mooring buoy, is known as rafting. This is a common method of making the most of the limited space in crowded harbors. Although it is not an ideal method of berthing, rafting alongside may be the only option available to you in a busy harbor. It is advisable, therefore, to learn how to raft safely, making sure that you do not damage your own or anyone else's boat. You also need to know how to leave safely from the inside of the raft, as well as from the outside. Rafting can be a straightforward procedure, as long as you follow a few basic strategies and observe certain courtesies to other members of the raft and to those arriving or leaving.

Rafting protocol
Always secure to the shore, pontoon, or piles with bow and stern lines, and to the boat next to you with springs and breast warps. Do not rely on your neighbors' shore lines to hold your boat—this is bad practice and also discourteous. Do not join a raft in which only the innermost boat has rigged shore lines. Such a raft will swing fore and aft under the effects of wind and tide, and will provide an uncomfortable and insecure berth.

A raft is more stable if the largest boat is on the inside and the smallest on the outside, so try to avoid rafting alongside a boat smaller than your own. When you join a raft, position your boat so that your mast is not in line with that of your neighbor. This will prevent them from clashing and causing damage as the boats roll. When going ashore across other boats in the raft, always cross by their foredecks, never their cockpits. This helps to preserve privacy.

Disadvantages of rafting
One of the main disadvantages of rafting is that it can restrict your freedom to leave when you wish. When you are on the outside, it is inconvenient if an inside boat wants to leave before you. If you are on the inside, you have to put up with crews from boats outside you crossing your decks to get aboard or ashore. In an exposed location, the boats may rub and roll against each other, causing discomfort and sometimes damage.

Joining a raft
Although joining a raft involves coming alongside another boat, the method you use is exactly the same as when coming alongside a dock or pontoon (*pp.262–263*). Plan your approach, taking into account the effects of wind and tide. Always head toward the element that will have the most effect on your boat as you stop alongside. It does not matter if you are not facing in the same direction as the boat you are going to be beside. Brief the crew and prepare fenders and warps in the usual way. You will need three sets of warps—bow and stern lines led to the shore, and breasts and springs attached to your neighbor.

Coming alongside another boat, rather than a pontoon or dock, is harder for the crew. They will have to climb over two sets of guardrails and make their way along the other boat's sidedeck to find suitable cleats to secure the bow and stern breast ropes. It is important that these warps are attached as soon

A TYPICAL RAFT
The boats are rafted with bow and stern breast lines, and springs between each boat. Bow and stern shore lines are also rigged, and the boats are arranged with masts staggered.

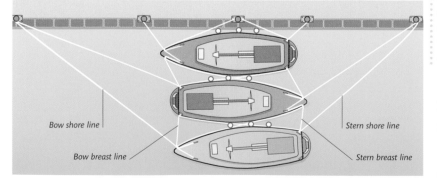

Bow shore line

Bow breast line

Stern shore line

Stern breast line

as possible, to bring the boat under control before rigging all the other lines.

The procedure can be made much easier if the other boat's crew are on deck. First, ask them for permission to come alongside. Then, if they are willing to help, your crew can hand them the ends of the bow and stern breast lines. Once they have been made fast, the lines can be adjusted from on board your boat. This means that your crew do not have to climb aboard the other boat. Rig the springs as quickly as possible, and then take your bow and stern lines ashore. Lead them outside all the boats between you and the shore or pontoon. Adjust them so that they are clear of the water, but have some slack in them.

Leaving a raft

If you are the outermost boat in the raft, leaving it is the same as leaving from a pontoon (*pp.260–261*), but you must recover your shore lines first. Before doing this, decide if the wind or tide is the strongest element, choose your exit strategy, and brief the crew. Then maneuver clear as you would if you were leaving an alongside berth.

When you are inside the raft, you must always leave with the strongest element. If you leave against it, there is a danger that the boats outside you will be at the mercy of wind or tide. To avoid problems, crew members may have to take control of other boat's warps as you leave. You will then have to pick the crew up at the outside of the raft once you are clear. Another raft close by may prevent you from departing until the boats outside you have left. If you are not sure that you can clear all nearby obstructions, either ask the outside boats to move to let you out or be prepared to wait until they leave.

LEAVING FROM WITHIN A RAFT

If you are on the inside or middle of a raft, leave with the strongest element—here, the tide. Otherwise, the boats outside you will become uncontrollable when their warps are released for you to leave.

❶ Check whether the wind or tide is the most significant factor and plan to leave downtide or downwind. Also, check carefully that there are no obstructions, such as another raft, in your line of departure. Next, recover your bow and stern shore lines so that your boat is now attached only to the boats either side of it.

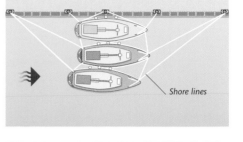

Shore lines

❷ Recover your warps from the boat that is outside you. Unfasten the outside boat's bow line and re-lead it around and behind your boat and back to the shore. Next, release your breast ropes and springs from the boat inside you, and allow your own boat to move out slowly with the strongest element.

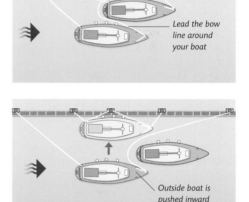

Lead the bow line around your boat

❸ As your boat moves downtide out of the raft, the shore line of the boat outside is pulled in and secured, and the boat is secured to the inshore boat with breasts and springs. If your crew have been on the raft helping to secure the outside boats, circle back and come alongside the outside boat to pick them up when they are ready.

Outside boat is pushed inward by the tide

RAFTING ON A BUOY

Boats are sometimes rafted on large mooring buoys, but usually only in areas where there are no significant tides or currents.

Mooring

Boats moor directly to the buoy and attach springs and breast warps to their neighbors. They leave stern-first simply by casting off. If necessary, a crew member stays on the raft to refasten the other boats' springs and breast warps, and is then picked up.

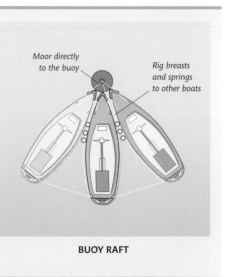

Moor directly to the buoy

Rig breasts and springs to other boats

BUOY RAFT

BERTHING BOW- OR STERN-TO

In areas without the complications of tide to consider, it is common to moor by the bow or the stern to a pontoon or dock. An anchor (or, occasionally, a pair of small piles) is used to hold the other end of the boat. This method saves space alongside, and makes it easier for individual boats to arrive or leave without disturbing others. When arriving, it is usually simpler to come in bow first, which also provides more privacy in the cockpit while you are berthed. However, you may find it easier to get to and from the shore if you berth stern-to the dock or pontoon.

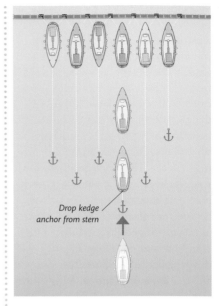

Drop kedge anchor from stern

Arriving bow-to

Brief the crew, and prepare the warps, fenders, and anchor well before you approach the berth. Hang fenders on both sides of the boat to protect it from contact with neighboring boats. For berthing bow-to, you will need two bow lines and the kedge anchor (p.278) with a long anchor warp or chain. The anchor must be ready to drop from the stern. If the kedge has a length of chain between it and the warp, stow the chain in a bucket to keep it clear of the deck as it runs out. Make sure that the chain and warp are led so that they run out under the pushpit and through a fairlead. Always lay the anchor clear of other boats' anchors. The best way to achieve this is by making a long approach with your boat lined up with the berth. This gives you time

BERTHING BOW-TO

Approach in a straight line from some way off. Drop the kedge anchor over the stern about three to five boat lengths from the berth. Stop just clear of the dock so the crew can take the bow lines ashore.

to adjust your line of approach, using tiller and throttle as needed, to give a steady and straight run into the berth.

TURNING USING WARPS

If you wish to moor stern-to but your boat does not handle well in reverse, you should first moor bow-to. You then have to use the anchor and the bow line to turn the boat while keeping it under complete control. Ensure that your crew understands how you intend to complete the maneuver, and keep an eye out for a cross wind that could push your boat onto its neighbors.

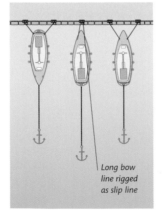

Long bow line rigged as slip line

1 Rig the bow line as a long slip line, making sure that you have enough rope to complete the maneuver.

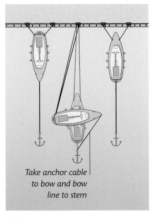

Take anchor cable to bow and bow line to stern

2 Pull on the anchor cable to move the boat clear. Take the anchor warp to the bow, and the bow line to the stern.

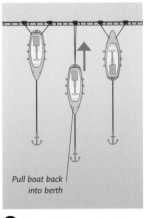

Pull boat back into berth

3 Turn the boat using the warps and pull it back into the berth stern first, easing out the anchor warp as you go.

When you are about three to five boat-lengths from the berth, drop the anchor over the stern and let its cable run free. Continue your approach until you are about half a boat length from the berth, then snub the anchor cable. This is done by taking a turn of the cable around a cleat or bollard and holding the end tightly enough to put some load on the warp, while allowing it to slip slowly around the cleat. This will set the anchor and slow down the boat. Put the engine in reverse if necessary to stop the boat just clear of the dock or pontoon, so that the crew can step ashore with the bow warps and secure the boat.

Arriving stern-to

If you wish to berth stern-to, you have two choices, depending on how well your boat handles in reverse. If it handles well in reverse, approach from some way off, reversing in a straight line toward the berth. Drop your bow anchor about three to five boat-lengths from the berth and allow the

cable to run out. As your stern approaches the dock or pontoon, snub the bow anchor and give a burst ahead on the engine to stop the boat. The crew can then step ashore with the stern warps and make them fast. If your boat does not handle well in reverse, but you still wish to berth stern-to, first berth bow-to and then turn the boat using the bow line and anchor cable (*opposite*).

Leaving

Leaving a bow- or stern-to mooring is usually straightforward. Simply release the shore lines and pull on the anchor cable to move the boat clear of the berth, using the engine to help if necessary. Then recover the anchor (*p.282*) and motor clear. If a strong cross wind makes it hard to hold the boat straight as you leave, rig a long slip line to the shore to help control the boat. Keep the line under low tension as you move clear to stop the boat from blowing downwind. Slip the line once clear of the berth.

When leaving a pile and pontoon berth, leave stern-first by simply releasing your bow warps and motoring out backward, provided you have good control in reverse and there is no strong cross wind. As you motor astern, release the pile lines as they come within reach.

If there is a strong cross wind, however, you should release only the downwind bow and stern lines, rigging the two remaining warps as slips. Next, take the stern line to the middle of the boat. Motor slowly astern, or pull the boat back on the stern warp, gradually easing the bow warp and keeping some tension on the bow warp to prevent the bow from blowing downwind. When the middle of the boat is level with the piles, slip the lines and motor clear.

If your boat does not handle well in reverse, rig both pile lines as slips and lead them forward to the middle of the boat. Release the bow lines and pull the boat back on the stern lines, slipping them when the piles are abeam and motoring clear.

PILE AND PONTOON BERTHS

Some harbors use a combination of piles and pontoons for berthing bow- or stern-to. Most resident berths have permanent lines attached to the pontoon and piles to make berthing easier. If you are entering a visitor's berth, however, you will have to use your own warps. These are best rigged as slips.

Arriving

Although it is possible to berth stern-to if you have good control in reverse, most sailing boats are easier to berth bow-to in this situation unless the wind is off the pontoon. Prepare two bow warps and two stern warps, with the latter rigged like springs, with the port stern line running to the starboard pile and vice versa. Brief the crew and have a boathook ready. Make the approach slowly under power. Be careful of any beam wind that could blow the bow downwind and spoil your approach.

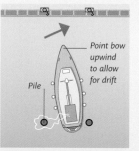

❶ If there is a cross wind, approach the upwind pile first under power. Lasso the pile with a loop of the stern line and leave slack.

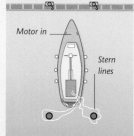

❷ Lasso the second pile with the other stern line. Then motor in, taking care to keep the lines clear of the propeller.

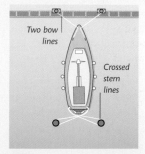

❸ Stop the boat just clear of the pontoon and make fast ashore using two bow warps. Position the boat just clear of the pontoon.

PILE MOORINGS

Some tidal harbors use pile moorings to provide fore and aft moorings along the edges of a channel, parallel to the main tide flow. Piles are large wooden or metal stakes driven into the seabed, with fittings to which mooring warps are tied. Boats often raft up between pile moorings, although there will usually be a limit to the number of boats allowed on each pair of piles. All the boats should be secured to both the piles and their neighboring vessels, when rafted between piles.

Mooring warp tied to ring

Ring slides on upright bar

Upright metal bar

Pile buried in seabed

PILE MOORING

UNDER POWER

Leaving a pile mooring is generally quite a simple procedure. The main thing to consider is your exit in relation to any nearby hazards.

Leaving under power

If you are lying alone between a pair of piles, leave into the tide, either bow or stern first. If you are inside a raft, recover your pile lines using the tender, then leave as for a raft (*p.269*). If you are the outside boat, recover your pile lines and leave as for an alongside berth (*pp.260–261*).

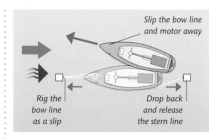

Slip the bow line and motor away

Rig the bow line as a slip

Drop back and release the stern line

LEAVE INTO THE TIDE
Pull the boat up to the uptide pile while paying out the other line. To leave bow first, rig the bow line as a slip, drop back to the stern pile, and release the stern line. Motor ahead and slip the bow line.

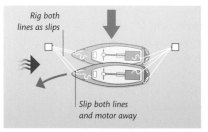

Rig both lines as slips

Slip both lines and motor away

STRONG WIND ON BEAM
If a strong wind on the beam threatens to cause difficulties, rig both bow and stern lines as slips. Ease both out to allow the boat to blow to leeward, then slip both lines and motor away into the tide.

Arriving under power

Picking up a pile mooring is quite simple. If you select empty piles, you will only need two mooring lines, and can complete the operation from on deck. If you choose to come alongside another boat, approach as for an alongside berth. You will need six warps, plus fenders, and you will have to use the tender to attach the pile lines. The skipper should plan to approach into the strongest element and should brief the crew in advance. Have a boathook handy, as well as the mooring lines, and appoint your quickest knot-tier to attach the lines.

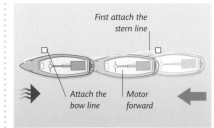

First attach the stern line

Attach the bow line

Motor forward

RUNNING MOOR
Approach into the strongest element. Stop the boat alongside the rear pile with the pile ahead of the shrouds. Attach the stern line. Motor forward to the bow pile and attach the bow line. Adjust both lines so you are positioned midway between the piles.

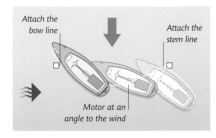

Attach the bow line

Attach the stern line

Motor at an angle to the wind

STRONG WIND ON BEAM
Approach the stern pile from the leeward side. Stop with the pile alongside the windward shroud. Secure the stern line. Motor forward with the bow angled to windward. Stop with the bow pile on the leeward bow. Secure the bow line and center the boat between the piles.

UNDER SAIL

If the immediate vicinity is not too crowded with other boats, you can often leave a pile mooring under sail.

Leaving under sail

It is a fairly easy maneuver to leave under sail if you are berthed alone between piles. If you are the outside boat in a raft on piles, you may be able to leave under sail if you are on the leeward side, after recovering your pile lines with the tender.

As pile moorings are usually found in tidal areas, it is best to leave bow into the tide; this gives you the most control. If you are lying stern to the tide, turn the boat using warps before you try to leave. With the bow pointing into the tide, your method of leaving will be determined by wind direction. As with other berthing

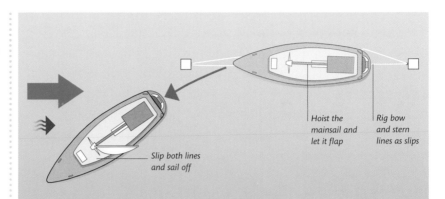

Slip both lines and sail off

Hoist the mainsail and let it flap

Rig bow and stern lines as slips

situations under sail, use the mainsail alone, or with the headsail, if the wind is forward of the beam, and the headsail alone if the wind is on or aft of the beam. Rig the bow and stern lines as slips before hoisting sails, and use them to turn the boat one way or the other if it helps you to sail off.

WIND FORWARD OF BEAM

Rig both pile lines as slips and prepare the mainsail for hoisting. Plan your exit route and brief the crew. Hoist the mainsail and let it flap freely, then cast off the stern line. Pull in on the bow line to give the boat steerage way, then slip the line and sail away.

Arriving under sail

If you choose to approach a pile mooring under sail, always make your final approach into the strongest element. This will usually be the tide. However, if a very strong wind opposes a very weak tide, you should plan your approach into the wind.

Brief the crew well in advance, and make a practice run, if necessary, to assess the situation. Prepare bow and stern lines and have a boathook to hand. Your method of final approach will depend on the relative direction of the wind. If the wind is ahead of the beam, then make your final approach under mainsail alone. Approach on a close reach and aim to stop alongside the bow pile. Make the bow warp fast, then lower the mainsail and drop back to the stern pile to attach the stern warp. Center the boat between the piles. If the

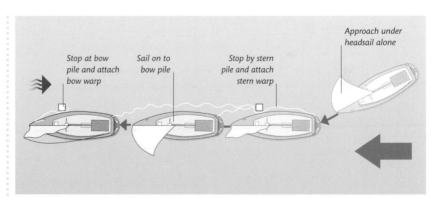

Stop at bow pile and attach bow warp

Sail on to bow pile

Stop by stern pile and attach stern warp

Approach under headsail alone

wind is on or aft of the beam, approach under headsail alone, using the jib sheet to control speed. In this case, use a running moor (*above*). Let the jib flap to stop by the stern pile first to attach the stern warp, before sailing on to the bow pile to attach the bow warp. If the wind is light and you cannot make way over the tide, hoist the top part of the mainsail to get extra drive.

WIND ON OR AFT OF BEAM

With the wind on or aft of the beam when you are pointing into the tide, sail upwind of the piles and lower the mainsail. Make your final approach under headsail alone, easing the sheet as necessary to spill wind and slow down. You should attach the stern line first, then sail on to the bow pile to attach the bow line.

MOORINGS

Keeping a boat on a mooring or using one for a lunchtime or overnight stay are both popular and practical options. Moorings are often laid in harbors, rivers, and bays to provide convenient securing points for yachts. They are often easier and less stressful to use than coming alongside in a busy harbor or crowded marina; however, they do require that you have a tender available for trips ashore, unless a water taxi is available.

About moorings

A mooring consists of one or more heavy anchors or weights on the seabed attached to a heavy-chain riser. This, in turn, is attached, sometimes by rope, to a floating buoy. Moorings intended for light craft usually have a single, small buoy that is picked up. The rope or chain underneath is passed through a bow fairlead and secured to a cleat. Other moorings have a larger buoy, either with a ring on top to which the boat is tied with a mooring line, or a separate, smaller pick-up buoy that is brought aboard to secure the boat. Moorings are often laid in rows, called trots, along the edges of river channels, usually in line with the tidal flow. In this case, the heavy chain riser of each individual mooring is connected to a long ground chain that is attached to a heavy anchor or weight at each end.

Choosing a mooring

When you visit a harbor with visitors' mooring buoys, choose a mooring suitable for your boat. Make sure the mooring is strong enough, that it is laid in water sufficiently deep so that your boat will still float at low tide, and that there is enough room to swing around the buoy with the wind and tide. You should also consider how sheltered the mooring is from both wind and swell, especially if you are planning an overnight stop. It is also important to think about how easily you will be able to approach and leave the mooring under power or sail, as well as the proximity of the

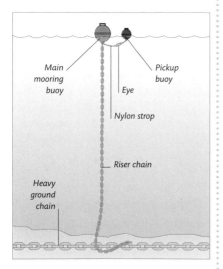

MOORING BUOY

This mooring is attached to a heavy ground chain that forms the base of a string of moorings in a "trot." The pickup buoy is attached to the chain riser under the main buoy by a strong rope, that often has an eye spliced into it so it can be quickly dropped over a deck cleat.

FORE-AND-AFT BUOYS

Fore-and-aft mooring buoys are usually laid in rows at the edges of tidal and river channels. You should use them just like pile moorings, and secure your boat between them.

Picking up buoys

Picking up fore-and-aft buoys is the same as picking up pile moorings (*pp.272–273*): before you pick them up, check that they are suitable for your size of boat. Reaching the buoys from the deck of a cruiser can be difficult. The crew may have to lie on the deck, so have a boathook handy. Some fore-and-aft buoys have smaller pickup buoys attached to them to make it easier to pick them up. When you leave, tie the pickup buoys together to make recovery easier. Come alongside the pickup buoys and take the forward buoy to the bow and the other to the stern. Check the quality of the line attaching them to the main buoys; if it is suspect, rig your own lines to the mooring buoys.

FORE-AND-AFT BUOYS

If the mooring buoys have lightweight pickup buoys attached to them, pick up the small buoys and take their lines to bow and stern. Otherwise, rig your own lines to the buoys.

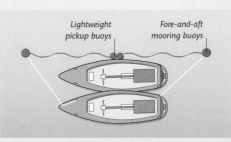

mooring to other boats and to the shore. Be careful not to pick up a permanent mooring, as its owner may return at any time and claim the berth. If you do have to pick up someone else's mooring, never leave your boat unattended in case the owner does appear. If possible, ask the harbormaster or a local sailor to advise you.

Securing to a mooring

It is simpler to pick up a mooring than to come alongside a pontoon or other boat, but be prepared before approaching. Detail one or two crew members to pick up the mooring; they should have a mooring line and boathook ready. Make a practice run up to the mooring to check the approach and inspect it closely, particularly its pickup arrangement. Check the depth of water and that there is room to swing.

On larger cruisers, the bow may be quite high out of the water, making it difficult to pick up the

PICKING UP A BUOY
The foredeck crew should be equipped with a boathook and have a mooring warp available. Hook the buoy with the boathook and tie up with a mooring line.

buoy or thread a mooring line. In this case, come alongside the buoy just forward of the shrouds, where the freeboard is usually less. As you make your final approach, the foredeck crew should indicate the position and distance of the buoy by hand signals, as the helmsman may lose sight of it in the last few yards. Hand signals are used because it is often impossible to hear spoken commands or information. Work out a system that suits your crew. A common method is for the foredeck crew to use the boathook to point continuously at the mooring.

DRYING MOORING
Be sure to check if a mooring dries out at low tide before securing to it. Here, a shoal-draft cruiser sits on the mud at low tide between its fore-and-aft mooring buoys.

Once the buoy is alongside, the foredeck crew can either pull the pick-up buoy on board and use the warp or chain underneath to secure the boat, or tie the mooring line to the ring on the buoy or to the chain under the buoy. Take a round-turn through the ring or chain, then tie a bowline with a long loop (p.47) so that it can be reached from the deck, which will make leaving much easier.

If a pickup buoy is pulled aboard, check the condition of the rope or chain between it and the main riser. If it looks at all suspect, use one of your own warps to tie to the main chain. Make sure that the mooring line is led through a fairlead or over the anchor roller. Ensure the foredeck crew signal to the cockpit when they have secured the boat. It is wise to rig a second, separate, mooring line so that the boat is not relying on one line alone.

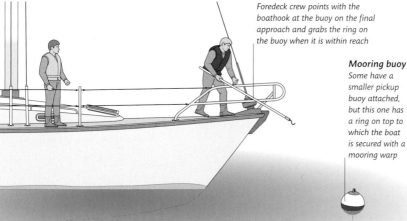

Boathook
Foredeck crew points with the boathook at the buoy on the final approach and grabs the ring on the buoy when it is within reach

Mooring buoy
Some have a smaller pickup buoy attached, but this one has a ring on top to which the boat is secured with a mooring warp

ARRIVING AND LEAVING

When arriving at a mooring, decide on a method and route of approach and brief the crew so that they know what is required of them. The aim is to proceed slowly, coming to a standstill with the mooring buoy at the bow or alongside the shroud.

Making the approach

The first step is to decide how your boat will lie once it is moored. Check how other boats in the vicinity are lying, and decide if the wind or tide will have most effect on the boat. The secret is always to approach into the strongest element of wind or tide to retain control and be able to stop. If in doubt, approach into the tide. If you are planning to approach under sail, you must decide whether to make your final approach under mainsail alone or headsail alone. The rule is: if the wind is forward of the beam for your final approach, use the mainsail only; if it is on the beam or farther aft, then approach under headsail only.

If the mainsail is used with the wind on or abaft of the beam, you will not be able to let it out far enough to spill all the wind, so you will not be able to slow down or stop. Sail around the area slowly to give yourself time to assess the situation and plan your approach and an escape route. If necessary, make a practice run at the chosen spot. Brief the crew and give them time to prepare a mooring line and station themselves with the boathook. They will also need time to lower or furl whichever sail is not going to be used.

If you decide to approach under power, lower and stow the sails in plenty of time. Then motor slowly around the area while you plan your approach. Make sure that the crew are fully briefed and understand your intentions. If there is a tidal stream present, make your final approach head to tide, motoring slowly up to the mooring buoy.

Arriving under sail

With the wind forward of the beam, approach under mainsail alone to keep the foredeck clear of a flapping headsail. If the wind is aft of the beam, sail upwind of the mooring, lower the mainsail, and sail slowly toward the mooring buoy under headsail alone. In strong winds, you may have to lower or furl the headsail and sail under bare poles. In light winds, you may have to partly hoist the top of the mainsail to create enough power to counter the tide.

LASSOING A MOORING
If it is difficult to grab the mooring with a boathook, it is possible to lasso the buoy by throwing a large loop of mooring warp so that it encircles the buoy. The line used must be one that sinks, such as nylon. Once it has encircled and sunk beneath the buoy, tighten the line so that it pulls against the chain underneath the buoy to secure the boat. Rig another line to the mooring buoy's ring and recover the first line from under the buoy by pulling on one end.

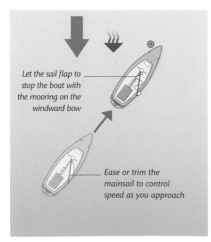

Let the sail flap to stop the boat with the mooring on the windward bow

Ease or trim the mainsail to control speed as you approach

WIND AHEAD OF THE BEAM
Approach on a close reach under mainsail alone. Let the sail flap in your final approach to stop the boat. As soon as the mooring is secured, drop the sail.

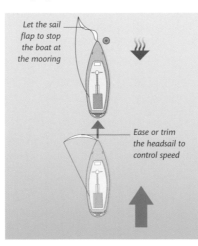

Let the sail flap to stop the boat at the mooring

Ease or trim the headsail to control speed

WIND AFT OF THE BEAM
Sail upwind of the mooring, lower the mainsail, and sail slowly back toward the mooring under headsail alone. Pick up the buoy and drop or furl the headsail.

Leaving under sail

The same rules apply to leaving under sail as to arriving. How you leave will be determined by the wind direction relative to the boat as it lies on the mooring. If the wind is from ahead of the beam, you should leave under mainsail only, or mainsail and headsail together. If it is on or abaft the beam, leave under headsail alone. Decide on the route you will take, check for obstructions, then brief the crew.

When you are lying on a mooring and wish to sail off, the boat can be given steerage way, and turned in the desired direction by pulling the buoy aft along one side of the boat before releasing it. This pulls the boat forward and creates steerage way.

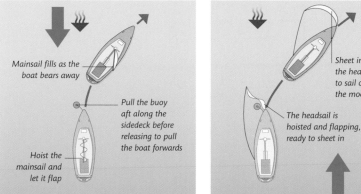

Mainsail fills as the boat bears away

Pull the buoy aft along the sidedeck before releasing to pull the boat forwards

Hoist the mainsail and let it flap

Sheet in the headsail to sail off from the mooring

The headsail is hoisted and flapping, ready to sheet in

WIND AHEAD OF THE BEAM

Hoist the mainsail and prepare the headsail. If the wind is light, or if your boat does not handle well under mainsail alone, hoist both sails. Drop the mooring and bear away to your chosen course.

WIND AFT OF THE BEAM

Hoist the headsail; when you are ready to drop the mooring, sheet it in and sail away. Sail into clear water before turning head-to-wind to hoist the mainsail and sailing off on your preferred course.

Arriving and leaving under power

Under power, approach the mooring into either the wind or the tide (whichever is the stronger). This will give you maximum control over where you stop. If you are not sure which is the stronger element, look at other boats of a similar type to yours that are moored in the vicinity. Plan your course clear of other boats or obstructions and have an escape route planned in case of unforeseen circumstances. Brief the crew and give them time to prepare.

When you leave the mooring, your boat will be pointing toward the wind or tide, whichever is stronger. This is the direction in which you will set off, unless an obstruction requires you to steer another course. As when you arrived, brief your crew to prepare them for departure.

To leave a mooring, the foredeck crew must prepare the gear to allow them to drop it immediately on command. If a pickup buoy has

been brought aboard, its line should be uncleated and held with a turn around the cleat. If a mooring rope has been tied to the buoy or chain, it should be led again as a slip line, with both ends on board; it can then be easily released and recovered. When the buoy is dropped, make

sure that it is thrown clear of the hull and away from the intended course. Retrieve all lines cleanly; mooring warps trailing through the water may catch around the keel or rudder; worst of all, they could foul the propeller and leave you stranded in a crowded mooring area.

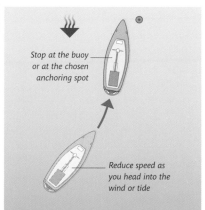

Stop at the buoy or at the chosen anchoring spot

Reduce speed as you head into the wind or tide

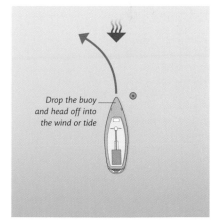

Drop the buoy and head off into the wind or tide

HOW TO APPROACH

Motor slowly into the wind or tide toward the mooring buoy or your chosen anchorage spot. Reduce speed until you are stationary alongside the buoy or at the anchoring spot.

HOW TO LEAVE

Drop the mooring buoy or motor forward to recover the anchor. Head initially into the wind or tide, whichever is stronger, as this will give you maximum control before turning to your preferred course.

ANCHORING

The ability to anchor easily and with confidence is a very important one for a cruising yacht, especially one that ventures off the beaten track and away from marinas. Anchoring is one of the fundamental techniques for a cruising sailor to learn, since it provides the yachtsman with the ability to secure his yacht to the seabed without relying on any outside facilities, such as a mooring. The cruising yachtsman must know how to anchor and should understand the advantages and disadvantages of the various types of anchor and the equipment needed to deploy an anchor efficiently.

Reasons for anchoring

Anchoring may simply provide a way to enjoy a quiet anchorage away from the bustle of a marina, or to stop for lunch or a swim, but it is also a vital skill to master as it allows a boat to wait out a foul tide or ride out a gale in shelter. It can hold a boat away from a dangerous lee shore and, should an engine fail on a windless day, it may be the only way to hold position rather than drifting into danger.

ANCHOR BOW ROLLER
Most cruisers carry their bower anchor on a bow roller for easy storage, deployment and recovery. If a headsail roller furler is fitted, it should be mounted high enough to clear the anchor when it is being dropped and recovered.

Anchoring equipment

All yachts should carry at least two suitably sized anchors, together with appropriate lengths of chain or rope cable. The choice of anchor and the decision whether to use chain or rope depend on the characteristics of your boat and the areas in which you normally sail. Suppliers of anchors and chain will suggest suitable sizes and weights for your boat, and you can also ask advice from experienced sailors. For serious offshore sailing, when it is likely that you will, at times, need to anchor in exposed anchorages, very strong tides, or bad weather conditions, it is sensible to increase the number of anchors, their size, and the amount of cable that you carry.

A typical setup for a coastal cruiser will include a main anchor, called the bower anchor, and a lighter anchor, called a kedge. The kedge is used for short stops in good weather, or for kedging-off after running aground (*pp.294–295*). The cable for the bower anchor may be rope with a short length of chain between the anchor and the rope to better resist the chafe of the seabed, or it may be

an all-chain cable. The kedge will usually have an all-rope cable with a short length of chain—about 6 ft (2 m)—at the anchor.

A long-distance cruiser should carry a more substantial inventory of anchors and cable to cope with a variety of anchoring situations. Four anchors would be typical, with a main bower anchor, a secondary bower of about the same weight but a different design (*opposite*) to cope with different bottom conditions, a kedge anchor, and a heavy storm anchor for exceptional conditions. A selection of chain and rope will be carried to allow the cruiser to anchor in deep water when necessary, and to set two or more anchors simultaneously.

Anchor design

Anchors vary from the classic Fisherman's anchor, which has several parts and can be dismantled, to single, one-piece anchors such as the Bruce. All anchors have one or more flukes that are designed to bury themselves into the seabed or hook onto rocks,

STERN ANCHOR STOWAGE
Some cruisers carry a stern anchor and this can be a good place to stow the kedge. This cruiser has an anchor and windlass mounted on the stern platform.

plus a shank to which the cable is attached. The flat anchor types, such as the Danforth and Fortress, have two large, flat flukes and a pivoting shank, together with a stock mounted at the crown. The plow type do away with a stock and may have a pivoting or fixed shank.

Some of the latest types are spade-like with a large, single fluke and a rigid shank. These designs try to maximize the fluke area and control the angle it presents to the seabed.

PARTS OF AN ANCHOR

All anchors have a shank, to which the cable is attached, and one or more flukes that dig into, or hook, the seabed. Some have a stock designed to turn the anchor so that the fluke(s) can dig into the bottom. The shank is attached to the fluke(s) at the crown. Some anchors (*below*) have only a single fluke and a shank.

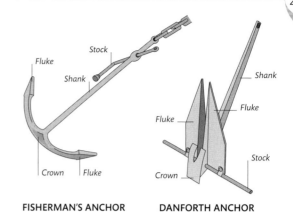

FISHERMAN'S ANCHOR **DANFORTH ANCHOR**

TYPES OF ANCHOR

The classic Fisherman's anchor is designed to hook the bottom with one of its flukes, but modern anchors are designed to bury themselves in the seabed. If the seabed is sand, gravel, or mud, this works well, but in rock or thick weeds, a modern burying anchor is often less effective.

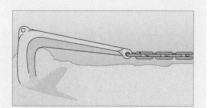

BRUCE ANCHOR
The Bruce anchor is solid with large flukes and no moving parts. It is a popular choice as a bower anchor and stows well on a bow roller. However, it does not hinge flat so it can be awkward to stow on deck.

PLOW ANCHOR
Plow-type anchors are very popular, especially the original CQR anchor. Most have a hinged shank but some have a solid construction. They stow well on a bow roller but are awkward to stow on deck.

SPADE ANCHOR
The Spade anchor is a newer anchor that is proving popular with cruisers. Available in aluminum, galvanized steel, or stainless steel, it stows well on a bow roller and can be dismantled for stowage in a locker.

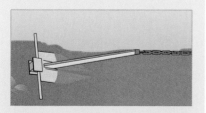

DANFORTH ANCHOR
The Danforth anchor uses a hinged plate to form the flukes and a stock to prevent it from rolling over. Because it lies flat it is easy to stow on deck or in a locker, but it is less suitable for stowage on a bow roller.

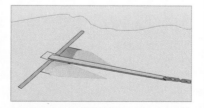

FORTRESS ANCHOR
The Fortress is a lightweight anchor made from aluminum. Like the Danforth, it has wide flat flukes, but their hinge angle can be adjusted to suit sand or mud bottoms. The Fortress can be dismantled.

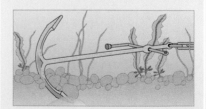

FISHERMAN'S ANCHOR
The Fisherman's anchor performs better than most other types of anchor in rock or weeds. However, it is much heavier than modern designs and, because of its shape, is very awkward to stow.

TYPE OF ANCHOR CABLE

Anchor cable can be made from rope or chain or a combination of both. Cruisers that do not anchor frequently often choose rope with a short length of chain but long-distance cruisers generally use chain for the bower anchor and rope for the kedge.

Chain cable

The best material for anchor cable is chain, as long as your boat is not very sensitive to weight and you can physically handle the weight when anchoring. Chain is stronger than rope and is much more resistant to chafe against the seabed. The weight of the chain itself provides some holding ability and also creates a catenary (curve) between boat and anchor. This catenary helps absorb shock loads as a wind gust must first straighten out the chain's catenary before the boat will snatch at its anchor. Because of its weight, the chain near the anchor lies on the seabed and transfers the load to the anchor in a horizontal direction, minimizing the tendency for the anchor to be pulled upward and out of the seabed.

Rope cable

If a rope cable is used, it should be nylon, which stretches well to absorb the shock loads from wind gusts and waves. When rope is used, it is normal to place a short length of chain (6–9 ft/2–3 m) between the anchor and the rope to take the chafe from the seabed. Always protect the rope where it passes through the anchor roller or fairlead with plastic tubing or other protection to avoid chafe, which can destroy a rope very quickly.

A nylon rope cable is particularly appropriate for the kedge as it may have to be used from the tender, where the lightness of rope will make the job much easier.

CHOOSING AN ANCHORAGE

When choosing an anchorage, you need to consider the amount of shelter from wind, swell, and waves, the depth of water now and throughout your stay, the type of seabed, swinging room, and the ease of approach and departure under sail or power. You should also consider the practical issue of getting ashore. If possible, try to anchor where the wind or tide will push you away from the shore if your anchor drags.

Changing conditions

An anchorage that is sheltered from the wind when you anchor can become untenable if the wind swings and the anchorage becomes exposed. The same may happen if a tidal stream changes direction and causes a change in the sea state. Check the weather forecast before you anchor, and take into account any predicted changes in wind direction or strength. Consult the tidal atlas and tide tables to see if any changes will affect your anchorage. If you are anchoring in shallow water, make sure there will be sufficient water at low tide to keep you afloat and to allow you to leave safely at any time.

Types of seabed

Check the chart or local sailing directions for a description of the type of seabed. Be careful when anchoring on rock, weeds, or coral covered by thin sand, as these bottoms provide poor holding for most anchors. Very soft mud also offers poor holding as the anchor is likely to pull through the mud. If possible, choose to anchor in sand or firm mud, which provide the best holding. Avoid anchoring near wrecks, areas of foul ground, or where underwater cables are present.

Anchor Scope

An anchor's holding power is dependent on the amount (scope) of cable you can pay out; this, in turn, will depend on the amount you can carry and the depth of water.

Estimate the maximum depth of water you expect during your stay and add the height of your bow from the water, then apply the following ratios. The absolute minimum scope for chain is 3:1 and for rope 5:1. However, you should aim for 5:1 for chain and 8:1 for rope. In rough conditions in an exposed anchorage, you may have to pay out ten or more times the depth of water to avoid dragging. Remember to allow for the rise of tide if you anchor at low water.

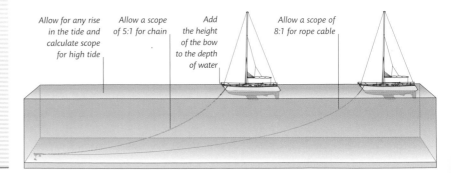

Allow for any rise in the tide and calculate scope for high tide　　*Allow a scope of 5:1 for chain*　　*Add the height of the bow to the depth of water*　　*Allow a scope of 8:1 for rope cable*

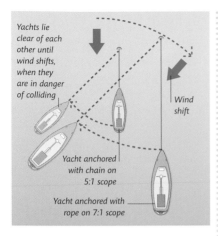

Yachts lie clear of each other until wind shifts, when they are in danger of colliding

Wind shift

Yacht anchored with chain on 5:1 scope

Yacht anchored with rope on 7:1 scope

AVOIDING OTHERS

Avoid anchoring close to other yachts, especially if they are of a different type or have a different cable or scope from yours.

Other boats

Before anchoring, consider any other boats that are already anchored, the likely position of their anchors, and the route you will take to approach and leave your chosen spot. Allow plenty of room between you and all the other boats, leaving enough space to swing clear of others if the wind or tide change direction. Try to anchor with boats of a similar type and size to your own, as they will react in much the same way as your boat to the effects of wind and tide. Remember that if your boat fouls another that was anchored before you arrived, it will be your responsibility to move to another spot.

Arriving and leaving

The techniques described for arriving and leaving a mooring (pp.276–277), by pointing into the strongest element of wind or tide, apply equally to anchoring except that anchoring does not require the precision of stopping at a mooring. It is, however, important to ensure that the boat stops moving through the water before the anchor is

lowered to the seabed and then moves slowly backward as the full scope of cable is paid out. This prevents the cable from piling up on top of the anchor and possibly fouling it. When arriving under power, it is a simple matter to slow down and stop at your chosen spot then slowly reverse to lay out the cable as the anchor is dropped. Under sail, you should also approach into the strongest prevailing element, under main or headsail alone (p.276). Aim to sail slowly to the drop zone, then stop the boat before dropping the anchor. Then lower the sails so that the boat begins to drift backward, away from the anchor.

When leaving under sail, steerage way can be provided by pulling the boat up to the anchor. When the wind is aft of the beam, break the anchor out (pp.282–283) before hoisting the headsail, then sail slowly while the anchor and cable are stowed before you hoist the mainsail. With the wind ahead of the beam, hoist the mainsail and sail slowly away, while stowing the anchor and cable.

Dropping an anchor

Prepare the anchor and cable before the final approach to the chosen spot. With the anchor stowed in its bow roller, release any lashings or securing pins and check the connection of the cable to the anchor. Also, make sure that the anchor cannot drop before you are ready. Check the depth of water using the depth sounder and calculate the amount of cable required. This length should be pulled on deck, so that it is ready to run without snagging, and then cleated. Anchor cables should be marked with paint or colored cable ties at predetermined intervals so it is easy to see how much has been deployed. When the boat reaches the chosen spot, and has stopped, or is moving astern, give the

order to let go. The anchor should be lowered under control, into the water, and the cable allowed to run out under control until the anchor reaches the seabed. Pay out the rest of the cable as the boat drifts away from the anchor, then snub it (take a turn on a cleat or engage the windlass brake) to set the anchor (make it dig into the seabed).

A better way to set the anchor is to apply reverse engine power with the cable securely cleated. Watch the cable, points ashore, and the water alongside the boat to see if the anchor is holding or dragging. A correctly set anchor should be able to hold full reverse thrust on most cruisers.

You can also check if the anchor is holding by putting your foot or hand on the chain. If you can feel any vibration or bumping, this suggests the anchor is dragging along the seabed.

When the anchor is set, take a series of bearings on two or more points on shore to make sure that the boat is not dragging its anchor. Re-check these bearings at regular intervals. If the anchor drags, let out more cable and repeat the setting procedure. If this does not work, weigh the anchor (pp.282–283) and try another spot.

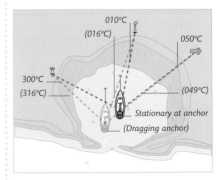

010°C
(016°C)

050°C

300°C
(316°C)

(049°C)

Stationary at anchor
(Dragging anchor)

ANCHOR BEARINGS

Once the boat is anchored, take at least two, and preferably three or more bearings on prominent shore features. Check these bearings periodically to ensure that the boat is not dragging its anchor.

WEIGHING ANCHOR

The ease with which an anchor can be weighed (recovered) depends on the weight of anchor and cable, the depth of water, wind and sea conditions, and the strength of the crew or the anchor windlass. The first step is to bring the boat over the anchor. In a small boat or good conditions, this can be done by pulling in the cable, but in a larger boat or stronger conditions, you will need the help of the engine or sails. A crew member should indicate the direction of the cable to the helmsman, who will be unable to see it from the cockpit. When the boat is over the anchor, the crew should inform the skipper that it is ready to break out. Stop the boat over the anchor and haul up the cable by hand or windlass until the anchor breaks out.

Alternatively, cleat the cable and use the engine to break out the anchor. When the anchor breaks out, motor or sail slowly until the foredeck crew has stowed the anchor and cable. If the anchor cannot be broken out by hand or windlass, you may have to haul the cable as tight as possible, then cleat it, and use the power of the engine or sails to break it out. The best way is to motor gently astern, increasing the power until the anchor breaks out. Do not motor forward or the cable may damage the bow or topsides, and the direction of pull may bend the anchor's shank.

Laying two anchors

To provide extra security, perhaps against predicted bad weather, lay two anchors, either both in line on one cable, or at a 30–45 degree angle to each other using two cables. This technique is especially useful if you are expecting heavy weather. To stop your boat from swinging far when the tide changes, lay two anchors ahead and astern of the boat. To do this, drop the main anchor and reverse the boat while paying out twice the length of cable needed. Drop the second anchor (the kedge) from the bow, and pull in the main cable while letting out the kedge cable to position the boat midway between the two anchors. Join the two cables with a shackle, and let out both to lower the join below the boat's keel. Secure both cables on cleats.

If you want to hold position, perhaps in a channel with a current or tide that reverses direction periodically, or in a very restricted anchorage, lay two anchors but lead the kedge cable to the stern.

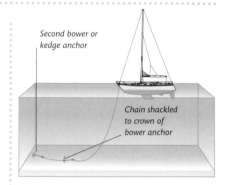

TWO ANCHORS IN LINE
Attach a second bower or kedge anchor, with a short length of chain (6–9 ft/2–3 m) to the crown of the bower anchor.

Second bower or kedge anchor

Chain shackled to crown of bower anchor

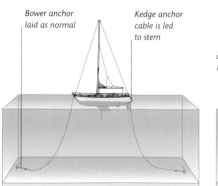

Bower anchor laid as normal

Kedge anchor cable is led to stern

HOLDING POSITION
Two anchors dropped ahead and astern with cables led to bow and stern will hold the boat in line with, say, a reversing current but will not allow it to swing.

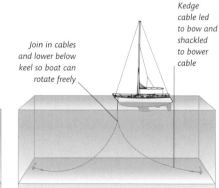

Join in cables and lower below keel so boat can rotate freely

Kedge cable led to bow and shackled to bower cable

REDUCING SWING
Two anchors dropped ahead and astern of the boat, and joined together at the bow, will restrict its swing to a very small radius compared with a single anchor.

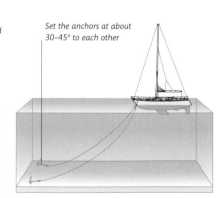

Set the anchors at about 30–45° to each other

TWO ANCHORS AND CABLES
For extra security, lay two anchors about 30–45° apart in the forecast wind direction. This system will tangle if a change in wind or tide direction causes the boat to swing.

ANCHOR WINDLASS
This windlass has a vertical gypsy with a rope drum above. The chain passes around the gypsy and down a chainpipe. The socket on top is for a manual handle.

Using a windlass

A windlass is a powerful winch with a horizontal or vertical gypsy (drum) designed to take the links of the anchor chain. Some models also have a smooth drum for winching rope. A windlass can pull the cable in or let it out under control, and can also be allowed to freewheel. The chain from the anchor runs from the bow roller to the windlass, over the gypsy and down a chainpipe that takes it through the deck and into a chain locker. Many windlasses can handle chain or rope cables, but only chain will self-stow in a locker due to its weight.

Windlasses are available in both manual, electric, or hydraulic models. The powered versions should have a manual facility in the case of power failure. Electric windlasses are common and very useful, but they do require a lot of battery power. Before using the windlass, start the engine so that its alternator can replenish the battery as the windlass is used.

Be careful when working with anchoring equipment. The gear is heavy and loads are high, so handle equipment carefully, wear good deck shoes, keep safety harnesses and loose clothing away, and don't stand where you could be hit should the system fail.

TRIPPING LINES

It is very easy for an anchor to become fouled by an obstruction on the seabed. Motoring around the anchor and pulling its chain from several directions may free it, but it is best to avoid the problem in likely areas of foul ground by using a tripping line.

Using a tripping line
A tripping line is a light line tied to the crown of the anchor. The other end of the line is either brought back on board, where it is left slack but secured on a cleat, or attached to a small buoy to float over the anchor.

Beware of using a buoy on the tripping line in crowded anchorages, as it may get caught by another boat's propeller or be mistaken for a mooring buoy and picked up. In such cases, it is better to bring the end back aboard, although a longer length of line will be needed.

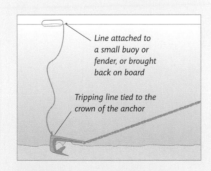

Line attached to a small buoy or fender, or brought back on board

Tripping line tied to the crown of the anchor

RETRIEVING A FOULED ANCHOR
If an anchor is fouled, it can be retrieved by pulling on the tripping line. This will capsize the anchor and retrieve it upside down.

USING THE TENDER
Sometimes it will be necessary to use the tender to lay or recover an anchor. This is easier to do with a solid dinghy than with an inflatable. It is also easier if rope cable is used rather than chain.

Laying an anchor
To lay an anchor from the tender, tie the tender securely alongside the cruiser and transfer the anchor and all the cable required into the dinghy. Coil the cable in the stern of the tender so that it will run out smoothly. Make the end fast aboard the cruiser. It is much easier to handle the anchor if it is hung over the tender's stern and held by a length of line tied to the thwart with a slip hitch. This allows you to release the anchor while seated and is much safer than trying to manhandle the anchor over the side. Row or motor the tender in the direction you want to lay the anchor. Then, when all the cable has run out, slip the retaining line to release the anchor. The crew left on board can now pull in the slack to set the anchor.

Retrieving an anchor
Sometimes you may have to recover an anchor using the tender, usually when you have set two anchors and you cannot recover them both from the yacht.

Recovering an anchor can be hazardous in an inflatable and is easier and safer in a rigid dinghy. Pull the tender along the anchor cable, with the cable running over the tender, until the cable leads vertically down into the water. The tender's buoyancy, combined with a strong pull on the cable, is usually enough to break out the anchor, which can then be pulled up and brought on board the tender. Return to the cruiser by pulling on the cable, coiling it into the tender as you go.

PASSAGE MAKING

There are few things more pleasurable for the cruising sailor than a well-executed passage culminating in a safe arrival at the destination. It does not matter if you arrive at a harbor you know well; the sense of satisfaction cannot be equaled by any other form of travel. As skipper, you alone are responsible for the safe handling of the yacht and the welfare of the crew. If your experience is limited, start with short day trips, building up to a longer cruise lasting several days or more.

Role of skipper

All aspects of the running of the yacht, its safety, and the crew's well-being are the skipper's responsibility. He or she should be comfortable with the sailing and navigation skills, inspire confidence in his crew, and be a good communicator. He should be able to keep on top of all his duties and give the crew tasks that are appropriate to their level of ability and experience so that they are neither underworked nor overburdened. Most importantly, he should be patient with inexperienced crew members and be able to run the yacht with a light touch while retaining respect and authority.

Role of crew

Good crew are worth their weight in gold. The most important qualities are a positive attitude, a sense of humor, and the ability to get along with others in the confined space aboard a cruiser. If the crew also have good sailing or navigation skills, the skipper can consider himself fortunate.

The crew should be fully involved in the boat's management and passage planning, and the skipper should always listen to their opinions. The crew must remember, however, that a vessel at sea might appear to be a democratic environment, but ultimately the skipper is in charge and must make the final decisions.

Skippers vary tremendously in their approach to running a yacht. Good ones demonstrate calm professionalism, while those unsure of their own abilities are often loud and tense. As crew you may encounter very different styles of boat management, and you will need to assess how you approach the idiosyncrasies of your skipper. No two skippers are alike in the way they operate a boat and the way they prefer jobs to be done. If you crew for a succession of skippers, you may even find that their ways of doing things are contradictory. If you aspire to become a skipper, then you will build up your own working practices—hopefully learned from the best skippers you have sailed with.

Learning to be a skipper

It is fairly easy to define the technical sailing and navigation skills required of a skipper, and you can learn these skills and obtain certificates at sailing

DISCUSSING PLANS
Plan your passage in detail before you set sail, and make sure that the crew are involved in the planning. Include backup plans to allow for bad weather.

CREW MORALE
If, at the end of the passage, the crew is healthy and happy, and can enjoy a chat in the cockpit reminiscing about the passage, then the skipper has done a good job

Do not undertake passages that are beyond your level of experience. Sailing is as much about the journey as the arrival and successful day trips will provide just as much pleasure for the skipper and crew as more ambitious passages. Short trips also involve more close-quarters boat handling with which to improve skills.

Although ultimate responsibility lies with the skipper, his job will be much easier if some of the crew have offshore passage-making experience. Passage making with an inexperienced crew puts great demands on a skipper, who may feel under immense pressure if there is not an experienced crew member to whom some tasks can be delegated. If you cannot find an experienced sailor to come with you, adjust your plans to suit the crew's level of experience.

schools. The ability to manage people aboard a small yacht and develop your crew's teamwork is, however, less easy to define and more difficult to acquire. If you have business management skills, these will help but you will need to modify your approach significantly, as running a boat is not like running an office. Crew members are not paid employees (unless you aim to be a commercial skipper) and are sailing with you for experience and fun, so they must be handled with consideration and understanding. Very often they are family or close friends, and your relationships can be harmed by stressful experiences afloat.

Your crew will feel more relaxed and confident if you are calm and show confidence, so try not to let your own nerves show or affect your behavior. Try to avoid high-stress situations by only attempting what you feel comfortable doing.

The technical sailing and navigation skills you learned at sailing school can be honed by regular use, so try to get as much experience as possible. Pre-plan each passage carefully and, if you feel at all unsure, ask a more experienced sailor to check your plans and confirm your interpretation of wind and tides.

If you are concerned about maneuvering your boat in tight spaces, seek advice from other skippers on similar boats or on similar moorings or marina berths. If you need a hand, then ask for it—this is a sign of a good skipper. If you have problems handling the boat in a crowded marina, well-stationed crew with roving fenders can often help avoid or soften a collision. Remember to perform berthing maneuvers slowly; this way, if you do have a collision, it will be a gentle one and only your pride may be damaged.

Becoming a better skipper

Try to always learn from the time you spend afloat, slowly building knowledge of the sea, weather, and your boat. Do not get disheartened or discouraged if something does not go according to plan; instead learn from it. Surprisingly quickly you will develop the skills and confidence necessary to undertake longer cruises lasting several days or more.

Although it is important to develop technical skills, focus on improving your interpersonal and crew management skills. Novice crew can be anxious about the passage ahead, while others may be overconfident and want to push too hard. A good skipper takes an interest in everyone on board and pays special attention to novice or nervous crew members. As an improving skipper, concentrate on ensuring that everyone has a safe and enjoyable experience.

PASSAGE PLANNING

Planning for a cruise or passage starts some time before the day of departure. The skipper, or navigator if there is one, prepares a detailed navigation plan (*p.358*). From this you can estimate the departure time, the number of hours or days for which you will be sailing, and whether the passage involves night sailing. Remember to have an alternative plan in case the weather or other factors require a change of plans. Also, on a cruise, build in days for rest and shoreside recreation, especially if there are children on board.

Using the cruise or passage plan, you will be able to work out your fuel, food, and water requirements, and can allow for stops to replenish supplies if necessary. Check your yacht's insurance details to be sure that you are covered for the passage and, if you are going abroad, make sure that all your crew bring their passports and make any visa arrangements that may be necessary.

If you will be sailing in foreign waters (even if you do not intend to enter port) check that your yacht's registration papers are on board. You should also carry paperwork confirming the yacht's tax status if you cruise in an area, such as Europe, that requires VAT or other tax to be paid on a boat. Failure to carry confirmation could result in a fine or even the yacht's being impounded.

It is also useful to have several photocopied crew lists with you. These provide authorities with details of who is aboard, next of kin, passport number, and contact details. Many countries now require a small-boat skipper to possess a certificate of competence, so make sure that you have it with you.

Coast guard services

In most countries with a coastline, a coast guard service is responsible for managing rescue operations at sea, either using its own resources or those of the navy, air force, lifeboat service, or any shipping in the vicinity.

Many coast guards operate a system in which a yacht setting out on passage can inform the coast guard of its passage plan, destination, and estimated date and time of arrival. On reaching the destination, the skipper then notifies the coast guard of his boat's safe arrival. This system allows the coast guard to begin a search-and-rescue operation if a yacht is overdue.

You can also preregister your boat's details with the coast guard so, in the event of an emergency call from your vessel, they immediately know the type of boat, its distinguishing features, what safety equipment you have, and other details. This will help them coordinate a speedy search and rescue. If the coast guard in your area operates such services, it is wise to take advantage of them. Always remember to inform the coast guard on arrival or if your plans change and you divert to another harbor.

Watch systems

When passage making, it is essential that all members of the crew, including the skipper, get sufficient rest so that they continue to perform at their optimum. Sailing offshore can be mentally and physically tiring, especially in rough weather.

If everyone is to enjoy the passage and be able to contribute to the sailing of the yacht, you need to ensure that the crew stay alert and are well fed and rested throughout. When setting out on a passage of more than a few hours, you should operate a defined watch system that allows all crew members to have time off watch for rest and sleep. A watch

KEEPING WATCH
The on-watch crew must keep a regular lookout because it is very easy to be taken unawares by a ship appearing over the horizon, especially from astern.

system divides the crew into two or more watches, one of which is responsible for the sailing of the yacht, while the other rests or prepares meals. Larger crews aboard bigger racing or cruising yachts are often split into three watches, each led by a watch leader. While one crew is on watch, a second is off watch, and the third is on stand-by to assist the on-watch crew and to undertake domestic tasks. With large crews, the skipper, navigator and, sometimes, a cook are left out of the watches.

The traditional, two-watch system has one watch on duty for four hours, followed by four hours off-watch. To prevent each watch from having the same periods on watch each day, the watches are staggered by two "dog watches" of two hours each in the late afternoon and early evening, during which everyone is usually awake.

Personalized systems

There is no need to use a traditional system. Many experienced skippers devise their own system to suit the particular needs and size of their crew and the length of the passage. What is important is that everyone gets sufficient rest, and that light and noise are kept to a minimum below when the off-watch crew is sleeping.

Whichever system you adopt, make sure that everyone fully appreciates how it will operate. Put a chart on the bulkhead above the chart table listing names and watch times if that helps. There is nothing less likely to induce sleep than lying in your bunk worrying about when you are next required to be on watch.

Keeping time

Make sure that everyone understands the importance of being on time for their watch. In the confines of a small yacht, when people are tired on

passage, it is very easy for tempers to fray if the watch on deck is not relieved on time because the new watch has overslept. The on-watch team should wake their colleagues about half an hour before they are needed on watch, to give them time to be fully alert and properly dressed for the prevailing conditions. This can take some time, as it may require putting on a full set of oilskins, life jacket, and safety harness in a confined and moving space.

It is courteous to prepare a hot drink for the new watch. This is also the time for the new watch to be briefed and receive standing orders and any instructions for the ongoing passage. Look out for each other's safety during the changeover—don't allow the new watch to come on deck at night without clipping on first, and be sure the new helmsman is comfortable with the course to steer and any other navigational issues before taking over.

When the crew is large enough, the skipper may stay outside the watch system but remain on call at all times. In such instances he will issue standing instructions as to when to be woken. Reasons will include an increase in wind strength, the approach of another vessel, the sighting of land or navigational marks, or when the crew is uncertain about anything. It can feel awkward waking the skipper, but don't delay; situations can develop very quickly and a good skipper would rather be woken unnecessarily than not be awake when a crisis unfolds.

Despite the best-laid plans, it may be that a crew member becomes overtired. If this occurs, they should be taken out of the system for a watch or two. The skipper may need to deputize for them until they are able to stand watch again.

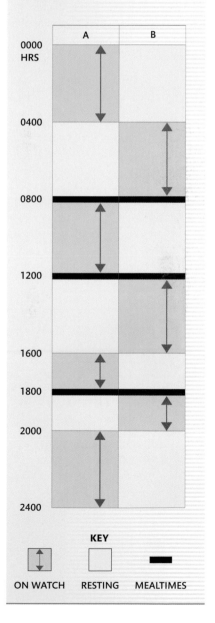

TRADITIONAL WATCH SYSTEM

Watch systems are arranged to run from midnight to midnight, splitting the 24 hours into periods of on-watch duty and off-watch rest. The traditional system uses four-hour watches at night, which may be too long when conditions are difficult.

KEY

ON WATCH   RESTING   MEALTIMES

LIFE ON BOARD

On longer passages, of about two days or more, a routine should be quickly developed, dictated by the needs of the boat and the need to maintain a fit crew. The crew, divided into watches, goes about their duties of sailing, navigation, and boat maintenance, and takes their rest as set by the watch pattern.

Two important factors when you are running a watch system are self-discipline and respect for each other, particularly for the off-watch crew's need for good-quality sleep.

The safety of the boat and crew depends on having an alert and efficient crew on watch, and this is not possible on a long passage if they do not get sufficient sleep. Where possible, the off-watch crew should sleep in berths away from the saloon, navigation station, and galley. Cabins forward and aft afford some privacy and relative quiet. This also allows for some lighting to be operated in the galley and navigational areas without disturbing the sleeping crew.

Unfortunately, cabins and berths at the ends of the boat are the least comfortable for sleeping, or even relaxing when sailing in waves. In rough conditions the only usable berths will be near the middle of the boat which, in a small cruiser, means the settee or pilot berths in the saloon. Berths farther aft, alongside the cockpit, may be tenable but often induce claustrophobia, and being close to the cockpit makes them noisy.

Minimizing noise

Noise is often a problem for crew trying to sleep, and the on-watch crew should try to keep it to a minimum. Noise can come from many sources—banging of hatches and lockers, whistling kettles (popular on boats), chatter from the cockpit, the VHF radio, instrument alarms, the whirring of winches, and even the water rushing past the hull. It is not possible to eliminate noise, but do remember how disturbing it can be to the crew trying to sleep.

Agree times in the watch system when everyone is awake, interacting, sharing meal times, and enjoying entertainment. At these times it is appropriate for the crew to be animated and for music to be played.

Domestic chores

It is important that the boat is kept clean and hygienic. A small boat at sea can very quickly degenerate into an unpleasant environment, which is bad for morale and for maintaining a healthy and motivated crew.

The galley, heads, and main accommodation areas should be thoroughly cleaned very frequently, probably on a daily basis, depending on the size of the crew and boat and the weather conditions. Antibacterial cleaning agents are useful for maintaining countertops and other hard surfaces. Cleaning tasks are unlikely to be popular, so make sure they are incorporated into the watch system routines and that each task is unambiguously allotted to one or more crew members.

Conserving water

In normal shoreside life, an unlimited water supply, and the high level of personal hygiene it affords, are taken for granted. On a boat, fresh water is in short supply, and there is rarely enough to allow daily or even frequent showers when on an offshore passage. In warm climates it may be possible to take a seawater

SECURE BERTHS
Bunks intended for use when sailing should have sturdy leecloths to hold the person in the berth when the boat heels. Some yachts have sleeping cabins with upper and lower berths, as here.

wash in the cockpit and rinse off with fresh water using a deck shower, but long, luxurious showers will have to wait until the next port is reached.

If you intend to allow swimming off the boat, you should enforce strict safety guidelines. Always stop the boat and trail the dinghy or long floating lines with fenders attached to act as safety lines for swimmers to grab if needed. Alternatively, insist that swimmers wear safety harnesses attached by lines to the boat. For each crew member swimming, make sure they have a "buddy" on board to keep watch over them and that someone competent in boat handling stays aboard. If in any doubt about the conditions, don't allow anyone to swim; instead, use a bucket on a rope to scoop up seawater. Remember, though, that a bucketful of water can easily be ripped out of your hand or pull you overboard if you try to fill it when the boat is moving. Tie the bucket's lanyard to a cleat and do not wrap it around your hand when you fill the bucket.

Keeping the boat tidy

Encourage crew members to keep their own personal belongings neat— it's all too easy for clothing and other items to spill across the boat as it heels or tacks. If this happens, the interior will quickly deteriorate into an unpleasant place that will discourage crew from going below when off watch.

Wet gear should be kept away from dry clothes. A dedicated wet locker for hanging oilskins is ideal if there is sufficient space; alternatively, use the heads compartment, as it usually has a sump into which the wet gear can drain.

Organize a rota to share domestic duties, and delegate crew to clean up immediately after each meal.

Cooking

Food preparation is often the least favorite task on board, unless you are fortunate enough to sail with a seagoing chef, but the importance of food and meal times is heightened at sea. It is important that meals are prepared at the correct times and that the crew is as well fed as possible under the circumstances.

Not everyone on board will consider themselves a good cook, and as a result some crew members may shy away from the galley. It is important, however, that as skipper, you don't allow the better cooks to feel put upon by having to do the majority of meal preparation, unless they are relieved of some other onerous duty such as dishwashing or cleaning. As with boat cleaning, meal preparation should be made a part of the watch system duties.

Food preparation is made easier if the boat has refrigerator or freezer facilities. For passages of a few days or less, meals can be prepared at home and frozen. They then simply need reheating. If that is not possible, select some simple but tasty recipes that won't be difficult to prepare at sea. Buy good-quality produce and check its expiration date. Keep fresh fruit and vegetables in a cool, dark, but well-ventilated locker if possible. Prepare a menu plan for enough days to cover your passage and any eventualities. Check any special requirements, allergies, or preferences your crew may have; feeding them their favorite food certainly helps morale. Bear in mind that if a long passage involves a change of climate, dietary requirements may change.

Always have some quick and easy convenience food standing by in case of heavy weather, and keep a container of chocolate, cookies, raisins, and other easy-to-eat snacks

PREPARING MEALS
The layout of the galley has a lot to do with whether cooking is a pleasure or a chore. A U-shaped galley with sufficient counter space allows the cook to work out of the way of other crew moving around the interior. Deep fiddles on galley counters keep items in place even when heeled, and secure storage space close to hand keeps the galley well organized.

handy for the on-watch crew. From the meal plan, make a shopping list so that you know exactly what you need. If you are shopping for a long passage, take a calculator to the supermarket with you to avoid going over budget.

Mealtimes should be communal, allowing both watches and the skipper to spend time together. Keep one person on deck as a lookout and rotate this task frequently. Mealtimes are a good time to discuss the passage and confirm future plans. It also gives the skipper a forum to pass on information, answer any queries, and set any standing orders.

AVOIDING COLLISIONS

The international regulations for Preventing Collisions at Sea (Col Regs) specify the responsibilities of all types of craft. They apply to all vessels on the high seas and connected waters, and it is essential that you learn the most common rules. As the skipper of a small boat, you have exactly the same responsibility for avoiding collisions as the skipper of the largest liner or supertanker. Ignorance of the rules is no defense and, quite apart from the dangers of collision to boat and crew, the penalties for lack of rule observance can be severe.

Rules of the road

In addition to the Col Regs, national governments and local authorities can impose their own regulations covering harbors, rivers, and inland waterways. Details of these additional regulations can be found in local pilot books. If you are preparing a passage plan, particularly in unfamiliar waters, be sure to check if there are local bylaws in place that may apply to you.

Make sure that you know and understand the basic "rules of the road" (pp.52–53). When you are out sailing, practice spotting who has right of way among the boats around you. Involve your crew in this exercise; as they should be involved in keeping a lookout, it will be useful for them to practice identifying potential collision situations. Study the full regulations for a more complete understanding, and have a reference guide to the rules on board. Radar and AIS (Automatic Identification System) (p.330) can provide invaluable backup, especially at night or when visibility is poor. Be sure to learn the rules that govern boats under power as well as those under sail. Remember that if your engine is running, and in gear and propelling the boat, your boat becomes a power-driven vessel, whether or not you have sails hoisted.

Daylight shapes and navigation lights

Always hoist the correct daylight shape (p.293) when you are motor-sailing to indicate that you are under power and sail. Also remember to hoist the appropriate shape when you are anchored. It can be a chore to find and hoist the correct daylight shapes, but they are an essential aid for others trying to identify your boat's status.

At night, be careful to show the correct lights when you are sailing or under power. Be careful not to show the lights for a sailing vessel if you are motor-sailing. This is an easy mistake to make if you have been sailing and turn on the engine to enter harbor. It is easy to forget to switch from your masthead sailing lights to your deck level navigation lights and steaming light required when you are under power (p.303). Unfortunately, the masthead combined light used on most sailing boats to conserve power is of no use in close quarters situations when low level lights are required.

Identifying the stand-on vessel

The concept of there being (at least) one give-way and one stand-on vessel in any potential collision situation is fundamental to an understanding and observance of the collision regulations. The rules are designed to identify which vessel should hold its course

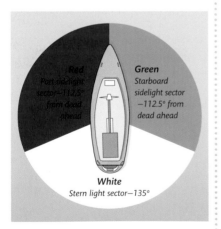

NAVIGATION LIGHT SECTORS
Under power at night, use the other power boat's light sectors to decide when you must give way. In the white or red sectors, give way; in the green sector, stand on.

Red
Port sidelight sector—112.5° from dead ahead

Green
Starboard sidelight sector—112.5° from dead ahead

White
Stern light sector—135°

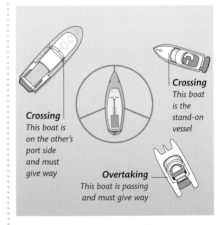

Crossing
This boat is on the other's port side and must give way

Crossing
This boat is the stand-on vessel

Overtaking
This boat is passing and must give way

STAND ON OR GIVE WAY?
In daylight, imagine the angles of the navigation lights to help assess the situation as you approach other boats on a potential collision course.

CLOCK-NOTATION SYSTEM
Use the clock-notation system to tell the skipper where an approaching vessel is in relation to your yacht—here, a large ship is at 10 o'clock and a motor yacht at 8 o'clock.

and speed and which should take avoiding action in any situation where vessels meet. Confusion sometimes arises when judging which boat is the stand-on or give-way vessel. When under power, this can be most easily understood by reference to the sectors of the basic navigation lights. Using this system it is easy to see that an overtaking boat is not just one approaching from directly astern, but is any approaching vessel within the sector covered by the stern light. Similarly, a vessel crossing from the port side in the port light's sector is a give-way vessel. A vessel crossing from the starboard side in the sector covered by the starboard light, is a

stand-on vessel. When under sail it is possible for the situation between two converging sailing vessels to be unclear. If one sailing boat is sailing upwind and the other, to windward, is sailing on a run on a converging course, it can be difficult to determine which tack the running boat is on. This only matters if the close-hauled boat is on port tack, in which case a boat running on starboard tack would be the stand-on boat. If the running boat was on port tack it would be the give-way vessel under the windward-boat-keeps-clear rule when two boats are on the same tack. In poor visibility, or at night, it can be difficult or impossible to determine the situation until the vessels get very close.

Other situations where it is difficult to identify which tack a sailing boat is on are when it is running under spinnaker alone, or when it is hove-to. In the former, the spinnaker pole will be set on the windward side of the boat and will identify which tack it is on. If the position of a hove-to yacht is uncertain, check which side the main boom is on.

In any situation where you cannot clearly identify the status of the other vessel, you should assume that you should keep clear and do so as early as possible.

Taking action

In some situations, especially when under sail, it can be considerate to alter course or speed, even if you have the right to stand on, if it is easy for you to do so but more difficult for the other boat. But if you decide to do so, always make your course alteration in plenty of time and make sure that your intentions are obvious so as not to confuse the other boat's helmsman. Equally, when you are the stand-on vessel, do not assume that the other

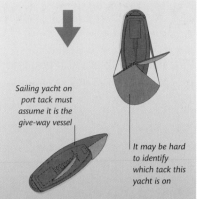

Sailing yacht on port tack must assume it is the give-way vessel

It may be hard to identify which tack this yacht is on

CONFUSING SITUATIONS AT NIGHT
Under sail at night, it can be hard to identify the give-way vessel, especially when one boat is sailing on a run and the other is close-hauled on port tack. The port tack boat must assume it has to give way.

crew has seen your boat or correctly interpreted the situation. It may be that they are just as sure as you are that they have the right to stand on. Or a boat you were expecting to give way may be hampered by other vessels or unable to change course because of a navigational hazard or shallow water.

Always be ready to take avoiding action, and remember that when a stand-on vessel finds itself so close that collision cannot be avoided by the action of the give-way vessel alone, the stand-on vessel must take any actions it can to avoid a collision.

A SAILING VESSEL UNDER WAY SHOULD KEEP CLEAR OF:
• A vessel not under command
• A vessel restricted in its ability to maneuvre
• A fishing vessel
• A vessel constrained by its draft

A POWER-DRIVEN VESSEL UNDER WAY SHOULD KEEP CLEAR OF:
• A vessel not under command
• A vessel restricted in its ability to maneuvre
• A sailing or fishing vessel
• A vessel constrained by its draft

CHANNELS AND TRAFFIC-SEPARATION ZONES

When sailing you will almost inevitably begin and end a passage in a narrow channel or river leading to a mooring or a marina. It is likely that you will be under engine rather than sail, so the rules that apply to power vessels will apply to you.

The rules for proceeding along a channel require all boats to stay on the starboard side of the channel, and you should remember to follow this requirement. Be aware of the possibility of boats entering the channel when you pass the entrances to marinas, rows of moorings, piles, or pontoons alongside the main channel. Obey any speed limits and be ready to reduce speed if the channel narrows, or you encounter boats maneuvering.

If you are in a line of traffic and wish to pass, remember that it is your responsibility to give the boat you are passing a wide berth and to keep clear until you have passed. Be aware of your wake and the effect that high speed and a large wake can have

on small boats or those moored alongside the channel. Always be considerate of other water users and keep your speed low. Look behind the boat occasionally and make sure you are not making a large wash.

Traffic lanes

When you cross a busy shipping lane for the first time, you will be amazed at just how much commercial shipping plies its trade along the coasts. Because of the volume of traffic, the size and speed of the ships, and the dangers of collision, traffic separation plans are used in busy areas, and in areas with significant navigational hazards, to bring some order to the traffic flow.

Shipping traffic is channeled into two lanes with a median strip, or "separation zone," which allows vessels to pass safely in opposite directions. These traffic-separation plans also keep local traffic apart from through traffic. Separation zones between the traffic lanes are restricted

to fishing vessels, ships in a state of emergency, and those crossing the lanes. Vessels entering a traffic lane should do so at the ends of the lane where possible, or at a shallow angle at other parts of the lane.

Local traffic must use the inshore zones and keep out of the lanes. If you must cross a traffic-separation area, the rules state that you should do so as quickly as possible on a heading that is at a right angle to the lane. Do not adjust your course to counter the effects of tide, as this will lengthen the time spent crossing the lane; steer a course at right angles to the lane and proceed across as quickly as possible.

If the visibility is poor, do not cross a lane unless it is essential to do so, or you have radar with which to spot the position of shipping. Commercial shipping often travels at over 20 knots, which means that a ship will cover one mile in three minutes. If visibility is only half a mile, you will have only 90 seconds between first seeing the ship and its being on top of you. Remember that as well as traveling quickly, commercial shipping takes a long distance to stop or to alter course by a significant amount.

When crossing a traffic separation lane, have sufficient crew on deck to maintain a full-time watch all around the horizon, and have someone manning the radar if you have one.

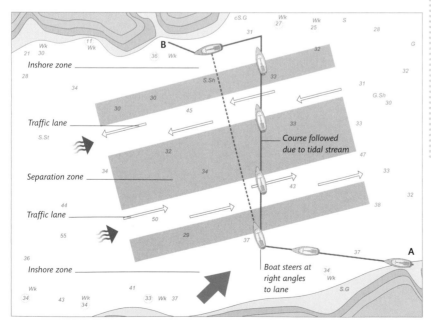

SEPARATION ZONES

From its departure point, A, the yacht travels along the inshore zone, then steers at right angles to the traffic lanes to get across as quickly as possible. It then proceeds to the destination, B, using the inshore zone. When crossing the lane, the yacht does not steer to counteract any tidal stream but steers directly across.

Keeping a lookout

The Col Regs state that all vessels should keep a proper lookout, by all available means, at all times. The crew should look, listen, and use radar if available. If you are sailing with a large headsail, then someone should sit near the leeward rail to cover the area masked by the genoa. As skipper, you should instruct your crew to alert you whenever an approaching vessel is seen. If you are uncertain if you are on a collision course, use a hand bearing compass (p.323) to take a bearing of the approaching ship. Record the bearing and then take a series of compass bearings, on the same part of the ship, at frequent intervals. If the bearing remains constant, then you are on a collision course. When you decide to take avoiding action, make a significant course change so that your intentions are obvious. Avoid crossing the bows of another craft, especially a large ship, which may be moving much faster than you think. Where possible, pass astern of the other vessel. If in doubt, turn onto a parallel course, in the same direction as the vessel, and wait for it to pass.

SOUND SIGNALS AND DAYLIGHT SHAPES

Sound signals are used in clear visibility to indicate that a vessel is carrying out a maneuver. When vessels under power are in sight of each other, and one is altering course, it must indicate its intentions by the use of horn signals. Most sailing boats keep an aerosol type foghorn aboard. This is ideal for producing loud sound signals, but be sure to have a spare reserved just for use during fog. At night, an all-around white light can be flashed the appropriate number of times.

During the day, vessels use daylight shapes hoisted in the rigging to make identification easier. For instance, when a yacht is under power but still has a sail hoisted, it should hoist an inverted cone shape up the forestay to indicate that it is motor-sailing. Another occasion when a yacht should use a daylight shape is when anchored; the regulations require you to hoist a ball shape in the fore-triangle. Refer to the Col Regs themselves for a full list of all the sound signals and daylight shapes.

SOUND SIGNALS	(■ = SHORT BLAST ; ▬▬ = LONG BLAST)	DAYLIGHT SHAPES	
■	Altering course to starboard	▼	Vessel under sail and power
■ ■	Altering course to port	●	Vessel at anchor
■ ■ ■	Engine going astern. Large ships take time to stop; they may still be moving ahead even when their engine is running astern	⧗	Vessel fishing or trawling
		▮	Vessel constrained by its draft
■ ■ ■ ■ ■	Vessel indicating that another's intentions are not clear	● ● ●	Vessel restricted in its ability to manoeuvre
		◆	Towing and towed
▬ ▬ ■	Wishes to pass another vessel on its starboard side in a narrow channel	● ●	Not under command
▬ ▬ ■ ■	Wishes to pass another vessel on its port side in a narrow channel	Mine clearance	Underwater operations / Vessel aground
▬ ■ ▬ ■	Vessel agreeing to be passed in a narrow channel		

RUNNING AGROUND

There are very few experienced sailors who have never run aground. In theory, careful navigation and good seamanship will avoid a grounding, but in the real world, it is an occupational hazard. Most groundings result in little more than wounded pride, but the situation is potentially dangerous. Quick and effective action is required to refloat the boat immediately if possible, or to minimize the danger and potential damage if you are stuck fast.

Assessing the situation

If you run aground, the amount of danger that your boat is in will depend on the bottom and on the sea state. Grounding on rocks in a heavy sea will wreck the strongest boat, but grounding on sand or mud in settled conditions should present little threat.

Check your charts and test around the boat with the spinnaker pole or boathook to find out what the bottom is like. If weather conditions are forecast to deteriorate, try everything possible to get the boat off quickly.

Taking action

First actions on running aground can be crucial if you are to get off quickly. It is important to know whether the tide is rising or falling. If it is rising, the situation is less serious: the tide will soon float you off, as long as you can prevent the boat from being driven farther into shallow water. If the tide is falling, however, you may have only a few moments to get off before you are stuck until the tide rises again. In the worst case—running aground at the top of a spring tide—you may have to wait two weeks or more until the tide returns far enough to float the boat. If you ground under sail, you must decide immediately if you can use the sails to help you get off. If you ground on a lee shore, the wind will push the boat into the shallows, and you will not be able to use the sails to get off.

When the sails cannot help, drop them and, under power, try backing off the way you went on. If the bottom is muddy, the keel will have plowed a furrow. It will be easier to reverse out than to turn the boat and motor off forward.

Grounding in channels

Grounding can easily occur when tacking up a channel with shallow water on each side. If you hold a tack too far, the boat will touch bottom. In this situation, you should immediately try to tack the boat so that it is pointing back into deep water. If you are successful, and the sails fill on the new tack, sheet them in very tight and the boat may heel far enough to reduce its draft and sail clear into deep water. You can

GETTING OFF
Fast actions are needed to get off if the tide is falling. Test the depth of water, heel the boat, and row out an anchor

Test depth
Test the depth all around the boat using a boathook

Heel the boat
Suspend a weight from the boom—here, a dinghy half-filled with water

Halyard
Lay an anchor and tie the cable to a halyard to heel the boat

Lay the kedge anchor
Use a tender to row the kedge anchor to deep water

avoid this situation by checking the depth sounder frequently when tacking along a channel.

Turning the bow

In a small boat with a shallow draft, you may be able to send a crew member over the side to push the bow around. If a crew member goes over the side, first check the depth of water around the boat with the spinnaker pole or boathook, and tie a line to keep him attached to the boat. Alternatively, you could try pushing off with a spinnaker pole or boathook from the deck.

Reducing draft

Sometimes, you may be able to reduce draft to enable the boat to sail or motor clear. If your boat has a centerboard, raise it immediately and head for deep water. In a deep-keeled boat, you can try heeling the boat to reduce its draft. If the wind is blowing off the shallows, try sheeting the sails in tightly to increase the heeling force. Alternatively, have the crew sit on the end of the boom and swing it out over the side of the boat. Make sure that the topping lift is strong enough before you do this, however. If the crew is reluctant to sit on the boom, try hanging a heavy weight, such as an anchor, from its end and swinging it over the side. This weight should be sufficient to heel the boat and reduce its draft. This may be enough to allow you to sail off.

Many boats have their deepest draft at the aft end of the keel. In this case, draft can be reduced slightly by putting all the crew on the bow to lift the stern. A bilge keel boat draws more when heeled than upright because of its keel configuration, so you should bring it upright in order to minimize its draft.

Returning tide

If you are stuck fast until the tide returns, try to lay the boat over with the mast pointing toward shallow water. If you have grounded on a slope and the boat lays over toward deep water, it may flood through the deck openings, such as hatches and ventilators, before the boat can rise on the returning tide. If the boat has already settled heeling the wrong way, try

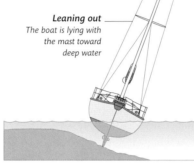

Leaning out
The boat is lying with the mast toward deep water

Leaning in
The boat is lying with the mast toward shallow water

LEANING THE WRONG WAY
If the boat is heeled with the mast lying toward deep water when the tide is rising, try to correct it or the boat may flood.

LEANING THE RIGHT WAY
If the boat is heeled with the mast lying toward shallow water, lay an anchor and wait until the tide rises and floats it off.

shifting weight to the side you want it to heel toward. Alternatively, push the bow or stern around, or pull it with an anchor line, to point the boat in the right direction. If the bottom is rocky or uneven, pad the outside of the hull before it lies on its side. This will help protect the hull from crashing on the seabed as it rises and falls on the returning tide. Use bunk cushions, sail bags, or a partly inflated dinghy.

USING A KEDGE ANCHOR

If the tide is not falling quickly, you may have time to launch the tender and row out the kedge anchor toward deep water. Try using it to winch the boat into water deep enough to float in.

Laying the anchor

Lay the anchor on the longest cable possible. Back aboard, take the cable to the bow or stern, depending on which end you are going to try to pull toward the deep water. Lead the cable through a fairlead and then to an anchor windlass or sheet winch. If necessary, lead the cable around two winches and wind on both of them. If your gear is strong enough, you may be able to winch the boat into deep water, recover the anchor, and motor or sail away. It can help to free the boat if the crew who are not required to winch the cable try to heel the boat, or rock it from side to side, to break the suction if the keel is trapped in mud.

Stuck fast

If you are stuck fast, lay the anchor as far as possible toward deep water to prevent the boat from being pushed further into the shallows by breaking seas, and to assist you in getting off when the tide returns.

MAN-OVERBOARD PROCEDURE

Having a man overboard is one of the greatest fears of any skipper. As soon as a person falls overboard, he is in very grave danger. Only the prompt and efficient action of the crew left on board can prevent a fatality. It is best to try to stop people from falling overboard in the first place: safety harnesses must be available and worn when necessary. If a man-overboard situation still occurs, it is vitally important to keep the person in sight, and to return to them and pick them up as quickly as possible.

The dangers

A man-overboard situation can transform a pleasant sail into a potentially fatal accident in a matter of seconds. To the inexperienced, a person falling over the side on a pleasant summer's day may appear little more than an unexpected swim, but even in perfect conditions a man-overboard incident has the potential to become a tragedy.

Whenever anyone falls overboard, they face the dangers of drowning, exposure or hypothermia, and impact injury. Drowning can occur quickly if the person is not wearing an automatic life jacket. A manually-inflated life jacket will not save someone who is unconscious, neither will a buoyancy aid if the person is face down in the water.

Even if the person is conscious, fit, and a strong swimmer, the shock of falling overboard may easily cause the person to swallow water, panic, and sink below the surface. If the water is cold, the natural reaction is to hyperventilate, causing blood pressure to soar. This in turn can lead to the dangers of stroke or heart attack.

If the person is wearing a functioning life jacket, he is still in danger. Exposure, followed by hypothermia and eventually death, is a real fear, even if the air and water temperatures are not cold. If a person's core body temperature drops by just 3.6°F (2°C), hypothermia sets in. Because the body loses heat 26 times faster in water than in air, a person overboard in water as warm as 75°F (24°C) still risks hypothermia. Since water temperature in temperate latitudes rarely reaches such a high temperature, survival time outside the tropics may be as little as a couple of hours even in summer. In the winter, survival time reduces to a few minutes.

Injury or death from impact is another serious danger for a person who falls over the side. First there is the danger of hitting the boat as you fall overboard, then there is the risk of being hit by other vessels—if the incident happens in congested waters such as the entrance to harbor—and finally there is the danger of being hit by the rescuing boat during the recovery procedure.

Priority actions

The immediate priority when a person falls overboard is to alert the rest of the crew, including those off-watch, with a cry of "man overboard," and to stop the boat or turn it onto a course from which it is easy to return to the person. It is vital to keep the casualty in sight, while deploying a lifebuoy and danbuoy immediately. Every second of delay in launching the lifebuoy will result in it being dropped farther away from the casualty, greatly reducing his chances of reaching it.

The next key step is to fix the person's position by eye, and any other means available. Returning to the person depends on knowing exactly where he is, and the best way to do this is to never lose sight of the

ON THE BOAT
If you can stop the boat close to the man overboard, a heaving line or, preferably, a rescue sling, as shown here, can be thrown.

IN THE WATER
If the man overboard is conscious and can reach the heaving line or rescue sling, he can be pulled back to the boat.

WEAR A HARNESS WHEN:

- Sailing at night or in fog
- The boat is reefed or when a reef may be needed
- In areas of rough water
- You are working alone on deck

person. On a fully crewed boat, one or more crew should be detailed to keep a continuous watch on the person overboard. In addition, they should point with outstretched arms toward the casualty. This is essential if you are to have any chance of a successful recovery. A person's head bobbing around in a sea, even with just a little swell, will easily get lost.

Other ways of marking his position should be employed as soon as possible. If the boat is equipped with a GPS set with a man-overboard (MOB) function, there should be a dedicated MOB button. When pushed, this records the position, and then the set can be used to guide the boat back to that position. If the boat takes too long to return to the position, the person is likely to have drifted due to wind, waves, tide, or current, but at least it provides a fixed spot from which to start a search.

Physical ways of marking the person's position include dye markers or even using cushions or fenders to mark the route back to the casualty. At night, floating light sticks are very useful. If the person is wearing a personal locator beacon (PLB), make sure the onboard receiver is working.

If the boat has sufficient crew, one should be detailed to plot the time and position on the chart and record the details in the logbook. This is a life-threatening situation, so another crew member should immediately initiate a mayday call (*p.423*).

PREVENTION

Clearly, the risks to a crew member who falls overboard are real and very serious, and it should always be treated as a life-threatening situation. The risk is so high, especially in rough conditions, when the difficulty of recovery increases dramatically, that the whole crew must focus on prevention and on learning appropriate recovery and survival techniques (*pp.298–299*). Often it is when least expected that an incident can occur. Offshore, and in heavy weather, everyone recognizes the danger and takes extra care, but inshore and when maneuvering in confined waters, attitudes to safety are often relaxed. It is wise to remember that many man-overboard situations occur in benign conditions when the crew is caught off guard.

Staying on board

Prevention includes wearing good nonslip footwear and learning the boat's deck layout so that you can move around confidently when it is upright, heeled, or pitching, and at night as well as day. If the deck layout does not work well or has hazardous areas, consider modifications to make it a safer working area. Often, safety bars can be installed near the mast to allow crew members to brace themselves securely when adjusting halyards and mast-mounted control lines. Make sure that there are sufficient handholds for all sizes of crew as they move between cockpit and foredeck.

Encourage your crew to get comfortable moving around on deck and explain to any novices how to move from handhold to handhold, always obeying the old adage of "one hand for the ship, one for yourself."

Using a safety harness

Each crew member should be issued with a safety harness, preferably of the type that is combined with an automatic life jacket (*p.217*). The harness tether is best clipped to jackstays (*p.216*) which should be installed permanently, or before each passage. If yours are made of webbing rather than plastic-covered wire (webbing does not roll underfoot if stood on), do not leave them permanently rigged or the stitching will rot quite quickly due to ultraviolet light.

In good weather and daylight, most skippers give experienced crew the freedom to decide for themselves when to wear their harness but require them to wear it at night and in other situations. They may ask novices to wear the harness and clip whenever they leave the greater safety of the cockpit. Some will be content if a novice wears a combined harness and life jacket without clipping on in good weather.

Even when a harness tether is used, it is still vital to maintain good handholds and avoid falling over. In fact, it is a good idea to crawl in rough weather or if you feel insecure.

Keeping your weight low means you are much less likely to be thrown over the side. Always keep your harness tether as short as possible, and when moving around on deck, try to do it along the windward side of a heeled boat. Then, if you do slip, your tether should keep you from sliding over the leeward side. Although it is better to be overboard but attached to the yacht, it is best by far not to be overboard at all.

RECOVERING THE MAN OVERBOARD

There are no set rules as to whether you recover a casualty under sail or power, although if you are already under power when the person falls overboard, you would return to him under power. Most training courses teach both methods. The size of the boat, the number and experience of the crew, and the weather will dictate the best course of action. However, unless you are supremely confident in the speed and accuracy of your sailing, the natural reaction is to start the engine, drop the sails, and motor back to the casualty. Whatever method you use, all that matters is that you keep the casualty within sight and return under full control, without hitting him with the boat as you approach.

Helmsman's first actions

When someone falls over the side, there are a number of things that must happen almost simultaneously (*pp.296–297*). How they are done and by whom will depend on the size and type of boat and the size and experience of the crew. The details should be included in the standing orders set by the skipper. The helmsman's actions are critical because they will have a major influence on the rest of the recovery procedure.

Usually, the skipper will take over the helm for the recovery, but the initial actions should be taken by the person steering or the person in charge of the watch if the yacht

is under autopilot. His actions should depend on whether the yacht is under power or sail and, if under sail, whether the standing orders call for a crash stop or a sail-away-and-return method.

If the boat is under power when the person falls overboard and the helmsman sees the person fall, he should immediately turn the bow toward the person in the water. This action will swing the stern away from the person and help keep them clear of the propeller as the yacht passes them. Having turned toward the person initially, the helmsman should then put the helm over the other way once the man overboard has cleared the stern. Swing the boat around in a tight circle and throttle back, and you should be in a position to maneuver alongside the person within seconds of their falling overboard.

Sail away and return

If you are under sail when the person falls overboard, and the standing orders call for the sail-away-and-return method, luff or bear away as necessary to turn to a beam reach. If you have a

spinnaker up, it must be dropped immediately. Even if you plan to pick up the man overboard under sail, start the engine anyway, leaving it in neutral so that it is ready if needed.

The sail-away-and-return method is the same as the man overboard recovery method taught for dinghies (*pp.116–117*) and is often taught for use in cruisers. It can work, especially with a full crew aboard, but has the disadvantage of taking you away from the person in the water to gain sea room, which means that you risk losing sight of the person. In very rough conditions or at night, it will be virtually impossible to keep the casualty in sight among the waves, and boat handling will be difficult.

Crash stop

Another method to consider is the crash stop. This has the advantage of keeping the boat close to the person in the water. With this technique, the helmsman should push the tiller hard to leeward as soon as the person goes over the side. Whatever the point of sailing you are on, this action usually results in the

SAIL AWAY AND RETURN
Sail away from the man overboard on a beam reach (to the apparent wind), tack around, and approach the person on a close reach, stopping to windward of him.

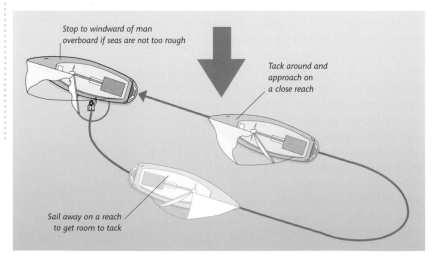

Stop to windward of man overboard if seas are not too rough

Tack around and approach on a close reach

Sail away on a reach to get room to tack

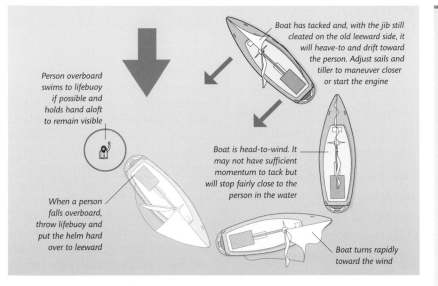

Boat has tacked and, with the jib still cleated on the old leeward side, it will heave-to and drift toward the person. Adjust sails and tiller to maneuver closer or start the engine

Person overboard swims to lifebuoy if possible and holds hand aloft to remain visible

Boat is head-to-wind. It may not have sufficient momentum to tack but will stop fairly close to the person in the water

When a person falls overboard, throw lifebuoy and put the helm hard over to leeward

Boat turns rapidly toward the wind

boat tacking or at least turning into the wind and stopping. If the boat tacks, leave the jib sheet cleated and the boat will end up hove-to (*p.245*). Push the tiller to the new leeward side to keep the boat stopped. There will be much flapping of sails and temporary disorder, but the boat will stop and lie relatively steady. Stopped in the water, the boat will drift in a way similar to the person, so you should not become separated too far. This method gives you time to assess the situation and plan what to do without sailing away from the man overboard. If you are sailing under spinnaker, the boat will almost certainly not tack when you crash stop, and the situation will be chaotic until you lower the spinnaker. Nevertheless, the boat will still be relatively close to the person.

After a crash stop, you may be close enough to throw the person a line. If not, try to work the boat closer by adjusting the sheets and tiller. Alternatively, lower the headsail, sheet the main in tight, and use the engine to approach the person overboard. Before starting the engine, make sure there are no lines in the water.

CRASH STOP
With this method, the helmsman should put the helm to leeward immediately so that the boat turns into the wind and stops, or tacks and heaves-to.

Final approach

Whichever method you use to return to the man overboard under sail, you should aim to make the final approach on a close reach. This allows you to adjust your speed easily by easing or trimming the mainsail. If possible, lower or roll up the jib to keep the foredeck clear of flapping jib sheets that can cause injury.

In moderate conditions, aim to stop with the bow to windward of the casualty so that it drifts to leeward as it slows down. This allows the casualty to be grabbed and brought aft to just behind the leeward shrouds.

In heavier conditions, it is safer to stop to leeward of the person in the water so that the boat is not pushed onto him by a wave, causing injury. Have a rope ready to throw in case you cannot get alongside, and have another ready to tie him to the boat as soon as you have contact with him.

GETTING THE PERSON ABOARD

Once you have maneuvered the boat alongside the person, immediately secure him to the boat with a line tied under his armpits using a bowline (*p.47*).

Factors to consider
How you get the person aboard will depend on his ability to help himself (if conscious), the height of the boat out of the water, and the crew strength on board. Bear in mind that it is much easier to recover a man overboard on the leeward side, where the boat's heel reduces the freeboard. In some circumstances it may make sense, as a first step, to get the person into the tender if that can be launched.

Lifting tackle
It is nearly physically impossible to pull a wet, heavy, and unconscious person out of the water, so some form of lifting tackle will be needed.

Make up a sling and tackle for this purpose, or buy a specially made system. Stow it where it can be reached quickly. The tackle can be attached to a spare halyard or to the end of the main boom. Use an arrangement appropriate for your boat, and practice using it before it is needed in a real-life situation.

Tail of tackle led to cockpit winch

Lifting sling under armpits

SLING AND TACKLE
A ready-to-use lifting sling and tackle is the best solution for lifting a person out of the water. The system should allow the weakest member of the crew to recover the heaviest person on board.

SAILING AT NIGHT

In good conditions, sailing at night can be very rewarding. It reinforces a sense of solitude and of being solely responsible for your boat and crew. Moonlight and phosphorescence can make for a beautiful nighttime passage, and dawn at sea is one of the most exquisite experiences afloat. To fully enjoy the experience, however, you and your crew must make preparations before darkness falls. For your first nighttime passage, try to have at least one crew member who has had experience of night sailing. At night, all vessels must display navigation lights according to their size and type. Make sure you have a suitable reference book aboard to look these up, since it can be difficult to remember all the possible light combinations.

Advance preparation

Before leaving on a passage that will include an overnight sail, check all your navigational lights, flashlights, and other electrical equipment. Replace broken bulbs and dead batteries. Carry a generous quantity of spares.

All crew who work on deck during the night must be familiar with the equipment they may need and be able to find and use it in the dark. Retaining night vision on deck is important. This is made easier if red lights, or at least very dim white ones, are used below in the galley and navigation area. Switch off all unnecessary lights.

Work out a watch system (*pp.286–287*) and make sure the crew knows exactly when they are on watch. Make sure that the crew understands the reasons for having a watch system and the importance of being on time when due on watch. Remind the crew of the importance of the off-watch getting adequate rest.

As skipper, make sure those on watch understand that they must call you if they are concerned about anything, or at any times or in any situations that you specify. Watch-keepers must dress warmly and wear waterproofs if necessary.

Wear safety harnesses and clip them on at all times when in the cockpit or on deck, even in calm weather. Before going on watch, use the toilet and take extra clothing, something to drink, and some snacks into the cockpit with you so that you avoid disturbing the off-watch crew if you get hungry or thirsty.

Before nightfall

Prepare and eat a hot meal before dark, and clean up immediately. Stow all loose gear below. Check the deck and stow any unnecessary equipment. Make sure that at least one flashlight and spare batteries are on hand in the cockpit. Take the foghorn, too; if the watch-keepers encounter a problem that is fully occupying them, they may not be able to summon the off-watch, but sounding the foghorn should wake those below.

Complete any sail changes before darkness makes the job harder. It can be helpful to change to a smaller headsail, or roll away part of a roller-reefing headsail, to improve the helmsman's visibility. Reducing sail

NIGHTFALL
As dusk falls, dress warmly and wear a safety harness, which should be clipped on at all times when in the cockpit or when working on deck.

area should certainly be considered, and undertaken while all hands are awake. Not only is it easier to reef with a full crew, but it will slightly de-power the boat so that it can sail more upright and provide a more stable platform for the off-watch crew to sleep. However, do not sail the boat under-canvassed in light weather. Sail with a spinnaker at night only if the crew is experienced, as spinnakers can be difficult to take down in the dark.

At dusk, switch on and check the navigation lights, update your position on the chart, and review your passage plan for the hours of darkness. Write standing instructions for the on-watch crew in the logbook or on a deck slate. Include the course to steer and any light that you anticipate being visible. Everything should be preplanned; watch-keepers are better on deck at night keeping a lookout rather than performing navigational duties down below. If you are a watch-keeper, write your own notes from the skipper's instructions and keep simple written navigational notes in the cockpit with you. Remember to have a copy of the Col Regs or other reference book to hand to help identify any lights you see around you.

Keeping a lookout

When sailing at night, especially in cold or wet conditions, it is very tempting to curl up in the shelter of a cockpit sprayhood, or inside a wheelhouse if your boat has one, but this should be avoided. Take a good look all around the horizon at least every five minutes if the visibility is clear and more frequently if the visibility deteriorates and there is a risk of being taken by surprise by an approaching ship.

Try to identify every light you see, deciding if it is a navigational, ship, or shore light. Make a note in the log, with the time, if you sight an important navigational mark. If you can see more than one lit navigational mark, consider taking the opportunity to get a visual fix with a handbearing compass and plot it on the chart as a valuable check for the GPS position.

If the boat is equipped with radar, keep it on standby and have an experienced crew member check it regularly. Alternatively, if electrical power is sufficient, have it in active mode and use its guard facility to help identify any approaching vessels. The radar can also help confirm the identity of any navigational buoys that you spot.

NIGHTTIME SHIPPING
Maintain a constant lookout at night and do not forget to look astern regularly—ships can appear quite unexpectedly.

COPING WITH THE DARK

It is important to know about some of the effects of night sailing. The boat's behavior does not alter, but the crew's perceptions of it may change. Conditions may feel rougher than they really are, and it will be more difficult to judge distances accurately. On the positive side, it can be easier to identify navigational marks, shore features, and other vessels at night when they are illuminated. Although it can be difficult to pick out an individual navigation mark against the light pollution of a populated coastline or harbor entrance, with practice you will develop a sharp eye for spotting lights.

Crew and helmsman

Inexperienced crew may feel nervous and disoriented at night. Wherever possible, they should be paired with a more experienced crew member. To avoid eye strain from staring at the compass, the helmsman should use a star, the moon, a cloud, or other reference point ahead of the boat to steer toward, checking the course by the compass at frequent intervals. The crew members on watch should be extra-supportive of each other at night. If someone needs to go below, perhaps to write the log, they should check their team members are happy for them to leave the cockpit.

Keep noise to a minimum; avoid slamming locker doors and moving around or talking unnecessarily.

Sail setting

Checking the set of the sails is much harder at night. Shine a flashlight on the luffs periodically to check that the sails are set properly. On larger boats this may mean someone needs to go forward to get a good view. Some boats have spotlights set into the deck near the forestay and shining upward to illuminate the luff of the headsail and the telltales.

At all times, stay clipped onto the boat by using the jackstays. Rather than shouting back to the cockpit, use predetermined hand signals, silhouetted against the illuminated sail, to communicate adjustments to the trim back to the cockpit crew.

Above all, avoid shining a light into someone's eyes, as this will ruin their night vision for up to 20 minutes.

UNDERSTANDING NAVIGATION LIGHTS

The International Regulations for Preventing Collisions at Sea (the Col Regs) specify the type, size, layout, arc, and distance of visibility of lights to be used by all types of vessels. Various combinations indicate, among other possibilities, whether a boat is anchored or under way, under sail or power, or fishing or trawling.

All vessels display basic navigation lights and may also show one or more steaming lights, which show a vessel is under power and making way. Navigation lights are required to be used from sunset to sunrise, and additionally at times of low visibility.

No extra lighting should be used in a way that will confuse identification or that impairs the ability to maintain a proper lookout.

When using your engine, even if a sail is hoisted as well, make sure that you display the correct lights for a vessel under power.

Make sure that you know all the common arrangements of lights and check that your own boat's lights conform to the Col Regs. The most common lights and their required arcs of visibility are shown here, but you should also carry a complete reference work on board.

BASIC NAVIGATION LIGHTS

WHITE LIGHT
A small dinghy (less than 23 ft/7 m) under sails or oars must carry a flashlight to show a white light when required.

ALL-ROUND WHITE LIGHT
A boat up to 23 ft (7 m) long, under power but capable of less than 7 kn, must have a fixed all-around white light.

MASTHEAD TRICOLOR LIGHT
Sailing yachts under 66 ft (20 m) may combine the sidelights and stern lights in a masthead tricolor light where its height offers greater visibility. A separate stern light and sidelights must still be installed for use under power, with a steaming light (*below*).

STERN AND COMBINED SIDELIGHTS
Sailing vessels over 23 ft (7 m) long must show red and green sidelights, each covering an arc of 112.5°. Under 66 ft (20 m), the sidelights can be combined in one lantern, but over 66 ft (20 m) they must be separate. The stern light must be visible over an arc of 135°. Alternatively, a tricolor light may be used (*left*).

SEPARATE LIGHTS
Yachts over 66 ft (20 m) are required to use two separate sidelights and a stern light. They may not use a tricolor masthead light (*left*), but they can choose to show the optional sailing lights (*opposite*) that are often used on large sailing vessels.

STEAMING LIGHTS

COMBINED STERN/ MASTHEAD LIGHT
A power craft under 66 ft (20 m) can combine its stern and masthead lights. Sidelights may be combined in a single bow-mounted light.

SINGLE STEAMING LIGHT
A power-driven craft less than 165 ft (50 m) long must show a masthead steaming light, visible over a 225° arc, positioned above the sidelights.

TWO STEAMING LIGHTS
Larger power vessels, over 165 ft (50 m) in length, must show two masthead steaming lights. The forward light should be positioned lower than the aft light.

RECOGNIZING NAVIGATION LIGHTS

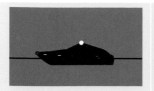

POWER VESSEL <66 FT (20 M)
A power vessel of less than 66 ft (20 m) has combined sidelights and a single masthead light.

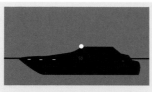

POWER VESSEL >66 FT (20 M)
A power vessel over 66 ft (20 m) has separate sidelights. If it was over 165 ft (50 m), it would need two masthead lights.

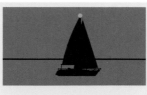

SAILING VESSEL <66 FT (20 M)
Under 66 ft (20 m), the sidelights and stern light can be combined in a single light at the masthead.

SAILING VESSEL OPTIONAL
Over 66 ft (20 m), separate stern light and sidelights plus optional all-around red over green lights.

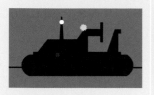

HOVERCRAFT
A hovercraft shows the same lights as a power vessel plus an all-around flashing yellow light.

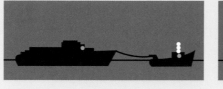

UNDER TOW (SIDE LIGHTS) (STERN LIGHTS)
A towing vessel shows two masthead lights in a vertical line (three if tow is over 655 ft/200 m) together with sidelights, stern light, and a yellow towing light above the stern light. The towed vessel shows sidelights and a stern light.

TRAWLING
A trawler making way shows all-around green over white lights, side, stern, and masthead lights.

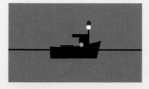

FISHING
A fishing vessel shows all-around red over white lights, plus side and stern lights when making way.

NOT UNDER COMMAND
Vessel not under command shows two all-around red lights plus side and stern lights when making way.

RESTRICTED MANEUVERABILITY
Vessel shows red, white, red all-around lights, plus masthead, stern, and side lights when making way.

MINE CLEARANCE
Minesweeper shows three all-around green lights plus side, stern, and masthead lights when making way.

UNDERWATER OPERATIONS
Restricted maneuverability plus two red lights on danger side and two green lights on side clear to pass.

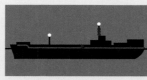

CONSTRAINED BY DRAFT
In addition to the lights for a power-driven vessel, three all-around red lights in a vertical line.

PILOT VESSEL ON DUTY
All-around white over red lights at the masthead plus stern and sidelights when underway.

AT ANCHOR
Vessel under 165 ft (50 m) has an all-around white light. Over 165 ft, two all-around white lights as shown.

SAILING IN FOG

Fog is possibly the greatest of all dangers a sailing craft can face. It can certainly represent a greater danger than rough weather to a small boat. Your visibility can be reduced to near zero, making you vulnerable to collision with another craft or with the shore. Do not put to sea unless you are absolutely sure that the fog is landbound and that conditions at sea are clear. When checking the forecast prior to sailing, be sure to listen for the visibility rating in your area. If you are at sea when fog forms, you must take steps to ensure your safety. Make sure you have a radar reflector mounted as high up as possible, use the appropriate sound signals, and avoid any other vessels in the vicinity.

FOG AT SEA
In fog, it is very difficult to estimate the size and speed of another boat and the direction in which it is traveling. When visibility is very poor, the risk of collision with another boat may be extremely high.

Type of fog

There are different causes and types of fog (*pp.376–377*) and when considering your options in fog it will be advantageous to know what type you are experiencing. Radiation fog may dissipate as the sun burns it off, whereas advection or sea fog may be much more persistent. Advection fog is by far the sailor's worst enemy. The prevailing weather in your sailing area will dictate at what times of year and in what conditions these different fog types will develop. In many waters, advection fog is more likely in the spring when water temperatures are at their lowest but air temperatures are rising.

Radar reflectors

All commercial vessels and many yachts use radar as a primary means of collision avoidance, so it is in your best interests to help them see you by using a reflector.

Radar reflectors are designed to increase the radar visibility of your boat. Other than the aluminum mast and spars, the most common materials

used in yacht construction, fiberglass and wood, are very poor reflective materials of radar signals. Radar reflectors work by using metal plates or film, combined in a geometric pattern, to reflect microwaves. Ideally, a radar reflector delivers a much bigger target for radar sets on other vessels than your yacht does without the reflector. In general, the larger the reflector and the higher it is mounted, the more efficient

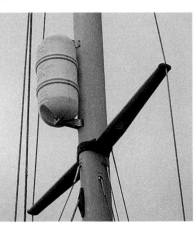

CYLINDER RADAR REFLECTOR
Cylinder-type radar reflectors have the advantage of being easy to mount permanently on the mast.

it is. However, when purchasing a radar reflector, it is worth checking its technical specifications. Reflectors come in a variety of shapes and sizes, and some work much better than others. The traditional octahedral metal plate variety looks unsophisticated, presents quite a lot of windage, and may snag and damage sails, but this simple and cheap reflector often performs better than more modern cylinder types. It is also easy to dismantle and stow below if required, although it is best if it is mounted permanently high up on the mast so it is always working to make the yacht more visible to mast.

Cylinder-type reflectors are easy to mount permanently on the mast, or can be hoisted when needed, and have no sharp edges to catch sails. However, many of these types have performed badly in comparative trials, so be sure that the one you choose has a good reputation and authenticated test reports. Active radar reflectors are the most effective. These powered units provide a much enhanced reflection that stands out on another vessel's radar display.

systems fail for any reason, you can move seamlessly to a manual plot on the paper chart.

Another instrument that can be a great help, especially if you do not have more sophisticated instruments, is a depth sounder. Knowing your depth can help pinpoint your position on the chart, and you can also use it to follow a depth contour. Thus, if you sail into shallow water to escape the risk from shipping, you may identify the 33-foot (10-meter) contour as a safe haven beyond which shipping will not venture. Work out the height of tide above chart datum (*pp.338–341*) and add that to the depth of the contour. Sail toward shallow water and monitor the depth sounder until you reach the depth you require. You are now on the depth contour, and you can use it, if necessary, as a position line which, together with one or more other position lines can give you a fix, or confirm a GPS fix.

Sound signals

Vessels in fog employ sound signals to indicate their presence to other boats (*right*). Many navigational aids, such as buoys and lighthouses, are also fitted with sound signal equipment to help you identify them. The type of signal that they emit is marked on charts and in pilot books.

Sound can be distorted by fog, so do not assume a direction for the sound. Stop to double-check, and proceed with caution. Craft indicate their presence, size, and activity with a combination of foghorn, bell, and gong signals. A boat under 39 ft (12 m) is required to carry only an "efficient sound signal." Most use some form of compressed air or aerosol foghorn (*p.305*). Larger boats, over 39 ft (12 m), must also carry a bell, and vessels over 328 ft (100 m) will also use a gong.

SOUND SIGNALS

In foggy conditions, you must make the appropriate sound signals, at the correct time intervals, to indicate whether you are sailing or motoring, aground, or at anchor. Foghorn signals are either prolonged (four to six seconds) or short (one second). A bell can be sounded as a single ring or as a rapid ringing for five seconds, while a gong is rung rapidly. The most common sound signals are shown here. You should also keep a reference book on board detailing the full list of signals as required by the International Regulations for Preventing Collisions at Sea.

KEY	FOGHORN	BELL	RAPID BELL-RINGING	GONG

	Under sail (and some other vessels): One long and two short foghorn blasts every two minutes.
	Making way under power: One long foghorn blast every two minutes.
	Under way but not making way: Two long foghorn blasts at two-minute intervals.
	Aground—under 328 ft (100 m): Three bells, rapid ringing, three bells, at one-minute intervals.
	Aground—over 328 ft (100 m): Three bells, rapid ringing, three bells, gong sounded aft, every minute.
	At anchor—under 328 ft (100 m): Rapid ringing of bell forward in boat at one-minute intervals.
	At anchor—over 328 ft (100 m): Rapid bell ringing forward, gong sounded aft, at one-minute intervals.
	Pilot boat on duty: Four short blasts (under way or making way) every two minutes.

ROUGH-WEATHER SAILING

The onset of heavy weather is a great test for the strength of the crew and the seaworthiness of the boat. The definition of rough weather depends less on the wind strength than it does on the experience of the crew, the type of boat, the state of the sea, and the course you are sailing. A novice crew in a small cruiser may have a rough ride upwind in a Force 5 against the tide, whereas an experienced crew in a large yacht would be comfortable in much heavier conditions. Every skipper must know the strengths and weaknesses of the boat, its gear, and its crew, and must have tactics for dealing with heavy weather.

Preparing the boat

As soon as you know that bad weather is on its way, begin preparing for it, even if you plan to get to a harbor before it arrives. Ready the boat for heavy seas by clearing the decks of loose gear and double-checking the lashings on the life raft and tender. Check the integrity of the jackstays and their deck securing points; they may be put under a lot of strain in heavy conditions. If jackstays are not permanently rigged, then rig them before the weather gets rough.

Close all deck hatches, and any ventilators that may leak—the Dorade type (*p.399*) can be left open longer than other types—and fit the washboards in the companionway. It is important to try to keep the living areas dry and, as there is a possibility that your boat will ship water, pump the bilges before bad weather arrives and then at regular intervals. Close all seacocks that may flood the galley sink or the heads if the boat heels far.

Navigation will be harder in rough weather, so bring the logbook up to date. Plot your position on a paper chart even if you have an electronic chart plotter and, by studying the chart and pilot book, decide on a course of action. Turn on navigation lights if visibility is poor. If you do not have a permanent radar reflector, hoist one

HEAVY SEAS
In heavy weather, rough seas are usually more of a problem than the wind strength. Here, a cruiser is sailing fast in rough seas with a small jib and reefed mainsail.

to increase your visibility (*p.304*). As the wind strength increases, be prepared to reduce the sail area to suit. Reef the mainsail, and change or reef the headsail (*pp.246–249*) to keep the boat moving quickly but without excessive heel. Remember to reef early. This will reduce strain on the gear, and the sooner you do it, the easier the operation will be. If conditions and sea-room allow, sail downwind while changing the headsail to provide the foredeck crew with a steadier working platform. Reef both sails to preserve balance and avoid excessive weather helm.

If you have storm sails on board, as you should if sailing offshore, make sure they are easily available and not buried at the bottom of a locker. Check that they have been stowed properly in their bags, complete with their sheets. Since it can be a difficult operation in bad conditions, be sure you have practiced rigging the trysail (*p.247*) and setting the storm jib.

Check all the safety gear, and ensure that anything that may be needed in a hurry, especially flares, are easily accessible and the crew knows their location and how to use them.

SAFETY HARNESS

Safety harnesses must be used in rough weather to ensure the safety of the crew. Adjust them so that they are comfortable, and clip the lifeline only to strong fittings.

Preparing the crew

A warm, dry, and neat cabin in which to rest, cook, navigate, and sleep is vital. Ensure that everything is stowed securely and make every effort to keep water from getting into the cabin.

Put on warm layers (and gloves and a hat in cold weather) and wear waterproofs and boots. If spray and rain are heavy, the helmsman may find it useful to wear clear ski goggles in order to maintain comfortable vision.

All crew must wear safety harnesses and clip on whenever they are in the cockpit or on deck. A strong securing point by the companionway should allow a crew member coming on deck to clip on before leaving the security of the cabin.

If possible, cook and eat a hot meal before the bad weather arrives, and prepare vacuum flasks of soup or hot drinks, together with nutritious

snacks for consumption during the storm. Issue anti-seasickness tablets to those who want them and try to give each crew member some rest before the worst of the weather arrives. The crew may be anxious, and the skipper should take time to reassure them.

If you have not been operating a watch system, impose one now. While maintaining a proper lookout, keep surplus crew out of the cockpit, where they are in more danger and may become cold.

If a crew member gets very cold, relieve them at once and have them warm up below. If a crew member in the cockpit feels the need to be sick, guide them, if possible, to the leeward side. Make sure they are clipped on at all times, as it is natural to lean out. Assign a "buddy" to comfort them until the sickness is passed. If the sick crew member is below, make sure they have a bucket available by their bunk.

STORM SAILS

They will be used very rarely, but when you are hit by severe weather, you will be grateful if your boat has a trysail and storm jib in its sail wardrobe.

TACTICS AND ACTION

Deciding on tactics

Your plan of action for rough weather should be based on the capabilities of the boat and crew, the severity of the expected weather conditions, and the proximity of any shoreline.

The most important thing to remember is to stay away from lee shores. In severe conditions it can be very difficult or impossible for even a modern cruiser to beat to windward away from a lee shore, and should the boat be driven ashore, it will quickly be destroyed.

Head for harbor only if you are certain your chosen refuge is safe to enter in strong winds and rough seas. Make sure there are no off-lying shallows or other navigational dangers, and that there is no risk that you could end up on a lee shore. A windward shore with a sheltered harbor or anchorage can offer protection, but you must be certain that the wind will not shift to turn it into a lee shore.

Seeking open water to ride out the bad weather clear of the shore is often the best option. Head offshore and get as much sea room as possible between your boat and any potential lee shore.

Taking action

If conditions become too rough to hold your chosen course, your aim should be to keep the boat as safe and comfortable as possible, while still making some progress toward your destination if feasible. The procedure you choose depends on the handling characteristics of your boat; however, the normal first step when conditions deteriorate too much to continue on course, especially when your chosen destination lies upwind, is to stop the boat by heaving-to.

Heaving-to

The normal procedure is to heave-to under a deeply reefed mainsail or trysail, and storm jib. Be sure to securely lash the tiller to leeward or tighten a wheel's friction lock to hold it to windward. Heaving-to involves balancing the forces on the boat so that it lies as close to the wind as possible while making little headway. The rudder and mainsail try to turn the boat toward the wind while the backed jib pushes it the other way.

Many cruisers will heave-to at an angle of about 60 degrees to the wind, their motion will be considerably reduced, and they will rise to the seas while drifting slowly to leeward. The relative amounts of headway and leeway vary with the boat and sea conditions. Depending on conditions and the type of boat, you can remain hove-to until or unless the boat starts being knocked down by the waves, at which point it will become too uncomfortable or dangerous.

Lying a-hull

As conditions deteriorate, consider lying a-hull. You will drift to leeward more quickly than when hove-to, so be sure you have sufficient sea room. To lay a-hull, take down all sails and lash the tiller to leeward (or wheel to windward). The boat will find its natural angle to the wind, normally somewhere near beam-on. As the boat drifts to leeward, roughly side-on to wind and waves, it will leave a flatter "slick" to windward.

The problem with lying a-hull however, is that it is dangerous when seas begin to break. Then, the boat is vulnerable to being hit by a breaking wave and rolled over, or falling down the face of a wave and landing on its side in the trough. This can

STORM TACTICS

Your choice of tactics will depend on the design of boat, the severity of the weather, and your proximity to the shore.

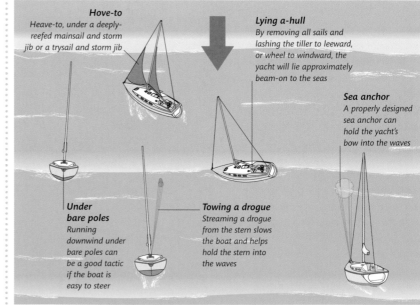

Hove-to
Heave-to, under a deeply-reefed mainsail and storm jib or a trysail and storm jib

Lying a-hull
By removing all sails and lashing the tiller to leeward, or wheel to windward, the yacht will lie approximately beam-on to the seas

Sea anchor
A properly designed sea anchor can hold the yacht's bow into the waves

Under bare poles
Running downwind under bare poles can be a good tactic if the boat is easy to steer

Towing a drogue
Streaming a drogue from the stern slows the boat and helps hold the stern into the waves

cause serious damage to even the strongest yacht. Portholes, windows, and even the cabin side on the leeward side could be damaged and flood the boat.

Running downwind

If you have plenty of sea room to leeward, consider running before the wind, either under bare poles or with a storm jib. Many modern, shallow-hulled, fin-keeled cruisers will surf downwind comfortably when steered by an experienced helmsman. If your chosen course is downwind, this might be the safest procedure.

However, if you have a heavier boat that does not surf easily, or a less experienced, or tired, helmsman you must slow it down as much as possible for safety (*right*). The danger is that the bow buries itself into a wave trough and a following wave, catching up with the boat, breaks over the stern and floods the cockpit.

Alternatively, the boat could broach (*p.257*) and end up on its side, broadside onto the waves and extremely vulnerable to the next breaking crest. In extreme conditions a wave could lift the stern so high that the whole boat could be thrown stern over bow, known as pitchpoling.

Using a sea anchor

Some long-distance cruisers prefer to use a sea anchor in storm conditions. A sea anchor is a large and strong parachute-like arrangement made of nylon and strong nylon webbing, connected to the boat by a long length of stretchy nylon rope. It is deployed from the bow and let out about 10–15 times the boat's overall length. To avoid chafe, it is best to attach the nylon rope to the end of the yacht's anchor chain and pay out a short length of the chain through

SEA ANCHOR
A sea anchor is deployed from the bow to hold the yacht's bow into the seas. A long nylon warp between sea anchor and boat helps absorb the shock loads by stretching.

the bow roller. Sea anchors are also used by fishermen and cruisers in less extreme conditions to hold position during a fishing or overnight stop. While lying to a sea anchor, the boat is held bow into the waves and its motion will be gentler than if left to drift.

SLOWING THE BOAT

A number of techniques can be used to slow the boat down when running before the wind, but all employ the same principle of creating more drag. The simplest technique is to trail warps. The most effective technique is usually to tow a very long warp in a loop from the stern (*below*). A drogue (similar to a small sea anchor) may also be trailed from the stern to increase the drag and help hold the boat's stern into the seas and prevent broaching. Experiment with various rough weather sailing techniques in less extreme conditions to discover how your boat might behave in a storm.

TRAILING WARPS
While running downwind without sail, or with just a small storm jib, secure your longest warp to the headsail winches and cleats, and trail the bight (loop) over the stern. This will slow the boat and help keep it in line with the seas.

Mainsail stowed on boom

Bight trailed a hundred yards (91 m) or more astern

NAVIGATION

To gain the true freedom of the seas, a sailor needs to learn the art of navigation. It may appear to be a complex subject, but anyone who can balance a checkbook will be able to cope with the mathematics required to navigate proficiently. The immense satisfaction gained when a planned destination appears out of an empty sea at the end of a sailor's first offshore passage is ample reward for the small effort involved.

STARTING TO NAVIGATE

You need to understand only a few basic concepts to begin navigating. Once you understand the meaning of some simple terms—such as position, direction, distance, and depth—you will be able to apply them to practical navigation. Then you will experience the great satisfaction all sailors feel when they complete a passage, perhaps out of sight of land, and reach a new destination through their own navigational efforts.

Position

The position of any spot on Earth's surface can be described accurately and unambiguously by reference to the lines of an imaginary grid laid on the planet's surface.

Imagine Earth covered by graph paper with the horizontal and vertical lines forming the reference grid. The lines running east to west are known as the parallels of latitude (the equator itself is 0° latitude). Now imagine cutting Earth along the parallels of latitude, in slices parallel to the equator. The farther away from the equator you cut, the smaller the slice and the shorter the circumference of its perimeter.

The lines that run north to south on the imaginary grid are called the meridians of longitude. The prime meridian (0° longitude) runs through the Greenwich Royal Observatory in England, from which it takes its name. Unlike a graph paper grid, Earth is not flat, so on the globe the meridians run between the North and South Poles where they converge, like the segments of an orange. Unlike the parallels of latitude, the meridians of longitude are of equal length, and cutting along any longitude line would result in two equal halves of the globe. This

makes each meridian a Great Circle, the term given to a section through Earth whose plane passes through the center of the planet. The perimeter of a Great Circle is actually the shortest distance between any two points on the perimeter. This is not the case for a segment that does not pass through Earth's center.

Theoretically it would be possible to describe a position on Earth's surface in terms of its distance in miles north or south from the equator and east or west from the Greenwich meridian; so, for instance, the location

of the Needles Lighthouse on the Isle of Wight in the UK could be uniquely defined as 3,039.7 nautical miles north (of the equator) and 60.9 nautical miles west (of Greenwich). This method of describing a position is not very convenient in practice. Because Earth is a sphere, not flat, there is an alternative and easier way to define a position—using an angular measurement. Latitude is the angle formed at the center of Earth between the position and the equator, while longitude is the angle formed at the center of Earth between the position and the Greenwich meridian. Latitude and longitude are measured in degrees (°), minutes ('), and tenths of a minute. There are 60' in 1°, and 360° in a circle.

Latitude and longitude on nautical charts

Navigational charts have latitude and longitude scales printed at their edges, with grid lines going across

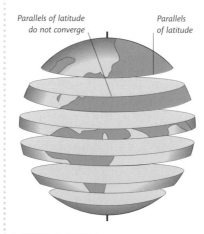

LATITUDE SLICES
If Earth was cut laterally along the parallels of latitude, the slices would be at their largest at the equator and their smallest at the poles.

Parallels of latitude do not converge

Parallels of latitude

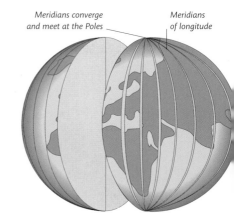

LONGITUDINAL SEGMENTS
Cutting Earth along a meridian of longitude will always result in two equal halves, as the resulting circle passes through the center of Earth.

Meridians converge and meet at the Poles

Meridians of longitude

MEASURING LATITUDE AND LONGITUDE ON A CHART

A position on the chart is measured using the latitude and longitude scales. Use dividers to transfer the distance from convenient grid lines to the scales at the chart edges. Measure longitude on the scale at top or bottom, and latitude at the sides.

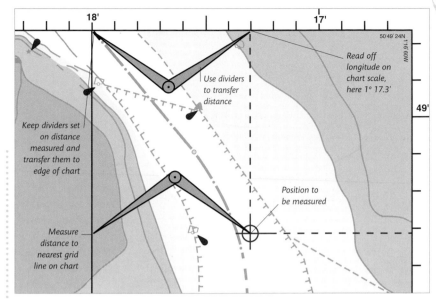

Use dividers to transfer distance

Keep dividers set on distance measured and transfer them to edge of chart

Measure distance to nearest grid line on chart

Read off longitude on chart scale, here 1° 17.3'

Position to be measured

them at regular intervals in the horizontal and vertical directions. The latitude scale runs along the two vertical sides and the longitude scale runs along the top and bottom of the chart. The scales allow positions to be easily measured or plotted on the chart.

When positions are described or written down, latitude is given first in °N or °S of the equator, followed by longitude in °E or °W of the Greenwich meridian. So, the position of the Needles Lighthouse is given as 50° 39'.7N, 01° 35'.5W.

When learning to navigate or using charts for the first time, practice accuracy when reading the latitude and longitude scales. It can be easy to misread, especially on larger scale charts where the whole number of

degrees may not be printed anywhere near the area of interest. Test your precision by reading off latitudes and longitudes of known marks then comparing them with published values. If you are inaccurate at first, repeat the exercise until you are confident that you are reading the scales correctly.

Be accurate when using dividers (p.326). Adjust them using the hinge screw so that the arms are snug.

Chart datums

Because Earth is not a perfect sphere, it is impossible to agree on a single location for the center of Earth that works everywhere across the globe. But latitude and longitude cannot be defined without reference to the center of Earth. Therefore, all surveys have to assume a position for Earth's center from which to measure their positioning data. As a result, a number of different chart datums exist and charts using these datums will give a different latitude and longitude for the same position.

Different manufacturers of paper and electronic charts may use different chart datums, but the most widely used datum currently in use is the satellite-based WGS 84 (World Geodetic Survey carried out in 1984).

All paper and electronic charts are marked clearly with the datum to which they refer, usually near their title (p.320). When using GPS, or other satellite or terrestrial positioning systems, make sure that the equipment is set to give positions relative to the same datum as the charts you are using.

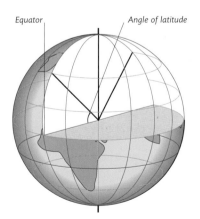

LATITUDE

The angle of latitude is measured at the center of Earth along the prime meridian from the equator (0°), and ranges from 0° to 90° north or south.

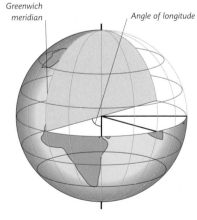

LONGITUDE

The angle of longitude is measured at the center of Earth along the equator from the prime (Greenwich) meridian (0°), and ranges from 0° to 180° east or west.

DIRECTION

When sailing in coastal waters, you will often find it easier to define a position with reference to a fixed sea- or landmark using direction and distance, rather than to use latitude and longitude. This method makes it easier to plot a position on the chart.

Direction is always measured clockwise as an angle relative to north. When describing the direction of an object in relation to your boat's position, or between two objects such as buoys, it is called a bearing. When describing the direction in which your boat is sailing, it is known as a heading.

North

Direction is usually defined relative to north. However, "north" can have three separate meanings: true north, magnetic north, and compass north. True north is the direction you would need to travel to eventually arrive at the geographic North Pole—at the very top of the globe. However, the most common way of finding north is by using a magnetic compass (pp.322–325). This utilizes a magnet that naturally aligns itself with the lines of magnetic flux surrounding Earth. In doing this, a magnetic compass points to magnetic north, the direction of the magnetic North Pole rather than to true north.

Because Earth's iron core—which generates the planet's magnetism—is molten, the magnetic North Pole is not in a fixed position but moves around, although at a known rate. The difference between magnetic and true north is known as variation (p.324). The amount of variation between magnetic and true north varies according to your position on Earth's surface.

In some parts of the world it is negligible; in others the amount is very significant.

A magnetic compass can also be influenced by local effects, particularly the close proximity of metallic objects. Compass north is defined as the direction in which your compass points. If there is no local magnetic interference, it will point to magnetic north, but if there is local interference, the compass needle will be deviated from magnetic north. The angular difference between compass north and magnetic north is known as deviation (p.325).

The lines representing the meridians of longitude printed on charts are aligned to true north, but the sailor guides his boat using a compass that points at compass or magnetic north. Therefore, navigators often have to convert between true, magnetic, and compass north (pp.324–325). Although this can seem complex initially, it should soon become straightforward, especially if you cruise the same

areas on the same boat. In this case, magnetic variation and deviation will not change over a sailing season and their application will soon become second nature.

Distance and speed

The unit of distance used at sea is the nautical mile, which is defined as one minute (1') of latitude. Because Earth is not a perfect sphere, the actual length of a nautical mile varies, being shorter at the equator (6,046 ft) and longer at the poles (6,108 ft). However, by international agreement it is standardized to 6,076 ft (1,852 m)—slightly longer than a statute mile.

The unit of speed used at sea (and in the air) is the knot. This is defined as one nautical mile per hour (equivalent to 1.15 mph).

Distance is measured on charts by reference to the latitude scale at the sides of each chart. The longitude scale, at the top and bottom of a chart, should never be used to measure distance because a degree

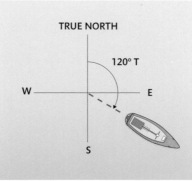

HEADINGS
A heading is the direction in which you steer your boat. This is always measured clockwise from north—either true, magnetic, or compass north. In this case, the boat's heading is 120°T.

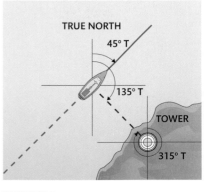

BEARINGS
The direction of an object from your position, or between two objects, is known as a bearing. Here the tower is on a bearing of 135°T from the boat. From the tower, the boat bears 315°T.

of longitude is only the same as a degree of latitude at the equator. As you move away from the equator, a degree of longitude decreases in distance until it falls to zero at the North and South Poles, where the meridians converge to a point.

Also, when measuring distance on a chart, it is important to use that part of the latitude scale on the sides of the chart that is level with the area of the chart where you are measuring the distance. This is particularly important when working on small scale charts that cover large areas of sea. This will avoid discrepancies due to the variations in the length of a nautical mile due to latitude.

Depth and height

Depth and height are measured in meters and tenths of a meter on most charts, although older charts may show depths in fathoms and feet. One fathom is equal to six feet.

Depths are indicated by spot measurements and by contour lines that join places with the same depth of water. Depth is shown on charts relative to a fixed datum, usually the lowest astronomical tide (LAT). This is the lowest water level ever expected. It is comforting to know that charts usually display the worst-case scenario for water depth. Although it is possible in certain weather conditions, it is unlikely that

you will find less water beneath you than the depth shown on the chart, and usually the water will be deeper than that shown because of the additional height of the tide (p.341).

Navigators also need to know the heights of objects both on dry land and at sea. For instance, the clearance under a bridge or power line at a particular state of the tide, or the extent to which rocks may be exposed by the falling tide are both items of information that may be critical to know when planning a passage. The datum from which heights are measured depends on whether the object is ashore or is sometimes covered by the tide (p.341).

NAVIGATIONAL TERMS AND SYMBOLS

A variety of terms and symbols are used to record information on charts and to write down bearings, headings, and other important navigational data. The symbols are recognized universally, eliminating (as far as possible) the risk of misunderstandings and enabling all navigators to understand the calculations. You need to know and understand these symbols to be able to navigate successfully.

SYMBOL	MEASUREMENT	DEFINITION
°T	Degrees true	Suffix attached to a direction measured relative to true north, e.g., 095°T.
°M	Degrees magnetic	Suffix attached to a direction measured relative to magnetic north, e.g., 135°M.
°C	Degrees compass	Suffix attached to a direction measured by the compass and not converted to °T or °M, e.g., 110°C.
M	Nautical mile	The unit of distance at sea. A nautical mile is equal to one minute of latitude (standardized at 6,076 ft/1,852 m). It is divided into 10 cables (ca) or tenths of a nautical mile. Each cable is 200 yd (185 m).
kn	Knot	The unit of speed used at sea. One knot is one nautical mile per hour.
m	Meter	The standard meter is used to display depth and height on charts. Meters are divided into decimeters; 7.1 m is shown on charts as 7_1.
fm	Fathom	The old unit of depth, equal to 6 ft (1.8 m), sometimes found on older charts. Parts of a fathom are shown in feet, e.g., 38 ft is shown as 6_2.

CHARTS

A chart is the essential tool for navigation at sea. Charts are produced by the hydrographic agencies of most maritime countries. They were originally produced for professional sea-goers. Today, many hydrographic agencies, and some specialty publishers, also produce special yachting charts, in paper and electronic form, that are derived from the official data but tailored to suit the yachtsman's needs. Often available in folios covering the most popular sailing areas, many include harbor plans and other useful local information.

Projection

A chart is a representation of a curved surface on a flat sheet of paper, which presents the cartographer with several problems. The main consideration is how best to represent (or project) the curve of Earth while minimizing distortion of the shape and size of land masses.

The Mercator projection is the most common form found on charts. It represents the parallels of latitude (*p.316*) as straight horizontal lines that are drawn farther apart toward the poles, while the meridians of longitude are represented as parallel, but equidistant, straight vertical lines. Some charts use the gnomonic projection.

These may be used for small-scale, ocean passage planning charts, or very large-scale harbor charts. On small-scale, gnomonic charts, the meridians are represented by straight lines that converge at the poles while the parallels of latitude are drawn as equidistant curved lines. On large-scale gnomonic charts, the area covered is so small that the meridians appear to be parallel.

Gnomonic charts are ideal for planning long voyages between distant ports, as a straight line drawn between two points on a gnomonic chart is a portion of a great circle and represents the shortest distance between the two points. In practice, to sail along the great circle track, it is necessary to transfer it to a Mercator chart on which it will be represented by a curved line between the two points (unless the course is north or south). Transfer the great circle track by plotting the positions where the track on the gnomonic chart crosses each meridian on to the Mercator chart and join up the positions with a smooth curve. On passage, small changes of course are needed at regular intervals to follow the curved track on the Mercator chart.

Scale

Charts are available at various scales. Small-scale charts cover whole seas or oceans. They are used for overall planning and for plotting position on long passages. Medium-scale charts are typically used to cover sections of coastline. These are useful for coastal and offshore information around your departure point and destination. Large-scale charts cover small areas in great detail. They are essential when you are entering an unfamiliar harbor or navigating a difficult stretch of water.

When on passage, always refer to your largest-scale chart of the area you are sailing through since it will provide you the most detailed information. Small-scale charts should only be used for plotting when far offshore.

Chart corrections

Charts are prepared from surveys conducted at regular intervals, depending on the importance to shipping of the area covered. As manmade features (and, occasionally, geographic ones) change, the chart is brought up to date with published corrections and a new one is issued periodically. Chart authorities issue regular corrections so you can update your charts, or you can return them to a chart agent for correction.

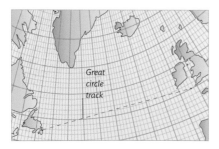

GNOMONIC PROJECTION
A gnomonic chart is used for planning long ocean passages and determining the shortest track (a great circle track) by drawing a straight line between two places.

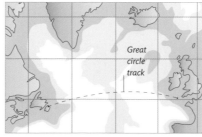

MERCATOR PROJECTION
On a Mercator chart, the shape of land masses is depicted differently due to the differences in projection. A great circle track is curved (except when north or south).

NAUTICAL CHART

An up-to-date chart is essential for safe navigation, especially in a confined and congested area. The area illustrated here is an extremely busy channel that is used by commercial shipping and yachts.

SYMBOLS

Symbols are used on charts to indicate dangers and areas of particular importance. Learn the most common ones and carry a reference guide to the complete list of symbols.

Danger
Limiting danger line

Eddies
Some water disturbance

Obstruction
Depth known

Obstruction
Swept to depth shown

Overfall, tide rips
Water surface disturbed

Rock awash
At chart datum

Rock ledge
Exact depth unknown

Traffic-separation scheme
One-way traffic lane

Wreck
Depth taken by sounding

Wreck
Depth unknown; thought safe

Wreck
Swept to depth shown

Wreck
Wreck showing hull

Wreck
Considered dangerous

Wreck
Not considered dangerous

Latitude and longitude

Horizontal lines of latitude and vertical lines of longitude are used to plot position. Distance is measured using the latitude scale at the sides of the chart. The grid formed by the lines of latitude and longitude can be used in conjunction with plotting instruments (pp.326–327) to measure direction

Tidal stream information

Tidal diamonds located at key points relate to an information panel on the chart. From this, you can calculate the direction and strength of the tide at the tidal diamond at any time

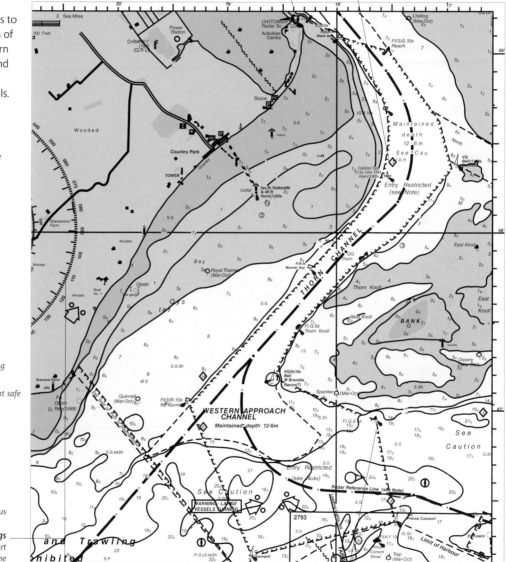

Depth soundings

Depths shown are related to chart datum (p.339), which are the lowest depths to which the water can usually be expected to drop. Contour lines join points of equal depth. Here, areas that dry out at low water are green, depths 0–15 ft (0–5 m) are blue, and depths 15–30 ft (5–10 m) are light blue. An underlined figure in areas that dry at low water indicates their drying height above chart datum

Compass rose

There are several compass roses located on the chart. They allow true (°T) and magnetic (°M) bearings to be read directly from them. Information given in the rose provides details of the magnetic variation (pp.324–325)

Buoyage

Buoys are marked on the chart, together with details of their light characteristics (pp.332–333). The direction of buoyage may also be marked, especially when two channels meet that could otherwise cause confusion

ELECTRONIC CHARTS

The development of electronic chart systems has produced a revolution in navigation that has impacted on even the smallest boats. Electronic charts provide information to dedicated chart plotters, or navigation software programs running on a laptop computer, tablet, or even a smartphone. They allow practical navigation to be conducted using a keyboard and mouse, plotter interface, or touchscreen.

Crucially, the plotter or computer program can also interface with other electronic instruments and display and make use of the data they provide.

Types of electronic chart

The two main types of electronic chart are the raster chart and the vector chart. The raster chart is created by scanning an existing paper chart and storing the information digitally. This process creates a digital picture, stored as millions of dots; the denser the dots, the better the quality of the electronic chart. A drawback of the raster chart is the size of the files, which use considerable disk space and which are often slow to load when required.

A vector chart is not scanned but traced from a paper original. Rather than being a single-layer picture of a chart, the data is stored on multiple layers. One layer might show the shape of the land, another depth information, another buoyage, and so on. Some information, such as a buoy's light characteristics, is concealed to reduce clutter but is revealed, in a popup box, when the cursor is clicked on or hovered over the object.

There is no limit to the information that can be added, including tidal graphs, pilotage notes, aerial photographs—anything the publishers feel is helpful. The layering of vector charts allows the navigator to select the information he requires and to remove the rest from view. There is usually also a facility for the navigator to add his own annotations, images, or comments on another layer.

Vector charts may be more user-friendly than their raster cousins, but there is more room for error in their origination because they are not cloned from an accurate master.

Features

Chart-plotting software, in either dedicated plotters or programs for personal computers, can be simple to operate, but most systems have a host of extra features that may or may not be useful, depending on your needs. At the minimum, the system allows the user to scroll and pan around the chart as well as zoom in and out.

With a vector system, zooming in may automatically call up additional levels of detail as the chart scale decreases. Waypoints can be entered, edited, and manipulated, and can be combined into routes. GPS data provides current position and track plotting, and data from other instruments can be shown, usually within boxes on the display. A radar picture can often be overlaid on the chart to compare features.

Some systems include tidal height data and may also have tidal stream data. The latter allow the software to plot courses allowing for tidal set and drift (*pp.344–345*). Most systems have a logbook function to record system data, and many are linked to an autopilot to steer the boat along the predetermined track. Some can also create polar performance curves from instrument data. With these, and weather files from downloaded from the Internet, routing software can calculate the best route to take. It is even possible to simulate night and day—showing the light characteristics

VECTOR CHART—BASIC DISPLAY
Because a vector chart is made up of a number of layers of information, layers can be turned on and off as desired.

VECTOR CHART—STANDARD DISPLAY
This system's standard display adds depth, buoyage, navigation light information, and some land features to the basic display.

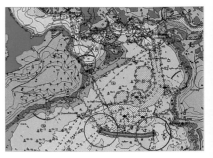

VECTOR CHART—FULL DISPLAY
The full display includes all depth soundings, land features, light details, and any personal, user-added information.

PERSONAL COMPUTER
A laptop is a popular choice for running navigation and chart plotting software and can be set up to interface with other electronic instruments on board.

of navigational marks, for instance—or to display 3D views of the land around you and the waters beneath.

Electronic charts, like paper ones, can be purchased singly or in folios. Charts are supplied on disk, by download, or on memory card, depending on the plotter system being used; PC-based software usually works with charts supplied on disk, while dedicated plotters generally use memory cards. When charts are purchased on disk, there are often many more charts on the disk than have been paid for. These can be accessed at a later date by purchasing access codes. Electronic charts need updating just like paper versions. How this is achieved, and the cost, depend upon your supplier. You should check what is included when choosing a chart system.

Dedicated plotter or computer software?

Electronic charts can be purchased to work with dedicated chart plotters and personal computers, tablets, or smartphones running plotting software. Dedicated chart plotters are designed to be robust and may be waterproof or splashproof. They

are usually designed to integrate easily with other onboard instrumentation, especially that from the same manufacturer.

A software plotter running on a laptop or tablet can be much more convenient and flexible. Passage planning can easily be done at home allowing practice with the system. Information from other instruments can often be integrated, and additional functionality can be added, such as weather routeing. Care is needed to keep the equipment dry, however, since non-marine computers are vulnerable to water damage.

Benefits and disadvantages of electronic charts

Electronic charts and plotting systems can display the information you need in one place and allow you to identify positions, courses, and distances simply by manipulating a cursor.

However, there is a real danger that a chart plotter will distract the skipper from the business of being in charge of his boat in the real, not virtual, world. Although paper-based chart work is more laborious, the fact that lines must be physically drawn, scales read off, and distances and angles measured by hand, makes for a safer self-checking process.

Electronic systems are costly and are vulnerable to power failure. Navigators must learn how to use them properly, and to interpret the information they provide. Digital systems give the impression of great accuracy, but this should never be assumed unless information can be checked using another source.

Under- or over-zooming an electronic chart is also a potential danger—information may be

missed or the impression given of greater accuracy and level of detail than actually exists.

Using these systems is not an alternative to learning to navigate using paper charts, which must still be carried on board. Always plot the boat's position on a paper chart and record information in a paper logbook at least hourly when close to land.

CHART TITLE AND INFORMATION

When you first use a new chart, begin by studying the information near its title. It will tell you a number of key things that you should know before you use the chart or plot positions derived from electronic fixing systems.

The information printed near the chart's title includes the scale of the chart, the datum it uses, the type of projection, units of measurement, and datum of depths (soundings) and heights. Essential information about pertinent navigational hazards and important regulations will also be displayed prominently.

The date of issue is also shown, often in the lower left margin of a paper chart, and any subsequent updates should be dated alongside the initial publication date.

The chart itself is a mine of information, depicting not only the land and sea areas, depths, navigational marks, and buoyage, but countless other useful details such as the nature of the seabed (useful when anchoring), areas of strong currents, eddies or disturbed water, tidal information, and suggested bearing lines for safe passage around hazards or for approaching harbor entrances.

Charts also include conspicuous shoreside features that are useful for taking compass bearings on to produce a position fix.

THE COMPASS

A compass is the most important navigation instrument on board a yacht. It is the primary means of identifying direction, enabling you to steer a course and to plot position by taking bearings of navigational marks and shore objects. The compass is also used to check the bearing of other vessels to help avoid collision. Two types of compasses are usually used—a steering compass for steering a course, and a hand bearing compass for taking bearings of objects and other vessels.

GETTING BACK ON COURSE

If you wander off course, it can be hard to know which way to turn to regain your course. Use this simple rule to avoid confusion. If the number on the compass is higher than the required course, turn to port. If the number on the compass is lower than the required course, turn to starboard.

Earth's magnetic field

If Earth did not have a magnetic field, navigation would be considerably harder than it is, not only for humans but for those birds and animals whose sensitivity to the magnetic field is thought to allow them to navigate over long distances.

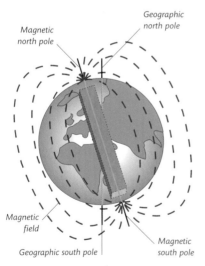

Geographic north pole

Magnetic north pole

Magnetic field

Geographic south pole

Magnetic south pole

EARTH AS A MAGNET
Earth acts as a huge magnet with lines of magnetic flux emanating from the magnetic north and south poles. The flux lines become more vertical the closer to the poles you are, but it is the horizontal component that is used by the traditional magnetic compass.

It helps to imagine Earth's magnetic field as being caused by a giant bar magnet running between the poles, but the real cause is believed to be the result of movement in the planet's iron core. The majority of the core is thought to be molten iron, but at the heart, the pressure is so great that the iron is crystallized into a solid ball. This ball is believed to rotate due to convection currents in the molten core and the rotation of Earth. It is the rotation of the solid core within the outer molten area that is believed to generate Earth's magnetic field which, at the surface, is quite weak.

The magnetic poles do not align with the geographic poles because Earth's magnetic axis is skewed slightly from the rotational axis. The angular difference between the direction of true north and magnetic north is known as variation (or declination) (*pp.324–325*).

The magnetic compass
In its simplest form, a magnetic compass comprises a small, light magnet, usually referred to as the compass needle, balanced on a nearly frictionless pivot. The compass needle aligns itself with the magnetic field

so one end points to the magnetic north pole and the other to the magnetic south pole. Near the poles, the lines of the magnetic field point downward, causing the compass needle to also try to point downward as you move toward a pole. The angle from the horizontal is called the angle of dip.

Because Earth's field is weak, a magnetic compass must be sensitive to detect it, which means it is also capable of detecting other weak magnetic fields such as those emanating from large metal objects (like a steel hull or a boat's engine) or from electrical wiring when current is flowing. The effects of local magnetic fields that deviate the compass needle from magnetic north is known as deviation (*p.325*).

Marine compasses
To operate correctly, a direction finding compass must be designed to react accurately to the horizontal element of Earth's magnetic field. To achieve this, it usually employs two or more bar magnets attached to the underside of a circular card, marked in degrees around its edge. The card is mounted on a pivot and is encased in a glass or plastic bowl filled with a damping liquid to slow

down its rotation. Internal or external gimbals keep the card level when the boat heels and pitches. A light should be installed to allow the compass to be used at night.

The compass aligns with the magnetic field and points at magnetic north and south. As the boat turns, the compass continues to point at magnetic north and south, while the boat's course, relative to magnetic north, can be read from the numbers on the compass card. The course, or bearing, is read with reference to the lubber line, which is a line marked on the inside of the bowl. The compass must be mounted with the lubber line parallel to the boat's fore-and-aft line.

Fluxgate compass

Electronic, fluxgate compasses dispense with cards, pivots, and liquids and use an electronic circuit to sense the lines of magnetic force or flux. Their reading is displayed as a digital readout to the nearest degree. A fluxgate steering compass may also have an analog readout that acts as a course pointer.

Fluxgate compasses can easily provide heading information to other electronic instruments. The apparent accuracy implied by a digital readout

ELECTRONIC COMPASS DISPLAY
An electronic, fluxgate compass comprises a fluxgate sensor mounted in a sealed box below decks, and a display head that is usually mounted in the cockpit within direct sight of the helmsman.

should be treated with caution since errors are not readily apparent, and there should always be a magnetic steering compass available.

Steering compass

Fit your boat with the best-quality magnetic steering compass you can afford. Choose one that has a large card, or display, with easy-to-read markings.

When siting the steering compass, it is important that it can be seen directly by the helmsman. It should be mounted with the lubber line on, or parallel to, the boat's fore-and-aft line. For these reasons, wheel-steered boats usually have the steering compass in a binnacle (casing) on top of the wheel pedestal. Tiller-steered boats often use one or two bulkhead-mounted compasses on the cabin bulkhead, to the sides of the companionway. In either case, in order to minimize the effects of deviation, the compass must be at least 6 ft (2 m) away from the engine. It must also be as far as possible from any other large ferrous-metal objects and the ship's wiring system. Keep movable magnetic items, such as some drinks cans, well away, too.

Despite your care in siting it, there is still likely to be some deviation; swing the compass (*p.324*) to identify the error before using it for navigation.

Hand bearing compass

Most steering compasses are not sited in a position that allows bearings to be taken all around the boat, so a portable hand bearing compass is often used. To use a hand bearing compass, line up the lubber line with the object for which the bearing is being measured, such as a vessel or buoy, and read off the bearing. With practice you will be able to take accurate bearings quickly. Do not move a magnetic compass around

STEERING COMPASS
This conventional steering compass is designed for bulkhead mounting, usually on either side of the companionway.

Lubber line

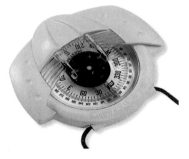

MINI HAND BEARING COMPASS
A small hand bearing compass is easy to use and convenient to carry in a pocket or hang around the neck. A magnifying prism enlarges the compass scale under the lubber line, making it easier to read.

violently since it will take time for the swinging card to come to rest. Brace yourself in a secure position away from metallic objects and keep your hands as steady as possible.

There are three types of hand bearing compasses: the traditional bowl compass with a handle, the smaller "mini" compass, and a hand-held fluxgate compass. The type you choose depends on personal preference; all will deliver good results if used properly. Try to use a few types afloat, preferably in rough conditions, to decide which suits you best before buying one.

VARIATION AND DEVIATION

There is nothing that you can do about variation (*below*) when using a magnetic compass other than allow for it when converting courses from magnetic to true or vice versa. Deviation, however, can be measured, minimized, and corrected (*right and opposite*).

Dealing with deviation

There are a number of specialist compass adjusters who will come aboard your boat and measure, very accurately, the deviation present in your steering compass. Once the deviation is known, and if it is excessive, a compass adjuster will use small magnetic correctors sited around the compass to reduce the deviation effects as much as possible. Employing a compass adjuster is usually only necessary if you have a steel-hulled vessel that creates a considerable local magnetic field. In some cases, the effect of deviation in a steel vessel can only be overcome by using a gyrocompass, which uses the properties of a gyroscope to point at true north, rather than magnetic north. However, these are expensive and complicated and are rarely used on small boats. Whatever the

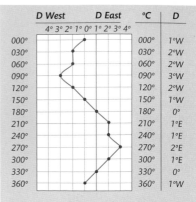

	D West						D East			°C	D
	4°	3°	2°	1°	0°	1°	2°	3°	4°		
000°										000°	1°W
030°										030°	2°W
060°										060°	2°W
090°										090°	3°W
120°										120°	2°W
150°										150°	1°W
180°										180°	0°
210°										210°	1°E
240°										240°	1°E
270°										270°	2°E
300°										300°	1°E
330°										330°	0°
360°										360°	1°W

Key: *D = Deviation, °C = Compass heading*

DEVIATION CARD
Measure the deviation on courses at least every 30° and note them down. Then plot a deviation curve using graph paper.

construction materials of your boat, it is rare that deviation can be eliminated altogether. So the amount of deviation must be measured, by a process called "swinging the compass," and a deviation card created from which the amount of deviation can be read off for each compass course.

Swinging the compass

You can employ a compass adjuster to swing your compass or you can do it yourself quite easily. There are several ways to do it, but the quickest and easiest is to have the helmsman steer due north (000°C) on the steering compass while another person uses a hand bearing compass to sight along the centerline of the boat while standing at the stern, well clear of any magnetic interference.

Make sure there is no deviation at your chosen spot, by taking a bearing of a charted transit and checking it on the chart (*p.332*). Note the course steered and the reading from the hand bearing compass, then turn to 030°C and repeat the procedure.

MAGNETIC VARIATION

The angular difference between magnetic and true north (*pp.316–317*) alters year by year. It is called variation, and its amount and direction—either east or west of true north—depend on where you are on Earth's surface. The movement of the magnetic poles is predictable and slow, and is marked on charts. Currently, the magnetic north pole is located in the Canadian Arctic.

Allowing for variation

All charts display a compass rose aligned with true north, along with a concentric inner rose aligned to magnetic north. Local variation and its annual rate of change are also marked on the rose. When shaping a course or plotting a position, you will often have to convert between true and magnetic bearings. Do this using the rose, or by simple addition or subtraction (*below*). Be consistent in your methods to avoid mistakes.

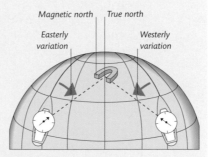

Magnetic north   True north

Easterly variation   Westerly variation

MAGNETIC VARIATION
The magnetic poles move over time, but their position and annual rate of change are known and can be allowed for.

TRUE TO MAGNETIC
ADD WESTERLY variation, or SUBTRACT EASTERLY variation
e.g., 150°T + 5°W = 155°M

MAGNETIC TO TRUE
ADD EASTERLY variation, or SUBTRACT WESTERLY variation
e.g., 155°M – 5°W = 150°T

Continue recording bearings every 30° until you have completed a full 360°. Plot the results on graph paper to produce a curve giving the amount and direction of deviation for each course steered.

If deviation exceeds about 6° on any course, employ a compass adjuster to correct the compass. Use the card to estimate deviation on any course when converting courses from compass to magnetic or vice versa (*right*).

Steering a course

When working in less than ideal conditions at a yacht's chart table, it is wise to recognize the level of accuracy that is achievable in practice. Even the most experienced helmsman cannot steer a course to single-degree accuracy, even in perfect conditions. The navigator should, therefore, expect the course actually steered to be no more accurate than plus or minus 5° of the course requested.

Even more inaccuracy is likely to occur in rough conditions, when sailing in darkness, or with an inexperienced helmsman. Try to give the helmsman a course to steer in increments of 5°—such as 030° or 035° rather than 033°. It is easier to remember and far easier to read on a conventional compass card which is clearly marked at 5° and 10° intervals.

PUTTING IT ALL TOGETHER

The navigator plots courses and bearings on charts that are aligned to true north. When calculating a course to steer, he will measure the true (or sometimes magnetic) bearing of the track. However, this must be converted to a compass bearing for the helmsman, who will use a magnetic compass to steer by.

Starting with a true bearing measured from the chart, the navigator must convert it to a magnetic bearing by allowing for variation. Then he must allow for deviation, if any. These corrections will result in a compass bearing, which is the course to steer by the steering compass to travel along the true bearing drawn on the chart (not allowing for leeway, *p.345*).

This may seem complex, but if you sail regularly on the same boat in the same sailing area, then you will quickly get used to the calculations. When working from true bearings to compass, or vice versa, it is helpful to follow a simple formula that combines each step into one calculation.

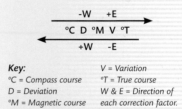

Key:

°C = Compass course	V = Variation
D = Deviation	°T = True course
°M = Magnetic course	W & E = Direction of each correction factor.

To convert a course from °C to °M or °T, the navigator simply works from left to right on the diagram (*above*), adding Easterly and subtracting Westerly corrections for deviation and variation. To convert a course from °T to °M or °C, the navigator works from right to left, adding Westerly and subtracting Easterly corrections for variation and deviation.

COMPASS DEVIATION

Compass alignment often differs from magnetic north due to on-board magnetic fields. This is called deviation. It varies with the boat's course, and is measured in degrees east or west of magnetic north. It may also be effected by the amount the boat is heeling.

Avoiding temporary deviation

On passage, avoid temporary effects by ensuring that beverage cans, eyeglasses with metal frames, personal music players, and all other metal or electrical equipment is kept well away from the compass. Be strict in enforcing this, since a magnetic item left close to the compass could cause very large errors.

Allowing for deviation

When shaping a course or plotting a position, convert between magnetic and compass courses by adding or subtracting the amount of compass deviation (*below*).

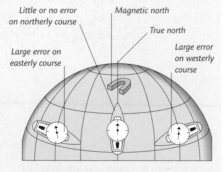

MAGNETIC DEVIATION
The amount of error depends on the boat's heading and the relative positions of the interfering magnetic materials (here, the engine), the compass, and magnetic north. It is largest on easterly or westerly courses.

MAGNETIC TO COMPASS

ADD WESTERLY deviation, or SUBTRACT EASTERLY deviation
e.g., 204°M + 4°W = 208°C

COMPASS TO MAGNETIC

ADD EASTERLY deviation, or SUBTRACT WESTERLY deviation
e.g., 208°C – 4°W = 204°M

PLOTTING EQUIPMENT

Before you can do any plotting work on paper charts, you will need to obtain a few navigation tools and learn how to use them. Practice with these basic tools leads to confident chart work and accurate navigation, which will give you great satisfaction.

A chart table

A secure place to work is a major help in navigation. The best solution is to have a permanent chart table with a horizontal surface large enough for a chart to be laid out with no more than one fold. A typical chart table has either a lifting top with chart storage space underneath, or a drawer. Either type should allow the charts to be stored flat when folded in half.

Siting a chart table

Some people prefer to stand up at a chart table that is arranged fore and aft, but, more usually, chart tables are built athwartships with a seat for the navigator. Ideally, the chart table is situated near the companionway, where there is least motion in the boat, with the seat facing forward. This position makes communication with the helmsman and access to the cockpit fairly easy. There should be shelf space for essential reference books, some of which will be quite large, and bulkhead space for instruments and communication equipment. A small compass, mounted with the lubber line fore and aft (*p.323*), is useful for keeping an eye on the course being steered.

If your boat is too small for a permanent chart table, use a flat board that is large enough to take a folded chart but that can be stowed away when not in use. Clip the chart to the board and use it on your knees, either down below or in the cockpit when conditions are suitable.

Lighting a chart table

The chart table should be lit so that the navigator can work on charts without disturbing sleeping crew or affecting the helmsman's night vision. A small, flexible gooseneck lamp can be useful for lighting the chart. Using a low-power red bulb can also help minimize loss of night vision.

Parallel rulers

A navigator uses parallel rulers to transfer a direction from the chart's compass rose to the part of the chart on which he is working. First, the ruler is lined up on either the true or the magnetic compass rose. Depending on its design, the ruler is then either rolled or "walked" across the chart to the appropriate area. Lines can then be drawn to indicate a course to steer or a bearing on an object.

When you are choosing a parallel ruler, it is best to try out a range of both roller and walking designs at sea, to find out which most suits you. Generally, roller types are impractical on a yacht and walking types can be awkward on small chart tables.

DIVIDERS   **COMPASS**

PLOTTER

CHART TABLE AND TOOLS
The chart table should be a secure spot to work, with space for spreading out a chart and mounting instruments within easy reach. A plotter, dividers, and a compass are all essential, basic tools.

LOGBOOK

A logbook is used for recording position, course, distance run, and other crucial information. You are required to keep one by maritime law, and might have to produce it in the event of an incident at sea.

Making a logbook

You do not need to buy a printed logbook. There is no standardized format for logbooks, and many commercial ones include space for unnecessary information. Many experienced navigators produce their own, simply by ruling a few columns in a notebook or on loose-leaf sheets inserted into a ring binder. The column headings can be adapted to suit your individual requirements.

Keeping records

Try to keep your entries as neat as possible because you may need to refer back to them. Record the key data half-hourly or hourly when you are cruising close to shore, and less often when you are well offshore. A rough notebook is handy for making notes and calculations; some skippers have a deck log for use by the crew on watch, and transfer the information at regular intervals to the main logbook.

Plotters

A plotter achieves the same result as a parallel ruler, and most people find it easier to use on a small boat. The Breton, Hurst, and Portland plotters are among the most popular brands.

All types of plotters are used in conjunction with the grid of latitude and longitude lines marked on the chart, rather than with the compass roses. The plotter is engraved with a compass rose and a square grid of lines, any of which are lined up with a line of latitude or longitude on the chart to orientate the plotter with true north. The plotter's straight edge is then lined up with the bearing to be measured, and the bearing is read off from the plotter's compass rose.

Some plotters allow variation and deviation to be set on their compass rose, thus allowing magnetic bearings to be read or plotted directly. A plotter does not need to be used in conjunction with a compass rose, so it does not have to be moved across the chart. This makes it easier to use and more accurate than parallel rulers.

Dividers

Used to measure distances on the chart, dividers are usually made of brass with steel tips. Buy a pair of dividers that is at least 6 in (15 cm) long so that it has a reasonable span. The single-handed type, which has a bowed top, is easier to use than the straight type, which needs two hands to open and close it.

Open the dividers to span the appropriate area, then read off the distance using the chart's latitude scale. If the span of the dividers is not large enough, set it to a convenient width using the latitude scale, then step the dividers across the area.

A simple drawing compass should also be carried for use when plotting curved lines of position (p.354).

Pencils

Use soft pencils, such as 2B, on charts to avoid permanently marking them. Hexagonal pencils are less likely than round ones to roll off the table when the boat heels. You will also need a pencil sharpener and a soft eraser.

REFERENCE BOOKS

Every navigator requires a selection of reference books to provide information that is not included on charts. These books should be stored somewhere conveniently close to the chart table for easy reference, and should be kept as up-to-date as possible.

Nautical almanac

The principal reference book you require is a current copy of the nautical almanac that covers your sailing area. This provides tidal information, harbor plans and details, and other useful material.

Pilot books

The navigator may want pilot books to cover the area being cruised. These vary from publications produced specifically for yachting, to those published by hydrographic agencies and intended for all types of seafarers.

Tidal atlases

Although tidal information is available from nautical almanacs and charts, tidal atlases of your sailing area showing the direction and rate of the tidal stream in pictorial form may be useful, depending on how you like to see the information presented.

Instruction manuals

Electronic navigation instruments are often quite complicated to use. Make sure you have a full set of instruction booklets and study them carefully to get the best out of your equipment.

Lights and radio signals

If you are sailing long distances, you may also want to carry published references for lists of lights and radio signals, especially if you do not have a full set of large-scale charts for the area.

NAVIGATION INSTRUMENTS

For successful navigation, you require some form of log to measure distance sailed. Along with your compass, this will give you the minimum information you need, although it is also prudent to carry a depth sounder. More sophisticated systems for performance measurement and position fixing are useful, but they do not remove the need to use the basic skills. Nor are they foolproof—you must always be prepared to double-check their readings, and be able to do without them if necessary.

Logs

Most yachts are equipped with some form of electronic log, nearly all of which avoid the trouble of towing a rotator behind the boat by having a transducer fitted through the hull or, sometimes, mounted inside. Transducers may be of the impeller, pressure, or Doppler types. Most electronic logs use a small paddle-wheel impeller mounted through the hull and connected to the electronics in the display head. The impeller is usually retractable so it can be cleared of weeds when necessary. As with any through-hull fitting, a wooden or rubber bung should be tied to the fitting so that if it should fail for any reason, the resulting hole in the hull can be plugged quickly. The vulnerability of the impeller to fouling is the main disadvantage of this type.

Pressure logs sense changes in pressure, which are proportional to speed. They have no moving parts outside the boat, but the tubes can get clogged. Doppler types measure the change of frequency in a signal emitted into the water flow next to the hull and proportional to speed. It has no moving parts and can be mounted inside the hull, against the skin.

A log's display unit is usually mounted in view of the steering position and/or at the chart table. Most units use a digital display, but analog instruments are also available. Many systems allow a repeater unit to be installed to allow two or more locations to be covered.

Even a simple log usually displays speed and total distance run, and has a trip meter that can be reset. More expensive units can also display other data, such as maximum speed achieved and average speed for the trip, and many have timer and countdown functions, which are particularly useful when racing. Remember that the log's transducer can only measure the speed at which water passes along the hull; it cannot measure the speed over the ground.

If a yacht is anchored or moored in a tidal stream, the log will show the speed of the water moving past the hull, and if the boat is sailing against the tide, the boat speed indicated by the log will be greater than the speed achieved over the ground. If the boat is sailing with the tide, the speed indicated by the log will be less than the speed over the ground. If a GPS set is installed (p.330) it will show your speed over the ground, and this can be compared with the log's display of speed through the water to estimate the set and drift of the tidal stream in which the yacht is sailing.

Depth sounders

A traditional lead line (a weighted line that is dropped over the side), about 50 ft (15 m) long, is the simplest and most reliable form of depth sounder. You should carry one even if you have an electronic depth sounder; it makes a useful backup and is handy for measuring depth all around the boat or for use from the dinghy.

Traditionally, a lead line is marked at specific depths with certain types and colors of material, but you can devise any marking system that suits you. The traditional lead has a hollow in the bottom that can

DEPTH AND SPEED

WIND

MULTIFUNCTION

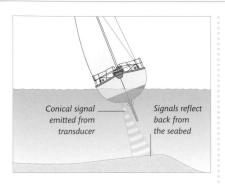

DEPTH SOUNDING SIGNAL

The depth sounder's transducer emits a conical signal, and errors can occur if the yacht heels significantly, or if false signals reflect back off the keel.

be armed (filled) with tallow or grease to collect a sample of the sea bed, which can be useful when selecting an anchorage.

Most modern yachts use an electronic depth sounder, which sends out conical pulses of sound toward the bottom and measures the time it takes for them to be reflected back. They can display depth in feet, meters, or even fathoms, and many have deep- and shallow-water alarm settings. It is prudent to add at least a meter or two to the boat's draft and set this as a shallow-water alarm. A deep water alarm can be useful for identifying a depth contour or for warning of a dragging anchor. The display head should be mounted in the cockpit where the helmsman can see it easily.

When the boat is heeled, the positioning of the transducer relative to the sea bed may change, thus affecting the depth reading. A soft sea bed may also cause errors, as may cavitation—when small air bubbles, often generated by a propeller, reflect the signal back. When reversing over your own wake, or passing across a power boat's wake, you may suddenly see the depth apparently drop dramatically.

Depth transducers are often mounted externally, although they have no moving parts, but most can be mounted internally. This does reduce their effective range but removes the risk of a hole through the hull.

Wind instruments

A wind instrument may be as simple as a small flag (burgee) on a pivoting support that is hoisted above the masthead on a burgee halyard, or a pivoting wind vane mounted on the top of the mast. Burgees and wind vanes are commonly used on dinghies and smaller boats and are equally useful on larger cruisers.

More sophisticated instrumentation consists of a small vane and anemometer placed at the masthead, connected to a display head in the cockpit. The display usually consists of an analog meter showing wind direction with a digital display for wind speed. On its own, a wind instrument will display the strength and direction of apparent wind (*p.33*) in relation to the yacht's head. When instruments are connected together to share their data, a wind instrument together with an electronic log will enable it to compute and display true wind strength and relative direction. If a fluxgate compass is added to the system, it will enable the wind instrument to calculate and display the actual direction, in degrees magnetic, of both the true and apparent wind.

Calibrating instruments

Electronic instruments, especially those with a digital display, give the impression of great accuracy when, in fact, the instruments can be wildly inaccurate unless their transducers are functioning properly and the instruments have been properly calibrated. Whatever type of log you use, it should be calibrated. Find a

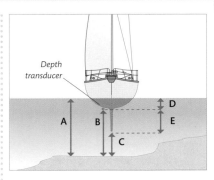

OFFSETS FOR DEPTH SOUNDER

The depth sounder will read the depth below it, B, unless corrected. Add D to give true water depth, A, or subtract E to give water depth under the keel, C.

measured distance on the chart and make two runs along it under power in opposite directions when the tidal stream is slack. Note the distance for each run from your log, add them together, and divide by two to get the average. The difference between this figure and the distance marked on the chart is the log error. Electronic logs can usually be adjusted by inputting the error correction; alternatively, you can simply record the observed error and apply it to each log reading.

The depth sounder also needs calibration. The vertical distance of the transducer from the waterline must be entered into the system as an offset so that the instrument can calculate the actual depth from the surface. Some sailors calibrate the other way, so that the instrument reads the depth below the keel. Make sure your crew knows which system you use.

Wind instruments also need to be calibrated to align with the ship's head. Racing boats mount their wind instruments on long wands to get them clear of the masthead and away from upwash effects that introduce errors. Cruising sailors do not require such accuracy but should calibrate their instruments according to the manual.

Satellite positioning

Radio positioning by satellite signal has revolutionized navigation on land and sea. The original, and most used, system is the US Global Positioning System (GPS). GLONASS (Russian), GALILEO (European), and COMPASS (Chinese) are similar systems in development. In each, a constellation of operational and standby satellites circles Earth, providing an orbital reference grid.

In the GPS system, at least four satellites are visible from anywhere on Earth. Each satellite permanently transmits a signal, giving any receiver in range a very accurate time signal and the position of the satellite. When a GPS receiver is in touch with three or more satellites, it has enough data to triangulate its own position (and altitude) on the surface of Earth.

The GPS system is freely available to anyone with receiving equipment and a GPS set will calculate its position within 49 ft (15 m) 95 percent of the time. More accurate DGPS sets (Differential GPS) receive additional signals from land-based stations that are used to correct errors in the GPS system. DGPS sets can achieve an accuracy of around 4 in (10 cm).

A GPS set can either be of the type that is permanently mounted, usually at the chart table, with an external aerial, or it may be a handheld set with a built-in aerial. Handheld GPS receivers are relatively cheap, have much of the functionality of larger units, and are often carried as a backup to the main set.

A GPS set requires setting up before use. Among the options, you can usually specify the chart datum for its reference position (*p.315*), your preferred unit of distance (statute or nautical miles), and whether to use true or magnetic north for bearings.

As with a visual three-point fix (*pp.352–353*), the accuracy of the calculated position is increased when the satellites are well spaced across the sky. The amount of spread is called the Horizontal Dilution of Precision (HDoP). Some GPS receivers display HDoP data so you can assess the accuracy of a fix.

GPS units can provide position information as a digital readout of latitude and longitude or as a bearing and distance from any chosen location. The latter is often easier to use for plotting position on a chart. Receivers can also be programmed with 100 or more waypoints—positions of charted objects, turning marks, or any other positions you choose. Routes, consisting of two or more waypoints, can also be stored in the unit's memory. GPS is a major navigation tool. However, the prudent navigator recognizes that GPS sets, or their power supply, can fail, or the signal can be degraded by many factors, or even jammed. You should always have another method of plotting your position.

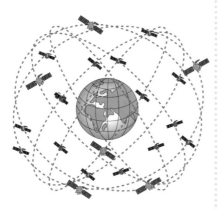

NETWORK OF SATELLITES
The positioning satellites circling above the earth form a network of orbits. Their orbits are arranged so that enough of them are visible from any point on the earth's surface to allow a receiving unit to calculate its exact location.

Radar

On boats larger than about 36 ft (11 m), radar can be the most useful electronic aid, and is the only one with position-fixing and collision-avoidance capabilities. Ideally, you should attend a course to learn to use radar properly.

A radar set consists of a display screen with controls, linked to an antenna usually mounted on the mast, or on an arch or pole at the stern, that transmits signals and receives reflections. These may be from the shore, buoys, other vessels, or anything else capable of adequately reflecting the signal. The radar then provides a bearing and distance between the yacht and a target shown on screen. If the object is fixed, and is marked on a chart, you can use the range and bearing to plot your position. However, radar is far more accurate at determining range than bearing, so the best radar fix uses three ranges of charted objects (*p.355*).

If the object is another vessel, you can determine its course and speed and whether it represents a collision risk. This is particularly useful in restricted visibility or in crowded shipping lanes when there may be multiple targets on the radar display.

RADAR DISPLAY
A radar display presents its information in picture form. Some displays can overlay the radar plot on an electronic chart or display them side by side, as here.

CHART PLOTTER
When connected to a GPS set, the chart plotter can display waypoints, and your boat's position and track, superimposed on the electronic chart.

If you have a chart plotter or an onboard PC with chart plotting software, then it is often possible to display the radar picture as an overlay on the chart plotter screen, or alternatively the chart on the radar screen. This makes it much easier to interpret the radar picture.

Communication systems

Most yachts carry a VHF (Very High Frequency) radio for short-range communication with shore stations or other boats. Cruisers sailing long distances also often have more sophisticated medium- and long-range ship radios or Ham (amateur radio) sets installed to allow them to stay in touch. Satellite systems are also available, for voice, data and fax transmissions, and for GMDSS signals.

GMDSS and DSC

First introduced in 1992, the Global Marine Distress and Safety System (GMDSS) provides efficient and enhanced communications and distress alerting. The system incorporates DSC (Digital Selective Calling) along with general broadcast marine radio communication, incoming weather and safety information as well as

emergency positioning indication equipment (EPIRB) (*p.423*). Most DSC VHF sets incorporate a prominent red distress button for emergency use. With these sets, the crew no longer needs to know the procedure for sending a verbal Mayday broadcast— they merely have to be able to hit the panic button in an emergency.

When a DSC VHF set is triggered to send a distress message, it automatically transmits pre-programmed information about your vessel together with your precise position derived from an onboard GPS set. This service is intended to be global and to operate without being restricted by language barriers.

AIS

AIS (Automatic Identification System) is an automated tracking system used on ships and some yachts, and by vessel traffic services (VTS), for identifying and locating vessels. AIS information supplements radar and visual lookouts, which are the primary methods of collision avoidance. An AIS display unit will show the position, speed, heading, and many other details about AIS equipped vessels in the area.

Navtex and Weatherfax

These radio systems (*pp.378–381*), sometimes combined into one unit, are very useful weather and safety information sources. Navtex provides up-to-date navigational, weather, and safety information for a selected sea area, and Weatherfax delivers weather forecasts and charts. If you connect an onboard PC to an all frequency radio receiver, Navtex and Weatherfax information can be received without the need for separate units. With a satellite communication system, you can also use the PC to obtain satellite weather images.

INTEGRATED SYSTEMS

The continuing trend toward integration of electronic aids gives the navigator information that would otherwise require considerable calculation, knowledge, and skill. Integrated systems can calculate course and speed, true wind speed and direction, velocity made good to windward or downwind, plus much other specialized data.

Unlimited possibilities

Most manufacturers offer systems that integrate log, wind, and depth instruments. Usually a fluxgate compass, GPS, a chart plotter, and a radar can be hooked in, too, so all the information is available to the computers in the individual instruments. It is also possible to add a PC with yet more calculation possibilities. The dedicated racing navigator will get much satisfaction from all this information, but the vast majority of it is not necessary for the cruising navigator who simply wants to enjoy sailing while being able to periodically fix his position and ensure a safe arrival at his or her destination.

SHARING INFORMATION
Integrated systems can share data between display heads, calculate additional useful information, and overlay or split screen information such as radar and chart images or, as here, multiple performance information.

PILOTAGE

Navigation by eye, compass, and chart, when in sight of land, is known as pilotage. The art of pilotage is to determine a series of safe tracks, in between hazards, that lead to your destination and to be able to confirm at any time that your boat is on or close to these tracks, without having to plot a position on the chart. Pilotage skills are used mainly when entering or leaving harbor; occasions when you do not have time to plot fixes on the chart and where an error of a few boat lengths can be critical.

Bearings

Two types of bearings are useful when piloting. One is the bearing of the safe track between hazards, and the other is a clearing line. The safe track is the course you follow through constricted water, while clearing lines define the boundaries of a safe zone and are used to keep the boat clear of potential hazards. Once they have been identified on a chart or harbor plan, bearings of a safe track or a clearing line can be measured using a hand bearing or steering compass (*pp.322–325*). Few steering compasses are mounted where they can be used to take bearings all around the boat, but if the boat can be pointed at the object, the steering compass can be used to take a bearing. Otherwise, the hand bearing compass must be used, so it should always be stowed within easy reach when piloting. However, using transits is quicker and simpler than taking compass bearings, and can be more accurate, so they are the first choice.

Transits

When two objects are in line, they are said to be in transit. If you see two objects in transit, your boat must be somewhere on the extension

---

CHOOSING AND USING BINOCULARS

A cruising yacht should have at least one pair of quality binoculars aboard. They are essential when you are in restricted waters and need to be able to navigate by eye rather than using a chart, and are very useful at other times when trying to identify navigation buoys or shore-side features.

Choosing binoculars

Buy the best binoculars you can afford, perhaps having a cheaper second pair for general crew use. Strong, waterproof binoculars with a rubber coating are best on yachts to protect against inevitable bumps. Binoculars are categorized by their magnification and the size of the object lens, which determines how much light is admitted. A pair of 7 x 50 binoculars makes a good choice. A magnification higher than 7 makes the binoculars difficult to hold steady, unless they have built-in stabilization, and an object lens smaller than 2 in (50 mm) will not work well in low light levels. Some types have a built-in compass and/or a range finder.

Using binoculars

When using binoculars on a moving boat, try to brace the lower half of your body and allow the upper half to move with the roll to keep the binoculars as steady as possible. The boat's companionway is often a good place to position yourself, as it allows you to brace yourself at waist height. If you wear glasses, make sure the binoculars you choose have rubber eyepieces that fit snugly against the glasses and exclude extraneous light.

Built-in compass   Moulded eyepieces

Resilient, waterproof casing

BINOCULARS

INTEGRAL COMPASS
Some binoculars have an integral compass and some have a range finder. These are handy for taking a bearing of an object and for determining how far away it is.

USING TRANSITS TO NEGOTIATE HAZARDS

One or more sets of transits can often be employed to navigate along safe tracks between hazards. Examine the chart to identify natural or manmade marks or features that can be used as transits or clearing lines. The appearance of rocks and headlands will alter with the tides; take this into account when using transits.

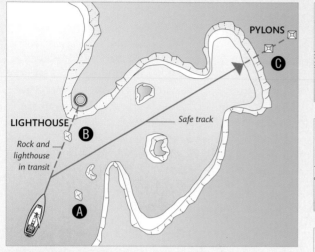

FOLLOWING A SAFE TRACK
To stay clear of rocks (A) at the entrance to the anchorage, keep the rock (B) closed, or in transit with the lighthouse. When the leading marks (pylons) come on transit (C), turn onto the safe track into the harbor.

CLOSED TRANSIT
The rock (B) is described as closed in relation to the lighthouse. In the diagram, this means that the yacht must be clear of the dangerous rocks (A) off the entrance.

IN TRANSIT
The rock (B) and the lighthouse here are in transit. If the yacht steers to keep them in transit, it will follow a safe track clear of the rocks (A) until it is able to turn into the harbor.

OPEN TRANSIT
The rock (B) is described as open in relation to the lighthouse. In the diagram, this means that the yacht could be in danger of hitting the rocks (A) off the entrance.

of the imaginary line that joins them. If the objects can be identified on the chart, you have a very useful single line of position. When you first acquire a chart for a new cruising ground, some major transits and bearing lines will already be printed on it, but you will be able to identify many other potentially useful transits as you study the chart. Draw lines connecting conspicuous features and see whether these lines could be used to define safe areas, turning points, or for any other navigational purpose. The nautical almanac and local pilotage guides will also identify useful transits.

Transits do not need to be in line to be useful. A clearing line can be defined by two objects not quite in line, said to be open or closed

(*above*). When using an open or closed transit as a clearing line, the boat is steered to keep the objects open or closed, as necessary, in order to avoid a danger to the side of the safe track.

Choosing transits

Transits are often manmade objects, such as posts or beacons, that are specifically constructed to mark safe passages (leading lines) into and out of harbor. Natural objects, such as rocks or headlands, may also be used as transits, as long as they are clearly visible and are identifiable on the chart. They must also be a reasonable distance apart from each other and not too close to your boat. If you select objects that are in the water, such as rocks or posts, you

must allow for their appearance to change with tide height. Remember, too, that individual rocks may be difficult to identify with any certainty in rock-strewn areas. Even manmade leading marks can be difficult to identify against the background clutter of shore-side buildings.

When studying a chart, try to develop the ability to visualize the coastline as it will appear to you in practice—horizontally from sea level rather than from the bird's-eye view a chart depicts. Some electronic chart plotting systems have the ability to present chart information, both above and below sea level, in a 3D view, taking into account tide height, which greatly aids the accurate interpretation of two-dimensional charts.

BUOYAGE

Although navigation marks can be found well offshore, they are mostly encountered near land, around shipping lanes, or in coastal waters where they are used to identify dangers and safe channels. The system of buoyage is organized by the International Association of Lighthouse Authorities (IALA).

There are, in fact, two systems: IALA system A is used in Europe, Africa, Australia, India, and most of Asia; IALA system B is used in North, Central, and South America, Japan, Korea, and the Philippines. The key difference between the two is in the color used for lateral marks. IALA system A uses red for port lateral marks and green for starboard lateral marks, whereas in IALA system B the colors are reversed.

Lateral marks

The edges of channels are indicated with lateral marks. These are arranged according to the direction of buoyage, which is marked on charts. In rivers and estuaries, buoyage is usually in the direction of the harbor from seaward, so, when traveling up a river (in IALA A), the port-hand buoys are red and the starboard-hand ones are green. Lateral buoys are often numbered, starting from seaward with even numbers on port hand marks and odd numbers on starboard marks.

Around coastlines, buoyage is typically arranged in a clockwise direction. If the direction of buoyage is not obvious, check on your chart; it will be marked using an arrow with two dots (*p.319*).

Preferred channel marks are modified lateral marks. They are used where a channel divides to indicate the direction of the main channel, which is usually the deepest or widest (*opposite*).

Cardinal marks

Large or individual hazards are indicated with cardinal marks. They are named after the points of the compass to indicate which side you should pass by them to avoid the danger. In other words, you should keep to the north of a north cardinal and south of a south cardinal. They are always pillar- or spar-shaped and are painted black and yellow. They all have two black cone top marks variously arranged one above the other, and at night their white lights flash in a sequence that indicates their quadrant (*opposite* and *p.336*).

LATERAL MARK
A red can is a port lateral mark in IALA system A. In system B, a can shape identifies it as a port lateral mark but the color would be green.

CARDINAL MARK
Cardinal marks have the same shapes, colors, and meanings in IALA system A and system B. A pillar buoy with a black band over yellow is a North Cardinal mark.

OTHER MARKS

In addition to the main lateral and cardinal marks, various other marks are used. An isolated danger mark is used to indicate a small, single danger with safe water all around. A safe-water mark indicates safe water around its position and is used for mid-channel or landfall marks. Other, special marks are used to indicate a special area or feature but are not primarily intended to assist in navigation. When lit, marks have specific light characteristics (*p.336*).

ISOLATED DANGER MARK
Light white, Fl (2).

SAFE-WATER MARK
Light white, Iso, Oc, or long Fl 10s.

SPECIAL MARKS
Light yellow, any rhythm but different from other buoys.

The shape of special marks is optional, but where cones, cans, or spheres are used, they show the side on which it is recommended to pass. So, a can shape is left to port, a cone to starboard, while a round shape can be left to either side.

LATERAL AND CARDINAL MARKS

Lateral marks define the edges of channels and show which, of two channels, is the preferred one. They may be lit (*p.336*), in which case the color of the light will be the same as the buoy's color—red or green. Cardinal marks define which side to pass a danger. At night, they display a white light in a specific sequence.

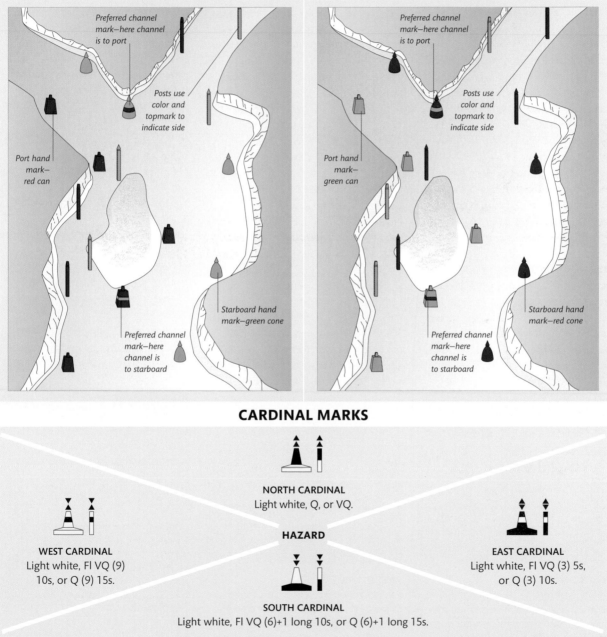

IALA A LATERAL MARKS

Preferred channel mark—here channel is to port

Posts use color and topmark to indicate side

Port hand mark— red can

Preferred channel mark—here channel is to starboard

Starboard hand mark—green cone

IALA B LATERAL MARKS

Preferred channel mark—here channel is to port

Posts use color and topmark to indicate side

Port hand mark— green can

Preferred channel mark—here channel is to starboard

Starboard hand mark—red cone

CARDINAL MARKS

NORTH CARDINAL
Light white, Q, or VQ.

HAZARD

WEST CARDINAL
Light white, Fl VQ (9) 10s, or Q (9) 15s.

EAST CARDINAL
Light white, Fl VQ (3) 5s, or Q (3) 10s.

SOUTH CARDINAL
Light white, Fl VQ (6)+1 long 10s, or Q (6)+1 long 15s.

BUOYAGE AT NIGHT

Navigation at night is made much easier through the use of lights that identify buoys, shore beacons, leading marks, and lighthouses. Buoys are usually lit with short-range lights, while medium-range lights may be found on shore beacons, and long-range lights are normally used on lighthouses. It can be difficult to identify marks at night, especially in the vicinity of ordinary shore lights.

To make it easier, different characteristics are used to light specific marks and aid identification. The characteristic of each light is noted on the chart of the area and in sailing directions. Usually, lights are white, red, green, or yellow, but purple, blue, and orange may also be used.

Light sequences

In addition to the color, the flashing pattern of the light and the time taken to complete one sequence are used as ways of identifying buoys. Using a stopwatch, check the timing of the flashing through three full sequences to be sure that you have correctly identified the light. Some of the most common light sequences are shown in the diagram (*right*). The abbreviations used in the diagram are also found on charts (*pp.318–319*). You should familiarize yourself with the abbreviations and the patterns associated with them. Some terms may be unfamiliar: "isophase" means that there are equal periods of light and dark in the sequence; "occulting" means that the periods of darkness are shorter than the periods of light—in effect, flashes of darkness.

Approaching a harbor at night with a lot of shore lights can make it tricky to pick out a buoy you are looking for. Using the hand bearing compass to sight along the expected bearing of a buoy, from a known position, can make it easier to find. Never assume that the light you see is the one you are expecting; you may not be where you think you are. Always double-check and, if possible, sail close to the buoy to identify it.

Lighthouses, and some other beacons, often use colored sector lights to indicate safe and dangerous areas. The chart will show details of the colors and sector angles. The edges of the sectors are often given in pilot books as bearings, and are from seaward toward the lighthouse in °T.

LIGHTS ON BUOYS
Lights with different colors and flashing characteristics are used to identify some buoys at night. Here, an IALA A starboard hand lateral mark has a green flashing light.

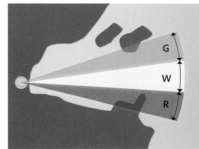

SECTOR LIGHTS
Some lighthouses have different colored lights in sectors. Seen from seaward, the navigator will see either the green, white, or red sector depending on his position.

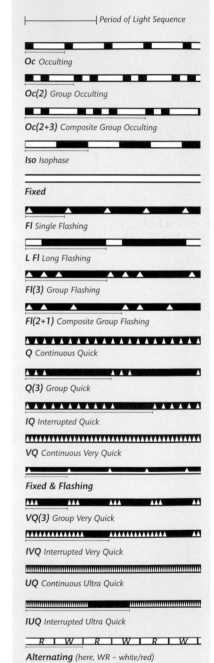

LIGHT SEQUENCES
Different light characteristics are used to allow the navigator to identify different navigation marks at night.

Period of Light Sequence

Oc Occulting

Oc(2) Group Occulting

Oc(2+3) Composite Group Occulting

Iso Isophase

Fixed

Fl Single Flashing

L Fl Long Flashing

Fl(3) Group Flashing

Fl(2+1) Composite Group Flashing

Q Continuous Quick

Q(3) Group Quick

IQ Interrupted Quick

VQ Continuous Very Quick

Fixed & Flashing

VQ(3) Group Very Quick

IVQ Interrupted Very Quick

UQ Continuous Ultra Quick

IUQ Interrupted Ultra Quick

R | W | R | W | R | W | R | W

Alternating (here, WR – white/red)

PLANNING

Pre-planning

The key to accurate and safe pilotage is to prepare thoroughly. Before you leave on a passage, prepare a pilotage plan. Study the chart, pilot books, and harbor plans to determine the safe tracks and find suitable transits near your course. The best and most prominent transits are usually marked on charts or shown in harbor plans.

Identify all the navigation marks you expect to see on the route, draw in your intended track, and check for dangers close to your course. When piloting at night, make a note of the characteristics of all the light buoys near your course. Do not trust your memory to retain all this information—jot down the key details for use in a pilotage plan.

Pilotage plans

When piloting, avoid using the chart on deck because it will be difficult to keep under control in a breeze and may quickly be damaged or even blown overboard. In addition, if your course is from north to south, it can be difficult to interpret the chart upside-down. The best solution is to prepare a pilotage plan for use on deck. Devise it to suit your particular way of working, and include courses to steer for each leg of the route, with distances between turning points, and details of navigation marks you expect to see.

Some people prefer to write a passage plan as a list of bearings, marks, and courses, while others can only visualize the situation if the pilotage plan is drawn in graphical form. Experiment with various ways of preparing a plan until you find one that suits you, then stick to that format. Use a suitable-sized notepad and protect it when on deck by

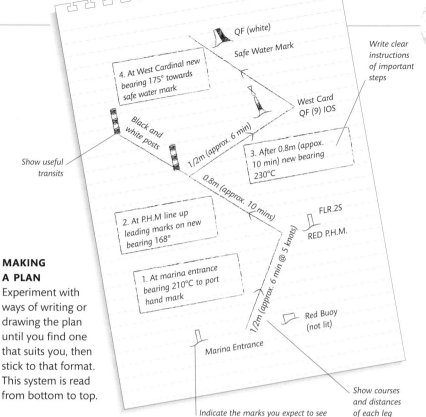

MAKING A PLAN
Experiment with ways of writing or drawing the plan until you find one that suits you, then stick to that format. This system is read from bottom to top.

Write clear instructions of important steps

Show useful transits

QF (white)
Safe Water Mark

4. At West Cardinal new bearing 175° towards safe water mark

West Card QF (9) IOS

Black and white posts

1/2m (approx. 6 min)

3. After 0.8m (approx. 10 min) new bearing 230°C

0.8m (approx. 10 mins)

2. At P.H.M line up leading marks on new bearing 168°

FLR.2S
RED P.H.M.

1/2m (approx. 6 min @ 5 knots)

1. At marina entrance bearing 210°C to port hand mark

1/2m (approx. 6 min @ 5 knots)

Red Buoy (not lit)

Marina Entrance

Indicate the marks you expect to see

Show courses and distances of each leg

placing it in a sealable plastic bag. If you use a list system, try starting the pilotage plan at the bottom of the page and working up. This way, the information on courses, navigation marks, and other important details, is clearly presented in relation to the direction in which you are traveling and may help you avoid confusion.

Write down all the navigation marks or other significant features you expect to see, together with their distance off the track. Also note the bearings of any clearing lines. If you are going to pilot at night, make a note of the characteristics of all the lit marks that are in the area.

Do not forget the value of back bearings. It is natural to look ahead along the track for marks and features to use as transits or clearing lines, but back bearings and back transits, using marks and features astern, can be just as useful. It is not unusual for there to

be a shortage of useful marks or features ahead, such as when leaving harbor, but if you look astern you will find they are in plentiful supply.

Once pilotage is underway, double-check each piece of information. Avoid complacency, and the temptation to make the facts fit your expectations. Aim to move only from one known safe location to the next so that you do not stray from the safe track.

A chart plotter mounted in the cockpit, linked to a GPS set, can make pilotage much easier, and it is then possible to watch the yacht's track moving across the chart on screen.

If you use an electronic system, do not rely on it as it may fail at the worst possible time. Always prepare a manual plan and double-check the information on the chart plotter by reference to your pilotage plan and visual observation of transits, safe track and clearing bearings.

TIDES AND TIDAL STREAMS

When you sail in tidal waters, knowing the height of the tide and the direction of the tidal stream is important for safe and accurate navigation. Some areas, such as Canada's Bay of Fundy, have enormous tidal ranges of 35 ft (11 m) or more, whereas others, such as the West Indies, have very small ones. Areas with large tidal ranges may seem daunting, but they are not difficult to cope with once you know the relatively simple procedures for calculating tidal heights and streams.

TIDAL INFORMATION

Tides are the vertical rise and fall of the surface of the sea, caused by the gravitational attraction of the Moon and, to a lesser degree, the Sun (*pp.56–57*). Earth's rotation causes a semi-diurnal tide in most parts of the world. In other words, there is a tide with two high waters and two low waters every 24 hours, 50 minutes (the length of the lunar day).

Some parts of the world, however, experience a different effect, due to the path of the Moon and other factors, and have only one high and one low water every day. This is called a diurnal tide and occurs mostly in the tropics. Diurnal tides usually feature small tidal ranges (vertical movement). A few other places experience a combination of diurnal and semi-diurnal tides, called mixed tides, in which there are two high and low waters every day but their heights vary considerably.

Changes in the height of the sea's surface are of little account in the open sea, but near coastlines they become crucially important. In some areas, the shape and orientation of the coastline cause very large tidal ranges, and these huge movements of water create powerful tidal streams.

Information sources

The navigator can find information on tide heights, ranges (difference in height between low and high tides), and times of high and low waters from a number of different sources. You can buy tide tables for local areas. These are often issued by harbor authorities and give tidal time and height information for every day of the year. National and international data is found in nautical almanacs, which provide the most comprehensive and authoritative information for their areas. Tidal predictions are also often included in chart-plotting software and there are many online sources of data. Remember, tidal predictions from different sources may differ due to different data sets or methods of computation. Also, natural effects (such as wind and pressure variations) can cause the observed tide to differ significantly from the predictions for both time and height.

A system of standard and secondary ports is used to cover all harbors within a particular area. The times and height of high and low water are given for each standard port for every day. A tidal curve (*p.340*) is also often given to allow the calculation of the height of tide at any time between high and low water, or the time that the tide will rise or fall to a particular height. Tidal information for secondary ports is given as corrections, known

FINDING THE TIME AND HEIGHT OF HIGH AND LOW WATER

The information on tide times and heights is provided in an almanac. If the place you require data for is a standard port, then the time and height can be read directly from the relevant page in your almanac (❶). In other cases, data is calculated using the corrections given in the almanac for secondary ports (❷). Here, time and height information is required for Ramsgate, which is a secondary port. The standard port is Dover, and the almanac includes corrections to be applied to the Dover high and low water times and heights to calculate the times and heights of high and low waters for Ramsgate (❸).

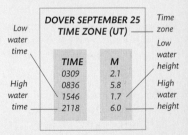

	DOVER SEPTEMBER 25 TIME ZONE (UT)		
Low water time →	**TIME**	**M**	← Time zone
	0309	2.1	← Low water height
High water time →	0836	5.8	
	1546	1.7	← High water height
	2118	6.0	

❶ Refer to your almanac to obtain the time and height of high water (HW) and low water (LW) at the standard port on the day you are interested in. Here, we require the time and height of the afternoon high water and low water on September 25 at Dover, which is the standard port.

as tidal differences. These can be applied to the time and height data from the standard port to find time and height at the secondary port. If the tide you are calculating falls between springs and neaps, you will have to interpolate between the figures given to achieve the best accuracy (*below*).

Time zones
Tide tables usually give the times of high and low water in the port's zone time or standard time, although some local tables show times already corrected for any daylight saving time. Make sure you know which system your tide table uses, and be prepared to convert to clock time if necessary.

Tide tables usually show their base time zone on each page. They also show the correction that must be applied to convert to local clock time.

When working out secondary port information from standard port data, do the calculations in zone time, then convert the answer to local time; otherwise, significant errors may occur.

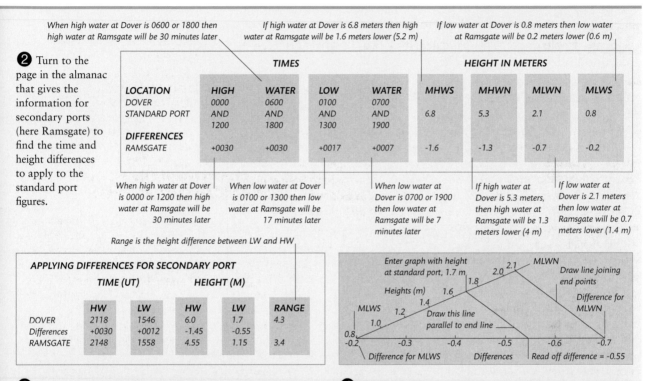

When high water at Dover is 0600 or 1800 then high water at Ramsgate will be 30 minutes later

If high water at Dover is 6.8 meters then high water at Ramsgate will be 1.6 meters lower (5.2 m)

If low water at Dover is 0.8 meters then low water at Ramsgate will be 0.2 meters lower (0.6 m)

❷ Turn to the page in the almanac that gives the information for secondary ports (here Ramsgate) to find the time and height differences to apply to the standard port figures.

	TIMES				HEIGHT IN METERS			
LOCATION	**HIGH**	**WATER**	**LOW**	**WATER**	**MHWS**	**MHWN**	**MLWN**	**MLWS**
DOVER	0000	0600	0100	0700				
STANDARD PORT	AND	AND	AND	AND	6.8	5.3	2.1	0.8
	1200	1800	1300	1900				
DIFFERENCES								
RAMSGATE	+0030	+0030	+0017	+0007	-1.6	-1.3	-0.7	-0.2

When high water at Dover is 0000 or 1200 then high water at Ramsgate will be 30 minutes later

When low water at Dover is 0100 or 1300 then low water at Ramsgate will be 17 minutes later

When low water at Dover is 0700 or 1900 then low water at Ramsgate will be 7 minutes later

If high water at Dover is 5.3 meters, then high water at Ramsgate will be 1.3 meters lower (4 m)

If low water at Dover is 2.1 meters then low water at Ramsgate will be 0.7 meters lower (1.4 m)

Range is the height difference between LW and HW

APPLYING DIFFERENCES FOR SECONDARY PORT

	TIME (UT)		HEIGHT (M)		
	HW	**LW**	**HW**	**LW**	**RANGE**
DOVER	2118	1546	6.0	1.7	4.3
Differences	+0030	+0012	-1.45	-0.55	
RAMSGATE	2148	1558	4.55	1.15	3.4

Enter graph with height at standard port, 1.7 m

Draw line joining end points

Difference for MLWN

Draw this line parallel to end line

Difference for MLWS

Differences

Read off difference = -0.55

❸ Create a table (or use a ready-printed one) to note the times and heights at the standard port (Dover), the differences to be applied, and the resulting times and heights at the secondary port (Ramsgate).

From the tide table (❶) HW Dover is 2118 at 6.0 m, and LW is 1546 at 1.7 m. From the secondary port data (❷) the correction for HW is +30 minutes, whatever the time of HW Dover.

The correction for LW depends on the time of LW Dover (❷). If LW Dover is at 0100 or 1300 the correction is +17 minutes. If LW Dover is at 0700 or 1900 the correction is +7 minutes. From the tide table (❶) LW Dover is at 1546—roughly halfway between 1300 and 1900. Therefore, the correction needed is +12 minutes, halfway between +7 minutes and +17 minutes.

The height difference for HW is easy to interpolate as the day's HW height (6.0 m) is about halfway between mean spring (6.8 m) and neap heights (5.3 m). By interpolating halfway between –1.3 m and –1.6 m we get a high water difference of –1.45 m.

❹ The LW difference is harder to interpolate, but we can use a graphical technique to find the answer. Using any convenient lined paper, draw a horizontal line and mark off the differences from the almanac at any convenient scale. Then draw another line, from the start of the first line and at an acute but arbitrary angle to it. On this, mark off the equivalent heights, again at any convenient scale. This scale need not be the same as the one used on the first line.

Join the end points of the two lines. Mark on the height scale the height at the standard port for which you need to find the difference at the secondary port (here, 1.7 m). From this mark, draw a line, parallel to the line you have just drawn to join the ends of the first two lines, to cut the differences scale. Read off the difference to apply, which here is –0.55 m.

You can use this graphical technique whenever you need to interpolate between figures that are not easy to interpolate by eye or by simple arithmetic.

TIDAL CURVES

Tidal curves can be used to calculate the time at which the water depth needed can be expected or to calculate the depth at a given time. The most accurate way to calculate depth of water and time is to use the tidal curves that are provided in the nautical almanac. Alternatively, software in a chart plotter, laptop computer, tablet, or smartphone can be used.

How tidal curves work

A tidal curve is represented on a graph that plots the progress of a tide over a complete tidal cycle. Where the cycle varies between spring and neap tides, two curves are shown. Spring tides are represented in the example (*right*) by a solid line, and neap tides by a dotted one. You can use the appropriate curve to find out what time the tide will reach a specific height, or what the tide's height will be at a specific time. When the range is between springs and neaps, estimate by eye where you expect the tidal curve to be. In some places, the time of low water can be more accurately predicted than that of high water. For these areas, tidal curves are based on low-water times. Use them in the same way as in the diagram, but substitute the time of low water for that of high water.

Secondary ports

The nautical almanac usually provides curves for each standard port. These can also be used to obtain the time or height of tide at the secondary ports, simply by entering the tidal data given for the secondary port. First calculate the time of high water, and the height of high and low waters at the secondary port. Then enter these into the tidal curve, and proceed exactly as for a standard port.

USING A TIDAL CURVE

Before using a tidal curve, use tide tables to find tide times and heights for the day. Here, the information for Ramsgate on the south coast of England is used (*p.339*). Then use the steps below to find the height of the tide at a specific time. To find the time the tide reaches a specific height, reverse steps 3–5: draw a line down from the desired height on the top scale; where this line intersects the diagonal line draw a horizontal line to the curve; at the curve draw a line down to the timescale grid and read the time.

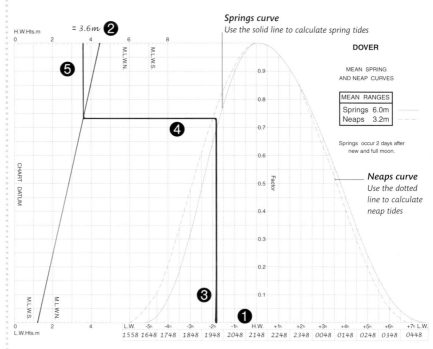

1 Enter the time of the day's nearest high water (*p.339*) in the timescale box marked HW and fill in the other time boxes, counting up and down from HW.

2 Enter the height of low water on the lower scale, marked LW Hts, and the height of high water on the upper scale, marked HW Hts. Draw a straight line to connect the two marks.

3 To find the height of tide at a particular time, enter the required time on the timescale grid. Then draw a line from this time up to the curve. If the day's tidal range is close to the spring range, draw the line to the spring curve. If it is close to neaps, take the line to the neap curve. If the day's tidal range is in between neaps and springs (as here), it is usually sufficient to interpolate by eye—estimating the position between the two curves according to the size of the day's range compared with the spring and neap ranges.

4 From the intersection of the curve and the vertical line, draw a horizontal line across to meet the angled line drawn in step 2.

5 From here, draw a line up to join the top scale. The figure at this point is the height above chart datum of the tide at the required time. To obtain the total depth of water at your position, you need to add this figure to the depth shown on the chart.

TIDE HEIGHTS AND CHART DATUM

The depth of water shown on charts, and drying heights, are calculated from chart datum, which is usually the lowest astronomical tide (LAT)—the lowest level to which the tide is expected to fall. Check the information near the chart title to confirm to which datum it refers.

Almanacs give figures for the height of an average spring (or large) tide's high and low waters—Mean High Water Springs (MHWS) and Mean Low Water Springs (MLWS). Almanacs also give the equivalent heights for an average neap (or small) tide's high and low waters—Mean High Water Neaps (MHWN) and Mean Low Water Neaps (MLWN).

Heights of objects on land are measured from the MHWS level. At all times other than MHWS, heights will be greater than shown, so the

DEPTHS AND HEIGHTS
Depths and drying heights are measured from chart datum while the heights of objects on land are measured from the level of Mean High Water Springs.

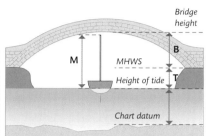

CHARTED HEIGHTS
The boat will pass under the bridge if the bridge height, B, (given above MHWS) plus the amount the tide is below MHWS, T, is greater than the height of the mast above water level, M.

navigator must be able to calculate the difference (*above right*). Remember that your calculations will provide you with a theoretically correct measurement, but they do not allow for any meteorological conditions that can affect the height of tide. For instance, a strong onshore wind may cause greater depths than your calculations suggest. Similarly, a deep low pressure system over the sailing area will cause the water to rise higher than usual. An increase or decrease in pressure of 34 millibars can cause a 1-ft (0.3-m) change in water level.

ESTIMATING TIDAL HEIGHTS
Tide tables show the height of the tide only at high and low water, and you will often need to know its height at other times. For an accurate figure, it is best to use the almanac's tidal curve (*opposite*), but for a rough guide you can estimate the height using the Rule of Twelfths.

The rule of twelfths
This method of estimating tidal height assumes that it rises and falls symmetrically and that the duration of the rise or fall is six hours. This is suitable for many areas where high accuracy is not required, but it should be used with caution.

The rule
The rule divides the tidal range (from high water to low water and vice versa) into twelve and assumes that the tide rises or falls as follows:
1st hour $\frac{1}{12}$ of the range
2nd hour $\frac{2}{12}$ of the range
3rd hour $\frac{3}{12}$ of the range
4th hour $\frac{3}{12}$ of the range
5th hour $\frac{2}{12}$ of the range
6th hour $\frac{1}{12}$ of the range

An example
To find the height of the tide at 15:15, or three hours after high water when the tide table gives HW at 12:15, 4.8 m high and LW at 18:20, 1.2 m high. First calculate the range 4.8 – 1.2 = 3.6 m, then divide it into twelfths:
• In the first hour (to 13:15) the tide drops 1/12 of 3.6 m = 0.3 m
• In the second hour (to 14:15) the tide drops 2/12 of 3.6 m = 0.6 m
• In the third hour (to 15:15) the tide drops 3/12 of 3.6 m = 0.9 m
• The tide will fall by 1.8 m (0.3 + 0.6 + 0.9) from HW by 15:15, so the height of tide (above chart datum) is 4.8 m – 1.8 m = 3.0 m

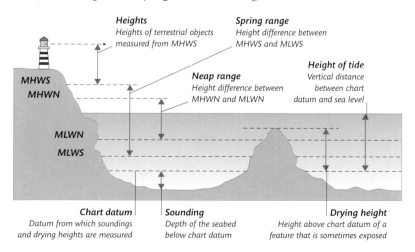

Heights
Heights of terrestrial objects measured from MHWS

Spring range
Height difference between MHWS and MLWS

Neap range
Height difference between MHWN and MLWN

Height of tide
Vertical distance between chart datum and sea level

Chart datum
Datum from which soundings and drying heights are measured

Sounding
Depth of the seabed below chart datum

Drying height
Height above chart datum of a feature that is sometimes exposed

TIDAL STREAMS

The rise and fall of the tide causes a horizontal flow of water known as a tidal stream. Tidal streams are at their strongest during spring tides and their weakest during neap tides.

The direction of the tidal stream at any time is called its set, and the strength of the stream is called its drift. A tidal set is always expressed as the direction in which it is running. For example, a westerly tide runs from the east to the west—the reverse of the way in which wind direction is described—a westerly wind blows from the west to the east.

Tidal streams alter direction and vary in strength on an hourly basis in many places, and when a navigator is shaping a course or plotting a position, he needs to know both the set and the drift for the area in which he is sailing and the time he is sailing. This information can be obtained from a chart, almanac, tidal atlas, electronic chart system, or software on a computer, tablet, or smartphone.

Tidal atlases

A tidal atlas provides tidal stream information for a specific area in the form of a separate page for each hour before and after high water at a standard port. Each page shows the set of the stream using arrows and indicates the drift at spring and neap tides in figures. Usually, a graphical indication of stream strength is given— the bigger and thicker the arrow line, the bigger the drift. Drift may be shown in knots and tenths of a knot, or it may simply be shown in tenths (thus 1.1 knots may be written as 1.1 or 11). The nautical almanac may also show tidal stream information using small chartlets that are similar to the pages in the tidal atlas.

Using a tidal atlas

In the tidal atlas, mark up the high water page with the time of high water for the day at the standard port, and then mark up each page before and after the high water page with the appropriate time. Turn to the page for the time you need and find the tidal arrow nearest your position. Measure its direction with a plotter (*p.326*) to find the set of the tide. Note the spring and neap rates shown by the arrow. If the tide is a spring or neap, use the appropriate rate given. If the day's tidal range lies in between the spring and neap ranges, interpolate between the two figures (*above right*).

An alternative to calculation is to use the computation of rates table in the tidal atlas. Alternatively, some chart plotters, and navigation software, include tidal data and do the calculations automatically.

INTERPOLATING BETWEEN SPRING AND NEAP RATES

To find the rate of drift during periods between spring and neap tides, use the formula: (range of tide for the day [HW – LW heights] ÷ spring range of tide) x spring rate of drift (from chart).

Using the chart

On charts, positions at which tidal streams have been measured are marked by a letter within a diamond, and are known as tidal diamonds (*p.319*). A table on the chart, usually near the title information, shows the set and drift for spring and neap tides at every

TIDAL ATLAS

Tidal atlases and almanacs show tidal stream information in pictorial form. Direction is shown by the arrows, with numbers indicating the speed.

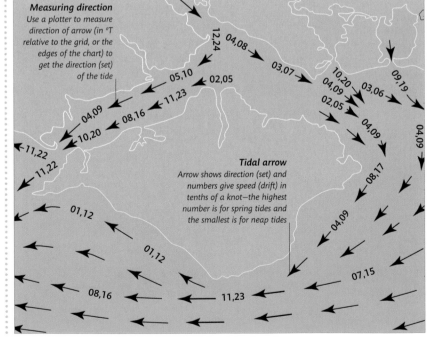

Measuring direction
Use a plotter to measure direction of arrow (in °T relative to the grid, or the edges of the chart) to get the direction (set) of the tide

Tidal arrow
Arrow shows direction (set) and numbers give speed (drift) in tenths of a knot—the highest number is for spring tides and the smallest is for neap tides

tidal diamond marked on the chart for each hour before and after high water at the standard port.

To use the information in the table, you need to know the time of high water at the standard port for the day in question and the tidal diamond that is closest to your position. High tide is shown as zero on the table. Select the hour in which you are interested, and read across the table to the column headed by your tidal diamond letter. Here, you can read off the rate of drift (written in knots and tenths of a knot) and the set of the stream, in °T. Select the spring or neap rate, or interpolate between the two rates if necessary (*opposite*). If your position on the chart is between two tidal diamonds, plot the results for both on the chart and interpolate between the two by eye.

			50°36'6N 2 24-3W		
		Ⓐ			
Hours before HW	-6	230		0.5	0.2
	-5	235		0.5	0.2
	-4	241		0.4	0.2
	-3	253		0.4	0.2
	-2	272		0.3	0.1
High water at standard port	-1	279		0.2	0.1
	0	287		0.1	0.0
	+1	-----		0.0	0.0
	+2	139		0.1	0.0
Hours after HW	+3	270		0.2	3.1
	+4	210		0.3	3.1
	+5	226		0.4	3.2
	+6	230		0.4	3.2

Tidal diamond marked on chart to show position the data refers to

Position of diamond

Tide direction —its set in °T

Tide strength— its drift— at springs (in knots)

Tide drift at neaps (in knots)

CHART INFORMATION

Tidal stream data is given on charts using tidal diamonds. These are marked on the chart and a table gives the strength and direction of the stream at that position for every hour of the tidal cycle related to the time of HW at the standard port.

WORKING THE TIDE

When planning a passage it is sensible to use the tide to your advantage. Aim to travel with the tide where possible and be aware of how a change in stream direction may affect conditions.

Tidal gates

In areas of strong tides you may encounter a "tidal gate." This may be a narrow passage, headland, or other obstruction to the tidal stream, where the stream is intensified as it meets the obstruction or constriction. At some tidal gates it may be difficult, impossible, or even dangerous to fight the tide, and there may be a number of hours in each tidal cycle when the gate is effectively closed. In these instances it is critical to time your arrival at the tidal gate to allow your onward passage, otherwise you may have no choice but to wait until the tidal stream moderates or changes.

At some gates, the stream may run for longer in one direction than in the other, making the timing more critical when going in the direction against the longest flow. Many almanacs and pilot books give information and advice about tidal gates in the area they cover.

Boat speed

Even in less difficult tidal situations, it is sensible to work the tide in a slow moving yacht, whether under sail or power. With a fairly typical boat speed of five knots, a two-knot stream running with you will give you a speed over the ground of seven knots, but only three knots if it is against you. If you have no option but to travel against a foul tide, then, if possible, stay in shallower water where the stream will be weaker. Conversely, if you have the benefit of the tidal stream, maximize the advantage by staying in deep water.

Sea state

Also be aware of the effect on sea state of the relative directions of wind and tide. A tidal stream running against even a moderate wind can create a steep and uncomfortable sea, while wind and stream running together result in much smoother sailing conditions.

WIND WITH TIDE
With the wind blowing with the tide the friction between wind and water is low and the sea remains fairly calm.

WIND AGAINST TIDE
With wind against tide, the friction between wind and water is greatly increased and waves are formed.

SHAPING A COURSE

The essence of navigating is setting a course to steer that will take you from your departure point to your destination. Known as shaping a course, this process is a vital skill for accurate and safe navigation offshore. To shape a course, the navigator requires a chart of the area, plotting tools, tidal-stream information, and a compass. He uses this equipment to plot the ground track he wants to achieve on the chart and to measure the bearings and distances for each leg of the trip. Finally, allowance must be made for tidal streams and leeway. Programming an electronic chart plotter may appear to be a simpler and quicker way to describe a course but the convenience factor is offset by potential pitfalls and traditional techniques should always be used as backup to electronic ones.

The ground track

The first step in shaping a course is to draw a line on the chart joining the departure point and the destination. This is called the ground track and is marked by two arrowheads. It is the course you want to follow, over the ground, to your destination. Check carefully along the line you have drawn to make sure that it does not pass over or near hazards or restricted areas. Next, measure the length of the track using the dividers to transfer the length of the line to the latitude scale at the side of the chart; never use the longitude scale (*p.315*).

If the length of the line to be measured is longer than the span of your dividers, set the dividers to a convenient length, using the latitude scale, and count the number of times you can step this length off along the line. Measure any odd length left over against the latitude scale. The length of the line, A–B (*opposite*), is the distance to your destination.

Next, assess how fast you believe your average speed will be. Studying the tidal streams and other factors you expect to encounter, together with familiarity with your boat's characteristics, will make this relatively straightforward. It is best to be pessimistic about your average boat speed; it is better to arrive early than to risk missing a tidal window or have to face a difficult landfall on a falling tide after dark.

Divide your total passage distance (A–B) by your anticipated speed to calculate the expected duration of your passage and hence an estimated time of arrival (ETA).

In the absence of tidal stream, or leeway, the ground track you have marked on the chart is the course you need to steer. You can measure its direction on the chart using a parallel ruler or plotter (*p.326*). You can use either °T or °M to measure direction, but be consistent in your choice and make sure that others involved in chart work know what you are working in. Write the distance and bearing of A–B alongside the line.

Course to steer

In the real world, it is rare that there are no external effects that you need to take into account. Even if there is no tidal stream, a sailing boat will always experience at least a small amount of leeway when sailing on upwind or reaching courses and this must be allowed for before you can give the helmsman a course to steer.

SYMBOLS

When plotting courses and positions on the chart, navigators use symbols in order to save space and avoid confusion. Standard symbols are shown below. You can devise your own if you wish, as long as everyone else doing chartwork on your boat understands your symbols and uses them consistently. Time is usually written using 24-hour-clock notation (e.g., 14:15) and should include the relevant time zone (e.g., 14:15 EST).

⊞	Waypoint
X	Dead reckoning position
△	Estimated position
→	Water track
→›	Ground track
→››	Tidal stream or current
⊙	Fix
←→	Position line
‹‹—››	Transferred position line

To allow for the effects of any tidal stream, you must obtain the set and drift of the stream from your chart or tidal atlas (pp.342–343). Plot these on the chart in what is known as a vector diagram (below).

This plotting exercise will give you the water track, marked by a single arrowhead, which denotes the course you want to follow through the water. Remember, however, that the boat does not actually follow the water track. It is important to have a mental picture of how your boat moves within the vector diagram. Your boat will not actually travel along the water track C–D, but will move, relative to the seabed, along the ground track A–B, while pointing in a direction parallel to the water track C–D as you steer to counteract the effect of the tidal stream pushing you off course. In the absence of leeway, the bearing of C–D is the course to steer.

Measure its bearing using a plotter or parallel rules, and convert to °C (p.325) before giving the course to the helmsman.

Allowing for leeway

If you are sailing with the wind forward of the beam, or are under power in strong beam winds, you will have to allow for the amount by which you are pushed sideways—your leeway. To estimate your boat's leeway angle, take a bearing on the boat's wake using the hand bearing compass (p.322). Compare this bearing with the reciprocal of your compass heading (add or subtract 180° to or from the compass heading). The difference is the leeway angle. Adjust the line C–D to windward by the amount of the predicted leeway angle. The angle is usually between five and ten degrees. By steering into the wind by this amount you will offset the leeway.

The amount of leeway will vary according to factors such as the shape of the hull, the type of rig, and the conditions. In practice, the adjustment is often made by calculation (above) rather than being drawn on the chart, but, to avoid confusion, you may wish to pencil in the wind direction and adjust C–D toward it. After you have allowed for leeway, apply any corrections required for variation and deviation to determine the compass course to steer in °C (pp.324–325).

ALLOWING FOR TIDAL STREAMS AND LEEWAY

In many situations, you will have to make allowances for a tidal stream. A tidal stream that is parallel to your ground track will not affect the course, but will affect the speed you achieve over the ground. For example, if your boat is sailing at 5 kn against a 2-kn tide, your speed over the ground will be reduced to 3 kn. On the other hand, a 2-kn tide running in the same direction as your course will give a speed over the ground of 7 kn. Quite often, the tide will be at an angle to your ground track, and you will have to adjust your course to avoid being pushed off track. This is done by drawing a vector diagram.

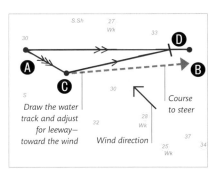

Draw the water track and adjust for leeway— toward the wind | Wind direction | Course to steer

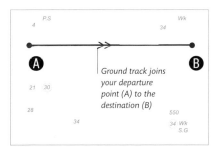

Ground track joins your departure point (A) to the destination (B)

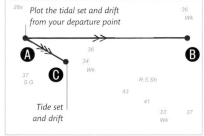

Plot the tidal set and drift from your departure point

Tide set and drift

❶ Draw a line from your departure point (A) to your destination (B). Mark it with two arrowheads. This is your desired ground track. Measure the distance A–B with dividers using the latitude scale at the side of the chart.

❷ With information from the tidal atlas, plot the direction of the tide's set, starting from point A. Use dividers and the latitude scale to measure along that line the expected drift in the next hour (C). Mark the line with three arrowheads.

❸ Open your dividers to the distance that you expect to sail within the next hour. Then place one point at C, and scribe an arc to cut through the line A–B at the point D. Now join together the points C–D and mark the line with a single arrowhead. This is the water track required to offset the effects of the tide in the next hour.

Now adjust the water track to windward by the amount of leeway to determine the course to steer. Finally, convert the calculation to °C. Do not make the common mistake of joining C to B rather than determining point D, with your dividers, on the ground track line A–B.

LONG PASSAGES

On a long passage in tidal waters you will encounter tidal streams that change hourly in set and drift. You can use one of two methods to deal with them.

Changing tides

If there are no hazards near the track, you can use a simple plotting process. First, estimate how long the passage will take. From your departure point (A), lay off the first hour of tide. Then, from the end of this line, lay off the next hour of tide and continue the process for as many hours as you estimate the passage will take. Open the dividers to the distance you expect to sail, then put one point on C and cut the track A–B. The line C–B is the water track for the whole passage. It can then be adjusted for leeway, variation, and deviation as normal.

If there are hazards close to your track, you will need to keep the boat close to the track at all times. Mark the first hour's tide and plot the course to steer for the first hour. From point D, lay off the second hour's tide and plot the course to steer for the second hour. Continue this process for the length of the passage. Each hour will require a different course to steer, but the boat will proceed along the desired ground track.

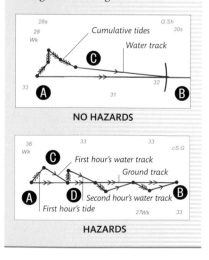

NO HAZARDS

HAZARDS

WAYPOINT NAVIGATION

If you have a GPS set available, you have the facility to use waypoint navigation techniques. In addition to continuously computing its current position, a GPS can store, as latitudes and longitudes, many (typically 100 or more) preprogrammed locations or "waypoints." When shaping a course a navigator may set up a "route" consisting of two or more waypoints.

A departure waypoint is set at a convenient location outside the departure harbor, and a destination waypoint is set in a safe location outside the destination harbor. In between, other waypoints can be defined at turning points, or to keep the yacht clear of hazards near the course. When on passage, the GPS can provide the navigator with the distance and bearing to the next waypoint, on a continuous basis.

Using waypoints

Before you start planning a passage using a GPS set, make sure it is set to the same datum as your paper or electronic chart (*p.315*). Draw the required course on the paper or electronic chart as a series of straight lines representing the safe ground track. Each change of direction is usually entered as a waypoint. Always take the time to run your eye along the ground track to ensure that it does not pass too close to any hazards. From the chart read off

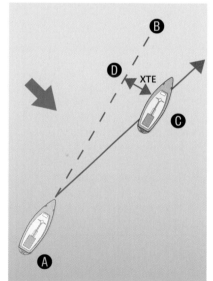

CROSS TRACK ERROR
The GPS can continuously monitor cross-track error (XTE). This is the amount the yacht has strayed laterally from its planned course due to poor steering, tidal stream effects, or leeway. Here, the plan was to travel from A to B but because of excessive leeway the boat has actually ended up at C. The GPS will display the XTE value CD.

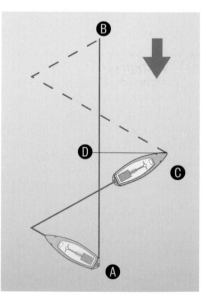

MEASURING VMG
VMG is the velocity with which you are closing on your objective. If this is upwind, you will be tacking and will not be able to point directly at your destination. However, VMG will indicate your progress. Here the destination is B. By dividing the "direct line" progress AD by the time elapsed to get to C, the GPS can calculate the VMG.

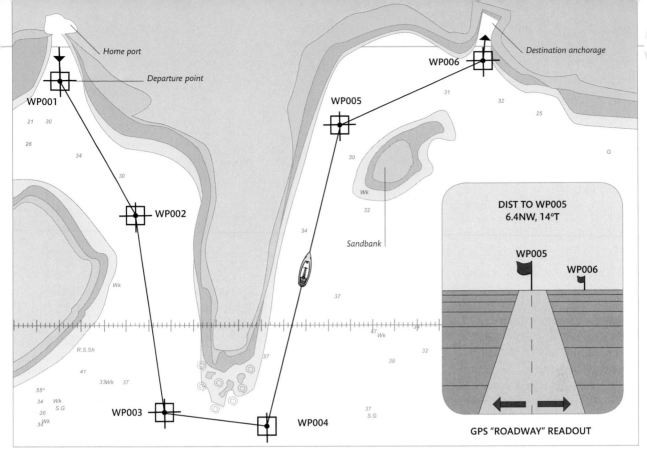

Home port

Departure point

WP001

21 30

28

34

30

WP002

Wk

R.S.Sh

41

3.3 Wk 37

55°

34 Wk S.G

36

34 Wk

WP003

WP004

WP005

30

Wk

32

34

Sandbank

37

47 Wk

37 S.G

38

32

31

32

25

G

WP006

Destination anchorage

DIST TO WP005
6.4NW, 14°T

WP005

WP006

GPS "ROADWAY" READOUT

FOLLOWING A ROUTE

Preprogrammed waypoints combine to form a route; they are the significant milestones on your passage that provide turning points and hazard avoidance marks. The GPS display can provide the navigator with a visual representation of progress, waypoint (WP) by waypoint.

the latitude and longitudes of each waypoint and program them into the GPS's memory. The GPS will calculate and display the bearing and distance between each waypoint, and a quick comparison against the chart will confirm that you have entered all the values correctly. It is easy to wrongly position a decimal point, transpose numbers, confuse longitudes east or west and latitudes north or south when entering the data, so double-check everything on the chart.

Many publications, including nautical almanacs, pilotage guides, and the yachting press, publish waypoint lists for navigational marks and popular locations. Be cautious about using published waypoints and do not enter them into your GPS set without checking them first (by plotting them on the chart) since typographical errors do occur. When creating waypoints, do not enter the charted position of a navigation mark but site your waypoint a short distance away, as otherwise there is a real danger you might actually hit the mark if an autopilot controlled by the GPS or chartplotter is steering the boat. Also, in busy cruising grounds other boats may be using the same waypoint, adding to the risk of collision. This is another reason not to use published waypoints but to select your own from the chart.

Do not forget that the GPS makes no allowance for tides, current, or leeway. It may seem easy to set the autopilot to follow the GPS to your destination, but it may result in a longer route that may take you some way from the required track. This is only acceptable if there are no hazards near the actual ground track. Another function available on the GPS can alert you to any deviation from the track. The GPS can measure cross track error (XTE) which is the lateral distance from the direct track between two waypoints. Knowing XTE allows you, or the autopilot, to continuously alter the heading to get back on track. The GPS can also monitor VMG—velocity made good—which tells you how fast you are proceeding toward the next waypoint. This may vary from your speed over the ground (SOG) due to tide, leeway, or if you are tacking upwind to your destination.

PLOTTING A POSITION

On any passage outside local waters, the prudent navigator must keep an accurate record of the course steered, distance run, times of course alterations, and the leeway experienced. These records are used to plot the position on the chart at regular intervals of about half an hour or an hour, unless you are well offshore where log intervals can be longer. This is very important even if electronic fixing aids are available; electrical systems and electronic equipment are vulnerable to failure on small boats.

Electronic instruments

A GPS set (*p.330*) can provide a continuous readout of the boat's position in latitude and longitude which, in most circumstances, is highly accurate. However, there are occasions when accuracy is degraded, and some instances of gross errors caused by serious system failures. These potential errors and risk of serious failure mean that the navigator must not rely exclusively on a GPS-derived position.

Even when the system is functioning accurately, a GPS display of latitude and longitude is of no use unless it is related to a chart. When using a GPS, regularly plot your position on a chart. Not only does this confirm that you are on course and proceeding according to plan, but it also provides an immediate backup navigational solution should the GPS fail. Wherever possible, confirm a GPS position using another method for fixing position (*pp.352–353*).

When a GPS set is connected to a chart plotter or PC, with appropriate navigational software (*p.321*), it will display your position continuously on an electronic chart. The plotter or navigation software can perform a range of navigational tasks, including showing your actual position compared to your intended track, and integrating with an autopilot to steer the boat along the required track. As helpful as these devices are, they cannot entirely replace conventional paper chart-based navigation. The paper-and-pencil approach needs no batteries, does not fail you when thrown around the saloon, and can even stand getting damp. It does not require sensitive equipment or sophisticated technology. By learning traditional navigational techniques you will have a deeper understanding of the forces at work since you will have assessed and applied them individually.

The logbook

The logbook is a vitally important record and must be kept up to date throughout the passage. Some electronic navigation systems automatically record an electronic logbook, which can be very useful,

Time Make log entries at regular intervals		*Course* Detail course required and course actually steered				*Remarks* Include any useful observations
TIME	**LOG**	**COURSE REQUIRED**	**COURSE STEERED**	**WIND**	**BARO**	**REMARKS**
2230	574	060°C	065°C	SW2	1005	Extremely misty and damp
0000	582	060°C	060°C	SW4	1005	Six knots regularly
0045	588	060°C	060°C	SW4	1005	Yacht in sight starboard bow
0200	594	060°C	060°C	SW4	1005	Watch change

Log Use the log reading to measure progress | *Wind* Record wind strength and direction | *Barometric pressure* Can be used to forecast weather

LOGBOOK
A simple ruled notebook will make a perfectly adequate logbook, or you can purchase a specially designed logbook.

but it is also essential to maintain a paper logbook as your primary record. Do not neglect log keeping or plotting your position on the chart because you trust your electronic aids. In the event of equipment failure, your written logbook will ensure that you can estimate your current position.

The logbook should be updated regularly and include distance run, course ordered and course achieved, estimated leeway, time of every course change, and details of fixes. The logbook must have two columns for course—required course and actual course—because it is often not possible to steer the ideal course to an objective. Each time the log is filled in, the helmsman should be asked for an honest assessment of the average course steered. Remember, you should only expect a helmsman to be able steer within 5 degrees or so of the required course.

If the destination is upwind, you will not be able to steer a direct course. In this case, you must log the course achieved and note the time, new heading, and log reading every time you tack.

Dead reckoning

The most basic way of estimating position is known as dead reckoning. It ignores any tidal or other factors and relies solely on the most basic information—your course and speed.

If you know your starting point and the speed and direction traveled, you can fix your position using dead reckoning. From your last known position, draw a line on the chart, using a plotter or parallel ruler, in the direction you have traveled since you were at that position. Be sure to convert the compass course to a true or magnetic bearing (depending on how you prefer to work on the chart) before you plot it on the chart. Mark

the line with a single arrowhead to show that it is the water track. Measure along this line, using a pair of dividers, the distance you have sailed from the last position, according to the log reading. This point is your dead reckoning (DR) position. Mark it with a short line across the track, and record the time and log reading beside it. If there is no tidal stream or current, this should be a reasonably accurate assessment of the yacht's position at that time.

In theory, the DR position should be plotted before allowing for leeway. However, in practice, it is easier to allow for it before plotting the course but after correcting for deviation and variation. Remember to apply the leeway correction to leeward of the course steered.

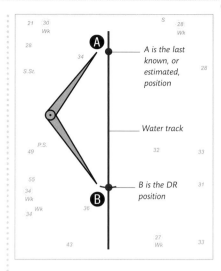

PLOTTING A DR POSITION
From known point (A), plot the water track and mark it with one arrowhead. Measure off the distance sailed according to the log and mark the DR position (B).

OTHER USES FOR THE LOGBOOK

The logbook is not merely used for navigational purposes; it also records other activities and data relating to the boat or passage. Before each trip note the date, where you are heading, where you are leaving from, and other related information. Record the names and onboard responsibilities of all crewmembers. Also record next of kin details. If you are traveling between countries, include crew information that you may be asked for by officials, such as passport numbers, dates and places of birth, nationality, etc.

Keeping a record

Each watch change should be noted so it is clear who is in charge at all times. You may also want to record barometer readings, wind direction and strength, cloud cover, and other general comments. Over time these observational details will confirm your impressions that conditions may be deteriorating or clearing up. The rate of change of barometric pressure, as shown by the pressure readings that are recorded every hour, will give you a good indication of the wind strength that you will soon encounter.

The logbook is also a good way of monitoring the hours of operation of engines, generators, water-makers, battery life, and other technical equipment. This will help you organize appropriate maintenance and servicing schedules. If you are concerned about a particular aspect of the boat's operation or systems, you can use the logbook to record and monitor the matter that is concerning you. For instance, if you believe you may have a slight water leak, you should make a point of inspecting the bilges each time you make a log entry; in this way you will become aware of the underlying trend and be able to make an informed assessment about the suspected problem. You might also record details each time you resupply with diesel and water. This will allow you to keep track of costs and could, potentially, identify leaks.

ESTIMATED POSITION

An estimated position (EP) is plotted from the DR position by applying the effects of any predicted tidal stream to the DR position. Using the tidal stream information on the chart or from a tidal atlas, work out the set (the direction the tide is moving) and amount of drift (distance the tide has flowed) since the time you were at your last known position. Then, from the DR position, plot the set of the tide by drawing a line on the correct heading and marking it with three arrowheads. Remember that tidal data is tabulated in °T. Using the dividers

and latitude scale on the chart, measure the amount of tide drift along the tide line. Draw a triangle with a dot in the middle to mark the point and record the time and the log reading alongside it. This is your EP at the time that the DR was recorded.

When in coastal waters you should record heading, distance, and other log information every half an hour or each hour, depending on the complexity of the navigation requirements. When you next record the distance sailed and heading, you should plot another DR and EP position. Plotting hourly works well as tidal information is based on hourly segments. If you can align the times of your data recording with the times of tidal change it makes it easier to plot the tidal information to create an EP.

To plot successive DRs and EPs, start from the previous EP position and plot the next DR, then plot the tidal set and drift to get the next EP.

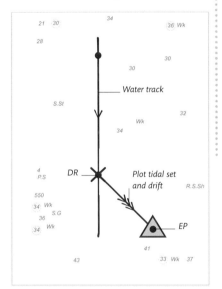

PLOTTING AN EP
Once you have plotted a DR position you can plot an EP by allowing for any tidal effect. From the DR position, plot the set and drift of the tide for the last hour to find the EP.

Predictive EP

Knowing your boat speed, heading, and prevailing tidal influence will not only allow you to precalculate where you expect to end up but also the track you will take to get there. This can be very useful if sailing near hazards as it can help confirm one way or the other whether you will approach a danger too closely and allow you to alter course in good time.

Errors

Navigation is not the exact science that electronic devices can make it appear; it is as much about assessing the likely level of accuracy at any time as it is about knowing the absolutes of your position and passage. Navigation errors arise for a variety of reasons—the difficulty of steering an accurate course, a log under-reading in calm conditions or over-reading in rough seas, uncalibrated instruments, or an inexperienced helmsman. Some arise from undue haste, misreading tables such as tidal diamond information, or forgetting to allow for local time corrections. Plotting errors can be minimized by using sharp, soft-leaded pencils—2B pencils are usually recommended as they can be sharpened to a good point and the lines they produce can be easily erased.

In all cases, double-check your workings, reread data and, above all, take your time. Errors are

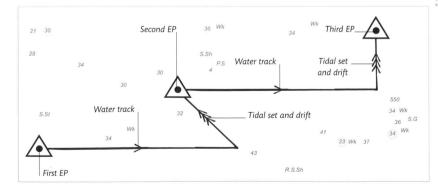

PLOTTING SUCCESSIVE EPS
Once you have plotted your first estimated position and are satisfied that you have taken into account possible errors, you can use it to plot subsequent EPs. Plot the water track since the last EP. Measure the distance sailed since then, before plotting tidal set and drift.

inevitable, so you must learn how to take them into account when navigating. Practice and hone your precision in reading tables and charts on dry land so that you are confident that you can be accurate without having to double check all your calculations.

Assessing errors

The longer the boat sails without a confirmed position fix (pp.352–357), the more important it is that errors are allowed for. Otherwise, the resulting EP could become very unreliable.

Make a list of possible errors and estimate their maximum effect, concentrating on course steered, distance sailed, leeway, and tidal information. Pencil in any errors you think are possible and use them to create a circular area of possible position. This is a much more realistic approach than assuming you are at the single point suggested by your EP. In heavy weather or when battling strong tides or against poor sea states, the diameter of this circle of uncertainty can be as much as 10 percent of

the distance traveled from the last known position. For safety, always assume that you are at the point within your circle of uncertainty closest to any nearby hazard and shape your next course accordingly. As the circle of uncertainty widens with distance, the clearance given to navigational hazards must also increase to ensure that even the most pessimistic prediction keeps you away from danger. Whenever you can, obtain a reliable and accurate fix to clarify your position and so eliminate the circle of uncertainty.

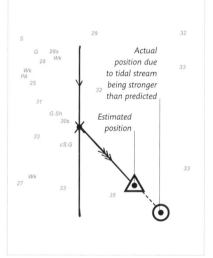

ESTIMATED AND ACTUAL

This fix reveals that the set of the tide is stronger than predicted. Use this new information to shape the next course and to plot the next EP.

Area of uncertainty
Plot your next course from the point closest to any hazards

PLOTTING ERRORS

Estimate possible errors in the course steered and the distance sailed. A course error would put you to one side or other of your track, whereas a log error would affect the distance you are along the track. Plot possible errors to get an area of likely position.

INCREASING CIRCLES OF UNCERTAINTY

Here, the yacht is on passage in rough weather and poor visibility. After 30 minutes the EP puts it 4 nm along the track with a circle of uncertainty of around ten percent of the distance traveled (i.e., a radius of 0.4 nm). At 1300 the increasing area of uncertainty suggests a position close to shallows. The EP is logged as being close to the danger. Later, the boat is passing rocks. By now the circle of uncertainty has opened up to a radius of 2.1 nm. Again, the worst-case scenario is assumed and the EP is plotted near the rocks. When a fix is obtained, the area of uncertainty can be eliminated.

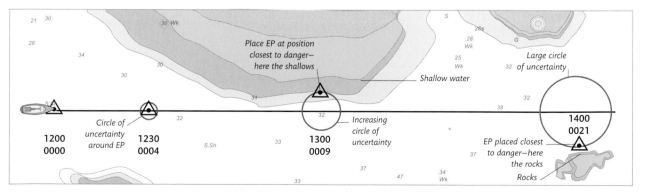

FIXING A POSITION

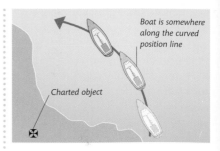

No matter how accurately you plot your estimated position (EP) on a passage, errors will always occur, making your exact position increasingly uncertain. To confirm position, a navigator periodically fixes the position of the yacht in relation to known objects. This is simplest to do when close to a charted sea- or landmark, when you can often determine your exact position by eye. In other cases, fixes can be obtained with a variety of instruments, such as a GPS set, radar, hand bearing compass, or even a depth sounder.

CURVED POSITION LINE
If the distance to a charted object (range) is measured using a rangefinder, a sextant, or a radar set, the position line is a curve, with its radius centred on the object.

Using electronic aids

Most cruising yachts today have a GPS set that offers the ability to obtain a continuous readout of position. However, it is vital that the navigator is able to fix the yacht's position without relying on the GPS in case the set, the boat's electrics, or the system should fail.

Even if the GPS is functioning properly, it is important to double-check its accuracy periodically and confirm your position using another means of fixing position. Learning to use other fixing techniques is also very satisfying and improves your skills. Try to obtain a fix using two or more methods whenever possible.

Position lines

If you are alongside a charted mark, you know exactly where you are and can confidently plot a fix on the chart. At other times, a navigator must obtain a fix by producing a minimum of two position lines. To do this, you need to measure either the bearing or the distance of a known object that is shown on the chart, and then plot the resulting line on the chart. Measuring the bearing of an object produces a straight position line (*below*), whereas measuring the distance of an object produces a curved one (*above*).

There are several ways in which a navigator can obtain position lines. These include using a hand bearing

compass, identifying a transit (*p.333*), watching a light just clearing the horizon, using the depth sounder, or using a GPS or radar set (*p.357*).

Single position lines

A single position line will not be sufficient to give you an accurate fix. You need to cross it with a second, and preferably a third, as an error check. However, a single line does tell you that the boat is situated somewhere along that line. Also, if the position line is at right angles to your track, it will confirm how far along the track you are, while if it is parallel to the track it will show if you are on the track or to

SINGLE POSITION LINE

A single position line can tell you only that the boat is located somewhere along the bearing drawn on the chart from the mark.

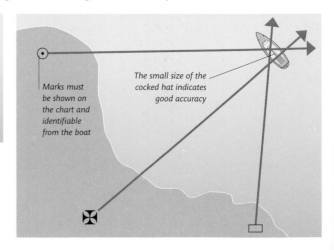

THREE-POINT FIX

Three visible objects that are also marked on the chart can be used to give you an accurate fix. If possible, choose objects that are about 60° apart, take their bearings, and plot the position lines from them on the chart. The size of the triangle ("cocked hat") that they form is a good guide to the accuracy of the fix.

one side or the other. Single position lines formed by a transit are very useful when you are less interested in your actual position but need an accurate direction along which to proceed. This is especially useful when entering harbors, or as a clearing line (p.333).

Choosing marks

Before you can plot a visual fix, you must identify two or three sea- or landmarks on the chart that are within sight. Nautical charts not only include buoyage but also show the locations of conspicuous chimneys, church spires, and other land-based objects. If these are in sight, use them in preference to buoys which can be physically moved, dragged in storms, or influenced by strong tidal streams.

It is preferable to use three marks, since any error is much more obvious. If you are using only two objects, try to pick marks that are about 90 degrees apart, as this will give the most accurate result. If you use three marks, it is best if they are about 60 degrees apart. Choosing marks that are quite close to the boat will increase your accuracy: if you are a long way from the mark, a typical error of just 3 degrees in the bearing will produce a significant positional error. If you are close to the mark, however, the error will be much less. It is vital that you identify the correct marks on the chart, or the fix will be worthless.

Compass bearings

Take bearings using the hand bearing compass from a point on the boat that is known to be free of deviation (p.325). Brace yourself securely and take three bearings on each mark; it is helpful if someone else writes down the bearings as you take them. Before you can plot the position lines, you must use the three readings to calculate the average bearing of each mark. If you plot in °T on the chart, you must correct the compass bearing by applying variation (p.324). Plot the position line on the chart by drawing a line through the object on the correct bearing.

Remember that the bearing from the object to the yacht is the reciprocal of the bearing you measured. Add or subtract 180 degrees from a bearing to calculate the reciprocal. You must work methodically but quickly to eliminate errors that may occur if you take your bearings some minutes apart. Clearly, the faster you are traveling, the less time you have to record all your data. However, there will be an obvious order in which to take your fixes; the bearing to a chosen mark ahead or astern of you will change less than one to the side of your course.

As the process will take a certain amount of time, the fix, when plotted, will already be historical as you will have moved farther down your track.

Cocked hat

When you take bearings of three marks, it is very unlikely that the three position lines will meet at one point. Instead, they will probably form a triangle. This is known as a "cocked hat." The size of the cocked hat is a good guide to accuracy—the smaller it is, the better. If your fix results in a large cocked hat, then a mistake has been made, either in selecting the correct mark, taking the bearings, or in plotting the bearings on the chart. Make sure you have plotted the bearings correctly, and if so, check that the marks you can see are really the ones shown on the chart. If so, repeat the procedure to obtain a new set of bearings. You will find that accuracy will improve with practice.

Draw a circle around the triangle and label it with the time and log reading. For added safety, assume that your position is at the corner of the triangle that lies closest to any hazard. You should then shape the next course from that point.

BEARING ERRORS

When you take a compass bearing of an object, there is always the possibility of errors because of the difficulty in holding a compass steady on a moving deck. Small bearing errors are inevitable, and will result in larger positional errors when the object is far away. Take bearings on closer objects, when possible, to minimize errors.

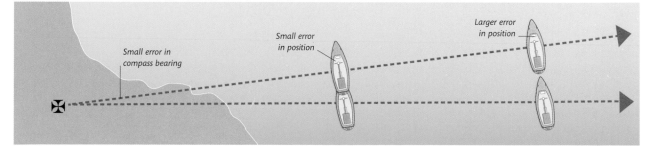

Small error in compass bearing

Small error in position

Larger error in position

A fix by GPS

A GPS set measures its precise position from three or more satellites and calculates the intersection point—your location—of the curved position lines obtained. A differential GPS set offers increased accuracy by using radio signals from a base station to refine the satellite signals and reduce built-in errors (*p.330*).

It is vital to be aware that GPS signals may be degraded and may sometimes be completely unavailable. It is essential that you do not rely on the availability or accuracy of GPS so always double-check the information against an EP or a fix obtained from another source. A GPS set displays the boat's position in degrees, minutes, and tenths of a minute of latitude and longitude. However, this is not usually the best type of display for the small-boat navigator. Plotting

a latitude and longitude position on the chart can be awkward and lead to errors. A better way is to find a suitable sea- or landmark near the track, and program its latitude and longitude into the GPS as a waypoint. The GPS can then be set to display the boat's position as a bearing and distance from the waypoint, which is much easier for the navigator to plot on the chart.

The chosen mark can be the center of a nearby compass rose which makes it very easy and quick to plot the resulting position. Once you have plotted the fix, mark it with a circle and dot, plus the time and log reading. Check the depth from your depth sounder to give a secondary confirmation of your position. Then take an overview look at the chart. Does the GPS fix seem reasonable?

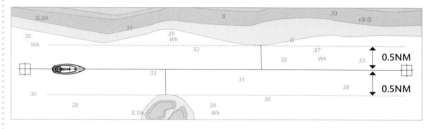

USING A CROSS TRACK ERROR LADDER

A cross track error (XTE) ladder can assist in keeping your craft away from dangers. Here, as the boat proceeds down a channel, an XTE alarm set at 0.5 nm will ensure that you follow the safe track and keep you clear of all potential obstructions.

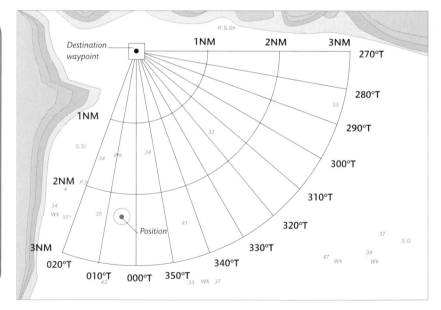

GPS DISPLAY

Even the simplest GPS can display much useful data. This handheld GPS set is showing an electronic compass, digital reading of heading, speed over the ground, total trip mileage, altitude (not really useful at sea), position, and time.

DRAWING A WAYPOINT WEB

A web of bearing lines and distance arcs drawn on the chart or pilotage plan in advance of your passage makes it very simple to plot your position quickly. This technique is invaluable if you are traveling fast or if you need to concentrate your attention on a difficult pilotage situation. If, in the example above, the GPS display shows a bearing of 005°T and distance of 2.5 nm to the destination waypoint, it is very easy to quickly plot your position on the web without drawing lines or measuring distances.

Does the depth tally with the charted value? Are you where you expect to be? Compare the GPS fix with the EP. If there is a discrepancy, check back through your workings for errors. If this does not reveal an answer, double-check your position by using another source of information.

Other ways of using GPS

The final waypoint of your passage may be in the mouth of your destination harbor. From that point draw a web of straight line bearings at suitable intervals—5° or 10°—and arcs of distance–between 0.25 nm and 1 nm is typical. As you approach your destination, set your GPS to display range and bearing to this waypoint and you have the means to fix your position very quickly. This technique is invaluable when you need to concentrate on visual pilotage to enter harbor safely.

Another technique uses the GPS's cross track error (XTE) facility. Draw a ladder of XTE either side of your track between two waypoints. By setting the GPS to display the distance to the next waypoint, or from the last one, together with the XTE, you can quickly fix your position on the chart. The XTE alarm will also help you avoid hazards.

If your GPS set is linked to an electronic chartplotter, the chartplotter will be able to continuously display the yacht's position on the chart, together with any waypoints that have been programmed into either the GPS or the chartplotter. Typically, the

RADAR OVERLAY ON CHART
Identifying objects on a radar screen takes skill and experience, and it is worth getting training in using the system. Having the facility of overlaying the radar picture on an electronic chart can make the identification of objects much easier.

boat's position is locked at the center of the screen and the chart display scrolls under the boat's position.

Using radar

A radar set is one of the most useful tools on a small boat since it assists with position fixing and avoiding collisions. Radar enables the navigator to measure bearings and distances of objects that are displayed on the radar screen. If the objects are fixed and can be positively identified on the chart a fix can be obtained. If the objects are other vessels, the operator can identify their course, the point of closest approach, and whether they represent a collision hazard.

Using radar effectively requires skill and experience, and it is worth taking a training course to develop your skills. Radar reflections from coastlines can be confusing, making identification of objects on screen difficult, and reflections from buoys can be hard to separate from the "clutter" created by a rough sea or heavy rain.

Radar bearings are not as accurate as radar ranges because the width of the radar beam causes the images of the objects it encounters to be stretched laterally. This makes it difficult to know exactly where to take the bearing from. A far better radar fix will result from using the system's ranging capabilities,

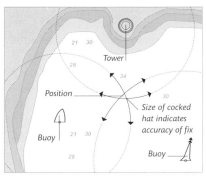

RADAR POSITION FIXING
By noting the ranges of three or more identifiable radar targets in quick succession you can fix your position where the three range arcs cross.

since radar is much more accurate at measuring distance. First, record the distance of two, or preferably three, objects that you can positively identify and which are shown on the chart. Then plot these ranges on the chart as curved position lines using a pair of drawing compasses. The boat's position is fixed where the curved lines of position intersect. The size of the cocked hat signals the accuracy of the fix. If your instrument system incorporates a radar set, and allows the radar image to be overlaid on the chart, it is much easier to identify objects and create a fix from radar ranges.

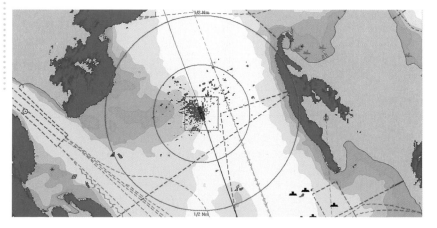

Distance off

When you know the distance of the boat from a mark, you can use it to plot a position line. Whereas a bearing on a mark produces a straight line of position, a distance off a mark gives a curved line of position. Curved position lines can be combined with other curved or straight position lines, obtained by any means, to give a fix.

Distance off can be obtained from a radar range (*p.355*) or by using a visual rangefinder or a sextant. At night, you can obtain distance off by observing the light from a lighthouse when it first appears or disappears over the horizon as you sail toward or away from it (*below*). Once you have obtained a distance off an object, set your drawing compass to the distance. With one point of the compass on the object on the chart, draw the curved position line.

Calculating height

On charts, the heights of lighthouses and other landmarks are given as height above mean high water spring tide (MHWS; *p.341*). To work out the object's actual height above sea level at any time, you must calculate the height of tide at that time (*p.340*). Deduct the height from the height of MHWS as shown in the almanac. Add the result to the charted height of the lighthouse or other object. If the height of tide is higher than the MHWS level, subtract the difference from the charted height.

Using depth soundings

A depth sounder is a useful but often forgotten device for checking on a fix deduced from other sources. On occasions, it can also be used to obtain a position line. Using a depth finder in this way is easiest if the instrument is set to show the water's depth from the surface. Check that yours is not set to measure the depth from the bottom of the keel or the transducer level.

Checking fixes with soundings

Before using the depth sounder for checking fixes, you must convert the depth observed to a sounding at chart datum (*p.315*). This is known as a reduction to soundings. To do this, use the tidal curves (*p.340*) for the nearest standard port to find out the current height of tide above chart datum. Subtract the current height of the tide from the observed depth to get the figure at chart datum. Now compare this with the sounding marked on the chart at your fix position. If they agree, you have a useful confirmation of your fix. If they are different, you should check your calculations and confirm the position using another information source.

A fix from soundings

Depth soundings can also be used to create a fix. Although this type of fix is not very accurate, it is valuable in fog or when other fixing aids are not available. This method works best when you are sailing into shallower or deeper water across the depth contours as marked on the chart. Note the time, course, and log reading, and take a depth sounding. Hold a steady course and take a depth sounding at regular intervals, noting the time and log reading on each occasion. Once you have a series of depths, reduce them to soundings as for checking fixes.

Now, you can use the results to plot your position. The easiest way to plot soundings is to lay a piece of tracing paper on the chart, aligning its edges with lines of latitude and longitude. Plot the boat's water track on the tracing paper between the first and last soundings. Then plot

LIGHTS RISING OR DIPPING

A light rising or dipping on the horizon can be used at night to obtain a position line or a fix. If you are approaching a charted lighthouse, note the time the light—not its loom (reflected light)—first appears above the horizon. When you first see the light, note the time and take a bearing on it with the hand bearing compass. You will need to know your height of eye above the water.

❶ Note the charted height of the light and allow for the height of tide to get the actual height. With your height of eye, and the light's height, use the almanac's tables to find your distance off the lighthouse.

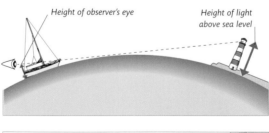

Height of observer's eye
Height of light above sea level

❷ Plot the bearing of the lighthouse on the chart and, with the dividers set to the distance off the lighthouse, scribe an arc (A) to cut the bearing. This is the boat's position at the time the light first rose above the horizon.

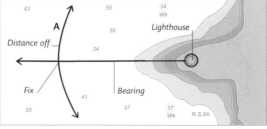

43   55   34 Wk
A   36   Lighthouse
Distance off   34
Fix   41   Bearing
33   37   37 Wk   R.S.Sh

the ground track by applying tidal set and drift. Mark the log readings along the water track. From these points, draw lines running parallel to the tidal vector and cutting the ground track.

At the points on the ground track, write the depth readings reduced to soundings. Slide the tracing paper over the chart until the first depth sounding is at the EP when the first sounding was taken. Keep the tracing paper aligned with the lines of latitude and longitude. The depth soundings should now agree with the charted depths. If they do not, move the tracing paper around until you find a good match. If there is no other good match nearby, the last depth reading indicates the position at the time of the reading.

TIME	LOG	DISTANCE BETWEEN SOUNDINGS	SOUNDINGS IN METERS
0640	55.1	–	46 m
0650	56.0	0.9	38 m
0700	56.9	0.9	25 m
0710	58.0	1.1	17 m
0720	59.1	1.1	10 m

FIX BY SOUNDINGS

On tracing paper, plot the water track and the tidal set and drift to obtain the ground track. Mark the log readings on the water track. Then draw lines parallel to the tide vector to cut the ground track. Write the depth soundings at these points. Position the tracing paper on the chart with the first depth sounding at the EP where the sounding was taken. The last depth reading indicates the position at the time the reading was taken.

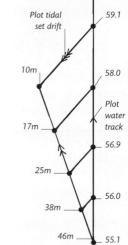

TRANSFERRED POSITION LINES

There are occasions, such as when you are sailing along a coastline, when there is only one identifiable sea- or landmark in sight. In such cases, it is possible to obtain a useful fix using two position lines taken at different times on the same mark. This is known as a running fix or a transferred position line.

Plotting and accuracy

This type of fix will be as good as your plotting skills and the accuracy that course, speed, and tidal data allows. It also relies on the helmsman to steer a steady course between the two bearings. Take the first bearing as you approach the mark, and the second one when you have passed it and its bearing has changed by up to 90 degrees. You must note the time and the log reading when you take each bearing. The use of GPS to fix position has reduced the need for this type of fix, but it is still a useful way of practicing essential skills.

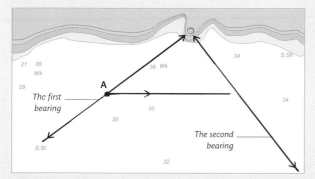

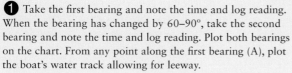

❶ Take the first bearing and note the time and log reading. When the bearing has changed by 60–90°, take the second bearing and note the time and log reading. Plot both bearings on the chart. From any point along the first bearing (A), plot the boat's water track allowing for leeway.

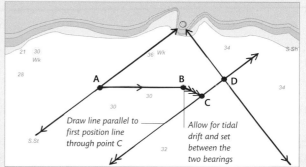

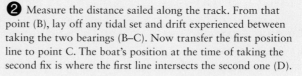

❷ Measure the distance sailed along the track. From that point (B), lay off any tidal set and drift experienced between taking the two bearings (B–C). Now transfer the first position line to point C. The boat's position at the time of taking the second fix is where the first line intersects the second one (D).

PASSAGE SKILLS

Once you have learned the individual navigational skills of pilotage, shaping and plotting a course, and fixing a position, you will be ready to navigate on an extended offshore passage. The navigator's job begins well before the cruise itself: you need to plan the trip carefully and make sure that you have all the relevant up-to-date charts, pilot books, and other references that you may need on passage. You must also prepare contingency plans to cope with rough weather or fog and to provide alternative harbors of refuge.

A complete passage

Navigation from one harbor to another starts with an outgoing pilotage plan for leaving harbor and reaching a safe, clear-water position, called the departure point. From this point, the navigator shapes the course required to reach the destination. During the passage, the navigator periodically works up an estimated position (EP; *p.350*), obtains fixes (*pp.352–355*), and evaluates any errors found, to check that the boat is staying close to the required ground track.

Once the boat reaches an offshore point close to its destination, the navigator commences in-going pilotage to guide the boat safely into harbor and to a berth. Navigation does not cease until the boat is tied up or at anchor. For instance, a harbormaster may allocate you a visitor's berth in an unfamiliar location and the navigator will need to quickly identify the location and assess prevailing currents and wind direction to suggest the best manner and direction of approach.

Planning a passage

To plan a passage, start with a small-scale chart that shows both the departure point and the destination.

Pencil the required tracks on the chart and identify the position of any point at which you will make a course alteration. If you have a GPS set, program these points into it as waypoints. Make sure that they are clear of hazards, and double-check their latitude and longitude.

Be sure to study the detail of any complicated or unfamiliar sections of your passage by referring to larger scale charts that show much more detail than small-scale charts. Never attempt to create a pilotage plan in or out of harbor from a small-scale chart, as important detail is likely to be missed.

Passage length

Consider the length of the passage and calculate approximately how long your journey will take. To do this you will need to estimate your likely boat speed. Always be pessimistic about this; it is better to arrive early and perhaps have to wait for the tide to rise sufficiently to enter harbor or berth in a marina, than it is to have to rush into harbor to catch the tide or to miss it completely.

Consider how the length of your passage fits in with the hours of daylight, and convenient departure and arrival times. Even if there is little chance that you will need to sail in the hours of darkness, check that all your navigational lights are functioning correctly.

Tide planning

Check the times of high and low water at the departure and destination ports and work out the strength and direction of the tidal streams during the time you will be on passage.

Work out whether the tidal stream will be a help or a hindrance to your journey. If you will have to fight a foul tide at some stage of your trip, is there a better time or place to be when this occurs? Perhaps you need to consider breaking your journey to avoid a period of foul tide. Review your information and consider whether any of it suggests a better time to leave, even if it means an early start or an overnight passage. You may discover that the trip would be better left to another day particularly if you need to negotiate a tidal gate (*p.343*). An alternative destination may be more suitable for the days you plan to sail.

Other considerations

Check the weather forecast for a few days leading up to your departure day. The trend in the weather is as important as the actual conditions. Is the weather favorable? Will the wind direction mean you have to beat to your destination? How is the wind likely to combine with the tidal drift? Will you encounter lengthy periods of choppy sea as the wind blows counter to the tide? If the weather is good, but has only recently moderated, has it left remnants of a big sea for you to contend with? If the weather is changeable, are you going to be able to sustain your course if the wind

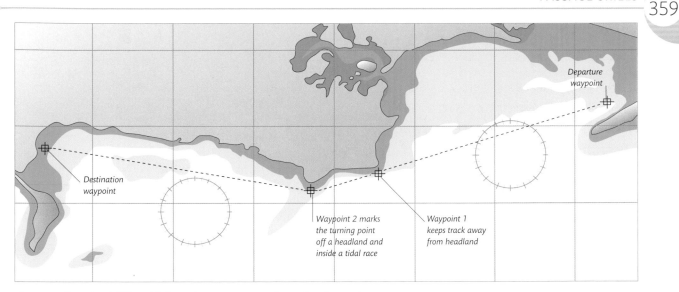

Destination waypoint

Waypoint 2 marks the turning point off a headland and inside a tidal race

Waypoint 1 keeps track away from headland

Departure waypoint

changes direction? What if there is no wind? How far can you, or are you prepared, to motor? Are there suitable safe harbors en route in case of emergencies, or for rest and shelter?

Finally, are the boat and crew prepared? Do you have enough food, water, fuel, and other supplies to get you comfortably to the next opportunity to restock? Is the boat sturdy enough for the passage? Are the crew up to the challenge?

There are many questions that need answering for a thorough passage plan, but it is important that you consider them all before finalizing your plans. Once you are sure that your plan is sensible and achievable then you can make your final preparations.

Ensuring a safe passage

Carefully check along your track on the chart to make sure that it is clear of dangers. Adjust it as necessary to keep away from any charted hazards such as shallows, overfalls, or tide races. Note any traffic separation areas and, if you have to cross one, plan to do so with the boat's heading at right angles to the lane. Make sure you consider the best time to cross a traffic zone

or pass through a hazardous area. Decide whether it is better to be in the area during daylight or night, and whether you will require all hands on deck at that time. Consider any implications for the watch system.

Making passage notes

Once you are satisfied with the track, transfer your plan to a notebook so that you can refer to it easily during the passage. A section of the logbook can be used for this purpose but a separate notebook is better as it can be taken on deck without risk to the logbook. Calculate the total distance of the passage and the distance between turning points or waypoints.

Note all track bearings between turning points and the details of all navigation marks that you expect to see along the way. Don't forget to jot down the light characteristics for buoys and other navigational aids you may encounter if there is any likelihood of being at sea in darkness.

List the times and heights of low and high water for each of the areas and days you will be sailing. Then mark up the tidal atlas with the correct times on each page, starting at the page for high water. Remember

SMALL-SCALE CHART
Whether using a paper chart or an electronic chartplotter, select a small-scale chart that shows both your departure point and destination. Pencil in the route on a paper chart or enter it onto an electronic chart, identify waypoints, and check for hazards near the track.

that the time for HW is considered to be the middle of the hour of high water. So, if the time for HW is given as 1200, the hour of high water runs from 1130–1230. Similarly, the hour HW+1 runs from 1230–1330.

Finally, make notes about your destination harbor from the pilot book. You should aim to be familiar with all aspects of the passage before you start. Consider what could go wrong and the consequences. If you need to take shelter in an intermediate harbor, have pilotage plans ready.

Check that all charts and reference books are on board, and that your VHF radio is working. Just before departure, inform the coast guard of your plans so that they can alert rescue services if you do not arrive as planned. Make sure you inform them when you reach your destination.

Navigating to windward

If your destination lies to windward, it will be impossible for the navigator to shape a course to steer as the boat will have to beat to windward. This means that the heading will be determined by the course that the helmsman can steer close-hauled, and it will change every time the boat tacks. In this situation, the navigator concentrates on recording the course steered, and periodically plots an estimated position, the accuracy of which will depend on how well the helmsman estimates the course sailed.

When you beat to windward, there is always a chance that the wind will shift to one side or the other. If you get too far to one side of the direct course, you may lose out because of an adverse shift. To minimize this risk and fully exploit gains from beneficial wind shifts, draw tack limiting lines on the chart and stay within them.

Using electronic aids

Modern chart plotters can store the whole passage plan for you, guide you from waypoint to waypoint, and even pilot you in and out of harbor. However, you should always have a backup system available and you should avoid becoming obsessed with the virtual rather than real world. Regard these electronic tools as extremely useful but understand that they may let you down. That said, their ability to utilize waypoints and an electronic track does offer new techniques that can be useful on passage. If you are passing a hazard, you can set the cross track error alarm to a distance that will alert you if you are drifting too far from the track or toward a hazard. Isolated dangers or large areas to avoid can be "cordoned off" with avoidance waypoints so that at all times you have a range and bearing to the nearest hazard.

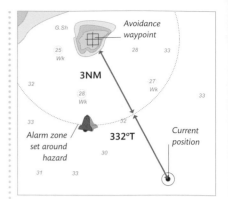

AVOIDANCE WAYPOINT

By plotting a waypoint on a charted hazard and monitoring the distance and bearing from it, you will always know your position relative to the danger. Here, an alarm has been set to ring if the distance falls below 3nm.

A strategically placed waypoint can also offer you an electronic clearing bearing, keeping you away from a potential danger. In these situations waypoints are used as warning marks, not as navigational marks to be aimed at. If you set up your system in this way, be sure your crew doesn't use the avoidance waypoints as targets to steer toward.

As the GPS continuously monitors your position it can derive your speed over the ground, rather than your speed through the water as shown by your log. This means it is easy to determine your real progress. If you are beating to windward in a series of long tacks it can be difficult to know how fast you are closing on your destination. However, the GPS can calculate this for you. The velocity made good (VMG) gives your actual straight-line speed toward the next waypoint. Knowing how well you are doing is vital on passage. If things are not going according to plan, it is good to know as soon as possible so contingencies can be considered.

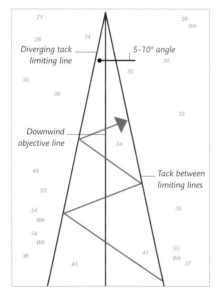

DIVERGING TACK LIMITERS

For sailing short distances to windward, draw a line on the chart downwind from the objective, then draw two lines on either side, diverging by 5–10° from the center line. Tack each time your EP or GPS fix reaches a tack limiting line.

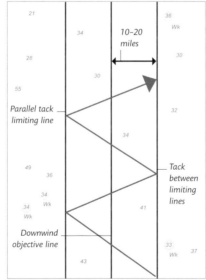

PARALLEL TACK LIMITERS

For sailing short distances to windward, draw a line on the chart downwind from the objective, then draw two lines on either side, diverging by 5–10° from the center line. Tack each time your EP or GPS fix reaches a tack limiting line.

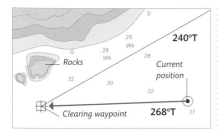

ELECTRONIC CLEARING BEARING
Place an electronic waypoint where it can provide a clearing bearing. Here the clearing bearing is 240°T. At the current position the waypoint bears 268°T which is safe, but if it drops below 240°T you could be in danger of running aground.

Rough-weather passages

In rough weather, the navigator has to work down below while the boat is pitching and heeling. Experience and a resistance to seasickness are great advantages in this situation. However, you should also try to limit the time you spend at the chart table by doing as much passage and contingency planning as possible before setting off.

Rough weather can quickly lead to tiredness, particularly in an inexperienced crew, which increases the risk of mistakes. Take time to double-check all information and remember to allow for steering errors and log errors, which tend to be more significant in difficult conditions.

When you plan a passage, you should always identify safe harbors along the route or within reach, and have an alternative plan in case weather conditions deteriorate. As a skipper you will find that your leadership and management skills are tested most in bad weather. You will have to monitor your crew's morale and well-being in these conditions and be prepared to head for harbor if necessary. You must know your crew's, and your own, limitations and avoid pushing beyond them.

Navigating in fog

The onset of fog prevents you from obtaining visual fixes to determine position. If possible, the skipper should head for shallow water to minimize the risk of collision with large ships. The navigator must be ready to navigate to a safe anchorage or harbour. A GPS set will continue to deliver position-fixing information. However, you must check this data against another source, and never rely on it alone. Probably the best electronic aid to have in these conditions is radar, as it will provide both position-fixing and collision-avoidance information. A GPS set together with a radar enable you to cross-check all information.

Fog and depth soundings

The depth sounder can provide valuable information when you are navigating through fog. By reducing the observed depth to soundings (p.357), a depth reading can confirm an EP or fix. Alternatively, a line of soundings can be used to fix a position (p.257). Depth soundings can also be used to follow a contour line on the chart. If you are trying to find a buoy at the entrance to a harbor, for instance, it may lie near a depth contour. In this situation, choose a suitable contour, making sure that there are no charted hazards along it. Calculate the height of tide to add to the depth at chart datum to get the actual depth of water at that time. Then you should plot your approach. You should try to cross the depth contour well to one side of the mark you are aiming for before turning toward it. Then steer a zigzag course that crosses and re-crosses the contour, checking the depth sounder regularly. This course will lead you to your destination.

USING DEPTH SOUNDINGS
Following a depth contour in shallow water in poor visibility has the advantage of getting you out of the big ship channel while providing you with a reference line you can follow toward your destination.

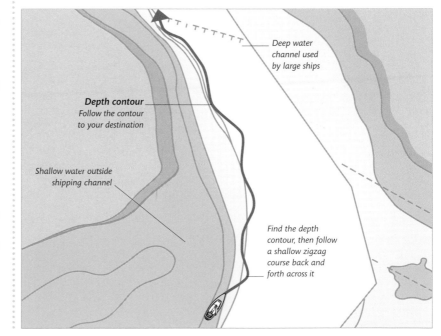

Deep water channel used by large ships

Depth contour
Follow the contour to your destination

Shallow water outside shipping channel

Find the depth contour, then follow a shallow zigzag course back and forth across it

WEATHER

The most awesome natural phenomenon on Earth is the weather. From light breezes to hurricanes, from spring showers to monsoon rains, it affects everything we do, yet we have no control over it. No one is more reliant on the weather than the sailor—without wind, there could be no sailing, yet too much of it makes sailing hazardous. Understanding weather systems, their causes and effects, forms an essential part of every sailor's skills.

CAUSES OF WEATHER

Weather occurs in a relatively narrow band of the atmosphere, called the troposphere. This extends about 10 miles (16 km) above Earth's surface at the equator, diminishing to half that thickness at the poles. As the Sun warms Earth's surface, some of the heat is transferred to the air above. This effect is greatest at the equator and least at the poles. Warm air tends to rise and cold air to sink, causing vertical movements of air and creating changes in air pressure. These movements and pressure changes take excess heat from the equator toward the poles, stabilizing global temperatures and preventing temperatures at the equator from becoming progressively hotter and those at the poles from becoming progressively colder.

Atmospheric pressure

Air exerts a downward force under the influence of gravity. This force, known as atmospheric pressure, is measured in millibars (mb). At all times, we experience atmospheric pressure that is equal to the weight of the column of air above us. The average pressure at sea level is about 1,013 mb, but pressure on Earth's surface varies widely from this mean figure because of differences in air temperature. Cold air is dense and heavy and tends to sink, resulting in high atmospheric pressure. Warm air is less dense and lighter and tends to rise, resulting in low pressure. Vast circulation systems develop around the planet, as warm air rises and cold air moves in to replace it.

Changes in atmospheric pressure are a significant indicator of changes in weather conditions. This makes a barometer or barograph (a barometer that provides a continuous record) an important forecasting aid aboard a yacht. If the pressure is rising, good weather may be on the way. If it is falling, stronger winds and poor weather may be imminent.

Isobars

Pressure is shown on weather maps by lines called isobars, which join areas of equal pressure in a similar way to contour lines on a map. In some places, isobars completely enclose areas of relatively high or low pressure, known as anticyclones and depressions, respectively (*pp.366–69*). The spacing between isobars on weather maps represents the pressure gradient between high and low in the same way that contours on a map indicate a shallow rise or a steep hillside. The closer the isobars, the steeper the pressure gradient and the stronger the wind in that area.

Dew point

Air contains water vapor, which it collects as water evaporates from Earth's surface. Air can hold large amounts of water, but it eventually becomes saturated. Warm air is capable of carrying far more water vapor than cold air, but it will become saturated if it cools down. When warm air cools, the excess water vapor condenses into droplets and forms clouds, mist, or fog. The temperature at which this occurs is known as the dew point. If air is cooled by its proximity to a colder surface, such as the sea, fog forms when the air reaches the dew point.

Clouds

There are three main ways in which clouds form: air is heated by radiation from a warmer area of land or sea and rises through convection currents; air is forced to rise when it meets obstacles such as mountains; or air rises over a mass of colder, denser air. As the air rises it cools. When it reaches its dew point, clouds form.

Clouds occupy three main layers: high cloud is usually above 20,000 ft (6,000 m); medium-level clouds are at 7,000–20,000 ft (2,100–6,000 m); and low cloud lies up to about 7,000 ft (2,100 m). Different types and shapes of clouds form (pp.370–71) within these bands. Clouds are an invaluable guide to the dominant weather system, and provide the best visual forecasting aid for assessing likely change.

Rain, hail, and snow

Water vapor can combine into droplets and fall as rain, hail, or snow. Droplets that form at higher altitudes in tall clouds freeze into snowflakes or hailstones. They will reach Earth's surface in that form if the air is cold at low levels. The capacity of a cloud to produce precipitation depends on its height and size. Expect heavy rain from large, tall clouds but little, if any, from a thin layer of low cloud.

Air masses

An air mass is an enormous volume of air with particular characteristics. Its type depends on whether it is warm or cold, wet or dry. When an air mass starts moving because of global pressure differences, it is known as an airstream. An airstream from a polar region is cold. If it has traveled over water to reach its present position, it will be relatively wet, but if it has traveled over land, it will be relatively dry. These differences lead to an airstream being classified as Polar, or Arctic, Maritime (cold and wet), Polar Continental (cold and dry),

Tropical Maritime (warm and wet), and Tropical Continental (warm and dry).

Hot or cold airstreams

When a cold airstream travels over warmer sea or land, it picks up heat in its lower levels. This forms convection currents that rise as air columns. If a column stays warmer than the surrounding air, it continues upward, creating unstable conditions that generally produce heaped clouds and good visibility. Wind is likely to be gusty as stronger, higher-altitude winds are drawn down to Earth's surface. The amount of cloud and rain depends on whether the air is wet or dry.

The opposite occurs when a warm airstream travels over colder land or sea. The air near Earth's surface cools, and any rising pockets of warmer air

quickly cool and stop rising. This is a stable airstream and features layer cloud, steadier winds, and reduced visibility.

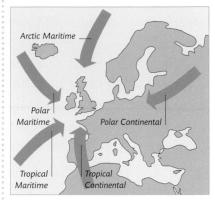

EUROPEAN AIRSTREAMS
Different types of airstreams converge on Europe, including cold, wet Polar Maritime airstreams, and warm, dry Tropical Continental airstreams.

WORLD WEATHER

The temperature differences that exist between the poles and the equator, together with the rotation of Earth, result in pressure being generally distributed in bands around the planet. These bands of relatively low pressure or high pressure create fairly stable wind systems over the oceans.

Pressure distribution
Lower-pressure bands are found at the equator and the mid-latitudes, and bands of higher pressure at the poles and the subtropics. The arrangement is disturbed by temperature changes caused by land masses, but over the sea, the bands of pressure result in semipermanent wind systems.

Wind direction
Air tries to move directly from an area of high pressure to an area of low pressure; this flow is felt as wind. The spinning of Earth makes the winds in the Northern Hemisphere bend to the right, whereas those in the Southern Hemisphere bend to the left.

WINDS AND PRESSURES
The spin of Earth deflects wind to the right in the Northern Hemisphere and to the left in the Southern Hemisphere.

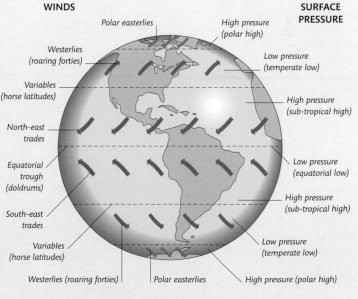

AIR CIRCULATION, WINDS, AND SURFACE PRESSURE

WEATHER SYSTEMS

The local weather conditions that we experience are part of larger weather systems—the patterns of weather distributed over the whole planet. Most pleasure-sailing takes place in the tropical and temperate zones. The tropics are dominated by the trade winds. The weather is usually fair, but with localized thunderstorms. Westerly winds predominate in temperate zones, although the weather is changeable because of the passage of depressions and anticyclones, and the influence of polar fronts.

Anticyclones

High-pressure areas are called anticyclones. They are shown on synoptic charts by pressure readings higher than the surrounding areas and by fairly widely spaced isobars (*p.364*).

Winds blow clockwise around an anticyclone in the Northern Hemisphere and counterclockwise in the Southern Hemisphere. The strongest winds blow around the outer edge; winds toward the center are lighter. Anticyclones can cover very large areas and usually move quite slowly. Sometimes they remain static for days or even weeks.

Anticyclones typically bring good weather, with light to moderate winds and clear skies. Thin layers of cloud may persist, but the clouds usually disperse. A temperature inversion (*p.371*) may form in anticyclonic conditions, and cause hazy weather or fog. A well-established and large anticyclone will interact with passing depressions, and may force them off course around its perimeter. Winds will increase between the anticyclone and the depression, where tightly packed isobars, squeezed between the two weather systems, indicate a steep pressure gradient. In this situation, strong winds under cloudless skies may be encountered.

Depressions

A depression is an area of relatively low pressure. They are shown on synoptic charts by pressure readings that are lower than the surrounding areas and by isobars that are closer together toward the center of the low-pressure area.

Winds blow clockwise around a depression in the Southern Hemisphere and counterclockwise in the Northern Hemisphere. The strongest winds are found near the center of the depression, and lighter winds around the outer edge. Depressions vary considerably in size, speed, and intensity, but they typically travel from west to east.

Depressions usually bring unsettled weather, strong winds, and heavy rainfall, with the worst weather near the center of the low pressure. Most depressions originate from activity at a polar front (*opposite*), although they can form in other circumstances, including very thundery conditions.

Wind and pressure systems

Air will attempt to move directly from high- to low-pressure areas, but it can do this only at the equator. Elsewhere, the rotation of Earth causes the wind to be deflected—to the right in the Northern Hemisphere and to the left in the Southern Hemisphere (*opposite*). This

NORTHERN HEMISPHERE
In the Northern Hemisphere, the wind blows clockwise around anticyclones and counterclockwise around depressions. This is because of the spin of Earth, which causes the wind to be deflected to the right.

SOUTHERN HEMISPHERE
In the Southern Hemisphere, wind blows counterclockwise around anticyclones and clockwise around depressions. This occurs because the spin of Earth deflects the wind to the left.

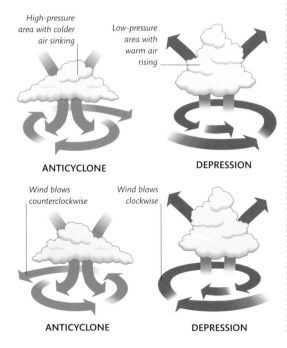

High-pressure area with colder air sinking

Low-pressure area with warm air rising

ANTICYCLONE

DEPRESSION

Wind blows counterclockwise

Wind blows clockwise

ANTICYCLONE

DEPRESSION

deflection causes the wind to blow in a circular pattern around the pressure systems.

Wind direction

The direction of the wind is always expressed in compass points (north or northeast, for example), which describe the direction from which the wind is blowing.

In the Northern Hemisphere, wind revolves clockwise around anticyclones and counterclockwise around depressions, with the isobars forming closed, concentric circles around both weather systems.

To find the approximate direction of a low-pressure system's center in the Northern Hemisphere, stand with your back to the wind; the low will be on your left. In the Southern Hemisphere, it will be on your right. The opposite applies to a high-pressure system. Above about 2,000 ft (600 m), the wind, known as the gradient wind, is more or less parallel to the isobars. At Earth's surface, however, friction will slow wind down and deflect it— in toward a depression, and outward away from an anticyclone. Over the sea, friction causes a deflection of 10–15 degrees; it can be double this over land. In unstable airstreams, wind brought down from higher altitudes can cause gusts, making the wind closer in speed and direction to the gradient wind.

The spacing of isobars indicates the gradient between high and low pressure, and hence the wind speed. This can be predicted by measuring the isobar spacing on a synoptic chart. Remember, however, that the wind speed is greater for a given isobar spacing when the isobars are curved around an anticyclone than when they are curved around a depression. Scales are given on synoptic charts to calculate wind speed from the isobars.

Polar fronts

A polar front is a demarcation line between two powerful and different airstreams—a warm airstream originating from a subtropical high, and a cold, polar one. When the airstreams meet, the cold, dense air pushes the warm air upward, forming a wedge under it. Activity at the front is the cause of depressions (p.368). Polar fronts twist their way around Earth, moving between about 35 and 60 degrees north and south, depending on the season.

SATELLITE IMAGE
Satellite images of weather systems are a useful forecasting aid. The position of weather fronts can be deduced from cloud cover. Here, an anticyclone is seen approaching the British Isles from the west.

PASSAGE OF FRONTS

Understanding the passage of a frontal depression and the associated changes in conditions is important for the offshore sailor. Depressions are often forecast in advance, but their speed and direction of movement can be unpredictable. It is an advantage if you can make your own judgments, based on observation. The type of weather you experience depends on where you are in relation to the center of the low. Here, an observer in the Northern Hemisphere is situated to the south of the low's center as it passes.

PASSING DEPRESSION

In this diagram a Northern Hemisphere depression passes from west to east, with its center north of the observer. There is an occluded front (p.369) near the center, but at the observer's position he sees the warm front, the warm sector (a trough of low pressure), and the cold front pass in turn. The photographs below show examples of the possible appearance of the sky at each numbered stage.

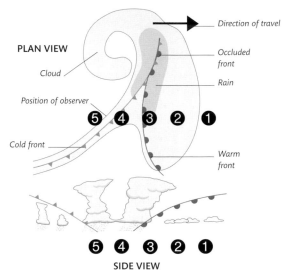

PLAN VIEW

Direction of travel

Occluded front

Rain

Cloud

Position of observer

⑤ ④ ③ ② ①

Cold front

Warm front

⑤ ④ ③ ② ①

SIDE VIEW

Frontal depressions

Along a polar front, a warm, westerly airstream meets a cold, easterly one. The warm airstream is lifted above the cold one, which slides underneath, creating unstable conditions that can lead to depressions.

Depressions are born along the polar front when a pocket of warm air encroaches on the neighboring cold airstream. This pocket creates a small wave in the front, with its crest on the polar side. In the middle of the wave, the air is warmer and rises faster, thus creating an area of low pressure and allowing cold air from the polar side to push in from behind to take its place. As the low-pressure area deepens at the crest of the wave, clearly defined fronts appear ahead of and behind the central trough of low pressure, curving out from the center of the low. These fronts form the demarcation line between the adjacent areas of warm and cold air.

❶ The presence of thin, high cirrus clouds, which are composed of ice crystals, indicates an approaching depression about 12–24 hours away. The speed and extent of the cirrus clouds are guides to the depth of the depression. The other clear indication of an imminent depression is the barometer reading, which will start to fall.

❷ Closer to the warm front, the cirrus cloud thickens into cirrostratus (high-layer cloud). A halo may appear around the sun or moon, caused by moisture in the upper atmosphere. The barometer will continue to record falling pressure. The wind will back (swing counterclockwise), often from westerly or southwesterly to southerly or southeasterly.

❸ On the approach of the warm front, the cloud thickens into altostratus and then nimbostratus with a lowering cloud base. The wind strength increases and often backs further, and the barometer drops more quickly as the center of low pressure moves closer. Visibility is reduced under the low cloud base, and rain begins to fall as the front moves closer.

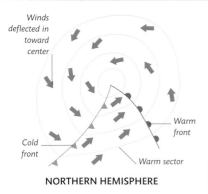

Winds deflected in toward center

Warm front

Cold front

Warm sector

NORTHERN HEMISPHERE

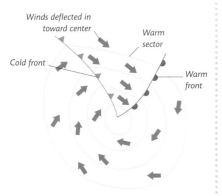

Winds deflected in toward center

Warm sector

Cold front

Warm front

SOUTHERN HEMISPHERE

FRONTAL DEPRESSION

Depressions typically form when a pocket of warm air encroaches into the neighboring band of cold air along the polar front. The front curls around the pocket, forming a wave with a warm, leading front and a cold, trailing one.

Warm and cold fronts

The leading front is called the warm front because it has warm air behind it, pushing over cooler air ahead. The trailing front is known as the cold front, and has cold air behind it. The cold front pushes under the warm air in the warm sector ahead. The cold front moves faster than the warm one.

Occluded front

As the cold front catches up with the warm front, the cold front pushes the warm-sector air off the surface, and the two fronts form an occluded front. Depending on whether the air behind the occluded front is colder or warmer than the air in front, it will be a cold-front type or a warm-front type. A cold occluded front is more active than a warm one, bringing heavier rainfall and higher gusts on the passage of the front.

Life span of depressions

Because cold fronts move more quickly and catch up with warm fronts, depressions have a limited life span. Secondary depressions can, however, form along the cold front of a dying depression. These are often smaller, develop faster, and can be more intense than the parent.

Depressions vary greatly in size, duration, and severity, but all continually change as they grow, interact with other weather systems, and eventually die. They can move at 50 knots or more, but those that cover a very large area tend to be much slower-moving.

Direction of depressions

Frontal depressions in temperate latitudes, in both hemispheres, tend to move from west to east, with the center of the depression toward the cold airstream on the polar side.

In the early life of a frontal depression, the low-pressure system tends to move in the same direction as the upper airstreams. This is approximately the same as the direction of the isobars in the warm sector (the area between the fronts). As the depression matures, it reaches higher into the high-altitude jet-stream winds and begins to move in their direction.

Toward the end of its life, the depression system will generally slow down. It may also change direction—usually to the north in the Northern Hemisphere, and to the south in the Southern Hemisphere.

❹ As the warm front passes over the observer, the wind veers, often to the southwest or west, and the barometer stops falling. The rain eases or stops, but visibility is poor with low cloud or mist. If the center of the low is some distance away to the north, the cloud layer is likely to be thinner, and breaks in the cloud cover may appear occasionally.

❺ The cold front is often marked by cumulus or cumulonimbus (huge heaped clouds). The pressure may drop again because of a trough of lower pressure ahead of the front. There may be heavy rain, fierce gusts and squalls, and sometimes thunderstorms. As the front passes, the wind usually veers sharply northwest and the pressure starts to rise.

DAILY CHANGES

If you are sailing near the coast in settled conditions, the weather you experience will change throughout the day. This effect is known as the diurnal weather variation. It is caused by the sun heating the land and, to a far lesser extent, the sea. Understanding diurnal effects enables you to predict wind speed and direction change during the day, and adjust your sailing plans accordingly. When sailing at night, you will understand when an inversion may form and bring light winds.

Morning to afternoon

As the land heats up with the rising of the sun, it warms the air above it. The warmed air rises through convection currents. As it goes higher into the troposphere, it gradually cools and sinks again. The convection currents are marked by cumulus clouds that form as water vapor carried in the cooling air condenses into droplets. As the convection currents grow in strength, they reach an altitude where the winds are stronger than they are at Earth's surface. The sinking currents then bring down parcels of upper air, causing an increase in wind strength and a possible change in wind direction at the surface. Convection currents reach their peak activity in the mid- to late afternoon, when clouds are at their highest and winds at their strongest. If the convection currents are particularly active, they may produce showers from rain-bearing clouds and thunderstorms may occur.

Evening to night

As the land cools in the late afternoon and evening, the convection currents stop and the wind drops in strength. On clear nights, an inversion effect may form (*opposite*). This is an indication of settled weather.

Tips for sailors

Study the weather forecast before you go afloat. If conditions seem stable and are being influenced by a nearby high-pressure system, check the clouds when you reach your sailing area. They will provide the clues to identify local heating of the land. If small cumulus clouds are evident in the morning, expect to see diurnal effects bringing stronger winds in the mid- to late afternoon.

THROUGH THE DAY

By studying the types of clouds that appear through the day, you can make many deductions about the kind of weather and wind conditions to expect. Practice observing clouds and making predictions to improve your skills.

CUMULUS
Early convection currents produce small cumulus clouds and variable winds. Deep clouds indicate that the good weather may not continue through the day.

ENLARGING CUMULUS
Cumulus may increase in size. Large clouds with high tops may produce rain showers. Stronger gusts with wind shifts are found near the clouds.

MIXED CUMULUS
Larger cumulonimbus sometimes develop among smaller cumulus. These are very active areas and can produce heavy showers and even hailstones.

UNDERSTANDING INVERSIONS

It is normal for the temperature of the air to cool as it rises. However, in settled weather, an inversion of this usual state of affairs may arise. Inversions occur when colder air becomes trapped under warmer air. This often happens in the evening or at night, when the land cools down quickly under clear skies, making the air near Earth's surface cool more rapidly than air at a higher altitude.

The inversion effect

When an inversion has formed, it separates low-level wind from wind at a higher altitude, preventing the two from mixing. This stops the usual effect of high-altitude wind speeding up low-altitude wind. The wind at surface level then slows down because of friction. The lightest winds occur around dawn, and fog patches may form when the air temperature reaches its lowest level.

Inversion breaking

When the sun rises, it heats the land and forms convection currents. These columns of warm air penetrate through the inversion layer, causing the surface winds and high-altitude winds to mix again.

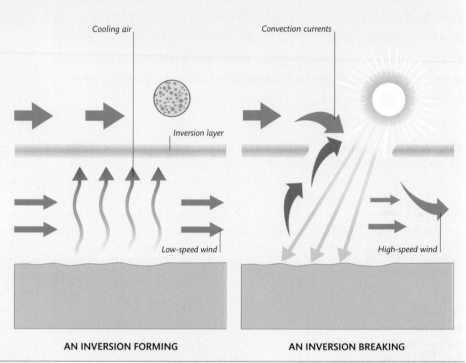

Cooling air

Convection currents

Inversion layer

Low-speed wind

High-speed wind

AN INVERSION FORMING

AN INVERSION BREAKING

THUNDERSTORMS
A rising air mass under a large cumulus or cumulonimbus cloud may produce a thunderstorm. Heavy gusts and big wind shifts occur at the base of the storm.

CLEAR SKIES
As the land cools, convection currents die and clouds disappear. With nightfall, the land cools quickly as there are no clouds to trap the heat. An inversion may form.

DAWN MIST
At dawn, winds will be very light or calm and fog may develop. Near land, the fog is likely to evaporate as the sun rises and warms the ground.

THE EFFECTS OF THE LAND

Understanding global weather patterns, depressions, and anticyclones is a great help when predicting changes in the weather, but the coastal or inland sailor also needs to understand how weather patterns can be influenced by the land. When you are sailing well offshore, you will experience wind conditions that are dictated by the nearest pressure systems; closer to land, local effects can interfere with the established pattern and cause localized changes in the weather.

Land and the weather

Land influences the wind and weather in a number of ways. Diurnal changes (*pp.370–371*), sea breezes, and land breezes all result from convection currents that are formed over the land. The effects are greatest in summer, when clear skies allow Earth's surface to heat and cool quickly.

Land and heat

Air is not warmed by the sun, but rather by the sea or land over which it travels. Land heats and cools far more rapidly than the sea, and different surfaces heat and cool at different rates. The topography and nature of the land determine how much heat it can absorb and radiate. Flat beaches and fields close to the coast heat up quickly in the morning, and large convection currents form above them. Steep hillsides and valleys stay cooler, whereas large urban areas can absorb considerable heat.

Land and wind

Land can alter the direction and strength of the wind. Wind blowing at a shallow angle onto a steep, high coastline will tend to be deflected parallel to the coast. River valleys also tend to deflect the wind up or down the valley. If the wind blows directly onto or off any coastline, however, it will be bent to blow at right angles to the shoreline. When wind blows over land, the increased surface friction slows it down. An onshore wind may be strong at the coast, but only a few miles farther inland its speed will be much reduced. An offshore wind will pick up speed as it leaves the coast and blows over the smoother sea. This is important for estimating the strength of the wind at sea.

Wind shadows

When you are sailing close to land, be aware of the effects of wind shadows (areas of reduced wind speed). An offshore sailor will notice the large wind shadows often found in the lee of large islands, and the coastal sailor will be affected by smaller features in harbors and rivers. Trees, buildings, ships, and high ground can all disrupt the passage of the wind and cause lulls, gusts, and wind shifts. Sailors who race on inland water need to be particularly aware of wind shadows and microclimate disturbances caused by very localized heating and small convection currents.

Sea breezes

One of the most obvious examples of winds caused by localized heating is the coastal sea breeze, common in stable weather conditions during the

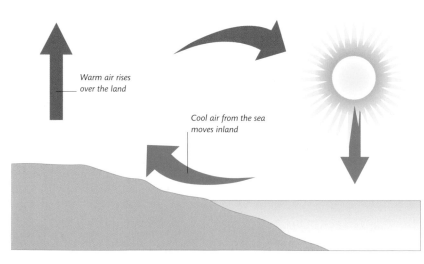

Warm air rises over the land

Cool air from the sea moves inland

DEVELOPMENT OF A SEA BREEZE

During the day, warm air rising from the land creates an area of low pressure that is filled by cold air coming off the sea, resulting in a sea breeze. The tops of the convection currents above the land are marked by cumulus clouds. Sea breezes die down when the land starts to cool.

KATABATIC WIND

In areas where there are steep cliffs or mountains on the coast, katabatic winds may occur. This often occurs on cloudless nights, when the land cools rapidly. Air moving over the cold ground becomes cooler and flows quickly downhill, pulled by gravity. When a land breeze effect combines with a katabatic wind, the resulting wind can be quite strong.

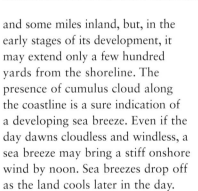

Cool air flows down coastal slopes

Land breeze combines with katabatic wind

Warm air rises from the water, causing a low-pressure area

MOON

summer. When coastal land is heated by the morning sun, large convection currents build up. As the air over the land heats up, it rises and the pressure drops. Over the sea, the air remains relatively cool and moves toward the low-pressure area to replace the rising air. A circulation system, driven by the convection currents, quickly develops, and a sea breeze is born.

Sea breezes and gradient winds

A sea breeze typically blows directly onto the coastline, but will be modified by any gradient wind (the wind caused by pressure systems). If the gradient wind is blowing onto the coast, the sea breeze will add to it, causing stronger winds in the middle of the day. If the gradient wind is offshore, the two may cancel out each other, and light winds or calm may result near the coast. A well-established sea breeze may be felt 5–10 miles (8–16km) offshore

and some miles inland, but, in the early stages of its development, it may extend only a few hundred yards from the shoreline. The presence of cumulus cloud along the coastline is a sure indication of a developing sea breeze. Even if the day dawns cloudless and windless, a sea breeze may bring a stiff onshore wind by noon. Sea breezes drop off as the land cools later in the day.

Land breezes

A land breeze is the direct opposite of a sea breeze. At night, under clear skies, the land cools quickly while the sea retains its heat. Air over the land cools and sinks, thus raising the pressure; air over the sea stays relatively warm and continues to rise. Once again, convection currents are

set up, but this time the wind blows off the land. Land breezes are usually lighter than sea breezes, but their effects may be felt several miles out to sea. They are typically stronger in the fall, when the sea is warmer than it is in spring or summer.

Katabatic winds

Sinking currents of air from mountains are known as katabatic winds. They may be experienced near mountainous coastlines where cool air, drawn down the slopes by gravity, causes a wind to blow down the slopes and out to sea.

Katabatic winds usually occur at night and may blow for several miles out to sea. A land breeze combined with a katabatic wind off a steep headland can bring strong gusts.

Zephyr winds

Zephyrs are gentle winds that occur when air over land is warmed and rises, allowing cooler air over the water to drift off the lake or river.

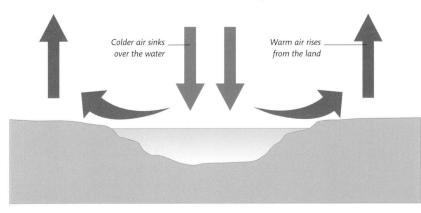

Colder air sinks over the water

Warm air rises from the land

CAUSE OF ZEPHYRS

In otherwise calm conditions, warm air rising from the banks of a river or edges of a lake creates an area of low pressure, into which cold air flows. This results in a zephyr wind, a gentle wind that can be exploited by inland dinghy sailors.

STORMS

Bad weather is caused by low-pressure systems and their ascending currents of air. When a large volume of humid air is forced rapidly upward, intense activity takes place and a revolving circulation of air is created. Frontal depressions (*p.368*) can cover very large areas and produce fairly strong winds, but smaller, yet more intense low-pressure systems, such as thunderstorms, tropical revolving storms, and tornadoes, are responsible for even more severe weather.

Thunderstorms

A thunderstorm is created by a very intense but localized area of low pressure that can produce very strong winds and heavy rain or hail. Thunder and lightning add to the drama. In tropical regions, thunderstorms are fairly common, often occurring at night. They are less frequent in temperate latitudes where they occur more often over large land masses such as North America. At sea, thunderstorms usually form along the line of a cold front.

Thunder clouds

A thunderstorm starts when a huge volume of air is forced upward by localized heating or by a wedge of colder air at a front. The large convection currents form huge banks of cumulus cloud that push upward and grow larger—a sign that a thunderstorm may develop. If the system becomes sufficiently active, cumulonimbus clouds form. These towering, dark, and forbidding clouds reach great heights and have characteristic anvil-shaped tops that point in the direction the storm is traveling. The higher the cloud top, the more intense the storm. Ice crystals form in the anvil top. They collide within the cloud and create static electricity, which discharges to the ground as lightning. Low rolls of cloud, created by violent internal air currents, form along the base of a storm, resulting in heavy rain or hail. This is also where the strongest winds and wind shifts are found. Behind the thunderstorm, the wind and temperature drop.

Safety at sea

If you are at sea when a thunderstorm approaches, the best course of action is to get out of its path. However, if the storm is going to pass over you, it is advisable to turn into it to get through it as quickly as possible. If you are heading in the same direction as a storm and are overtaken by it, you will spend longer within the storm.

Revolving storms

Tropical revolving storms are known by different names in different parts of the world: in the Atlantic they are hurricanes, in the western Pacific they are typhoons, and in the Indian Ocean they are cyclones. They are born in low latitudes and are marked by enormous banks of clouds that reach to the limit of the atmosphere, indicating a very intense depression. The depression covers a much smaller area than a frontal depression but the

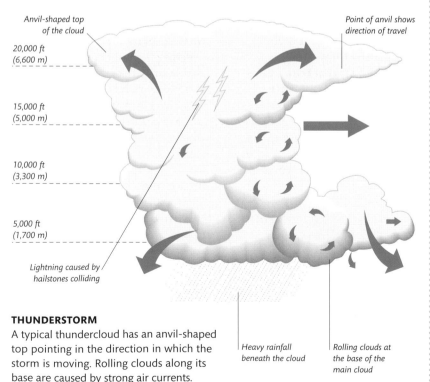

Anvil-shaped top of the cloud

Point of anvil shows direction of travel

20,000 ft (6,600 m)

15,000 ft (5,000 m)

10,000 ft (3,300 m)

5,000 ft (1,700 m)

Lightning caused by hailstones colliding

THUNDERSTORM
A typical thundercloud has an anvil-shaped top pointing in the direction in which the storm is moving. Rolling clouds along its base are caused by strong air currents.

Heavy rainfall beneath the cloud

Rolling clouds at the base of the main cloud

pressure gradient is much steeper, causing winds in excess of Force 12, and very heavy and steep seas.

Wind characteristics

During a revolving storm, the winds spiral inward toward the center of the depression at all heights through the storm, instead of blowing along the isobars at higher levels, as they do in a normal depression. The winds revolve counterclockwise in the Northern Hemisphere and clockwise in the Southern Hemisphere. At the center of the storm there is an "eye" in which the wind is temporarily calm, but the seas are rough and confused without the controlling influence of the wind. The clouds may clear for a short time but the respite will be brief as the opposite wall of cloud approaches, containing more violent winds. The wind is at its strongest close to the eye and visibility is seriously reduced, often to zero, as the air fills with flying foam and spray.

Storm origins

Tropical storms usually develop on the eastern side of oceans, and mature as they travel westward or northwest-ward in the Northern Hemisphere, or westward or southwestward in the Southern Hemisphere. In their early stages, they usually move at 10–15 knots, later increasing to 25 knots or more. As they near the western side of the ocean, they may curve north or northeasterly in the Northern Hemisphere, or south or southeasterly in the Southern Hemisphere.

Forecasting storms

Most tropical storms occur in fairly predictable seasons, such as July to September in the Atlantic, but they can develop at other times, too. The birth, growth, and development of tropical storms are monitored by forecasters using weather satellites, and sailors may receive warnings issued by radio and Weatherfax. When sailing in tropical latitudes, a drop in barometric pressure of 5 mb or more is a warning of an approaching storm. Other signs include a large ocean swell, significant changes in wind speed and direction, and cloud building from high cirrus through altostratus to heaped cumulus.

Safe refuges

Sailors who think they are in the path of a tropical storm should try to avoid being caught in the most dangerous semicircle, which is to the north of the center in the Northern Hemisphere, and to the south of the center in the Southern Hemisphere. A tropical storm is extremely dangerous to all craft but especially to small yachts. Safe refuges, known as hurricane holes, can be found in areas vulnerable to these storms, but most harbors present as many dangers as being at sea.

Tornadoes

A tornado is the most violent small-scale disturbance and is far more common over land than at sea, occurring most frequently on the central plains of North America. Forming in hot, humid, thundery conditions, tornadoes are created by severe convection currents that occur in large cumulonimbus clouds. A tornado's diameter is usually only a few hundred yards, and it will rarely travel more than a few miles. In that distance, however, it can cause more destruction than almost any other natural phenomenon. Winds at the center may reach 200 knots, and the exceptionally low pressure can rip houses apart and throw cars in the air.

WATERSPOUT
Strong convection currents produce a funnel-shaped extension at the base of cumulonimbus clouds. The powerful revolving motion of the wind in this cloud draws water off the surface of the sea, creating a spinning mass of spray.

Waterspouts

A waterspout is a type of tornado that is found at sea. It forms under heavy cumulonimbus clouds that contain strong convection currents. As a waterspout forms, a funnel-shaped cloud extends from the base of the cumulonimbus cloud toward the sea. Its revolving motion causes a spinning mass of spray to rise from the sea. If the waterspout continues to develop, the end of the funnel meets the spray cloud and forms a spinning column between cloud base and sea. The top and bottom of the column travel at different speeds so it quickly takes up a slanting position and eventually breaks up. A waterspout is a very localized and short-term event but can present a serious danger to small craft in the vicinity. It is less severe than a tornado, typically lasts less than 30 minutes, and covers an area 100 ft (30 m) in diameter. Waterspouts move slowly, but can be erratic, and are more common in tropical than temperate latitudes.

FOG

When you sail in a small boat, your safety and enjoyment depend on your ability to see all around you and avoid any potential hazards or collisions. Fog, therefore, can be a significant problem at sea. Although there are four main types of fog, all are basically cloud that has formed at Earth's surface. Three types of fog are caused by air being cooled to the point where it can no longer hold its moisture in vapor form, so some condenses into water droplets. The fourth type is caused by air that remains at the same temperature but picks up more water until it reaches saturation point, when some of the water condenses. It is helpful to know the types and causes of fog in order to predict its duration and extent.

During the early hours of the morning, it may extend several miles out to sea, but will disperse if the water temperature is higher than that of the land. In general, radiation fog poses little hazard to sailors, apart from in rivers and estuaries, where it may persist for some hours. Radiation fog quickly disperses when the sun rises—the land heats up, warming the air, raising its dew point, and lifting the fog. However, if overcast conditions come in at dawn, the land takes longer to heat up and the fog may persist.

Radiation fog

Often called land fog, radiation fog forms over land at night in clear conditions. During the night, the land cools rapidly by radiating its heat upward. Since there are no clouds to trap the heat, the air in contact with the land cools. When the temperature at Earth's surface falls below the dew point of the adjacent air, it becomes saturated and water vapor condenses to produce fog.

Radiation fog will only form when land cools rapidly under a warm, moist airstream that will probably have come off the sea. This type of fog requires low wind speeds; otherwise, vertical mixing warms the air at the surface. It commonly forms under high-pressure systems that bring settled weather and clear skies.

Radiation fog forms first as mist in low valleys, gradually thickening and deepening as more air is cooled.

Advection fog

Also called sea fog, advection fog is the type that is normally found at sea. It is caused by warm, moist air blowing over cooler water. It is most common during winter and spring, but may also occur in summer. Localized areas of sea turbulence that bring cold water to the surface may also produce advection fog.

A warm, moist airstream moving from temperate to polar latitudes will form large banks of sea fog along a wide front as it is gradually cooled by moving over cold water. An example is the Grand Banks of Newfoundland,

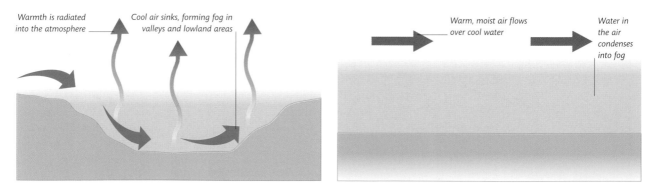

RADIATION FOG
Radiation fog is formed at night during clear conditions, when rapidly cooling land cools the air above and makes water vapor condense into droplets. The fog forms first as mist in low valleys, and spreads and thickens as the air continues to cool.

ADVECTION FOG
When warm, moisture-laden air passes over cold water, it cools down to its dew point, the water vapor in the air condenses, and advection fog forms. Also known as sea fog, advection fog can be persistent, requiring a dry wind to disperse it.

where a warm airstream that has picked up moisture from the warm Gulf Stream meets the cold waters of the Labrador Current.

Advection fog poses the greatest potential hazard to sailors. It can be very thick and persistent, even when there is a strong wind. Sea fog will disperse only when a change of wind brings drier air. In this situation, it is very important to determine the boat's position as accurately as possible.

Frontal fog

As its name implies, frontal fog occurs along the warm front of a depression. Warm air rises over cold air (p.366) and then cools rapidly to below its dew point to form a long, narrow strip of fog along the front. Frontal fog is often seen as low cloud, which can fall to sea level. It can also develop as high-level fog above otherwise clear conditions, obscuring high land and headlands from view. Frontal fog is not particularly persistent, but it can cause problems with pilotage (pp.334–337) if the navigator wants to use landmarks such as transits or lighthouses.

FOG FORMING
A bank of advection fog forms where a warm and moist airstream flows over cold water. As the air cools, the moisture it contains is condensed to form fog.

Sea smoke

Sea smoke is usually found in arctic and polar regions. Unlike other forms of fog—which form when warm, moist air cools—sea smoke occurs when cold air absorbs moisture as it passes over a warmer sea. The excess moisture cannot be absorbed by the cold air, so it immediately condenses into fog. At the same time, however, the air is being warmed by the sea so its dew point rises and the fog next to the sea disperses. The warmer air then rises to be cooled again by the air higher up, so the fog reappears. This type of fog produces an effect that resembles the appearance of smoke, as it quickly forms, disperses, and re-forms. Sea smoke is not a particularly serious problem for sailors. It lasts only a short time, until the air is warmed by the sea sufficiently to eliminate the effect.

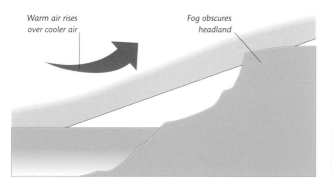

FRONTAL FOG
Frontal fog develops when warm, moist air at the front of a depression rises over colder air. This causes the temperature of the warm air to fall below its dew point. Frontal fog causes most problems for sailors when it obscures landmarks.

SEA SMOKE
Cold air flowing over a warmer sea absorbs and immediately condenses any water evaporating off the sea, forming fog. The water warms the air, raising the dew point and dispersing the fog. Higher up, the air cools again and the fog re-forms.

FORECASTING

Weather forecasting is a very complex subject. Although you can learn how to make general assessments of conditions and reasonably good predictions of what to expect in the near future, you will also need to take advantage of any suitable published forecasts that are available to you before you sail or while on passage. You can then compare these forecasts with your own observations to produce an overall picture that you can use when planning a sailing trip or during an offshore passage.

Weather information

The modern mariner is spoiled in terms of the availability of weather data. Only a few years ago, the primary source of weather information was via radio broadcasts based on data usually supplied by national meteorological organizations. Using these broadcasts, mariners would construct weather maps on which a forecast could be based. Today, weather information based on advanced computer models and satellite information is available from a range of providers, and via every form of media, giving mariners a level of detail that would previously have been thought impossible.

Internet

The Internet provides an enormous range and depth of weather information for the mariner—in fact, part of the skill in using it is finding the information you need. It is possible to subscribe to special

sites for weather information but it is not necessary, as with a little effort you will be able to find free information. Typically, weather sites on the net provide a summary of frontal systems, a breakdown of expected weather conditions covering system movement, wind speed and direction, visibility, precipitation, and pressure tendency.

In addition to this basic information, many sites provide detailed weather charts and satellite imagery showing forecast frontal system movement over a large area. Studying these charts enables a sailor to make informed judgments on conditions likely to be experienced during a passage. Some Internet sites also provide a more detailed analysis of publicly available data.

In addition to synoptic charts showing barometric pressure and position of frontal systems (wind speed and direction can also be interpreted from these charts), many weather sites provide infrared satellite images, from which cloud cover can be observed and position of fronts confirmed. Other charts may be available showing wind speed and direction over the area in which you are interested.

Most Internet sites provide weather charts for short range (1 to 3 day) and long range (4 to 7 day) forecast periods, but the latter have

SYNOPTIC CHART

Synoptic charts can be downloaded from the Internet and show information such as the movement of fronts, pressure systems, and wind strengths and directions.

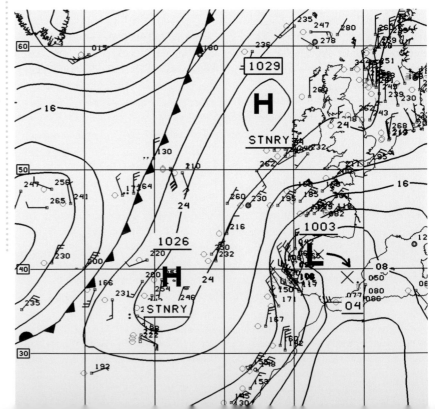

a greater degree of uncertainty. Some sites also provide upper atmosphere (500 mb/500 hPa) charts that enable the skilled user to evaluate how the upper atmosphere may influence the behavior of frontal systems and hence the weather that is experienced at sea or on land.

Although interpreting weather charts may sound complicated, if you practice by studying the forecast weather charts for your location over, say, a 48- or 72-hour period, and then compare your expectation with the weather you actually observe, you will quickly hone your skills.

For the vast majority of mariners, the Internet is only accessible close to shore, at best, and therefore will form the backbone of predeparture weather information. Once underway, mariners must rely on other sources of weather information unless they have a satellite internet connection.

Weatherfax

This service provides mariners with access to a range of weather information including gale warnings, surface analysis, ocean frontal positions, forecasts up to 96 hours from time of issue, as well as charts of quality similar to the ones available on the Internet.

This information can be received while on passage, either via a dedicated receiver or by Weatherfax software installed on a PC linked to a suitable radio receiver. Most marine electronics retailers should be able to advise on a suitable solution to meet your needs and budget.

Navtex

The Navtex system is used for the automatic broadcast of localized Maritime Safety Information (MSI) using Radio Telex (also known as Narrow Band Direct Printing, or NBDP). The system mainly operates in the Medium Frequency radio band just above and below the old 500 kHz Morse Distress frequency. System range is generally 300 nautical miles or so from the transmitter. Major areas of Navtex coverage include the Mediterranean Sea, the North Sea, and coastal areas around Japan and the North American continent.

A Navtex receiver is normally a compact unit, with an integrated printer, display, and keyboard, although some units have a larger LCD display rather than a printer. The user selects the areas for which he wishes to receive information, and programs in the types of information he wants to receive.

Once set up, the unit can then be left unattended as messages will be received automatically and printed on the integrated printer or stored in memory for later display on screen.

Navtex broadcasts can also be received on a PC with suitable software installed and connected to a radio capable of receiving the Navtex frequencies. The software solution for Weatherfax is often also able to receive Navtex information, providing an attractive proposition where budgets are tight.

GRIB files

Gridded Binary (GRIB) data files are output files generated by computer weather forecasting models. They provide information on wind speed and direction, ocean currents, sea state, and sea surface temperature.

GRIB files have the big advantage that they are much more compact than regular weather charts that are transmitted for Weatherfax (about 10Kb in size for large regions and about 4Kb for the Caribbean). Because of their small size they are very well suited

NAVTEX RECEIVER
A Navtex receiver can be programmed to display just the information and areas you require. Some, as here, have built-in printers and others use only an LCD screen to display incoming information that is stored in memory until required.

for download via wireless means such as through an HF receiver or satellite phone system.

The largest producer of GRIB weather is the National Oceanic and Atmospheric Administration (NOAA), although other organizations also generate GRIB files. NOAA GRIB files are best suited for marine forecasts, but you should be aware that human forecasters do not review the data before it is published and therefore some knowledge and awareness is required by the end user. Also, NOAA uses several models to generate GRIB files with different strengths and weaknesses. It is best to familiarize yourself with the GRIB files from each model for the area you travel in and compare these forecasts with other reliable weather sources before depending on them.

GRIB forecasts can be extremely accurate and, in remote parts of the world, possibly the only source of weather forecasting. You will require a software application to view GRIB files but many software chart-plotting programs have the ability to read GRIB files and use them in their routing facility. Some providers of navigation software make daily GRIB files available from their Internet sites.

Radio forecasts

Weather information via radio broadcasts is available to all sailors via a standard ship's radio. Most countries with a coastline broadcast marine or shipping forecasts, usually with forecasts split into sea areas. Typically, these forecasts include gale warnings, general synopsis of weather systems and any expected change over the next 24 hours, forecast of wind strength and direction, and weather and visibility for the next 24 hours.

Some countries also broadcast reports of actual weather from a series of reporting stations around the coast. This usually includes information on observed wind direction and force, present weather, visibility, and sea level pressure tendency. This information is invaluable as it allows you, together with the forecast information, to create your own weather chart from which a reasonable short term forecast can be derived. Details of the timing and frequency of radio broadcasts can be found in most almanacs or in an official List of Radios Signals.

It is very worthwhile to learn the terminology and abbreviations used in these broadcasts so that you are able to note them down. With this information you can then draw your own weather chart. By comparing your charts with professional forecast weather charts and your observations of actual weather, you will soon develop your skills and the confidence to use them.

Weather observation

All of the sources of weather information are invaluable in terms of providing sailors with detailed forecast information derived largely from advanced computer models. However, these are still only forecasts, and there is no substitute for the direct observation and recording of weather information at sea to enable the sailor to determine the most likely short-term weather in the locality and to evaluate the accuracy of the forecast information available. There are several key characteristics of the weather that can be directly observed at sea and used by the sailor to give a valuable insight into forthcoming weather events.

Barometric pressure

The most useful forecasting tool aboard a small yacht is a good-quality barometer. Traditionally, this would have been an aneroid barometer, which is a mechanical device with metal bellows that move according to changes in atmospheric pressure. A variation, the barograph, records the pressures on a paper chart on a revolving drum.

The aneroid barometer and barograph have now largely been superseded, for use aboard yachts, by electronic barometers, most of which have the ability to record hourly readings for 24 hours, and show change to one decimal place or more. As they have no moving parts or metal bellows, they are much less susceptible to corrosion from dampness on board.

However, with either type, it is very important to calibrate your barometer by checking its readings against those from a reliable external source, such as the nearest coast guard station or harbormaster's office.

When underway, pressure readings should be recorded in the ships log every hour and the skipper or watch leader should keep a close eye on the rate of change. The actual pressure reading

ELECTRONIC BAROMETER
An electronic barometer displays pressure and changes over time on a graphical display that can also show temperature, humidity, time, and other information.

is less important than the direction of change and, especially, its rate of change—rising or falling pressure and the speed of change is an indicator of imminent weather changes.

You must take into account the "diurnal variation" in pressure, which is the natural rise and fall in pressure around the mean barometric pressure over a 24-hour period, and allow for it when observing changes over time.

In weather forecasts, the rate of change is given over a three-hour period, providing an indication of the trend in terms of direction and rate of change.

If barometric pressure falls or rises by, say, 4 to 5 millibars over three hours, then you could expect wind speeds of between 17 knots to 27 knots; a change of 6 millibars or more over three hours is a strong indication that gale-force winds are imminent.

Wind speed and direction

Observing changes in wind speed and direction while you are afloat is key to determining likely changes in weather conditions in the short term.

Onboard a sailing boat, the wind speed is usually recorded using an anemometer that is fixed to the top of the mast and linked to an output display (p.328), which provides details of the apparent wind speed and direction. If these units are connected to an electronic log so that they receive boat speed, they can also show the true wind direction.

If you use a handheld anemometer, the wind-speed readings should be taken from the windward side of the vessel, and the wind direction measured using a hand bearing compass. Remember, too, that handheld instruments only provide apparent wind direction and strength, so you must record boat speed and heading to calculate the true wind speed and direction. This information should be recorded in the ship's log book every hour along with the barometric pressure.

Before the introduction of measuring instruments, wind strengths were expressed on the Beaufort scale (*pp.382–383*). This was devised by Admiral Francis Beaufort in 1805 to describe the effects of wind. At first, the Beaufort scale related the wind strength to the amount of sail a tall ship could carry. This was later modified to include the effects of wind observed on land and at sea. The Beaufort scale is still used to define wind strengths at sea, and the Beaufort forces are now defined as

HANDHELD ANEMOMETER
Wind speed can be obtained using a handheld unit, which is handy for small-boat sailing as the unit is small and light and can be kept in a pocket. Cruisers often have a fixed instrument giving speed and direction.

speed in knots. The descriptions are just as useful now as they were originally, allowing an observer to judge wind speed on land or at sea without the use of instruments.

Sea surface temperature

Taking observations of sea surface temperature is of greater use to sailors in tropical regions as it gives an indication of the likely degree of convection activity in relation to the development of tropical depressions.

In temperate latitudes, sea surface temperature also gives an indication of the likely risk of fog. Most modern electronic logs are made with a temperature sensor built into the transducer. This allows the user to note sea temperature.

In temperate latitudes, measuring sea surface temperature is more useful when it is used in conjunction with readings from a psychrometer. A traditional psychrometer has a dry bulb thermometer for measuring temperature and a wet bulb thermometer for measuring humidity. It is used in conjunction with tables that enable you to predict the dew point temperature of the air. By comparing dew point information and the sea temperature, you can make a much more accurate assessment of fog risk (*pp.376–377*). Modern versions utilize electronic sensors for measurement, then calculate and display the results on a screen.

Using observation

If you are unable to receive useful forecasts at sea, you will be reliant on your own observations to monitor the weather. Once you become used to the normal weather for the area in which you normally sail, you will be able to predict the speed and severity of approaching fronts. If you are in

tropical latitudes, you should monitor the barometer and expect to see gradual diurnal changes. However, if the pressure starts to drop significantly, while high altitude cloud increases and a building ocean swell appears, expect an approaching storm with the center in the direction from which the swell is coming.

When in temperate latitudes, approaching depressions are signaled by falling barometric pressure and a wind direction that backs, initially, under building high cloud.

Wherever you are in the world, you can use clouds to forecast weather. High clouds are associated with weather systems up to six hours away. If they are wispy and white, fine weather is imminent. Clouds that are lifting and dispersing also indicate that good weather is approaching. Lower level clouds relate to current weather. If they are dark, heavy, and lowering, poor conditions and rainfall are likely to be on their way.

Another way of forecasting rain is to observe whether there is a halo around the sun or moon. This haze is caused by the refraction of light by ice crystals carried in moisture-laden clouds from which rain may fall.

PSYCHROMETER
A psychrometer is used to measure temperature and humidity to calculate the dew point and predict fog. Small handheld units are available that use electronic sensors and have an easy-to-read LCD screen. Some electronic barographs also display humidity and temperature.

BEAUFORT SCALE

FORCE	MEAN SPEED	DESCRIPTION	ASHORE	DINGHY SAILING
0	Less than 1 knot	Calm	Smoke rises vertically and flags hang limp.	Drifting conditions. Heel the boat to assist sail efficiency. Make gentle movements.
1	1–3 knots	Light air	Smoke drifts slightly, indicating wind direction.	Gentle forward movement. Flatten sails and balance boat bow down and heeled.
2	4–6 knots	Light breeze	Light flags and wind vanes move slightly.	Steady speed is possible. Sail upright with full sails for maximum power.
3	7–10 knots	Gentle breeze	Light flags extend outwards.	Hull speed possible. High-performance dinghies may plane. Ideal for learners.
4	11–16 knots	Moderate breeze	Paper lifted off the ground. Small branches move.	Planing on most points of sailing. Crew fully extended. Beginners should head for shore.
5	17–21 knots	Fresh breeze	Small trees sway visibly and tops of trees move.	Ideal conditions for experienced crews, otherwise capsizes are common.
6	22–27 knots	Strong breeze	Large trees sway and wind whistles in power lines.	A dinghy sailor's gale. Only experienced crews with good safety cover should race.
7	28–33 knots	Near gale	Whole trees are in motion. It is difficult to walk against the wind.	Most dinghies remain on the shore. If they are taken afloat, they are likely to be overpowered and damaged.
8	34–40 knots	Gale	Twigs are broken off trees. Progress on foot very much impeded.	Dinghy sailing not possible. Dinghies should be securely tied down ashore.
9	41–47 knots	Severe gale	Chimney pots and slates blown off roofs. Fences blown down.	Dinghy sailing not possible.
10 to 12	48+ knots	Storm to hurricane	Trees uprooted and considerable structural damage likely. Extremely rare inland.	Dinghy sailing not possible.

CRUISER SAILING	WAVE HEIGHT	SEA STATE IN OPEN WATER
Becalmed. Use engine.	0 ft (0 m)	Mirrorlike water.
Very slow sailing upwind. Downwind spinnaker hard to keep filled.	Less than 3 in (0.1 m)	Ripples form on the water.
Slow sailing upwind with little heel. Spinnaker fills downwind.	Up to 1 ft (0.3 m)	Small wavelets with smooth crests.
Pleasant sailing. Spinnaker fills and sets well downwind.	Up to 3 ft (0.9 m)	Large wavelets with crests starting to break.
Hull speed achieved by most yachts. Some small cruisers start to reef.	Up to 5 ft (1.5 m)	Small waves and frequent whitecaps.
Medium-sized cruisers start to reef. Crew wear and clip on safety harnesses.	Up to 8 ft (2.5 m)	Moderate waves and many whitecaps.
Most cruisers reefed. Wear and clip on harness. Seek shelter if inexperienced.	Up to 12 ft (4 m)	Large waves, white foamy crests. Spray likely.
Seek shelter or sail away from land to ride out any forecast storms. Family crews may have problems coping. Most cruisers deep-reefed.	Up to 20 ft (6 m)	The sea heaps up and waves break. Much spray.
Use a deep-reefed mainsail and small headsail. Close and secure hatches and companionways against water. Only essential crew should be on deck.	Up to 25 ft (8 m)	Moderately high waves of greater length that frequently break.
Danger of knockdown. Some crews may continue to sail; others heave-to or run before. Depending on the sea state, a trysail could be set.	Up to 30 ft (10 m)	High waves with breaking crests and flying spray.
Stay well away from coastlines. Survival conditions. Danger of 90° knockdowns and full capsizes.	30–52 ft (10–16 m)	Very high waves. Sea becoming heaped up and white. Visibility affected.

PRACTICAL BOAT CARE

The level of maintenance a boat requires depends on its age, size, type, and complexity, and the amount of care an owner wishes to lavish on his pride and joy. Whereas the owner of a general-purpose dinghy need only give his boat an occasional wash and check over, the owner of a cruiser should be able to service and maintain a variety of onboard systems.

THE HULL

The amount and type of maintenance that a hull requires depends on the material used in its construction. Glass-reinforced plastic (GRP) combines strength with relatively low maintenance. It is also ideal for high volume production and is used for almost all production-built boats. Wood in the form of plywood, veneers, or strip planking combined with epoxy resins makes strong, light, molded hulls that are aesthetically pleasing, but traditionally-built wooden hulls require considerable maintenance. Steel or aluminum hulls are very strong and resilient but are far less common than GRP.

If they are well cared for, boats have the potential for a very long life—perhaps more akin to a building than to a car. Like either, they need regular maintenance and, like a house, occasional refurbishment or modernization during their life-span.

General maintenance

Always check underwater surfaces every time you dry out or lift the boat ashore, and repair any damage immediately. Check the topsides regularly, and repair even minor damage as soon as possible, especially with steel and wooden boats. All boats that are kept afloat should be given one or two coats of antifouling paint at least once a year to combat underwater fouling from weed and barnacles. Check with other boat owners to see what is recommended in the area in which you plan to sail, because there because there may be a special formulation that is designed to be most effective against the weed and other sources of fouling in your sailing area.

Most hull materials benefit from being brought ashore during the winter and allowed to dry out.

GRP hulls

Production-built GRP boats are finished with a smooth gel coat that protects the underlying laminate and produces a shiny surface. The gel coat is quite easily damaged by impact or abrasion, and repairs must be made

quickly to stop water from penetrating the laminate. This is not usually a difficult job, but it can be tricky to match the color and blend the repair with the existing gel coat, especially if the color of the gel coat has faded over time, which is most likely with a dark color.

Routine maintenance is simply a matter of cleaning and polishing the gel coat to restore the shine. Polishing with abrasive cleaners gradually reduces the thickness of the gel coat, which will also age from exposure to ultraviolet light. Eventually, the time will come when a coat of paint is needed for cosmetic purposes, although there are plenty of 30-year-old yachts still looking good with their original gel coat finish.

GRP is inherently a long-lasting material—the oldest boats made of it are now about 50 years old, with many still giving good service. The biggest, potentially serious problem that a GRP boat may succumb to is osmosis—water ingress leading to gel-coat blistering and, if left unchecked, the eventual weakening of the whole structure. Most modern boats are now molded with isopthalic resins, which are resistant to osmosis, so the problem is mainly restricted to older vessels. One cause of osmosis is flaws in the molding, so once a boat reaches a certain age—over 10 years or so—the likelihood of its occurring is reduced, as is the speed at which it spreads.

Minor patches of osmosis, or isolated blisters, can be treated individually by grinding out the

ANTIFOULING PAINT
Applying antifouling paint is one of the least popular maintenance chores, but it is essential to prevent underwater fouling, which will slow the boat considerably.

OLD GRP HULL
If the underwater areas have blisters on the surface, it may be a sign of osmosis, or it could be confined to the antifouling layer.

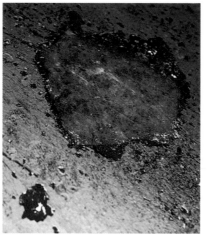

EXPOSE THE GEL COAT
Scrape off a patch of antifouling to reveal the gel coat (here a clear type) to check if the blisters are in the laminate.

PEEL THE GEL COAT
If osmosis is diagnosed, a good solution is to remove the gel coat, using a handheld peeling machine, to dry out the laminate.

affected area, drying the laminate thoroughly, and rebuilding with epoxy resin. Many boat owners have found that having done this they experience few, if any, further blisters. However, if osmosis is extensive, the gel coat must be peeled off the entire underwater area of the hull, which must be allowed to dry fully (often with infrared lamps). The hull is then filled and faired (smoothed), before applying several coats of epoxy resin as a waterproof barrier to replace the original gel coat. This work is costly, but a five-year warranty is usually included.

Steel and wooden hulls

Both steel and wooden hulls are protected by a paint layer. Minor collisions usually result in nothing more than damage to the paint. This is easily rectified, but the repair should be done as quickly as possible, before water penetrates the wood or surrounding paint system. If a steel hull weeps rust, this is an indication that the paint system has broken

down, allowing moisture and air to attack the steel. This may require sandblasting to remove the old paint and surface rust. Modern paints make it much easier to obtain a lasting finish on steel, but it is vital that the surface is thoroughly prepared and that the paint supplier's instructions are closely followed. Two-pack polyurethane paints are much harder and longer-lasting than the single-pack types, but require more work if small areas need to be touched up. They are not, however, suitable for traditionally constructed wooden hulls, which need the greater flexibility of single-pack types. A quality two-pack polyurethane paint that is applied properly should last about five years, with an annual polish; a single-pack polyurethane may need renewing every year or two.

Aluminum hulls

Aluminum is strong and lighter than steel, and hulls made of this material need paint only for cosmetic reasons.

For low maintenance, it makes sense to leave an aluminum hull bare, as its surface will form an oxidized layer that turns matt-gray. If painted, the surface must be carefully prepared according to the paint supplier's instructions and a hard, two-pack polyurethane should be used.

Ferro-cement hulls

A number of yachts were built, mostly in the 1970s and 1980s, using concrete plastered over a steel and wire mesh frame. Many were home-built, with the standard of construction varying considerably, although a few were professionally built to a high standard. Problems with ferro-cement hulls, such as rusting of the steel framework, can be difficult to detect, so they are an unpopular secondhand buy. For this reason they can be very cheap, but such a boat may not be the bargain it appears. If you are tempted by a ferro-cement boat, a thorough survey by a specialist in the material is absolutely essential.

Repairing minor damage

If you sail a GRP boat, always carry some epoxy filler and polyester gel coat of the appropriate color aboard to repair minor chips and grazes. Clean out the damaged area, degrease it, and dry it thoroughly. If the damage is quite deep, fill with epoxy filler to just below the surface, allow it to cure, then apply gel coat, leaving the surface slightly raised. For shallow grazes use only gel coat, which should be mixed with 1–2 percent wax to ensure that it hardens fully when in contact with air. Otherwise, cover the repair with plastic film taped in place and wait for the gel coat to cure. Once hard, it can be rubbed back using fine wet-and-dry paper and a rubbing paste to finish the job and polish the surface. More serious damage can be repaired by a skilled owner using a glass cloth or mat, but it is usually better to employ professional help.

If your boat has a painted hull, carry some topside paint on board to touch up minor damage before water can penetrate the paint system.

Fill deep scratches with an epoxy filler before painting. Hard, two-pack paints can be polished like gel coat. Minor dents to aluminum and steel hulls can also be filled and painted, but more serious damage will probably require expert skills.

Through-hull fittings

Many modern yachts have a large number of through-hull fittings for engine-cooling water, toilet intake and discharge, galley and shower sump pumps, and so on. All of these holes in the hull are potential causes of water intake, so the fittings must be checked regularly.

Damage to metal through-hull fittings is often caused by a process called galvanic corrosion (*opposite*). Check metal through-hull fittings by withdrawing a fastener. Consider removing and checking the entire fitting if there is any sign of corrosion on the fastener. Grease all seacocks at least once a season, and open and close them regularly to ensure that they do not seize. Similarly, the plastic transducers for speed and distance

logs and depth sounders should be checked for damage each time the boat is hauled ashore or dried out. If you are planning to build a new boat, minimize the number of through-hull fittings by using standpipes to which all inlets and outlets are connected.

Keel construction

The construction of the keel varies depending on the design of the boat. Many older GRP production cruisers have their keels encased in the GRP molding, using lead or iron in the keel cavity to provide the necessary weight. Other craft have a fin or bilge keels, made of iron or lead, bolted onto the hull structure, and their fastenings occasionally need to be checked for corrosion.

If your cruiser has an external keel that is bolted onto the hull, withdraw one or two bolts every few years to check for corrosion. If leaks occur at the junction of keel and hull, the keel should be removed and re-bedded on new sealant. A skilled amateur with the right tools can do this job; otherwise, get expert help.

REPAIRING GEL COAT DAMAGE

Gel coat repairs are within the abilities of a reasonably practical boat owner. Clean and degrease the surface and allow to dry thoroughly before starting the repair, and make sure the temperature is moderately warm to help the new gel coat mix to cure fairly quickly.

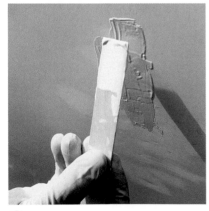

❶ Mix the gel coat and hardener in a suitable container and apply to the scratches using a disposable wooden spatula. Use disposable gloves to protect your hands. Do not expect to achieve a smooth surface at this stage.

❷ Use a piece of acetate film to keep air off the gel coat while it cures. Cut the film oversize, smooth over the repair to eliminate air, and fix with masking tape.

❸ Peel back the acetate to test the hardness of the new gel coat with a finger nail. If not yet cured, re-cover with the acetate and leave until it has hardened.

❹ When the repair has cured, remove the film, and wet sand the repair with fine wet-and-dry paper. Finish off with a rubbing paste to polish the surface.

If your boat has an encapsulated keel, check that any grounding damage has not worn away the gel coat (or even the GRP laminate) at the bottom of the keel. Check also that there is no way in which water could penetrate the GRP and reach the ballast.

Rudder and bearings

Rudder bearings should be checked annually. This is done by grasping the bottom of the rudder and trying to move it fore and aft and from side to side. Movement indicates that there is wear in the bearings. Worn bearings should be replaced as soon as possible.

A transom hung rudder is easier to check than one situated under the boat and its fittings are accessible for inspection. They are usually hung using variations on the dinghy system of pintles and gudgeons (*p.84*) which are bolted through the transom. There should be a strong backing pad and the fastenings should be checked regularly as they take high loads.

Rudders on GRP boats are usually molded GRP with a foam core. These can absorb water if they sustain damage, and the foam core can become sodden. Check yours carefully for signs of delamination or for water leaking out of the seam that joins the two halves.

Propeller, shaft, and bearings

Check the propeller-shaft bearings by vigorously pushing the propeller from side to side. If there is any significant movement, the bearings or the shaft may need to be replaced. Check the propeller itself for any corrosion or impact damage. If a propeller blade is damaged, replace or repair it as soon as possible. An unbalanced propeller can cause increased vibration, which may lead to premature failure of the shaft bearings.

PREVENTING GALVANIC CORROSION

Galvanic corrosion occurs because different metals, when in close proximity and immersed in sea water, tend to form an electric cell. A current flows, and one of the two metals is eaten away. Metals are ranked by their position in the galvanic series.

Zinc anodes

The higher in the galvanic series a metal is (*right*), the more prone it is to galvanic corrosion; and the farther apart two metals are in the series, the faster the rate of corrosion. Protection against galvanic corrosion is doubly important for metal hulls and for traditionally constructed wooden boats, as the boat itself (or the fastenings in a wooden boat) may be slowly corroded by galvanic action.

Many boats have fittings made of several different metals on the underwater part of the hull—a bronze propeller on a stainless steel shaft, for instance. To protect these from galvanic corrosion, you should fit one or more sacrificial anodes. These are made from zinc, which is attacked before any of the other metals used in boat building; it will therefore protect them from corrosion. Zinc anodes must not be painted and should be replaced when half their bulk has been eaten away.

Galvanic series

**CORRODED END
(ANODIC – LEAST NOBLE)**

Magnesium
Zinc
Galvanized steel
Aluminum alloys
Cadmium
Mild steel
Wrought iron
Cast iron
304 Stainless steel (active)
316 Stainless steel (active)
Aluminum bronze
Naval brass
Yellow brass
Red brass
Tin
Copper
Admiralty brass
Aluminum brass
Manganese bronze
Silicon bronze
Bronze G
Bronze M
401 Stainless steel
Lead
Nickel 200
304 Stainless steel
(passive)
316 Stainless steel
(passive)
Titanium
Platinum

**PROTECTED END
(CATHODIC – MOST NOBLE)**

Strap for bolting anode to the hull

Pear-shaped anode for fitting to hull with minimum resistance to water flow

SACRIFICIAL ANODE
These are fittings made of zinc in various shapes and sizes. They are fastened near skin fittings, the rudder, and the propeller shaft to protect these important fittings from corrosion.

THE DECK

In most cases, the deck of a yacht is made of the same material as the hull, although a few have a wooden deck with, for instance, a GRP or steel hull. On larger or more expensive yachts, a GRP or metal deck may be overlaid with teak for its appearance and good nonslip properties. All equipment attached to the decks should be securely fastened with through-bolts, and should have substantial backing plates underneath the decks to spread the load through the structure.

GRP decks

On all but the very smallest cruisers, most decks are made of sandwich construction with two layers of GRP separated by a core material, usually closed-cell foam or end-grain balsa wood. This creates a rigid but light structure. GRP decks require little maintenance, apart from the occasional clean and polish of the "shiny" areas; do not polish the nonslip areas.

Surface damage—often consisting of star-crazing around highly stressed areas such as stanchion bases—is repaired in the same way as for a GRP hull (*p.388*). However, if the deck has a nonslip pattern molded into the gel coat, it will require professional help to reproduce the pattern.

Deeper damage may let water into the foam or balsa core. If this is allowed to happen the core may start to delaminate from the GRP skins and slowly reduce the strength of the

structure. More major repairs, therefore, may require the removal of a section of the core and drying of the whole area, before replacing the core material and then making good the GRP skin, first with fiberglass cloth, then with gel coat.

Where new deck fittings are bolted through a sandwich deck, a section of the core material must be replaced with stronger material so that the compression created when the nuts are tightened does not crush the core and weaken the deck. This is usually done from underneath to preserve the appearance of the deck. The area removed can be replaced with marine plywood, and the exposed edges of the core material sealed with epoxy filler.

Steel decks

Steel decks are strong but heavy and add weight high up in the vessel, so they are mostly found on larger

yachts. Steel decks must be protected with a good paint system, preferably with epoxy base layers. A nonslip finish is provided with a top coat of gritted paint, nonslip sheeting applied in the working areas with glue, or a laid teak deck.

Aluminum decks

Although they do not need covering for protection against corrosion, aluminum decks are rarely left bare as some kind of nonslip coating is needed for the safety of the crew. Most boats have paint or nonslip sheeting, as with steel boats, although a laid teak deck is popular.

One advantage of aluminum decks is that many fittings can be welded to the deck or fastened with machine screws in blind tapped holes so that there are no through-deck holes, thus removing a major cause of leaks in other deck materials.

Wooden decks

It's vitally important to keep the paint or epoxy system of wooden decks in good condition, as ingress of fresh (rain) water will result in rot or delamination setting in more quickly than if salt water—which is a mild preservative—gets into the timbers.

Traditionally planked decks need to have a flexible paint coating (unless they are teak, in which case they can be oiled or left bare) to accommodate movement in the timbers. The caulking between

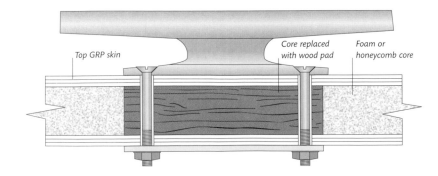

Top GRP skin   Core replaced with wood pad   Foam or honeycomb core

SANDWICH DECKS

All deck fittings should be through-bolted with a substantial backing pad. In sandwich construction decks, the core must be reinforced or replaced to prevent it being crushed when the bolts are tightened. Sometimes, the lower skin and core are removed, the core is replaced with a plywood pad, and the lower skin replaced.

planks should be maintained in good condition to prevent fresh water from leaking through the decks and rotting the timber. In hot climates, planked decks will dry out and shrink under the heat of the sun. Thoroughly wetting the decks with sea water early morning and late evening will slow this effect and reduce the amount of damage sustained.

Plywood decks are best coated with a hard two-pack polyurethane paint system, which should be maintained in good, watertight condition. Any damage should be made good as quickly as possible, bearing in mind the need to dry the wood before painting so that moisture is not sealed in.

Laid teak decks

Teak decks have the image of luxury and are often fitted over GRP or metal decks for cosmetic reasons. Teak was originally used for traditionally laid decks because it is stable and long-lasting and can be left bare or oiled. A modern teak deck, on the other hand, is usually installed only for its appearance. However, it adds significant weight, creates the risk of leaks if fasteners are used, is expensive, and gets hot underfoot in tropical conditions. Furthermore, since thin strips of teak are used when being laid on a subdeck, the teak can wear out quite quickly in high-traffic areas.

Windows and hatches

Most boat windows and hatches are made of polycarbonate, which slowly degrades and crazes in UV light, so they may need replacing every 10–15 years. The strongest windows are the type that bolt directly through the sides of the coachroof, although the type with aluminum frames are a common alternative and have a neat

DECK HATCHES
Some modern cruisers have several deck hatches. All must be well fitted and the gaskets should be checked periodically.

appearance. Windows and hatches are a potential source of deck leaks and should be checked periodically to ensure they are watertight. Also check the condition of hinges and catches, as well as the rubber sealing gasket of opening ports.

Sealing deck fittings

All deck fittings are potential sources of leaks, which may let water into the balsa or foam core of a GRP deck, or into the timbers of a wooden deck. The weak point is often where the gear is attached to the deck.

Aluminum craft can have much of their gear welded directly to the deck; on other types of boat it is through-bolted and bedded down on a marine adhesive sealant to eliminate leaks. Over time, fittings may loosen and sealant will harden and crack. Check deck fittings for movement, and tighten fastenings if necessary. At the first sign of any deck leaks, remove the fitting and re-bed it on fresh sealant. Inspect the fitting and its fasteners for signs of corrosion. If water finds its way through the deck and gets to the interior, it can damage fabrics and finishes.

CARING FOR WOOD

Woodwork requires a good deal of care, especially if it is above deck, where it is exposed to the elements. The best way to reduce your workload is to get rid of all woodwork on deck, but for many sailors its aesthetic attraction justifies the long hours of maintenance it needs.

Varnishing wood

Varnishing is necessary at least annually in temperate climes and as often as every few weeks in the tropics. Single-pack polyurethane varnishes are appropriate for traditional wooden construction, but a harder, two-pack varnish is better on stable, molded wood surfaces or plywood.

To get an excellent finish, the wood must be dry and sanded to a very smooth finish with progressively finer grades of sandpaper. At least ten coats of varnish must be applied, starting with one or two thinned coats. The surface must be sanded with very fine sand- or emery paper between each coat for maximum adhesion and gloss. Only apply varnish in warm, dry, and calm weather conditions.

Coating wood

An alternative to varnish is to use a wood oil or polymer coating, which can seal the wood very effectively and give an acceptable finish while requiring little maintenance.

BARE TEAK DECKS

THE RIG

Whatever the size of your craft, the condition of its rig and related fittings is critical for handling efficiency and safety. Most of the equipment should require little in the way of maintenance, but it must be checked regularly for wear and the appearance of small cracks that indicate stress damage. This will involve at least an annual trip to the masthead, unless you unstep the mast when you lay up the boat for the winter.

INSPECTING THE RIG
If the yacht is not kept ashore each winter with its rig removed, it is essential to do a thorough check of every component of the rig at least once every season.

Rig components
The rig comprises the mast (or masts in a ketch, yawl, or schooner), boom, standing rigging, running rigging, and the sails. In addition, other hardware—including winches, cleats, and jammers—is fitted to the mast, boom, and deck to help control or secure halyards, sheets, and control lines. Every component must be of a suitable size for the loads involved and must be maintained properly. Most good-quality marine gear will give many years of reliable service as long as it is the correct size for the loads involved.

Stainless-steel fittings
Many fittings and fasteners are made of stainless steel, which is resistant to rust because of a protective layer that forms on its surface in the presence of oxygen. However, if a stainless-steel fastener is sealed from the air, corrosion can occur in small crevices.

Salt water speeds up the corrosion process, so if a stainless steel fastener is sealed from air within timber that is allowed to become wet with salt water, it is to be expected that the fastener will corrode. High-quality marine fittings are polished after welding to remove surface

irregularities. If they begin to rust, they can be buffed up to remove the surface damage at the source of the corrosion.

Rope clutches
Clutches are commonly used to secure halyards, reefing lines, and other control lines. They are often mounted ahead of a winch so that once the clutch has been engaged to lock the rope, it can then be removed from the winch. Clutches require little maintenance—just an occasional check that the springs are intact and functioning properly. Lines are often led aft from the mast through deck-

mounted turning blocks called deck organizers. These should also be checked occasionally to make sure the sheaves are running smoothly and their fasteners are secure, as these fittings often take considerable load.

Wire running rigging
Halyards are often made of wire with a rope tail, so stretch is eliminated in the part under load. Alternatively, low-stretch ropes, such as Spectra and Vectran, can be used. They are more expensive, but are lighter and easier to handle. Wire halyards can be made of flexible galvanized or stainless steel.

SERVICING A WINCH

Winches are long-lasting items, but should be serviced annually to keep them working efficiently. Remove the drum, having first released the circlip or removed the Allen screws at the top. A dust sheet hung on the guardrail will stop small items such as pawl springs from rolling overboard. Remove all components, clean them thoroughly in kerosene, and inspect for wear. Each item should be lightly coated with winch grease before being

replaced; most winches that stick or gum up have been too heavily greased.

DISMANTLING A WINCH
Learn how your winches come apart and service them at least once a season. A dust sheet will stop parts from falling overboard.

Stainless wire is more common since it is less prone to rust, but, unlike galvanized wire, any damage can be hard to spot and the wire may fail suddenly and unexpectedly. Damage in wire halyards usually occurs where they pass over sheaves (pulley wheels) in the mast that are too small in diameter. Watch out for broken wire strands, which indicate likely failure, and check the rope-to-wire splices.

Rope running rigging

Rope halyards, sheets, and control lines should be checked regularly for chafe. Most damage occurs when a highly loaded rope rubs slightly against another rope, shroud, or lifeline. Make sure that all sheets and halyards have a fair lead and cannot rub on anything when under load.

If damage occurs at or near the end of a rope, it can be cut off and the rope shortened; if it occurs in the middle, the best you can hope for is two much shorter ropes. Periodically end-for-ending (reversing) a rope, especially sheets, can lengthen its life. Make sure rope ends are sealed or whipped to prevent fraying (*p.222*).

Wash all your ropes in warm, soapy water from time to time to remove the dirt and salt that makes them stiff and accelerates wear.

Standing rigging

Shrouds, forestays, and backstays are usually made of stainless steel wire (or galvanized wire on some older traditional craft). Solid stainless steel rod rigging is also used on larger cruisers and racing boats, and some racing boats use high-performance, low-stretch rope for standing rigging because it is much lighter than wire.

Wire standing rigging needs little maintenance other than periodic checks for broken strands. If you find any, replace the wire because any weakness compromises the strength of the entire rig.

Occasionally wiping down the rigging will also remove dirt and salt crystals that can accelerate crevice corrosion, especially where wire enters the end terminals. Similarly, check that guardwires and jackstays are in good condition with no broken strands of wire, and that their attachment to the boat is secure.

All rigging screws should have toggles fitted between them and the chainplates so that they are free to move in any direction without bending. Inspect them carefully for any signs of hairline cracks, which indicate stress damage. Check also the condition of split pins and clevis pins, as well as the security of locking nuts. Do not use split rings to secure clevis pins used on standing rigging; they are not as secure as split pins. If your standing rigging is over ten years old (less for a racing boat), replace it, even if there are no obvious signs of defects.

Spars

Most boats today have aluminum spars, although wooden masts and booms are still used, and the use of carbon fiber is increasing. Aluminum spars have anodized surfaces that are eventually roughened by salt crystals and contaminants in the air. Wash them off and finish the surface with a wax polish. Spars should be checked annually for corrosion around fittings (especially if stainless fasteners have been used) and for any hairline cracks. Pay special attention to the mast-step area, spreader roots, and rigging attachment points. Spreader ends should be checked to be sure they are smooth and will not damage genoas that sweep across them when tacking, and that they have not damaged the shroud passing through them.

At the masthead, check that the halyard sheaves run smoothly and lubricate them with silicon spray. Check also the condition of the gooseneck fitting and the vang and mainsheet attachment points.

Wooden masts require varnishing, oiling, or painting at least annually and possibly even more frequently in the tropics. Check for splits in the wood and signs of rot.

Carbon masts on large cruisers and high performance race boats are usually painted with a hard two-pack polyurethane and should be checked and cleaned like aluminum.

ROPE CLUTCHES

A bank of clutches is often found in front of coachroof-mounted winches to allow one winch to handle several lines.

THE SAILS

The sails are the driving force of a sailing boat, and they are expensive to replace, but they are often ignored in terms of regular inspection and maintenance. The old cliches—"a stitch in time saves nine" and "prevention is better than cure"—are nowhere more applicable than in sail care. Make it a habit to scan your sails every time you hoist, lower, and trim them to try to pick up minor damage before it develops into a major failure. Protect your sails and they will have a long life.

The stitching is where most damage occurs, so check along seams, batten pockets, and around high-load areas such as corners and the leech. Scan these areas every time you hoist or lower a sail.

When you are sailing, walk around the deck to check which areas of the sails can rub on any part of the mast, standing rigging, or guardrails. If the genoa snags on the stanchions when tacking, then fit small rollers to the lifelines each side of the stanchion to help the sail "skirt" itself over the rail. This saves a crew member from doing it by hand. Small areas of damaged stitching are easily dealt with by hand sewing using the original needle holes. Damage to stitching is usually caused by chafe, often against the shrouds and spreaders. If the source of the chafe cannot be moved, or the sail retrimmed to avoid it, fit self-adhesive anti-chafe patches at strategic points to protect the sail.

A small rip in the middle of a panel can quickly develop into a large tear in a sudden gust. Early action with a needle and thread can prevent damage from spreading rapidly. Larger areas of damage can be repaired temporarily using adhesive tape and hand stitching, but should be dealt with by a sailmaker as soon as possible.

Sails should be washed thoroughly in fresh water as often as is practical to remove salt crystals and dirt, as these abrade the cloth. Always cover sails when they are not in use—long exposure to sunlight will quickly weaken and destroy the cloth, especially in Mediterranean and tropical climates. Roller reefing headsails should have a sacrificial strip of cloth along the leech and foot to protect the sail itself from ultraviolet (UV) degradation. If this strip degrades, it can be replaced relatively cheaply.

Stretching and flogging

All sails, whether they are traditionally constructed of woven Dacron, or high-tech laminates of film and low-stretch fibers, will suffer if allowed to flap or flog excessively, as this causes the material to gradually weaken and break down. For this reason, sail handling operations should be carried out efficiently; reefing or changing the headsail should be done in good time so wind does not need to be spilled from the sail to prevent the boat from being overpowered.

When motor-sailing to windward for long periods, lower the mainsail or steer a few degrees off the wind to keep the sail full rather than flogging. Rough handling when stowing the sail will also cause damage. Handle the sail as gently as possible and do

SAIL LOADS
When a boat is fully powered up and well heeled, the loads on a sail become very high, especially at the head, clew, and tack, where extra reinforcement is essential. Check the stitching regularly in these areas.

not jerk the sail to pull out creases, as this is harmful to the finish of a Dacron sail as well as to the integrity of a laminate sail.

Dacron sails will stretch with use, especially if the boat is not reefed sufficiently in strong winds. As a sail ages and the cloth weakens, this stretch may reach a point where the sail will no longer drive the boat efficiently to windward. Laminate sails have negligible stretch, even near the end of their useful life, but are even more susceptible to damage caused by flogging and rough handling, which cause the material to break down and delaminate. When these sails fail, it tends to be sudden and dramatic.

Downwind sails

Spinnakers, asymmetrics, and cruising chutes are made from lightweight nylon that is easily ripped if it snags on a sharp part of the boat or rigging. To protect all sails, check that all split pins and other sharp items on the rigging and lifelines are adequately taped over. If small nicks or tears are found in the spinnaker, a temporary patch can be made with spinnaker repair tape, after any salt has been washed away with fresh water and the sail allowed to dry thoroughly. A permanent stitched repair should always be made as soon as possible. More serious damage will need to be repaired by a sailmaker.

Valeting

Most sailmakers offer a service where they will examine a sail for damage to the cloth or stitching, make any minor repairs necessary and launder the sail. An annual valet may seem expensive but it will help deal with potential problems early, before more

RIPPED SPINNAKER
A small rip in a spinnaker can grow very rapidly, especially when the sail abruptly fills with wind after collapsing. The shock load can turn a small tear into a destroyed spinnaker in seconds.

serious and costly damage is done to the sail, and will keep the sail looking good for as long as possible.

Sail damage at sea

If a sail rips when it is in use, you must get it down as soon as possible; otherwise, the damage will quickly get worse and the sail will be destroyed.

If the damaged sail is a headsail, replace it with another and stow the damaged sail until you reach port. If it is the mainsail, lower it completely, unless it is possible to reef the sail so that the damaged area is not exposed.

If the sail cannot be used, replace it with the trysail if you have one. If you are on a long passage and if conditions allow, take the mainsail off the mast and boom and repair it down below. A repair at sea need only be good enough to allow you to reach port. Once ashore, however, the damage should be assessed by a sailmaker as soon as possible and professionally repaired. If long-distance cruising, especially on a boat with a roller reefing headsail, it makes sense to carry an old suit of sails as spares.

PATCHING A SAIL

You should be able to undertake minor sail repairs at sea. This usually involves either replacing seam stitching or patching rips in a sail panel. High-tech laminate sails made of low-stretch fibers cannot be stitched—repairs can only be made by gluing patches to the sail.

SEWING KIT

A sailmaker's palm (*p.220*), needles, waxed thread, sailcloth, and glue or sticky-backed sail repair material.

❶ Cut a patch to cover the tear. Trim the corners, and turn the edges under.

❷ Glue the patch centrally so that it covers the tear on all sides.

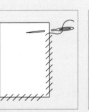

❸ Oversew neatly around the turned-under edges of the patch.

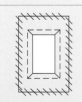

❹ Turn the sail over, and then trim the torn area to make a rectangle.

❺ To finish the repair, oversew around the edges of the rectangle.

THE INTERIOR

Many different materials are used in the interior of a yacht. These range from the wood and soft furnishings that make a cabin into a comfortable living area, through to the electrical and mechanical gear used for operating the boat. These items are fitted into an environment that is often poorly ventilated and exposed to a wide range of temperatures and humidity conditions. They need to be looked after carefully and checked regularly or they will quickly deteriorate, especially when a boat is not used frequently.

Wooden surfaces

Wood is the traditional material for boat interiors. It is popular because it is easy to work with and looks warm and natural; even boats with GRP or metal hulls often have a considerable amount of wood down below.

It is also traditional for most interior wood to be varnished. A varnished finish looks very attractive if the wood is good-quality and has been fashioned by an expert shipwright. However, varnish must be well applied in a sufficient number of coats to produce a deep gloss. On stable wooden surfaces, such as plywood or laminates made up with veneers, a two-pack polyurethane varnish gives the hardest and most durable finish, which should last for at least five years. Wood in older boats will probably have been finished with tung oil or single-pack polyurethane varnishes. These require annual revarnishing to stay in good condition.

If the quality of the wood or existing varnish is not perfect, consider using a matt or eggshell varnish; this will hide far more flaws than a high-gloss finish, which exaggerates defects.

Varnish care

Revarnishing is best done during the spring or fall, when conditions are warm and dry but not too hot. Cold, humid conditions produce a much poorer finish. During the sailing season, wipe down varnished surfaces occasionally, and touch up any small scratches when they occur to prevent moisture from getting under the varnish and penetrating the wood.

Painted and GRP surfaces

Although painted surfaces are easier to maintain than varnished ones, they are not as common aboard yachts. As with varnishes, conventional and single-pack polyurethane paints need more regular repainting than two-pack finishes and are softer and more vulnerable to scratching. However, they are cheaper and easier to use, especially when you need to touch up an area of minor damage.

Some GRP craft have a molded interior, designed to give smooth surfaces that are easy to clean and do not require painting. Interior moldings are practical in the heads where wet oilskins are often hung to dry, and a shower is usually fitted.

THE GALLEY
A U- or L-shape (pictured) is a practical galley arrangement. The stove has a grab bar in front, which is an important safety feature. The sinks are supplied with both pressure hot and cold water.

CHART TABLE

A navigation area with chart table and seat is often located between the saloon and the companionway ladder. This location is handy for quick access to the cockpit and for easy communication between the navigator and the helmsman.

Deckheads and hull sides

Many deckheads and hull sides are lined with plywood panels covered in foam-backed vinyl or fabric to provide extra insulation and hide constructional features. Because they usually need to be removable to allow access to fasteners, wiring, or plumbing, the panels are often held in place with small amounts of Velcro, although self-tapping screws may be used for larger headlining panels.

After a few years the panels may sag or become completely detached, or the foam backing may break down with age. Such panels can be replaced quite easily, or re-covered and refastened with more substantial strips of Velcro or positive push fasteners.

Soft furnishings

Bunk cushions on boats are usually a compromise because most bunks have to double as seating during the day. Bunk cushions that are comfortable to sleep on are often too soft for good seating, and good seats are usually too narrow to be used as bunks. Many production cruisers are built within a stringent budget, and savings are sometimes made in soft furnishings. When the time comes to upgrade or refit an older boat, improvements can often be made in this area.

Open-cell foam is generally used for bunk cushions, while closed-cell foam (which does not absorb moisture but is much harder) is more common for cockpit cushions that may get wet.

A wide range of fabrics can be used for covering cushions. Vinyl is sometimes used as it is water-resistant, but it is uncomfortable to sit on, especially in hot weather. In small yachts, where there is a greater risk of water finding its way below, vinyl can be used on the underside of cushions with fabric on the top. Turn the cushions over if there is a danger of their getting splashed, but use them the right way up at other times. In any case, upholstery fabric should have a high percentage of synthetic content so that it does not absorb moisture. If bunk cushions do get wet, both the foam and the cover will need to be cleaned thoroughly to remove the salt, otherwise the cushion will never dry out completely and will be unpleasant to sit or sleep on.

Many owners brighten up their yacht's interior with curtains, carpets, and scatter cushions. Take these off the boat when laying up for winter, otherwise they will get damp and may develop mold. Carpets can be pleasant in port, but should be taken up at sea if there is any likelihood that water will get below, remembering that wet foul-weather gear can carry quite a quantity of water below. Waterproof carpet is highly effective and, although it is expensive, only a little is needed to cover the cabin sole of a small yacht.

Have somewhere dry and out of the way to stow loose furnishings when you go to sea, or they will end up in a soggy mess on the cabin sole. If possible, stow anything vulnerable to moisture in waterproof bags.

SLEEPING CABINS

Many yachts have a forecabin with a double V-berth or two-single berths. They are not practical for sleeping at sea, but are useful in port. Stowage space is often available underneath the berths.

Refrigeration

Installing refrigeration on board cruising boats is increasingly popular, despite the system's being the largest single power drain found on most yachts. For the system to function efficiently, the refrigerator must be well insulated—4 in (10 cm) of good-quality insulation all around is ideal for a refrigerator, with more being needed if a freezer is required.

The best types are compressor-driven and incorporate a holding plate that is cooled to a low temperature when surplus electrical power is available, such as when the engine is running. Once the liquid in the holding plate has been pulled down to a low temperature, it sustains the temperature in the box. Limiting the number of times the lid of the refrigerator is opened will reduce the amount of power required.

An alternative is a similarly well-insulated box into which block ice is put at the beginning of a passage. Place a frozen, five-liter water container in the ice box and surround it with items that have already been chilled. This system is common in the tropics but less so in temperate areas. An ice box will work surprisingly well for up to four or five days, even in hot weather.

If you have refrigeration in a temperate area, and you intend to sail to a hot climate, make sure the unit has sufficient cooling capacity and insulation to cope with the increased demands that will be placed on it.

Heating

Installing cabin heating of some kind will extend your comfortable sailing season if you sail in temperate latitudes; indeed, it will even allow you to use the boat all year should you choose to do so. Combined with good ventilation, a heater will also help to keep the interior dry and free of mildew.

The most popular and effective heaters are the ducted warm-air central-heating type, usually fueled by diesel, but occasionally by gas. Advantages of this type of system are that heat can be ducted to outlets in each cabin, warmup time is very short, temperature control is easy, and operation is simple and mess-free—you just flip a switch. The forced passage of warm air through the boat is also very effective at drying out a wet interior. Drawbacks are a significant electrical drain, high initial cost, space consumption, and a fairly complicated installation. A

similar alternative, but one that does not require so much space for large diameter ducting, is a diesel-fired hot-water system that feeds small radiators, which may be fan-assisted, through small-bore piping.

At the other end of the spectrum, a charcoal heater mounted on the saloon bulkhead can be installed in a couple of hours and will provide ample heat to the main parts of the boat in all but the coldest weather. The disadvantage is that charcoal is potentially messy and bulky to stow in large quantities, but these heaters are ideal for occasional use.

Kerosene and drip-feed diesel are other popular types of traditional-style heaters. The fuel is easy to carry, and, if it is a diesel heater, it uses the same fuel as most yacht engines. Also, these traditional-style heaters are reliable, virtually maintenance-free, last almost indefinitely, and create a cozy ambience in the cabin.

Improving stowage

Many production boats have relatively little stowage volume, and what is provided may be poorly organized. An owner with basic woodworking skills can add fiddles or shelves, convert wasted space into useful lockers, and provide custom stowage for items that need to be accessed easily. Long-distance cruisers often store fruit and vegetables in netting above bunks. This allows good ventilation, so the food stays fresh for longer.

GALLEY COUNTER
This yacht has a galley that runs fore and aft along one side of the saloon. The counter contains a top-loading refrigerator, a gimballed stove with removable cover, and twin sinks with pressurized hot and cold water. Lockers are installed under the sinks and above the counter, under the sidedecks.

VENTILATION

Adequate ventilation is essential for comfort aboard a boat in all conditions. It can be provided through hatches, opening ports, or dedicated ventilators. Boats without enough ventilation will stay damp inside, accelerating deterioration and encouraging mold. If your boat is kept somewhere with access to domestic electricity over the winter, it is often worth investing in a dehumidifier, which will keep the interior of a yacht completely dry at a very modest cost. Whether or not you are using a dehumidifier, cabin doors and locker doors should be left open wherever possible to allow air to circulate.

Hatches

Deck hatches can bring a welcome flow of air in hot conditions, but in most cases, they need to be closed at sea. In hot climates, a wind scoop—effectively a large fabric funnel set over the hatch—is a useful addition to increase the flow of air on light wind days.

Opening ports

Ports that can be opened are useful, especially if they open from a stern cabin into the cockpit where they will be protected in all but heavy weather. Those fitted in the hull or cabin sides should be shut when under way.

Ventilators

The best ventilators are of the Dorade type, which allow air in but divert any water back to the deck. These can be left open most of the time but should be closed off in very severe conditions. Mushroom ventilators are very popular, and work with any wind angle, but need to be closed off if water is coming over the decks.

The type that incorporates a solar-powered fan is particularly effective at forcing a flow of air into the boat. Simple cowl ventilators work well on boats kept on swing moorings, as they will be head-to-wind much of the time.

When under way the cowl can be pointed into the wind to funnel maximum airflow, but in rough conditions the cowls should be pointed downwind, or blanked off, to prevent spray from getting below. Ideally, cowl ventilators should be used in conjunction with a Dorade box, to allow water to escape back on deck.

Louvers in doors and cutouts in furniture can be used to encourage air to circulate around lockers. A louver fitted in the washboards will allow air channeled into the cabin by ventilators farther forward to escape, helping to promote a through draft.

OPENING PORT

MUSHROOM VENTILATOR

LOUVERED WASHBOARD

COWL VENTILATOR

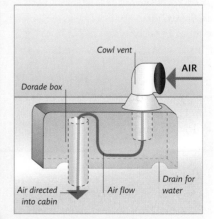

HOW A DORADE VENT WORKS

A Dorade vent, so called because the first example was fitted on a yacht called *Dorade*, provides the best chance of achieving good ventilation in a yacht while keeping water out of the interior. Air and water can both enter the cowl vent, but the water drops to the floor of the box and runs out of the drain holes, while air can flow up to the top of the high inlet tube and into the yacht's interior.

ELECTRICS

Most cruising yachts rely heavily on their electrical system. Electricity is used to run navigation and communications equipment, lighting, entertainment systems, and refrigeration. Consequently, there is a need to generate and store sufficient power to operate the gear. Although modern boats tend to be reasonably dry down below in most conditions, electrical equipment must be of good marine quality and should be well installed and maintained, otherwise it can deteriorate very quickly. If you sail a small boat, you should not rely totally on its electrical supply. There should always be a backup system that will allow the boat to be sailed and navigated, and the crew to be kept comfortable, in the event of a total power failure.

BATTERY TYPES
Proper traction batteries, here 2-volt cells that are wired in series to produce a 12-volt bank, are most suitable for domestic power needs and will last much longer than an automotive-style battery.

DC systems

Small- and medium-sized yachts typically use 12- or 24-volt direct current (DC) systems, with the power supplied by a bank of batteries. These are often stored in or near the bilges to keep their considerable weight as low as possible. Batteries are designed for specific purposes; the automotive type, often seen aboard small boats, is not designed for marine use. An automotive battery delivers a short burst of high current to a car's starter motor. Once the engine is running, an alternator meets the needs of the car's electrical system. On a boat, batteries start the engine, but they are also needed to power electrical gear for many hours when the engine is not running.

Batteries

The best batteries for marine use are deep-discharge or traction batteries. Both these heavy-duty types are designed to be "deep-cycled." This means that they can be discharged to a relatively low percentage of their capacity and subsequently recharged

when the engine is running. A good marine battery will be able to handle many hundreds of charge-discharge cycles, which would quickly destroy an automotive battery. It is good practice to have one battery for engine-starting and another for the domestic loads, so the engine battery is never discharged by running the boat's systems. If your batteries are stowed low in the bilge, consider having a smaller one higher up to run the radio equipment in an emergency, such as if the main batteries were flooded by an ingress of seawater.

Battery care

Unless they are of the sealed type, batteries require occasional topping off with distilled water to replace

SELECTING EQUIPMENT

It is extremely important to use the best-quality electrical gear that has been designed specifically for use in boats. No other equipment will be as reliable or as safe in marine conditions.

battery fluid that evaporates when the battery is charged. They give off hydrogen gas, which is lighter than air, when they are being charged, so the top of the battery compartment should be well ventilated.

Gel batteries, in which the electrolyte is a gel rather than a liquid, require no maintenance and cannot spill battery fluid. They are totally sealed and do not give off hydrogen gas. They are more expensive than conventional batteries, but have obvious advantages for use on boats. Some types can withstand more charge-discharge cycles than conventional deep discharge batteries.

All batteries should be fastened down securely so they cannot come loose in the event of a knockdown, and conventional batteries should be mounted in a drip-tray to catch any spills of electrolyte. The state of charge of a conventional battery can be checked with a hydrometer, which measures the specific gravity of the electrolyte. If you are leaving the boat unattended for some time, be sure that the batteries are fully charged as they will slowly discharge over time. Do not leave them heavily discharged for long, as this will shorten their life. The voltage across a battery also gives an indication of its state of charge. In theory, a 12V battery will deliver 13.2V when fully charged, although in practice 12.9V is the highest figure you are likely to obtain. At 12.5V there is around 75 percent of the charge remaining, and at 12.2V, 50 percent charge is left. Once the voltage falls to 11.8V, the battery has only 25 percent of its charge remaining. However, discharging to this level will shorten the life of even deep-discharge batteries—ideally, they should be charged before the voltage drops below 12.2V.

Charging systems

The most common charging system aboard small boats uses an alternator mounted on the engine and driven by a belt from the flywheel. Whenever the engine is run, the alternator supplies power to the batteries, with the amount of power delivered being controlled by a regulator.

So-called "smart" regulators are far more efficient than the simple type built into most alternators. These sense the condition of the battery, its temperature, state of charge, and the voltage delivered by the alternator, and they automatically adjust the output from the generator to deliver the best charge to the batteries. Using a smart regulator significantly improves the performance of your batteries and reduces recharging times.

Wiring

Only marine wiring should be used aboard a boat. The best type of wiring has good-quality insulation surrounding multiple strands that have been tinned by drawing them through a solder

CURRENT DRAW OF POPULAR ITEMS

It is easy to add new equipment that requires electricity and to forget the extra load that it will put on your battery capacity. If your domestic battery bank and charging ability is not sufficient, you will end up having to run your engine for long periods just to replace the electrical energy the equipment consumes.

How big a battery bank?

To calculate the size of battery bank needed for your boat, start by working out the total daily power usage (multiply current in amps by the length of time for which you expect to use each item), using the table (right) as a guide. Assuming you charge batteries once a day and do not want to discharge them beyond 50 percent of total capacity, your battery bank should be at least twice the size of your estimate daily power usage. It is rarely worth skimping when specifying the size of battery banks and charging systems. Well-cared-for batteries will last many seasons, but those that are regularly run nearly flat because they are too small for the task may fail in the first year or two.

ITEM	TYPICAL CURRENT DRAW
Anchor light	1 amp
Tricolor light	2 amp
Interior lights (each)	1 amp
Log/depth sounder	0.5 amp
GPS	<0.5 amp
VHF	<0.5 amp
CD player	1–5 amp
Autopilot	4–10 amp
Warm-air heater fan	1–2 amp
Refrigerator	4 amp

bath. Untinned copper wire in a marine environment quickly develops a green coating that extends inside the insulation, increasing the wire's resistance to the flow of electricity and making it more brittle. All wiring should be well secured and is best run in plastic conduit and hidden behind headliners or hull paneling.

A yacht's wiring must be able to handle the maximum current drawn by the equipment with as small a voltage drop as possible between the battery and the equipment. Wires that carry high loads, such as those between the batteries and the starter motor, or that lead to an electric windlass or other high power equipment, should be of an adequate size and as short as possible to minimize voltage drop. If in doubt, use oversized wire as this will reduce

energy lost as heat in the wiring system. If you are considering buying a boat that is more than five years old, look carefully at the electrical system. If the best materials were not used initially, they may need replacing. It is also likely that extra electrical equipment has been added to the original system, which could cause problems in the future if the system was not designed, and did not have spare capacity, for additional items to be added.

Many older boats have each wiring circuit protected by a fuse on the switch panel. These are fine until a fuse blows, when a new one of the correct rating has to be found. This may be simple in daylight, but could be a different matter at night in a heavy sea. It is, therefore, worth installing a switch panel with circuit breakers, since these can be reset after they have tripped.

Extending the system

Unless you have a thorough understanding of your boat's electrical system, you should consult an expert before making modifications or adding new gear. Most problems with electrics on boats arise because the system was badly installed, poor-quality materials were used, or additional equipment was installed without considering the extra loads placed on the system.

Some new boats are built with an electrical system that can be extended without difficulty, but in others the system can be hard to access and expand. Ideally, a boat's electrical system should have spare contact breakers on the switch panel to accommodate new equipment, and the battery and charging system should be capable of handling more equipment.

A good sign that a new boat's electrical system is capable of being expanded is the presence of spare contact breakers on the panel and "mousing" lines in the electrical conduit to pull through additional wires. These simple items allow additional equipment to be easily installed, whereas the lack of them can make the same job much more difficult and expensive.

Installation

Always turn off the batteries at their isolating switches before starting work on the electrical system. If you are installing new gear that draws a high current, consider whether you need to increase the capacity of your battery bank or your charging system. Also, you must ensure that wiring and terminals of a suitable size for the current load are used, and that there are appropriately sized circuit breakers or fuses in the new circuit.

All equipment should be connected to the positive and negative bus bars at the boat's distribution panel with a fuse or, preferably, circuit breaker for each item. Wiring runs should be well secured, and preferably run through a conduit. Make sure that the size of the wiring is sufficient to cope with the current needed by the equipment and the distance over which the current must be delivered.

High current and long distances require a larger cross-section wire to avoid significant voltage drop between the panel and the item of equipment. Using wire that is too small will reduce the power available to the item, and will cause the wiring to heat up, possibly leading to the insulation melting and causing a fire hazard.

Maintenance, replacement, and the addition of new electrical equipment will be made much easier if you have a wiring diagram of your boat's 12-volt and 240-volt systems. If one was not supplied, consider having an electrician draw one for you, and always update it to include new equipment when it is installed.

Power-usage monitors

If your yacht has a lot of electrical equipment, or if you use it for serious cruising, it is helpful to add a monitor of the type that measures the total charge delivered to the batteries, and the total power used by the boat's systems. These monitors give a precise indication of how much charge is left in the batteries, and when they will next need charging.

Controlling usage

Unless you spend a lot of time living aboard, it is very easy to forget to conserve electrical power, with the result that you have to run the engine for many hours to replenish the batteries. Your time spent cruising will be less noisy, cheaper, and simpler if you restrict your use of electrical equipment as much as possible. Ways to minimize electrical consumption include replacing light bulbs with LED bulbs that require a fraction of the power and last far longer. Turn off equipment when not required, open the refrigerator as little as possible, and only run your instruments and radar when needed on passage. Also, on passage, turn off a pressurized water system to save both power and water.

AC systems

Larger yachts often run an alternating current (AC) generator to power onboard domestic electrical systems. An AC generator can also be used to charge the DC battery bank, which

DISTRIBUTION PANEL
An electrical distribution panel, usually mounted at the chart table (*top*), provides control of the 12-volt and 240s electrical systems and allows you to monitor consumption and the state of the batteries. It is best if the panel hinges open (*above*) to give access to the rear so that wiring can be organized neatly and new equipment can be added more easily.

Control panel with on/off switch

Small size allows easy mounting

Connections for 12-volt input and 240-volt output

INVERTER
A small inverter can provide AC power by converting the DC power supplied by the batteries. Modern inverters are efficient and are useful when there is a need to run equipment that needs AC power without installing an AC generator.

avoids reliance on the main engine for charging. However, the vast majority of small and medium-sized cruisers have little need for an AC generator, which is expensive and can also be noisy unless it is well installed.

The most common, and simplest, AC system plugs into a shore-based supply when the boat is in a marina. This is often used when alongside to run a battery charger and to provide power to run domestic equipment.

An AC system must be kept totally separate from the onboard DC system and must be installed and maintained properly to avoid potentially fatal electric shocks. If AC power is needed to run small appliances when the boat is not plugged into shore power, an inverter can be installed to convert the DC supply to AC. On a small boat, these are most suitable for powering low-current devices such as laptop computers; high-current items such as hair dryers and microwaves will draw so much power that they will rapidly discharge all but the largest battery.

ALTERNATIVE ENERGY
Some cruising boats, particularly those used for long-distance sailing, make use of alternative forms of energy production. Wind generators, solar panels, and water generators are all popular means of delivering charge to the batteries without running the engine. All have their benefits and shortcomings, and their use depends on where you sail and how you use your boat. An additional benefit of these generators is that charging is often continuous over several hours, so the batteries' discharge cycle is shorter than if the engine is used to charge just one or two hours a day.

Wind and water power
Many cruisers use a wind generator to help keep batteries fully charged without needing to run the engine. Wind generators vary in size and efficiency. Small ones put out little power in most wind strengths but are useful for maintaining batteries when the boat is unattended. In windy regions, large wind generators can comfortably supply a boat's entire power requirements. Water generators are towed behind the yacht when it is under way. They tend to be very powerful, but their drag can slow the boat a little.

Solar power
Solar panels are an increasingly popular choice as an environmentally friendly means of providing additional electrical power on cruising yachts—in particular, for those sailing in tropical areas with long hours of sunshine.

As with small wind generators, a small solar panel will have a low output, even in direct sunshine, and can do little more than maintain the batteries in good condition when the boat is left unattended.

Larger panels, however, can produce enough charge to, for instance, power a refrigerator in a Mediterranean climate. Long-distance cruisers sometimes mount panels on brackets so that they can be angled to face the sun for maximum power.

WIND AND SOLAR POWER
A wind generator and solar panels are mounted on an aft gantry where they are out of the way and unobstructed.

PLUMBING

On boats, plumbing can be quite complex and must be constructed with gear designed for marine use. It must be properly installed and regularly serviced. Freshwater systems store and deliver water for sinks in the galley and heads, and for showers. They often include a hot-water supply. Separate systems are used for bilge pumping, engine cooling, flushing the heads, and draining the shower sump. You should understand how each system works and the maintenance it requires, and carry spare parts on board since pumps are susceptible to failure.

Freshwater systems

Water tanks may be made from GRP, stainless steel, rigid polyethylene, or flexible plastic. They should be mounted to keep their weight as low as possible and, where possible, away from the bow or stern sections of the hull for efficient weight distribution.

Many boats have tanks under the saloon bunks, which is ideal for weight distribution, although the two tanks need isolation valves so that when heeled the water from the windward tank does not flow into the downwind one. In metal-hulled boats tanks can be welded in, thereby creating a double bottom and using space efficiently. If space cannot be found for rigid tanks, flexible ones can be used in small or inaccessible spaces, but must be protected from chafe. All tanks and piping must be properly supported and secured against movement of any kind. Tanks should have inspection covers for access and cleaning. They must also have vents to allow air to escape as they are filled. If possible, take the vent up under the deck in a high loop before leading the end into the bilge. This will prevent water from overflowing when the tank is full. It is worth installing a charcoal filter in the drinking-water supply to the galley.

Hoses and manual pumps

Various types of plumbing hose are available. Avoid clear plastic, as algae will grow inside the pipe where light penetrates. Rigid plastic piping is ideal and offers a range of easy-connect valves, couplings, and junctions to make the plumbing system easy to install and maintain.

If hot water is used in the system, make sure that the piping you select can handle the heat. You should also choose the correct piping for each purpose—for example, food quality for the plumbing to the galley, and sanitation piping for the sea toilet and holding tank. When installing the piping, secure it at frequent intervals, with securing points near all junctions and fittings, to prevent vibration or movement from weakening the joints and causing leaks.

The simplest fresh water system uses a manual pump at the galley and heads sinks. Manual pumps require no power, are very reliable, and discourage high water consumption.

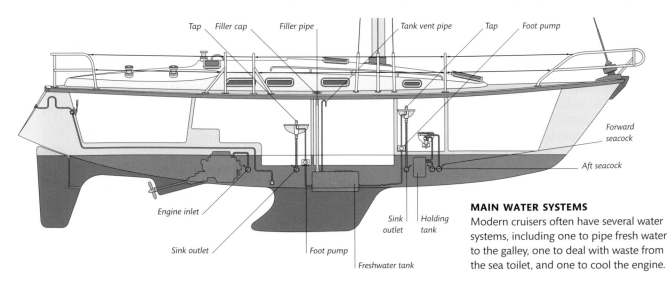

Tap Filler cap Filler pipe Tank vent pipe Tap Foot pump

Forward seacock

Aft seacock

Engine inlet

Sink outlet

Sink outlet

Foot pump

Freshwater tank

Sink outlet Holding tank

MAIN WATER SYSTEMS

Modern cruisers often have several water systems, including one to pipe fresh water to the galley, one to deal with waste from the sea toilet, and one to cool the engine.

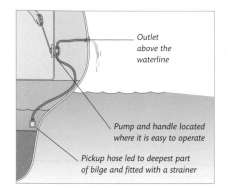

MANUAL BILGE PUMP
The bilge pump can be vital in a flooding emergency, so it must be well maintained and the hose fitted with a strainer to keep it from becoming blocked by debris.

ELECTRIC BILGE PUMP
Electric pumps often incorporate a strainer in their body and use an external, as here, or internal float switch to control automatic operation.

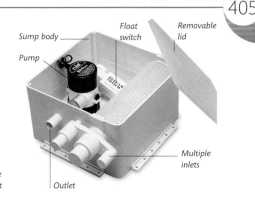

SHOWER SUMP PUMP
Shower water collects in the sump and is pumped overboard or into a holding tank. Waste water from the wash basin or other sources can also be piped into the sump.

If sited properly, they are easy to maintain and repair. A high-capacity foot pump is easy to operate and leaves both hands free.

Pressure pumps

Increasingly, even quite small yachts have a pressurized hot and cold water system. Although convenient, these increase water and electricity consumption, as well as running costs and maintenance. For reliability, choose a good-quality pump that is suitable for the job, and include an accumulator tank in the system.

Pressure pumps work by sensing the pressure drop when a tap is opened. If an accumulator tank is fitted in the system, its pressure reservoir smooths the operation of the system and frees the pump from having to repeatedly switch on and off to maintain pressure. This extends the pump's life and makes the system quieter. Most pumps are quite noisy, however, but rather than using sound insulation to eliminate the noise, it is useful to be able to hear when the pump is operating. Then, if a leak occurs, you have a chance of noticing that the pump is operating for an

unusually long time before it transfers all your fresh water from the tank to the bilge. A manual fresh water pump should always be fitted in the galley in case the pressure system or electrics fail and to use on passage when you wish to conserve water and electricity.

Bilge pumps

A yacht should have at least two bilge pumps, one of which must be manually operated and should be sited in the cockpit within reach of the helmsman. If your boat is holed below the waterline, your pumps can gain you vital seconds while you make emergency repairs. Most of the time, however, they are used to remove water that accumulates in the bilge.

The pickup hose should lead to the deepest part of the bilge and should have a strainer fitted to prevent debris from blocking the pump; an item as small as a matchstick can hold the valve of a pump open, rendering it useless. Shallow bilges may require two pickup hoses—one to port and one to starboard—so that the pump can operate with the boat heeled. Any

separate watertight compartments must have their own pumps, or be plumbed to the main one.

Electric bilge pumps can be used to supplement the manual unit and can be fitted with float switches that automatically activate the pump when the bilge water rises. When choosing an electric pump, specify the largest that will fit the available space. An 800-gallon-per-hour pump may sound as if it will move an impressive amount of water, but this rating does not allow for pumping the water up to a higher level, or for the friction encountered in a long run of narrow diameter pipe. On a large boat these effects can reduce an 800-gph flow to a mere trickle. For this reason, offshore cruisers often fit a very high capacity damage-control pump, which can remove large amounts of water in the event of a holing.

Shower sumps are normally kept separate from the main bilge and are generally cleared with an electric submersible pump. An efficient filter must be used to prevent hair from clogging the pump. An alternative is to use a manual sump pump. This will save electrical power.

Sea toilets

Make sure that every member of the crew understands how the sea toilet works and impress on them that they should never put anything into it, apart from toilet paper, that is not human waste. Allowing anything else to be put into the system is a sure way of causing a blockage—an event that will require the pump to be dismantled and cleared by hand.

Having to clear a blocked toilet pump at sea, and in the confined space of a yacht's heads compartment, is an experience that no one will wish to repeat, so it is an effective punishment for the person responsible for causing the blockage.

Most sea toilets are operated by hand, with a pump drawing in sea water to flush the bowl and pump out waste. Larger yachts may fit electrical toilets, but a manual pump should always be available in case of failure. Always use reinforced flexible hose for the pump's inlet and outlet,

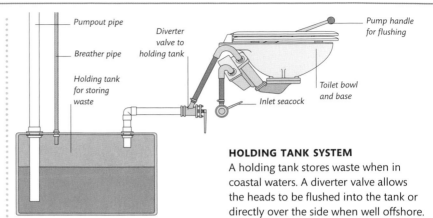

HEADS COMPARTMENT
Most production cruisers use interior moldings for the heads compartment as they are easy to clean and are not damaged by water from the shower.

both of which must be fitted with seacocks. If the hose is not reinforced, there is a danger that it may collapse on the suction side, or burst on the pressure side if there is a blockage. Use toilet-grade hose and avoid clear or translucent hose, which encourages microbe growth and leads to bad odors in the heads compartment.

Some countries prohibit the discharge of sewage from yachts within a certain distance of the shore, usually several miles. In this case, you will require a holding tank into which all waste is pumped. When the holding tank is full, it can be emptied at a marina pump-out station or by the toilet's own pump (or a dedicated pump) when you are well offshore. Chemical treatments are available to put into the tank to help keep the system odor-free and to assist in the breakdown of waste.

The flexible hoses that run between the seacocks and the heads, on both the inlet and outlet sides of the pump, should be led in a loop to the level of the underside of the deck, and should be fitted with anti-siphon valves. This will prevent sea water from siphoning back into the toilet bowl and flooding the yacht, especially when the yacht heels under sail. The pump for the heads should be serviced at least annually, and an

HOLDING TANK SYSTEM
A holding tank stores waste when in coastal waters. A diverter valve allows the heads to be flushed into the tank or directly over the side when well offshore.

additional service kit carried on board in case of emergency. When servicing the pump, smear the rubber O-rings and seals with a little Teflon-based grease to prolong their life. Do not use household bleaches or toilet cleaners as these will attack the rubber components in the pump—only products specifically designed for use with marine toilets should be used. Heads compartments are usually

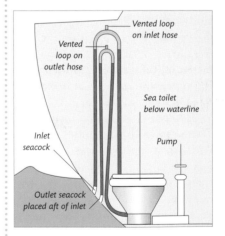

PREVENTING FLOODING
If the sea toilet is near or even below the waterline, which it is on most small cruising yachts, the inlet and outlet hoses cannot be led directly to their seacocks or the bowl will fill with water and could flood the boat. Lead the hoses up as high as possible under the decks and fit an anti-siphon fitting—a vented loop—at the highest point.

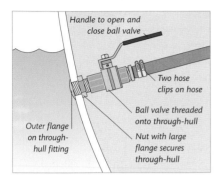

THROUGH-HULL FITTING

A through-hull fitting should be made of a corrosion resistant metal such as bronze, or a plastic approved for underwater marine use. A separate ball valve is usually screwed on to the threaded shank of the fitting.

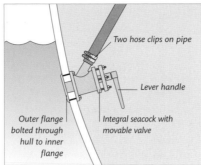

TRADITIONAL SEACOCK

A traditional seacock incorporates a valve operated with a lever handle. The fitting is usually bolted through the hull rather than using a threaded tube as with the standard through-hull fitting (*left*).

small and can become unpleasant if bad odors are allowed to develop. Clean the compartment frequently, insist that everyone uses the toilet sitting down, and try to ensure adequate ventilation via a small hatch, opening porthole or effective ventilator. When leaving the boat unattended, prop the heads door open to encourage a through-flow of air, make sure that the compartment is thoroughly clean, and remember to close the seacocks.

Through-hulls and seacocks

Although it is best to have as few holes through the hull as possible, some are unavoidable, and they must be fitted with traditional seacocks or good-quality through-hull fittings fitted with ball valves.

Seacocks, or the valves fitted to through-hulls, should be of the type with a tapered plug valve or a ball valve. Sometimes gate valves are fitted, but these are unsuitable for marine use. Many gate-valves are made of brass, which is very susceptible to corrosion in the marine environment. It is not

possible to see at a glance whether the valve is open or closed, and just a small amount of debris stuck within the body of the valve can prevent it from being fully closed.

All types of valves should be opened and closed regularly to stop them from seizing in position. They should also be cleaned and greased on a regular basis.

All hoses attached to through-hull inlets or outlets below the waterline should be fitted with two stainless-steel hose-clips for safety. If one should fail, the other remains in place. Make certain that the hose clips are made from marine-grade stainless steel or they will rust and eventually disintegrate.

It is also good practice to carry a set of soft wooden plugs of varying sizes. A plug of the appropriate size should be tied to every seacock or through-hull fitting so that in the unlikely, but potentially disastrous, event that a fitting fails, the plug can be hammered into the hole to stop or reduce the leak. Once wet, the softwood plug will swell and it will create a surprisingly good seal.

GAS SYSTEMS

Bottled gas is the most popular fuel for on-board stoves and is sometimes used for heaters. The gas system must be made from the best-quality materials and be checked and serviced regularly. When not in use, the bottle must be turned off to prevent leakages. All marine gas installations should be fitted and maintained by a qualified installer.

Gas safety precautions

As bottled gas is heavier than air, any gas that leaks from the system will seep into the bilges, where it will form an explosive mixture with air. Always store gas bottles in a sealed locker, preferably above deck, that drains overboard so any leaks cannot accumulate in the bilge. Use good-quality marine gas piping with flexible hose used for the final connection to a gimbaled stove. Make sure there is no risk of chafe on the flexible hose and that there is some slack in the hose to allow the stove to swing freely.

Consider fitting a remote-controlled solenoid valve near the bottle, with the control switch by the stove, so that the gas can be easily turned off at the bottle when not in use. Check all the joints for leaks using soapy water. A gas detector is an important precaution. It should be fitted with its sensor in the bilge, fitted above the level at which bilge water accumulates.

SELF-DRAINING GAS LOCKER

ENGINES

The majority of cruisers are fitted with an auxiliary engine that provides a charging facility for the boat's electrical system in addition to motoring capability. Today's marine engines are light and comparatively reliable. As well as using them for motoring, or motor-sailing when the wind is not fair, many sailors exclusively use engines in preference to sails for entering harbor and berthing. The drawback with this approach is that some sailors fail to become adept at handling a boat in close quarters under sail and then are likely to get into trouble when the engine fails. Sailors who rely on their engine for boat handling and for running a complex electrical system must fully understand their engine installation, be able to maintain it in good condition, and carry a comprehensive set of spares to carry out repairs at sea.

Diesel engines

The most common type of marine engine is an inboard diesel that drives the boat via a gearbox and propeller shaft. Diesels ignite their fuel using the heat created when air is compressed in the cylinder. An injector pump and fuel injectors spray precisely measured amounts of diesel into the combustion chamber at high pressure, and at exactly the right point in the compression stroke.

Very high compression ratios are required to achieve the temperature needed to ignite the fuel, so a diesel engine has to be tougher than a gasoline engine (and therefore heavier). Older designs of diesel engines typically ran at lower revs than modern units

and were much heavier than later engines. Modern diesel engines are still heavier than a gasoline engine of equivalent power, but their performance has become much more similar. For starting from cold, many diesel engines have electric preheating coils in the inlet manifold which need to

warm up for ten seconds or so before starting. Diesel engines are more expensive to purchase than gasoline engines, but they are cheaper to run, more reliable, and do not rely on an explosive fuel.

Diesel-electric hybrid engine

A new approach that is likely to prove popular on long-distance cruisers is the hybrid diesel-electric engine. A standard diesel engine drives the shaft, which also drives an electric motor/generator. A large battery bank is also installed. The boat can be powered by the diesel or the electric motor and the batteries can be charged by the diesel engine, wind, water, or solar power sources.

Gasoline engines

Marine gasoline engines are similar to car engines and are common on high-speed power boats. They need an electrical circuit to provide a spark to ignite the fuel, which can be a problem because electric ignition systems are vulnerable to damp. Gasoline engines operate at lower compression ratios and are lighter than diesel engines. Unlike diesel,

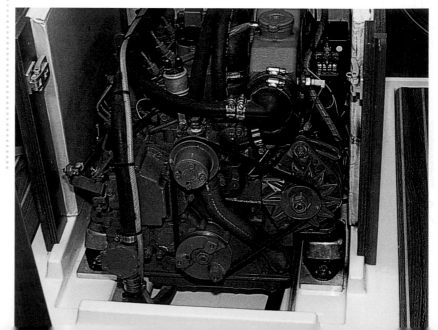

INBOARD DIESEL ENGINE
Most small yachts have an inboard diesel engine, which is often located under the companionway steps. The steps are removable to allow access to the engine.

STARTING PROBLEMS

If a diesel engine will not start, make sure clean fuel is reaching the injectors and there is no air in the system. Learn to bleed the injectors to remove trapped air from the fuel supply. Also check that the battery is sufficiently charged to turn the starter motor fast enough to fire the engine.

gasoline is an explosive fuel. However, as long as the engine is properly installed and operated, the risk of explosion should be low.

Operating gasoline engines

If a gasoline engine is fitted, the fuel tank must have a shutoff valve that is closed when the engine is not in use. A non-sparking extractor fan, ducted to the lowest part of the engine compartment, is needed to extract gasoline fumes. It should be linked to the ignition so that the engine cannot be run without the fan operating.

OUTBOARD ENGINE
An outboard engine is commonly used on a cruising yacht to power the tender. When not in use it is stored in a deep locker or, frequently, mounted on a pad secured to the pushpit.

Always run the fan for five minutes before the engine is started and all the time it is running.

Outboards

Most older outboards are gasoline two-stroke units, but four-strokes are now widely available. Four-stroke units tend to be more reliable, fuel efficient and smoother than two-strokes, but heavier and less portable. Outboards are sometimes used on very small cruisers as the primary means of propulsion, but they are most likely to be carried for use on the tender. They are ideal for this role as they are relatively light, portable, and self-contained, and can be easily tilted up when in shallow water. Their main disadvantages are that they can be expensive to run and are vulnerable to theft. When buying an outboard, pick one that is the size recommended by the tender supplier. An outboard that is too large will be heavy, consume more fuel and may overload the boat; one that is too small will not have the power to push the tender at a reasonable speed when fully loaded.

Caring for outboards

Although they are often clamped to a block on the pushpit when not in use, outboards are better stored away from the elements, preferably in a cockpit locker that is sealed from the interior. Two-stroke outboard motors need an oil-and-gasoline mix. It is important that the correct oil is used and mixed in the ratio specified in the manual. Always use fresh fuel and discard old fuel at approved points in harbors or marinas. Most outboards are water-cooled, pumping sea water through their leg and around the engine head. You should check that the cooling water is flowing freely, otherwise the engine will overheat.

LAYING UP AN ENGINE

If you lay up your boat ashore for the winter, you should take measures to protect the engine from deterioration while it is not being used.

Winterizing an engine

• Change the engine and gearbox oil (run the engine for a few minutes beforehand to heat and thin the old oil; this makes it easier to pump out).
• Change the oil filters.
• Clean out the fuel line's water-separation filter.
• Top off the fuel tanks to reduce the chance of condensation forming in the tank.
• Remove diesel injectors (if you have a diesel engine) or spark plugs (if you have a gasoline engine) and inject oil in the bores while turning the engine over by hand.
• Thoroughly clean the outside surfaces of the engine, starter motor, and alternator.
• Grease all moving parts lightly or spray them with a water repellent such as WD40.
• Drain the cooling water system and flush through with an antifreeze mixture.
• Remove the impeller from the water pump, place it in a plastic bag, and tie it to the pump so that you do not lose it.
• Disconnect the battery and grease the terminals.
• Store the battery somewhere warm and dry, charging it occasionally during the winter.
• Tie a note to the engine to remind yourself what needs to be done before the engine can be started in the spring.
• During the winter, turn the engine over by hand occasionally, and oil the bores.
• After winterizing your outboard, store it in a warm, dry place to protect it until you next use it.

FUEL, COOLING, AND EXHAUST SYSTEMS

Diesel engines are inherently reliable if well cared for, but a thoroughly clean fuel supply is crucial to their well-being. Water, dirt particles, or bacteria (which feed on condensation in fuel tanks) will, at best, clog filters. At worst they will wreck the injector pump—the most expensive single component of a diesel engine.

The fuel system should be designed to provide as clean a supply of fuel as possible, although on many boats the system falls short of ideal. Keep the tank topped up as much as possible to reduce condensation, clean and change the filters regularly, and use antibacterial and water-absorbing additives to keep the fuel clean. For maximum reliability and longevity, make sure the manufacturer's service recommendations are carried out at the specified intervals, and carry out daily engine checks.

Diesel fuel system

Fuel tanks should have an inspection hatch to allow for periodic draining and cleaning. The fuel takeoff pipe should enter at the top of the tank and run down inside to just above the bottom of the tank to avoid sucking up dirt and sediment. A fuel shutoff valve should be fitted

in an accessible location, so the supply can be shut off in the event of a fire.

A combined primary fuel filter and water separator should be fitted to isolate larger particles of dirt and water. Any water in the fuel will appear at the bottom of the glass bowl as an opaque layer and can be drained out by loosening the drain plug. The primary filter and water separator is not supplied with the engine and is often missing in marine fuel systems. The water separator bowl should be checked daily and after every five hours of engine use.

The next component is the lift pump, a low pressure pump that sucks fuel out of the tank and delivers it to the injector pump. Lift pumps usually incorporate a lever to allow manual pumping of fuel when bleeding air out of the system.

The secondary fuel filter, mounted on the engine, is designed to remove microscopic particles of dirt—as small as 0.00039 in (0.01 mm) across. This measurement gives an indication of exactly how important clean fuel is. The top of the filter housing should have a bleed screw that is used to remove air.

The injector pump is a delicate precision instrument and the most complex component in the fuel system. It has three functions—metering exactly the right amount of fuel to send to the injectors (often less than one-hundredth of a milliliter at a time), timing the precise moment it is delivered, and increasing the pressure of the fuel to several hundred pounds per square inch (psi).

Always take care when working on the high-pressure side of the fuel system—diesel at this pressure can penetrate the skin. Fuel is delivered to the combustion chamber through injectors that convert the pressurized fuel into a very fine spray, which burns cleanly. A fuel return pipe returns unused fuel to the fuel tank.

Cooling system

Most inboard engines (gasoline or diesel) are cooled by water. In the simplest systems, raw salt water is pumped around the engine and used to cool and silence the exhaust system.

PARTS OF THE FUEL SYSTEM
Clean fuel is essential for the reliable service of a diesel engine. Always include a separate primary filter in the system.

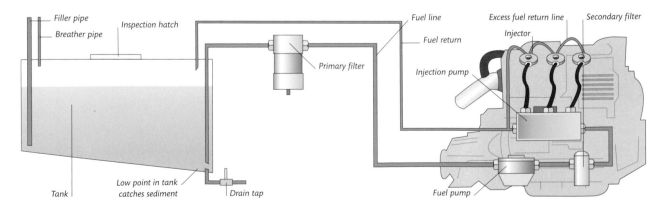

Filler pipe   Breather pipe   Inspection hatch   Fuel line   Excess fuel return line   Secondary filter   Injector   Fuel return   Primary filter   Injection pump   Tank   Low point in tank catches sediment   Drain tap   Fuel pump

This has two disadvantages—the engine must be run at a lower than optimum temperature (approximately 145°F/63°C), leading to more wear, and pumping hot sea water around the engine increases corrosion in the water channels. A filter ensures debris is not drawn into the cooling system from the sea. Sacrificial zinc anodes in the cooling system protect the engine from the potentially devastating effects of corrosion caused by pumping hot salt water through the system.

A better system is a car-type, closed cooling system, with a mix of fresh water and antifreeze circulating around the engine. In place of a car's radiator there is a heat exchanger that uses pumped sea water to cool the fresh water and antifreeze mixture. The sea water is then discharged through the exhaust system.

A freshwater-cooled system allows the engine to run at its optimum temperature of about 185°F (85°C). You should check the level of coolant in the expansion tank daily. Sea water is pumped around both types of cooling system by an engine-mounted impeller pump. In freshwater-

COOLING AND EXHAUST SYSTEM
Most modern diesels have a freshwater cooling system in which the fresh water is cooled by sea water in a heat exchanger.

cooled systems, a centrifugal pump is often used for the fresh water. If a blockage occurs in the sea water system, the water flow is reduced or stopped and the engine will overheat. The impeller pump is also likely to be damaged. Make sure there is a good flow of water through the cooling system by cleaning the seacock's weed trap on a regular basis. Carry a spare impeller and learn how to change it.

Exhaust system
The simplest exhaust system is a funnel, but yachts normally route their exhaust system to expel the exhaust gases at the stern. Because the gases are very hot, most systems inject the engine's cooling water into the exhaust immediately behind the engine. The water helps cool and quiet the gases.

After the water injection, the gas and water mixture is usually led through a silencer, then routed to the stern, where it exits the boat through a seacock in the transom or counter. A siphon-break should be fitted before the seacock to reduce the risk of the engine being flooded by sea water.

Some systems incorporate a water separator to expel the water out below the waterline with the cooled gases exiting through the topside or transom.

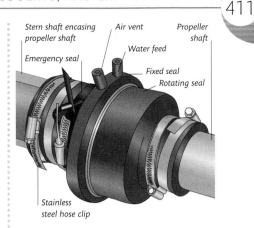

Stern shaft encasing propeller shaft · Air vent · Propeller shaft · Water feed · Emergency seal · Fixed seal · Rotating seal · Stainless steel hose clip

STERN GLAND
A stern gland seals the gap where the propeller shaft runs into the stern tube that passes it through the hull. Modern glands are virtually maintenance free.

Stern glands
A stern gland is the seal that prevents water from entering the boat around the propeller shaft. Traditionally, a stuffing box with turns of lightly greased packing is used. If the stuffing is well maintained and the propshaft is perfectly aligned, this system can work well. Modern alternatives to the traditional stuffing box offer the benefit of being virtually maintenance-free. Some rely on water lubrication, so when the boat is launched, air may need to be purged from the seal by squeezing it tightly with both hands until water starts to flow.

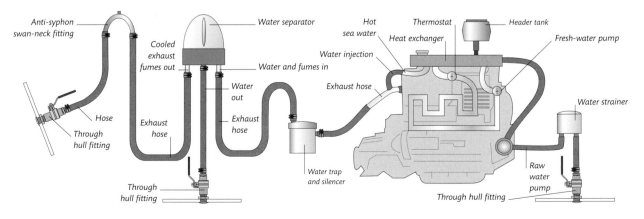

Anti-syphon swan-neck fitting · Cooled exhaust fumes out · Water separator · Water and fumes in · Water out · Hot sea water · Thermostat · Header tank · Heat exchanger · Water injection · Fresh-water pump · Hose · Through hull fitting · Exhaust hose · Exhaust hose · Exhaust hose · Water strainer · Through hull fitting · Water trap and silencer · Through hull fitting · Raw water pump

BASIC ENGINE MAINTENANCE

The best way to ensure a trouble-free engine system is to learn how to carry out basic maintenance and repair tasks. Most can be carried out at sea, or alongside, with only a small toolkit and handful of spare parts, and will enable you to deal with the majority of common engine failures.

Learn to handle the basic tasks on your engine by attending an engine maintenance course run by your engine supplier or a sailing school. Alternatively, employ a mechanic to show you how to do the jobs on your own engine and to help you put together a toolkit and set of spares.

Raw water filter

A filter must be fitted on the seawater inlet for the engine cooling system (p.411). Its job is to prevent seaweed and other floating material from finding its way into the engine cooling system. There are two types of filter that are commonly fitted. The first is a tubular mesh filter that fits within a long cylinder that is part of the seacock. To check and unblock this type, stop the engine, close the

REMOTE WATER FILTER
This type of water filter can be positioned remotely from the water inlet and makes it easy to check that water is flowing.

seacock, and unscrew the top of the cylinder. Withdraw the filter mesh, clear any debris, and replace. Make sure you remember to open the seacock before starting the engine.

The second type of filter is contained in a plastic bowl that is usually fitted partway between the seacock and the water pump. Access to the filter is obtained by removing the lid of the bowl. Most types have transparent lids, which makes it easy to check the water flow and to see if the filter is blocked. When replacing the lid, make sure it seats properly on its rubber seal. If your engine is cooled by freshwater, always check the freshwater header tank when you check the filter on the raw water side of the system. Be careful if the engine has been running as the water in the system will be hot. If the water level is low, top off with fresh water mixed with antifreeze as recommended by the engine manufacturer.

Replacing an impeller

The impeller is the part of the water pump that actually moves the sea water around the raw water side of the cooling system. The impeller rotates on a drive shaft within the pump housing and forces the water through the pump. Impellers are made of rubber or neoprene and rely on the flow of water for lubrication. They should be replaced at intervals recommended by the engine manufacturer, but they occasionally fail in service. If the engine is run dry—because the inlet seacock is left shut or debris blocks the inlet or filter—for longer than a minute or so, some damage to the impeller on the sea water pump is likely.

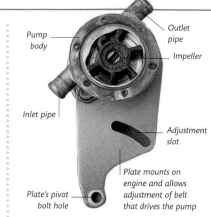

Pump body

Outlet pipe

Impeller

Inlet pipe

Adjustment slot

Plate's pivot bolt hole

Plate mounts on engine and allows adjustment of belt that drives the pump

IMPELLER PUMP
A belt-driven impeller pump is mounted on the engine. A rubber impeller rotates within the pump chamber and forces water from the "in" to the "out" pipe.

If the flow of water through the raw water side of the system reduces or stops, or if the engine overheats, check the raw water filter first to see if it is blocked, then check the pump impeller. To replace the impeller, turn off the water inlet seacock, remove the faceplate from the water pump, and gently pry out the old impeller. Remove all traces of the old gasket from the faceplate and pump housing, and fit a new gasket. Press the new impeller in place, refit the faceplate, open the seacock, and check for leaks.

Bleeding the fuel system

It becomes necessary to bleed the fuel system if air gets into it, perhaps during filter replacement, or if the engine runs out of fuel. Most modern diesel engines are self-bleeding, which means they should only need to be bled on the low-pressure side of the system, although if the engine stopped because it ran out of fuel, it may be necessary to bleed the high pressure side as well.

The principle of bleeding a diesel is quite straightforward. The aim is to remove air by opening each bleed screw in turn, starting at the one closest to the tank and working toward the injector pump. If all the bleed screws are below the level of the fuel in the tank, the job is simple, since gravity will cause the fuel to flow through the piping. Undo the bleed screw on the primary filter a couple of turns and watch the fuel and air bubbles seep out. When clean fuel without air bubbles flows from the screw, tighten it again. Move on to the next bleed screw, usually on the secondary filter and repeat the process. Then do the same at the bleed screw on the injector pump.

If the bleed points are above the level of fuel in the tank, you will need to use the manual handle on the fuel pump to pump fuel through the system as you bleed each screw in turn. Sometimes the primary filter contains a lift pump that can be used instead of the engine fuel pump.

Get used to bleeding your engine so that you can do it quickly. Mark each bleed screw with a dab of bright paint so it can be found easily in a dark engine compartment, and fasten the right-sized wrench or screwdriver close to each bleed screw point.

FUEL PUMP
The fuel pump mounted on the engine usually has a manual lever that is used when bleeding the system.

Replacing fuel filters

All engines come with an engine-mounted fuel filter—usually called the secondary or fine filter—but all systems should also have another filter mounted between the tank and the engine to remove the majority of the dirt and water that accumulates in the fuel in the tank. This first filter is usually called the primary or pre-filter.

Most primary filters contain a filter cartridge and have a lower bowl, usually transparent, in which water and dirt collects. The primary filter should be checked every few hours of engine running. Drain water and dirt from it by loosening the drain screw at the bottom of the bowl until clean diesel runs out, then tighten the screw again. If the primary filter contains a replaceable filter cartridge, replace it at least once a season.

Most secondary filters have a disposable filter element that should be changed at least once a season. Some also have a water trap that should be drained in the same way as the primary filter. Before changing the filter, turn the fuel off and clean around the filter to keep dirt from getting in while it is dismantled. Unscrew the body of the filter if it is the spin-on type, or unscrew the central bolt of a cartridge type. Replace the new filter, seals and O-rings. Before fitting the new seals or O-rings, smear a little diesel on their surfaces— this will help make a good seal. Put the new filter in place and tighten the securing bolt, making sure the seals seat properly. Open the fuel tap, bleed the air out of the system, and check for leaks when the engine is running.

Drive belts

The alternator and, on some engines, seawater impeller pump are powered by drive belts. These should be

PRIMARY FUEL FILTER
The top part of the unit contains a cartridge filter, while water and sediment collects in the lower, transparent bowl, from where it can be drained.

checked regularly to be sure they are in good condition and adequately tight—if you press your thumb on the center of the longest run, the belt should deflect by about 0.5 in (10–15 mm). Do not overtighten belts since this will damage the alternator or pump bearings. A shiny surface on the sides of the belt indicates it has been slipping and should be replaced.

Checking lubrication

Always check the oil level before using the engine, and every three to four hours while it is running. The engine manual will tell you which type of oil to use and how often to change it. If you do not use the engine much, change the oil more regularly than is recommended and consider installing oversized oil filters to keep the oil clean. This helps prolong the life of diesel engines, which suffer from short periods of use at low loads followed by long periods of idleness—a typical pattern of use for most yacht engines.

The gearbox requires a special oil that will be specified in the manual. Include the gearbox oil level in your pre-start engine checks.

RUNNING REPAIRS

Every cruising yacht should have sufficient tools and spare parts on board to allow basic repairs to be carried out at sea so that the boat can get back to harbor. The selection of spare parts you need to carry depends on the type of boat you own and the distances you sail. It is all too common for an emergency to develop from a small initial failure, so it is imperative that the skipper is capable of carrying out running repairs as and when they are required.

Spare parts

You will not require many spares if you tend to day-sail close to your home port. However, if you are long-distance cruising, you should carry sufficient spares to keep all essential systems operable. Some items are not possible to repair at sea, such as an electronic autopilot. If the failure of such an item would have a significant impact on the voyage, it is advisable to carry full replacement units.

Essential spares

Opinions as to what spare parts are essential will vary according to the experience of the skipper and the crew. A novice skipper may consider the engine to be a vital piece of equipment, whereas someone who is very confident in his own skills and the boat's performance under sail will be less concerned about loss of engine power. This is especially true if the boat has an alternative system for charging the batteries, or if there are oil lamps and other simple facilities that will allow the cruise to continue without the need for electrical power.

Every skipper should make sure he knows exactly what items of equipment are essential for the safety of his crew and his boat, and he should be able to identify items that will significantly affect its ability to complete a passage.

He should also know which items are useful but could be dispensed with if necessary.

Tools

You should carry a selection of tools to repair all essential equipment, together with the instruction manuals where available. Go through your boat and examine every piece of equipment and how it is secured. If you might need to remove it at some stage, check the size and type of fasteners and make sure you have the right screwdriver, wrench, or socket for the job. Check the engine manufacturer's recommendations for the engine toolkit and, again, ensure that you are carrying all the necessary wrenches, sockets, and Allen keys to work on the engine. Also, make sure that you have wrenches to service seacocks, and check that there is enough room around each seacock in which to use them.

Storing tools

The best way to store tools is to use purpose-designed plastic toolboxes. These have compartments of various sizes to keep everything neat, and are easy to secure. A comprehensive tool kit could be split among several boxes, according to the type of tool

CONTENTS OF A BASIC TOOL KIT

Tools for use aboard your boat should be of the best possible quality, otherwise they will quickly deteriorate in the damp conditions prevalent at sea.

They should be kept lightly oiled and stored securely. The following list is an example of the contents of a tool kit that would be useful for making basic repairs.

- Screwdrivers—all head types and sizes, including electric screwdrivers
- Wrenches—an assortment, including an adjustable wrench
- Socket set
- Mole wrench
- Electrical wire terminal crimper

- Wire cutter
- Hacksaw and spare blades
- Wood saw
- Power drill (12V), drill bits and screwdriver bits
- Hand drill and bits
- Brace and bits

- Pliers and electrical pliers
- Hammers and a mallet
- Set of chisels
- Files
- Flashlight
- Mirror (to see into confined spaces)
- Bolt cutters

and how frequently it is required. This will make it quicker to find the tool that you need, and makes arranging storage easier. It is a good idea to obtain boxes that have individual compartments for small items. These can be useful for frequently used spares such as tape or split rings, shackles, or fasteners.

Repairs at sea

Repairs are much simpler to carry out in harbor, but it is sometimes necessary to do them at sea. In this case the job will be much easier if you have somewhere to work where you can spread out your tools and hold the item you are working on securely. Some long-distance cruising boats incorporate a small workbench. This is an ideal solution, but most yachts do not have the space. A useful alternative is to have a strong piece of wood that is cut to fit across the cockpit, between the seats, and to which you can fasten a small portable vise to hold the work securely.

USEFUL SPARES

Some of the vital and most useful spares and kits are listed below. You should also consider carrying replacement units for items that are essential to the running of your boat but are not repairable.

ENGINE SPARES	ELECTRICAL SPARES
• Spark plugs and coil (gasoline engine) • Injectors (diesel engine) • Repair kits for fuel and water pumps with seals and impellers • Set of hoses • Oil filters • Fuel filters • Sets of gaskets, seals, and O-rings • Fuel • Oil and grease • Fuel antibacterial additives (diesel) • Spare ignition key	• Fuses – all types used on board • Bulbs – including navigation lights • Terminal fittings • Connecting blocks • Soldering iron and solder • Wire – assorted sizes • Tape – insulating and self-amalgamating • Batteries (for torches and so on) • Distilled water (for topping up batteries) • Hydrometer (for checking batteries)

ASSORTED SPARES	
• Sail repair kit (p.392) • Sticky-backed sail repair tape • Piston hanks • Whipping twine • Mainsail slider • Rope—spare lengths of various sizes • Shackles—assorted • Bottlescrew • Clevis pins • Split pins and rings	• Bulldog clamps and rigging wire—a length equal to longest on board • Marine sealant • Underwater epoxy • Waterproof grease • Petroleum jelly • Paint and varnish (minor repairs) • Epoxy glue and fillers • Fiberglass tape and cloth • Nails, screws, and bolts—assorted • Wood—assorted pieces

MAINTENANCE PLANNING

Use a notebook to record all items and equipment that need repairs or regular maintenance. This makes it quick and easy to identify the most important work and to plan time and materials for the job.

Scheduling repairs

Maintenance jobs are much easier and more pleasant to carry out when the weather is good. Try to schedule regular maintenance sessions and keep your list of repairs as short as possible during the sailing season.

Making a list

Make time to take the occasional tour through your boat, checking all possible sources of problems and making a list of repairs as you go. Once you have checked structural fixtures above deck, work your way through the interior. Run all electrical and mechanical systems to be sure they work and have not been affected by moisture.

What to look for

• Check structural items to make sure that their fastenings have not loosened. Sailing to windward in large waves can put a considerable load on the forward parts of the boat and the main bulkhead. Take a look down below when the boat is sailing hard to see if there is any movement of the hull or bulkheads.
• Check the chainplates and look for signs of leaks around them.
• Look for any leaks around fittings, windows, or hatches.
• Check along the hull-to-deck joint for signs of water leakage.
• If water regularly appears in the bilge of a GRP or metal boat, try to track its source and seal the leak.
• In GRP boats, check the decks for signs of star-shaped crazing around fittings that is caused by stress.

STAYING **SAFE**

Sailing is generally safe despite the potentially hostile environment in which it takes place. If safety is to be maintained, however, it is crucial that participants understand the risks, accept responsibility for their own well-being, and sail within the bounds of their experience. Staying safe depends as much on attitude, seamanship, and common sense as on equipment.

EMERGENCY REPAIRS

A cruising yacht's crew must be prepared to deal with all eventualities once they cast off and head out to sea. Although most passages will be enjoyable and uneventful, the crew will occasionally be presented with an unwelcome challenge, such as a hole in the boat, dismasting, loss of steering, a fouled propeller (which renders the engine useless), or even a fire. All skippers must plan for such contingencies, carry the right spares and equipment, and drill the crew in emergency procedures.

Holing and leaks

If the boat is holed above the waterline, perhaps in a collision, you have some time to assess the situation and take action. If the damage is below the waterline, however, immediate action is required to prevent the boat from sinking. Your priorities must be to eliminate or minimize the inrush of water, and to start pumping to keep the boat afloat.

First, turn on all electric bilge pumps, and the damage control pump if installed, and have a crew member work the manual pump. If you have spare crew members and the water is already over the cabin sole, instruct them to use buckets in order to scoop water through the companionway into the cockpit. You may be able to add to the pumping capacity by removing the engine-cooling water inlet hose from its skin fitting and putting the end in the bilge.

Sometimes the source of the water is not obvious—in which case, suspect a broken engine-cooling water hose or toilet hose, or a failed seacock or through-hull fitting. If the leak is from a hose, turn off the seacock. All seacocks should have a wooden plug tied to them so that if a seacock fails, you can quickly use the tapered plug

to block the hole. If the inrush of water is from a hole in the hull skin, it should be easy to locate unless it is behind paneling, in which case you may have to pry interior furniture away to expose the source of the leak.

Your objective is to block the hole as effectively as possible by whatever means available. Bunk cushions, sail bags, or any other soft material can be pushed into the hole and held in place

BLOCKING A HOLE
It is important to block the hole, particularly below the water line, as quickly as possible and by whatever means you can. Push soft furnishings (folded as many times as possible) into the hole, and hold in position with a brace such as the boathook or fender board.

with a brace, such as the fender board or other suitable length of wood. You can purchase an umbrella-like piece of equipment that is pushed through the hole and opened on the outside. Water pressure then seals it against the hull and stops the leak. Whatever material you use, you need to be innovative and act quickly to block the hole before the inrush of water overwhelms your pumps. Once the hole is blocked from the inside, you may be able to lower a sail over the hole on the outside using lines led under the hull to secure it. Fasten the lines at suitable strong points on deck, such as handrails.

The size of the hole and how deep it is below the waterline determine the amount of water coming in. Water pressure increases rapidly with depth, so a hole low down will create a high-pressure jet of water that will be difficult to stop.

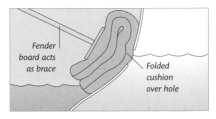

Fender board acts as brace

Folded cushion over hole

USING A BUNK CUSHION

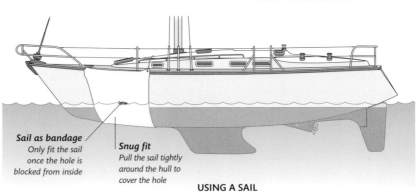

Sail as bandage
Only fit the sail once the hole is blocked from inside

Snug fit
Pull the sail tightly around the hull to cover the hole

USING A SAIL

If the hole is near the waterline, you may be able to heel the boat to raise the hole out of the water or at least reduce the pressure. If you cannot stem the inflow, and if your boat does not have watertight compartments, your best hope lies in the ability of your pumps to keep up with the flooding. Assess the situation quickly, and if it is clear that you will not be able to keep the yacht afloat, you must commence the procedure for abandoning ship (*pp.426–427*). If your boat is near shallow water and the tide is falling, another option may be to deliberately ground the vessel. This will allow you to patch the damage before the tide rises again.

Dismasting

The loss of a mast usually occurs when a piece of rigging or a terminal fitting gives way. This usually happens in rough conditions, but can occur in calm weather if the fitting has been weakened earlier and suddenly gives way. The mast will fall roughly downwind as the sails pull it over the side. As soon as this happens, the motion of the boat will change dramatically as it loses the inertia of the rig high above the hull. The motion will be quick and jerky and it will become difficult to stand and work on deck. The immediate priority is to prevent the broken pieces of mast, still attached to the boat by rigging, halyards, and control lines, from damaging the hull or decks. Ideally, try to recover as much of the broken mast as possible for use in constructing a jury rig (a makeshift rig to get you to safety). Recovery is often impossible in rough weather; you will usually have to cut away the rig to prevent it from holing the hull. You will need a hacksaw or a large pair of bolt cutters to cut standing rigging; the alternative—

DISMASTED YACHT
The priority is to get the broken pieces on board or cut away so that they cannot damage the hull. The boat's motion will be jerky without the mast, so there is an increased risk of falling overboard.

disconnecting the standing rigging at the chainplates—is difficult in rough conditions.

Assess the situation once you have cut away or recovered the gear. You may be able to reach port under power if you have sufficient fuel, but do not start the engine until you have checked and rechecked that there are no ropes in the water that may foul the propeller. If motoring is not an option, then attempt to improvise a jury rig—perhaps using the spinnaker pole and a storm jib—that will allow you to sail downwind, albeit slowly.

Steering failure

Loss of steering occurs most frequently aboard wheel-steered boats as a result of a steering-cable failure, which can often be prevented by regular checks and maintenance. Tiller-steered boats have simpler systems with less to go wrong, but it is wise to carry a spare tiller for use in case of a breakage. Rudder hangings or bearings rarely fail—if a problem does occur, it is generally in the rudder-control system. An emergency tiller must be available in a wheel-steered boat, and you should practice using one before it is needed. Deck layout may necessitate the use of relieving tackles to control the makeshift tiller. Undertake a practice run to try these out to make sure you know how to rig and use such a system if necessary.

If the rudder or its fittings fail, you will have to find another way of steering. An emergency sweep can sometimes be constructed by bolting the spinnaker pole to a floorboard and lashing it to the pushpit or stern rail. Alternatively, you may be able to tow two small drogues off each quarter and adjust these to steer the boat. How the boat balances under sail will determine whether you can steer in this way, but you will have to reduce sail to keep the boat under control.

Fouled propeller

Fouled propellers are quite a common occurrence, especially in busy sailing areas with many moorings, fishing nets, and lobster-pot lines to snag the unwary. Propellers are usually fouled by a rope caught and wrapped around the propeller shaft. Synthetic materials often melt and fuse because of the heat generated by friction. This creates a solid mass around the propeller and shaft, which stops the engine.

Prevention is far better than cure. Be alert to ropes in the water, and make sure your own ropes do not fall over the side: there is little worse than being immobilized by your own warp.

Another effective preventative measure is to fit a shaft cutter. These are mounted ahead of the propeller. They have a serrated edge with sharp teeth that catch and cut any rope or plastic that comes near the propeller.

If, despite all your precautions, a rope does foul the propeller, you are likely to have a difficult task freeing it. If the engine was turning at low speed and you can still reach an end of the rope, you may be able to free it by turning the engine slowly, by hand if possible, in the opposite direction to that in which the propeller was turning, while pulling on the rope.

It is more likely, however, that the only remedy is to cut the tangled or fused material away. This may require someone to go over the side with a sharp knife, something that is both difficult and hazardous to do at sea. This should be attempted only in calm weather by someone wearing a wetsuit and with a safety line tied around them. In harbor, you may be able to dry out alongside or heel the boat, or trim it down by the bow sufficiently to reach the prop from the dinghy. Always be sure the engine is stopped if anyone is working near the propeller.

Firefighting

Fire on board is most typically the result of a cooking accident, an electrical fault, or an explosion in the gas or fuel supply. There is little to be done in the event of an explosion, as it is likely to destroy the boat. Prevent such an eventuality by fitting and maintaining the gas and fuel supply properly, and install a gas detector with a loud warning bell. Avoid bringing naked flames near gas appliances, and do not run the engine or other machinery when refueling or when working on the engine.

Fire must be combated as soon as it starts if it is to be brought under control with the minimum of damage. It is essential to ensure that there are fire extinguishers of appropriate types in all the key areas of the boat. Test them regularly to be certain that they work and make sure the crew understands their use.

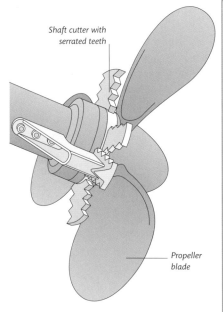

Shaft cutter with serrated teeth

Propeller blade

SHAFT CUTTER
Fitting a shaft cutter to the propeller shaft ahead of the propeller is a good way to minimize the risk of a fouling.

WHICH FIRE EXTINGUISHER?

Mount foam or dry powder extinguishers close to the galley and engine compartment and fit others in the forecabin and a cockpit locker. Equip enclosed engine compartments with a remote fire extinguisher, either manually or automatically operated. Pressure-test all extinguishers regularly and invert dry powder extinguishers monthly to prevent the powder inside from compacting in the bottom. Know how and when to use each of the different extinguishers, and brief the crew thoroughly in their use.

TYPE OF FIRE	METHOD OF EXTINGUISHING FIRE
Combustible materials	Foam or dry powder extinguisher. Aim extinguisher at the base of the fire.
Engine fire	CO_2, foam, or dry powder extinguisher. Turn off fuel supply at tank.
Electrical fault	CO_2 or dry powder extinguisher. Turn off battery system at isolating switch.
Cooking fire	Foam or dry powder extinguisher, or fire blanket. Use the blanket to smother flames.

BEING TOWED

If your boat has been disabled and you have been able to summon assistance, you may have to accept a tow from another vessel. Towing at sea is difficult and must be handled correctly if the tow is to be successful and not result in further damage to your boat. Be aware that taking a tow may make you liable for a salvage claim by the towing vessel. Try to negotiate and agree a fee before accepting a tow, and supply your own tow rope. If possible, agree on a destination and speed of tow with the other vessel's skipper.

Towing a sailing dinghy

Sailing dinghies sometimes take a tow in light winds or before or after a race. When you are being towed, lower the mainsail and pull the centerboard almost fully up. Leave the rudder in place and steer to follow the wake of the towing boat. A dinghy can be towed alongside or astern. Several dinghies can be towed together in line astern or herringbone fashion.

Towing a cruiser

Towing a cruiser places high loads on both the towed and towing vessels, but the towed yacht is especially vulnerable if it is being towed by a much larger vessel. Ships often cannot travel at a slow speed without losing steerage way, and their minimum speed will often impose very high strains on the yacht being towed. Avoid taking a tow from a much larger vessel unless there is no alternative. If the tow is to take place in rough seas, or if you have to be towed for some distance, rig a towing bridle made up of one or more heavy warps, attached to the strongest parts of the yacht to distribute the loads throughout the structure. Use a long, springy nylon warp, or the anchor chain, to form the tow rope. Make sure it is long enough to reduce snatching loads on the warp, otherwise it may break.

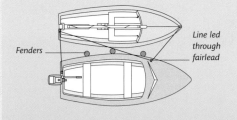

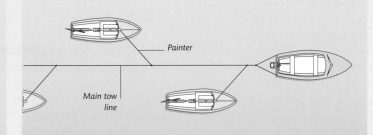

TOWING A DINGHY ALONGSIDE

If a single dinghy is being towed in calm conditions, it can be towed alongside as above. Otherwise, tow astern to avoid damage—tie a painter around the mast and lead it through a fairlead at the bow.

TOWING HERRINGBONE FASHION

If several dinghies are being towed, they will be arranged either one behind the other or in a herringbone tow, as shown. In the latter, each boat uses its rudder to steer, and the painter is led directly from the mast to the main tow line, not through the bow fitting, and fastened with a rolling hitch (p.221).

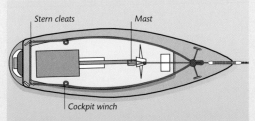

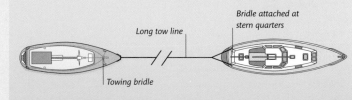

TOWING BRIDLE

Rig your mooring warps to form a towing loop at the bow with the warps leading from the bow cleats back to the cockpit winches, stern cleats, and mast. Attach the towing warp or chain to the towing loop and use plenty of chafe protection on the warp at the fairlead.

TOWING A CRUISER

A long tow rope in a rough sea will reduce shock loading and reduce the danger of the towed yacht's overrunning the warp if it surfs down waves. If this is still a danger, the yacht under tow should trail a warp astern to help stop it from surfing on waves. Steer the yacht in the wake of the towing boat to stop it from sheering to one side, which dramatically increases towing loads.

DISTRESS SIGNALS

If an emergency on board has developed beyond the ability of the crew to deal with it, the time has come to ask for help. Distress signals are only ever used when a boat or crew member is in grave and imminent danger and immediate assistance is required. If you see or hear a distress signal, you are legally required to render speedily all possible assistance. The small-boat and cruising sailor is most likely to use radio, emergency position indicating radio beacon (EPIRB), or flares to signal for help.

Calling for assistance

You should not hesitate to use a recognized distress signal to call for assistance if you find yourself in a situation where either your boat or you or your crew are in grave and immediate danger. If the situation is urgent but does not warrant a distress signal, and the full-scale rescue operation that it will set in force, you can use your radio to broadcast an urgency signal to inform other vessels and the coast guard of your situation. However, you should know that distress signals are not intended to be used in situations that are simply inconvenient—such as being becalmed when on a tight schedule. Many common situations, such as an engine failure or running out of fuel, can be dealt with by a call to the coast guard to request a referral to a commercial tow or repair service.

When you do need to attract attention and call for assistance, there are a number of methods to choose from, ranging from the most sophisticated Global Maritime Distress and Safety System (GMDSS) equipment, through voice-only radio, flares, sound signals, shapes, flags, and even arm-waving. Recognized distress signals have developed over the centuries, but most of the old ones remain valid and may still save your life—make sure you know them all.

GMDSS

The GMDSS has been developed by the International Maritime Organization (IMO) to create an integrated, worldwide distress and safety communications system for commercial and recreational vessels. GMDSS regulations are compulsory for commercial vessels over 300 gross tons and for some classes of passenger and fishing vessels but are voluntary for pleasure craft. In the short term, existing distress alert procedures for small craft—in particular the use of VHF Channel 16 and the Mayday signal (*opposite*)—will continue to operate alongside GMDSS but will eventually be phased out.

GMDSS is designed primarily to be a ship-to-shore and ship-to-ship distress alerting system while also delivering urgency, safety, and routine communications, including weather forecasts, navigational warnings, and search and rescue messages. Ashore, distress messages are routed to rescue coordination centers, that coordinate the rescue response and communicate with Search and Rescue services and other vessels and organizations involved in the rescue.

GMDSS makes use of Digital Selective Calling (DSC) (*p.331*) via conventional radio or satellite systems to provide an automatic means of sending (and receiving) distress alerts. DSC communication is faster and more reliable than a manually operated radio and provides the receiving station with the identification of the vessel in distress and, when the DSC unit is connected to a GPS set, the position of the vessel. As well as communicating distress alerts by radio, GMDSS also provides for alerts and locating signals to be sent using emergency position indicating radio beacons (EPIRBs) and search and rescue radar transponders (SARTs) (*p.424*).

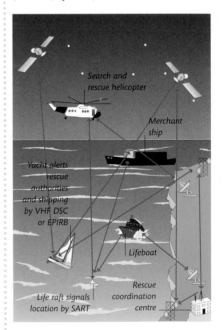

Search and rescue helicopter

Merchant ship

Yacht alerts rescue authorities and shipping by VHF DSC or EPIRB

Lifeboat

Life raft signals location by SART

Rescue coordination centre

GMDSS INTEGRATION
GMDSS provides an automatic means of sending and receiving distress alerts, by using conventional radio or digital signals, that can tell the rescue authorities both who you are and where you are.

EPIRB

Units have a unique serial number that you must register with your national authority. They can be operated manually or automatically—with a float-free bracket to release if the vessel sinks.

Radio

Sending a distress call by radio is often the most practical way of seeking help when the electricity supply is working or if a battery-operated handheld VHF radio is available. Most yachts carry a very high frequency (VHF) radio; some also use medium frequency (MF) radio and a few long-distance cruising yachts use high frequency (HF) radio. VHF radio is limited to line-of-sight operation between the transmitting and receiving aerials. In practice, this means reception of about 40 miles (65 km) from a coastal radio station with a high aerial or 10 miles (15 km) between two yachts at sea. An MF set has a longer range of about 200 miles (320 km) but is more expensive and requires more power. A ship's license is required to install a VHF, MF, or HF radio, and the user needs an operator's license.

If you have a modern DSC VHF set that conforms to GMDSS, it will have a dedicated distress button, usually colored red and protected by a cover to prevent accidental triggering. A shore station receiving a DSC distress signal also receives the unique Maritime Mobile Service Identity (MMSI) number that identifies the vessel and, if the DSC set is connected to a GPS unit, will receive the position of the vessel. If you do not receive a response from a coast guard shore station or ship

within 15 seconds, then you should repeat the distress call by voice in exactly the same way as you would if you have a pre-DSC set.

With an older set, distress, urgency, and safety signals are transmitted by international agreement on VHF Channel 16 (or 2,182 kHz on an MF transmitter). The recognized radiotelephony distress signal is the word MAYDAY and indicates that a vessel is in grave and immediate danger. Use of the distress signal imposes general radio silence, which must be maintained until the emergency is over and the distress signal is canceled by the authority controlling the emergency response.

Sending a distress signal

To send a distress signal (without using DSC), make sure the VHF (or MF) set is turned on and has power. Switch to high power to transmit. The form the message takes is vital (*right*). Listen for a reply which, in coastal waters, should come at once. If no reply is heard, check that the set is transmitting and try again. Once you have made contact, it is important to repeat your position.

Urgency signals are used to send an urgent message concerning the safety of the boat or a crew member, but when you are not yet in grave and imminent danger. It may be that a crew member has been injured and requires medical assistance or your boat has been rendered helpless and is drifting, but is not in danger of sinking. In such cases the PAN PAN signal is used, repeated three times. The PAN PAN message is usually broadcast initially on Channel 16 or 2,181 kHz, but if the message is long you should switch to a working

channel once contact has been made. The PAN PAN signal takes priority over all but a MAYDAY message. The safety signal, which consists of the word SÉCURITÉ spoken three times in succession, indicates that an important safety, navigational, or weather warning is about to be sent.

EPIRB

Another radio aid common aboard yachts that sail offshore is an emergency position indicating radio beacon (EPIRB). This transmits a distress signal to satellites that are part of the GMDSS, locating the EPIRB's position and relaying the information to a rescue coordination center. On purchasing an EPIRB, it is registered with the name and details of the vessel so that rescue services have this information if the EPIRB is activated.

MAYDAY

Mayday is the internationally recognized radio distress signal. It is essential that all crew members know exactly how to call, should the need ever arise.
"MAYDAY, MAYDAY, MAYDAY THIS IS...."
[name of yacht, repeated three times, plus MMSI if available]
"MAYDAY...."
[name of yacht spoken once]
"MY POSITION IS....."
[give position in latitude and longitude, or bearing, and distance from a known point]
"I AM...." [Give the nature of the emergency]
"I HAVE...." [Give the number of people on board, whether they are taking to the life raft, firing flares, or any other useful information]
"I REQUIRE IMMEDIATE ASSISTANCE" [Or other type of assistance that is required]
"OVER"

424

SART

A search and rescue transponder (SART) is a small, battery-powered receiver and transmitter that operates on the 9GHz frequency, which is the frequency of X-band radar sets. This system is designed to provide a locating signal and is primarily intended to be used from a life raft, although it could also prove invaluable on board the yacht if it is disabled but still afloat.

When a SART is switched on and is in range of an X-band radar, the SART responds by producing a distinctive series of 12 blips on the radar screen of the ship or aircraft whose radar signal triggered the SART's response. At sea level, as in a life raft, a SART will produce a contact when a ship is within about 5 miles (8 km).

An aircraft's radar display will see the contact at up to about 30 miles depending on its altitude. The 12-blip echo produced by a SART on a radar screen shows as a line of blips running outward from the SART's position along its line of bearing. As the rescue craft gets closer to within about 1 nm, the blips change to arcs of a circle, and when the target is very close the arcs change to complete circles. A SART should have sufficient battery life for about 96 hours of standby operation and 8 hours' transmission. When using a SART, it is best not to deploy a radar reflector at the same time as this can mask the SARTs signal. If a SART is switched on by accident, inform the coast guard immediately in case the signal has been picked up by a nearby ship which has then initiated a search.

TYPES OF FLARES

All boats that sail on the sea, or large inland waters, should carry flares. The type and number depend on the distance you sail from shore. A dinghy may carry a couple of handheld red flares, whereas a cruiser sailing offshore will need a larger selection. Keep them dry and replace them before their renewal date.

PARACHUTE FLARE

RED FLARE
Fires a bright red flare up to 1,000 ft (300 m) that burns for about 40 seconds. Use when some distance from help. In low cloud, fire downwind under the cloud.

BUOYANT SMOKE

ORANGE SMOKE FLARE
Once ignited, is dropped into water to leeward of boat and emits dense orange smoke for about three minutes. Highly visible from air and indicates wind speed and direction.

MINI-FLARES

MINI-FLARES
Meant for personal use and kept in jacket pocket. Ideal for small boats such as dinghies. Fires eight red flare cartridges, for day or night use, visible for 5–10 miles (8–16 km).

HANDHELD FLARES

WHITE FLARE
Not a distress signal but a way of warning other vessels of your presence. Burns for about 40 seconds. Always stow one within easy reach of the helmsman.

RED FLARE
Burns with a bright red light for about 60 seconds with a range of about 3 miles (5 km). Use to indicate your exact position when within sight of assistance.

ORANGE SMOKE FLARE
Handheld flare emits bright, dense orange smoke and burns for about 60 seconds. It is intended for use in daylight and good visibility, and is best in light winds.

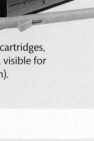

FIRING A FLARE
Handheld flares emit burning embers, so always hold them downwind, at arm's length and tilted away from your body. Avert your eyes in order to avoid being temporarily blinded by the bright light.

Using flares

Flares are used to attract attention, raise the alarm to a distress situation, and pinpoint your boat's position. Make sure that you carry sufficient flares of the various types (*opposite*) and make sure that they are within their expiration date. Old flares can be kept aboard for, say, a year after their expiry date as extras, but always have enough fresh flares on board. Old flares are likely to burn less brightly and generally become less reliable. Store flares where they can be kept dry but are instantly available. It is a good idea to clip a few flares (including a couple of white flares) near the companionway for immediate use with the others stored in a waterproof flare canister. Read the instructions so you and your crew know how to use the flares and, if possible, attend a course on flare use.

When firing a parachute flare, stand with your back to the wind and fire the flare downwind at an angle of about 15 degrees to the vertical. The flare will turn into the wind as it rises. However, if there is low cloud, fire the flare at about 45 degrees to keep it under the cloud base where it can be seen. Never fire a parachute flare if there is a helicopter nearby.

OTHER SIGNALS

Although the GMDSS system components—DSC radio and satellite communication, EPIRBs and SARTs—together with non-DSC radio and the use of flares, are the main ways of signaling distress or urgent situations, there are older systems that should not be forgotten and could be life-savers if the electrical system fails and renders the sophisticated equipment useless. Flags, shapes, sound signals, and physical waving can all be used to indicate distress when in sight of another vessel or the shore.

Flags and shapes

Flags are one of the oldest means of human communication, and the system of international code flags includes signals for indicating distress and requesting assistance. Even in today's technological world, signals by flags and shapes are still used. Even if you do not carry a full set of code flags, it is worth carrying the ones needed for use in a distress or urgency situation. If you do carry flags, make sure that they are large enough to be seen from a distance.

Sound and visual signals

Sound signals can be made using a horn powered by mouth, electricity, or compressed air. The classic sound distress signal is SOS, but the rapid sounding of a horn is also a recognized distress signal.

If you are in a small boat—a dinghy, perhaps—in sight of help and have no other signals available, the easiest international distress signal to use is to slowly raise and lower your outstretched arms.

CODE FLAGS N OVER C
Code flag N hoisted over code flag C indicates "I am in distress and require assistance." Flags are made of cloth, but painted boards can be used.

CODE FLAG V
This code flag signals "I require assistance."

CODE FLAG W
Hoisting this flag signals "I require medical assistance."

BLACK SQUARE OVER BLACK BALL
These shapes indicate "I require assistance."

SIMPLE DISTRESS SIGNAL
Stand facing in the direction of potential assistance and slowly raise and lower your outstretched arms from down by your sides to above the shoulders. Keep repeating the signal until you receive an acknowledgment. You can combine this signal with others, such as sounding SOS on a foghorn, to attract attention.

● ● ● ▬ ▬ ● ● ●
SOS SIGNAL

ABANDONING SHIP

If an emergency situation develops to the point where you may have to abandon ship, the decision to do so must be carefully considered. Unless the yacht is in imminent danger of sinking, you will be safer staying aboard than taking to a life raft. Whether the skipper accepts an offer of rescue from a helicopter or another vessel, the decision ultimately to abandon ship will depend on his confidence in the yacht, his crew, and his own ability to get the yacht to port.

Abandon ship preparation

Speed is vital if you have to abandon a sinking yacht and your life raft is the only option open to you. First, prepare the life raft for launching and ensure that the crew dresses in their warmest clothing, with full oilskins, harnesses, and life jackets.

If time allows, the crew should gather together items that may be useful in the life raft. Fill sealable containers with extra drinking water, and collect cans of food and a can opener in case you are in the raft for a long time. A chart, compass, and plotting tools will also be useful, as will a handheld GPS, a portable VHF radio, extra red flares, a signaling flashlight, and a knife. An offshore yacht should have a panic bag containing these items ready for just such an emergency. This bag should be kept close to the companionway.

Once everything is prepared, do not rush to launch the raft, but do everything possible to save the yacht.

The life raft

The term "life raft" suggests that it is a guaranteed life-saver. In reality, rafts often do not fulfill these expectations.

A life raft should be of a style approved by your national authority for the type of sailing you intend to do, and should be large enough to hold every member of the crew. Try to take a short course in using the raft to familiarize yourself with the inflation mechanism, the difficulty of boarding from the water, and how to right the raft if it inverts. Life rafts are packed in a solid container or in a flexible case and should contain emergency equipment to help you survive in the raft. However, this equipment is the minimum required; check what yours contains and prepare your panic bag accordingly. If possible, supplement with equipment salvaged from the yacht before you abandon ship.

LAUNCHING THE LIFE RAFT

When you are ready to launch the raft, cut or untie its lashings but leave its painter tied to a strong point on the vessel as this is needed to inflate the raft.

Be careful not to lose your footing

❶ Launch the raft by throwing its container over the leeward side. A sharp tug on the painter will inflate it.

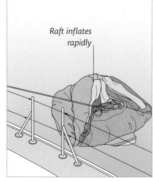

Raft inflates rapidly

❷ The raft will take about 30 seconds to inflate. If the raft inflates upside down, you must right it before boarding.

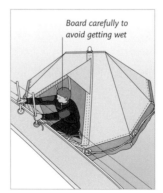

Board carefully to avoid getting wet

❸ As soon as the raft is inflated, the first crew member boards. Rig an additional mooring line in rough seas.

Help any crew in the water into the raft

❹ Once all the crew are aboard, release or cut both painters. Bail out water and shut canopy openings.

If you are forced to use a life raft, always stream the drogue—a mini-underwater parachute—as soon as you have boarded. Trailing this beneath the raft will slow down its drift and help to prevent a capsize.

It is important that life rafts are serviced regularly in accordance with the manufacturer's instructions.

Helicopter rescue

When the boat is within flying range of the coast, helicopters are frequently used for search-and-rescue operations. The helicopter's crew decides how to rescue the yacht's crew, and if possible will communicate directly using marine VHF. Always follow their orders exactly and help them complete the rescue as quickly as possible; the time they are able to spend hovering at the scene will be limited. Where possible, position the boat head-to-wind (or nearly so), with all its sails lowered, and make sure all crew are wearing life jackets. If you can, motor slowly into the wind or, if you are drifting, slow the rate of drift by streaming a drogue from the bow or lowering the anchor and chain.

The helicopter will not hover directly over the yacht because of the danger of becoming entangled in the rig. Depending on the circumstances, the rescue may take place in one of the following three ways: from a dinghy towed behind the yacht, from the water, or by using a Hi-Line technique. If it is to be a dinghy rescue, connect it to the yacht with a long warp of about 100 ft (30 m) and put only one person in it at a time. The helicopter will lower a lifting strop or send a winchman down to assist the crew.

HELICOPTER RESCUE
Using the Hi-Line technique, the helicopter first lowers a nylon line across the yacht before moving to hover to one side. The line is used to pull in the winchman.

If no dinghy is available, or the conditions are too rough, you may have to be picked up from the water. In this case, each crew member in turn is tied to a long warp and enters the water to drift astern of the yacht from where he is retrieved by the helicopter.

Alternatively, the helicopter may use a Hi-Line method. A long nylon line, carrying a weight on the lower end with its the upper end attached to the helicopter's recovery hook, is lowered across the yacht so that the crew can grab it. Once the yacht's crew has the line, the helicopter moves off to one side of the yacht. The line must not be made fast on board but should be pulled in as the helicopter lowers the winchman or lifting strop. The line is attached to the lifting hook by a weak link designed to break if the line snags. Pull in the line until the winchman or lifting strop is within reach, and flake it down so that it cannot snag and is free to run. Be careful not to touch the winch wire until its end has been earthed by the sea or winchman, because static electricity can give an unpleasant shock. Once the winchman is on board, follow his instructions. When the winchman and the first crew are being lifted off the yacht, the nylon

line is fed out. Keep hold of the end if further casualties are to be lifted and the procedure repeated.

Ship rescue

If a ship or lifeboat comes to your assistance, you should follow its skipper's instructions as to how he intends to recover your crew. In rough seas it is extremely hazardous to come alongside another vessel, especially if your rescuer is a large ship. A lifeboat will normally come directly alongside, and your crew should be ready to board it quickly under instruction from the lifeboat crew.

A large ship may lower a boat if the size of the seas permits, but in very rough seas it will probably stop to windward of the yacht to create a smoother area in the ship's lee. This is hazardous as the ship will drift downwind rapidly, and the yacht and its crew will be vulnerable to a hard collision. The ship's crew will lower a ladder or scrambling net over the side, which the yacht's crew must climb. If you have to jump for a ladder or net, wait until the yacht is on the top of a wave to lessen the danger of being crushed between ship and yacht, and climb up as quickly as possible.

FIRST AID

The crew's welfare afloat is the responsibility of the skipper. He should be aware of any existing medical conditions among his crew, and whether specific medicines or treatment are required. Each crewmember must inform the skipper of any condition that may affect his performance and ability to contribute to the sailing of the yacht. The skipper should ensure that a suitable first-aid kit and good first-aid manual are aboard. At least one crew member should have some first-aid training.

Be prepared

Fortunately, sailing is a healthy and relatively safe sport and serious injuries are rare. Most commonly, sailing accidents result in simple cuts and bruises. However, you must be prepared to deal with more serious accidents if you are to be truly responsible for the welfare of your crew. First-aid kits are commercially available to suit all types of sailing. When planning long voyages, consult your doctor, who can arrange for you to carry prescription drugs such as strong painkillers and antibiotics.

SEVERE BLEEDING

Deep cuts and severe bleeding require prompt action to stem the blood loss. Pressure must be applied to the wound using a sterile dressing if possible. Treat for shock (*p.430*) and seek medical help.

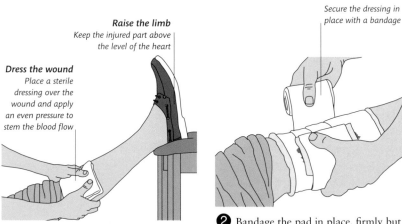

Raise the limb
Keep the injured part above the level of the heart

Dress the wound
Place a sterile dressing over the wound and apply an even pressure to stem the blood flow

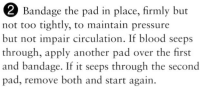

Secure the dressing in place with a bandage

❶ If the wound is deep and bleeding is severe, apply pressure directly over the wound, preferably over a sterile or clean dressing pad. Raise the injured part above the level of the victim's heart.

❷ Bandage the pad in place, firmly but not too tightly, to maintain pressure but not impair circulation. If blood seeps through, apply another pad over the first and bandage. If it seeps through the second pad, remove both and start again.

Cuts and grazes

Small cuts and abrasions are the most common form of injuries afloat. Treatment aims to stop the bleeding and preventing infection. Raise the injured part and rinse the wound under fresh running water to remove dirt. Use sterile gauze swabs to clean around the wound, then gently pat the area dry. If a cut or graze is small, cover it with an adhesive bandage (take care not to touch the sterile pad). For larger wounds, use a sterile dressing held in place with a bandage.

Sprains, strains, dislocations, and fractures

A strain occurs when the muscles or their tendons are stretched or torn. A sprain occurs when the ligaments that support a joint are damaged. The former can be especially painful and may be mistaken for a broken bone. Swelling develops and pain will be made worse by movement—the victim may not be able to move the limb. Later, bruising develops. In both cases rest and raise the injured limb. Place a cold compress over the area to cool it and minimize bruising. Wrap the injured area in padding and apply a support bandage that extends from the joint below the injury to the joint above.

A dislocation is caused by a twisting strain that displaces the bones of a joint. The victim may describe a sickening pain and be unable to move the joint. The area will look deformed and will swell. Immobilize the limb in the most comfortable position for the victim; use a sling or improvise with pillows and rolled towels.

If a broken bone is suspected, avoid unnecessary movement and immobilize the limb, then seek medical aid. Splint the arm or leg to an uninjured part of the body.

Immobilize
*Use a bandage
or tape for
strapping*

FRACTURE

A broken finger can be held immobile by using a bandage or tape to strap it to an adjacent finger.

Support an arm injury with a sling. For a leg injury, bring the uninjured leg to the injured leg. Place padding between the legs and rolled towels on either side. For extra support, secure folded triangular bandages around the knees and ankles. If there is a wound or a bone end is protruding, cover with a sterile dressing before immobilizing the limb.

Burns

Burns are a hazard on boat, especially in the galley and around the engine. A burn may be superficial, or affect part or the full thickness of the skin. They can be extremely painful and there is a risk of shock developing through fluid loss. For all but small superficial burns seek medical advice as soon as possible. Immediately cool the area by flooding it with cold water for about 10 minutes or until pain ceases. While waiting for medical attention, cover the injury with plastic kitchen wrap or a loose sterile dressing that extends well beyond the injury.

Head injury

A blow to the head is always potentially serious, since it can result in unconsciousness. On a boat it usually occurs when a person is struck by the boom. It can cause a scalp wound, skull fracture, concussion (a short period of unconsciousness followed by full recovery), or injury to brain tissues. Always watch the victim carefully for signs of deterioration, such as drowsiness, nausea, vomiting, and dilated or uneven pupils, which may not develop for some hours. Avoid letting the victim sleep until you are quite certain that he has completely recovered. If he was knocked unconscious or shows any of the signs of deterioration, seek urgent medical assistance.

FIRST-AID KIT

If you day-sail in coastal waters and are close to medical help in the event of an emergency, a basic first-aid kit will suffice. For long passages away from immediate help, keep a more comprehensive kit to allow you to treat victims of accidents and injuries. Below are the suggested contents for a basic first-aid kit.

Essential supplies

A basic first-aid kit should contain:
• Assorted sterile dressings
• Sterile gauze pads
• Assorted adhesive bandages
• Crepe and conforming bandages
• Triangular bandages
• Bandage clips, tape, and safety pins
• Scissors and tweezers
• Sterile wipes for wound cleaning
• Latex-free disposable gloves
• Diarrhea medication
• Painkillers
• Antiseptic cream
• Eye bath and lotion
• Thermometer
• Good first-aid manual

SEASICKNESS

Few sailors have claim never to have suffered from seasickness. You should always carry an anti-seasickness medications, or alternatives, such as medicated patches, acupressure bands, or electronic stimulation wristbands, and ensure sufferers use a preventive remedy before sailing or the onset of rough weather. If you sail regularly, experiment to find which treatment suits you best. Some anti-seasickness medications can cause drowsiness.

Minimizing sickness

Seasickness, like all motion sickness, is caused by disturbance to the balance mechanism in the inner ear. You can do several things to help prevent its onset. Preventative treatments take time to work and will not be effective once seasickness has begun: take them several hours before sailing. Get plenty of rest before you sail and avoid rich food and alcohol. If you start to feel sick, sit where you can get a good supply of fresh air and keep your eyes on the horizon—this helps the sense of balance. Take your mind off your feelings of sickness through involvement in sailing the boat. Avoid working at the chart table or galley if possible, as the motion down below often makes the feelings worse. Avoid getting cold or damp, and eat dry food to settle the stomach. If you go below, lie down if possible until you feel better. Most people suffer only mild seasickness, which soon passes. If a crew member is suffering badly, they can become weak and immobilized. In this case, the skipper should return to harbor as speedily as possible. Once in calm waters, the problem will usually disappear quickly.

SHOCK

This life-threatening condition can develop after any serious injury, especially severe bleeding or burns. Take action as described below in this situation.

Dealing with shock

Initially, the victim will have a rapid pulse and pale, clammy skin. Later, breathing becomes shallow, the pulse weakens, skin becomes gray-blue, and the victim may complain of nausea and thirst. He will become restless, will be gasping for air, and will eventually lose consciousness. Get medical help as soon as possible or seek advice via radio. Lay the victim down on a blanket. Raise and support his legs above the level of his heart and loosen tight clothing at the neck, chest, and waist. If possible, attend to any injury. Cover him to keep him warm. Do not leave him alone or allow him any food or liquid. If he is thirsty, moisten his lips with water. Monitor his pulse and breathing while waiting for help.

Sunburn

Prevention is better than cure, so always use sunblock and wear a hat and long-sleeved shirt. If you do get sunburned, cool the area with fresh water, cover the skin with light clothing, and move into the shade. Take frequent sips of fresh water to avoid dehydration. If the sunburn is mild, apply anesthetic cream or calamine lotion to soothe your skin.

Heat exhaustion

This is caused by extreme loss of salt and water through prolonged sweating. The symptoms include headaches or cramps, pale and moist skin, a fast, weak pulse, and a raised temperature. Move the affected person into the shade. Lay him down and raise his legs. Give him plenty of water to drink; oral rehydration salts or isotonic drinks can help, but do not give him salted water.

Heatstroke

This is a life-threatening condition that can occur when the body's temperature control system fails—for

example, after prolonged exposure to extreme heat and humidity. Signs include restlessness, headache, dizziness, flushed and hot skin, a fast, strong pulse, and raised body temperature (above 104°F/40°C). If left untreated, the affected person will lose consciousness. Lower his body temperature quickly and seek urgent medical assistance. Lay the affected person down in a cool place and remove his clothes. Cover him with a cold, wet sheet and fan him—re-wet the sheet regularly. Continue until his temperature falls below 99.5°F (37.5°C), then replace the sheet with a dry one.

Hypothermia

Hypothermia occurs when the body's temperature drops below 95°F (35ºC). The first signs are intense shivering and difficulty speaking. As hypothermia progresses, shivering decreases and the affected person becomes clumsy, irritable, and slurs his speech. Further heat loss leads to an inability to reason, lack of muscle control, and breathing and pulse rates

RECOVERY POSITION

If a victim is unconscious but still breathing, he should be put in the recovery position so that he is supported in a stable position and cannot choke on his tongue or vomit. You may be able to do this on a bunk or on the cabin sole, or in the cockpit if the victim's injuries make it unwise to move him below.

Moving the victim into position

With the victim on his back, open the airway and straighten his legs. Place his arm closest to you alongside his body. Bring his other arm across his body and hold the back of his hand against his cheek. With your other hand, pull up his far leg, holding it just above the knee. Roll him toward you until he is lying on his side by pulling on his leg, while keeping his hand pressed against his cheek. Check that the airway is still open. Bend his upper leg at the knee so that it is at right angles to his body. Monitor the victim's breathing and pulse every few minutes until you can obtain medical assistance.

Head faces arm at right angles to the body

RECOVERY POSITION
The victim is placed on his side in a stable position with his airway open.

become very slow. Eventually, he will lose consciousness and the heart may stop. You must prevent further heat loss and warm the person gradually. Move him into a sheltered area. Replace wet clothes with dry ones, if possible (do not sacrifice the clothes you are wearing). Wrap the person in a space blanket and/or sleeping bag, and keep his head warm. If he is fully conscious, give him warm drinks and high-energy food. Do not warm him with a hot water bottle. Get medical help as soon as possible.

Drowning

If you recover someone from the water who is unconscious, check his breathing. If he is not breathing, begin CPR immediately (*right*). If he is breathing (or once breathing has been reestablished following CPR), place him in the recovery position (*opposite*). If possible, replace his wet clothes with dry ones (*above*). If the person is conscious and has been in cold water or immersed for a while, he will be suffering from hypothermia, so treat as at left.

Unconsciousness

If a person collapses you must establish whether he is unconscious. Gently shake his shoulders and talk to him—speak loudly and clearly. If there is no response, he is unconscious and you need to check his breathing. Place one hand on the forehead and tilt the head, then place your other hand on the chin to lift it (step 3, *right*). Place your ear near the mouth, listening and feeling for breaths, and look along the chest, checking for movement. If he is breathing normally, place him in the recovery position (*opposite*) to keep his airways open and clear. If the person is not breathing, or is gasping for breath, begin resuscitation immediately (*right*).

RESUSCITATION

If an unconscious victim has stopped breathing, begin cardiopulmonary resuscitation (CPR), a combination of chest compressions and rescue breaths. Ask someone else to call for medical help while you give CPR and make sure he or she requests an automated external debfibrillator.

1 Kneel beside the victim, level with his chest. Place the heel of one hand on the center of his chest (*below*) then place the heel of your other hand on top of the first and interlock your fingers.

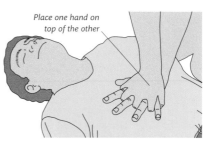

Place one hand on top of the other

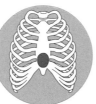

COMPRESSING THE CHEST
Find the spot where the bottom rib meets the breastbone.

2 Lean forward over the victim. Keeping your arms vertical and straight, press down onto his breastbone, depressing the chest by 2–2½ in (5–6 cm). Release the pressure and allow the chest to come back up, but do not move your hands. Repeat to give 30 compressions at a rate of at least 100 per minute.

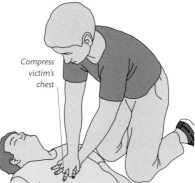

Compress victim's chest

3 Move to the victim's head and open the airway. Place one hand on the forehead and gently tilt the head back. Place the fingertips of your other hand on the victim's chin and lift it.

4 Move the hand on the victim's forehead down slightly to pinch the nostrils closed, and let the victim's mouth fall open. Take a normal breath, place your lips over the mouth, and blow steadily into the mouth until the chest rises. Remove your mouth and watch the chest fall. A complete rescue breath should take about one second. Repeat to give two breaths.

5 Repeat the cycle of 30 chest compressions followed by two rescue breaths. Continue until medical help arrives, the victim starts to breathe normally, or you are too exhausted to continue. If the person starts to breathe normally, place him in the recovery position (*opposite*).

GLOSSARY

A

ABAFT Behind, at, or toward the stern of a boat.

ABEAM At right angles to the fore-and-aft line.

AFT Toward, at, or near the stern.

AHEAD In a forward direction.

AIRFLOW Movement of air across the sails.

ALTOSTRATUS Mid-level cloud in the form of a sheet or layer totally or partly covering the sky.

AMIDSHIPS At, near, or toward the center of a vessel.

ANCHOR A eavy device attached to a boat by a rope (anchor warp) or chain cable and lowered overboard to secure a boat to the bottom.

ANCHORAGE An area with good holding ground where it is sheltered and safe to drop anchor.

ANCHOR WINDLASS A manual or motor-driven mechanism used on some cruisers to raise the anchor by winding the rope or chain around a drum or barrel.

ANCHOR CABLE The chain or rope used to attach an anchor to the boat. See *warp*.

ANEMOMETER An instrument that measures wind speed.

ANGLE OF VANISHING STABILITY (AVS) The angle of heel at which a boat's righting moment reaches zero.

ANODES Sacrificial zinc shapes that are fastened near underwater metal fittings, such as the propeller shaft, to protect them from corrosion through electrolysis. The anodes corrode first.

ANTICYCLONE Area of relatively heavy, sinking air which results in high pressure.

ANTIFOULING PAINT Special paint applied to the hull to prevent underwater fouling from weeds and barnacles, which would slow the boat.

APPARENT WIND The combination of true wind (that which we feel when stationary) plus the wind produced by motion.

ASTERN Backward. Outside, and abaft the stern.

ASYMMETRIC SPINNAKER Downwind sail that does not use a pole but requires a bowsprit.

ATHWARTSHIPS Across a boat, from side to side.

AUTOPILOT Mechanical helmsman that steers the boat relative to a compass course or a wind angle.

B

BACKING THE JIB To sheet the jib to windward; used when sailing away from a head-to-wind position and sometimes when tacking.

BACKSTAY Wire leading from the masthead to the stern. It prevents the mast from falling forward and is used to tension the forestay.

BACKWIND When a mainsail is let out beyond its best trim, or if the jib is sheeted in too tight, the mainsail flutters in its front portion.

BAILER Device to remove water from a boat.

BALANCE A boat is balanced when it is upright, both fore-and-aft and athwartships.

BALANCED HELM When a boat has a balanced helm, it will have little tendency to turn. If you let go of the tiller, it will continue on a straight course. See *weather helm* and *lee helm*.

BAROGRAPH A recording barometer, which creates a continuous reading of air pressure on a paper graph.

BAROMETER Instrument that registers atmospheric pressure.

BATTEN A light wooden, fiberglass, or plastic strip that slots into a pocket sewn into the aft edge (leech) of a sail to support the roach.

BEAM REACH Sailing with the wind blowing directly over the side of the boat.

BEARING The direction of an object from your boat, or between two objects. Both are measured in degrees relative to north. See *heading*.

BEARING AWAY Turning the boat away from the wind; opposite of *luffing* (or luffing up).

BEATING Tailing to windward close-hauled, and zigzagging to reach an objective to windward.

BEAUFORT SCALE A descriptive scale used for measuring wind strengths.

BENDING ON The traditional term used to describe fitting the sails onto the boat.

BERMUDAN SLOOP A rig with a triangular mainsail and a single headsail.

BERTH A place to park alongside a dock or pontoon or in a marina.

BERTHING The process of parking a boat in its berth.

BIGHT (1) Bend in the shore making cove, bay, or inlet. (2) Bend in a rope.

BILGE (1) The rounded parts of the hull where the sides curve inward to form the bottom. (2) The area where water collects inside the boat.

BILGE KEEL A twin keel, used on boats designed to be able to dry out sitting upright. Sometimes used in conjunction with a shallow central keel.

BILGE PUMP Manual or electric pump to remove water that accumulates in the bilge.

BIMINI A removable sun screen over the cockpit.

BINNACLE A pedestal in which a compass is installed, often with magnets to compensate for magnetic deviation, and on which the wheel is usually mounted.

BLADE The flat part of an oar or propeller.

BLOCK A pulley through which a rope is passed.

BOAT HOOK Pole with hook used to pick up mooring buoy or ring when mooring or berthing.

BOLTROPE A reinforcing rope along a sail's edge.

BOOM A horizontal spar or pole, used to extend the foot of a sail and to help control the sail's angle in relation to the wind.

BOOM VANG (or kicking strap) A tackle that prevents the boom from rising under the pressure of wind in the mainsail.

BOTTLESCREW A fitting to adjust the tension in the standing rigging.

BOW The forward end of a boat; opposite of *stern*.

BOW-FITTING Fitting to which the forestay and jib tack are attached.

BOW SPRING Rope running from the bow of the boat aft to another boat or pontoon when berthed to prevent the boat from moving ahead.

BOW WAVE The wave that the bow of a vessel creates as it travels through the water.

BOWER ANCHOR The main anchor on a boat.

BOWLINE (pronounced "bow-lynn") Knot used to make a loop in the end of a rope or to tie to a ring or post.

BOW LINE Also known as the head rope, the bow line is a mooring warp that runs from the bow to a point ashore ahead of the boat; opposite of *stern line*.

BOWSPRIT A spar projecting from the bow of some boats, allowing sails to be secured farther forward, thus extending the sail plan.

BREAST ROPE A mooring rope running at right angles to the boat, from bow or stern, sometimes used in addition to the four main warps to hold the boat alongside.

BRIDGE DECK A raised area that separates the cockpit from the cabin.

BRIDLE Wire span for attaching forestay to hulls on catamarans, or a rope span sometimes used to secure lower mainsheet block on dinghies that do not use a mainsheet traveler.

BROACH When a boat turns inadvertently broadside to the waves. This may occur when a boat is sailing in strong winds, and the sails are not properly balanced or the boat heels a lot.

BRUCE (anchor) A type of burying anchor.

BROAD REACH Sailing with the wind coming over the port or starboard quarter of the boat.

BULKHEAD Below-deck partition separating one part of a boat's interior from another.

BUNG A plug used to close a drain hole.

BUOY A floating marker used for navigation.

BUOYAGE A system of navigation marks used to identify hazards and safe channels.

BUOYANCY BAGS (tanks) Removable and inflatable bags (or sealed compartments) that provide buoyancy so that the boat will float if capsized or swamped.

BURGEE A small triangular flag flown from the top of a mast, serving as an indicator of apparent wind.

C

CABIN The living quarters below deck.

CAM CLEAT A device with two moving and spring loaded cams that secures a rope.

CANTING KEEL A keel that can be pivoted from side to side. In use is pivoted to windward to increase the righting moment of the keel.

CAP SHROUDS The outer shrouds. See *shrouds*.

CAPSIZE When a boat tips over to 90° or 180°.

CARDINAL MARKS Forms of buoyage, used to indicate large or individual hazards in the water.

CATAMARAN A twin-hulled boat consisting of two narrow hulls connected by two beams and a trampoline or rigid deck.

CENTER OF EFFORT The point on a sail at which all the forces acting on the sail's surface can be thought of as being concentrated.

CENTERBOARD A plate that pivots around a pin inside a centerboard case, and is lowered below the hull of a sailing boat to resist leeway. See *daggerboard*.

CHAIN PLATES Metal fittings on each side of the boat, and at the bow and stern, to which the bottlescrews on the shrouds, forestay, and backstay are attached.

CHART A nautical map.

CHART DATUM The level from which soundings (depths) and drying heights are measured.

CLAM CLEAT A cleat that secures a rope in a grooved, V-shaped body.

CLEARING LINE Used in navigation to keep the boat clear of potential hazards by defining the boundaries of a safe zone. See *safe track*.

CLEAT A wooden or metal fitting that is used to secure ropes. See *cam, clam,* and *horn cleat*.

CLEW The lower aft corner of a fore-and-aft sail.

CLEW OUTHAUL The rope or wire that adjusts the position of the clew and the tension in the foot of the mainsail.

CLOSE REACH The point of sailing between close-hauled and a beam reach.

CLOSE-HAULED Sailing as close to the wind as possible, with the sails pulled in tight.

CLOVE HITCH A knot used for short-term mooring to a ring or post, or for hitching fenders to a rail.

COACHROOF The raised cabin trunk in the middle of the boat.

COAMING A vertical piece around the edge of a cockpit, hatch, etc. to prevent water on deck from running below.

COCKPIT The working area, usually toward the stern of a boat, from which the boat is steered.

COIL Method of securing ropes for stowage.

COMPANIONWAY A ladder or steps leading down from the cockpit to the cabin.

COMPASS NORTH The direction in which a compass points. If there is no local magnetic interference (see *deviation*), it will point to magnetic north.

CONTROL LINE A rope or line that adjusts a sail or part of the rig—such as the cunningham.

CONVECTION CURRENTS Air currents formed due to the land's heating up and cooling down.

COURSE MADE GOOD The course achieved after allowing for leeway and tidal set and drift.

COURSE STEERED The course actually steered by the helmsman and read off from the compass.

CREW Either everyone on board, or everyone else except the helmsman. To "crew" means both to work as a member of the crew (including the helmsman) and, in a small boat, to work alongside a helmsman with your own tasks.

CRINGLE A metal or plastic eye sewn into a sail.

CROSSING TURN Term used when one part of a rope crosses another; start of knot sequence.

CRUISING CHUTE See *gennaker*.

CRUTCH(ES) See *oarlocks*.

CUDDY A small shelter; access to a covered area in a small boat usually used for stowage.

CUNNINGHAM A control line for adjusting tension in the luff of a mainsail or jib.

CUTTER A single-masted yacht with two headsails, a staysail (inner headsail), and a jib (outer headsail).

D

DACRON Woven cloth often used for sails.

DAGGERBOARD A plate that is raised and lowered vertically inside its case, and is used to resist leeway. See *centerboard*.

DANBUOY A loating marker pole with flag that is attached to a lifebuoy to improve visibility.

DANFORTH (anchor) Type of burying anchor.

DAVIT A cranelike device equipped with a tackle for suspending or lowering a tender.

DEAD RUN See *running*.

DEPRESSION Area of low pressure.

DEPTH Distance from the seabed to the surface.

DEPTH SOUNDER Device to measure distance from the sea bed to the instrument's transducer.

DEVIATION The difference between magnetic and compass north due to the effect of local magnetic fields acting on the boat's compass. Deviation varies with the boat's course, and is measured in degrees east or west of magnetic north.

DINGHY A small boat, powered by sail, oars, or an outboard motor; usually designed to be used by one or two people.

DIP-POLE JIBE Method of jibing a spinnaker on larger cruisers and cruiser-racers.

DIRECTION Measured clockwise as an angle relative to north. See *heading* and *bearing*.

DIRTY AIR Term used to describe airflow when sailing in the wind shadow of another boat.

DISMASTING When the mast breaks, usually because a piece of rigging or a terminal fitting has given way. See *jury rig*.

DISPLACEMENT The weight of the water displaced by a floating hull.

DISTANCE Measured in nautical miles.

DIURNAL Variation in weather during the day.

DODGERS Weather cloths that can be laced along the lifelines for added protection in the cockpit.

DORADE A type of ventilator that feeds air to the interior while keeping water out.

DOWNHAUL A rope for hauling down sails or for controlling a spar such as the spinnaker pole; opposite of *uphaul*.

DOWNWIND (or offwind) All courses that are farther away from the wind than a beam reach are known as downwind, or offwind, courses; opposite of *upwind*.

DR Dead reckoning position. It is plotted on a chart by drawing the course steered from the last known position and measuring off the distance sailed according to the log. See also *EP*.

DRIFT The strength of a tidal stream; the distance the stream will move a floating object in an hour.

DROGUE An object towed, usually over the stern of a boat, as a way of reducing its speed in heavy weather.

E, F

EBB TIDE When the tide is going out, between high and low water; opposite of *flood tide*.

EDDIES Circular current, the area of reversed current which forms behind a rock or headland in a current or tidal stream.

EP Estimated position. A DR (dead reckoning) position plus tidal set and drift. EPs are plotted at regular intervals on a chart and compared with a fix to identify any errors in plotting.

EPIRB Emergency position indicating radio beacon that transmits distress signals to satellites that are part of the GMDSS.

FAIRLEAD A bolt, ring, or loop that guides a rope.

FAIRWAY A channel; unobstructed water.

FATHOM An old unit of length for measuring water depth. One fathom is 6 feet.

FEATHER (oars) To turn oar blades parallel to the water's surface in between strokes to prevent the blades from catching in the waves.

FENDER A protector hung over the side between the boat and a pontoon or another vessel.

FERRO-CEMENT Concrete boat-building material.

FIDDLES Used below deck, fiddles are the raised lips on horizontal surfaces such as tables, to stop objects falling off them when the boat heels.

FIGURE-EIGHT A stopper knot, used to prevent a rope end from running out through a block or fairlead.

FIN KEEL A single, central, fixed, ballasted keel.

FISHERMAN'S ANCHOR Traditional hooking anchor.

FLOOD TIDE Tide that is coming in.

FLUKE The barb or hook of an anchor.

FOILS A collective term for the keel, centerboard (or daggerboard), and rudder.

FOOT The bottom edge of a sail.

FORE At, near, or towards the bow.

FORE AND AFT In line from bow to stern; also on, or parallel to, the centerline.

FOREDECK The deck nearest the bow.

FOREGUY On large boats, the downhaul for the spinnaker pole pulls the outer end of the pole forward as well as down.

FOREMAST Forward mast in all vessels with more than one mast, except yawls and ketches.

FORESTAY A stay that leads from the mast to the bow fitting. A foresail may be attached to it.

FORTRESS (anchor) A type of anchor made from aluminum, with fluke angles that can be adjusted to suit sand or mud bottoms.

FOUL TIDE A tidal stream from an adverse direction.

FRACTIONAL SLOOP A sloop in which the forestay joins the mast at a point some distance below the masthead. See *masthead sloop*.

FREEBOARD A boat's freeboard is the height of the topsides out of the water.

FREER (lift) A wind shift; when the wind moves aft you are freed; opposite of a *header*.

FRONT (weather) Meteorological term used to describe the boundary between warm and cold air masses.

G

GAFF RIG A rig with a four-sided mainsail.

GALLEY A boat's kitchen.

GENNAKER A sail that is a cross between a genoa and a spinnaker. Sometimes called a cruising chute.

GENOA A large headsail that overlaps the mast and usually sweeps the deck with its foot. See *jib*.

GIMBALS Fittings that allow an object (such as a galley stove) to swing so as to remain upright when the boat heels.

GMDSS (Global maritime distress and safety system) A set of standards to which modern radio sets, satellite communication systems, and EPIRBs conform.

GOOSENECK The universal-joint fitting fixed to a mast, which attaches the boom to the mast.

GOOSEWINGING Sailing directly downwind (running) with the mainsail set on one side and the foresail (e.g., the jib or genoa) set on the other.

GPS A global positioning system receiver that uses information from a network of satellites to determine a boat's position accurately.

GRAPNEL A light anchor for small boats.

GRIB Gridded binary data files; small files of weather data easily transmitted over the internet.

GROUND TRACK The course followed, relative to the sea bed. See *water track*.

GRP Glass-reinforced plastic (fiberglass), from which many boat hulls are made.

GUARDRAILS Safety rails or wires fitted around the deck edge, supported by stanchions.

GUNWALE (pronounced "gunnel") The top edge of the side of the hull.

GUY A rope that controls the spinnaker on the windward side. It runs through the end of the spinnaker pole.

GYPSY The drum of a windlass.

H

HALYARD A rope or wire that is used to hoist a sail (or to hoist a flag or other signal).

HAND BEARING COMPASS A portable compass for taking bearings on objects.

HANK A metal or plastic hook that is used to secure a sail to a stay, such as a jib's luff to the forestay.

HATCHES A cover over an opening on deck.

HEAD The top corner of a triangular sail, or the top edge of a four-sided sail.

HEADBOARD The reinforced top corner of a Bermudan mainsail, to which the halyard is attached.

HEADER A wind shift; when the wind moves forward you are "headed"; opposite of a *freer*.

HEADFOIL An aluminum grooved tube that slides over the forestay and holds the luff of the headsails.

HEADING The direction in which you are steering the boat measured by a compass. See *bearing*.

HEADS Often used to mean only the sea toilet, but can also mean the compartment containing the toilet, washbasin, and shower.

HEADSAIL A sail set on the headstay; a jib.

HEAD-TO-WIND The point at which the boat is heading straight into the wind with the sails luffing; when you pass through head-to-wind, you are tacking. See *tacking*.

HEAVING-TO Bringing a boat to a halt, usually by sheeting the headsail to windward. After the event, a boat is described as "hove-to."

HEEL (1) When a boat tilts over to one side, it heels. (2) The heel of the mast is its bottom end.

HELMSMAN The person who steers the boat.

HOIST To raise a sail or flag.

HORN A sound-signaling device.

HORN CLEAT A metal, wooden, or plastic cleat with two horns around which the rope is wrapped to create sufficient friction to hold the rope fast.

HOUNDS The position at which the shrouds and forestay are attached to the mast if not at the masthead.

HULL The main body of a boat.

I-K

IALA International Association of Lighthouse Authorities, which organizes buoyage.

IN-IRONS Stuck head-to-wind with sails luffing and no steerage.

INJECTOR Part of an engine which delivers fuel under pressure into the combustion chamber.

INVERSION (1) Weather—when warm air lays on top of cold air. (2) Boat—capsizing so mast points vertically down.

ISAF International Sailing Federation—the international governing body of sailing.

ISOBARS Lines shown on weather maps to indicate pressure. They join areas of equal pressure in a way similar to contour lines on a chart.

JACKSTAYS Lengths of webbing or wire that run the length of both sidedecks, to which the crew attaches their lifelines when working on deck.

JIB A triangular headsail (a sail set in front of the foreward mast).

JIB SHEETS Ropes used to trim or "sheet" the jib.

JIBING Turning the stern of the boat through the wind; opposite of *Tacking*.

JURY RIG A makeshift rig that you construct to get you to safety following a dismasting.

KATABATIC WINDS Sinking currents of cold air running down mountain slopes.

KEDGE ANCHOR A lighter anchor than the main (or bower) anchor.

KEDGING-OFF Pulling a boat out of shallow water with an anchor when it has run aground.

KEEL The lowest part of a sailing boat, and used to resist sideways drift (leeway).

KETCH A two-masted yacht with the aft mast (mizzen mast) smaller than the main mast and stepped ahead of the rudder post. See *yawl*.

KICKING STRAP See *boom vang*.

KNOT The unit of speed at sea, defined as one nautical mile per hour.

L

LAID A method of rope construction where three strands are twisted together to make the rope.

LATITUDE The angular distance north or south of the equator. The lines of latitude are the grid lines on a map or chart running east to west, and parallel to the equator. See *longitude*.

LAZYJACKS Restraining lines rigged from the mast to the boom to retain the mainsail when it is lowered and stowed on the boom.

LAZY GUY A leeward guy left slack (not in use) when using a spinnaker on a larger boat.

LEAD LINE A line with a weight attached used to measure the depth of water.

LEEBOARDS (LEECLOTHS) Wooden boards (or canvas cloths) fitted along the inboard edge of a sea berth, to prevent the occupant from being thrown out of the berth in rough conditions.

LEECH The aft edge of a sail.

LEE HELM If a boat turns to leeward when you let go of the tiller, it has lee helm. See *weather helm* and *balanced helm*.

LEE-OH Call made by the helmsman when executing a tack.

LEE SHORE A shore onto which the wind is blowing; opposite of *weather shore*.

LEEWARD Away from the wind; opposite of *windward*.

LIFELINE (1) A term sometimes used instead of *guardrails*. (2) The tether of a safety harness that is attached to strong points, such as *jackstays*.

LIFT A wind shift; when the wind moves aft you are "lifted." Also called a *freer*. See *header*.

LOCKER A storage or stowage compartment.

LONGITUDE The angular distance west or east of the Greenwich meridian. The lines of longitude are the grid lines on a map or chart running north to south. See *latitude*.

LUFF (1) The forward edge of a triangular sail. (2) A sail luffs, or is luffing, when its luff shakes due to the sail not being pulled in sufficiently. (3) To turn towards the wind.

LUFFING (1) When a sailing boat is turned toward the wind (also luff and luff up). (2) When the luff of a sail shakes or flaps.

LYING A-HULL Drifting with all sail stowed, usually in heavy weather.

M

MAGNETIC NORTH The direction to which a magnetic compass points. Magnetic north differs from true north and moves over time.

MAGNETIC VARIATION The angular difference between magnetic north and true north, which alters year by year as the magnetic poles move.

MAINSAIL (pronounced mains'l) The principal fore-and-aft sail on a boat.

MAINSHEET The rope attached to the boom and used to trim (or adjust) the mainsail.

MAINSHEET TACKLE A system of blocks through which the mainsheet is run, to make it easier for the helmsman to hold and adjust the sheet.

MARLINSPIKE A pointed tool used to loosen knots and assist in splicing rope.

MAST A vertical pole to which sails are attached.

MAST GATE The point where the mast passes through the deck of a dinghy or small keelboat. Called *partners* on larger boats.

MAST SPANNER A device on catamarans, used to control the angle of a rotating mast.

MAST STEP A recessed wooden block or metal frame, which receives the heel of the mast.

MASTHEAD The top of a mast.

MASTHEAD SLOOP A sloop in which the forestay joins the mast at the masthead.

MAYDAY The internationally recognized radio distress signal for use when you are in grave and imminent danger. It takes priority over any other kind of message. See *PAN PAN*.

MEAN DIRECTION The term used to describe the average wind direction.

MERCATOR PROJECTION The most common projection of the globe used when making charts.

MERIDIAN A line of longitude that runs from north to south poles.

MIDSHIPS In the middle of the boat, fore and aft and athwartships.

MIZZEN MAST A smaller aft mast on a ketch or yawl. See *ketch* and *yawl*.

MOORING A permanent arrangement of anchors and cables to which a boat can be secured.

MULTIHULL A boat with more than one hull; a *catamaran* or a *trimaran*.

MYLAR A film material often used in high-performance sail manufacture.

N, O

NAUTICAL ALMANAC A reference book giving annual information, such as tidal data, for a wide area.

NAUTICAL MILE The unit of distance at sea, defined as one minute (1') of latitude. It is standardized to 6076 ft (1852 m), slightly longer than a statute mile.

NAVIGATION LIGHTS Lights shown by a boat that indicate relative course, position, and status such as sailing, fishing, or towing.

NEAP TIDES These tides have the smallest range between high and low water; opposite of *spring tides*.

NO-SAIL ZONE Boats cannot sail directly into the wind; there is a no-sail zone on either side of the direction of true wind. The closest most boats can achieve is an angle of 45° on either side.

OARLOCKS U-shaped fittings used to support the oars and act as a pivot when rowing. Fitted into sockets in each gunwale.

OCCLUDED When a cold front overtakes a warm front, the front becomes occluded.

OCTAHEDRAL REFLECTOR A simple type of radar reflector.

OFFSHORE WIND A wind that blows off the land.

OFFWIND See *downwind*.

ONSHORE WIND A wind blowing onto the land.

OVERFALLS Rough water caused by the tide pouring over a rough or precipitous bottom.

OUTBOARD ENGINE An engine mounted externally, usually used on small boats.

OUTHAUL A rope, such as the mainsail clew outhaul, which adjusts the tension in the foot.

P, Q

PAINTER A rope attached to the bow of a dinghy or small boat that is used to moor the boat.

PAN PAN An internationally recognized distress signal that takes priority over all except a *MAYDAY* message.

PARALLEL RULER A rolling or sliding device for plotting a course or bearing on a chart.

PARTNERS The hole where the mast passes through the deck of a cruiser or cruiser-racer. Called *mast gate* on dinghies and small boats.

PASSAGE A journey between two ports.

PASSAGE PLAN The plan constructed to help a crew to navigate safely from one port to another.

PILE MOORINGS Large wooden or metal stakes (piles) driven into the seabed, with fittings to which mooring warps are tied.

PILOTAGE Navigation by eye, compass, and chart, when in sight of land.

PINCHING Sailing too close to the wind inside the no-sail zone.

PISTON HANKS A form of hank. See *hank*.

PITCHPOLING Capsizing stern over bow.

PLANING The motion of a boat when it lifts partly out of the water and increases speed by reducing its drag.

PLOTTER A device for plotting a course on a paper chart, used in conjunction with the grid of latitude and longitude lines marked on a chart.

POINTS OF SAILING The direction in which a boat is being sailed, described in relation to its angle to the wind. Collectively, these angles are known as the points of sailing.

POLING OUT Method of holding the headsail out to windward to increase downwind speed.

PONTOON A floating platform to which boats can be moored.

PORT The left-hand side of a boat, when looking forward.

PORT TACK A boat is on port tack when the wind is blowing over the port side and the main boom is out to starboard. See *starboard tack*.

POSITION LINE A straight or curved line on a chart drawn with the aid of a compass bearing or the distance off a charted object.

PRAM BOW A cut-off, square bow in small boats.

PRE-BEND The amount of fore-and-aft bend set in a mast before sailing.

PRESSURE GRADIENT The difference between high and low pressure that causes wind to blow.

PROP WALK The paddlewheel effect of a turning propeller. Prop walk pushes the stern of the boat sideways in the same direction in which the propeller rotates.

PULPIT An elevated and rigid metal rail around the bow of a boat.

PUSHPIT An elevated and rigid metal rail around the stern of a boat.

R

RAKE The amount that a mast leans aft from vertical.

RAM'S HORNS Inverted hooks onto which a mainsail's luff cringles are fixed when reefing.

RATCHET BLOCK A type of pulley, containing a ratchet, to reduce the load the crew has to hold.

REACHER A lightweight sail designed to be used on reaching courses.

REACHING Sailing with the wind approximately abeam. See *beam reach* and *broad reach*.

REACHING HOOK On a dinghy, a hook fitted just aft of the shrouds to hold the guy down.

READY ABOUT Term used to warn the crew that the helmsman is about to tack.

REEF To reduce sail area when the wind becomes too strong to sail comfortably under full sail.

REEF KNOT A knot that is used for tying the ends of rope of equal diameter, such as a sail's reef points when putting in a reef.

REEF POINTS Light lines sewn to the sail to tie up the loose fold in a sail when it is reefed.

RIG The arrangement of the sails, spars, and masts on a boat. To rig the boat is to step the mast and bend on the sails. See *rigging*.

RIGGING The system of wires and ropes used to keep the mast in place and work the sails.

RIGGING LINK An item of equipment that is used to attach the shrouds and stays to the chainplates.

RISER CHAIN The chain that attaches the mooring buoy to a ground chain.

ROACH The curved area on the leech of a sail, outside a straight line from head to clew.

ROLL TACKING A fast way of tacking in which crew weight is used to roll the boat during a tack.

ROLLER FURLING A mechanical system to roll up a headsail or mainsail.

ROLLER REEFING A mechanical system to reef a headsail or mainsail.

ROUND TURN A complete turn of a rope or line around an object.

RUDDER A movable underwater blade that is used to steer the boat, controlled by a tiller or wheel.

RULES OF THE ROAD See *Col Regs*.

RUN/RUNNING Sailing directly downwind (that is, with the wind right behind you, or nearly so) on either a port or starboard tack. A dead, or true, run is slightly different from a *training run*.

RUNNING MOOR To moor up to a pile mooring or fore-and-aft buoys under sail.

RUNNING RIGGING All of the moving lines, such as sheets and halyards, used in the setting and trimming of sails.

S

SAFE TRACK The course you follow through constricted water. See *clearing lines*.

SAILMAKER'S PALM Used for pushing needles through rope or sail cloth.

SAMSON POST A strong vertical post usually at the bow of a boat and used for mooring warps.

SCHOONER A sailing vessel with two or more masts with the tallest mast stepped aft.

SCULLING A method of propelling a dinghy by manipulating a single oar over the stern in a figure-eight pattern.

SEACOCK A valve that can be shut to close a through-hull fitting.

SEIZING Binding two lines together, or a rope to a spar, or a loop in a rope, using a light line.

SETTING SAILS The process of bending-on and hoisting sails ready for sea.

SHACKLE A U-shaped link with a screw pin, used to connect ropes and fittings.

SHEET Rope attached to the clew of a sail, or to a boom, which can be tightened or eased to trim (adjust) the sail.

SHEET BEND A knot used to join two ropes.

SHEAVES The pulley wheels in *blocks*.

SHOALING (1) The water is said to be shoaling as the boat sails into shallow water. (2) Shifting sand, silt, or sediment causing shallow areas; a problem in some channels.

SHOCK CORD An elastic "rope" useful in limited stowage situations.

SHOCK LOADS Sudden loads on sails, sheets, and rigging caused by gusts of wind or a sudden slowing caused by burying the bow into a wave.

SHORELINE Where the land meets the water.

SHROUDS The wire ropes on either side of the mast, which support it sideways.

SIDE DECK The deck at the side of a boat.

SINGLE UP Taking in all ropes not required, so that only a minimum number of ropes will require casting off when leaving a berth or buoy.

SKEG A projecting part of the hull that supports the rudder.

SKEG-HUNG RUDDER A rudder supported by a part of the hull called a skeg. See *spade rudder*.

SLAB REEFING Reduces the area of the mainsail by partially lowering the sail and tying up the loose fold (slab) of sail created.

SLEEVED SAIL A sail with a sleeve at the luff that encloses the mast. Usually found on small dinghies.

SLIP LINE A doubled line with both ends made fast on the boat so that it can be released and pulled from on board.

SLIPWAY A launching ramp.

SLOOP A single-masted boat with only one headsail set at any one time.

SLOT The gap between the luff of the main and the leech of the jib.

SOCK (spinnaker) A light nylon tube used to stow, hoist, and lower some spinnakers and cruising chutes.

SPADE RUDDER A rudder supported only by its stock (rudder tube) and not by a skeg.

SPAR A general term for masts, booms, yards, gaffs, etc.

SPINNAKER A large, light, downwind sail set from a spinnaker pole.

SPINNAKER POLE A pole used to extend the spinnaker tack away from the boat.

SPLICE The joining of two lines, or the forming of a loop in one, by interweaving their strands.

SPREADERS Small poles extending outward from one or more places on the mast. Shrouds run through the outer ends to provide additional support to the mast.

SPRINGS Mooring warps to help prevent the boat from moving ahead or astern when moored.

SPRING TIDES Tides that have the largest range between high and low tides.

STANCHION An upright post used to support the guardrails.

STANDING PART The part of a rope that is not being used to tie a knot.

STANDING RIGGING The shrouds and stays that support the mast(s).

STARBOARD The right-hand side of a boat, when looking forward.

STARBOARD TACK The course of a boat when the wind is blowing over a boat's starboard side and the main boom is out to port. See *port tack*.

STAY A wire running fore or aft (forestay or backstay) to support the mast.

STAYSAIL A triangular sail flown from an inner forestay or loose-luffed (not attached to a stay) from the middle of the foredeck.

STEERAGE WAY Having enough speed through the water so that the rudder can be used to steer.

STEM The main upright or sloping structure at the bow.

STEMHEAD FITTING The metal fitting at the bow of the boat to which the forestay is usually attached. Cruisers usually have an anchor roller incorporated into the fitting.

STERN The rear or after part of a vessel; opposite of *bow*.

STERN LINE A mooring warp that is run from the stern of the boat to a point on shore astern of the boat. See *bow line*.

STERN QUARTERS The aft corners of a boat.

STERN SPRING The mooring line that leads from the stern forward to another boat or pontoon when berthed to prevent the boat from moving astern. See *bow spring*.

STOW To place equipment in its storage place.

STORM JIB A small, strong headsail used in very strong winds.

SWELL Succession of long and unbroken waves generally due to wind some distance away.

T

TACK (1) The forward lower corner of a fore-and-aft sail. (2) Under sail, a boat is either on starboard tack or port tack. See *tacking*.

TACKING Turning the bow of the boat through the wind so that the boat turns from one tack to the other. See *jibing*.

TACKLE An arrangement of a line led through two or more blocks to create mechanical advantage, in order to move heavy objects or handle large loads.

TAIL To pull on the free end (the tail) of a sheet or halyard when winching.

TELLTALES Light strips of fabric or wool, sewn or glued to sails to show the wind flow and the best sail trim.

TEMPERATURE INVERSION An increase in temperature with height above the Earth's surface, a reversal of the normal pattern.

TENDER A small boat used to ferry people and provisions to and from a larger boat.

THROAT The forward upper corner of a four-cornered, gaff mainsail.

THWART A seat fixed across a small boat.

TIDAL ATLAS Small charts showing tidal stream directions and rate of flow.

TIDAL CYCLE The period of tidal flow from one high water to the next.

TIDAL DIAMOND Symbol shown on a chart which relates to information, in a panel on the chart, giving the speed and direction of the tidal stream, at that point, through the tidal cycle.

TIDAL DRIFT The strength of a tidal stream.

TIDAL RACE An area of disturbed water and increased tidal stream due to a constriction that accelerates or diverts the tidal stream.

TIDAL RANGE The difference between a tide's high and low water levels.

TIDAL SET The direction of a tidal stream.

TIDAL STREAM A horizontal flow of water caused by the rise and fall of the tide.

TIDE The regular rise and fall of the sea's surface caused mainly by the moon's gravitational pull (and to a lesser degree the sun's).

TIDE RIP Term for a tidal stream when it is running fast around rocks, shallows, or headlands, causing a disturbance at the surface.

TIDE TABLES A record of the times and heights of high and low water for every day of the year.

TILLER Rod by which the rudder is controlled, for steering.

TILLER BAR A rod that connects the two tillers on a boat with twin rudders, such as a catamaran.

TILLER EXTENSION A light pole attached to the tiller with an universal joint to allow the helmsman to steer from either side of the boat.

TOESTRAPS Straps of webbing under which a dinghy crew hooks their feet when sitting out.

TOPSAIL A triangular sail set above the gaff on a gaff-rigged boat.

TOPPING LIFT A rope running from the masthead to the boom end used to support the boom when the mainsail is not hoisted.

TOPSIDES The sides of the hull between the water line and the deck edge.

TRAINING RUN Sailing downwind, 5–10° off a true run.

TRAMPOLINE A strong nylon mesh that stretches between the hulls of a catamaran or trimaran.

TRANSIT Also called a range. Two prominent marks separated in distance so that they can be aligned to determine that a boat lies on a certain line.

TRANSOM Flat vertical surface at the stern of a boat.

TRANSOM FLAPS Flaps in the transom through which unwanted water can escape.

TRAPEZE A wire used in high-performance dinghies to enable the crew to place their weight farther outside the boat than they would if just sitting out.

TRAVELER A slide that travels along a track, used for altering sheet angles.

TRIM To let out or pull in a sheet to adjust a sail.

TRIMARAN A vessel with three hulls.

TRIP To release a rope, such as releasing the spinnaker pole from the guy or the guy from the spinnaker.

TRIPPING LINE A line attached to the end of an anchor to help free it from the ground when weighing anchor.

TRI-RADIAL SAIL A sail construction technique where radial panels emanate from all three corners of the sail.

TROT A line of mooring bouys.

TRUE BEARING A bearing measured relative to true north.

TRUE NORTH The direction of the true North Pole. See also *magnetic north* and *compass north*.

TRUE WIND The speed and direction of the wind you feel when stationary. The motion of a boat will cause the wind to appear to be in a different direction and speed, which is known as apparent wind.

TRYSAIL A small, strong replacement for a cruiser's mainsail used in severe weather.

TWINNING LINE A small block with a light line attached to it, used instead of reaching hooks when flying a spinnaker.

TWIST The difference in angle to the wind between the top and bottom of a sail.

U-Z

UNIVERSAL JOINT A hinge that allows articulation in all directions.

UNSTAYED MAST A mast without standing rigging.

UPHAUL A rope for adjusting the height of the spinnaker pole; opposite of *downhaul*.

UPWIND All courses that are closer to the wind (heading more directly into it) than a beam reach are called upwind courses; opposite of *offwind* or *downwind*.

VARIATION See *magnetic variation*.

VECTOR A line drawn to indicate both the direction and magnitude of a force, such as a tidal stream.

VHF (Very high frequency radio) A common radio system used on boats, but its range is limited to line-of-sight.

VICTUALING Provisioning a boat for a passage.

WAKE Waves generated astern by a moving vessel.

WARP Any rope used to secure or move a boat.

WASHBOARDS Wooden or plastic shutters that close off the companionway.

WATCH (1) A division of crew into shifts. (2) The time each watch has duty.

WATER TRACK The course to steer through the water to achieve a ground track after allowing for the effects of any tidal stream.

WAYPOINTS Positions, in latitude and longitude of turning or other important points along your route. Usually programmed into a GPS set or chart plotter.

WEATHER HELM If the boat, under sail, turns to windward when you let go of the tiller, it has weather helm. See *lee helm* and *balanced helm*.

WEATHER SHORE When the wind blows off the land, the shore is called a weather shore; opposite of *lee shore*. See *offshore wind*.

WHIPPING To bind the ends of a rope with thin cord (whipping twine) to keep it from unraveling.

WHISKER POLE Pole for holding out the jib when *goosewinging*.

WINCH Device to provide mechanical advantage for pulling in sheets and halyards.

WINDAGE The drag caused by the parts of the boat and crew exposed to the wind.

WINDLASS A mechanical device used to pull in a cable or chain, such as an anchor rode.

WINDWARD Toward the wind; opposite of *leeward*.

WORKING END The part of a rope used for tying a knot.

YAWL A two-masted yacht with the mizzen mast stepped aft of the rudderpost. A *ketch* is similar, but its mizzen mast is forward of the rudderpost.

ZEPHYR Gentle winds on a still day, often on the edge of lakes or other inland waters, caused when air over land is warmed and rises, pulling in cooler air from over the water.

INDEX

ACKNOWLEDGMENTS

THE AUTHOR would like to thank SF for inspiration.

Grateful thanks for editorial contributions to the second edition are due to **Rupert Holmes** (for help with Practical Boat Care), **Andy Rice** (Advanced Small Boat Sailing), **Tim Robinson** (Cruiser Sailing and Navigation), and **Simon Hay** (Forecasting). Thanks are also due to **Magic Marine** for assistance with images and clothing, and to **Spinlock** for assistance with images and DeckVest.

Thanks are due for help with the second editon to **Nigel Vick** of the Oxford & District Sailing Centre and the Oxford Sailing Club for their assistance with photography. Also, **Alice Kingham** and **Tariq Melhem** for their assistance with dinghy sailing. The **Laser Centre** kindly provided facilities and boats for photography, and **Sally-Ann Johnson** and **Chris Blackburn** kindly assisted with photography.

Opal Marine kindly loaned a Bavaria 38 Match and **James Blackburn** helped with cruiser photography. **Michelle Fisher** and **Carl Blenkinsop** kindly loaned their Dart 15 and assisted with photography. Thanks are also due to the **UKSA** (United Kingdom Sailing Academy) for help with photography and to **Alison Burton** and **Eddie Sherwin** for help with clothing photography. Clothing for cruiser photography was kindly provided by **Musto**. Musto is a registered trademark of Musto Ltd.

Thanks for help with the first edition of this book are due to **Gary Pearson, Mark Elson, Will Upchurch,** and **Ben Willows** of UKSA for assistance with dinghy-sailing photography, **Rival Bowman Yachts Ltd** for the use of a Starlight 35, and **Julian Fawcett** from Rival Bowman for his sailing assistance. Thanks are due to **Martin Pass** at Audi UK, Milton Keynes, for organizing and providing the cars for the photoshoot.

DORLING KINDERSLEY
would like to thank the following people.
Design: **Joanne Clark.**
Editorial: **Nidhilekha Mathur, Pankaj Deo, Suparna Sengupta, Sreshtha Bhattacharya,** and **Priyanka Chatterjee.**
Picture library: **Martin Copeland** and **Susie Peachey.**
The publisher would like to thank the following for their kind permission to reproduce their photographs and reference material. (Abbreviations: t=top, b=bottom, r=right, l=left, c=centre, a=above.)
Alamy Images: Keith Shuttlewood 145; **Alubat & Northsea Maritime:** 403 br; **Arun Sails:** 394; **Audi:** 50; **Avon:** 232; **Jim Baerselman:** 192; **Beken:** 127 br, 264, 257 bc; **Alan Jacobs Gallery, London:** 12; **Blue Water Supplies:** 216; **Broadblue Catamarans:** 195 br; **Nick Champion:** 124 br; **Christal Clear:** 63 ca, 82 bl, 102, 129 bc, 167 tc, 175, 195 tr; **Corbis:** Chris Hellier 15, Gerry Penny/EPA 53, Randy Lincks 190–191, 198; **Peter Danby:** 101; **Dehler Yachts:** 195 bl, 205, 300; **Julie Dunbar:** 63 tc; **D14 Dundee Satellite Receiving Station, University of Dundee:** 367; **Dubarry:** 215 bl; **Dufour Yachts:** 195 cl; **Patrick Eden:** 5cr, 6, 13, 18, 183 tl; **Jeremy Evans:** 14, 54, 62, 184 bc, 203, 250, 396 bl, 397 tl, br; **Elan Yachts:** 208; **Finnclass.org:** 157 tr; **Frank Lane Picture Agency:** 370 bc, B&D Hosking 377, Brian Cosgrove 368 bc, Chris Demetrion 371 br, Francois Merlet 368 br, H Hoflinger 375, Larry West 370 bl, Martin Smith 304 tr, Maurice Nimmo 371 bl, S. McCutcheon 369 bl, bc, 370 br, R Thompson 368 bl; **Garmin Ltd.:** 322 clb, 328 bl, bc, br; **Geoscience Features:** 371 bc; **Getty Images:** 416–417, Abner Kingman 308, Mike Hewitt 362–363; **Steve Gorton:** 29 r, 80 tr, 80 bl, 117, 206–207 all, 210–211, 212–213, 226, 228, 230, 238, 241, 243, 245, 248, 255, 256, 257 tc, 326 bl; **Helly Hansen/Jon Nash:** 125 t, 138; **iStockphoto.com:** 384–385; **ITT Industries/Rule/Jabsco:** 405 ct, tr; **J/Boats UK:** 251; **Kos Picture Source:** 120–121, 201, 239, 289, 309 tl, 312–313; David Williams 284; F Salle 158 bl; **Laser Centre:** 5 c, 63 bca, 152 br, 157 tl; **Laser Performance:** 63 cla; Peter Bentley: 5 c, 20–21, 110; **LDC Racing Sailboats:** 36, 38, 51, 60, 61, 63 bc, 77br, cr, 124 cl, 157 cl, cr, 161 cb; **Mach2boats:** Thierry Martinez 124 bl; **Mannix:** 381 br; **Magic Marine:** 98, Thierry Martinez 122, Richard de Jonge 183 br; Ingrid Abery 185 br, **Mastervolt:** 400, 402 bl, 403 tl; **Maxsea:** 321; **McMurdo:** 217 cl, bl, 219 tl, 423, 424 all; **Damien Moore:** 26 tr, 326 br, cr; **Musto:** 4–5 main, 8, 66, 67 bl, bc, br, cr, 125 b, 137 tc, 139, 209, 215 cr, 217 bc; **Ocean Images:** 37cl, 63 cr, 142, 176, 181 br; Richard Langdon: 63 cr, 154, 161 bl; **Ovington Boats:** 63 br, 124 cla, bc; **Para-Tech Engineering Co:** 311; **Petticrow:** 161 cl, bc, 323 tr, br, 381 bl; **PPL:** Alan Taphouse 111; Alastair Black 129 bl, 246, 427; Barry Pickthall 68, 119, 419; Bob Fisher 167 tr; Gary John Norman 214, 391 br; Gilles Martin-Raget 170; Ingrid Abery 141, 180, 181 tc; Jamie Lawson-Johnston 195 tl; Jon Nash 196; Jono Knight 152 tr; Nick Kirk 174; Peter Bentley 128 tr, 129 tl, 153, 167 tl, 386; **Phileas Boats:** 161 br; **Raymarine:** 323 bl, 331 tl; **Patrick Roach:** 22, 57br; **Rohan Veal / M. Poitevineau:** 157 bl; **RS Sailing:** Riki Hooker 124 cra; **Seasure:** 137 bc, br; **Secumar:** 217 cr, br, 296 bl, br, 425; **Simrad:** 305 tr; **Steve Sleight:** 19, 37 tr, 195 cr, 259, 304 cb, 330, 331 tl, br, 380, 379; **Steiner:** 332 bl, br; **Sunsail/Pat Collinge/ Richard Neall/Jonathan Smith:** 1, 2, 234, 242, 285; **TKZ photography:** Gary Ombler: 28–29 bl, tl, tr, 71 all, 73 all but br, 74 t, 75 tc, tr, cl, cr, Patrick Eden: 26 l, 28 br, 33, 35, 42 tr, 63 bla, 64, 65, 67 tl, cb, ca, tc, 72 tr, tc, tl, 112 ct, cb, 114, 118 bl, bc, br, 132, 135 bl, tr, 146, 151 cl, bl, 161 cla, clb, c, 162, 163, 165 bl, bcl, bc, bcr, br, 168 all, 182, 215 tl, cl, tr, cr, 240, 276, 288, 334 cb, 336, 348, 388 bl, bcl, bcr, br, 393 bl, 395, 398, 399 cr, 406, 407; Sara Coombes: 392 tr; Steve Sleight: 70 cr, 73 br, 131 tl, br, 147, 164 tr, bl, 165 tc, 169 all, 218 bl, tr, 219 br, 251, 275, 278 bl, br, 283, 301, 305 tl, 305 bc, 334 bl, 387 tl, tc, tr, 391 tc, 392 bc, 399 cl, bl, bc, 409, 412 bl, tr, 413 bl, tr; **Rick Tomlinson:** 5cl, 10–11, 244, 251; **Turtle Photography:** 63 tl, tlb, clb, tcb, cb, 58–59, 76 bl, 81, 82 tl, 82 tc, 124 tl, clb, tc, c, cb, 161 ca, 184/185; **UK Sailmakers:** 309 br; **UKHO:** 286, 320 bl, bc, br 'Reproduced from Admiralty chart 2040 by permission of the Controller of Her Majesty's Stationery Office and the UK Hydrographic Office (www.ukho.gov.uk)'; **UKSA:** 286; **UltimateSailing.com:** Sharon Green 16; **US National Weather Service:** 378; **Volvo Ocean Race:** Dan Armstrong 17 tr; **William Payne Photography:** 402 br, 408; **Paul Wyeth:** 18, 152 bl, bc, 161 cr.

Illustrations from the first edition by **Peter Bull Art Studio.** Additional illustrations by **Phil Gamble, David Ashby, Martin Woodward, Quo Kong Chen, Robert Campbell, Claire Pegrum, Steve Cluett.**
All other images © Dorling Kindersley.
For further information see
www.dkimages.com